Behavioral Law and Economics

People are frequently both unselfish and overly optimistic; they have limited willpower and limited self-control; and they often rely on mental shortcuts and rules of thumb. What do these traits have to do with law? This is the question considered in *Behavioral Law and Economics*, the first book to analyze law by looking at how people actually behave. Marking the birth of a new field, one that combines the study of law with cognitive psychology and behavioral economics, the book offers a useful new perspective on many of our most disputed current legal issues, such as labor strikes, environmental protection, and punitive damages. It explores the impact of human nature on legal matters ranging from tax compliance and voting behavior to corporate finance and crime. Ultimately it shows how, with a clearer knowledge of human behavior, we might be better able to predict the actual effects of law and to assess the real, and potential, role of law in society.

Cass R. Sunstein is Karl N. Llewellyn Distinguished Service Professor at the University of Chicago Law School and Department of Political Science. His many books include *Free Markets and Social Justice, One Case at a Time: Judicial Minimalism on the Supreme Court,* and *Legal Reasoning and Political Conflict.*

Cambridge Series on Judgment and Decision Making

The purpose of the series is to convey the general principles of and findings about judgment and decision making to the many academic and professional fields to which these apply. The contributions are written by authorities in the field and supervised by highly qualified editors and the Publications Board. The series will attract readers from many different disciplines, largely among academics, advanced undergraduates, graduate students, and practicing professionals.

Behavioral Law and Economics

Edited by

Cass R. Sunstein
University of Chicago Law School

CAMBRIDGE UNIVERSITY PRESS
Cambridge, New York, Melbourne, Madrid, Cape Town, Singapore, São Paulo

Cambridge University Press
32 Avenue of the Americas, New York, NY 10013-2473, USA

www.cambridge.org
Information on this title: www.cambridge.org/9780521661355

First published 2000
Reprinted 2001, 2003, 2005, 2007

Printed in the United States of America

A catalog record for this publication is available from the British Library.

Library of Congress Cataloging in Publication data
Behavioral law and economics / edited by Cass R. Sunstein.
p. cm. – (Cambridge series on judgment and decision making)
ISBN 0-521-66135-8 (hb.) – ISBN 0-521-66743-7 (pbk.)
1. Law and economics – Psychological aspects. I. Sunstein, Cass
R. II. Series.
K487.E3B435 2000
330′.01′9 – dc21 99-31294
CIP

ISBN 978-0-521-66135-5 hardback
ISBN 978-0-521-66743-2 paperback

Contents

Contributors

Linda Babcock *is Professor of Economics at the H. John Heinz III School of Public Policy and Management at Carnegie Mellon University. Her research uses insights from psychology to improve economic models and analyses, particularly in the domain of negotiation and dispute resolution.*

Jonathan Baron *is Professor of Psychology at the University of Pennsylvania. Author of* Thinking and Deciding *(2d ed. 1994) and* Judgment Misguided *(1998), he is interested in utility measurement and nonconsequentialist judgments.*

Ward Farnsworth *is an associate professor at the Boston University School of Law. He attended law school at the University of Chicago and has served as a law clerk to Judge Richard A. Posner of the United States Court of Appeals for the Seventh Circuit and to Justice Anthony M. Kennedy of the United States Supreme Court.*

Christine Jolls *is Assistant Professor of Law at Harvard Law School and Faculty Research Fellow at the National Bureau of Economic Research. She holds a law degree from Harvard Law School and a Ph.D. in Economics from the Massachusetts Institute of Technology. She writes and teaches primarily in the areas of employment law and behavioral law and economics.*

Daniel Kahneman *is Eugene Higgins Professor of Psychology and Professor of Public Affairs at Princeton University. He has worked in diverse areas of experimental psychology and at the intersection of psychology, decision theory, and economics.*

Mark Kelman *is the William Nelson Cromwell Professor at Stanford Law School. He has written in the fields of law and psychology, law and economics, antidiscrimination law, tax policy, and criminal law.*

Jack L. Knetsch *received degrees in Soil Science and Agricultural Economics from Michigan State University, and in Public Administration and Economics from Harvard University. After holding academic, government, and other noncademic positions in the United States, Malaysia, and Australia, he has been Professor of Economics and Professor of Resource Management at Simon Fraser University, in Canada, for twenty-five years. Much of his research and teaching has been in behavioral economics, environmental economics, law, and policy.*

Russell Korobkin *is an assistant professor at the University of Illinois College of Law and University of Illinois Institute of Government and Public Affairs.*

James E. Krier *is the Earl Warren DeLano Professor at the University of Michigan Law School. Before moving to Michigan he taught at UCLA and Stanford University.*

Timur Kuran *is Professor of Economics and King Faisal Professor of Islamic Thought and Culture at the University of Southern California. His publications include* Private Truths, Public Lies: The Social Consequences of Preference Falsification *(Harvard University Press).*

Donald C. Langevoort *is Professor of Law at Georgetown University Law Center, Washington, D.C. His principal research interests are in corporate and securities law, with special focus on the application of social psychology and organization theory to marketplace behavior.*

George Loewenstein *is Professor of Economics and Psychology at Carnegie Mellon University. His research focuses on applications of psychology to economics, and specific interests include decision making over time, bargaining and negotiations, law and economics, the psychology of curiosity, and "out of control" behaviors such as impulsive violent crime and drug addiction.*

Edward J. McCaffery *is the Maurice Jones, Jr. Professor of Law, University of Southern California Law School, and Visiting Professor of Law and Economics, California Institute of Technology. He is the author of many articles on tax, property, and legal theory, and the book* Taxing Women *(University of Chicago Press, 1997).*

Roger G. Noll *is the Morris M. Doyle Centennial Professor of Public Policy in the Department of Economics, Stanford University. His teaching and writing focus on public policies toward business, including the application of the economic theory of politics to understanding legal processes.*

Jeffrey J. Rachlinski *received a J.D. and a Ph.D. in Psychology from Stanford University. He is an assistant professor of law at Cornell Law School, where he studies the application of psychology to the legal system.*

Ilana Ritov *is a senior lecturer at the Hebrew University of Jerusalem. Her research interests include cognitive determinants of individual biased decisions.*

Yuval Rottenstreich *is Assistant Professor of Managerial and Organizational Behavior, Center for Decision Research, University of Chicago Graduate School of Business. His research interests include the normative and descriptive analysis of judgment and choice.*

David Schkade *is Professor of Management and the William W. Spriegel Fellow at the University of Texas, Austin. His research interests include the psychology of judgment and decision making, jury decision making, the psychology of well-being, environmental resource valuation, and psychological aspects of decision support systems.*

Matthew L. Spitzer *is William T. Dalessi Professor of Law at the University of Southern California and Professor of Law and Social Science at the California Institute of Technology. He writes in the areas of telecommunications regulation, administrative law, and law and economics.*

Cass R. Sunstein *is Karl N. Llewellyn Distinguished Service Professor, Law School and Department of Political Science, University of Chicago. He is the author of many books, including* Free Markets and Social Justice *and* Democracy and the Problem of Free Speech.

Richard H. Thaler *is the Robert P. Gwinn Professor of Economics and Behavioral Science and Director, Center for Decision Research at the Graduate School of Business, University of Chicago.*

Amos Tversky *was a professor of psychology at Stanford University and a pioneer in the fields of cognitive psychology and behavioral economics.*

Edna Ullmann-Margalit *teaches philosophy at the Hebrew University of Jerusalem and is a member of its Center for Rationality and Interactive Decision Theory.* Reasoning Practically, *which she edited, will be published by Oxford University Press later this year.*

Acknowledgments

Many people contributed to the production of this book; I single out a few of them here. For overall help, special thanks to my colleague and coauthor Richard Thaler, who taught me a great deal about economics and behavioral economics, and who provided a lot of helpful advice. Christine Jolls, another coauthor, offered valuable suggestions about how to organize the book. Richard Posner, in many ways a skeptic about behavioral law and economics, provided both probing criticisms and valuable encouragement. Thanks too to Daniel Kahneman and David Schkade for helpful discussions on many of the topics of this book. Gary Becker provided an illuminating discussion of the basic idea of "rationality." Brian Lehman did a wonderful job of putting the manuscript in shape. Julia Hough was an enthusiastic and extremely helpful editor. To all of you, and to others not mentioned here, I am extremely grateful.

The chapters in this book borrow from previous work. There has, however, been substantial condensing of many chapters, and several chapters have been revised and updated. I am grateful to the following journals for permission to reprint as follows (noting that in some cases, there have been significant revisions as well):

Chapter 1 is republished with permission of the *Stanford Law Review*, 559 Nathan Abbott Way, Palo Alto, CA 95305. Jolls, Sunstein, and Thaler, "A Behavioral Approach to Law and Economics," vol. 50, 1998. Reproduced by permission of the publisher via Copyright Clearance Center, Inc.

Chapter 2 was originally published in 25 *J. Legal Stud.* 287 (1996); it is republished with permission of the *Journal of Legal Studies*. Copyright, *Journal of Legal Studies*.

Chapter 3 was originally published in 65 *U. Chi. L. Rev.* 571 (1998); it is reproduced with permission from the University of Chicago Law Review.

Chapter 4 borrows, with permission, from Russell Korobkin, "The Status Quo Bias and Contract Default Rules," 83 *Cornell L. Rev.* 609 (1998), and

"Inertia and Preference in Contract Negotiation: The Psychological Power of Default Rules and Form Terms," 51 *Vanderbilt L. Rev.* 1583 (1998).

Chapter 5 is reproduced with permission from 146 *U. Pa. L. Rev. 101*. Copyright, *University of Pennsylvania Law Review*.

Chapter 6 was originally published in 3 *J. Behavioral Decision Making* 263 (1990). Copyright, John Wiley & Sons Limited. Reproduced with permission.

Chapter 7 is reproduced from *Ethics* (1999). Copyright 1999, the University of Chicago. All rights reserved.

Chapter 8 was originally published in 98 *J. Polit. Econ.* 1325 (1990); it is reprinted with permission of the University of Chicago Press. Copyright, University of Chicago Press.

Chapter 9 is reprinted by permission of the Yale Law Journal Company and Fred B. Rotman & Company from the *Yale Law Journal*, vol. 107, pp. 2071–153.

Chapter 10 is reprinted with permission of the *Virginia Law Review*, from 81 *Va. L. Rev.* 1341 (1995).

Chapter 11 is reprinted from 51 *Vanderbilt L. Rev.* 1653 (1998), with permission of the *Vanderbilt Law Review*.

Chapter 12 is reprinted from 66 *U. Chi. L. Rev.* 373 (1999), with permission of the *University of Chicago Law Review*.

Chapter 13 is reprinted from 19 *J. Legal. Stud.* 747 (1991), with permission of the *Journal of Legal Studies*. Copyright 1991, *Journal of Legal Studies*.

Chapter 14 is reprinted from 11 *J. Econ. Persp.* 109 (1997), with permission of the American Economic Association.

Chapter 15 is republished with permission of the *Stanford Law Review*, 559 Nathan Abbott Way, Palo Alto, CA 95305. Kuran and Sunstein, "Availability Cascades and Risk Regulation," vol. 51, 1999. Reproduced by permission of the publisher via Copyright Clearance Center, Inc.

Chapter 16 was originally published in 41 *UCLA L. Rev. 1961*, Copyright 1994, the Regents of the University of California. Reprinted with permission; all rights reserved.

Introduction

Cass R. Sunstein

How does law actually affect people? What do people do in response to the law? Why is the law as it is? How can law be enlisted to improve people's lives? This book attempts to provide some answers. It is also the first general effort to bring behavioral economics to bear on the analysis of law.

In the last two decades, social scientists have learned a great deal about how people actually make decisions. Much of this work requires qualifications of rational choice models, which have dominated the social sciences, including the economic analysis of law. Those models are often wrong in the simple sense that they yield inaccurate predictions. People are not always "rational" in the sense that economists suppose. But it does not follow that people's behavior is unpredictable, systematically irrational, random, rule-free, or elusive to social scientists. On the contrary, the qualifications can be described, used, and sometimes even modeled.

The purpose of this book is to bring new and more accurate understandings of behavior and choice to bear on law. The purpose of this introduction is to say something about the field and about the book's structure and content.

Constructed Preferences

Human preferences and values are constructed rather than elicited by social situations.[1] People do not walk around with menus in their heads: "[O]bserved preferences are not simply read off some master list; they are actually constructed during the elicitation process.... Different elicitation procedures highlight different aspects of options and suggest alternative heuristics, which give rise to inconsistent responses."[2] Human beings do not generally consult a freestanding "preference menu" from which selections are made at the moment of choice; preferences can be a product of procedure, description, and context at the time of choice: "Alternative descriptions of the same choice problems lead to systematically different preferences; strategically equivalent elicitation procedures give rise to different choices; and the preference between x and y often depends on the choice set within which they are embedded."[3]

Analysis of law should be linked with what we have been learning about human behavior and choice. After all, the legal system is pervasively in the business of constructing procedures, descriptions, and contexts for choice. Most obviously, the legal system creates procedures, descriptions, and contexts in the course of litigated cases. For example, the alternatives (selected to be) placed before a jury or judge may matter a great deal; liability or conviction on some count A may very much depend on the nature of counts B, C, and D (as suggested by Chapter 2). In this respect the preferences and values of judges and juries can be constructed, not elicited, by the legal system. Certainly this is true for the award of damages, where special problems may arise. But similar points hold outside of the courtroom. The legal system's original allocation of entitlements, and the structures created for exchange (or nonexchange) by law, may well affect people's preferences and values (as suggested by a number of papers in Part II). Thus law can construct rather than elicit preferences internally, by affecting what goes on in court, and externally, by affecting what happens in ordinary transactions, market and nonmarket.

We might distinguish among three different tasks of those interested in law: positive, prescriptive, and normative. Positive work is concerned with predictions. What will be the effects of law? Why does law take the form it does? If, contrary to conventional assumptions, people dislike losses far more than they like equivalent gains, predictions will go wrong insofar as they rest on conventional economic assumptions. As we will see, this point has important implications for positive analysis of law, prominently including the Coase Theorem, for which Ronald Coase received the Nobel Prize; indeed, behavioral law and economics shows that the Coase Theorem is often wrong (See chapters 8 and 10).

Prescriptive work is concerned with showing how society might actually reach our shared goals. If we want to decrease poverty, or save more lives, or decrease pollution, how can we do it? Consider the following information campaigns, which conventional analysis deems equivalent. (1) If you use energy conservation methods, you will save $X per year. (2) If you do not use energy conservation methods, you will lose $X per year. It turns out that information campaign (2) is far more effective than information campaign (1).[4] As we will see, important features of human judgment, properly understood, undermine conventional thinking about what will work best; they help explain, to take just one example, precisely why the public service advertising slogan "Drive defensively; watch out for the other guy" is particularly ingenious.

Normative work is of course concerned with what the legal system should do. Recent revisions in understanding human behavior greatly unsettle certain arguments against paternalism in law. They certainly do not make an affirmative case for paternalism, but they support a form of anti-anti-paternalism. If, for example, people use heuristic devices that lead to systematic errors, their judgments about how to deal with risks may be badly misconceived. If people are unrealistically optimistic, they may run risks because of a factually false belief in their own relative immunity from harm, even if they are fully aware of the statistical facts. And if people's choices are based on incorrect judgments about their experience *after choice*, there is reason to question whether respect for choices, rooted in those incorrect judgments, is a good way to promote utility or welfare. None of these points make a firm case for legal paternalism, not least because bureaucrats may be subject to the same cognitive and motivational distortions as everyone else. But they suggest that objections to paternalism should be empirical and pragmatic, having to do with the possibility of education and likely failures of government response, rather than being a priori in nature.

Heuristics and Biases

The first part of the book is concerned with heuristics and biases. It is now well established that people make decisions on the basis of heuristic devices, or rules of thumb, that may work well in many cases but that also lead to systematic errors. It is also well established that people suffer from various biases and aversions that can lead to inaccurate perceptions. Here is a very brief description of several biases and heuristics of particular relevance to law.

Biases

Extremeness Aversion. People are averse to extremes. Whether an option is extreme depends on the stated alternatives (See Chapter 2). Extremeness aversion gives rise to *compromise effects*. As between given alternatives, most people seek a compromise. Almost everyone has had the experience of switching to, say, the second most expensive item on some menu of options, and of doing so partly because of the presence of the most expensive item. In this as in other respects, the framing of choice matters; the introduction of (unchosen, apparently irrelevant) alternatives into the frame can alter the outcome. When, for example, people are choosing between some small radio A and a midsized radio B, most may well choose A; but the introduction of a third, large radio C is likely to lead many people to choose B instead. Thus the introduction of a third, unchosen (and in that sense irrelevant) option may produce a switch in choice as between two options.

Extremeness aversion suggests that a simple axiom of conventional economic theory – involving the irrelevance of added, unchosen alternatives –

is wrong. It also has large consequences for legal advocacy and judgment, as well as for predictions about the effects of law. How can a preferred option best be framed as the "compromise" choice? When should a lawyer argue in the alternative, and what kinds of alternative arguments are most effective? This should be a central question for advocates to answer. Juries and judges may well try to choose a compromise solution, and what "codes" as the compromise solution depends on what alternatives are made available. And in elections, medical interventions, and policy making, compromise effects may matter a great deal.

Hindsight Bias. According to a familiar cliché, hindsight has 20-20 vision. The cliché turns out to hold an important truth, one with considerable relevance to law. A great deal of evidence suggests that people often think, in hindsight, that things that happened were inevitable, or nearly so. The resulting "hindsight bias" can much distort legal judgment if, for example, juries end up thinking that an accident that occurred would inevitably have occurred. Judgments about whether someone was negligent may well be affected by this bias. Chapter 3 discusses hindsight bias in detail.

Optimistic Bias. Human beings tend to be optimistic. By itself this seems to be good news; but it can lead them to make big mistakes. Even factually informed people tend to think that risks are less likely to materialize for themselves than for others. Thus there is systematic overconfidence in risk judgments, as the vast majority of people believe that they are less likely than other people to be subject to automobile accidents, infection from AIDS, heart attacks, asthma, and many other health risks.[5] Reflecting illusions about their own practices, gay men appear systematically to underestimate the chance that they will get AIDS, even though they do not lack information about AIDS risks in general.[6] As Chapter 1 suggests, unrealistic optimism creates a distinctive problem for conventional objections to paternalism in law. If people tend to believe that they are relatively free from risks, they may lack accurate information even if they know statistical facts. As Chapters 5 and 11 suggest, optimistic bias is relevant to a number of areas of law and has some surprising implications.

Status Quo Bias. People tend to like the status quo, and they demand a great deal to justify departures from it. More specifically, people evaluate situations largely in accordance with their relation to a certain reference point; gains and losses from the reference point are crucial. This is a central finding of prospect theory. In law, an ordinary reference is the status quo, which produces status quo bias, an important phenomenon for the law; Chapter 4 discusses the relationship between contract law and status quo bias.

Heuristics

Behavioral economists and cognitive psychologists have uncovered a wide array of heuristic devices that people use to simplify their tasks.

Availability. People tend to think that risks are more serious when an incident is readily called to mind or "available." If pervasive, the availability heuristic will produce systematic errors. Assessments of risk will be pervasively biased, in the sense that people will think that some risks (of a nuclear accident, for example) are high, whereas others (of a stroke, for example) are relatively low. The availability heuristic appears to affect the demand for law (see Chapters 1, 13, and 15).

Anchoring. Often people make probability judgments on the basis of an initial value, or "anchor," for which they make insufficient adjustments.[7] The initial value may have an arbitrary or irrational source. When this is so, the probability assessment may go badly wrong. Jury judgments about damage awards, for example, are likely to be based on an anchor; this can produce a high level of arbitrariness.

Case-based Decisions. Because it is often difficult to calculate the expected costs and benefits of alternatives, people often simplify their burdens by reasoning from past cases,[8] and by taking small, reversible steps. This form of "case-based decision" plays an important role in courts, which tend to think analogically (see Chapter 7).

The various biases and heuristics raise a large question: Can individuals and institutions make metadecisions, or second-order decisions, that will make it more likely that things will go well? Chapter 7 discusses a number of possibilities.

Valuation

The second part of the book deals with valuation. How do people react to gains and to losses? The legal system frequently deals with dollars; can people think well about dollars? What are the characteristics of their thinking?

Loss Aversion. People are especially averse to losses. They are more displeased with losses than they are pleased with equivalent gains – roughly speaking, twice as displeased. Contrary to economic theory, people do not treat out-of-pocket costs and opportunity costs as if they were equivalent.

Loss aversion has important implications for positive analysis of law. It means, for example, that the Coase Theorem is in one respect quite wrong. Recall that the Coase Theorem proposes that when transaction costs are zero, the allocation of the initial entitlement will not matter, in the sense that it will not affect the ultimate state of the world, which will come from voluntary bargaining. The theorem is wrong because the allocation of the legal entitlement may well matter, for those who are initially allocated an entitlement are likely to value it more than will those without the legal entitlement. Thus workers allocated a (waivable) right to be discharged only for cause may well value that right far more than they would be if employers were allocated a (tradable) right to discharge at will. Thus breathers of air may well value their (tradable) right to be free from air pollution far more than they would if polluters had been given a (tradable) right to emit polluting substances into the air. The legal entitlement creates an *endowment effect*, that is, a greater valuation stemming from the mere fact of endowment. Chapters 8, 10, 12, and 13 relate this finding to a number of legal issues.

There is a further point. People are averse to losses, but whether an event "codes" as a loss or a gain depends not on simple facts but on a range of contextual factors, including how the event is framed. The status quo is usually the reference point, so that losses are understood as such by reference to existing distributions and practices; but it is possible to manipulate the frame so as to make a change code as a loss rather than a gain, or vice versa. Consider a company that says "cash discount" rather than "credit card surcharge," or a parent who says that for behavior X (rather than behavior Y) a child will be rewarded as opposed to saying that for behavior Y (rather than for behavior X) a child will be punished, or familiar advertisements to the effect that "you cannot afford not to" use a certain product. In environmental regulation, it is possible to manipulate the reference point by insisting that policy makers are trying to "restore" water or air quality to its state at time X; the restoration time matters a great deal to people's choices.[9]

For present purposes, the most important source of reference points is the law – where has the legal system placed the initial entitlement? Much of Part II discusses the effects of this initial allocation.

Loss aversion also raises serious questions about the goal of the tort system. Should damages measure the amount that would restore an injured party to the status quo ante, or should they reflect the amount that an injured party would demand to be subject to the injury before the fact? Juries appear to believe that the amount that would be demanded pre-injury is far greater than the amount that would restore the status quo ante. The legal system appears generally to see the compensation question as the latter one, though it does not seem to have made this choice in any systematic way. Chapter 10 treats this issue in detail.

Mental Accounting. A simple and apparently uncontroversial assumption of most economists is that money is fungible. But the assumption is false. Money comes in compartments. People create "frames" that result in mental accounts through which losses and gains, including losses and gains in simple monetary terms, are not fungible with each other. A glance at ordinary practice shows that people often organize decisions in terms of separate budgets and accounts. Thus some money is for retirement; some is for vacation; some is for college tuition; some is for mortgage or rental payments. Mental accounting is an important aspect of financial self-control, and the practice of mental accounting has a range of implications for law and policy. It suggests, for example, that government may be able to create certain mental accounts by creative policy making. It also suggests that there may be a demand for publicly created mental accounts, perhaps as a self-control strategy, as, for example, with Social Security and other programs with an apparent paternalistic dimension. Some statutes that appear to prevent people from making choices as they wish may be best understood as responsive to the widespread desire to have separate mental accounts. Of course, there are private mechanisms for accomplishing this goal, but lawyers will not understand those mechanisms well unless they see that money itself is not fungible. Chapter 11 deals with mental accounting in the context of legal rules.

The Difficulty, Outside of Markets, of Mapping Normative Judgments Onto Dollars. Often the legal system requires judges or juries to make judgments of some kind and then to translate those judgments into dollar amounts. How does this translation take place? Can it be done well? Chapter 9 suggests that in many contexts, normative judgments of a sort are both predictable and nonarbitrary. With respect to bad behavior that might produce punitive damages, for example, people come up with relatively uniform judgments on a bounded numerical scale. Similar findings have been made for environmental amenities in the context of contingent valuation. But the act of mapping those normative judgments onto an unbounded dollar scale produces considerable "noise" and arbitrariness. When people are asked how much they are willing to pay to protect two thousand birds, or how much a defendant should be punished for reckless conduct leading to personal injury, the numbers they generate seem to be stabs in the dark.

The legal system, however, frequently relies on just those stabs. Thus the award of damages for libel, sexual harassment, and pain and suffering is affected by severe difficulties, as is the award of punitive damages in general. An understanding of those difficulties may well lead to concrete reform proposals. Perhaps the "mapping" can occur by a legislative or regulatory body that decides, in advance, on how a normative judgment made by a bounded numerical scale can be translated into dollars.

The Demand for Law

The third part of the book deals with the demand for law. Why is law as it is? Behavioral law and economics provides some distinctive answers.

Self-serving bias. People's judgments about fairness are self-serving, and they tend to be both unrealistically optimistic and overconfident about their judgments. In any random couple, it is highly likely that addition of answers to the question "What percentage of the domestic work do you do?" will produce a number greater than 100 percent. The point bears on the otherwise largely inexplicable phenomenon of bargaining impasses (see Chapter 14). Why don't more cases settle? Why does the legal system spend so much on dispute settlement? Part of the answer lies in the fact that self-serving bias – a belief that one deserves more than other people tend to think – affects both parties to a negotiation, and this makes agreement very difficult.

Cooperation, Fairness, Spite, and Homo Reciprocans. Economists sometimes assume that people are self-interested, in the sense that they are focused on their own welfare rather than that of others, and in the sense that material welfare is what most concerns them. This is sometimes true, and often it is a useful simplifying assumption. But people also may want to be treated fairly and to act fairly, and, perhaps even more important, they want to be seen to act fairly, especially but not only among nonstrangers. For purposes of understanding law, what is especially important is that people may sacrifice their economic self-interest in order to be, or to appear, fair. Rather than being *homo economicus*, people may be *homo reciprocans*.[10]

Consider, for example, the ultimatum game (discussed in Chapter 1). The people who run the game give some money, on a provisional basis, to the first of two players. The first player is instructed to offer some part of the money to the second player. If the second player accepts that amount, he can keep what is offered, and the first player gets to keep the rest. But if the second player rejects the offer, neither player gets anything. Both players are informed that these are the rules. No bargaining is allowed. Using standard assumptions about rationality, self-interest, and choice, economists predict that the first player should offer a penny and the second player should accept. But this is not what happens. Offers usually average between 30 and 40 percent of the total. Offers of less than 20 percent are often rejected. Often there is a 50-50 division. These results cut across the level of the stakes and also across diverse cultures.

The results of the ultimatum game are highly suggestive. Perhaps people will not violate norms of fairness, even when doing so is in their economic self-interest, at least if the norm violations would be public. Do companies always raise prices when circumstances create short-term scarcity? For example, are there social constraints on price increases for snow shovels after a snowstorm, or for umbrellas during a rainstorm? It may well be that contracting parties are reluctant to take advantage of misfortune, partly because of social constraints on self-interested behavior. Here there is much room for future work. Experimental work shows a high degree of cooperation in Prisoner's Dilemma situations, especially when people are speaking with one another.[11] Chapter 12 shows that acrimony, or spite, can play an important role in determining legal outcomes.

Availability Again and Social Influences. We have seen that people make judgments about probability on the basis of judgments about available or easily retrievable instances. Moreover, the availability heuristic operates in an emphatically social environment. People often think and do what (they think) other people think and do. Partly this is because when a person lacks much personal information, he will sensibly rely on the information of others. If you don't know whether pesticides cause cancer, or whether hazardous waste dumps are a serious social problem, you may as well follow what other people seem to think. And partly this is because of reputational influences. If most people think that hazardous waste dumps are a serious social problem, or that laws should ban hate crimes, you might go along with them, so that they do not think that you are ignorant, malevolent, or callous. These points have a wide range of implications for the content of law. They help explain the supply of, and the demand for, government regulation. "Availability cascades" help drive law and policy in both fortunate and unfortunate directions (see Chapter 15).

The Future

Behavioral law and economics is in its very early stages, and an enormous amount remains to be done. Some of the outstanding questions are foundational and involve the nature of economics itself: Can behavioral economics generate a unitary theory of behavior, or is it an unruly collection of effects? Is it too ad hoc and unruly to generate predictions in the legal context? As compared with approaches based on ordinary rationality assumptions, does behavioral economics neglect the value of parsimony? In what sense is behavioral economics a form of economics at all?

Many unanswered questions are empirical, and these remain to be studied in both real-world and experimental settings. An especially important issue has to do with the possibility of increasing cooperative behavior and decreasing spiteful behavior. What are the preconditions for the two? When does law produce one or the other? From another direction, it would be highly desirable to have a full data set of jury awards in cases involving injuries that are hard to monetize (libel, pain and suffering, sexual harassment, and intentional infliction of emotional distress), and to see what factors account for high or large awards. Whether normative judgments are widely shared, and dollar awards widely divergent (as found in Chapter 9), is an intriguing issue in numerous areas of the law.

A very large question involves the extent to which education can counteract cognitive and motivational distortions, so as to eliminate some of the effects described above. (Some of these effects of course should not be considered distortions; people who care about reciprocity can keep themselves out of a lot of trouble.) Is it possible for those involved in law to "debias" people, in the process, perhaps, lengthening human lives? What institutions work best at reducing the effects of biases? Would a broader understanding of behavioral economics produce learning, and thus make it less necessary to use behavioral economics?

Despite its length, this book is intended above all as a beginning – to new and improved understandings of the real-world effects of law, and ultimately to better uses of law as an instrument of social ordering.

Notes

1 See Paul Slovic, The Construction of Preference, 50 *Am. Psychol.* 364 (1995); Amos Tversky, Rational Theory and Constructive Choice, in *The Rational Foundations of Economic Behavior* (Kenneth Arrow et al. eds., 1996).
2 Amos Tversky, Shmuel Sattath, and Paul Slovic, Contingent Weighting in Judgment and Choice, 95 *Psychol. Rev.* 371 (1988).
3 Tversky, supra note 1, at 186.
4 See Elliot Aronson, *The Social Animal* 124–5 (6th ed. 1996).
5 See Neil Weinstein, Optimistic Biases About Personal Risks, 246 *Science* 1232 (1989).
6 Laurie Bauman and Karolyn Siegel, Misperception Among Gay Men of the Risk for AIDS Associated with Their Sexual Behavior, 17 J. *Applied Soc. Psychol.* 329 (1987).
7 See David Kahneman and Amos Tversky, Judgment Under Uncertainty: Heuristics and Biases in Judgment Under Uncertainty 3 (David Kahneman et al. eds., 1982).
8 See Itzhak Gilboa and David Schmeidler, Case-Based Decision Theory, 110 *Q.J. Econ.* 605 (1995).
9 See Robin Gregory, Sarah Lichtenstein, and D. MacGregor, The Role of Past States in Determining Reference Points for Policy Decisions, 55 *Org. Behav. & Hum. Decision Processes* 195 (1993).
10 See Ernst Fehr and Simon Gachter, How Effective Are Trust- and Reciprocity-Based Incentives, in *Economics, Values, and Organization* 337 (Avner Ben-Ner and Louis Putterman eds., 1998).
11 See *The Handbook of Experimental Economics* 111–73 (John H. Kagel and Alvin E. Roth eds., 1995) for an overview. There is thus a close relation between some behavioral research and the growing and apparently independent interest in regulation via social norms. See also R. Ellickson, *Order Without Law* (1991). I believe that ultimately these two lines of inquiry will merge into a unitary field of inquiry.

Part I

Overview and Prospects

1 A Behavioral Approach to Law and Economics

Christine Jolls, Cass R. Sunstein, and Richard H. Thaler

Our goal in this chapter is to advance an approach to the economic analysis of law that is informed by a more accurate conception of choice, one that reflects a better understanding of human behavior and its wellsprings. We build on and attempt to generalize earlier work in law outlining behavioral findings by taking the two logical next steps: proposing a systematic framework for a behavioral approach to economic analysis of law, and using behavioral insights to develop specific models and approaches addressing topics of abiding interest in law and economics. The analysis of these specific topics is preliminary and often in the nature of a proposal for a research agenda; we touch on a wide range of issues in an effort to show the potential uses of behavioral insights.

We suggest that an approach based on behavioral economics will help with the three functions of any proposed approach to law: positive, prescriptive, and normative. The positive task, perhaps most central to economic analysis of law and our principal emphasis here, is to explain both the effects and content of law. How will law affect human behavior? What will individuals' likely response to changes in the rules be? Why does law take the form that it does? The prescriptive task is to see how law might be used to achieve specified ends, such as deterring socially undesirable behavior. The normative task is to assess more broadly the ends of the legal system. Behavioral analysis suggests problems with conventional economic arguments against paternalism – based on the view that citizens invariably understand and pursue their own best interests – but also problems with many forms of government intervention, since bureaucrats are, after all, behavioral actors too.

Foundations: What Is "Behavioral Law and Economics"?

In order to identify, in a general way, the defining features of behavioral law and economics, it is useful first to understand the defining features of law and economics. As we understand it, this approach to the law posits that legal rules are best analyzed and understood in light of standard economic principles. Gary Becker offers a typical account of those principles: "[A]ll human behavior can be viewed as involving participants who (1) maximize their utility (2) from a stable set of preferences and (3) accumulate an optimal amount of information and other inputs in a variety of markets."[1] The task of law and economics is to determine the implications of such rational maximizing behavior in and out of markets, and its legal implications for markets and other institutions.

What then is the task of behavioral law and economics? How does it differ from standard law and economics? These are the questions we address below.

Homo Economicus and Real People

The task of behavioral law and economics, simply stated, is to explore the implications of actual (not hypothesized) human behavior for the law. How do "real people" differ from *homo economicus*? We will describe the differences by stressing three important "bounds" on human behavior, bounds that draw into question the central ideas of utility maximization, stable preferences, rational expectations, and optimal processing of information.[2] People can be said to display bounded rationality, bounded willpower, and bounded self-interest.

All three bounds are well documented in the literature of other social sciences, but they are relatively unexplored in economics (although there is a burgeoning recent literature). Each of these bounds represents a significant way in which most people depart from the standard economic model. While there are instances in which more than one bound comes into play, at this stage we think it is best to conceive of them as separate modeling problems. Nonetheless, each of the three bounds points to systematic (rather than random or arbitrary) departures from conventional economic models, and thus each of the three bears on generating sound predictions and prescriptions for law.

Bounded Rationality. Bounded rationality, an idea first introduced by Herbert Simon, refers to the obvious fact that human cognitive abilities are not infinite.[3] We have limited computational skills and seriously flawed memories. People can respond sensibly to these failings; thus it might be said that people sometimes respond rationally to their own cognitive limitations, minimizing the sum of decision costs and error costs. To deal with limited memories we make lists. To deal with limited brain power and time we use mental shortcuts and rules of thumb. But even with these remedies, and in some cases because of these remedies, human behavior differs in systematic ways from that predicted by the standard economic model of unbounded rationality. Even when the use of mental shortcuts is rational, it can produce predictable mistakes. The departures from the standard model can be divided into two categories: judgment and decision making. Actual judgments show systematic departures from models of unbiased forecasts, and actual decisions often violate the axioms of expected utility theory.

A major source of differences between actual judgments and unbiased forecasts is the use of rules of thumb. As stressed in the pathbreaking work of Daniel Kahneman and Amos Tversky, rules of thumb such as the availability heuristic – in which the frequency of some event is estimated by judging how easy it is to recall other instances of this type (how "available" such instances are) – lead us to erroneous conclusions. People tend to conclude, for example, that the probability of an event (such as a car accident) is greater if they have recently witnessed an occurrence of that event than if they have not.[4] What is especially important in the work of Kahneman and Tversky is that it shows that shortcuts and rules of thumb are predictable. While the heuristics are useful on average (which explains how they become adopted), they lead to errors in particular circumstances. This means that someone using such a rule of thumb may be behaving rationally in the sense of economizing on thinking time, but such a person will nonetheless make forecasts that are different from those that emerge from the standard rational-choice model.

Just as unbiased forecasting is not a good description of actual human behavior, expected utility theory is not a good description of actual decision making. While the axioms of expected utility theory characterize rational choice, actual choices diverge in important ways from this model, as has been known since the early experiments by Allais and Ellsberg.[5] There has been an explosion of research in recent years trying to develop better formal models of actual decision making. The model offered by Kahneman and Tversky, called prospect theory, seems to do a good job of explaining many features of observed behavior, and so we draw on that model here.[6]

Bounded Willpower. In addition to bounded rationality, people often display bounded willpower. This term refers to the fact that human beings often take actions that they know to be in conflict with their own long-term interests. Most smokers say they would prefer not to smoke, and many pay money to join a program or obtain a drug that will help them quit. As with bounded rationality, many people recognize that they have bounded willpower and take steps to mitigate its effects. They join a pension plan or "Christmas Club" (a special savings arrangement under which funds can be withdrawn only around the holidays) to prevent undersaving, and they don't keep tempting desserts around the house when trying to diet. In some cases they may vote for or support governmental policies, such as Social Security, to eliminate any temptation to succumb to the desire for immediate rewards. Thus, the demand for and supply of law may reflect people's understanding of their own (or others') bounded willpower; consider "cooling off" periods for certain sales and programs that facilitate or even require saving.

Bounded Self-interest. Finally, we use the term bounded self-interest to refer to an important fact about the utility function of most people: They care, or act as if they care, about others, even strangers, in some circumstances. (Thus, we are not questioning here the idea of utility maximization, but rather the common assumptions about what that entails.) Our notion is distinct from simple altruism, which conventional economics has emphasized in areas such as bequest decisions. Self-interest is bounded in a much broader range of settings than conventional economics assumes, and the bound operates in ways different from what the conventional understanding suggests. In many market and bargaining settings (as opposed to nonmarket settings such as bequest decisions), people care about being treated fairly and want to treat others fairly if those others are themselves behaving fairly. As a result of these concerns, the agents in a behavioral economic model are both nicer and (when they are not treated fairly) more spiteful than the agents postulated by neoclassical theory. Formal models have been used to show how people deal with both fairness and unfairness; we will draw on those models here.

Applications. When is each bound likely to come into play? Any general statement will necessarily be incomplete, but some broad generalizations can be offered. First, bounded rationality as it relates to judgment behavior will come into play whenever actors in the legal system are called upon to assess the probability of an uncertain event. Second, bounded rationality as it relates to decision-making behavior will come into play whenever actors are valuing outcomes. Bounded willpower is most relevant when decisions have consequences over time; our example is criminal behavior, where the benefits are generally immediate and the costs deferred. Finally, bounded self-interest (as we use the term) is relevant primarily in situations in which one party has deviated substantially from the usual or ordinary conduct under the circumstances; in such circumstances the other party will often be willing to incur financial costs to punish the "unfair" behavior.

Testable Predictions

Behavioral and conventional law and economics do not differ solely in their assumptions about human behavior. They also differ, in testable ways, in their predictions about how law (as well as other forces) affects behavior. Behavioral law and economics is, we claim, law and economics with a higher "R^2" – that is, greater power to explain observed data. To make the differences between the behavioral and standard approaches more concrete, consider the three "fundamental principles of economics" set forth by Richard Posner in his *Economic Analysis of Law*,[7] in a discussion that is, on these points, quite conventional. To what extent would an account based on behavioral law and economics offer different "fundamental principles"?

The first fundamental principle for the conventional approach is downward-sloping demand: total demand for a good falls when its price rises. This prediction is, of course, valid. However, confirmation of the prediction of downward-sloping demand does not suggest that people are optimizing. As Becker has shown, even people choosing at random (rather than in a way designed to serve their preferences) will tend to consume less of a good when its price goes up as long as they have limited resources.[8] This behavior has also been demonstrated with laboratory rats.[9] Thus, evidence of downward-sloping demand is not evidence in support of optimizing models.

The second fundamental principle of conventional law and economics concerns the nature of costs: "Cost to the economist is 'opportunity cost,'" and "'[s]unk' (incurred) costs do not affect decisions on prices and quantity."[10] Thus, according to traditional analysis, decision makers will equate opportunity costs (which are costs incurred by foregoing opportunities – say, the opportunity to sell one's possessions) to out-of-pocket costs (such as costs incurred in buying possessions); and they will ignore sunk costs (costs that cannot be recovered, such as the cost of nonrefundable tickets). But each of these propositions is a frequent source of predictive failures. The equality of opportunity costs and out-of-pocket costs implies that, in the absence of important wealth effects, buying prices will be roughly equal to selling prices. This is frequently violated, as is well known. Many people holding tickets to a popular sporting event such as the Super Bowl would be unwilling to buy tickets at the market price (say $1,000), yet would also be unwilling to sell at this price. Indeed, estimates of the ratio of selling prices to buying prices are often at least two to one, yet the size of the transaction makes it implausible in these studies to conclude that wealth effects explain the difference.[11] As described below, these results are just what behavioral analysis suggests.

The traditional assumption about sunk costs also generates invalid predictions. Here is one: A theater patron who ignores sunk costs would not take into account the cost of a prepaid season pass in deciding whether to go out on the evening of a particular performance;[12] but in a study of theater patrons, some of whom were randomly assigned to receive discounted prices on prepaid passes, the patrons who received discounts were found to attend significantly fewer performances than those who did not receive discounts, despite the fact that (due to random assignment) the benefit-cost ratio that should have mattered – benefits and costs going forward – was the same on average in the two groups.[13] In short, sunk costs mattered; again, the standard prediction proved invalid.

The third fundamental principle of conventional law and economics is that "resources tend to gravitate toward their most valuable uses" as markets drive out any unexploited profit opportunities.[14] When combined with the notion that opportunity and out-of-pocket costs are equated (see fundamental principle two), this yields the Coase Theorem – the idea that initial assignments of entitlements will not affect the ultimate allocation of resources so long as transaction costs are zero.[15] Many economists and economically oriented lawyers think of the Coase Theorem as a tautology; if there were really no transaction costs (and no wealth effects), and if an alternative allocation of resources would make some agents better off and none worse off, then of course the agents would move to that allocation. Careful empirical study, however, shows that the Coase Theorem is not a tautology; indeed, it can lead to inaccurate predictions (see Chapter 8). That is, even when transaction costs and wealth effects are known to be zero, initial entitlements alter the final allocation of resources. These results are predicted by behavioral economics, which emphasizes the difference between opportunity and out-of-pocket costs.

Consider the following set of experiments (described more fully in Chapter 8) conducted to test the Coase Theorem; let us offer an interpretation geared to the particular context of economic analysis of law. The subjects were forty-four students taking an advanced undergraduate course in law and economics at Cornell University. Half the students were endowed with tokens. Each student (whether or not endowed with a token) was assigned a personal token value, the price at which a token could be redeemed for cash at the end of the experiment; these assigned values induce supply and demand curves for the tokens. Markets were conducted for tokens. Those without tokens could buy one, while those with tokens could sell. Those with tokens should (and do) sell their tokens if offered more than their assigned value; those without tokens should (and do) buy tokens if they can get one at a price below their assigned value. These token markets are a complete victory of economic theory. The equilibrium price was always exactly what the theory would predict, and the tokens did in fact flow to those who valued them most.

However, life is generally not about tokens redeemable for cash. Thus another experiment was conducted, identical to the first except that now half the students were given Cornell coffee mugs instead of tokens. Here behavioral analysis generates a prediction distinct from standard economic analysis: Because people do not equate opportunity and out-of-pocket costs for goods whose values are not solely exogenously defined (as they were in the case of the tokens), those endowed with mugs should be reluctant to part with them even at prices they would not have considered paying to acquire a mug had they not received one.

Was this prediction correct? Yes. Markets were conducted and mugs bought and sold. Unlike the case of the tokens, the assignment of property rights had a pronounced effect on the final allocation of mugs. The students who were assigned mugs had a strong tendency to keep them. Whereas the Coase Theorem would have predicted that about half the mugs would trade (since transaction costs had been shown to be essentially zero in the token experiments, and mugs were randomly distributed), instead only 15 percent of the mugs traded. And those who were endowed with mugs asked more than twice as much to give up a mug as those who didn't get a mug were willing to pay. This result did not change if the markets were repeated. This effect is generally referred to as the "endowment effect"; it is a manifestation of the broader phenomenon of "loss aversion" – the idea that losses are weighted more heavily than gains – which in turn is a central building block of Kahneman and Tversky's prospect theory.

There are at least three important lessons here. First, markets are indeed robust institutions. Even naive subjects participating at low stakes produce outcomes indistinguishable from those predicted by the theory *when trading for tokens*. Second, when agents must determine their own values (as with the mugs), outcomes can diverge substantially from those predicted by economic theory. Third, these departures will not be obvious outside an experiment, even when they exist and have considerable importance. That is, even in the mugs markets, there was trading; there was just not as much trading as the theory would predict. These lessons can be applied to other markets; we offer some examples below.

The Role of Market Forces

In some (fairly unusual) circumstances, such as futures trading, market forces are strong enough to make the three "bounds" irrelevant for predictive purposes. The point is important; it suggests that while human beings often display bounded rationality, willpower, and self-interest, markets can sometimes lead to behavior consistent with conventional economic assumptions. Then the question becomes when, exactly, do market forces make it reasonable to assume that people behave in accordance with those assumptions? What circumstances apply to most of the domains in which law and economics is used?

In this regard it is instructive to compare the market for futures contracts with the market for criminal activity. Consider the proposition that a potential criminal will commit some crime if the expected gains from the crime exceed its expected costs.[16] Suppose a criminal mistakenly thinks that the expected gains outweigh the expected costs, when in fact the opposite is true. First notice that no arbitrage will be possible in this situation. If someone is unfortunate enough to commit a crime with a negative expected value, then there is no way for anyone else to profit directly from his behavior. Outside of financial markets (and not always there), those who engage in low-payoff activities lose utility but do not create profit opportunities for others. Nor do they typically disappear from the market. (Even poorly run firms can survive for many years; consider GM.) Being a bad criminal is rarely fatal, and except possibly for organized crime, there is little opportunity for "hostile takeovers." Finally, the decision to enter a life of crime is not one that is made repeatedly with many opportunities to learn. Once a teenager has dropped out of high school to become a drug dealer, it is difficult to switch to dentistry.

Parsimony

A possible objection to our approach is that conventional economics has the advantage of simplicity and parsimony. At least – the objection goes – it provides a theory. By contrast, a behavioral perspective offers a more complicated and unruly picture of human behavior, and perhaps that picture will make prediction more difficult, precisely because behavior is more complicated and unruly. Everything can be explained in an ex post fashion – some tool will be found that is up to the task – but the elegance, generalizability, and predictive power of the economic method will be lost. Shouldn't analysts proceed with simple tools? We offer two responses. First, simplicity and parsimony are indeed beneficial; it would be highly desirable to come up with a model of behavior that is both simple and right. But conventional economics is not in this position, for its predictions are often wrong.

Second, to the extent that conventional economics achieves parsimony, it often does so at the expense of any real predictive power. Its goal is to provide a unitary theory of behavior, a goal that may be impossible to achieve. By itself the notion of "rationality" (the centerpiece of traditional analysis) is not a theory; to generate predictions it must be more fully specified, often through the use of auxiliary assumptions. Indeed, the term "rationality" is highly ambiguous and can be used to mean many things. A person might be deemed rational if her behavior (1) conforms to the axioms of expected utility theory; (2) is responsive to incentives, that is, if the actor changes her behavior when the costs and benefits are altered; (3) is internally consistent; (4) promotes her own welfare; or (5) is effective in achieving her goals, whatever the relationship between those goals and her actual welfare. We observe departures from most of these definitions; thus, with respect to (1), scholars have documented departures from expected utility theory for nearly fifty years, and prospect theory seems to predict behavior better. With respect to (4) and (5), people's decisions sometimes do not promote their welfare or help them to achieve their own goals; and with respect to (3), behavioral research shows that people sometimes behave in an inconsistent manner by, for example, indicating a preference for X over Y if asked to make a direct choice, but Y over X if asked to give their willingness to pay for each option.[17] Many of our examples will thus show that people are frequently not rational if the term is understood to mean (1), (3), (4), or (5). As for (2), without some specification of what counts as a cost and a benefit, the idea of responsiveness to incentives is empty. If rationality is used to mean simply that people "choose" what they "prefer" in light of the prevailing incentives, then the notion of rationality offers few restrictions on behavior. The person who drinks castor oil as often as possible is rational because she happens to love castor oil. Other self-destructive behavior (drug addiction, suicide, etc.) can be explained on similar grounds. It is not even clear on this view whether rationality is intended as a definition of "preference" or as a prediction.

If such a notion of rationality allowed for good predictions, then perhaps there would be no reason for complaint; the problem, however, is that so high a degree of flexibility leaves the theory with few a priori restrictions. A theory with infinite degrees of freedom is no theory at all. For example, consider whether it is a paradox (as many economists think) that so many people vote (despite the virtual certainty that no one person's vote will alter the outcome). If it is a paradox, so much the worse for the rationality assumption; if it is not a paradox, what does the assumption predict? Does it merely predict that people will respond to changes in conditions – for example, fewer people will vote when it is snowing? If so, the prediction is not bad, but surely it would be possible to say, after an unusually large vote amid the storm, that more people voted simply because voting seemed especially valiant in those circumstances (so much for predictions based on this form of rationality). Conventional economics sometimes turns to stronger forms of rationality in response, and those forms provide stronger predictions in some cases; but those predictions are often inaccurate, as described above and as illustrated by the examples considered below.

We now turn to positive, prescriptive, and normative issues. Our purpose is not to settle all of them, but to show the promise of behavioral economics in casting light on a wide range of questions. A great deal of work would be necessary to justify authoritative judgments on most of these questions. What follows should be taken partly as a proposal, perhaps in the spirit of the early economic analysis of law, for a research agenda to be carried out with a new set of tools.

Behavior of Agents

The Ultimatum Game and Fairness

The Game and Its Sunk-Cost Variation. We begin with bounded self-interest, the third bound described above. A useful first example of this bound is agents' behavior in a very simple bargaining game called the ultimatum game. In this game, one player, the Proposer, is asked to propose an allocation of a sum of money between herself and the other player, the Responder. The Responder then has a choice. He can either accept the amount offered to him by the Proposer, leaving the rest to the Proposer, or he can reject the offer, in which case both players get nothing. Neither player knows the identity of his or her counterpart, and the players will play against each other only once, so reputations and future retaliation are eliminated as factors.

Economic theory has a simple prediction about this game. The Proposer will offer the smallest unit of currency available, say a penny, and the Responder will accept, since a penny is better than nothing. This turns out to be a very bad prediction about how the game is actually played. Responders typically reject offers of less than 20 percent of the total amount available; the average minimum amount that Responders say they would accept is between 20 and 30 percent of that sum.[18] Responders are thus willing to punish unfair behavior, even at a financial cost to themselves. This is a form of bounded self-interest. And this response seems to be expected and anticipated by Proposers; they typically offer a substantial portion of the sum to be divided – ordinarily 40 to 50 percent.[19]

Economists often worry that the results of this type of experiment are sensitive to the way in which the experiment was conducted. What would happen if the stakes were raised substantially, or if the game was repeated several times to allow learning? In this case, we know the answer. To a first approximation, neither of these factors changes the results in any important way. Raising the stakes from $10 per pair to $100, or even to more than a week's income (in a poor country) has little effect; the same is true of repeating the game ten times with different partners.[20] (Of course, at some point raising the stakes would matter; probably few people would turn down an offer of 5 percent of $1,000,000.) We do not see behavior moving toward the prediction of standard economic theory.

Thus, the factors that many economists thought would change the outcome of the game did not. But, as we learned in a study conducted for this chapter, a factor that economic theory predicts will not have an effect, namely the introduction of a sunk cost, does have an effect. As noted above, economics predicts that decision makers will ignore sunk costs in making their choices (see fundamental principle two above); but in fact decision makers often do not behave in this way. Do sunk costs alter behavior in the ultimatum game? To find out, we asked classroom volunteers to bring $5 – what would become a sunk cost for them – to class. Students were given a form asking them how they would play both roles in an ultimatum game in which the $10 to be divided was contributed half by the Proposer and half by the Responder. They were told that their role would be determined by chance, so they had to decide first what offer to make if they were chosen to be a Proposer and then what minimum offer they would be willing to accept if they were a Responder.[21] We also ran a version of the standard ultimatum game (without sunk costs by the students) as a control.

Although economic theory says that the sunk-cost variation of the ultimatum game will have no effect on behavior (since the $5 collected from each student is a sunk cost and should therefore be ignored by the players), we predicted that in this domain sunk costs would matter. In particular, we anticipated that Responders would feel that they had an "entitlement" to the $5 they had contributed to the experiment and would therefore be reluctant to accept less. This is precisely what we found. In the original version of the game, when the $10 to be divided was provided to subjects by the experimenter, the average minimum amount demanded by Responders was $1.94. In the sunk-cost version, where the students each paid $5 to

Table 1.1. *Ultimatum Game Results*

	Average Demand	Percent Demanding $4.00	Percent Demanding $5.00
MIT MBA	$3.21	61%	32%
UC MBA	3.73	67	40
UC Law	3.35	47	23

participate, the average demand was $3.21 for a group of MIT MBA students, $3.73 for a group of University of Chicago (UC) MBA students, and $3.35 for a group of UC Law students (see Table 1.1). Each of these means is significantly different from the control value of $1.94 under any conventional measure of statistical significance. Looking past means, 61 percent of the MIT students demanded at least $4.00, and 32 percent demanded a full refund of their $5.00. For UC MBA students, 67 percent demanded at least $4.00, and 40 percent demanded $5.00. The UC Law students were slightly less extreme: 47 percent demanded at least $4.00, and 23 percent demanded $5.00.

Note that our emphasis here, as well as in the ordinary ultimatum game, is on the fairness behavior of Responders, not on affirmative concerns for fairness on the part of Proposers. (As noted above, their behavior appears fully consistent with financially maximizing responses to Responders' fairness behavior; other experimental results support this conclusion.)[22] We do know, however, that in other contexts people appear to display affirmative concerns for fairness.[23]

The fairness results obtained in various experimental settings, such as the ultimatum game, cannot be explained on grounds of reputation. The parties are interacting anonymously and in a one-shot fashion. Of course, many real-world situations may reflect a combination of reputational and fairness factors. The ultimatum game results show that people will often behave in accordance with fairness considerations even when it is against their financial self-interest *and no one will know*. Thus, for instance, most people leave tips in out-of-town restaurants that they never plan to visit again.

Fairness, Acrimony, and Scruples. *Theoretical considerations*. How can economic analysis be enriched to incorporate the behavior observed in the ultimatum game and its sunk-cost variant? As we have indicated, the first step is to relax the assumption, common to most economic theorizing, of "unbounded self-interest." This assumption implies that Proposers should offer the smallest sum possible, and Responders should accept. An alternative view is offered in the following account:

In the rural areas around Ithaca it is common for farmers to put some fresh produce on a table by the road. There is a cash box on the table, and customers are expected to put money in the box in return for the vegetables they take. The box has just a small slit, so money can only be put in, not taken out. Also, the box is attached to the table, so no one can (easily) make off with the money. We think that the farmers who use this system have just about the right model of human nature. They feel that enough people will volunteer to pay for the fresh corn to make it worthwhile to put it out there. The farmers also know that if it were easy to take the money, someone would do so.[24]

We emphasize that this is not a story of simple altruism. As noted, such altruism is sometimes recognized in conventional economics; our account, in contrast, is a more complicated story of reciprocal fairness. A concern for fairness is part of most agents' utility function. The results of the ultimatum game, like the behavior of the Ithaca shoppers, cannot readily be explained on grounds of simple altruism. First of all, the games are played between anonymous strangers. What reason is there to believe that these people care about one another? (Most of us give little of our wealth to anonymous strangers whom we have no reason to believe are any worse off than we are. Similarly, most people driving by a farm do not pull over and stuff two dollars through the mail slot, even in Ithaca. Fairness behavior is probably reciprocal.) Second, we observe not only apparently "nice" behavior (generous offers) but also "spiteful" behavior (Responders turning down small offers at substantial cost to the Proposers). In the ultimatum game, people appear simultaneously nicer and more spiteful than conventional assumptions predict.

The sort of balanced conception of human nature suggested by the ultimatum game results and the practices of farmers in Ithaca need not be informal or ad hoc. It is possible to incorporate material and nonmaterial motives, such as the desire to be fair (to those who have been fair) and also to be spiteful (to those who have not been fair), in a rigorous analysis. An elegant formal treatment is offered by Matthew Rabin in a model of fairness.[25] Rabin's framework incorporates three stylized facts about behavior. Stated simply and nonformally:

A. People are willing to sacrifice their own material well-being to help those who are being kind.
B. People are willing to sacrifice their own material well-being to punish those who are being unkind.
C. Both motivations (A) and (B) have a greater effect on behavior as the material cost of sacrificing becomes smaller.[26]

Rabin shows how these assumptions about behavior can explain the behavior observed in the ultimatum game as well as other games of cooperation such as the Prisoner's Dilemma. Related work, bearing on the appropriate role of law, has shown the role of such behavior in helping to produce norms that solve collective action problems.[27]

Rabin's theory can be viewed as a theory of manners and principles. Generalizing from Rabin's treatment, we might say that people can be understood as having preferences for (1) their own material payoffs and (2) those of some others they know well, and in addition they have preferences about (3) the well-being of some strangers whose interests are at stake, (4) their own reputation, and (5) what kind of person they wish to be. A person's willingness to cooperate or to help others can be seen as a function of these variables. The last factor is important and especially easy to overlook; the desire to think of yourself as an honest, principled person helps explain why most of us (though not all) do leave tips in strange restaurants and would leave money in the box at the roadside stand. As Rabin says, people are willing to sacrifice their own material well-being to help those who are being or have been kind. Of course, these desires compete with others in a world of scarce resources. We don't recommend that Mercedes dealers adopt the roadside stand selling technique.

Thus behavioral economic agents have manners and scruples that can lead them to be "nice" in some settings. But, as we observe in the ultimatum game, people can also be provoked to be spiteful. Sometimes the fact that another person will lose, in a material or other sense, is a benefit to the agent; these are the conditions for spite. An agent may calculate that the costs of benefiting another person argue strongly against a deal, even if the agent would benefit materially. Thus Responders who receive (relatively) small offers are willing to decline them in order to punish the rude Proposers who tried to grab too much for themselves, even when the small offer is a substantial amount of money. Notice that this spiteful behavior is also "principled": People are willing to pay to punish someone who has been unfair. This is the same behavior that drives boycotts, in which consumers refrain from buying something they normally enjoy in order to punish an offending party. Conventional economics has sometimes recognized such behavior, but it has received little attention in law and economics, where, unfortunately, it may often be quite relevant.[28]

Spiteful behavior is common under conditions of acrimony, such as during a fight or argument. Under these circumstances, even married couples will say and do things to hurt the other party; under bad conditions, the hurting, material or otherwise, is part of the agent's gain. A loss to another is a gain to oneself; even the idea of thinking of oneself as a certain kind of person (not a doormat or a dupe) can lead in the direction of inflicting losses. (Concern with not establishing a reputation as a doormat or a dupe may also play a role.) This is of course the converse of circumstances of cooperative behavior. Unfortunately, acrimony is particularly prevalent in many legal settings, before, during, and after litigation. Much protracted litigation – cases that fail to settle early and amicably – may arise precisely because the two sides were unable to deal with matters in a more friendly manner. (Divorces that end up in court are, almost by definition, acrimonious.) We suspect that spiteful behavior is frequently observed in conditions of acrimony even when reputational concerns are unimportant; for example, we think that the average contestant in a divorce case that ends up in court would be likely, in the role of Responder in the ultimatum game playing against his soon-to-be-ex-spouse, to reject low offers, not wanting the Proposer to benefit greatly.[29]

What is "Fair"? Absent acrimony, spiteful behavior – such as rejection of small offers in the ultimatum game – is typically observed in situations where one party has violated a perceived "norm of fairness." This raises an obvious question: What is "fair"? In the ultimatum game, most people regard an offer of, say, a penny to the Responder as "unfair." This perception is an illustration of a more general pattern: People judge outcomes to be "unfair" if they depart substantially from the terms of a "reference transaction" – a transaction that defines the benchmark for the parties' interactions.[30] When the interactions are between bargainers dividing a sum of money to which neither is more entitled than the other (and this is common knowledge), the "reference transaction" is something like an equal split; substantial departures are viewed as unfair and, accordingly, punished by Responders. If parties are bargaining over the division of money and both have reason to view one side as more entitled than the other, then the "reference transaction" is a split that favors the more-entitled party.[31] And if the parties are a consumer and a firm in the market, the "reference transaction" is a transaction on the usual terms for the item in question.[32] We will have much more to say about this last context below. For now our goal is simply to offer our general definition of what is "fair" and to make clear that we do not view the term as a vague and ill-defined catch-all. Rather, we view it as having a reasonably well-specified meaning that can generate useful predictions across a range of contexts.

Norms. Fairness-related norms are a subset of a large category of norms that govern behavior and that can operate as "taxes" or "subsidies." An analysis like that above could be undertaken for many decisions in which people care not only about material self-interest but also about their reputations and their self-conception – for example, through purchasing books, suits, and vacation spots, or through smoking, recycling, and discriminating on the basis of race and sex, or through choosing friends, restaurants, and automobiles. A better understanding of the ingredients of individual utility could help a great deal with both the positive and prescriptive analysis of law. For example, it might help us understand more about (and be better able to predict in related contexts in the future) the massive changes in behavior that have followed largely unenforced bans on smoking in public places – the phenomenon of "compliance without enforcement."[33]

Bargaining Around Court Orders

Coasian Prediction. As noted above, an important aspect of law and economics is the Coase Theorem, which says that the assignment of a legal entitlement will not influence the ultimate allocation of that entitlement when transaction costs and wealth effects are zero. A straightforward application of this idea is that when a court enters a judgment, whether in the form of an injunction or a damage award, the parties are likely to bargain to a different outcome if that outcome is preferable to what the court did and the transaction costs and wealth effects are small. (Thus, for instance, if the court enters a prohibitively high damage award but the activity in question is efficient, the parties should bargain for a lower damage level, since this would increase the surplus to be shared between them.) To whom an entitlement is allocated after litigation, and how it is protected (by a property rule or a liability rule), are irrelevant to the ultimate allocation of the entitlement in these circumstances.

Behavioral Analysis. Influenced by behavioral economics, many legal commentators have observed that in light of the endowment effect described above (an aspect of prospect theory, and thus an instance of bounded rationality), the assignment of a legal entitlement may well affect the outcome of bargaining, even when transaction costs (as conventionally defined) and wealth effects are zero. This conclusion is suggested by the mugs experiments described above, as well as by a substantial body of other evidence on the endowment effect.[34] Although the endowment effect suggests generally that the assignment of a legal entitlement may affect the outcome of bargaining, such an effect is especially likely when the entitlement is in the form of a court order obtained after legal proceedings between opposing parties (our focus here). This is so for several reasons.

First, the process of going through litigation may strengthen the endowment effect. Experimental evidence suggests that there is an especially strong endowment effect when a party believes that he has earned the entitlement or that he particularly deserves it.[35] Of course someone who has received a court judgment in his favor will believe that he has earned it. Such a person may also believe strongly that this outcome is fair, based on the self-serving bias discussed in the following section.

Bounded self-interest, and specifically the acrimony notions developed above, provide an additional reason we might expect less bargaining in real-world settings than in law and economics texts. Even if there are financial gains from making a deal, it is difficult to bargain without communication, and litigants are often not on speaking terms by the end of a protracted trial. Even if communication is possible, bargains are unlikely to be struck when both sides take pleasure in making the other side worse off; in such circumstances it can be difficult to reach agreements on settlements even if they would substantially improve the lot of both parties. For all of these reasons, behavioral research suggests that injunctions and damage awards may stick even with low transaction costs (as conventionally defined).

It is of course true that most cases settle, so that those which do not, and which thus produce court orders, may be atypical in some respects. But that does not mean they are unimportant objects of study for purposes of positive analysis. With conventional law and economics, behavioral analysis is concerned with the fact (and the consequences of the fact) that some cases proceed to trial.[36]

Evidence. Conventional economic theory and behavioral analysis thus generate distinct predictions about what happens after trials. These theories can therefore be tested with empirical evidence. What happens once a court judgment has been entered? How often do the parties bargain to a different outcome? Consider the set of cases where the court has assigned an entitlement to the party who values it less. In these circumstances, the standard theory would predict contracting around the court order whenever transaction costs (as conventionally defined) and wealth effects are small. (The possibility of asymmetric information is discussed below in connection with the existing empirical findings.) The behavioral theory predicts that even in such cases, there will often be no recontracting. Since it is unlikely that court orders are, across the board, uniquely efficient, it should be possible to test these differing predictions.

Even without this detailed type of information, data gathered by Ward Farnsworth suggest that there is much less posttrial bargaining than the economic model would predict (see Chapter 12). Farnsworth interviewed attorneys from approximately twenty nuisance cases in which injunctive relief was sought and either granted or denied after full litigation before a judge. In not a single case of those Farnsworth studied did parties even attempt to contract around the court order, even when transaction costs were low, and even when an objective third party might think that there was considerable room for mutually advantageous deals. Conventional analysis might attribute failures to reach an ultimate agreement to asymmetric information; but under such analysis it is difficult to explain the complete failure even to negotiate. It is also interesting to note that the lawyers interviewed said that the parties would not have reached a contractual solution if the opposite result had been reached. (This last point also means that the no-bargaining result cannot be explained by supposing that the court orders entered were uniquely efficient.)

The lawyers' explanations for these results are behavioral in character. Once people have received a court judgment, they are unwilling to negotiate with the opposing party, partly because of an unwillingness by victorious plaintiffs to confer advantages upon their opponents. Having invested a great deal of resources in pursuing the case all the way to court and through a trial, victors perceive themselves as having a special right to the legally endorsed status quo, and they are unlikely to give that right up, especially to their opponent, for all, or most, of the tea in China.

Failed Negotiations

Even among the well-mannered, fair-minded agents that populate behavioral economics, self-interest is very much alive and well. For often there will be room for disagreement about what is fair (or, equivalently, what is the appropriate reference transaction) – and thus there will be the opportunity for manipulation by self-interested parties. These parties may tend to see things in the light most favorable to them; while people care about fairness, their assessments of fairness are distorted by their own self-interest. This is a form of bounded rationality – specifically, a judgment error; people's perceptions are distorted by self-serving bias.

This form of bias can help to explain the frequency of failed negotiations. It is quite common, in cases involving divorce, child custody, and even commercial disputes, to see protracted litigation in circumstances in which it might be expected that the parties would be able to reach negotiated solutions (although it of course remains the case that most suits settle). On the standard account, the existence of such protracted litigation is somewhat of a puzzle. With a good sense of the expected value of suit, parties should settle more than they do. It may be possible to explain some of the observed behavior in terms of asymmetric information and signaling, which may interfere with settlement prospects. However, this account is difficult to test. By contrast, the effects of self-serving bias in negotiations have been tested empirically (see Chapter 14), and the results support our account here.

Mandatory Contract Terms

Wage and Price Effects. One of the most frequent claims in the economic analysis of law is that the imposition of mandatory terms on parties to a contract will make both parties worse off; it will operate as an effective tax on their transaction. For example, rules granting employees a particular level of workplace safety, or tenants the right to a habitable apartment, will make employers and employees, or landlords and tenants, worse off. In this section, we suggest that bounded rationality, in particular the endowment effect, casts doubt on the conventional law and economics claim. Our analysis here parallels that offered by Richard Craswell several years ago in the context of mandatory product warranties;[37] we build upon Craswell in emphasizing the employment setting and in drawing upon a recent empirical study of the effects of mandatory contract terms.

The conventional argument against mandatory terms such as those just mentioned has two steps. First, since the parties did not bargain for the term in question when left to their own devices, the cost of the term must exceed its benefit (otherwise they would have agreed to it on their own). The second step in the conventional argument is that imposing a mandatory term in these circumstances will operate as a tax on the parties, causing the wage to fall (or, in the case of a habitable apartment, the price to rise) by somewhere between the benefit and the cost of the term, and causing the number of profitable trades to fall. This analysis assumes an upward-sloping (not vertical) labor supply curve, but, at least for the worker group discussed below in connection with the existing empirical evidence (female employees), this assumption is clearly reasonable.

The conventional account thus offers sharp predictions about the effects of imposing mandatory contract terms. Do the data bear out these predictions? The leading study in this area is by Jonathan Gruber; Gruber examines the effects of imposing mandatory coverage of childbirth expenses in employer-provided insurance policies.[38] Imposition of the mandatory health-insurance term – which represented a substantial departure from the usual contractual arrangements prior to the mandate – caused the wages of affected workers (most prominently, married women of childbearing age) to fall by at least the cost of the mandated coverage according to most of the author's estimates. The study also found that the hours of employment of these workers were either unchanged or slightly higher with the mandate and that their probability of being employed was either unchanged or slightly lower. In sum, "[t]he findings consistently suggest shifting of the costs of the mandates on the order of 100 percent, with little effect on net labor input."[39] These findings are not easy to reconcile with the conventional account, which predicts a fall in wages less than the cost of the benefit. (If the wage were going to adjust by the full cost of the benefit, then some substantial fraction of employers should have offered the benefit even prior to the mandate.)

Behavioral Analysis. Departures from the assumptions of expected utility maximization by unboundedly rational agents suggest a different account of the effects of imposing mandatory contract terms, one that is consistent with the empirical findings just described. As noted above, the endowment effect implies that people are often less willing to sell entitlements that are given to them than to buy entitlements that they do not already possess; if given a mug, they will not sell it for three dollars, but if not given a mug, they will not buy one for that price. Thus, the fact that an employee (say) chooses not to purchase a particular workplace benefit if he is not granted an entitlement to it does not imply that he would want to sell the entitlement (if he could) once it has been granted. The corollary of this observation is that imposing a mandatory term may have different effects than the standard analysis predicts. In supply-and-demand terms, imagine a labor supply curve prior to the imposition of the mandate, reflecting willingness to work at different wage levels given provision of the benefit; the consequence of the endowment effect may be that this curve is shifted to the right once the mandate is imposed, and this move may more than compensate for the backward shift in the employer's labor demand curve as a result of the mandate. If this occurs, then the wages of the affected worker will fall by as much as or more than the cost of the benefit. This is precisely what the Gruber study of mandated childbirth coverage finds.

Three caveats are important here. First, while the endowment effect is consistent with complete or more than complete adjustment of the wage or price, it is also possible to have less than complete adjustment of the wage or price in the presence of the endowment effect. Perhaps workers are not any more willing to supply labor in exchange for a given wage plus the benefit in question once they have an entitlement to the benefit; it may be just that they would be even less willing to supply labor in the absence of the benefit. It is also possible that conventional economic analysis, by incorporating a market failure such as adverse selection (a possibility generally ignored by the above-mentioned critics of mandatory contract terms), can explain the empirical findings discussed above.[40] Our point is just the modest one that the behavioral account can predict an instance of observed behavior that is inconsistent with the standard law and economics account of mandatory terms. Future empirical work could attempt to address the adverse selection possibility by examining the effects of mandatory contract terms in a setting in which (in contrast to the health insurance context) adverse selection is unlikely to be a significant force.

The second qualification is that the endowment effect may not operate in contexts in which the beneficiaries of a mandatory term must give up a preexisting level of income, since they may be highly averse to such a loss. This qualification applies only to situations in which there is a financial loss relative to some preexisting expectation; thus it would not apply to, for example, a consumer's purchase of a durable good at a higher price due to the inclusion of a warranty. The final qualification here is that our analysis in this section is purely positive, concerned with the effects of imposing a mandatory contract term. The endowment effect does not necessarily imply that, from a normative perspective, mandatory terms are desirable; they may be efficient, in the sense that they would not be undone (if they could be) once imposed, but the situation without such terms is also efficient, for the same reasons given by the standard account, and there is no obvious means by which the two situations can be compared. Unlike several of the scenarios discussed in the last section, in which we think there is often a relatively strong argument for choosing one normative benchmark over another (say because people are likely to underestimate certain objective probabilities based on some form of judgment error), here there does not seem to be a clear basis for such a decision.

Our emphasis, then, is the positive question of the effects of imposing mandatory contract terms. The primary point is that there is a substantial research agenda to test various hypotheses; what we wish to suggest is that the conventional view cannot be accepted a priori and that there is reason to think that behavioral law and economics points in helpful directions.

The Content of Law

In this section we argue that law and economics explanations of the content of law need to be modified by incorporating the ideas of bounded self-interest (in the form of fairness norms) and bounded rationality developed above. As we will try to show, many laws on the books appear to be difficult to justify on efficiency grounds (for example, those that prohibit mutually beneficial exchanges without obvious externalities) and seem to benefit groups that do not have much lobbying power (such as the poor or middle class). We argue that the explanation for the "anomalous" laws is typically a quite simple one: most people think the result is fair. We also suggest that some laws we observe reflect neither efficiency nor conventional rent seeking but, instead, aspects of bounded rationality.

The mechanisms underlying our behavioral economic account of the content of law are simple and conventional. With the existing analysis, we assume (for present purposes, and insofar as statutory rather than judge-made law is concerned) that legislators are maximizers interested in their own reelection. Legislators interested in their own reelection will be responsive to the preferences and judgments of their constituents and those of powerful interest groups. If constituents believe that a certain practice is unfair or dangerous, and should be banned or regulated, self-interested legislators will respond, even if they do not share these views. We suspect that a full account of the content of law would have to incorporate legislators' independent judgments about fairness or risk, which play an occasional role; but we do not discuss that point here because for the examples we consider, public and interest-group perceptions seem to provide a good (and the most parsimonious) account of the laws we observe.

Bans on Market Transactions

This section discusses the demand for the law insofar as that demand is affected by people's bounded self-interest and in particular by their taste for fairness as they understand it. We do not mean to defend the laws that we describe; we suggest more modestly that people's commitment to fairness is part of the causal mechanism that establishes those laws. Fairness norms interact with other forces to produce some of the seemingly anomalous laws we observe. "Fairness entrepreneurs" may play a role, mobilizing public judgments to serve their (selfish or nonselfish) interests.

Bans on Economic Transactions.

Puzzle. A pervasive feature of law is that mutually desired trades are blocked. Perhaps most puzzling amid this landscape – which includes bans on baby selling and vote trading, discussed below – are bans on conventional "economic" transactions, such as usurious lending, price gouging, and ticket scalping. Usury, or charging an interest rate above a certain level, is prohibited by many states in consumer lending transactions. Price gouging, or the charging of "grossly excessive" or "unconscionable" prices, is prohibited during "states of emergency" (as after a flood or other natural disaster) in many states that have had recent experience with such events. Finally, ticket scalping, or the resale of tickets at prices well above face prices (in excess of a modest margin to cover ticket brokers' costs), is prohibited by roughly half of all states, including New York (with its heavy theater population).

Not surprisingly, economists and economically oriented lawyers often view these laws as inefficient and anomalous.[41] The laws also do not generally seem well explained in terms of conventional rent seeking by a politically powerful faction. One might argue that ticket-scalping laws are an exception to this last point, on the ground that ticket sellers (who may be politically powerful) might lobby in favor of the laws because moderate prices are necessary to create demand, which in turn certifies quality and makes the product more desirable.[42] (Thus, for example, the argument would be that restaurant owners do not raise prices when waits develop for tables, and if a secondary market in restaurant reservations were to develop with very high prices for tables, restaurateurs might wish to outlaw it.) The difficulty with this form of argument as applied here is that it cannot explain the application of ticket-scalping laws to perennially popular events whose quality is known from TV and whose attractiveness to the public would not decrease significantly even with some diminution in demand – a category that includes many professional sporting events. Our point here is actually a more general one: Although it may be possible to offer efficiency or conventional rent-seeking explanations for certain sorts of laws banning economic transactions, there does not seem to be a general theory or set of theories that can explain all or even most of these laws on traditional grounds.

Behavioral account. By contrast, laws banning usurious lending, price gouging, and ticket scalping when such activities are prevalent are a straightforward prediction of the theory of perceived fairness developed above. (We assume here that self-interested legislators are responsive to citizens' or other actors' demand for the content of law.) In the case of each of these bans, the transaction in question is a significant departure from the usual terms of trade in the market for the good in question – that is, a significant departure from the "reference transaction." Behavioral analysis predicts that if trades are occurring frequently in a given jurisdiction at terms far from those of the reference transaction, there will be strong pressure for a law banning such trades. Note that the prediction is not that all high prices (ones that make it difficult or impossible for some people to afford things they might want) will be banned; what we predict will be banned are transactions at terms far from the terms on which those transactions *generally occur in the marketplace*.

Consider this example:

> A store has been sold out of the popular Cabbage Patch dolls for a month. A week before Christmas a single doll is discovered in a store room. The managers know that many customers would like to buy the doll. They announce over the store's public address system that the doll will be sold by auction to the customer who offers to pay the most.[43]

Nearly three-quarters of the respondents judged this action to be either somewhat unfair or very unfair, though, of course, an economic analysis would judge the auction the most efficient method of assuring that the doll goes to the person who values it most. Although the auction is efficient, it represents a departure from the "reference transaction," under which the doll is sold at its usual price. (Of course, there would be no need for a law banning such behavior, since it does not appear to be prevalent.) As in the doll example, if money is loaned to individuals at a rate of interest significantly greater than the rate at which similarly sized loans are made to other customers, then the lender's behavior may be viewed as unfair. Since lumber generally tends to sell for a particular price, sales at far higher prices in the wake of (say) a hurricane, which drives demand sky high, are thought unfair. Tickets to sporting events or the theater often sell for around the face price of the ticket, so large markups over that amount are judged unfair. Consistent with this last suggestion, subjects asked whether a team should allocate its few remaining tickets to a key football game through an auction thought that this approach would be unfair; allocation based on who waited in line longest was the preferred solution.[44] Of course, waiting in line for tickets is precisely what happens with laws against ticket scalping. Thus, pervasive fairness norms appear to shape attitudes (and hence possibly law) on usury, price gouging, and ticket scalping.

Private Behavior. It is interesting to note that these transaction-banning laws often mimic, rather than constrain, the behavior of the firms they regulate. Consider first usury: It is a well-known puzzle of lending markets that lenders often refuse to loan money to risky borrowers even at above-market interest rates; rather, someone either qualifies for a loan at the offered rate or does not qualify for a loan at all.[45] This is true even when a modest increase in the interest rate would not violate usury laws. (Adverse selection considerations may also explain this behavior, but they cannot easily explain the existence of laws against such behavior.) Price gouging and ticket scalping are similar in terms of private actors' behavior. Thus, when Hurricane Andrew hit Florida and the demand for lumber and other building supplies skyrocketed, Home Depot, a major national chain, continued to sell these goods at its usual prices, despite the fact that the stock could have been sold at an enormous (short-term) profit, and despite the fact that no law banned price increases. More generally, economists have often remarked on the failure of firms to increase prices in response to temporary increases in demand.[46] Likewise, an interesting feature of ticket-scalping laws is that they will keep prices down only to the extent that firms choose to sell tickets at reasonable prices in the first place; but in fact firms routinely do this. For example, during the 1997 NBA playoffs, the Chicago Bulls sold some tickets to the general public at prices that were somewhat higher than regular season games but a fraction of the price the tickets commanded on the (legal in Illinois) ticket broker open market. As the head of a major theater company explained, "there's a strong public relations argument" against raising prices for tickets for very popular shows (and presumably sporting events as well) – despite excess demand for seats at the going prices – because the public already believes "that Broadway ticket prices are too high."[47] Consistent with the foregoing analysis, recent evidence of price stickiness shows that firms' behavior seems to be affected greatly by their customers' perceptions of unfair price increases.[48] Note that this is not a standard reputation story; fairness considerations are the reason that raising prices harms the firm's reputation.

Why then are the laws necessary? Some of the relevant actors will not be constrained by fairness norms in the absence of a law. Noninstitutional lenders may be willing to lend at exorbitant rates; suppliers selling lumber out of the back of pickup trucks will often charge whatever the market will bear (as occurred after Hurricane Andrew); ticket scalpers, who are typically anonymous actors engaged in one-time transactions, have no reason to keep prices down. It is these actors who are regulated by the law. The more powerful mainstream firms will tend to support, or at least not oppose, rules banning unfair transactions. (Note, though, that their support would not be predicted by the standard account.)

Other Bans. Laws banning economic transactions are just a species of a broader form of regulation of transactions. Many deals are blocked, across a wide range of contexts. People may not buy and sell body parts. They cannot sell their votes. In some states, commercial surrogacy is prohibited, and baby selling is banned in all states. People may not contract around bans on race and sex discrimination, as for example through written agreements. Blocked trades can be found in every American jurisdiction.

Bans of this variety raise serious normative questions; those questions have been well ventilated. Doubtless reasonable distinctions can be drawn between bans in different areas; sometimes externalities are readily apparent. We make a simple positive point here: Behavioral analysis suggests that pervasive judgments about fairness may account for many such bans on voluntary deals. Whether or not those judgments make sense, they seem to be widespread, and they help to explain the persistence of legislation that is often difficult to explain by reference to an efficiency or rent-seeking account. In banning certain deals, legislators may be responding to community sentiments about what kinds of things are properly subject to market arrangements. The reference transaction in these areas is generally "no transaction"; just as the norm or benchmark is the usual or face price of the ticket, or an equal division of the amount to be divided in the ultimatum game, the norm or benchmark here is "no market exchange." Departures from that norm are viewed as unfair and are prohibited.

Prior Restraints on Speech

Another instance in which fairness-related norms, and in addition bounded rationality, may affect law involves one of the enduring puzzles in First Amendment law: the special judicial hostility to "prior restraints" on speech, most notably injunctions.[49] A court may well refuse to issue an injunction against speech even if it would allow subsequent punishment of that same speech. The puzzle is that a prior restraint involves subsequent punishment too; what an injunction means is that a violator will be subject to (subsequent) sanctions. Why is a criminal statute any less problematic than an injunction whose violation produces criminal penalties?

Conventional economic analysis provides no satisfying answer to this question. True, the injunction might be thought to create the prospect of a greater total punishment for the speech, but no one has suggested that the First Amendment imposes limits on the severity of punishment for speech that the government is entitled to criminalize. In any case, many criminal statutes impose greater punishments than many injunctions, and the latter are nonetheless more troublesome than the former.

Can behavioral analysis explain the law's special treatment of prior restraints? As noted earlier in this chapter, court-ordered remedies are likely to create special forms of attachment for their beneficiaries; individuals will typically be reluctant to forego rights granted by such remedies, due to the perceived unfairness of that outcome and the type of attachment created by the endowment effect. This is apt to be as true for prosecutors as for everyone else. A prosecutor who has sought an injunction may be particularly insistent on ensuring that punishment occurs. A criminal statute, standing by itself and unaccompanied by an injunction, is likely to produce a different response on the part of the prosecutor. Reasonable defendants know the difference. Hence it is especially important for a court to ensure that any injunction imposed on speech is not issued *in advance of an accurate judgment that the speech involved is unprotected by the First Amendment.*

As it happens, this account matches the most sophisticated defenses of the special barrier to prior restraints.[50] Those defenses urge that the real purpose of the prior restraint doctrine is to ensure that no regulation is imposed without a reliable judgment that the First Amendment does not protect the speech at risk. The doctrine is difficult to explain on conventional economic principles but is a natural inference from behavioral ones.

Anecdote-Driven Environmental Legislation

Judgment errors by boundedly rational individuals also play a significant role in predicting and explaining the content of law. In particular, people seek law in areas such as environmental protection on the basis of their judgments about the probabilities associated with certain harmful activities. Their judgments about probabilities will often be affected by how "available" other instances of the harm in question are, that is, by how easily such instances come to mind.[51]

Here is a familiar example of availability: Individuals asked how many seven-letter words in a two-thousand-word section of a novel end in "ing" give much larger estimates than individuals asked how many words in such a section have "n" as the second-to-last letter, despite the fact that objectively there are more words that satisfy the latter criterion than the former.[52] Reliance on how "available" instances of the event in question are is a form of judgment error, but the error is fully rational – in the sense of reflecting optimizing behavior – for people with limited information. Still, it can lead to systematic errors in probability assessment. In the context of environmental legislation, it encourages the well-known "pollutant of the month" syndrome, where regulation is driven by recent and memorable instances of harm. When beliefs and preferences are produced by a set of probability judgments, made inaccurate by the availability heuristic, legislation will predictably become anecdote-driven. Many illustrations come to mind; consider the outcry over Agent Orange and Times Beach,[53] or the strict regulation of asbestos in schools after a large amount of media attention.[54] The same phenomenon may occur in other areas of regulatory law; an example here is the move toward heavy regulation of school bus safety in the wake of media coverage of school bus accidents in which children were killed.[55]

What determines how available a particular environmental hazard is? Two factors are particularly important: the observed frequency of the hazard and its salience. Thus, if a particular hazard has materialized recently, people are likely to attach a higher probability to its occurring in the future. And this is particularly true if the hazard has a high degree of salience – as, for instance, with the discovery of asbestos in schools, where many children are present. Apart from the nature of the event, salience is heavily influenced by the way the event is packaged by the media, organized interest groups, and politicians.

Interested actors in the private and public sectors can be expected to exploit the availability heuristic for their own purposes. These actors are amateur behavioralists, operating strategically to promote their selfish or nonselfish goals. "Availability entrepreneurs" will thus focus attention on a specific event in order to ensure that this event will be salient and available to many members of the public (see Chapter 15).

The availability heuristic can lead to under- as well as overregulation. People sometimes (although not always) underestimate the likelihood of low-probability or low-salience events because these threats simply do not make it onto people's "radar screens"; many health and environmental risks (such as the health threats from poor diet and exercise) may fit this description with some parts of the population. But when a particular threat, even an unlikely one, becomes available, as when, for example, asbestos is discovered in schools, then regulation will be demanded. The behavioral account thus predicts a patchwork of environmental laws characterized by both over- and underregulation, with overregulation when a particular risk has recently materialized, particularly if the harm in question is highly salient.

Prescriptions

In this section we shift our focus from the positive to the prescriptive. Our claim in each context that we consider is that attention to behavioral insights can improve the law's ability to move society toward desired outcomes.

Negligence Determinations and Other Determinations of Fact or Law

Background. Frequently juries are called upon to determine the probability of an event that ended up occurring; a prominent example is the negligence standard, which (in the formulation favored by the economic analysis of law) requires jurors to assess the costs and benefits of the defendant's course of action from an ex ante perspective, and thus to determine the probability that harm would end up coming of that action. These determinations are made with the "benefit" of hindsight; jurors know at the time they make their decision that the event in question did in fact occur. Jurors' determinations are thus likely to be afflicted by "hindsight bias" – the tendency of decision makers to attach an excessively high probability to an event simply because it ended up occurring.[56]

Hindsight bias will lead juries making negligence determinations to find defendants liable more frequently than if cost-benefit analysis were done correctly – that is, on an ex ante basis. Thus, plaintiffs will win cases they deserve to lose. Hindsight bias has been observed in a wide range of contexts across many studies and is likely to be present whenever juries make negligence determinations.

A threshold issue raised by the hindsight-bias account of negligence determinations is whether hindsight bias is simply a countervailing weight to a tendency on the part of defendants to underestimate the likelihood of being sanctioned. A common feature of human behavior is overoptimism: People tend to think that bad events are far less likely to happen to them than to others. Thus, most people think that their probability of a bad outcome is far less than others' probability, although of course this cannot be true for more than half the population.[57] If defendants exhibit such overoptimism, then they will be underdeterred by a correct application of the negligence standard; overestimation of the probability of harm based on hindsight bias might then be a desirable countervailing factor. We think that defendant overoptimism is likely to be a much smaller factor for firms than for individual defendants, since firms that make systematic errors in judgment will be at a competitive disadvantage. And for individuals, the role of overoptimism is likely to vary significantly with context. In a case in which the threat of being found liable is highly salient, individuals may tend to overestimate the likelihood of being sanctioned, for reasons discussed in connection with our account of Superfund above. Hindsight bias, in contrast, seems to be an across-the-board phenomenon; it has been observed in a wide range of contexts across many studies and is likely to be present whenever a jury makes a negligence determination.

In fact, the law in areas such as patent law already takes clear steps to address the problems caused by hindsight bias. Thus, as Jeffrey Rachlinski has recently pointed out, patent courts are required to guard against hindsight bias in determining whether an invention was "nonobvious" at the time of invention – despite its now (perhaps) seeming obvious – by looking to such "secondary considerations" as "commercial success, long felt but unsolved need, [and] failure of others";[58] this is in effect a limited form of debiasing of the decision maker. (Thus, the law seems to acknowledge that *judges*, like juries, may exhibit hindsight bias – although there is evidence that the bias is less for judges than juries.)[59] But in the area of tort law the existing responses are partial and incomplete at best. Hindsight bias seems to be so deeply ingrained in the tort system that even when it is called to a court's attention, it may be difficult for the court (never mind a juror) to recognize or address it. How might the law respond to hindsight bias in tort cases?

An obvious response is the use of jury instructions that inform jurors of the bias and tell them to focus on the ex ante situation. Unfortunately, such debiasing techniques appear either to have no effect on decisions or to reduce hindsight bias by only a limited degree, leaving a significant gap between ex post and ex ante decision making.[60] The findings on the limited effect of debiasing techniques suggest that attempts by lawyers to employ such techniques may also be of limited effectiveness, although there is room here for future research on the role of lawyers. Because of the apparent limits on debiasing, we propose two alternative prescriptions – one simple and clear-cut, but limited to certain sorts of cases, and the other general and giving rise to important avenues for future research.

Prescriptions.

First prescription: Manipulate the information given to jurors. One means of responding to the problem of hindsight bias in tort cases involves manipulating the set of information given to jurors. Suppose that a food-processing company is claimed to have decided in a negligent fashion to use a particular chemical in its production process; imagine that the chemical ended up causing cancer in a small number of residents who live near the company's plant. The company claims that *not* using the cancer-causing (as it turned out) chemical would have carried significant risks to residents in terms of bacterial contamination. Imagine that jurors are not told that the company decided to use the chemical; rather they are told only about the ex ante decision facing the company (whether to use the chemical). They learn about the benefits and costs of that strategy and must determine whether either pursuing it or failing to pursue it would have been negligent. In this scenario the jurors would be transformed into ex ante decision makers. Their probability estimates for each type of harm – and their resulting assessment of whether either decision by the company would have been negligent – would be untouched by hindsight bias.

In some cases, it might not be possible to keep the defendant's choice from the jury; the fact of the suit will make clear what that choice was. For example, in the well-known case of *Petition of Kinsman Transit Co.*,[61] in which a bridge operator failed to lift the bridge in time to prevent an accident, apparently because he was at a tavern, the fact of a suit may provide a strong indication that the bridge was not lifted. In this sort of setting, a possible prescription (offered previously in the literature) involves bifurcation of trials, so that jurors deciding on liability do not learn any of the details of what happened until an initial determination of liability is made.[62] Although we think this is a sensible prescription in such settings, we note that it will not eliminate the effects of hindsight bias, since (as proponents of bifurcated trials recognize) "the jury will undoubtedly *know* that they are not being asked simply to engage in an academic exercise,"[63] and that (because a trial is being held) "a bad outcome must have occurred."[64] In contrast, in cases in which jurors need not know (because they cannot infer from the fact of a lawsuit) what choice the defendant made, it may be possible to eliminate the hindsight bias completely. And there are many such situations: cases in which either of two options facing a physician could have caused harm or death to a patient; cases in which either the use or the failure to use a new technology could have led to harm; cases in which either revealing or failing to reveal suicide threats by a psychiatric patient could have resulted in suicide.

Second prescription: Alter the evidentiary standard. The result of hindsight bias, as described above, is that jurors will overestimate the probability that harm will occur (since harm did, in fact, occur). The determination of the probability of harm would conventionally be made under a "preponderance of the evidence" standard: If jurors think it more likely than not, based on the evidence, that the probability of harm was above the threshold level required for liability, they are to find the defendant liable. One might imagine counteracting the effects of hindsight bias by raising the evidentiary standard (as an alternative, not in addition, to the previous proposal; the two together would produce overcorrection and, thus, underdeterrence). Thus, for example, if the jurors were to find the defendant liable only if the evidence suggested at least a 75 percent likelihood – rather than merely a 51 percent likelihood – that the critical harm probability threshold was met, then they might well reach the correct conclusion about liability: They would overestimate the likelihood attached to the critical threshold, but the overestimate might well be below the new required level.

The highest evidentiary threshold known to our legal system – the "beyond a reasonable doubt" standard – is used only in criminal cases. However, in civil cases an intermediate standard (higher than the preponderance standard, but less demanding than the "beyond a reasonable doubt" standard) is the "clear and convincing evidence" standard. This, of course, would be likely to be a second-best solution; in some situations defendants might be found not liable when, under a perfectly functioning system with no hindsight bias and no heightened evidentiary standard, they would be found liable. This need not be the case, however, and even if it is, we might well tolerate a crude measure that produced some errors so long as it represented an improvement over the current system. Most importantly, there is much room for research focused on determining whether altering the evidentiary threshold would represent a desirable response on balance – either across the board or in particular categories of cases. Our goal is to suggest the value of research on this issue, rather than to urge an immediate change in policy based on what we now know.

Other Applications. The discussion to this point has focused on tort cases decided under the negligence standard, but similar issues may arise in other areas of law in which juries (or judges) must determine whether an ex ante standard was met while armed with the knowledge that a negative event in fact materialized. One example is securities fraud litigation, whose perceived excesses prompted Congress to enact the Private Securities Litigation Reform Act of 1995.[65] In a typical securities fraud case, decision makers are confronted with a company whose stock price experienced a dramatic fall, and they are required to assess whether a particular issue or problem facing the company, whose disclosure prompted the fall, should have been disclosed at an earlier stage (typically before it had become an issue or problem). Decision makers in such a case are required to make an after-the-fact determination of whether a reasonable ex ante decision maker would have thought the prospective issue or problem "material" to the average shareholder based on the information available at the time.[66] The problem is that this determination must be made against the backdrop of knowledge that the issue or problem in fact materialized, and produced a large drop in the company's stock price. In this situation, a decision maker will likely find it difficult to see how a reasonable ex ante decision maker might have thought the prospective issue or problem other than material. Consistent with this analysis, the main predictor of whether a securities fraud action is brought seems to be whether there has been a large change in the company's stock market value, not whether the company's behavior was reasonable from an ex ante perspective.[67]

Another example here involves damage suits for violations of the Fourth Amendment. A risk in such suits is that if the allegedly illegal search did in fact produce damaging evidence (say, drugs or other contraband), then decision makers are likely to conclude that the law enforcement agency's behavior was reasonable. This will be true even if, from an ex ante perspective (without knowing the eventual outcome), this behavior would not have been found reasonable.

Information Disclosure and Government Advertising

Background. Suppose it is agreed that individuals lack adequate information on a given subject – for example, workplace safety, appliance energy efficiency, or the effects of drug use. In some such instances the government may seek to foster comparison shopping and informed decision making (as in the federal truth-in-lending law, which requires lenders to announce interest rates, measured the same way);[68] in other instances the government may have a specific policy goal (reducing drug use, encouraging the use of energy-efficient refrigerators). Conventional economics acknowledges the possible desirability of each of these goals (the second in the case of phenomena such as externalities), and it often advocates, as a means of achieving them, providing additional information to citizens, either through a mandate to the relevant private actors (for instance, employers), or through provision of information by the government itself.[69]

The prescription to "provide more information" is striking in its spareness. Behavioral analysis suggests that this prescription is far *too* spare. "Provide more information" says nothing about the *way* in which the information will be provided, and yet we know that this will matter a great deal.

That presentation matters has several implications. One is "antiprescriptive": Prescriptions directed toward fostering comparison shopping – the first government goal mentioned above – will often be incomplete and may even be paralyzing, since there is often no "neutral" way to present information. The second implication is that effective prescriptive strategies for achieving the second goal mentioned above – discouraging particular types of behavior – must take behavioral factors into account. It is not enough simply to "provide information." We discuss several examples of this below.

Antiprescription. Consider the following example of a government attempt to foster informed decision making. In the case of defined contribution plans such as 401(K)'s, the Labor Department, the relevant government authority, has ruled that employers must give employees investment alternatives and must provide information about those alternatives (such as risk and returns); but firms are not allowed to offer "advice" as to how to invest. We think that such spare guidelines place employers in a very difficult position. The reason is that the way firms decide to describe and display information on investment alternatives will have a powerful impact on the choices employees make.

Consider in this connection a recent study of the division of retirement savings by university staff employees between two different funds, a safe one (bonds) and a risky one (stocks).[70] All the employees were shown actual historical data on the returns of the two funds, but this information was displayed in two different ways; one group was given the distribution of one-year rates of return, while the other was given a simulated distribution of thirty-year rates of return. Those shown the thirty-year returns elected to invest nearly all their savings in stocks, while those shown the one-year returns invested a majority of their funds in bonds. Our point is not that one of these outcomes is better. Our point is simply that in the real world, she who provides information ends up giving advice.

This is an example in which the prescription to "provide more information" may be paralyzing; in other instances it may simply be incomplete. Thus, suppose that the prescription is that certain private actors be required to provide "information"; what does this mean? If it means that those who expose people to a dangerous substance or product in the workplace (say benzene) must provide them with accurate information about the danger, this leaves open a tremendous range of possibilities. The actors subject to the mandate will often have an interest in providing the least scary, most pallid version of the information possible (for example, "benzene has been associated with a statistical increase in risk"), while regulators might want the most scary, salient message available (say, "exposure to benzene will increase your risk of getting CANCER and other FATAL diseases"). Of course, the best message in this case, if the goal is accurate knowledge, may well be somewhere in between. An important goal of the analyst's task in making prescriptions in this area is to say *how* the information should be provided – not just *that* it should be provided.

In still other contexts, such as ones in which the presentation of information will affect people's preferences rather than just their perceptions of risk, it is not clear in theory what is meant by ensuring "informed decision making." It is not even clear that there are steady or stable background preferences that might be "informed." The preferences can themselves be an artifact of the method of informing. For instance, one of the central features of Kahneman and Tversky's prospect theory is that people evaluate outcomes based on the change they represent from an initial reference point, rather than based on the nature of the outcome itself; also, losses from the initial reference point are weighted much more heavily than gains.[71] This aspect of prospect theory (like its other features) is based on evidence about actual choice behavior.[72] The evaluation of outcomes in terms of gains and losses from an initial reference point, coupled with the special aversion to losses, means that it matters a great deal whether something is presented as a gain or a loss relative to the status quo; a perceived threat of a loss relative to the status quo weighs more heavily than a perceived threat of foregoing a gain. In such cases it is difficult to say which individual is "informed" – the one who is told of the perceived threat of a loss or the one who is told of the perceived threat of foregoing a gain. In this and other contexts, preferences are not preexisting but rather "constructive, context-dependent," analogous to the balls or strikes that do not predate the situation of choice and that "ain't nothing till" the umpire calls them.[73]

Prescriptions. Suppose now that the agreed-upon goal is not to foster "informed decision making," but to discourage particular types of behavior. Quite obviously, some ways of providing information are more effective than others.

First prescription: Exploit loss aversion. As just noted, individuals tend to weight losses far more heavily than gains. As a result, framing consequences in terms of losses rather than gains is likely to be far more effective in changing behavior. A well-known illustration of this sort of framing effect is a study involving breast self-examination; pamphlets describing the positive effects of breast self-examination (for example, women who undertake such examinations have a greater chance of finding a tumor at a treatable stage) are ineffective, but there are significant changes in behavior from pamphlets that stress the negative consequences of a refusal to undertake self-examinations (women who fail to perform such examinations have a decreased chance of finding a tumor at a treatable stage).[74] Note that this example illustrates how the provision of information may be a more natural tool than taxation or regulation for discouraging some forms of behavior (such as the failure to perform a self-examination).

Second prescription: Exploit salience. Effective prescriptive strategies need to take account of the fact that vivid and personal information will often be more effective than statistical evidence. This sort of information has a high degree of salience, and, as a result of the availability heuristic, people will tend to respond to it by attaching a higher probability to the event in question. Thus an antidrug advertisement, showing a frying egg with the announcer's voice claiming, "This is your brain on drugs," appeared to have a significant effect on behavior.[75] Availability suggests that the ad produced a higher perceived probability of negative effects than a flatter ad would have.

Third prescription: Avoid the pitfalls of overoptimism. As noted in the previous section, a common feature of human behavior is overoptimism. This behavior is not specific to the young, although it may be diminished as people move beyond middle to old age, as Richard Posner has suggested.[76] What does this feature of behavior imply about government provision of information? Consider the choice between a safe-driving campaign focused on drivers' own driving and the ingenuous campaign actually adopted by the government: "Drive defensively: Watch out for the other guy." The government's campaign, perhaps self-consciously, responded to the fact that most people tend to believe that they are unusually safe drivers. This is a model of the sort of prescriptive approach advocated by behavioral analysis.

Behavior of Criminals

Background. Our discussion of prescriptive analysis has thus far focused on bounded rationality. But bounded willpower may also play a role. Consider the question of deterring criminal behavior. Economic analysis of this question typically starts from the premise that potential offenders will be deterred from criminal acts if the expected costs of those acts exceed their expected benefits. Potential offenders are imagined to make at least a rough calculation of these costs and benefits in the process of making their decisions. Bounded rationality suggests that people may make systematic (as opposed to random) errors in computing these costs and benefits; for example, as described above, individuals tend to judge the likelihood of uncertain events (such as getting caught for a crime) by how available such instances are to the human mind, and this may depend on factors unrelated to the actual probability of the event. This analysis suggests the desirability, from a prescriptive standpoint, of making law enforcement highly visible, holding constant the actual probability that offenders will be caught; it suggests, for example, the good sense of the familiar method of parking-ticket enforcement – sticking a large, brightly colored ticket that reads "VIOLATION" in large letters on the drivers' side window, where it is particularly noticeable to drivers passing by – as opposed to a less costly approach (putting small, plain tickets under the windshield wiper on the curb side of the street, convenient for the parking officer to reach). Another example here is "community policing," now widely practiced across the country; by making more visible and memorable the presence of police (as, for example, by having them walk their beats rather than ride in patrol cars), authorities can, it is suggested, increase the deterrence of potential criminals without altering the actual probability of apprehension.

But even if one assumes that potential offenders can accurately compute the costs and benefits of crime, bounded willpower suggests that they will often behave in ways at odds with conventional economic analysis, due to problems of self-control. A central feature of much criminal behavior is that the benefits are immediate, while the costs (if they are incurred at all) are spread out over time – often a very long time. Economic analysis assumes that such future costs are discounted to present value, and A. Mitchell Polinsky and Steven Shavell have recently suggested that potential criminal offenders may have unusually high discount rates, so that years in prison far in the future will be discounted very heavily.[77] Behavioral economic analysis carries this idea further by incorporating self-control issues often emphasized by criminologists.[78]

Prescriptions. As just noted, the existing economic analysis assumes a constant discount rate (although perhaps a high one); this means that the difference between the attractiveness or aversiveness of a reward or punishment today versus tomorrow is the same as the difference between a year from now and a year and one day from now. In contrast to this theory, there is considerable evidence that people display sharply declining discount rates.[79] This means that impatience is very strong for near rewards (and aversion very strong for near punishments), but that each of these declines over time – a pattern referred to as "hyperbolic discounting."[80]

What does hyperbolic discounting imply for effective deterrence of criminal behavior? With this sort of bounded willpower on the part of potential offenders, the difference between not getting caught and being imprisoned for, say, a year differs dramatically from the difference between being imprisoned for ten years and being imprisoned for eleven years (even apart from any fixed costs that may accompany the fact of conviction). While the standard theory says that these two things differ only insofar as the costs of imprisonment in year eleven must be discounted to present value in order to be compared with the loss of wages and personal freedom in year one, behavioral economic analysis (and basic common sense) tells us that this is not so. Short punishments will thus have much more effect than long punishments as a result of the "priority of the present"; adding years onto a sentence will produce little additional deterrence.[81]

Normative Analysis: Anti-Antipaternalism

In its normative orientation, conventional law and economics is often strongly antipaternalistic. The idea of "consumer sovereignty" plays a large role; citizens, assuming they have reasonable access to relevant information, are thought to be the best judges of what will promote their own welfare. Yet many of the instances of bounded rationality discussed above call this idea into question – and also, as we will emphasize below, call into question the idea that intervention by government actors, who themselves may face the same cognitive or motivational problems as everyone else, can improve matters. In this way bounded rationality pushes toward a sort of anti-antipaternalism – a skepticism about antipaternalism, but not an affirmative defense of paternalism. We also note (although we do not explore this point here) that while bounded rationality may increase the need for law (if government's failings are less serious than citizens'), bounded self-interest may reduce it, by creating norms that solve collective action problems even without government intervention.[82]

Citizen Error

Many of the forms of bounded rationality discussed above call into question the idea of consumer sovereignty. For example, overoptimism leads most people to believe that their own risk of a negative outcome is far lower than the average person's. Similarly, the effect of salience may lead to substantial underestimation of certain risks encountered in everyday life (for example, the risks from poor diet), since these harms may not be very salient. When overoptimism is combined with salience, people may underestimate risks substantially. We emphasize that these problems are not ones of insufficient information per se; they are ones of insufficient ability to process accurately the information one possesses insofar as that information bears on one's own risks. Thus, for example, people may have reasonably adequate information about the risks of smoking,[83] but this does not at all imply that they have adequate perceptions of the risks of smoking that they themselves face.[84] Even if people can obtain accurate statistical knowledge, statistical knowledge may not be enough to inform actual choices.[85] It does not follow from this that information is useless; it is just that having information per se does not automatically imply optimal behavior.

Further questions about the idea of consumer sovereignty arise from the gap between "decision" and "experience" utility. The utility of actual experience may diverge from the anticipated utility as revealed by people's decisions.[86] The identity of decision and experience utility in conventional economics is often treated as an axiom, or at least as a proposition that could not be falsified. But behavioral research shows that people's judgments about their future experience at the time of decision can be mistaken, in the sense that people are sometimes unable (even apart from the sorts of informational issues recognized by conventional economics) to assess what the experience will actually be like. Thus, for example, people appear not to predict accurately the consequences of becoming seriously ill or disabled.[87] They tend to underestimate their ability to adapt to negative changes, a point that may bear on law and policy in such areas as global climate change.[88]

But this suggestion about adaptation raises a complex normative question: Is a person's measure of welfare after (for example) becoming ill the appropriate measure of value? Perhaps people, through coping mechanisms, are able to adapt to disease better than they anticipate in advance, but does this mean that disease is a less severe problem than prior attitudes would have suggested? On conventional utilitarian grounds, the answer is probably affirmative; the subjective experience is what counts. But a well-established challenge to utilitarian analysis suggests the possibility of a negative answer, on the ground that subjective experience may not be all that counts.[89] What we mean to suggest here is a simple point: People sometimes do mispredict their utility at the time of decision, and on conventional grounds this phenomenon raises serious problems for the idea of consumer sovereignty.

Behavioral Bureaucrats

Any suggestion that the government should intervene in response to people's mistakes raises the question whether the government will be able to avoid such errors. The prospects for productive and useful intervention may be smallest in the case of populist government; the actions of such a government, based heavily on pressures coming from citizens, may tend to be subject to the very same biases and errors that afflict citizens. (Thus behavioral analysis complements existing accounts of the problems with populism.) Irregular perceptions of risk by ordinary people may tend to produce irregularities in regulation, as the cognitive errors that ordinary people make are replicated in statutory and administrative law.[90] The effects of social interaction may even make government action worse, and more dangerous, than individual errors. Our earlier discussion suggests a possible mechanism: Availability entrepreneurs in the private sector can heighten the demand for regulation, and public-sector availability entrepreneurs can take advantage of, and heighten, this effect, by advocating anecdote-driven policy. Thus public choice accounts of legislation can work productively with behavioral accounts; there is a good deal of synergy between behavioral mechanisms and interest group leaders, many of whom are amateur (or professional?) behavioral economists. The pollutant-of-the-month syndrome in environmental law is paralleled by many measures responding to the crisis-of-the-month. These difficulties with populist government also point to problems with the referendum process.

But populist government is not the only worry. Government will often be subject to cognitive and motivational problems even if it is not populist. (Bureaucrats may also lack appropriate incentives to make decisions in the public interest.)[91] Thus, for example, there is no necessary reason to think that government officials are, by virtue of their offices, able to avoid overoptimism or predict experience utility. On the other hand, a degree of insulation from populist pressures, combined with knowledge of behavioral economics, might produce some improvement. New institutions may play a role; consider Justice Breyer's plea for an insulated body of specialized civil servants, entrusted with the job of comparing risks and ensuring that resources are devoted to the most serious problems;[92] Howard Margolis's behaviorally informed suggestion that government should be required to ensure that all initiatives "do no harm";[93] even proposals for cost-benefit analysis, understood in a behavioral light as an attempt to overcome biases and confusions in both perception and motivation.[94] We also emphasize that government intervention need not come in highly coercive forms; perhaps distortions in people's decision making can be overcome by information campaigns falling well short of coercion. For instance, in the contexts of risks such as smoking, might debiasing techniques work to link the statistical evidence with the personal reality?

All of the foregoing ideas raise many complexities; and we have not even touched upon the complicated philosophical literature on the legitimacy of paternalism. Application of these ideas to any specific topic in law would require a much fuller development of many issues than the space in this chapter permits. But we need not leave the ideas in purely abstract form; consider the following simple illustration of their application. Imagine that sunlamps are being sold in an unregulated market and that it is learned that many consumers fall asleep under the lamps, burning themselves badly. Consumers make this mistake in spite of warnings included on the package and in the instructions, perhaps because they fail to anticipate that lying in a warm place with one's eyes closed is likely to induce sleep. Let's call this an "unintended risk," meaning a risk that consumers fail to appreciate. The existence of this unintended risk leaves open the possibility of welfare-enhancing regulation. Suppose, for example, that an automatic timer can be added to the sunlamp at a cost of twenty-five cents, and that manufacturers have not included this feature because consumers do not anticipate that they will need it. We do not discuss here the issues raised by the possibility that a government mandate of the timer interferes with freedom, rightly conceived. Nor do we address possible distributive issues (all will pay more for sunlamps, although perhaps only some failed to appreciate the risks of falling asleep). All we suggest is that an important part of the analysis involves asking whether the cost of requiring this safety-promoting feature (twenty-five cents per customer) is less than the cost of the unanticipated burns.

A central point of this example is that from the perspective of behavioral law and economics, issues of paternalism are to a significant degree empirical questions, not questions to be answered on an a priori basis. No axiom demonstrates that people make choices that serve their best interests; this is a question to be answered based on evidence. Of course the case for intervention is weakened to the extent that public institutions are likely to make things worse rather than better. What we are suggesting is that facts, and assessment of costs and benefits, should replace assumptions that beg the underlying questions.

Conclusion

Traditional law and economics is largely based on the standard assumptions of neoclassical economics. These assumptions are sometimes useful but often false. People display bounded rationality: They suffer from certain biases, such as overoptimism and self-serving conceptions of fairness; they follow heuristics, such as availability, that lead to mistakes; and they behave in accordance with prospect theory rather than expected utility theory. People also have bounded willpower; they can be tempted and are sometimes myopic. They take steps to overcome these limitations. Finally, people are (fortunately!) boundedly self-interested. They are concerned about the well-being of others, even strangers in some circumstances, and this concern and their self-conception can lead them in the direction of cooperation at the expense of their material self-interest (and sometimes spite, also at the expense of their material self-interest). Most of these bounds can be and have been made part of formal models.

In this chapter we have sketched some of the implications of enriching the traditional analysis by incorporating a more realistic conception of human behavior. We have insisted on the value and importance of using the three bounds in the economic analysis of law; more tentatively, we have explored a series of legal problems in which the bounds may be significant. Obviously there is a great deal of research to be done, and one of our principal goals has been to outline areas that could benefit from further work, both analytic and empirical.

We do not doubt that replacing the simple maximizing model of economics with a more complicated psychological treatment comes at some cost. Solving optimization problems is usually easier than describing actual behavior. It has been said (we believe by Herbert Simon) that economics makes things hard on agents, but easy on economists; behavioral economics, we suggest, does the opposite. We recapitulate here some of the reasons we think the enriched model is worth the trouble for those interested in the economic analysis of law.

1. Some of the predictions of the standard model are simply wrong. For example, people can be both more spiteful and more cooperative than traditional analysis predicts, and this matters a great deal to law. It is also important to know that even in a world without transaction costs and wealth effects, the assignment of property rights alters the ultimate allocation of those rights, and that this may be particularly true for certain forms of property-rights assignment (such as court orders). These features of the world matter greatly for making predictions and formulating policy.

2. In other cases economics makes no predictions (or incorrect predictions of no effect). Prominent in this category are the effects of presentation; since economic theory assumes that choices are invariant to the manner in which a problem is framed, it falsely predicts that the language of a media account or advertisement has no effect on behavior, holding the information content constant. In contrast, it is well established that people react differently to potential outcomes depending on whether they are perceived as foregone gains or out-of-pocket costs (losses), and that they are likely to think, mistakenly, that salient events are more common than equally prevalent but more subtle

ones. These points bear on the supply of and the demand for law, and on the behavior of agents in their interactions with the legal system.

3. Standard economic theories of the content of law are based on an unduly limited range of potential explanations, namely optimal (or second-best) rules set by judges and rent-seeking legislation determined by self-interested log rolling. Behavioral economics offers other sources of potential explanation – most prominently, perceptions of fairness. We have tried to show that many laws which are seemingly inefficient and do not benefit powerful interest groups may be explained on grounds of judgments about right and wrong.

4. A behavioral approach to law and economics offers a host of novel prescriptions regarding how to make the legal system work better. Some stem from the improved predictions mentioned in point 2 above. Cognitive difficulties and motivational distortions undermine or alter conventional economic prescriptions about the jury's role, most notably in the context of assessing negligence and making other determinations of fact or law. We have taken some preliminary steps in suggesting ways to reduce the costs of some of these problems.

5. A behavioral approach to law and economics produces new questions about possible mistakes by private and public actors. On the one hand, it raises serious doubts about the reflexive antipaternalism of some economic analyses of law. On the other hand, it raises equivalent questions about whether even well-motivated public officials will be able to offer appropriate responses to private mistakes and confusion.

We hope that this chapter will encourage others to continue the inquiry and research, both theoretical and empirical, that will be needed to flesh out the behavioral approach for which we have argued here. This approach will use traditional economic tools, enhanced by a better understanding of human behavior. Thirty years from now, we hope that there will be no such thing as behavioral economics. Instead we hope that economists and economically oriented lawyers will simply incorporate the useful findings of other social sciences, and in so doing, transform economics into behavioral economics, and economic analysis of law into one of its most important branches.

Appendix: Framework and Summary of Applications

This appendix summarizes our framework for behavioral law and economics. It also lists the law and economics issues we analyze within each category of the framework. The specific behavioral mechanisms we draw upon, which are summarized here, do not constitute an exhaustive list of the mechanisms that might be relevant to law and economics; they simply reflect the mechanisms we have used here. For each mechanism, we provide a reference to the literature, as an overview of or entry to the existing research; we refer the interested reader to the text of the chapter for additional references on each topic.

Bounded Rationality

Judgment Errors

Self-serving Bias. Reference: Linda Babcock and George Loewenstein, Explaining Bargaining Impasse: The Role of Self-serving Biases, 11 *J. Econ. Persp.* 109 (winter 1997).

Our applications: bargaining around court orders; failed negotiations.

Availability Heuristic. Reference: Amos Tversky and Daniel Kahneman, Judgment Under Uncertainty: Heuristics and Biases, in *Judgment Under Uncertainty* 3 (Daniel Kahneman, Paul Slovic, and Amos Tversky eds., 1982).

Our applications: environmental legislation, government advertising, anti-antipaternalism.

Hindsight Bias. Reference: Baruch Fischhoff, Hindsight $\neq$ Foresight: The Effect of Outcome Knowledge on Judgment Under Uncertainty, 1 *J. Experi. Psychol. Hum. Perception & Performance* 288 (1975).

Our applications: negligence determinations; other determinations of fact or law.

Overoptimism. Reference: Neil D. Weinstein, Unrealistic Optimism About Future Life Events, 39 *J. Personality & Soc. Psychol.* 806 (1980).

Our applications: government advertising, anti-antipaternalism.

Inability to Predict Experience Utility. Reference: Daniel Kahneman, New Challenges to the Rationality Assumption, in *The Rational Foundations of Economic Behaviour* 203 (Kenneth J. Arrow, Enrico Colombatto, Mark Perlman, and Christian Schmidt eds., 1996).

Our applications: anti-antipaternalism.

Decision-Making Behavior

Loss Aversion. Reference: Daniel Kahneman and Amos Tversky, Prospect Theory: An Analysis of Decision Under Risk, 47 *Econometrica* 263 (1979).

Our applications: government advertising.

Endowment Effect (a Corollary of Loss Aversion). Reference: Daniel Kahneman, Jack L. Knetsch, and Richard H. Thaler, Experimental Tests of the Endowment Effect and the Coase Theorem, 98 *J. Pol. Econ.* 1325, 1327 (1990).

Our applications: bargaining around court orders, mandatory contract terms, prior restraints on speech.

Bounded Willpower

"Hyperbolic" Discounting. Reference: David Laibson, Golden Eggs and Hyperbolic Discounting, 112 *Q.J. Econ.* 443 (1997).

Our applications: criminal behavior.

Bounded Self-interest

Fairness Behavior and Spitefulness. Reference: Colin Camerer and Richard H. Thaler, Anomalies: Ultimatums, Dictators, and Manners, 9 *J. Econ. Persp.* 209 (spring 1995).

Our applications: bargaining around court orders; bans on market transactions; prior restraints on speech.

Notes

1 Gary S. Becker, *The Economic Approach to Human Behavior* 14 (1976).

2 For a further elaboration of this view, see Richard H. Thaler, Doing Economics Without *Homo Economicus*, in *Foundations of Research in Economics: How Do Economists Do Economics?* 227, 230–5 (Steven G. Medema and Warren J. Samuels eds., 1996).

3 Herbert A. Simon, A Behavioral Model of Rational Choice, 69 *Q.J. Econ.* 99 (1955).

4 Amos Tversky and Daniel Kahneman, Judgment Under Uncertainty: Heuristics and Biases, in *Judgment Under Uncertainty* 3, 11 (Daniel Kahneman, Paul Slovic, and Amos Tversky eds., 1982).

5 See Colin Camerer, Individual Decision Making, in *Handbook of Experimental Economics* 587, 619–20, 622–4 (John H. Kagel and Alvin E. Roth eds., 1995) (describing the Allais paradox); Daniel Ellsberg, Risk, Ambiguity, and the Savage Axioms, 75 *Q.J. Econ.* 643 (1961).

6 Daniel Kahneman and Amos Tversky, Prospect Theory: An Analysis of Decision Under Risk, 47 *Econometrica* 263 (1979). For a survey of empirical tests of this and other models, see Camerer, supra note 5, at 626–43. John D. Hey and Chris Orme, Investigating Generalizations of Expected Utility Theory Using Experimental Data, 62 *Econometrica* 1291 (1994), conclude that expected utility theory performs fairly well, but they do not consider prospect theory as an alternative. An alternative to prospect theory for modifying expected utility theory is offered by Itzhak Gilboa and David Schmeidler, Case-Based Decision Theory, 110 *Q.J. Econ.* 605 (1995).

7 Richard A. Posner, *Economic Analysis of Law* 4 (5th ed. 1998).

8 Gary S. Becker, Irrational Behavior and Economic Theory, 70 *J. Pol. Econ.* 1, 4–6 (1962).

9 John H. Kagel, Raymond C. Battalio, and Leonard Green, *Economic Choice Theory: An Experimental Analysis of Animal Behavior* 8, 17–19, 24–5 (1995).

10 Posner, supra note 7, at 6, 7.

11 See Daniel Kahneman, Jack L. Knetsch, and Richard H. Thaler, Experimental Tests of the Endowment Effect and the Coase Theorem, 98 *J. Pol. Econ.* 1325, 1327 tbl. 1 (1990) (summarizing studies).

12 See Robert Nozick, *The Nature of Rationality* 22 (1993).

13 Hal R. Arkes and Catherine Blumer, The Psychology of Sunk Cost, 35 *Org. Behav. & Hum. Decision Processes* 124, 127–8 (1985).

14 Posner, supra note 7, at 11.

15 R. H. Coase, The Problem of Social Cost, 3 *J.L. & Econ.* 1 (1960).

16 See, e.g., Steven Shavell, Criminal Law and the Optimal Use of Nonmonetary Sanctions as a Deterrent, 85 *Colum. L. Rev.* 1232 (1985).

17 Amos Tversky, Rational Theory and Constructive Choice, in *The Rational Foundations of Economic Behavior* 185, 189–91 (Kenneth J. Arrow et al. eds., 1996).

18 See Werner Guth, Rolf Schmittberger, and Bernd Schwarze, An Experimental Analysis of Ultimatum Bargaining, 3 *J. Econ. Behav. & Org.* 367, 371–2, 375 tbls. 4–5 (1982); Daniel Kahneman, Jack L. Knetsch, and Richard H. Thaler, Fairness and the Assumptions of Economics, 59 *J. Bus.* S285, S291 tbl. 2 (1986).

19 See Guth et al., supra note 18, at 371–2, 375 tbls. 4–5; Kahneman et al., supra note 18, at S291 tbl. 2.

20 See Colin Camerer and Richard H. Thaler, Anomalies: Ultimatums, Dictators, and Manners, 9 *J. Econ. Persp.*, spring 1995, at 209, 210–11; Vesna Prasnikar and Alvin E. Roth, Considerations of Fairness and Strategy: Experimental Data from Sequential Games, 107 *Q.J. Econ.* 865, 873–5 (1992); Robert Slonim and Alvin E. Roth, Learning in High Stakes Ultimatum Games: An Experiment in the Slovak Republic, 66 *Econometrica* 569, 573 (1998). When repetition is combined with very high stakes, however, offers decrease somewhat, although they are still far above what the standard analysis would predict. See Slonim and Roth, supra, at 573, 588 fig. 3A.

21 This experiment is profitable for the experimenter if any offers are rejected by Responders (because the experimenter has collected $10 from each pair of bargainers, which the bargainers forfeit if the Proposer's offer is rejected). To solve this "problem," we conducted another experiment right after in which the winner of a game was awarded any profits earned by the experimenter in the first round.

22 See Elizabeth Hoffman, Kevin McCabe, and Vernon L. Smith, Social Distance and Other-Regarding Behavior in Dictator Games, 86 *Am. Econ. Rev.* 653, 653–4 and fig. 1 (1996) (finding that Proposers typically offered no more than 10 percent of the sum to be divided – and over 60 percent offered nothing – when (1) the Responder had no choice but to accept the Proposer's offer and (2) anonymity was guaranteed).

23 See Ernst Fehr, Georg Kirchsteiger, and Arno Riedl, Does Fairness Prevent Market Clearing: An Experimental Investigation, 108 *Q.J. Econ.* 437 (1993).

24 Richard H. Thaler and Robyn M. Dawes, Cooperation, in *The Winner's Curse: Paradoxes and Anomalies of Economic Life* 6, 19–20 (Richard Thaler ed., 1992).

25 Matthew Rabin, Incorporating Fairness into Game Theory and Economics, 83 *Am. Econ. Rev.* 1281 (1993).

26 Ibid. at 1282.

27 Robert Axelrod, *The Evolution of Cooperation* (1984); Axelrod, *The Complexity of Cooperation* (1997).

28 The concepts of revenge and retribution, which are related to spite, have been discussed by Posner. See Richard A. Posner, Retribution and Related Concepts of Punishment, 9 *J. Legal Stud.* 71 (1980).

29 Cf. Robert Gibbons and Leaf Van Boven, Multiple Selves in the Prisoner's Dilemma (Nov. 16, 1997) (unpublished manuscript, on file with the Stanford Law Review) (finding that subjects are more likely to engage in cooperative behavior in games when they have a positive impression of their opponent than when they have a negative impression).

30 See Daniel Kahneman, Jack L. Knetsch, and Richard Thaler, Fairness as a Constraint on Profit Seeking: Entitlements in the Market, 76 *Am. Econ. Rev.* 728, 729–30 (1986).

31 See Elizabeth Hoffman and Matthew L. Spitzer, Entitlements, Rights, and Fairness: An Experimental Examination of Subjects' Concepts of Distributive Justice, 14 *J. Legal Stud.* 259, 261 (1985).

32 See Kahneman et al., supra note 30, at 729–30.

33 See Robert A. Kagan and Jerome H. Skolnick, Banning Smoking: Compliance Without Enforcement, in *Smoking Policy: Law, Politics, and Culture* 69 (Robert L. Rabin and Stephen D. Sugarman eds., 1993).

34 See Kahneman et al., supra note 11.

35 See George Loewenstein and Samuel Issacharoff, Source Dependence in the Valuation of Objects, 7 *J. Behav. Decision Making* 157, 159–61 (1994).

36 Conventional law and economics attributes failures to settle primarily to informational differences among parties. There is a large body of literature on this topic, which is summarized in Bruce L. Hay and Kathryn E. Spier, Settlement of Litigation, in 3 *The New Palgrave Dictionary of Economics and the Law* 442 (Peter Newman ed., 1998).

37 Richard Craswell, Passing on the Costs of Legal Rules: Efficiency and Distribution in Buyer-Seller Relationships, 43 *Stan. L. Rev.* 361, 388–90 (1991).

38 Jonathan Gruber, The Incidence of Mandated Maternity Benefits, 84 *Am. Econ. Rev.* 622 (1994).

39 Ibid. at 623.

40 See ibid. at 626 n. 9.

41 See, e.g., John Tierney, Tickets? Supply Meets Demand on Sidewalk, *N.Y. Times*, Dec. 26, 1992, at A1 (quoting New York University economist William J. Baumol criticizing laws against ticket scalping).

42 See Gary S. Becker, A Note on Restaurant Pricing and Other Examples of Social Influences on Price, 99 *J. Pol. Econ.* 1109, 1110 (1991) (offering quality-certification argument).

43 See Kahneman et al., supra note 30, at 735.

44 See Kahneman et al., supra note 18, at S287–8.

45 See, e.g., Keith N. Hylton and Vincent D. Rougeau, Lending Discrimination: Economic Theory, Econometric Evidence, and the Community Reinvestment Act, 85 *Geo. L. J.* 237, 258 (1996) (discussing the residential mortgage lending market); Board of Governors of the Federal Reserve System, *Report to the Congress on Community Development Lending by Depository Institutions* 34 (1993) (same).

46 See David D. Haddock and Fred S. McChesney, Why Do Firms Contrive Shortages? The Economics of Intentional Mispricing, 32 *Econ. Inquiry* 562, 562–3 (1994) (surveying the economic literature).

47 Peter Passell, If Scalpers Can Get So Much, Why Aren't Tickets Costlier? *N.Y. Times*, Dec. 23, 1993, at D2 (quoting Gerald Schoenfeld, head of the Shubert Organization).
48 Alan Blinder, Elie R. D. Canetti, David E. Lebow, and Jeremy B. Rudd, *Asking About Prices: A New Approach to Understanding Price Stickiness* 9–10, 149–64 (1998).
49 See, e.g., Geoffrey R. Stone, Louis M. Seidman, Cass R. Sunstein, and Mark V. Tushnet, *Constitutional Law* 1183–96 (3d ed. 1996).
50 See Martin H. Redish, The Proper Role of the Prior Restraint Doctrine in First Amendment Theory, 70 *Va. L. Rev.* 53, 55 (1984).
51 See W. Kip Viscusi, *Rational Risk Policy* 96 (1998) (discussing role of availability); Roger G. Noll and James E. Krier, Some Implications of Cognitive Psychology for Risk Regulation, 19 *J. Legal Stud.* 747, 762 (1990) (same); Cass R. Sunstein, Congress, Constitutional Moments, and the Cost-Benefit State, 48 *Stan. L. Rev.* 247, 265–6 (1996) (same).
52 Amos Tversky and Daniel Kahneman, Extensional Versus Intuitive Reasoning: The Conjunction Fallacy in Probability Judgment, 90 *Psychol. Rev.* 293, 295 (1983).
53 See, e.g., Keith Schneider, Fetal Harm Is Cited as Primary Hazard in Dioxin Exposure, *N.Y. Times*, May 11, 1994, at A1, A20.
54 See *Asbestos Hazard Emergency Act of 1986*, 15 *U.S.C.* §§2641–56 (1994); Margo L. Stoffel, Comment, Electromagnetic Fields and Cancer: A Legitimate Cause of Action or a Result of Media-Influenced Fear, 21 *Ohio N.U. L. Rev.* 551, 590 (1995) (referring to an ABC news special on how media reports "heightened anxiety over . . . asbestos in schools").
55 See Jerry L. Mashaw and David L. Harfst, *The Struggle for Auto Safety* 141–6 (1990).
56 See Baruch Fischhoff, Hindsight ≠ Foresight: The Effect of Outcome Knowledge on Judgment Under Uncertainty, 1 *J. Experimental Psychol. Hum. Perception & Performance* 288 (1975).
57 See Neil D. Weinstein, Unrealistic Optimism About Future Life Events, 39 *J. Personality & Soc. Psychol.* 806 (1980); Neil D. Weinstein, Unrealistic Optimism About Susceptibility to Health Problems: Conclusions from a Community-Wide Sample, 10 *J. Behav. Med.* 481 (1987).
58 Jeffrey J. Rachlinski, A Positive Psychological Theory of Judging in Hindsight, 65 *U. Chi. L. Rev.* 571, 615 (1998) (quoting *Graham v. John Deere Co.*, 383 U.S. 1, 17–18 [1966]).
59 See Reid Hastie and W. Kip Viscusi, What Juries Can't Do Well: The Jury's Performance as a Risk Manager (May 21, 1998) (unpublished manuscript, on file with the Stanford Law Review).
60 See, e.g., Martin F. Davies, Reduction of Hindsight Bias by Restoration of Foresight Perspective: Effectiveness of Foresight-Encoding and Hindsight-Retrieval Strategies, 40 *Org. Behav. & Hum. Decision Processes* 40, 61–4 (1987); Baruch Fischhoff, Perceived Informativeness of Facts, 3 *J. Experi. Psychol.* 349, 354–6 (1977); Kim A. Kamin and Jeffrey J. Rachlinski, Ex Post ≠ Ex Ante, 19 *Law & Hum. Behav.* 89, 96–8 (1995).
61 338 F.2d 708 (2d Cir. 1964).
62 Hal R. Arkes and Cindy A. Schipani, Medical Malpractice v. the Business Judgment Rule: Differences in Hindsight Bias, 73 *Or. L. Rev.* 587, 633–6 (1994); Norman G. Poythress, Richard Wiener, and Joseph E. Schumacher, Reframing the Medical Malpractice Tort Reform Debate: Social Science Research Implications for Noneconomic Reforms, 16 *Law & Psychol. Rev.* 65, 105–11 (1992); David B. Wexler and Robert F. Schopp, How and When to Correct for Juror Hindsight Bias in Mental Health Malpractice Litigation: Some Preliminary Observations, 7 *Behav. Sci. & L.* 485, 496 (1989).

63 Wexler and Schopp, supra note 62, at 494 (emphasis in original).
64 Arkes and Schipani, supra note 62, at 635.
65 Pub. L. No. 104-67, 109 *Stat.* 737 (1995) (codified in scattered sections of 15 *U.S.C.*).
66 See Robert Charles Clark, *Corporate Law* §8.10.4 (1986).
67 See Janet Cooper Alexander, Do the Merits Matter? A Study of Settlements in Securities Class Actions, 43 *Stan. L. Rev.* 497, 511–13 (1991); James Bohn and Stephen Choi, Fraud in the New-Issues Market: Empirical Evidence on Securities Class Actions, 144 *U. Pa. L. Rev.* 903, 935–40, 979–80 (1996).
68 See Edward L. Rubin, Legislative Methodology: Some Lessons from the Truth-in-Lending Act, 80 *Geo. L. J.* 223, 235–6 (1991).
69 See, e.g., Joseph E. Stiglitz, *Economics of the Public Sector* 90–1 (1986).
70 Shlomo Benartzi and Richard H. Thaler, Risk Aversion or Myopia? Choices in Repeated Gambles and Retirement Investments (Nov. 8, 1997) (unpublished manuscript, on file with the Stanford Law Review).
71 See Kahneman and Tversky, supra note 6, at 277–9.
72 See ibid. at 273 (outcomes are viewed differently depending on whether they come in the form of gains or losses from a perceived status quo); ibid. at 279 (citing Eugene Galanter and Patricia Pliner, Cross-modality Matching of Money Against Other Continua, in *Sensation and Measurement* 65 [Howard R. Moskowitz, Bertram Scharf, and Joseph C. Stevens eds., 1974]) (losses are weighted more heavily than gains). Another feature of how outcomes are viewed, both empirically and under prospect theory, is that a given change produces less reaction the further a decision maker is from her reference point. Thus, for example, the value difference between $10 and $20 is greater than the value difference between $1,000 and $1,010, both for gains and for losses, assuming a reference point of $0. See ibid. at 278. In terms of the shape of the "value function" for decision makers (a function giving the value of each outcome; this is prospect theory's counterpart to the utility function), this suggests a function that is concave for gains and convex for losses; only with that shape are both gains and losses viewed as less significant the further the decision maker is from her reference point. See ibid. This shape of the value function is further supported by evidence of attitudes toward risk: People appear generally (though there are exceptions) to exhibit risk-averse attitudes toward gains but risk-seeking attitudes toward losses, and these attitudes imply concavity of the value function for gains and convexity for losses. See ibid. This pattern of concavity and convexity has received considerable empirical support. See ibid. at 268, 278; Peter C. Fishburn and Gary A. Kochenberger, Two-Piece Von Neumann–Morgenstern Utility Functions, 10 *Decision Sci.* 503, 509–10 (1979).
73 Amos Tversky and Richard H. Thaler, Preference Reversals, in *The Winner's Curse: Paradoxes and Anomalies of Economic Life* 79, 91 (Richard Thaler ed., 1992).
74 Beth E. Meyerowitz and Shelly Chaiken, The Effect of Message Framing on Breast Self-examination: Attitudes, Intentions, and Behavior, 52 *J. Personality & Soc. Psychol.* 500, 505 (1987).
75 See Douglas Herring, Comment, Getting High from South of the Border: Illicit Smuggling of Rohypnol as an Example of the Need to Modify U.S. Response to International Drug Smuggling After NAFTA, 18 *Loy. L. A. Int'l & Comp. L. J.* 841, 863 (1996) (citing Mathea Falco, Toward a More Effective Drug Policy, 1994 *U. Chi. Legal F.* 9, 15).
76 See Neil D. Weinstein, Unrealistic Optimism About Susceptibility to Health Problems: Conclusions from a Community-Wide Sample, 10 *J. Behav. Med.* 481 (1987) (overoptimism apparent in the general public); Richard A. Posner, *Aging and Old Age* 104–6 (1995).

77 A. Mitchell Polinsky and Steven Shavell, On the Disutility and Discounting of Imprisonment and the Theory of Deterrence 12–13 (Harvard Law School, John M. Olin Center for Law, Economics, and Business, Discussion Paper no. 213, 1997).

78 See, e.g., Michael R. Gottfredson and Travis Hirschi, *A General Theory of Crime* 85–120 (1990) (emphasizing role of lack of self-control in criminal behavior); James Q. Wilson and Allan Abrahamse, Does Crime Pay? 9 *Just. Q.* 359, 372–4 (1992) (similar).

79 See George Loewenstein and Richard H. Thaler, Intertemporal Choice, in *The Winner's Curse: Paradoxes and Anomalies of Economic Life* 92, 95–6 (Richard Thaler ed., 1992) (discussing studies).

80 See David Laibson, Golden Eggs and Hyperbolic Discounting, 112 *Q.J. Econ.* 443, 445–6 (1997).

81 Cf. Robert D. Cooter, Lapses, Conflict, and Akrasia in Torts and Crimes: Towards an Economic Theory of the Will, 11 *Int'l Rev. L. & Econ.* 149, 154 (1991) (concluding that short but highly probable sentences are optimal in a model in which potential offenders experience "lapses" in self-control).

82 A standard argument for law under the conventional economic approach is that self-interested people will create collective irrationality; if people are boundedly self-interested, however, this problem may tend to disappear.

83 See W. Kip Viscusi, *Smoking* 4 (1992).

84 See Paul Slovic, Do Adolescent Smokers Know the Risks? 47 *Duke L. J.* 1133, 1136–7.

85 See Cass R. Sunstein, Behavioral Analysis of Law, 64 *U. Chi. L. Rev.* 1175, 1184 (1997).

86 See Daniel Kahneman, New Challenges to the Rationality Assumption, in *The Rational Foundations of Economic Behaviour* 203 (Kenneth J. Arrow, Enrico Colombatto, Mark Perlman, and Christian Schmidt eds., 1996).

87 See Philip Brickman, Dan Coates, and Ronnie Janoff-Bulman, Lottery Winners and Accident Victims: Is Happiness Relative? 36 *J. Personality & Soc. Psychol.* 917 (1978); George Loewenstein and David Schkade, Wouldn't It Be Nice? Predicting Future Feelings, in *Well-being: The Foundations of Hedonic Psychology* (Ed Diener, Norbert Schwartz, and Daniel Kahneman eds., 1999).

88 See George Loewenstein and Shane Frederick, Predicting Reactions to Environmental Change, in *Environment, Ethics, and Behavior: The Psychology of Environmental Valuation and Degradation* 52, 64–5 (Max H. Bazerman, David M. Messick, Ann E. Tenbrunsel, and Kimberly A. Wade-Benzoni eds., 1997).

89 See Jon Elster, *Sour Grapes: Studies in the Subversion of Rationality* (1983); Amartya Sen, *Commodities and Capabilities* (1985).

90 See W. Kip Viscusi, *Fatal Tradeoffs: Public and Private Responsibilities for Risk* 149 (1992); W. Kip Viscusi, *Rational Risk Policy* 85–8, 94–7 (1998); Noll and Krier, supra note 51, at 747, 760–72.

91 See Robert C. Clark, Contracts, Elites, and Traditions in the Making of Corporate Law, 89 *Colum. L. Rev.* 1703, 1719–20 (1989).

92 Stephen Breyer, *Breaking the Vicious Circle: Toward Effective Risk Regulation* 55–81 (1993).

93 Howard Margolis, *Dealing with Risk* 165–89 (1996).

94 *Risk vs. Risk* (John D. Graham and Jonathan Baert Wiener eds., 1995). Each of the solutions stated in the text may also be attractive to conventional economists on a variety of grounds.

Part II

Heuristics and Biases: Shortcuts, Errors, and Legal Decisions

2 Context-Dependence in Legal Decision Making

Mark Kelman, Yuval Rottenstreich, and Amos Tversky

Normative analyses of choice commonly assume value maximization: a numerical value or utility is associated with each option such that, given a set of options, the decision maker chooses the one with the highest value. An immediate consequence of value maximization, called context-independence, is that the relative ranking of any two options should not vary with the addition or deletion of other options.[1] A person who prefers chicken over pasta should not change this preference on learning that fish is also available.[2] Despite its intuitive appeal, there is evidence[3] that decision makers do not always satisfy this condition. In this chapter we test the descriptive validity of context-independence in legal settings and discuss its prescriptive implications.

Two types of violations of context-independence – compromise effects and contrast effects – have recently been demonstrated. "Compromise effect" refers to the finding that the same option is evaluated more favorably when it is seen as intermediate in the set of options under consideration than when it is extreme. Consequently, compromise implies that the relative ranking of two options depends on the presence or absence of other options. Salespeople sometimes exploit this tendency by showing both bare bones and fancy products in order to induce customers to buy an intermediate product. Several experiments have demonstrated compromise effects. In one experiment subjects first reviewed several available Minolta cameras in a catalog. One group chose between a midlevel Minolta camera and a low-end camera; 50 percent chose each camera. Another group could also choose a third, high-end camera. In this group, of those choosing either the midlevel or low-end camera, 72 percent chose the midlevel camera.[4]

"Trade-off contrast," or simply "contrast," refers to the observation that the same option is evaluated more favorably in the presence of similar options clearly inferior to it than in the absence of such options. Contrast effects, more generally, are ubiquitous in perception and judgment. The same circle appears larger when surrounded by small circles and smaller when surrounded by large ones. Similarly, the same product may appear attractive on the background of less attractive alternatives and unattractive on the background of more attractive ones.[5] Real estate agents interested in selling a particular home sometimes show customers a similar home that is clearly less attractive. Experimental studies also demonstrate contrast effects. Given the choice between $6 and a Cross pen, only 36 percent of subjects chose the Cross pen. However, when given the choice between $6, the Cross pen, and a less attractive pen, the percentage choosing the Cross pen rose to 46 percent (only 2 percent of subjects chose the other pen, confirming its inferiority).[6]

Our goal was to test compromise and contrast in two types of legal decisions. First, we investigated the degree to which decision makers made contested legal judgments (grading or sentencing decisions in criminal law) independently of the set of available judgments. Second, we investigated the degree to which consumers of heavily legalized products (plaintiffs or their lawyers facing distinct settlement offers) chose between such consumption bundles independently of the set of options available.

We report five experiments. Two tested for compromise and one for contrast in legal judgments, two for contrast in choices between heavily legalized products. The experimental methodology was as follows. Subjects read case summaries and made decisions. Each subject read one or two cases. The case summaries (reprinted in the appendix) contained (1) a presentation of established facts, (2) a list of possible options (verdicts for experimental jurors, sentences for experimental judges, settlement offers for experimental lawyers acting as client advisors), and (3) legal definitions where relevant (for example, definitions of offenses for jurors selecting an appropriate verdict). Subjects read individually, spent about ten minutes on each case, and did not discuss the cases with others. Subjects reading the first two cases were students in "Introductory Psychology" at Stanford University and San Jose State University, as well as random persons recruited in two public places (White Plaza at Stanford and downtown Palo Alto) to participate in exchange for a lottery ticket. Cases 3 and 5 were read only by students in Stanford's "Introductory Psychology" class. Case 4 was read only by students enrolled in a "Psychology of Gender" class at Stanford. Subjects in the classroom settings participated for course credit and were recruited by methods normally used at the two schools. Since the responses in the distinct settings were extremely similar, we report aggregated data. The experimental results were inconsistent with the context-independence condition implied by value maximization. We present the experiments, detail limitations of the data, and discuss implications of the results.

Experimental Tests of Compromise

Case 1

Subjects first read the following summary of facts:[7]

On January 1, 1993, at 9:00 A.M., the Defendant gave her second husband a cup of coffee into which she poured twenty crushed sleeping pills. He died within hours of drinking it. You should take it as given that he suffered a great deal of physical pain in the last several hours of his life. The Defendant concedes that after she gave him the coffee, she typed a suicide note on his computer screen in the basement and that she did so hoping that the police would believe she had nothing to do with his death. She concedes, too, that she gave him the coffee and ground-up pills hoping that he would die. The prosecution concedes that at 8:05 A.M. the Defendant had overheard her seventeen-year-old daughter from her first marriage sobbing on the phone. The daughter was telling her best friend that her stepfather (the deceased) had "once again" attempted to molest her sexually the previous evening. At the same time, the prosecutor argues, and the Defendant concedes, that she stood to inherit a large amount of money from the deceased, and that she had been involved with another man for more than six months prior to her husband's death.

One group of subjects was told the incident occurred in the District of Columbia; members of this group were told to choose either murder or manslaughter as the verdict since there is no category of special circumstances murder in the jurisdiction. A second group of subjects was told the incident occurred in California; members of this group were given the additional option of choosing the verdict of special circumstances murder and told that potentially relevant special circumstances were (1) that the defendant killed for financial gain; (2) that she killed in an exceptionally heinous fashion, manifesting exceptional depravity (and that that finding was appropriate if the crime were conscienceless or pitiless and was unnecessarily torturous to the victim); and (3) that the defendant killed by the administration of poison.[8]

Jurors should choose the manslaughter verdict if they believe the defendant was acting under the influence of extreme emotional disturbance for which there is a reasonable explanation and an available murder verdict otherwise. The choice between manslaughter and the other verdicts should not be sensitive to whether, if the defendant were acting deliberately, she killed for financial gain, or in a heinous fashion, or using something that would be considered poison. Thus, context-independence requires a juror who prefers manslaughter over murder in the two-option condition to prefer manslaughter over both murder and special circumstances murder in the three-option condition,[9] implying, in the aggregate, that manslaughter will be chosen by as many jurors facing a two-option choice set as jurors facing a three-option choice set. Compromise, however, predicts that a smaller proportion of jurors will select manslaughter in the three-option choice set than in the two-option choice set. The logic follows directly from the definition of compromise. If each person is more likely to choose murder than manslaughter when a third option, involving still more serious penalties than murder, is present, that tendency should be revealed in the aggregate.

Table 2.1. *Choices of Subjects Reading Case 1*

	Percentage Choosing Manslaughter	Percentage Choosing Murder	Percentage Choosing Murder with Special Circumstances	N
Group 1 (D.C.)	47%	53%	–	167
Group 2 (California)	19	39	42%	183
Group 3	52	48	–	151

Note: See text for explanation.

The data show that 47 percent of 167 subjects chose manslaughter when given only murder and manslaughter as options; when special circumstances murder was also present, only 19 percent of 183 subjects chose manslaughter ($\chi^2 = 32.96$, $p < .0001$).[10]

It is possible that the presence of the special circumstances option communicated relevant information about the appropriateness of choosing murder rather than manslaughter. A fact finder forced to focus (by the presence of the special circumstances instruction) on the fact that the defendant used particular means to kill (poison) and may have had a particular motive (greed) may be more likely to adopt the view that the murder was premeditated and planned, rather than committed "in the heat of passion." To respond to this concern, a third group of subjects read about special circumstances murder, so that they received the information potentially describing the defendant's form of killing but were told that special circumstances murder was not an available option in their jurisdiction. The hypothesis that the finding is attributable to relevant information available to one, but not both, experimental groups was not borne out by the data; 52 percent of the 151 subjects in the third group chose manslaughter, a rate comparable to that of the two-option group and substantially higher than that of the initial three-option group ($\chi^2 = 40.61$, $p < .0001$) (see Table 2.1).

Case 2

Subjects were told to take the following as proven:

Donald Dewey, the defendant, who is an African American, is walking in the inner courtyard of a shopping mall well after all the shops have closed. However, the mall is still open. Fifteen minutes earlier, one of the jewelry shops in the mall was burglarized, but not by Dewey. Nonetheless, a security guard, an off-duty policeman hired by the owners of the mall, approaches Dewey and asks whether he would mind if he patted him down, telling him that there had been a burglary.

The guard intended to check both for burglar's tools and for some of the cash and the missing jewelry. The guard realized he had no probable cause to detain Dewey. Nonetheless, when Dewey refused, the guard reached out to grab him, and felt a bulge, which proved to be a gun, in his coat pocket. Dewey tried to spin away from the guard's hold, screaming, "You've got no business stopping me!" The guard then shouted a racist epithet. Dewey was able to break the guard's grip and knock him over. While the guard was lying on the ground, he shot him with his gun, killing him. All sides concede that Dewey purposely killed the victim.

Subjects were informed that special circumstances murder, murder, voluntary manslaughter, and involuntary manslaughter were possible verdicts; that involuntary manslaughter would be appropriate only if the defendant subjectively, but unreasonably, believed he was entitled to defend himself;[11] and that the distinction between murder and special circumstances murder depended solely on whether the off-duty policeman acting as a guard should be treated as an officer acting in the line of duty since the murder of officers was sufficient grounds for the finding of special circumstances. Note that the question of whether Dewey committed murder or voluntary manslaughter depends only on whether the defendant was, in the minds of the fact finder, adequately provoked (to use common-law language) or "acting under the influence of severe emotional disturbance for which there is a reasonable explanation" (to use the portions of the Model Penal Code language that subjects were in fact given). The distinction between special circumstances murder and murder is irrelevant to this question. The possibility of involuntary manslaughter is likewise orthogonal.[12]

One group was told the judge had ruled, as a matter of law, that off-duty police employed as private security guards are not "police officers in the performance of their duties" so that they could not grade the homicide as special circumstances murder. A second group was told the judge had ruled, as a matter of law, that Dewey was not entitled to use deadly force and that there was no evidence that he subjectively believed, even unreasonably, that he was defending himself; thus they could not grade the homicide as involuntary manslaughter. Since every subject was initially informed about all four possible verdicts, differences across groups do not involve information about the existence of possible alternatives.[13]

The proportion of subjects choosing voluntary manslaughter rose from 31 percent among those choosing from the "upper set" of special circumstances murder, murder, and manslaughter to 55 percent among those choosing from the "lower set" of involuntary manslaughter, manslaughter, and murder. The proportion choosing murder fell from 57 percent in the upper set to 39 percent in the lower set (χ^2 for murder vs. all other verdicts was 7.66, $p < .01$). This pattern indicates a strong compromise effect.

It seems reasonable to assume in this case that the options are naturally ordered in terms of "severity." (Special circumstances murder is more severe than murder, which is more severe than voluntary manslaughter, which is more severe than involuntary manslaughter.) Consider any subset consisting of three of the options. Preferences satisfy betweenness if someone who prefers one of the extreme options in the subset over the intermediate option in the subset is more likely to prefer the intermediate option over the other extreme option than someone who does not. In the Dewey case, betweenness is natural: someone preferring special circumstances murder to murder would almost surely prefer murder to voluntary manslaughter.[14] Someone preferring murder to voluntary manslaughter would almost surely prefer voluntary manslaughter to involuntary manslaughter.

Given betweenness, context-independence requires that the ratio of murder verdicts to voluntary manslaughter verdicts be lower in the upper group than in the lower group. To see why, take choices in the upper group as given and consider how these choices should be translated into the lower group. Anyone choosing special circumstances murder should select murder. Any movement to involuntary manslaughter should come from voluntary manslaughter. Thus, as we move from the upper to the lower group, the number of murder verdicts should rise, and the number of manslaughter verdicts should decline.

Compromise predicts the opposite pattern. In the set of available options, murder is the intermediate option for the upper group, voluntary manslaughter is the intermediate option for the lower group. Thus, compromise predicts that murder will be seen more favorably in the upper group and manslaughter will be seen more favorably in the lower group. If this holds for each individual, it will be reflected in the aggregate. Consequently, the ratio of murder to manslaughter verdicts will be higher in the upper rather than in the lower group.

The data support the compromise prediction. Of 103 upper-group subjects choosing either murder or manslaughter, 65 percent chose murder. Of 100 lower-group subjects choosing either murder or voluntary manslaughter, only 41 percent chose murder ($\chi^2 = 11.79$, $p < .001$). Thus, an option does better by being intermediate in the choice set presented, in violation of the requirement that preference between two options be independent of the presence or absence of other options (see Table 2.2).

Experimental Tests of Contrast

Case 3

Subjects read the following established facts:

The defendant has been convicted of violating a section of the state's criminal code. Any licensed real estate broker who knowingly conceals a substantial and material defect from a purchaser of residential property shall be adjudged in violation of the Code. The Code provides that brokers need not necessarily make efforts to ascertain the condition of the dwelling units they offer. However, brokers must

Table 2.2. *Choices of Subjects Reading Case 2*

Choices	Upper Group ($N = 118$)	Lower Group ($N = 107$)
Murder with special circumstances	13%	–
Murder	57	38%
Voluntary manslaughter	30	55
Involuntary manslaughter	–	7
Proportion of manslaughter/murder[a]	35	59

Note: See text for explanation.
[a] The proportion of manslaughter to murder is voluntary manslaughter divided by voluntary manslaughter plus murder.

inform buyers of all substantial and material defects of which they have been apprised. Additionally, in those cases in which the brokers make no efforts to learn about the dwelling unit's condition, they must inform buyers that they have made no such efforts. In this particular case the broker had in his possession at the time of sale a four-month-old engineer's report indicating that the house he was representing had sustained substantial dry rot damage to the foundation. The report indicated that the damage would cost close to $100,000 to repair. The broker did not inform the would-be buyers of this fact, and they purchased the house for $200,000, which was estimated by appraisers to be within $10,000 of the fair market value of the home without dry rot. At trial, the broker claimed that he believed the report was dated. He testified that he surmised that the foundation had probably been repaired during the six weeks time between the time the engineer's report was prepared and the time the house was first listed by his real estate agency. The jury apparently did not believe this claim for they convicted the defendant of knowingly withholding material information.

Subjects were instructed to act as the judge in the case and to sentence the defendant. One group was asked to choose either the prosecutor's recommendation of a $2,500 fine and one month in jail or the probation department's recommendation of a $2,500 fine plus six months' probation during which the defendant would perform fifty hours of community service. A second group was given these choices plus the additional alternative of selecting a distinct probation recommended by the probation department as an additional option for the judge's consideration: a $2,500 fine plus six months' probation during which the defendant would undergo "50 hours of counseling sessions . . . [focusing] on the importance of ethical business practices and the connection between dishonesty and impaired self-esteem." We tested the hypothesis that the community service probation recommendation would be seen more favorably when contrasted with the counseling probation. We believed most subjects would be skeptical of the utility of counseling for an offender seemingly motivated by greed. Thus we suggest that the community service probation option dominated the similar counseling probation option.

Table 2.3. *Decisions of Those Subjects Choosing Either Community Service Probation or Jail in Case 3*

	Percentage Choosing Community Service Probation	Percentage Choosing Jail	*N*
Two-option group	74%	26%	73
Three-option group	88	12	85

Note: An inferior probation option was also available to subjects in the three-option group. See text for further explanation.

Assuming context-independence, the ratio of community service probation choices to jail choices should be higher in the two-option group than in the three-option group. To see why, take choices in the three-option set as given and consider how they should be translated into the two-option set. Anyone choosing either community service probation or jail from the three-option set should do so from the two-option set as well. Those choosing counseling probation from the three-option set hold one of two rank orders of the three options.[15] We expect few people to hold the rank order counseling probation, jail, community service probation. The alternative rank order – counseling probation, community service probation, jail – is far more likely. Those choosing counseling probation from the three-option set are more likely than not to choose community service probation from the two-option set. As a result, under context-independence, the ratio of community service probation choices to jail choices should be higher in the two-option group than in the three-option group.

Contrast predicts the opposite pattern. If community service probation is evaluated more favorably when contrasted with the inferior counseling probation, that effect should be reflected in a higher ratio of community service probation choices to jail choices in the three-option set than in the two-option set. The data support the contrast prediction. 74 percent of the 73 subjects chose the community service probation over jail in the two-option set; in the three-option set 88 percent of the 85 subjects choosing either community service probation or jail chose community service probation ($\chi^2 = 4.55$, $p < .05$) (see Table 2.3).

Case 4

Subjects were asked to act as lawyers evaluating a series of settlement offers proffered by the defendant and to recommend one of the offers to their clients. Subjects read the following background facts:

The Economics department of a major university voted, two years ago, to recommend that your client, then an associate professor at the university, not be promoted to a tenured position. She claims that she was discriminated against on account of her gender. She notes, first, that male colleagues with parallel publication records had been promoted though none had, like her, received undergraduate teaching awards. She notes, second, that the department had neither hired nor promoted a number of qualified women it had considered over the past two decades.

Your client is interested in (1) being compensated for wrongs done to her and in (2) having the university publicly admit guilt in her case. At the same time, your client is very interested in the progress of women generally and wants (3) to do her part to push for affirmative action plans that would help women in Economics. Your client is not sure how to weigh and compare these three interests. The university counsel's office has contacted you and asked you to communicate settlement offers to your client.

One group of subjects faced three settlement offers. One bound the university to an affirmative action plan for the Economics department without admitting guilt or paying damages. A second consisted of a public admission of guilt and $45,000 in damages. A third consisted of a public admission of guilt, plus a donation of $35,000 in the client's name to her favorite charity. We predicted that few subjects would select the third proposal; it appears inferior to the proposal in which the university pays $45,000 in damages. The professor could always accept the $45,000, give $35,000 to charity and keep $10,000 for herself.[16] However, the third proposal is not clearly inferior to the affirmative action proposal. A second group of subjects faced only the first two options. Additionally, all subjects were given information about the client's underlying preferences, her financial condition, her charitable giving plans, and her estimates of the possibility that the affirmative action plan would be adopted with or without her intervention.

Contrast predicts that subjects are more likely to prefer, and hence recommend, the $45,000 proposal over the affirmative action proposal when the third inferior proposal is offered than when it is not. Context-independence implies that an option can never be "more popular" in a three-option offered set than in a corresponding two-option offered set.[17]

Thus, if the percentage of people choosing the $45,000 proposal is actually larger when three options are available, it is clear that violations of context-independence, attributable to contrast effects, are prevalent.

The data indicate a strong contrast effect. Only 50 percent of 36 subjects chose the $45,000 proposal from the two-option set, while 76 percent of 31 subjects chose it when the option clearly inferior to it was also available ($\chi^2 = 4.54$, $p < .05$). The presence of an inferior option leads to a markedly more favorable evaluation of a similar but superior option[18] (see Table 2.4).

Table 2.4. *Choices of Subjects Reading Case 4*

	Percentage Choosing \$45,000	Percentage Choosing \$35,000 for Charity	Percentage Choosing Admission of Guilt	*N*
Two-option group	50%	–	50%	36
Three-option group	74	6%	20	31

Note: See text for explanation.

Case 5

Once more, subjects were asked to advise a client selecting among settlement offers. The client, Mr. Wells, is the sole neighbor of a nightclub. The nightclub is excessively noisy on weekends, and the owner concedes that were Wells to file a nuisance suit, he would and should prevail in court. The club owner thus communicates a number of settlement offers.

One group received two offers: (1) the club would not lower the noise level but would pay for Wells to stay in a fancy hotel each weekend and give him \$120 a week, or (2) the nightclub would reduce the noise level. Another group received an additional proposal: (3) the nightclub would pay for Wells to stay in a fancy hotel and give him \$40 in cash plus \$85 of vouchers per week redeemable at several nightclubs. The third proposal is clearly inferior to the hotel/unrestricted cash proposal but is not clearly inferior to the noise-reduction proposal. That \$85 in "restricted" money plus \$40 in cash is inferior to \$120 in cash was highlighted by noting that Wells attended nightclubs only three times a year and spent only \$50 per visit when alone and \$90 when accompanied by a date. We hypothesized that the presence of the hotel/vouchers proposal creates a contrast in which the hotel/money proposal looks more favorable than it does when standing alone.

As in case 4, the presence of contrast and a belief that few people will choose the hotel/vouchers option gives rise to a prediction that the overall popularity of the hotel/money option will rise with the addition of the latter option. Recall that context-independence implies that no option can become more popular with the introduction of additional options.

The results show a marked increase in overall popularity of the hotel/money option. This option was chosen by 47 percent of the 32 subjects in the two-option condition and by 74 percent of the 31 subjects in the three-option condition ($\chi^2 = 4.91$, $p < .05$). The presence of an inferior option again leads to a more favorable evaluation of the similar superior option (see Table 2.5).

Table 2.5. *Choices of Subjects Reading Case 5*

	Percentage Choosing Weekend Lodging	Percentage Choosing Inferior Weekend Lodging	Percentage Choosing Sound Decrease	*N*
Two-option group	47%	–	53%	32
Three-option group	74	0%	26	31

Note: See text for explanation.

Interpreting the Data

There are two distinct interpretive issues. The first issue concerns the validity of our findings. Do the experiments demonstrate the presence of genuine compromise or contrast effects that undermine our faith that decision makers will make context-independent decisions? This question turns both on whether the experimental subjects actually made context-dependent decisions (an internal validity question) and whether the experimental setting permits us to make reasonable inferences about decision makers in ostensibly parallel real-world settings (an external validity question).

The second issue concerns the response to the presence of context-dependent decision making. The present findings, we suggest, provide at least prima facie evidence that the decisions of judges or juries may be prone to compromise and contrast effects. It could be argued that this conclusion is of limited practical significance either because the observed biases are not particularly troubling from a normative standpoint or because there is little that can be done to reduce or eliminate them. We shall discuss these issues in turn.

Have We Demonstrated Genuine Context-Dependence in Legal Decision Making?

Preferences are said to be context-dependent only if the choice between two options is affected by the presence of a third option that does not provide new information about the relative merits of the remaining options. It is important to consider whether preferences we labeled "context-dependent" can be explained on the basis that the additional options conveyed "added relevant information" that could reasonably cause preferences to change. We have addressed this issue in discussing the experiments in turn, but we thought it important to systematize prior discussions.

The results of our experiments closely parallel results of experiments in consumer choice where no meaningful information was conveyed about the options present. For instance, the presence of an unattractive pen does not convey additional information about the attractiveness of a Cross pen. Similarly, we argue that no additional relevant information was provided by the added options in the second, fourth, and fifth experiments. This might be true for formal or procedural reasons, as in the second (Dewey) experiment, where all subjects read all four possible verdicts and were simply told to rule out one of the extreme ones. This might also be true for substantive reasons, that is, because focusing on the additional option does not lead one to reconsider any features of the other options that are salient in reaching a decision. In the Dewey case, for instance, the choice between murder and manslaughter, given the prevailing definitions of the two offenses in the experiment, turns only on the presence or absence of "extreme emotional disturbance for which there is a reasonable explanation." Directions either to attend to (or ignore) whether a security guard is a police officer acting in the line of duty or whether the defendant was acting in imperfect self-defense are irrelevant to that question.[19] In case 4 one does not learn more about the value of $45,000 in untied money by being presented with the option of $35,000 in tied money. Similarly, in case 5 one would not learn more about the value of $120 a week by being presented with the option of receiving $40 plus $85 in vouchers.[20]

In the first and third studies, it is plausible that subjects substantively "learned" about the core options by being offered additional ones. One could argue that in the first experiment (in which the wife killed her husband), the presence of the special circumstances murder instruction alerts readers to three features of the case that are more consistent with the claim that the defendant was a premeditated murderer than one who acted in something resembling the "heat of passion": first, that she had a long-term motive (financial gain); second, that she killed by administering poison; and, third, that she arguably killed in a torturous manner, all of which seem less consistent with the standard model of manslaughter in which the defendant simply lashes out. (The argument that the experiment involving group 3 [in Table 2.1] does not cure this defect, by exposing all subjects to this account of the crime, is that they have not been asked to apply this account to the particular facts if they are in the experimental group that chooses only between murder and manslaughter. Subjects may, thus, pay less attention to this account of the killing. In a sense they have been told that "authorities" – experimenters in our cases, judges in a courtroom – do not credit such an account of the case.) Similarly, in the third experiment (in which a judge is asked to choose between incarceration and probation for the real estate agent) one could argue that subjects given the "inferior" probation option (counseling) in addition to the superior one (community service) choose some probation more often because the presence of the counseling option suggests that the real estate agent acted not out of the maliciousness some might think necessary to justify imprisonment but out of psychological pathology.

In summary, the second, fourth, and fifth experiments most strongly suggest that subjects' preferences are context-dependent, while the first and third experiments are consistent with this conclusion, although they are more open to alternative accounts.

Finally, it might be argued that the behavior of jurors and judges in real trials is quite different from the behavior of students in experimental situations. The question, however, is not whether our experimental task captures the essential features of legal decision making but whether compromise and contrast effects observed in our studies are likely to disappear in a real-world setting. Although this possibility cannot be ruled out, it is not supported by available data.[21] There is evidence to suggest that the qualitative patterns observed in hypothetical studies are generally replicated in more realistic conditions involving real payoffs and significant consequences.[22] Thus, we believe the present findings provide at least prima facie evidence that context effects are likely to influence jurors and judges.

How Should We Respond to Context-Dependent Decision Making?

There are two separate questions policy makers might pose if they believed context-dependent decisions were commonplace. First, they must ascertain whether such decisions are problematic, harming some cognizable interests of some party. Second, they must determine whether the decisions they deem harmful can be avoided by reducing the decision makers' authority, "educating" them about their tendencies, or designing procedures to reduce context-dependence.

Do Context-Dependent Decisions Cause Harm? Violations of context-independence may be more troubling in legal decision making than in consumer choice. Unlike consumer choice, where the decision maker does not have clearly defined ends, legal processes have been designed with specific purposes in mind. Legal rule makers (legislatures, administrative agencies) typically state, rather explicitly, a set of goals to be met by legal judgment in particular cases. It is, therefore, easier to argue that the failure to meet those goals efficaciously is troublesome. Once we declare, for instance, that the purpose of differentiating murder from manslaughter is, for instance, to show a certain level of mercy to those acting in atypically stressful circumstances, then we have failed to meet that stated goal if we differentiate defendants on some other basis (for example, the presence of an option in which we condemn murderers of policemen more than ordinary murderers). Whether a violator deserves "reasonable" probation or imprisonment should similarly turn on some explicit set of policy judgments: If the decision is likely to be different when we learn facts unrelated to those policy judgments (that is, that we could choose between reasonable and "silly" probation), it is far less likely that we are attending to the set of policy judgments we have declared relevant.[23]

Because consumers do not have explicit "policies" or goals, it is less clear in what sense differential evaluation of options on the basis of context hinders consumers' interests. The notion that the consumer harms herself by breaches of context-independence is grounded in two observations. First, we suspect that the consumer herself would be prone to reevaluate (if not alter) her decision if she became aware of the fact that she made it on the basis of nonprobative facts. In this sense, a pragmatic test of the problematic nature of context-dependent choices is simply that such choices are prone to be ones the decision maker would prefer to reconsider or revisit.[24] Second, to the extent that people do not have a stable, context-independent preference order, their choices can be manipnulated by the composition of the set of options under consideration. As we have noted, such manipulations are common in the marketplace. They suggest that harm befalls context-dependent consumers since someone manipulated into choosing the option favored by another party, with her own set of interests, is less likely to maximize his own well-being.[25]

Going beyond the question of possible harm, it is perfectly possible to read the experiments as (1) describing a regular pattern in human behavior, and (2) giving lawyers (like marketers of consumer goods) information about how better to manipulate those they deal with (or defend themselves from manipulation). A lawyer prefers that the party suing her accept one of two realistic settlement offers: Knowledge of contrast effects permits her to increase the probability that her adversary will accept her preferred offer.

We have little doubt that some lawyers already implicitly incorporate informal intuitions about context-dependence, even if unaware of the formal category. "Compromise" effects are well known to both district attorneys and defenders: As a tactical matter, one side and/or the other might choose not to request that judges instruct jurors to consider lesser included charges,[26] hoping to force the jury to elect between acquittal and conviction of a serious charge, believing that the jury will otherwise be unduly prone to pick the compromise judgment, even if that judgment would attract little support in a two-option set (against acquittal alone, or against conviction of the serious offense alone, assuming one could decide to convict and then, sequentially, grade). That clients are rarely able to challenge the competence of lawyers who fail to ask for instructions on lesser included offenses, even when conviction of those offenses would have been legally tenable, reflects not only generally high burdens in challenging lawyer competency[27] but also the recognition that the decision to offer a compromise verdict diminishes the probability of acquittal and is, as a result, a tactical judgment[28] that the client must make in consultation with his attorney.[29]

Can We Reduce Context-Dependence and Improve Legal Decision Making? The experiments do not tell whether an experimental group alerted to the existence of contrast or compromise effects avoids them any better than an experimental group not so alerted. Thus it is not clear whether we can "educate" people to avoid context-dependent decisions, even one effect at a time, let alone whether more general education would lead to context-independence more globally.

We can, of course, eliminate irrelevant options when we have a substantive theory of irrelevance and, more interestingly, weigh the value of including a relevant option against the costs that will be borne because inclusion shifts preferences among other options for irrelevant reasons. However, if we believe, for instance, that it is impossible to eliminate compromise biases because people might still implicitly consider an unstated option more extreme than one or the other pole in the option set, then the goal of eliminating irrelevant options may not be achievable. It would appear, though, that we should retain at least presumptive faith that eliminating explicit irrelevant options will reduce context-dependent decisions.

The question appears most salient and obvious in relation to the issue of "lesser included offenses," offenses in which the underlying act might be consistent with a variety of criminal charges but in which culpability is differentiated for some reason (mental state, motivation, deliberativeness, victim status, and so on). Presumably, the legislative decision to subdivide a potentially unified offense and the judicial decision to instruct a jury to consider all subdivided offenses are based on policy decisions about each additional subdivided offense. In the absence of context-dependent decision making, the legislature should subdivide an offense when it believes that distinctions in defendant conduct within a historically unified (or conceptually unifiable) category reasonably differentiate offenders (along dimensions like blameworthiness, deterrability, signaling dangerousness, and so forth). Similarly, the judge should instruct the fact finder to consider convictions for an additional category that the legislature has created so long as she believes a reasonable jury could find beyond a reasonable doubt that the defendant committed the (contested) suboffense, rather than some other suboffense (even if the judge herself believes the other suboffense a more plausible conviction pigeonhole).[30]

Given context-dependent decision making, though, it appears that neither of these decision rules is adequately complete. A legislature that adds capital murder to the list of crimes and attempts to distinguish it from "ordinary" murder (and manslaughter) must understand that it is not only creating a new substantive category – based on the substantive belief that certain killings are morally more reprehensible, or harder to deter in the absence of aggravated punishments, or socially more harmful – but it must also understand that it is altering the balance of convictions between murder and manslaughter (though the legislature might not intend to alter the substantive grounds for distinguishing, say, provoked, partly mitigated homicides from unprovoked murders). This will be true, at least arguably, both because murder will more frequently become a compromise verdict between capital murder and manslaughter and because it may frequently be the case that murder clearly dominates capital murder (or vice versa) and that the "murders" thus benefit (as a result of contrast effects) relative to manslaughter. To put the point more generally, a legislature must recognize that, in establishing what one might concede, at least for argument's sake, is a substantively distinguishable new category, it may alter substantive judgments among other categories even when the substantive lines between those categories have formally remained constant.[31]

Similarly, when a judge decides that a reasonable jury might convict a defendant of a particular option – even though the judge believes that rather unlikely – she must recognize that she has altered the probability of convicting the defendant of yet another option (that would have been offered the jurors in any case, uncontroversially). A judge's decision, say, to refuse to instruct on special circumstances murder might not appear reasonable if we focus solely on the question of whether special circumstances murder is a plausible charge, but it may appear more reasonable if we understand the judge must weigh what we will accept as one form of loss in decision-making capacity (the refusal to let the jury hear an option that it might in fact accept) against what might be perceived as a larger gain (preventing the jury from making the choice between options it is more likely to consider seriously on grounds that are irrelevant to the distinction between these options).[32]

Conclusion

Past research has demonstrated context-dependence in consumer choice. We extended this work to legal decision making and showed that violations of context-independence are prevalent in this domain. We have argued that, from a normative standpoint, context-dependence is more problematic in legal decision making than in consumer choice because legal decision makers, unlike consumers, are guided by explicit principles declaring certain factors to be relevant and others to be irrelevant. Moreover, legal decision makers make choices that invariably affect others, while consumers routinely make only self-regarding decisions. Given the fact that context-dependent decision making is problematic when actors make legal judgments, it would appear that both legislatures and judges (instructing jurors) must carefully consider the option sets available to decision makers. They must account for the fact that, whether it is their intention to do so or not, additional alternatives will not only introduce what may seem a substantively plausible decision option but will alter the choice patterns among other options.

Appendix

Experimental Materials

Below are the full experimental materials from all five cases. In each of the five cases, all subjects read the same background, introductory materials. Materials read by only certain experimental groups are clearly marked.

Case 1

Below is a description of a homicide case. Please read the summary of the facts and the potential verdicts. Then, please indicate which verdict you think is the correct one.

You should take the following facts as proven:

On January 1, 1993, at 9:00 A.M., the Defendant gave her second husband a cup of coffee into which she had poured twenty crushed sleeping pills. He died within hours of drinking it. You should take it as a given that he suffered a great deal of physical pain in the last several hours of his life. The Defendant concedes that after she gave him the coffee, she typed a suicide note on his computer screen in the basement, and that she did so hoping that the police would believe she had nothing to do with his death. She concedes, too, that she gave him the coffee and ground-up pills hoping that he would die. The prosecution concedes that at 8:05 A.M. the Defendant had overheard her seventeen-year-old daughter from her first marriage sobbing on the phone. The daughter was telling her best friend that her stepfather (the deceased) had once again attempted to molest her sexually the previous evening. At the same time, the prosecutor argues, and the Defendant concedes, that she stood to inherit a large amount of money from the deceased, and that she had been involved with another man for more than six months prior to her husband's death.

Your Task

All the other jurors believe that the defendant is guilty of homicide, the unlawful killing of another human being. You believe your task, at this point, is simply to grade the unlawful homicide, to determine the level of culpability.

Group 1 Subjects Were Given the Following Materials

This trial is being held in the District of Columbia. In the District of Columbia there are two grades of homicide that are relevant to this case:

A. MURDER

B. MANSLAUGHTER

On the next page you will find a summary of the legal code relevant to deciding upon a grade for the homicide in question. We then ask you to indicate which verdict you would choose.

Relevant Law

District of Columbia law provides in part:

A. Murder. (1) Murder is the unlawful killing of a human being when there is manifested malice, a deliberate intention unlawfully to take away the life of a fellow creature. A defendant found guilty of murder shall receive a penalty of confinement in prison for a term of from twenty-five years to life with the possibility of parole.

B. Manslaughter. (2) Criminal homicide constitutes manslaughter when a homicide which would otherwise be murder is committed under the influence of extreme mental or emotional disturbance for which there is reasonable explanation or excuse. The reasonableness of such explanation or excuse shall be determined from the viewpoint of a person in the actor's situation under the circumstances as he believes them to be. A defendant who has had an adequate period to cool off following a severe disturbance will be presumed not to act under the influence of such disturbance. Manslaughter shall be punished by a term in prison of eight years.

Group 2 Subjects Were Given the Following Materials

This trial is being held in the State of California. In the State of California there are three grades of homicide that are relevant to this case:

A. SPECIAL CIRCUMSTANCES MURDER

B. MURDER

C. MANSLAUGHTER

On the next page you will find a summary of the legal code relevant to deciding upon a grade for the homicide in question. We then ask you to indicate which verdict you would choose.

Relevant Law

California law provides in part: (1) Murder is the unlawful killing of a human being when there is manifested malice, a deliberate intention unlawfully to take away the life of a fellow creature.

A. Special Circumstances Murder. (2) The penalty for a defendant found guilty of murder shall be either death or confinement in prison for a term of life without the possibility of parole in any case in which one or more special circumstances are found.

(3) The potentially relevant special circumstances are: (a) The murder was intentional and carried out for financial gain. (b) The murder was exceptionally heinous, atrocious, or cruel, manifesting exceptional depravity. You should find this to be the case if the crime is conscienceless or pitiless and is unnecessarily torturous to the victim. (c) The defendant intentionally killed the victim by the administration of poison.

(4) If you, as juror, find that the defendant has committed murder with special circumstances, there shall be a separate hearing to determine whether the defendant is sentenced to death or simply to life imprisonment without possibility of parole. You do not have to attend to the bases for that decision.

B. Murder. (5) A defendant found guilty of murder and not of murder with special circumstances shall receive a penalty of confinement in prison for a term of from twenty-five years to life with the possibility of parole.

C. Manslaughter. (6) Criminal homicide constitutes manslaughter when a homicide which would otherwise be murder is committed under the influence of extreme mental or emotional disturbance for which there is reasonable explanation or excuse. (a) The reasonableness of such explanation or excuse shall be determined from the viewpoint of a person in the actor's situation under the circumstances as he believes them to be. A defendant who has had an adequate period to "cool off" following a severe disturbance will be presumed not to act under the influence of such disturbance. (b) Manslaughter shall be punished by a term in prison of eight years.

Group 3 Subjects Were Given the Following Materials

Other Jurisdictions

In some jurisdictions, special circumstances murder is a possible verdict. Here is a summary of legal code pertaining to special circumstances murder:

(a) Murder is the unlawful killing of a human being when there is manifested malice, a deliberate intention unlawfully to take away the life of a fellow creature. (b) The penalty for a defendant found guilty of murder shall be either death or confinement in prison for a term of life without parole when one or more special circumstances are found. (c) The potentially relevant special circumstances are:

(i) The murder was intentional and carried out for financial gain.

(ii) The murder was exceptionally heinous, atrocious, or cruel, manifesting exceptional depravity. You should find this to be the case if the crime is conscienceless or pitiless and is unnecessarily torturous to the victim.

(iii) The defendant intentionally killed the victim by the administration of poison. (d) If it is found the defendant has committed murder with special circumstances, there shall be a separate hearing to determine whether the defendant is sentenced to death or simply to life imprisonment without parole.

This Jurisdiction

This trial is being held in the District of Columbia where special circumstances murder is not part of the law. Thus, the only possible grades for the homicide in question are:

A. MURDER

B. MANSLAUGHTER

On the next page you will find a summary of legal code defining murder and manslaughter. Please indicate which of these two verdicts is the appropriate one for this case.

Relevant Law

A. Murder. (1) Murder is the unlawful killing of a human being when there is manifested malice, a deliberate intention unlawfully to take away the life of a fellow creature. A defendant found guilty of murder shall receive a penalty of confinement in prison for twenty-five years to life with the possibility of parole.

B. Manslaughter. (2) Criminal homicide constitutes manslaughter when a homicide which would otherwise be murder is committed under the influence of extreme mental or emotional disturbance for which there is reasonable explanation or excuse. The reasonableness of such explanation or excuse shall be determined from the viewpoint of a person in the actor's situation under the circumstances as he believes them to be. A defendant who has had an adequate period to cool off following a severe disturbance will be presumed not to act under the influence of such disturbance. Manslaughter shall be punished by a term in prison of eight years.

Case 2

Below is a description of a legal case. Please read the summary of the facts and the potential verdicts. Then, please indicate which verdict you think is the correct one.

The defense and prosecution agree that the following is an accurate depiction of the event in question:

Donald Dewey, the defendant, who is an African American, is walking in the inner courtyard of a shopping mall well after all the shops have closed. However, the mall is still open. Fifteen minutes earlier, one of the jewelry shops in the mall was burglarized, but not by Dewey. Nonetheless, a security guard, an off-duty policeman hired by the owners of the mall, approaches Dewey and asks whether he would mind if he patted him down, telling him that there had been a burglary. The guard intended to check both for burglar's tools and for some of the cash and missing jewelry. The guard realized he had no probable cause to detain Dewey. Nonetheless, when Dewey refused, the security guard reached out to grab him, and felt a bulge, which proved to be a gun, in his coat pocket. Dewey tried to spin away from the guard's hold, screaming, "You've got no business stopping me!" The guard then shouted a racist epithet. Dewey was able to break the guard's grip, and knock him over. While the guard was lying on the ground, he shot him with his gun, killing him.

All sides concede that Dewey purposely killed the victim.

Your Task

Homicide is defined generally as the unlawful killing of another human being. There are four grades of homicide in this jurisdiction:

A. SPECIAL CIRCUMSTANCES MURDER

B. MURDER

C. VOLUNTARY MANSLAUGHTER

D. INVOLUNTARY MANSLAUGHTER

Given the facts of the case, your task as a juror at this trial is simply to grade the unlawful homicide. That is, you must decide of which of the different grades of homicide Donald Dewey is guilty.

Grades of Homicide – Definitions and Relevance to This Case

Upper Group Subjects

A. Special Circumstances Murder. A person is guilty of Special Circumstances Murder if he purposely or knowingly kills another human being and if the victim of the killing is a police officer who is in the course of performing his official duties. The penalty for Special Circumstances Murder is either life imprisonment without the possibility of parole or death (exactly which is determined later in a separate hearing). The District Attorney (DA) argues for Special Circumstances Murder in this case on the basis that the guard was acting with the authority he would have had as a police officer and thus should be deemed a police officer acting in his official capacity. Although he was not formally on duty at the time, police officers always have the rights of officials to make arrests.

B. Murder. A person is guilty of Murder if he purposely kills another human being. The penalty for Murder is imprisonment for a term of twenty-five years to life with the possibility of parole.

C. Voluntary Manslaughter. A homicide is to be graded as Voluntary Manslaughter when it would otherwise be considered Murder but is committed under the influence of extreme mental or emotional disturbance for which there is a reasonable explanation. The penalty for manslaughter is imprisonment for a term of up to eight years. The DA maintains that Dewey was not sufficiently provoked to warrant a decision of Voluntary Manslaughter. That is, the DA maintains that Dewey was not under the influence of extreme mental or emotional disturbance. Dewey's lawyer argues that his defendant was provoked to kill by both the illegal, unwarranted arrest, and by the guard's use of a racist epithet. That is, Dewey's lawyer maintains that the unwarranted arrest plus racist epithet constitute sufficient cause for extreme mental or emotional disturbance.

D. Involuntary Manslaughter. If a person kills another human being when he subjectively but unreasonably believes he is entitled to use deadly force to defend himself, a judgment of Involuntary Manslaughter is appropriate. However, the judge has ruled that as a matter of law, Dewey is not entitled to use deadly force against an unwarranted arrest, and finds that there is no credible evidence to back a claim that Dewey believed that he was legally entitled to use deadly force to defend himself. Thus, this homicide cannot be graded as an Involuntary Manslaughter.

Lower Group Subjects

A. Special Circumstances Murder. A person is guilty of Special Circumstances Murder if he purposely or knowingly kills another human being and if the victim of the killing is a police officer who is in the course of performing his official duties. The penalty for Special Circumstances Murder is either life imprisonment without the possibility of parole or death (exactly which is determined later in a separate hearing). However, the judge has ruled that as a matter of law, off-duty police employed as private security guards are not police officers in the performance of their official duties. Thus, the homicide in question cannot be graded as a Special Circumstances Murder.

B. Murder. A person is guilty of Murder if he purposely kills another human being. The penalty for Murder is imprisonment for a term of twenty-five years to life with the possibility of parole.

C. Voluntary Manslaughter. A homicide is to be graded as Voluntary Manslaughter when it would otherwise be considered Murder but is committed under the influence of extreme mental or emotional disturbance for which there is a reasonable explanation. The penalty for manslaughter is imprisonment for a term of up to eight years. The District Attorney maintains that Dewey was not sufficiently provoked to warrant a decision of Voluntary Manslaughter. That is, the DA maintains that Dewey was not under the influence of extreme mental or emotional disturbance. Dewey's lawyer argues that his defendant was provoked to kill by both the illegal, unwarranted arrest, and by the guard's use of a racist epithet. That is, Dewey's lawyer maintains that the unwarranted arrest plus racist epithet constitute sufficient cause for extreme mental or emotional disturbance.

D. Involuntary Manslaughter. If a person kills another human being when he subjectively but unreasonably believes he is entitled to use deadly force to defend himself, a judgment of Involuntary Manslaughter is appropriate. The judge has ruled that as a matter of law, Dewey is not entitled to use deadly force against an unwarranted arrest. However, if you judge that Dewey mistakenly believed that he was entitled to use deadly force to defend himself, you should then grade the homicide as Involuntary Manslaughter. Dewey's lawyer argues just such a position. He states that Dewey believed he was entitled to use deadly force to resist an illegal arrest and that, in addition, Dewey feared the guard would seriously injure or kill him.

Case 3

The Situation

Take the following as given:

The defendant has been convicted of violating a section of the state's criminal code. Any licensed real estate broker who knowingly conceals a substantial and material defect in a dwelling unit from a purchaser of residential property shall be adjudged in violation of the Code. The Code provides that brokers need not necessarily make efforts to ascertain the condition of the dwelling units they offer. However, brokers must inform buyers of all substantial and material defects of which they have been apprised. Additionally, in those cases in which brokers make no efforts to learn about the dwelling unit's condition, they must inform buyers that they have made no such efforts.

In this particular case, the broker had in his possession at the time of sale a four-month-old engineer's report indicating that the house he was representing had sustained substantial dry rot damage to the foundation. The report indicated that the damage would cost close to $100,000 to repair. The broker did not inform the would-be buyers of this fact, and they purchased the home for $200,000, which was estimated by appraisers to be within $10,000 of the fair market value of the home without dry rot. At trial, the broker claimed that he believed the report was dated. He testified that he surmised that the foundation had probably been repaired during the six weeks between the time the engineer's report was prepared and the time the house was first listed by his real estate agency. The jury apparently did not believe this claim for they convicted the defendant of knowingly withholding material information.

Your Task

You are the judge. You must decide upon a sentence for the offender in this case. On the next page is a short summary of recommended sentences.

Your Options

Below are sentences recommended by the prosecutor's office and the county probation department:

Two-Option Group

A. Prosecutor's Recommendation. The prosecutor has recommended that the defendant be imprisoned for one month and fined $2,500.

B. Probation Department's Recommendation. The probation department recommends that the defendant be fined $2,500 and placed on probation for six months. During his probation the defendant would perform fifty hours of community service, largely working to find new dwelling places for persons displaced by redevelopment in the city in which he lives.

The Additional Option Available to the Three-Option Group

C. Probation Department's Recommendation. Alternatively, the probation department recommends that the defendant be fined $2,500 and placed on probation for six months, during which time he would be asked to report for fifty hours of counseling sessions. The counseling sessions would focus on the importance of ethical business practices and the connection between dishonesty and impaired self-esteem.

Case 4

Imagine that you are an attorney working for the plaintiff in the legal case described below. Please indicate which course of action you would take.

Background

The Economics Department of a major university voted, two years ago, to recommend that your client, then an associate professor at the university, not be promoted to a tenured position. She claims that she was discriminated against on account of her gender. She notes, first, that male colleagues with parallel publication records had been promoted though none had, like her, received undergraduate teaching awards. She notes, second, that the department had neither hired nor promoted a number of qualified women it had considered over the past two decades.

Your client is interested in (1) being compensated for the wrongs done her and in (2) having the university publicly admit guilt in her case.

At the same time, your client is very interested in the progress of women generally and wants (3) to do her part in helping to push for affirmative action plans that would help women in economics.

Your client is not sure how to weigh and compare these three interests.

The university counsel's office has contacted you and asked you to communicate three distinct settlement proposals to your client.

The Situation

Your client asks you to recommend one of the settlement proposals. The proposals appear on the back.

Two-Option Group: The Proposals

Offer including admission of guilt by the university:

Proposal 1. (a) The university would pay your client $45,000 in damages. (b) The university would publicly admit guilt in your client's case.

Note. Your client now has a job at another university making $70,000 per year. She would find the $45,000 helpful but not utterly life changing.

Offer including a plan to increase female representation in economics:

Proposal 2. (a) The university would agree to what your client would feel is an acceptable affirmative action plan to increase female representation in the department. (b) The university, though, would not admit guilt in your client's case.

Note. It is conceivable that the university might enact an affirmative action plan whether or not your client agrees to this settlement proposal.

The Additional Option Available to the Three-Option Group.

Proposal 3. (a) The university would contribute $35,000 in your client's name to her favorite charity. (b) The university would publicly admit guilt in your client's case.

Note. Your client would probably not wish to contribute such a large amount of money. Also, your client could always contribute a portion of the money she receives from Proposal 1.

Case 5

Imagine that you are a lawyer. Which choice would you make in the case below?

Background

Your client, Wells, is the sole neighbor of a dance club that stays open until 3 A.M. The club owner acknowledges that the noise levels from midnight to three exceed levels that Wells should have to tolerate; he concedes that the activity would be judged a "nuisance" if Wells sued him in court.

The club owner would prefer not to be forced to diminish the noise too radically, especially on Friday and Saturday nights, and he communicates three offers to your client.

Your client asks you to advise him. Which settlement offer would you recommend that he take?

Two-Option Group

Sound Decrease Alternative: Proposal X. The club owner would (a) lower the sound system by ten decibels and (b) plant a hedge outside the club that would muffle away more of the sound. Wells would usually no longer be bothered by the noise. Every now and then he would still hear the loud music from the club and find it aggravating.

Weekend Lodgings Alternative: Proposal Y. The club owner would (a) put Wells up at a nearby plush hotel every Friday and Saturday night, and (b) pay Wells $120 per week in cash. Wells would enjoy staying at the hotel although he may get tired of it after a while. If some time he didn't want to go to the hotel, he could stay home. Wells makes $25,000 per year and the $120 would be helpful.

The Additional Option Available to the Three-Option Group.

Proposal Z. The club owner would (a) put Wells up at a nearby plush hotel every Friday and Saturday, and (b) pay Wells $40 in cash per week and give Wells $85 per week in credit for use at this or three other dance clubs. Wells would enjoy staying at the hotel although he may get tired of it. Wells attends the clubs where he would have credit about three times a year, spending $50 if alone and $90 if on a date. He probably would not go to these clubs every weekend.

Notes

1 This condition is often called independence of irrelevant alternatives.

2 We exclude the case where availability of the third option may convey relevant information about the relative merits of the other two. For instance, the availability of veal parmesan might suggest that the restaurant specializes in Italian dishes.

3 See, for example, Joel Huber, John W. Payne, and Christopher Puto, Adding Asymmetrically Dominated Alternatives: Violations of Regularity and the Similarity Hypothesis, 9 *J. Consumer Res.* 90 (1982); Joel Huber and Christopher Puto, Market

Boundaries and Product Choice: Illustrating Attraction and Substitution Effects, 10 *J. Consumer Res.* 31 (1983); Itamar Simonson and Amos Tversky, Choice in Context: Tradeoff Contrast and Extremeness Aversion, 29 *J. Marketing Res.* 281, 282 (1992); and D. A. Redelmeir and E. Shafir, Medical Decision Making in Situations That Offer Multiple Alternatives, 273 *J. Am. Med. Ass'n* 302 (1995). Discussions and attempts to model the phenomena appear in Amos Tversky and Itamar Simonson, Context-Dependent Preferences, 39 *Mgmt. Sci.* 1179 (1993); and Eldar Shafir, Itamar Simonson, and Amos Tversky, Reason-Based Choice, 49 *Cognition* 11 (1993).

4 Simonson and Tversky, supra note 3, at 290.

5 If one considers the choice between options that vary along two dimensions and assumes that neither option dominates the other, the comparison between them involves an evaluation of differences along the two attributes. Consider a consumer evaluating two personal computers: the first has 64 MG memory and costs $1,200, while the second has 32 MG memory and costs $1,000. The choice between the two depends on whether the consumer is willing to pay $200 more for an additional 32 MG of memory. The contrast hypothesis implies that the tendency to prefer the first over the second will be enhanced if the decision maker encounters other choices in which the exchange rate between price and quality is higher than that implied by the two computers. Ibid.

6 Ibid.

7 The full text of the experiments is in the Appendix.

8 The precise legal definitions subjects saw are reprinted in the Appendix.

9 The "two-option" set is indeed a two-option set, not a three-option set in which acquittal is an option (and manslaughter intermediate between acquittal and murder) since the subjects are told that all the jurors believe the defendant is guilty of homicide and that their only task is to grade the unlawful homicide.

10 More specifically, the data support the prediction that manslaughter will be chosen less frequently when it is an "extreme" choice than when there are simply no extreme choices because there are only two options. The proportion of people choosing murder in the two-option study was 53 percent, and it fell to 39 percent in the three-option set because 42 percent of the people chose special circumstances murder. We suggest that people become more predisposed to find murder than manslaughter when murder is seen as a compromise choice, rather than an extreme one, and they are less predisposed to find manslaughter when it is an extreme choice than when there simply are no extreme choices. Then, subjects decide between murder and special circumstances murder. In this case, it strikes us that finding murder at all, rather than special circumstances murder, once one has found murder rather than manslaughter, is explicable only as a compromise verdict: The defendant almost certainly killed the victim by administering poison. (While it is plausible to find that other special circumstances existed – to determine that the killing was done in a heinous fashion or was done for financial gain – these findings are not so uncontroversial that one would expect anyone who finds murder rather than manslaughter to accept them unquestioningly.)

11 The actual instructions on involuntary manslaughter appear from a lawyer's vantage point to blur together "mistake of law" and "mistake of fact" issues that would almost surely be differentiated in an actual case. (If one looks at the experimental jury instructions, it appears that Dewey would be guilty of involuntary manslaughter whether he unreasonably believed the guard physically threatened him or if he unreasonably believed it to be permissible to use deadly force to resist illegal detention.) In most American jurisdictions, though, a mistake about the scope of

justification norms would be considered a mistake about the governing norm; no mistakes about the content of governing norms are deemed exculpatory (unless the legislature intends such a "mistake of law" defense or unless due process constitutional norms preclude convicting a defendant ignorant of a particular norm). It may well be the case that one could construct an argument that the defendant in such a case simply makes a (potentially exculpatory) mistake about some legal circumstance attendant to the definition of the offense, but such an argument would, for a wide variety of reasons, appear to be unavailing. Unfortunately, the initial instructions (in the pretest experiment), which paid heed to these subtle distinctions, were too difficult for experimental subjects to cope with in the short time frame of these experiments.

12 In a real case, jurors might conceivably have been instructed to find the defendant guilty of voluntary manslaughter if he had either acted under extreme emotional disturbance or if he recklessly believed that he was entitled to use force to defend himself against the deceased. (One should recognize that, even in a jurisdiction in which such a reckless belief in the need to use deadly force would result in a manslaughter conviction, many judges would, in this case, refuse to give such an instruction.) What is critical, however, is that the "experimental judge's" refusal to allow one experimental group to consider involuntary manslaughter should not affect a juror's choice between murder or manslaughter. The judge's refusal to credit the possibility that Dewey subjectively believed he was defending himself is irrelevant to the form of voluntary manslaughter the decision makers are asked to consider. If voluntary manslaughter could be predicated on a form of imperfect self-defense (one in which the defendant took a conscious risk that he was not entitled to defend himself), then one possible criticism might hold that voluntary manslaughter is less plausible once it has been concluded that the defendant did not subjectively though unreasonably believe there was a substantial risk that he might not be entitled to defend himself. The criticism does not hold here, however, since, for our subjects, grading the killing as voluntary manslaughter is appropriate only when the defendant acted under the influence of explicable emotional disturbance.

13 It is remotely plausible, though not necessary to consider in reviewing our results, that more, not fewer, subjects should choose manslaughter when told by the judge, in effect, that the off-duty policeman is not clearly a person acting without official state penal authority (for these purposes, that is the relevant message of allowing the jury to consider special circumstances murder). One would think that jurors would find it (very marginally) more reasonable and explicable for a person to "act under the influence of extreme emotional disturbance" when confronted by official, rather than private, racism and unreasonableness in making decisions to detain so that the judge's instruction to consider special circumstances murder might serve as a (weak) informational reminder of the official status of the victim.

14 To the limited extent that some subjects reacted as we discussed in note 13 supra, focusing on the official status of the victim so that they felt the relevant choice was between those categories in which official status was arguably salient (special circumstances murder or manslaughter) versus those in which it was not (murder), then we should not expect all experimental subjects who are "deprived" of the chance to choose special circumstances murder to choose murder, rather than manslaughter. Still, the "betweenness" hypothesis we detail in the text appears overwhelmingly more plausible.

15 For convenience, we exclude the possibility of ranking two options as tied.

16 It is conceivable that some people would prefer to direct a lower sum of money to charity rather than receive a larger sum, which they could personally donate to charity, in order to demonstrate to the defendant university that some people (including the plaintiff herself) make decisions without any regard to selfish concerns. Our ex ante prediction, borne out in fact, was that the number of people who want to demonstrate such selflessness, and believe one would better demonstrate it if one never controlled the funds at all, would be very small.

17 We again exclude the possibility that the presence of the third option communicates information relevant to the assessment of the others.

18 We doubt that the results here reflect a combination of contrast and compromise effects. It is difficult to see the second option as "intermediate" along salient dimensions. It is possible that the options could be aligned in terms of how costly they are for the university to implement. However, it cannot be clear to subjects whether the affirmative action plan is more or less expensive than the $45,000 settlement, although the $45,000 settlement is clearly more expensive for the defendant than the $35,000 donation. Likewise, if the options are to be "aligned" in accord with the degree to which the defendant gains from the settlement, they appear incommensurable in significant ways.

19 See note 13 supra for a qualification, but one that implies that the "informational" role of the added option is to make manslaughter seem more attractive to those exposed to the special circumstances murder charge.

20 The substantive barriers appear more meaningful to us than the formal ones in assessing the probative value of the experiments. One could argue, reasonably plausibly, that reading the full option set is not the sole way subjects gather information about options so that "formal" or "procedural" techniques to ensure that no information is gained by altering option sets are, in the final analysis, never quite adequate: It may well be the case that subjects reasonably "tilt" in a particular direction when certain options are "on the table." The fact that an option is "on the table" may signal that the perspective embodied in the option is a serious one, and the substantive positions that underlie it should be embodied, at least to some extent, in any final judgment.

21 One might reasonably argue that internal and external validity issues are related in the following sense: If experimental jurors or experimental consumers are not like real jurors or real consumers, they may not be seeking the same goal as their real counterparts. Experimental subjects may always seek, for instance, simply to give the "answer" they anticipate the experimenter wants to hear, or the answer that is "correct" or smart in some sense. If that is the case, the consumer is not trying to express her authentic preferences. However, it is not the least bit clear what answer is the "correct" answer (or the one experimenters expect). It might be that what we see as compromise and contrast effects are efforts to pick up on clues about the experimenters' wishes. Naturally, it is also possible that the real counterparts face quite parallel complex agendas (real jurors may be trying to guess what the judge wants; real consumers may be trying not to look foolish in front of the salesman); if this were the case, though, one would say that the experiments are externally valid (real actors behave like experimental actors) but that we have not demonstrated context-dependence so much as the possibility that people's goals are less straightforward than they might appear.

22 See, in particular, Colin Camerer, Behavioral Decision Theory, in *The Handbook of Experimental Economics* (John H. Kagel and Alvin E. Roth eds., 1995).

23 In a similar vein, social choice theorists have discussed the distinction between relevant and irrelevant grounds for social choice: It is deemed worrisome that agenda setting (whether deliberate or inadvertent) determines political outcomes. See Kenneth Arrow, *Social Choice and Individual Values* (2d ed. 1963). For further discussions, see, for example, Frank Easterbrook, Ways of Criticizing the Court, 95 *Harv. L. Rev.* 802, 823 (1982). What we have noted is that even for individual decision makers, inadvertent or manipulative agenda setting (presentation of distinct option sets) may alter substantive outcomes.

24 The proposed pragmatic test suggests that one is more likely to express a "true" preference when irrelevant options are eliminated, that is, from two-option choice sets. However, even if contrast effects are monumentally fleeting – so that the consumer's preferences may change each time we expose her to new option sets – it is not clear that any of these short-lived choices is inferior to a preference revealed in some initial two-option set, precisely because we lack a theory of what inferiority would mean here.

25 One possible account would hold that forming preferences is itself a costly activity so that rules of thumb reducing that cost could be globally optimal, even if such rules mandated inclusion of informationally valueless clues on particular occasions. Thus, it might be that we have learned that we are most typically satisfied if we pick the compromise good from a range of alternatives or that we make decisions with least stress if we rely on contrast.

Two aspects of such an account should be stressed. First, it is important to recognize that the notion of costly preference formation represents a major departure from the standard model. In the traditional picture, preferences are the starting point of analysis: The decision maker is assumed to know her preferences. Second, it is far from clear that any theory holding that departures from the normative standard are the result of "thinking costs" can account for the remarkable lability of preferences, which are not only context-dependent but also sensitive to the way a choice problem is described or "framed" and to the mode of response used to express preference (see Paul Slovic, The Construction of Preference, 50 *Am. Psychologist* 364 [1995], for an excellent, though brief, review).

26 Lesser included offenses are offenses composed of elements already contained in the charged offense or that must be committed during the perpetration of the charged offenses. Only North Carolina, Tennessee, and Oklahoma require that lesser included offense instructions be raised *sua sponte*: in other jurisdictions, one of the parties must request the instruction before it can be given. The judge must then grant the request by either party for the lesser included offense instruction so long as there is some evidence that would justify conviction of the lesser offense and the proof of the element or elements differentiating the two crimes is sufficiently in dispute that the jury may consistently find the defendant innocent of the greater, but guilty of the lesser included offense. Initially, the lesser included offense doctrine was developed as a way for the prosecution to obtain a conviction in cases in which it had overcharged or was unable to prove some element of the crime (for example, premeditation in the homicide context) while proving others (for example, causing death intentionally in that same homicide context). Defendants, though, began to request the instructions, hoping that it might allow jurors to temper convictions when they were sympathetic to the defendants but still felt them culpable to some extent. For basic discussions of lesser included offense law, see *Beck v. Alabama*, 447 U.S. 625, 700 S.Ct. 2382, 65 L.Ed. 2d 392 (U.S. Ala. 1980); Note, Improving Jury Deliberations: A Reconsideration of Lesser Included Offense Instructions, 16 *U. Mich. J.L. Ref.* 561

(1983) (Michael Craig); Tracy L. Hamrick, Looking at Lesser Included Offenses on an "All or Nothing" Basis: *State v. Bullard* and the Sporting Approach to Criminal Justice, 69 *N.C. L. Rev.* 1470 (1991); Janis L. Ettinger, In Search of a Reasoned Approach to the Lesser Included Offense, 50 *Brook. L. Rev.* 191 (1984); Edward G. Mascolo, Procedural Due Process and the Lesser Included Offense Doctrine, 50 *Alb. L. Rev.* 263 (1986); Comment, Jury Deliberations and the Lesser Included Offense Rule: Getting the Courts Back in Step, 23 *U.C. Davis L. Rev.* 375 (1990) (David F. Abele).

27 See *Strickland v. Washington*, 466 U.S. 668 (1984).

28 *Van Alstine v. State*, 263 Ga. 1, 426 S.E. 2d 360 (1993); *Wisconsin v. Hollsten*, 170 Wis. 2d 734, 492 N.W. 2d 191 (1992). The lawyers' refusal to request a lesser included offense instruction may be successfully challenged only in situations in which the court has a reason to doubt that it was tactically motivated, most obviously in situations in which the lawyer is paid contingent on acquittal, either as a result of a formal contingency fee contract or some factual equivalent. See, for instance, *United States v. Murphy*, 349 F. Supp. 818 (E.D. Pa. 1972) (lawyer's fees to be paid out of insurance proceeds that were payable only if defendant acquitted; lawyer's decision not to inform client that prosecutor had offered to cap charges at second-degree murder if client plead guilty before trial or to seek lesser included charge instructions at trial constituted incompetent assistance).

29 See *ABA Standards for Criminal Justice*, Rule 4-5.2 (comment at 4) (client must ultimately make the decision whether to seek a lesser included offense instruction).

30 See, for example, *Sansone v. United States*, 380 U.S. 343, 351 (1965); *Beck v. Alabama*, 447 U.S. 625, 636 n. 12 (1980) (citing state and federal cases supporting the proposition that a defendant is entitled "to a requested lesser included offense instruction if the evidence warrants it"); *United States v. Thompson*, 492 F.2d 359, 362 (8th Cir. 1974) (lesser included offense charge must be given when there is some evidence that would justify conviction of the lesser included offense and the proof on the element or elements differentiating the two offenses is sufficiently in dispute so that the jury may consistently find the defendant innocent of the greater and guilty of the lesser included offense).

31 While the model applies most readily to subdivided criminal offenses, it applies in rather obvious fashions to any situation in which the legislature increases the option set of decision makers entitled to respond to a particular set of behaviors or to situations in which the judge must choose whether to allow fact finders to choose from the full menu of options a lawmaker has provided. Thus, decisions about whether to increase the range of remedies available in a class of civil cases may be analyzed "traditionally" (that is, the legislature should increase the remedy range if additional remedies seem apt for a subclass of cases and the court should instruct the jury to consider any remedy that a reasonable juror could find fits the legislatively established criteria to apply that remedy) and/or in light of context-dependence (the legislature and judge must consider the effect of additional options on choices among the options that might more frequently be chosen as well).

32 Currently, when judges instruct jurors to consider lesser included offenses, they indeed make some efforts to "separate" decisions, to try to ensure that jurors do not look at their actual menu of choices as an option set. Thus, typically, judges instruct that the jury must acquit the defendant, unanimously, of the most serious offense he is charged with committing before considering the lesser included offense. See, for example, *Nell v. State*, 642 P.2d 1361, 1367 (Alaska App. 1982); *Stone v. Superior Court of San Diego County*, 31 Cal. 3d 503, 646 P.2d 809, 183 Cal. Rptr. 647 (1982) ("The jury must be cautioned, of course, that it should first decide whether the

defendant is guilty of the greater offense before considering the lesser offense, and that if it finds the defendant guilty of the greater offense, or if it is unable to agree on that offense, it should not return a verdict on the lesser offense." 646 P.2d at 820). Still other states attempt to separate decisions on the distinct charges by submitting each charge to the jury in guilty/not guilty form. See, for example, *State v. Dippre*, 121 Ariz. 596, 592 P.2d 1252 (1979). Finally, in some states, jurors are informed that they should not consider lesser included offense charges unless they have reasonable doubts about whether the defendant is guilty of the higher charge, but there appears to be no requirement in such states that the jury as a whole unanimously vote to acquit (that is, unanimously shares such reasonable doubts) before considering the lesser included offenses. See, for example, *People v. McGregor*, 635 P.2d 912 (Colo. App. 1981); *State v. Santiago*, 516 P.2d 1256 (Haw. 1973). While it is possible that the first and third procedure produce distinct jury dynamics – a juror or jurors committed to convicting the defendant of the higher charge would seem to have more leverage under the first procedure – the fact remains that jurors informed, as they are in the third class of states, that "[i]f you are not satisfied beyond a reasonable doubt that the defendant is guilty of an offense charged, or you entertain a reasonable doubt of the defendant's guilt, you may consider whether he is guilty of a lesser offense" (*McGregor*, 635 P.2d at 914) may interpret the charge to do no more or less than remind them that juries are supposed to acquit of offense (whether "higher" charges or the only charge) when they are not satisfied beyond a reasonable doubt that the charges have been proven. Thus, in some jurisdictions, the courts explicitly disclaim the idea that the first and third instructions are significantly distinct. See, for example, *People v. Padilla*, 638 P.2d 15 (Colo. 1981). The jury instructions read: "If you are not satisfied beyond a reasonable doubt that the defendant is guilty of the offense charged, he may, however, be found guilty of any lesser offense" (ibid. at 17). The court notes that it is unclear whether the jury would have first had to acquit the defendant of the higher charge before considering the lesser offense (ibid.) but notes that, even if the instruction does require a finding of acquittal, it withstands the defendant's challenge (ibid.). See also *State v. McNeal*, 288 N.W.2d 874 (Wis. App. 1980) (while instructions seem to require that the jury acquit the defendant first of the greater charge before considering the lesser included offense, the court describes the instructions as allowing the jury to consider the lesser included offense if it fails to find the defendant guilty).

In any case, it is by no means clear that any effort to make the jurors consider each charge in isolation from context will succeed. Each juror who favors the compromise position (the lesser included offense) that he knows is available once the lesser included offense instruction has been given will be more prone to vote to acquit on the more serious charge.

We should note, though, that a judge-imposed rule of the sort we suggest in the text is quite invasive of the jury's traditional fact-finding role. To protect the jury from making a context-dependent decision, the judge, in essence, refuses to give instructions about the requisite elements of a crime although it is a concededly plausible option to convict of that crime. Obviously, distrust of juror capacity drives a good deal of restrictiveness in admitting evidence (one can think of the suggestion that judges be more circumspect in giving lesser included offense instructions as a variant on the traditional idea that certain information is likely to be more prejudicial than probative). One would be hard-pressed, though, to find a situation in which the jury is not told of a legal option that the jury formally possesses for fear that they would misuse the information, but jurors are indeed sometimes left unaware of salient features of the legal system for fear that they will perform their fact-finding function less capably if they are more informed. For instance, in capital trials, jurors may not hear that each executive will have the power to commute what are formally labeled "life sentences" without possibility of parole (or, for that matter, that the executive at the time of scheduled execution could commute a death sentence), presumably on the supposition that they will make the choice between life imprisonment and the death penalty on the basis of an inadequately policy-salient fact: the risk of the sentence not being carried out.

3 A Positive Psychological Theory of Judging in Hindsight

Jeffrey J. Rachlinski

Nothing is so easy as to be wise after the event.[1]

Everyone is familiar with the feeling that they "knew it all along." Events, especially tragedies, often feel as if they were predictable. Folk wisdom admonishes us to distrust this sensation. We all know that hindsight vision is "20/20" and that "Monday morning quarterbacking" exaggerates one's ability to know the future. Learning how the story ends makes the outcome seem inevitable, thereby distorting our perception of what could have been predicted. Despite this well-known obstacle to assessing the predictability of events accurately, the law constantly requires courts to make such assessments. Numerous legal judgments, from determining whether a tort defendant failed to take reasonable care to whether a corporate officer committed securities fraud by knowingly making false statements, require that a judge or jury ignore what they have learned in hindsight. If the folk wisdom is correct, these judgments should be distrusted. Our legal system apparently must rely on faulty judgments.

Psychological Research on Judging in Hindsight

The Hindsight Bias

Research by cognitive psychologists supports the folk admonition against trusting judgments made in hindsight. Beginning with the work of Baruch Fischhoff, psychologists have demonstrated repeatedly that people overstate the predictability of past events,[2] a phenomenon that psychologists have termed the "hindsight bias." Fischhoff described the bias as follows: "In hindsight, people consistently exaggerate what could have been anticipated in foresight. They not only tend to view what has happened as having been inevitable but also to view it as having appeared 'relatively inevitable' before it happened. People believe that others should have been able to anticipate events much better than was actually the case."[3]

Baruch Fischhoff provided the first systematic demonstration of this phenomenon.[4] In his study Fischhoff gave undergraduate subjects a description of an unfamiliar, nineteenth-century war between the British and the Nepalese Gurkhas. His materials consisted of a 150-word description of the conflict, including the strengths and weaknesses of each army. This description listed four possible outcomes of the conflict (British victory, Gurkha victory, stalemate with no peace settlement, and stalemate with a peace settlement). The remainder of Fischhoff's materials split into five different conditions. The materials either stated that one of the four possible outcomes had actually occurred or provided no information about the actual outcome. Subjects read the materials and then answered the following question: "In light of the information appearing in the passage, what was the probability of occurrence of each of the four possible outcomes?" Subjects who were told that one of the outcomes had occurred made inflated estimates of the ex ante likelihood of that outcome (as compared to subjects who were given no information about the outcome). In fact, the mean probabilities that subjects assigned to the supposed outcome of the conflict summed to 170 percent, whereas they would have summed to approximately 100 percent if knowing the outcome had not influenced the subjects. In this study, and in the replications that Fischhoff ran with other scenarios, providing subjects with an outcome increased their estimates of the likelihood of that outcome by between 6.3 and 44.0 percentage points.

It is important to distinguish between the hindsight bias and the more ordinary process of learning from experience. In most circumstances, learning an outcome *should* cause people to update their estimates of an event's likelihood. If Fischhoff had asked his subjects to estimate the probabilities of the possible outcomes of a *future* conflict between the British and the Gurkhas, it would have been appropriate for the subjects to suppose that history might repeat itself. Fischhoff did not ask his subjects to predict a future event, however; he asked them to judge the predictability of past events as if they were ignorant of the known outcome. His subjects behaved as if they were supposed to learn from the outcome, even though that was not their chore.

Researchers have also used a wide range of different materials to document the hindsight bias. The research on judging in hindsight, taken as a whole, strongly supports Fischhoff's conclusion that "[f]inding out that an outcome has occurred increases its perceived likelihood."[5] "The overwhelming verdict . . . is that the hindsight bias is a robust phenomenon that is not easily eliminated or even moderated."[6] Across a wide variety of tasks and materials, a sizeable and consistent bias clouds judgments made in hindsight.

Causes of the Hindsight Bias

Why is a known outcome so difficult to ignore? Psychologists have proposed three principal theories to explain the hindsight bias. Two theories are motivational, meaning that they attribute the bias to people's needs or desires, and one theory is cognitive, meaning that it attributes the bias to the mental strategies that people rely upon when making judgments in hindsight. Of the three, the cognitive theory provides the best account of the hindsight bias, although motivational factors probably also influence judgments made in hindsight.

Fischhoff's phrase "creeping determinism" itself describes the cognitive theory that best explains the hindsight bias.[7] According to this theory, people naturally integrate an outcome and the events that preceded it into a coherent story.[8] In so doing, they attribute the outcome to some of the precipitating circumstances, making these circumstances seem more significant than they appeared in foresight. People also downplay the importance of other antecedents that would have been likely to lead to alternative outcomes. For example, in Fischhoff's original study using the British-Gurkha conflict, subjects told that the British had won rated the British advantages (better weapons and training) as more relevant to the outcome than the Nepalese advantages (better motivation and familiarity with the terrain). These subjects probably also concluded that training and weapons are more important to a military victory under these circumstance than motivation and familiarity with the terrain and perhaps are more significant in warfare generally. These subjects naturally relied upon these inferences to judge the likely outcome of the conflict. Even if people can suppress specific knowledge of the outcome, they are unable to forget the insights inferred from that outcome. Consequently, the actual outcome seems more likely after it is known than beforehand.

The creeping determinism theory has other support in the literature. Materials that directly attribute the outcome to an occurrence unrelated to any of the antecedents do not produce a hindsight bias.[9] For example, subjects reading about the British-Gurkha conflict who were told that the Nepalese won because of a freak snow storm did not rate a Nepalese victory as more likely than subjects who were not told the outcome of the conflict. Creeping determinism also explains why adding more information sometimes increases the size of the bias;[10] the more antecedent facts that can be integrated into an explanation for the outcome, the more inevitable it will seem. This theory also accounts for the finding that materials describing the occurrence of an event produce a larger hindsight bias than materials stating that an event did not occur;[11] occurrences are generally easier to explain than nonoccurrences. Fischhoff's original hypothesis seems to account adequately for the pattern of data in the literature on the hindsight bias.

The bias also results, to a lesser extent, from two motivational factors. First, many people want to see the world as a stable and predictable place.[12] If a tragedy was foreseeable, then, logically, it could have been prevented by careful people. Thus, the hindsight bias makes the world seem more stable and controllable than it actually is. Second, subjects in psychology experiments, as in most social settings, try to avoid looking foolish. Consequently, subjects in the hindsight studies might be asserting that *they* could have predicted outcomes even if *others* could not as part of an effort to show the experimenter (or other subjects or themselves) that they are intelligent. Because subjects in some of the studies of the hindsight bias actually end up looking more foolish when they express the bias, however, this theory cannot adequately account for all of the data. Overall, "motivational factors do not appear to play a large role" in explaining the hindsight bias.[13]

Debiasing

Fischhoff's demonstration of the hindsight bias was followed by a series of efforts to find a successful debiasing strategy, a way of evaluating the predictability of past events accurately. These efforts have been unsuccessful. Because motivational factors only partly account for the bias, attempts to increase people's incentives to make accurate judgments, such as paying subjects for correct estimates or urging them to "try harder," reduce the bias only slightly.[14] The bias is a product of cognitive processes, and only procedures that alter the mental strategies used to make judgments in hindsight have any chance of producing unbiased evaluations.

Psychologists have tried a number of different cognitive strategies to avoid the hindsight bias. Simple remedies, such as informing people about the bias or giving them repeated attempts to make judgments with feedback, have no effect.[15] Several studies have reliably reduced the bias by restructuring the decision-making task so as to force people to "unlearn" what the outcome has taught them about the antecedent events.[16] Because the subjects in these experiments, judging in hindsight, still knew that there was but a single reality, they assigned more weight to that reality and the inferences that it inspired. As a result, these techniques reduced the size of the hindsight bias but did not produce completely unbiased judgments. Complete elimination of the bias has eluded psychologists.

Thus, the psychological research demonstrates that the hindsight bias is an extremely robust phenomenon. It influences judgments made in many different settings by many different types of people. The bias is also large enough to have an important impact on the legal system and has been shown to affect the two kinds of decision makers upon which the legal system relies – groups[17] (juries) and experienced decision makers (judges).[18] The bias is a product of the normal process of integrating feedback into our understanding of the world and updating our beliefs. As such it resists efforts to avoid it. No matter how a judgment made in hindsight is restructured, the feeling that an outcome was both inevitable and predictable is impossible to avoid.

The Hindsight Bias in Legal Decisions

The Hindsight Bias and Legal Culpability

Because courts primarily judge in hindsight, the bias might exert tremendous influence on judgments in the legal system. When a court must determine what someone "knew or should have known," it is especially likely to fall prey to the hindsight bias. Consider the assessment of negligence in a tort action as an example. A defendant's conduct was negligent if it created an "unreasonable risk of harm" to others, "which the actor should have recognized at the time of his action or inaction."[19] The determination of whether a defendant's conduct was unreasonable is necessarily made *after* the consequences of an actor's conduct are known, but this knowledge is not supposed to influence the determination of reasonableness.

Several studies have demonstrated that the hindsight bias influences negligence judgments.[20] These studies show that a decision not to take a precaution can seem reasonable before an accident occurs and yet seem negligent after an adverse outcome results. For example, Kamin and Rachlinski compared judgments of the reasonableness of a precaution in foresight and in hindsight. Under the facts that they used, only 24 percent of the subjects in foresight found that a precaution was necessary, but in hindsight, 75 percent of the subjects judged that the failure to take this precaution was negligent. Similarly, fully one-quarter of the subjects in a study by LaBine and LaBine found the actions of a psychotherapist to constitute negligence, even though all psychotherapists, judging in foresight, concluded that the psychotherapist's actions were appropriate under the circumstances. In short, people judging in hindsight believe that people "should have known" more than was perhaps possible.

Fairness and the Hindsight Bias

The hindsight bias would seem to produce unjust results; it ensures that potential defendants cannot rely on the legal standard to avoid liability. Hindsight, in effect, raises the bar after an accident. The bias converts an announced negligence rule into what is almost a strict liability rule in application. An incongruence "between the rules as announced and their actual administration"[21] such as this smacks of injustice. Several considerations, however, mitigate the apparent injustice of determining liability in hindsight.

First, the availability of comparative negligence as a defense might result in a process that is influenced by the bias but that nevertheless produces unbiased judgments. If the negligence of both parties is at issue, then the defendant might benefit from the bias in roughly the same proportion as the plaintiff. A judge or jury might condemn both litigants in a tort suit for failing to have apprehended the true probability of potential injury, thereby leading, on balance, to an unbiased assignment of fault. Thus, in cases judged under a comparative fault rule, the hindsight bias might not have much impact on judgment.

Second, the influence of the bias can be blunted by other factors. For example, in tort cases, although the bias probably makes it easier for plaintiffs to prevail, tort plaintiffs generally face fairly significant hurdles to filing a lawsuit and building a case. Tort plaintiffs also might face other psychological biases in the courtroom that make it difficult for them to prevail.

Third, potential defendants should understand that if their actions injure another, a court will necessarily judge them in hindsight. Potential defendants either can adjust their level of care to avoid liability by taking a slight excess of precautions, or can act as if they will be judged under a standard of strict liability. Although the hindsight bias creates an incongruence between the law as announced and the law as applied, it is neither an unpredictable nor an unexpected incongruence. Biased assessments in hindsight are well understood, and it is therefore not necessarily unfair to subject potential defendants to them.

Economic Consequences of the Hindsight Bias

Intuitively, treating parties as if they were negligent even though they took reasonable precautions seems likely to have adverse economic consequences. Holding defendants who were not negligent liable, however, is nothing more pernicious than a system of strict liability. In effect, the hindsight bias converts the negligence standard into a de facto system of strict liability. Negligence judgments influenced by the hindsight bias should therefore have economic consequences similar to those of a system of strict liability.

Strict liability does not create incentives for potential defendants to take an excess of precautions.[22] Under both negligence and strict liability, potential defendants minimize their costs by taking all socially efficient precautions. Both systems would appear to create adequate incentives to take efficient precautions. There are, however, two caveats. First, the possibility that the defendant or the ultimate trier of fact will make errors in determining due care might, in a negligence system, cause potential defendants to undertake an inefficient excess of precautions. Defendants experience a sharp benefit from increasing their precautions from just below reasonable care to just above it. Therefore, if there is any uncertainty about what constitutes reasonable care, defendants should err in favor of an excess of precautions.[23] Second, because strict liability forces potential defendants to pay for *all* of the injuries that result from an activity, as opposed to only those that result from negligence, an activity is more expensive under strict liability than under negligence. With the exception of these two issues, however, the classic law and economics models of liability suggest that a system of strict liability would closely resemble a system of negligence.

The hindsight bias changes the economic comparison between negligence and strict liability. A system of negligence judged with the hindsight bias is similar to, but not quite the same as, a system of strict liability; it is essentially a "quasi-strict" liability rule. The bias causes courts to hold defendants who took reasonable care liable, much as they would under a strict liability rule. But, because even a biased assessment of reasonable care can result in a finding that the defendant was not negligent, the two systems differ somewhat. Defendants who have taken precautions that are far greater than reasonableness requires (as determined in foresight) probably still will be free from liability, in spite of the bias. Defendants who have taken precautions that are barely adequate probably will be found negligent because of the hindsight bias. The amount that potential defendants will have to spend beyond the socially efficient level of care to be free from liability depends upon the size of the bias, the costs of the excess precautions, and the impact of these precautions on the probability of an adverse outcome. If the savings that potential defendants realize from taking enough precautions to be immune from "quasi-strict" liability exceed the costs of these precautions, then defendants will take this socially excessive level of precautions. A negligence rule judged in hindsight will not necessarily produce a socially inefficient result, however. When the costs of the excess precautions are greater than the savings from being found not liable, potential defendants will minimize their costs at the socially efficient level of precautions, even though they will have to pay for the damages that the plaintiffs suffer.

Figure 3.1 depicts this by graphing the costs that the liability system, judged in hindsight, will likely impose on potential defendants. The X-axis

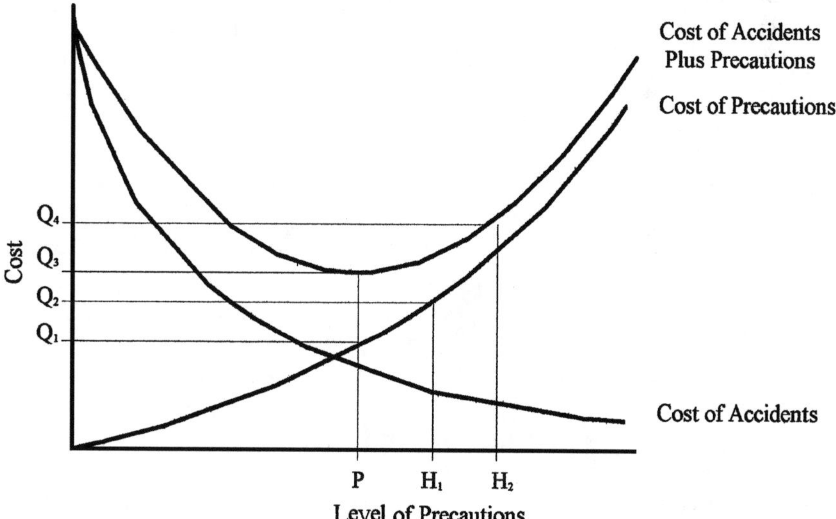

Figure 3.1. Costs of Accidents and Precautions.

represents the level of precautions the defendant may take, and the Y-axis indicates the cost of accidents and precautions. Defendants who are judged nonnegligent pay only for the costs of the precautions, while defendants who are judged negligent pay for the cost of the precautions plus the damages caused to the plaintiffs. Total social costs (the cost of the accident plus the cost of the precautions) are at their lowest at point P on the graph. Under the conventional economic analysis, defendants are not negligent if they take a level of care of at least that marked by point P. They minimize their costs at point P under either a negligence or strict liability rule, the only difference being that under a negligence rule, their costs are Q_1 while under a strict liability regime their costs are Q_3.

The hindsight bias increases the point at which courts judge defendants not negligent. Therefore, if the bias moves this point to H_1, defendants who take only the socially efficient level of care (P) will have to pay for both the cost of the precautions and the cost of the accident (Q_3) just as defendants do in strict liability. If defendants take the higher level of care (H_1), however, they will be required to pay only for the cost of the precautions (Q_2). Thus, because their overall costs will be less, the defendants will take the higher level of care (H_1). The private savings that these defendants realize from taking an excess of precautions outweigh the private costs of these precautions, leading to incentives for defendants to be inefficient. If the effect of the hindsight bias is more influential than this, however, and courts exonerate only defendants who take a level of care of at least that marked by point H_2, defendants will now minimize their costs at the efficient level of P. This is because, at H_2, defendants pay Q_4 in costs for precautions, which exceeds Q_3.

Thus, the presence of the hindsight bias in the negligence system has an indeterminate effect on incentives to take adequate precautions. If the consequences of the bias are so severe as to make negligence resemble strict liability, it might produce incentives to be efficient. Under different conditions, however, it might also create incentives to take an excess of care. Neither common law judges nor legislators are likely to have the capacity to distinguish which of these two situations any class of cases follows. It would take a wealth of econometric data on the cost of accidents and precautions, along with a precise quantification of the hindsight bias and its relationship to these precautions, to determine whether judging negligence in hindsight creates incentives to take an excess of precautions in any given context. It would be difficult, if not impossible, for a court to determine whether negligence judged in hindsight creates inefficient incentives. Therefore, retaining a negligence system, despite its biases in judgment, might be the optimum, albeit imperfect, alternative for courts to pursue.

A system that produced unbiased judgments would, therefore, avoid one of two adverse economic consequences of the hindsight bias. First, unbiased judgments would avoid the possibility that the hindsight bias would create incentives to undertake an excess of precautions. Second, in those circumstances in which judging negligence in hindsight produces the same incentives as strict liability, the costs of de facto strict liability might make the underlying activity undesirably expensive. Regardless of whether the cost of excess precautions exceeds the savings in liability to the defendant, judging negligence in hindsight is inferior to an unbiased system.

Adaptations in the Legal System

Long before empirical studies proved its existence, the hindsight bias has been part of folk wisdom. Therefore, it is likely that the legal system has developed adaptations to the bias's influence. Avoiding the influence of the hindsight bias altogether is probably impossible. Because the bias is so deeply ingrained into the human judgment process, psychologists have been unable to develop a way to induce people to make unbiased ex post judgments of ex ante probabilities. Even if courts understand that judging liability in hindsight generates biased results, they might be powerless to do anything about it. Although general procedures that avoid the bias in all cases are unlikely to be available, in some specific circumstances the courts have opportunities to reduce the bias's influence. In most cases, however, because the bias makes accurate judgments unavailable, the courts must struggle to develop a second-best method of assigning liability.

General Procedures to Avoid Biased Judgments

Judicial instructions, suppression of evidence, and the standard of persuasion are the usual "quality control" mechanisms for judgment in the courtroom. To aid a jury in reaching a rational decision, the judge structures the trial and provides instructions on how to decide the case. Judges also suppress evidence deemed to be misleading.[24] The standard of persuasion is also set so as to advance rational functioning of the legal system. None of these methods, however, can be used to ameliorate the hindsight bias.

Psychologists have uncovered no way to instruct people on how to evaluate decisions in hindsight in a way that completely avoids the hindsight bias. Judicial instructions are unlikely to include a mechanism that would fare any better. The Kamin and Rachlinski study tested debiasing instructions in a trial context.[25] The materials in this study warned half of the subjects in the trial (hindsight) condition of the difficulty of determining liability in hindsight and that they should therefore consider "all the ways in which the event in question may have happened differently or not at all."[26] This debiasing procedure had no effect. Passive debiasing instructions such as those used by Kamin and Rachlinski are insufficiently intrusive to counteract the hindsight bias. The effective strategies that psychologists have used to reduce the bias all require invasive procedures that are unsuitable for the courtroom. Even if a debiasing technique could be successfully shoe-horned into the trial context, it would still only partly reduce the effect. No strategy has been found for completely avoiding the bias.

In fact, courts do not attempt to use judicial instructions as a means of debiasing jurors. Instructions typically ask for unbiased ex post judgments of ex ante probabilities without providing any suggestion as to how to accomplish this complex cognitive task. Jury instruction manuals lack general instructions on how to avoid the hindsight bias, even though they include instructions that require juries to make judgments that will almost certainly be biased.[27]

One other common legal mechanism for avoiding bias and prejudice – suppressing evidence – probably cannot cure the hindsight bias. To avoid the influence of the bias, the evidence that needs to be suppressed is the very fact that some adverse event led to a lawsuit. Courts have used juries to make findings of fact in the absence of both the injured parties and descriptions of their injuries.[28] Even in these bifurcated trials, however, juries cannot remain completely unaware of the existence of injured plaintiffs. In some circumstances, courts do suppress evidence that would exacerbate the impact of the hindsight bias on judgment; evidence that would create the conditions for biased judgment, however, cannot be eliminated from the trial process. Hiding the extent of injuries will not eliminate the hindsight bias, because the severity of the outcome does not alter the bias's influence on assessments of responsibility.[29] The mere fact of the adverse outcome creates a biased judgment, and this fact cannot be suppressed from evidence or eliminated from the jury's knowledge by a special procedure.

Raising the standard of persuasion by requiring "clear and convincing evidence" for findings that the bias is likely to affect might undo its impact on the judgment. Raising the standard would make it more difficult for a party relying on the hindsight bias to win a case, but this reform would treat the symptom and not the disease. The effect of increasing the standard would be unlikely to match the effect of the hindsight bias perfectly. It might overcompensate for the bias, thereby creating the potential for more errors in judgment than the hindsight bias caused. It is perhaps not surprising then that courts do not manipulate the standard of persuasion as a means of avoiding the hindsight bias.

Remedies for the Hindsight Bias in Specific Circumstances

The usual methods for promoting rational decision making in the courtroom are unlikely to eliminate the influence of the hindsight bias on judgments. Courts do not even attempt to issue instructions that might reduce the bias, they could not suppress enough evidence to avoid the bias, and increasing the burden of proof risks increasing the likelihood of error. This is not to say that the courts are ignorant of the hindsight bias or completely impotent to respond to it. In certain circumstances the courts can, and do, use techniques to avoid rendering biased judgments or to reduce the effect of the hindsight bias. Several examples support the theory that courts do understand the hindsight bias and correct for it when it is possible to do so.

Compliance with Ex Ante Norms. A reliable judgment of reasonable care that was made before an accident has occurred is sometimes available. Many customary practices within an industry or a profession are attempts to identify precautions that constitute a reasonable level of care. So are many government safety regulations. In such cases, rather than conducting an open-ended inquiry into whether a defendant took reasonable precautions, a court could assess whether the defendant complied with the relevant custom or regulation. Under this rule, only a determination that the defendant had not complied with the ex ante norm could support a conclusion that the defendant was negligent. This decision rule would avoid the need to determine the probability of an accident in hindsight, thereby eliminating much of the hindsight bias's influence on the judgment.

Despite this advantage, the law does not recognize compliance with either custom or regulation as a complete defense to liability.[30] Courts treat compliance with a custom or regulation as evidence that a tort defendant's actions were not negligent, but courts independently assess the reasonableness of the defendant's actions. Merely introducing evidence that conduct complied with custom or regulation might reduce the impact of the hindsight bias, but because the judge or jury still assesses the ex ante probability of the adverse event, the bias will still influence the judgment.

The failure to rely on regulation or custom as a complete defense to a determination of negligence does not mean that courts are ignorant of the hindsight bias. Rather, the status of custom and regulatory compliance as defenses is the result of other considerations. As to regulations, courts are concerned that the agencies that create regulations might craft inadequate regulations because they are "captured" by the targets of regulation, lack adequate resources, or are subject to political pressures to produce lax regulations.[31] Furthermore, because federal law is the source of many safety regulations, whereas state law governs common law tort liability, adoption of a strong version of the regulatory compliance defense would turn much of state law over to federal control.

As to the use of custom as a defense, the courts have worried that customary practices might reflect a habit or even result "from the kind of inadvertence, carelessness, indifference, cost-paring and corner-cutting that is normally associated with negligence."[32] Although manufacturers and professionals face incentives to develop customs that reflect reasonable care, an industry or profession is only likely to develop such customs if the transaction costs between the entity that provides the product or service and everyone who may be injured by the product or service are low, and if consumers have the same bargaining power, ability to identify efficient precautions, and risk preferences as the entity providing the product or service.[33] Few transactions have such characteristics. Consequently, the cautious approach to custom that the courts have followed makes economic sense.

In one class of cases – medical malpractice – courts have acknowledged that the profession's ex ante custom is probably superior to their ex post judgment.[34] Doctors who have followed customary medical procedure are not to be considered negligent. The courts believe that the conditions necessary for the development of efficient customs exist in the medical profession and that these customs are more accurate measures of reasonable care than ex post assessments by a court.[35] This exception to the general rule shows that the courts do distrust the value of second-guessing ex ante decisions.

The refusal to rely more heavily on either regulatory compliance or custom presents a lost opportunity to avoid a biased assessment of liability. As discussed, however, there are good reasons to suppose that regulations and customs might not actually reflect an appropriate analysis of reasonable precautions. Where there is strong reason to believe that the ex ante norm is identical to reasonable care, as in the case of medical malpractice, the courts have relied on it as a gauge of negligence that is superior to their ex post judgments.

Good Evidence of an Ex Ante Assessment – The Case of Patent Law. Hindsight problems are not restricted to the common law. The federal courts, for example, have long struggled with the problem of judging the validity of patents in hindsight and have worked to develop a sensible resolution to the hindsight bias. For a device or technique to merit patent protection, not only must it be a novel and useful advance, it must actually be an invention – it must be a "nonobvious" advance in an art.[36]

The determination of nonobviousness is likely to be affected by the hindsight bias, although this has not been tested empirically. Even a truly novel idea might seem obvious after it has been revealed. The law requires that nonobviousness be determined "at the time the invention was made,"[37] although "hindsight is often difficult to avoid in determining obviousness of inventions."[38] Courts have recognized the problem of hindsight and have expressed concern that they "must be continually on guard against the natural tendency to treat as obvious something which appears simple in the light of hindsight, but which may not actually have been so at the time of the invention."[39]

Partly in response to the influence of hindsight, the Supreme Court added "secondary considerations" to the test for nonobviousness. In addition to the inquiry into the technical aspects of the invention, the Court also requires lower courts to analyze "such secondary considerations as commercial success, long felt but unsolved need, failure of others, etc., [that] might be utilized to give light to the circumstances surrounding the origin of the subject matter sought to be patented."[40] The Court observed that determining nonobviousness by reference to these secondary considerations helps courts to avoid conducting technical inquiry that they might be incompetent to undertake and "guard[s] against slipping into the use of hindsight."[41] The mere fact of an invention will not color a court's evaluation of the evidence of the invention's commercial success or its resolution of a long-felt unresolved need, whereas the mere fact of the invention might make the inventor's technical achievements seem obvious. Secondary characteristics have grown in importance since the Court first introduced them into the test for nonobviousness. The Federal Circuit ultimately held that an inquiry into secondary characteristics may, by itself, support the conclusion that an invention was not obvious.[42] Thus, rather than make a technical evaluation of how the inventor arrived at his or her alleged innovation, courts determining nonobviousness may look to considerations that are not as susceptible to the hindsight bias.

The situation here resembles medical malpractice. Part of the reason that courts rely on custom in medical malpractice and secondary evidence of nonobviousness in patent law is a recognition of their limited ability to understand technical or scientific subject matters raised by such cases, but the courts also recognize that judgments made in hindsight are biased. The law in both cases represents an attempt to find reliable ex ante evidence of an appropriate judgment, so that trial courts need not rely on judgments made in hindsight that are influenced by outcome knowledge.

No "Liability by Hindsight." Although no general remedy for the hindsight bias is available, courts have used the burden of production to blunt the benefit that the hindsight bias confers upon plaintiffs in negligence cases. Because of the bias, a plaintiff could rely exclusively on the mere fact of an adverse outcome to convince a judge or jury that the defendant's actions were negligent. To prevent this possibility, courts require more evidence than the mere fact of injury.[43] As the Oregon Supreme Court described this doctrine: "With hindsight's 20/20 vision, it is easy to see that [the defendant] should have foreseen . . . a risk to the public at large. [But, p]roof aided by hindsight . . . is insufficient to establish negligence."[44]

The federal courts have adopted a particularly vigorous prohibition against liability based solely on hindsight in cases alleging violations of the federal securities laws. To win a federal securities case, a plaintiff must allege and prove that a defendant has intentionally misrepresented material facts about a publicly traded company in an effort to defraud investors.[45] As in all fraud cases, in order to survive a motion to dismiss brought under Rule 9(b), plaintiffs must make additional allegations of specific instances of intended fraud.[46] Courts have held that, in a case of alleged securities fraud, this heightened pleading requirement means that a plaintiff must do more than merely allege that some prediction made by the defendant ultimately failed to come true:[47] "There is no 'fraud by hindsight,'"[48] Plaintiffs who can allege specific circumstances of fraud in addition to the defendant's failed predictions still benefit from the hindsight bias, however. The "fraud by hindsight" doctrine guards only against a severe abuse of the hindsight bias; it does not entirely purge the system of the bias's influence.

Subsequent Remedial Measures. Although suppressing evidence is not generally a useful way to avoid the influence of the hindsight bias, courts can sometimes suppress evidence that would, if admitted, exacerbate the bias's impact on the judgment. For example, the rule that a defendant's postaccident remedial measures are not admissible to prove negligence[49] can be traced to the hindsight bias. Injurers often update their safety precautions after an accident, and wisely so. An accident can teach an injurer much about how to avoid causing future harm. Nevertheless, such subsequent remedial measures are almost irrelevant to a determination as to whether the defendant was negligent with respect to the initial accident. These measures only reveal insights gleaned from the adverse outcome itself and do not speak to what was predictable beforehand.

The liberal rules of relevance in contemporary evidence law, however, probably support admitting evidence that a defendant has taken subsequent remedial measures. Defendants should, in principle, have no fear of this evidence. If the evidence that the defendant took subsequent remedial measures is virtually irrelevant, then a rational fact finder should give it no weight. The evidence should have no effect on the outcome.

Nevertheless, courts have worried that evidence that the defendant has taken subsequent remedial measures will have a dramatic effect on a jury.[50] They worry that juries will mistakenly assume that "because the world gets wiser as it gets older, therefore it was foolish before."[51] This is essentially an assertion that juries' assessments of defendants' adoption of subsequent remedial measures will be influenced by the hindsight bias. If juries do overreact to the defendants' taking subsequent remedial measures, then defendants will be loath to undertake them. The increased probability of paying for the accident that already occurred might overwhelm the benefits to the defendant of reducing the prospects of future liability, at least until the trial is over. Courts worry that admitting evidence of subsequent remedial measures would induce juries to hold defendants liable when they actually took reasonable care. This would discourage defendants from taking subsequent remedial measures. To avoid this problem, courts have deemed such evidence inadmissible.[52]

In cases involving subsequent remedial measures, the courts suppress evidence that would magnify the hindsight bias's influence on the judgment, thereby averting an unwanted incentive structure. Admitting such evidence would not only leave the defendant subject to the ordinary version of the hindsight bias – the accident occurred, so the defendant's actions appear less reasonable than they would in foresight – but it also would tempt the jury with more detailed evidence of the defendant's decision-making process on precautions. The fact of the accident cannot realistically be suppressed, but evidence that would aggravate the bias can be. Courts' response to the problem of subsequent remedial measures reveals a good understanding of the hindsight bias and the judicial ability to respond to it.

Adopting a "No Liability" Rule

The courts have thus proven remarkably adept at pursuing opportunities to avoid or to reduce the impact of the hindsight bias on judgments of liability. These opportunities are restricted to isolated circumstances, however, and the lack of a generally applicable remedy leaves a great many cases subject to the bias's influence. In some circumstances, the adverse consequences of biased judgments are both unavoidable and intolerable. In these situations, rather than subject defendants to biased judgments of liability, the best option might be to refuse to hold defendants liable, even if their actions seem negligent in hindsight. A rule of "no liability" might have fewer adverse consequences than a rule of negligence judged in hindsight. Indeed, in certain circumstances, courts have adopted just such a rule.

The best example of such a situation is probably the business judgment rule in corporate law. The business judgment rule refers to the standard for judicial review of decisions by corporate officers and directors.[53] The rule varies across jurisdictions and is difficult to state precisely, but an officer or director who is informed about a transaction and is not interested in the transaction "fulfills the duty [of care to the shareholders] if . . . he rationally believes that the business judgment is in the best interest of the corporation."[54] Officers and directors who satisfy the elements of the rule are not liable to the shareholders for decisions that turn out badly, even if these decisions seem negligent in hindsight: "Whereas automobile drivers who make a mistake in judgment . . . will likely be called upon to respond in damages, a corporate officer who makes a mistake in judgment . . . will rarely, if ever, be found liable for damages suffered by the corporation."[55]

But is judicial deference to business decisions attributable to the hindsight bias? There are several justifications for the rule, but the principal ones boil down to the relative institutional competence of corporate managers as compared to the courts. Corporate managers have much more expertise than courts do at making business decisions, a justification that has nothing to do with the hindsight bias. Expertise, however, is not a sufficient account of the business judgment rule; the courts have no problem holding other experts, such as doctors, lawyers, and accountants, liable for negligent decisions. Courts evaluating business decisions also mistrust their perspective: "[C]ourts recognize that after-the-fact litigation is a most imperfect device to evaluate corporate business decisions. The circumstances surrounding a corporate decision are not easily reconstructed in a courtroom years later. . . . [A] reasoned decision at the time made may seem a wild hunch viewed years later against a background of perfect knowledge."[56] The business judgment rule arises from the concern that even a good decision can produce an undesirable result and can be judged unfairly in hindsight: "Courts recognize that even disinterested, well-intentioned, informed directors can make decisions that, in hindsight, were improvident."[57]

This rationale, however, also applies to potential tort defendants, especially in cases of professional liability.[58] Indeed, the similarities between corporate managers and other professionals are striking. All professionals could merit deference from judicial second-guessing of their decisions, particularly as the second-guessing is done in hindsight. Nevertheless, both equitable and economic factors provide some grounds for distinguishing the business judgment context from other professional liability. Immunizing professionals from liability for negligence would create a greater injustice for the potential plaintiffs than the business judgment rule inflicts upon shareholders. Shareholders can fire incompetent managers either directly through a shareholder vote or indirectly by selling their holdings in the corporation. Although patients and clients can fire incompetent lawyers or accountants, the harm that is inflicted in the meantime may be more personally significant. Incompetent managers will cost their shareholders only their money, after all. To be sure, this distinction is a slight overgeneralization: The loss of a personal investment in a business could exceed the financial loss from legal or accounting malpractice. Shareholders, however, can diversify their risk of loss in a manner that is not possible in the professional service context. The likely nature of the damages in each context distinguishes between corporate liability and the liability of other professionals.

Economic grounds provide a better explanation for the different liability standards in corporate governance as opposed to other professions. The bias converts the negligence standard into a quasi-strict liability rule, which if applied to corporate managers would either induce them to take an excess of precautions or act as if they operated under a system of strict liability. If it mimicked strict liability, then fewer people would be willing to become corporate managers than if they were subject to an unbiased negligence system. This concern might account for the business judgment rule, and it does run through the early business judgment cases in the nineteenth century.[59]

Furthermore, the possibility that quasi-strict liability would create incentives to take an excess of precautions would undermine the basic functioning of corporate managers more severely than other professionals. Investors want corporate managers to make risk-neutral business decisions, because investors already control their overall investment risk through diversification.[60] Ensuring that managers effectively represent this concern and do not avoid business decisions that have a high expected payoff but also carry a high degree of risk is a central problem of corporate governance.[61] Liability for negligence judged in hindsight would only exacerbate this problem. Investors do not need the security of being able to hold their managers strictly liable, and they certainly do not want them taking an excess of precautions against losses. As the court in *Joy v. North* put it, "[I]t is very much in the interests of shareholders that the law not create incentives for overly cautious corporate decisions."[62] We might want doctors, lawyers, or accountants to guarantee their work with a system of de facto strict liability, or take an occasional excess of precautions, but corporate managers operating under such a regime will be apt to betray the real interests of their shareholders.

Without the hindsight bias, it is difficult to explain why corporate managers are immune from liability for negligence and other professionals are not. Arguably all professionals have sufficient incentives to avoid negligent conduct; they need to do so in order to retain their patients or clients. Therefore, all professionals could argue that they should be immune from liability for negligent conduct. Alternatively professionals have much more information than their clients, patients, and shareholders and are in the best position to respond to reduce the social costs of their actions. Therefore, all professionals (corporate managers included) should be subject to liability. When negligence judged in hindsight is revealed to be a system of quasi-strict liability, however, the distinction becomes clear. Strict liability is a perfectly defensible, even laudable, form of liability: It creates incentives to be efficient and spreads the risk of injury, reducing the possibility that a single individual will experience a catastrophic loss. But adopting a system of strict liability raises the costs of any activity, which might create some unwanted consequences. The consequences of a system of strict liability are particularly undesirable to shareholders in a corporation. Shareholders already spread their risks through diversification, and even without a system of quasi-strict liability, they must worry that their managers make risk-averse decisions. With decades of experience in the matter and a basic understanding of the foibles of judging in hindsight, courts seem to have realized this and carved out the business judgment rule for corporate managers alone among professionals.

Conclusion

The legal system has a good understanding of the hindsight bias and its effects on judging liability after the fact. Generic debiasing strategies are unlikely to be available, and the courts do not attempt to use them. Instead they have developed mechanisms for taking advantage of specific circumstances that allow them to reduce the influence of the hindsight bias. In those cases in which the bias cannot be avoided, the courts have pursued sensible second-best strategies that are sensitive to the consequences of biased judgments for both economics and justice.

The development of rules on judging liability in hindsight speaks to two different schools of legal theory: law and economics and law and psychology. To the law and economics community, especially those developing positive theories of law, it shows not only that a cognitive bias can persist in the system, but also that the system itself can recognize the bias and adapt to it. In fact, a legal academic armed with an understanding of the limits of human judgment is in a better position to explain the pattern of case law than one without such understanding. As for the law and psychology tradition, a close look at the legal system's response to the bias suggests that the law is well equipped to address the cognitive limitations of judges and juries. Although an understanding of cognitive biases may reveal patterns in the case law, not every bias needs a new reform. The law might have figured it out all on its own.

Notes

1 *Cornman v. The Eastern Counties Railway Co.*, 157 *Eng. Rep.* 1050, 1052 (Exch. 1859).

2 See Baruch Fischhoff, Hindsight ≠ Foresight: The Effect of Outcome Knowledge on Judgment Under Uncertainty, 1 *J. Exper. Psychol.* 288 (1975) (first describing the effect). For reviews of research on the hindsight bias, see Jay J. Christensen-Szalanski and Cynthia Fobian Willham, The Hindsight Bias: A Meta-analysis, 48 *Org. Beh. & Hum. Decision Processes* 147, 147–8 (1991); Scott A. Hawkins and Reid Hastie, Hindsight: Biased Judgments of Past Events After the Outcomes Are Known, 107 *Psychol. Bull.* 311, 312 (1990).

3 Baruch Fischhoff, For Those Condemned to Study the Past: Heuristics and Biases in Hindsight, in *Judgment Under Uncertainty* 335, 341 (Daniel Kahneman, Paul Slovic, and Amos Tversky eds., 1982) (offering a thorough analysis of potential causes of the bias).

4 See Fischhoff, supra note 2.

5 See Christensen-Szalanski and Willham, supra note 2, at 155. The quotation is originally from Fischhoff, supra note 2, at 297.

6 Stephen J. Hoch and George F. Loewenstein, Outcome Feedback: Hindsight and Information, 15 *J. Exper. Psychol.: Learning, Memory, & Cognition* 605, 606 (1989).

7 Fischhoff, supra note 2, at 288.

8 See Fischhoff, supra note 2, at 297; Hawkins and Hastie, supra note 2, at 312 (although they argue that this process is not automatic).

9 See David Wasserman, Richard O. Lempert, and Reid Hastie, Hindsight and Causality, 17 *Personality & Soc. Psychol. Bull.* 30, 34 (1991).

10 See Michelle R. Nario and Nyla R. Branscombe, Comparison Processes in Hindsight and Causal Attribution, 21 *Personality & Soc. Psychol. Bull.* 1244, 1252 (1995); Donald C. Pennington, The British Fireman's Strike of 1977/78: An Investigation of Judgments in Foresight and Hindsight, 20 *Brit. J. Soc. Psychol.* 89, 93–5 (1981); Neal J. Roese and James M. Olson, Counterfactuals, Causal Attributions, and the Hindsight Bias: A Conceptual Integration, *J. Exper. Soc. Psychol.* 197, 205–18 (1996).

11 See Christensen-Szalanski and Willham, supra note 2, at 154–5.

12 See generally, Michael J. Lerner and Dale T. Miller, Just World Research and the Attribution Process: Looking Back and Looking Ahead, 85 *Psychol. Bull.* 1030 (1978).

13 Hawkins and Hastie, supra note 2, at 317.

14 Martin F. Davies, Reduction of Hindsight Bias by Restoration of Foresight Perspective: Effectiveness of Foresight-Encoding and Hindsight-Retrieval Strategies, 40 *Org. Beh. & Hum. Decision Processes* 50, 51–64 (1987); Baruch Fischhoff et al., Fault Trees: Sensitivity of Estimated Failure Probabilities to Performance Representation, 4 *J. Exper. Psychol.: Hum. Perception & Performance* 349, 354–6 (1978); Wolfgang Hell et al., Hindsight Bias: An Interaction of Automatic and Motivational Factors? 16 *Memory & Cognition* 533, 535–6 (1988).

15 See Fischhoff et al., supra note 14, at 354–6; Rudiger F. Pohl and Wolfgang Hell, No Reduction in Hindsight Bias After Complete Information and Repeated Testing, 67 *Org. Beh. & Hum. Decision Processes* 49, 51–5 (1996).

16 See, e.g., Paul Slovic and Baruch Fischhoff, On the Psychology of Experimental Surprises, 3 *J. Exper. Psychol.: Hum. Perception & Performance* 544, 549 (1977) (asking subjects to consider alternative outcomes); Baruch Fischhoff et al., supra note 14 (having subjects draw out "fault trees" to consider alternative outcomes).

17 Ed Bukszar and Terry Connolly, Hindsight Bias and Strategic Choice: Some Problems in Learning from Experience, 31 *Acad. Mgmt. J.* 628, 631 (1988); Dagmar Stahlberg et al., We Knew It All Along: Hindsight Bias in Groups, 63 *Org. Beh. & Hum. Decision Processes* 46, 51–5 (1995).

18 John C. Anderson et al., Evaluation of Auditor Decisions: Hindsight Bias Effects and the Expectation Gap, 14 *J. Econ. Psychol.* 711, 730 (1993); Marianne M. Jennings et al., Outcome Foreseeability and Its Effects on Judicial Decisions (unpublished manuscript on file with U. Chi. L. Rev.).

19 *Restatement (Second) of Torts* §§282, §282 cmt. g (1965).

20 Kim A. Kamin and Jeffrey J. Rachlinski, Ex Post ≠ Ex Ante: Determining Liability in Hindsight, 19 *Law & Hum. Beh.* 89 (1995); Susan J. LaBine and Gary LaBine, Determinations of Negligence and the Hindsight Bias, 20 *Law & Hum. Beh.* 501 (1996).

21 Lon L. Fuller, *The Morality of Law* 39 (rev. ed. 1969).

22 See William M. Landes and Richard A. Posner, *The Economic Structure of Tort Law* 64 (1987); A. Mitchell Polinsky, *An Introduction to Law and Economics* 40–2 (2d ed. 1989); Steven Shavell, Strict Liability Versus Negligence, 9 *J. Legal Stud.* 1, 2–9 (1980).

23 See John E. Calfee and Richard Craswell, Some Effects of Uncertainty on Compliance with Legal Standards, 70 *Va. L. Rev.* 965 (1984). But see Mark F. Grady, A New Positive Economic Theory of Negligence, 92 *Yale L. J.* 799 (1983) (arguing that the negligence system accommodates this uncertainty).

24 See, e.g., Fed. R. Evid. 403.

25 Kamin and Rachlinski, supra note 20.

26 Ibid. at 97.

27 See, e.g., BAJI §3.11 (7th ed. 1986) (California); 1A *New York Pattern Jury Instructions – Civil* §2:20 (3d ed. 1997); 3 Edward J. Devitt et al., *Federal Jury Practice and Instructions – Civil* §80.07 (4th ed. 1987).

28 Fed. R. Civ. Pro. 42(b) (allowing bifurcation of issues); In re *Richardson–Merrell, Inc. "Benedectin" Products Liability Litigation*, 624 F. Supp. 1212 (S.D. Ohio 1985), aff'd sub nom., Hoffman v. Merrill Dow Pharmaceuticals, Inc. (In re Benedectin Litigation), 857 F.2d 290 (6th Cir. 1988), cert. denied, 488 U.S. 1006 (1989).

29 Elaine Walster, "Second Guessing" Important Events, 20 *Hum. Rel.* 239, 244–7 (1967).
30 See *Restatement (Second) of Torts* §288C (1965) (regulatory compliance); *Restatement (Second) of Torts* §295A (1965) (custom).
31 See Richard C. Ausness, The Case for a "Strong" Regulatory Compliance Defense, 55 *Md. L. Rev.* 1210 (1996) (outlining these problems; although Ausness ultimately concludes that a strong version of the regulatory compliance defense is still tenable).
32 W. Page Keeton et al., *Prosser and Keeton on the Law of Torts* §33, at 194 (5th ed. 1984).
33 See Landes and Posner, supra note 22, at 132–3 (transaction costs must be low); James A. Henderson Jr. and John A. Siliciano, Universal Health Care and the Continued Reliance on Custom in Determining Medical Malpractice, 79 *Cornell L. Rev.* 1382, 1389–95 (1994) (identifying other problems with custom).
34 See Keeton et al., supra note 32, at §33.
35 Richard A. Posner, *Economic Analysis of Law* 169 (4th ed. 1992). But see Henderson and Siliciano, supra note 33, at 1389–1400 (arguing that courts' assumption that appropriate custom will develop in medical practice may be incorrect).
36 35 *U.S.C.* §103(a) (1994). See also 2 Ernest Bainbridge Lipscomb III, *Lipscomb's Walker on Patents* §6.1 (3d ed. 1985).
37 35 *U.S.C.* §103(a).
38 *Ellicott Mac. Corp. v. United States*, 405 F.2d 1385, 1390 (Ct. Cl. 1969).
39 *Teleflex Inc. v. American Chain & Cable Co.*, 273 F. Supp. 573, 587 (S.D.N.Y. 1967).
40 *Graham v. John Deere Co.*, 383 U.S. 1, 17–18 (1966).
41 *Graham*, 383 U.S., at 36, quoting *Monroe Auto Equipment Co. v. Heckthorn Mfg. & Supply Co.*, 332 F.2d 406, 412 (6th Cir. 1964).
42 *Vandenberg v. Dairy Equip. Co.*, 740 F.2d 1560, 1567 (Fed. Cir. 1984).
43 See Keeton et al., supra note 32, §39, at 242.
44 *Cain v. Rijken*, 300 Or. 706, 720, 717 P.2d 140, 149 (1986).
45 See generally *Basic v. Levinson*, 485 U.S. 224, 231 (1988) (stating elements of a violation of §10[b] of the Securities Exchange Act of 1934).
46 Fed. R. Civ. Pro. 9(b).
47 See William S. Feinstein, Pleading Securities Fraud with Particularity – Federal Rule of Civil Procedure 9(b) in the Rule 10b–5 Context: *Kowal v. MCI Communications Corporation*, 63 *Geo. Wash. L. Rev.* 851, 857–8 (1995); Elliott J. Weiss, The New Securities Fraud Pleading Requirement: Speed Bump or Road Block? 38 *Ariz. L. Rev.* 675, 684 (1996).
48 *Dileo v. Ernst & Young*, 901 F.2d 624, 628 (7th Cir. 1990), quoting *Denny v. Barber*, 576 F.2d 465, 470 (2d Cir. 1978) (Friendly, J.).
49 See Fed. R. Evid. 407; David P. Leonard, *Selected Rules of Limited Admissibility, The New Wigmore* §§2.3.4, 2.5 (1996) (only two states, Maine and Rhode Island, regularly admit such evidence to prove negligence). Subsequent remedial measures are admissible for other purposes, "such as proving ownership, control, or feasibility of precautionary measures, if controverted, or impeachment." *Fed. R. Evid.* 407.
50 See Leonard, supra note 49, §2.2, at 2–14.
51 *Hart v. Lancashire & Yorkshire Ry.*, 21 L.T.R. (n.s.) 261, 263 (Ex. 1869).
52 See *Flamino v. Honda Motor Co., Ltd.*, 733 F.2d 463, 471 (7th Cir. 1984) (Posner, J.) ("It is only because juries are believed to overreact to evidence of subsequent remedial measures that the admissibility of such evidence could deter defendants from taking such measures").

53 See Dennis J. Block et al., *The Business Judgment Rule: Fiduciary Duties of Corporate Directors* 3–4 (4th ed. 1993).

54 American Law Institute, *Principles of Corporate Governance: Analysis and Recommendations* §4.01(c), at 181–2 (1992).

55 *Joy v. North*, 692 F.2d at 885 (citations omitted).

56 Ibid. at 886.

57 *Washington Bancorp. v. Said*, 812 F. Supp. 1256, 1267–8 (D.D.C. 1993).

58 See generally, Hal R. Arkes and Cindy A. Schipani, Medical Malpractice v. the Business Judgment Rule: Differences in Hindsight Bias, 73 *Or. L. Rev.* 587, 633–6 (1994) (comparing the liability of corporate mangers to doctors).

59 See, e.g., *Percy v. Millaudon*, 8 Mart. (n.s.) 68, 77–8 (La. 1829).

60 *Joy v. North*, 692 F.2d at 886 n. 6.

61 See Posner, supra note 35, at 405.

62 692 F.2d at 886.

4 Behavioral Economics, Contract Formation, and Contract Law*

Russell Korobkin

The Coase Theorem,[1] on which much of the edifice of "law and economics" is built, posits that when transaction costs are zero the initial allocation of a legal entitlement is irrelevant to its eventual ownership. If an entitlement is first granted to Amy, she will keep the entitlement if she values it more than does Beth, but Amy will sell the entitlement to Beth if it is Beth who values it more. If the entitlement is originally granted to Beth, on the other hand, she will sell it to Amy if Amy places a higher value on it. The power of the Coase Theorem, and indeed its veracity in the real world, depends on its underlying behavioral assumption that an individual's valuation of entitlements does not depend on ownership; that is, Amy values an entitlement neither more nor less if she is initially allocated that entitlement than if it is initially given to Beth.

The assumption that preferences are exogenous to entitlement allocations is testable, and it has been demonstrated to be false, at least under some conditions. The contrary evidence, often labeled the "status quo bias" or the "endowment effect," instead suggests that the initial allocation of legal entitlements can affect preferences for those entitlements. The consequence is that completely alienable legal entitlements will be "sticky" – that is, tend not to be traded – even when such stickiness cannot be explained by transaction costs. The evidence thus describes a substantial weakness in the edifice of traditional law and economics. The principal goal of one branch of the discipline of "behavioral law and economics" is to explore the implications of this weakness for legal theory.

This chapter describes experimental evidence of the effect that the status quo bias can have on the negotiation of contract terms. The analysis is

* Substantial portions of this chapter are reprinted from Russell Korobkin, "The Status Quo Bias and Contract Default Rules," 83 *Cornell L. Rev.* 608 (1998), and Russell Korobkin, "Inertia and Preference in Contract Negotiation: The Psychological Power of Default Rules and Form Terms," 51 *Vanderbilt L. Rev.* 1583 (1998). The protocols for and statistical analysis of the experiments discussed here can be found in these articles.

both positive and prescriptive. On the positive side, the evidence suggests that the preferences of negotiating parties for contract terms depends on the extent to which the terms in question are perceived as being part of the status quo state of the world, in contradiction to predictions of traditional law and economics analysis derived from the Coase Theorem. On the prescriptive side, the evidence suggests strategies for lawyers and other negotiators seeking to maximize the profits of their clients, and strategies for legal policy makers concerned with adopting rules of contract law that optimally encourage private parties to maximize allocative efficiency through their transactions.

The chapter proceeds in the following steps. The first section contrasts the received wisdom of traditional law and economics literature on the nature of preferences for contract terms with evidence from research in psychology and experimental economics that demonstrates the effect of the status quo bias on preferences for property rights and other legal entitlements. The second section then presents new experimental evidence that suggests the preferences of negotiating parties can also be affected by their perceptions of which contract terms represent the status quo. It describes how, under some conditions, legal default terms – contract terms that govern parties who fail to stipulate to other terms – can embody the power of the status quo bias, whereas in other cases terms contained in "form contracts" can be seen as constituent parts of the status quo. The third section develops a theory of why the status quo bias exists in negotiations over contract terms, arguing that theories consistent with traditional approaches to law and economics are far less plausible than psychological theories that rely on emotion and desire to avoid future regret over current choices. Finally, the fourth section considers the implications of the status quo bias's effect on contract negotiations for lawyers who advocate on behalf of clients in negotiations and for legal policy makers concerned with selecting rules of contract law that will best encourage efficient private ordering.

Preference Exogeneity and the Status Quo Bias

Rational Choice Theory and Preference Exogeneity

Approaches to the study of contract negotiation that rely on traditional law and economics analysis rest on the following fundamental premise: Contracting parties' intrinsic preferences for contract terms are exogenous to contextual factors that frame the negotiations. For example, the content of default terms that will govern the parties by operation of law if the parties do not explicitly contract around them should not affect parties' preferences, nor should the interpersonal dynamics of the bargaining table.

The reason for the persistence of this "preference exogeneity assumption" is embedded deeply in the behavioral model of rational choice theory, which underlies the economic analysis of law. Rational choice theory presumes parties will act so as to maximize their expected utility, which involves comparing end states that might result from alternative behaviors discounted by their likelihood of occurring. In economic analysis of law – at least in the field of contracting behavior – this presumption is usually simplified by assuming that parties will act to maximize their expected wealth.

Under the standard application of this theory, contracting parties are assumed to compare the expected financial costs and benefits of alternative contract terms and to base their preference on which term will provide the greatest differential of benefits over costs. Under this common application of rational choice theory to contracting behavior, contextual features of the negotiation might affect what terms parties *ultimately reach* agreement upon. For example, an intrinsically preferable term might be disfavored by a party because the term is more expensive to draft or negotiate, or because bargaining for the term might convey information that the party wishes to keep secret. But the context of the negotiation should not affect parties' underlying *preferences* for contract terms.

The Status Quo Bias

The analytical power of rational choice theory makes the preference exogeneity assumption attractive, but there is a significant body of empirical and experimental data that suggests that the assumption, as applied to contract terms, might be false. Research demonstrates that individuals will often place a higher value on an entitlement or property right if they own it than if they do not. Put slightly differently, individuals favor maintaining the status quo state of affairs to adapting to alternative states, assuming all other things are equal.

In a well-known experiment conducted by Daniel Kahneman, Jack Knetsch, and Richard Thaler (Chapter 8 of this book),[2] subjects were randomly divided and given either a coffee mug or $6 in cash. "Mug owners" were asked to reveal the minimum amount they would be willing to accept to sell the mug (their "WTA" value), while the cash holders were asked to reveal the maximum amount they would be willing to pay for one of the mugs (their "WTP" value). Subjects were told that the experimenters would calculate the market-clearing price for the mugs based on the WTA and WTP data elicited and execute trades between the mug holders who preferred the cash market value of the mugs and cash holders who preferred the mug to dollars at that price. While the traditional assumption of preference exogeneity leads to the prediction that 50 percent of the mugs would trade hands (because there was no reason to think subjects in one group valued mugs more than subjects in the other group), mug owners actually valued the mugs at roughly twice as high a price as did cash holders, which caused very few trades to occur.

In a similar set of experiments, Jack Knetsch and J. A. Sinden[3] gave some subjects a ticket for a lottery with a $50 cash prize and others $3 in cash, and then offered to buy the tickets back from the subjects who had them for $3 and to sell tickets to the subjects without them for $3. Eighty-two percent of the ticket holders kept their tickets while only 38 percent of the cash holders purchased a ticket, implying that those endowed with tickets valued them more than those who were not endowed with tickets. These results have been replicated in numerous other experiments using relatively inexpensive consumer goods, and similar results have been observed in real-world quasi experiments in which individuals have more of their personal wealth at risk.

Making a similar point with a different experimental design, William Samuelson and Richard Zeckhauser[4] found that subjects were more likely to express a preference for one entitlement from a list of choices when that entitlement was described as consistent with the status quo. In one test, for example, subjects were presented with four investment options, each with a different risk profile – a high-risk stock, a moderate-risk stock, a treasury bill, and a municipal bond – and asked to choose one in which to invest a sum of money. Subjects in one subgroup were told only that they had recently inherited the money, and that they now needed to invest it (the neutral frame). The others were told that they had inherited a portfolio of securities dominated by one of the four investment vehicles, and that they had to decide whether to leave the investments where they were or switch them to one of the other categories, with zero transaction costs of switching. Each of the investment vehicles was selected by subjects most often when it was the status quo investment and least often when one of the other choices was the status quo investment.

Consistent with these data, many studies have demonstrated that individuals place a higher value on preserving environmental resources when they are told that preservation is the status quo or that the public is entitled to block development than when they are told that development is legally protected. To summarize, in a great many circumstances, "whether people have a preference for a good, a right, or anything else is often in part a function of whether the government, or the law, has allocated it to them in the first instance."[5]

Can the Status Quo Bias Affect Preferences for Contract Terms?

The experiments discussed above demonstrate that, in at least some contexts, preferences can be dependent on how a decision maker perceives entitlements relative to the status quo or a reference position. This insight suggests that the preference exogeneity assumption, embedded in traditional law and economics scholarship on contract formation, might be incorrect. Just as individuals, on average, appear to place a higher value on mugs, lottery tickets, and investment instruments if they possess those items than if they do not, contracting parties might place a higher value on a particular contract term if they perceive it to be consistent with the status quo than if they perceive it to represent a change from the status quo.

On the other hand, there is also a reason to hypothesize that the status quo bias might not affect preferences for contract terms in the way that it appears to affect preferences for property rights or other legal entitlements. Before a party enters into a contract, a contract term cannot be viewed as providing the party with a vested entitlement. At that point in time, no contract term – no matter how strongly identified with the status quo – confers any benefit on a potential contracting party. Rather, the benefit that one party might derive from a contract term is contingent on that party's ability to convince another party to enter into a contract and to accept the term at issue. Because parties engaged in contractual negotiations are not endowed with any benefits from contract terms, it is a plausible hypothesis that the parties' valuation of such terms will not be affected by their perception of which terms are consistent with the status quo. If this is the case, the preference exogeneity assumption might, in fact, be accurate in this context.

Inertia and Preference for Contract Terms

To investigate whether negotiating parties' preferences for contract terms are dependent on their perceptions of the status quo, I conducted a series of experiments in which subjects were asked to respond to hypothetical contract negotiation scenarios. The first hypothesis tested was that subjects' preferences for specific contract terms would be affected by identifying those terms as the legal default terms. The second hypothesis tested was that preferences would also be affected by identifying terms as part of a "form contract" that the parties agreed would serve as a basis for negotiation. The experimental results supported both of these hypotheses. This section first describes the experimental methodology used and then considers, in turn, the data supportive of the two hypotheses.

Methodology

Subjects for the series of experiments were students at the University of Illinois College of Law who had completed a basic course in contract law. Subjects were asked to play the role of a lawyer and provide advice to a client on the negotiation of a commercial contract.

Each subject was provided the following background information about their client, the general content of the negotiations between their client and one of its customers, and the objectives the subject should pursue:

You represent a company called "NextDay" that specializes in overnight delivery of packages (similar to FedEx). NextDay has reached an agreement in principle to provide shipping services for a company called "Gifts, Inc." (which markets gifts by catalog and ships orders overnight around the country) for a fixed per-package charge, regardless of the size, value, or destination of the package. The company that handled Gifts, Inc.'s shipping last year charged it $20 per package; the price that Gifts, Inc. will pay NextDay has not yet been finalized.

You are currently engaged in negotiations with Gifts, Inc. over certain provisions of the contract. NextDay's management has asked you to provide recommendations concerning certain issues that have arisen and will almost certainly rely on your advice. At the end of the year, NextDay will review how it fared under the contract you negotiate and decide whether to retain you as their attorney in future dealings, so you have a strong personal stake in making sure that the contract serves the needs of NextDay *and* reflects well on your judgment and ability.

In each negotiation scenario, subjects were told that they were engaged in negotiations with Gifts, Inc. over which of two contract terms would be adopted by the parties to deal with a certain problem or contingency. Each subject was randomly assigned to one of two or more experimental conditions that differed from each other in only one way: the information provided suggested that either one of the possible terms or the other was consistent with the status quo. The strength of the subjects' preferences for the alternative contract terms was then measured by eliciting the monetary value they would place on a contract that included one term rather than the other but was identical in every other way. Conclusions were drawn by comparing the valuations provided by subjects who responded to the different versions of the scenarios.

Default Terms as the Status Quo

Three experiments tested the hypothesis that subjects' preferences for contract terms would be dependent, in part, on whether terms are identified as legal default terms or alternatives to the legal default terms. The results of all three supported the hypothesis; two are described here.

The first experiment ("Consequential Damages") dealt with a contract term delineating the amount of damages for which the subject's client, NextDay, could be held liable if it failed to deliver a Gifts, Inc. package on time. All of the subjects participating in this experiment were told that Gifts, Inc. would prefer a contract term that would hold NextDay liable for all damages caused by its failure to meet its delivery obligations. NextDay, in contrast, would prefer a contract term limiting its potential liability to damages that were "reasonably foreseeable" at the time that NextDay took possession of the package in question. Subjects were advised that NextDay's accountants had estimated that there was a 95 percent chance that a contract including the broader, "full liability" damages clause would cost NextDay, on average,

\$0–\$10 more per package than would a contract with the narrower, "limited liability" damages clause.

Subjects randomly assigned to condition 1 ("Limited Liability") of the experiment were told that the limited, "reasonably foreseeable" damages term was the legal default term in their state. They were asked how much money per package Gifts, Inc. would have to agree to pay NextDay above what the contract price would otherwise be before they would recommend that NextDay agree to contract around the limited liability default in favor of a full liability term. In contrast, subjects assigned to condition 2 ("Full Liability") of the experiment were informed that the default term was one of full liability. They were asked how much of a per-package reduction in the contract price (below what it would otherwise be) they would recommend NextDay be willing to accept for shipping if, in return, Gifts, Inc. would agree to include a limited liability term in the contract.

The mean valuations were significantly affected by condition. Subjects in condition 1 ($N = 26$) recommended, on average, that NextDay demand a minimum surcharge of \$6.96 per package before agreeing to include a full liability term in the contract. Condition 2 subjects ($N = 28$), on the other hand, recommended, on average, that NextDay be willing to offer a maximum discount of \$4.46 per package for Gifts, Inc.'s agreement to include a limited liability term in the contract. The difference between the mean responses of subjects in the two conditions can be understood as one measure of the strength of the bias for terms that are identified as the default over those identified as alternatives to the default.

The second experiment ("Impossibility Excuse") made use of the same background facts but changed the subject matter of the negotiation. Rather than being asked to value the difference between a contract with a full liability term versus a limited liability term, subjects were asked to value the difference between a contract that would excuse NextDay on the ground of impossibility or impracticability and one that would not. In the former case, NextDay would be excused from its contractual obligations if an unforeseen contingency beyond its control were to occur that rendered performance of its obligations "commercially impracticable." In the latter case, NextDay would be forced to perform its obligations or pay damages, regardless of the occurrence of any contingency in or out of NextDay's control, foreseeable or not. Unlike the Consequential Damages experiment, the Impossibility Excuse experiment did not provide subjects with expert estimates of differences in costs NextDay might expect to incur under a contract that recognized the impracticability excuse and one that did not.

Mirroring the design of the Consequential Damages experiment, approximately half of the subjects in the Impossibility Excuse experiment were randomly assigned to condition 1 ("Excuse"). These subjects were told that the default legal rule provided for the impossibility/impracticability excuse and were asked to recommend the minimum amount NextDay should demand before agreeing to insert a "no excuse" clause in the contract. The other half of the subjects, assigned to condition 2 ("No Excuse"), were told that the default rule was one of "no excuse." They were asked for the maximum amount NextDay should be willing to discount the contract price if Gifts, Inc. would agree, in return, to include in the contract a clause providing for an impossibility/impracticability excuse.

Again, although the preference exogeneity assumption would lead to the prediction that subjects' responses would not depend on the condition to which they were assigned (and thus what term they were told was the default), defining the default contract term differently had a significant effect on subjects' valuations. Subjects assigned to condition 1 ($N = 22$) recommended, on average, that NextDay demand a side payment of at least $188,000 before agreeing to include a "no excuse" term in the contract. Subjects assigned to condition 2 ($N = 25$) recommended, on average, that NextDay be willing to pay no more than $56,000 to convince Gifts, Inc. to add an "excuse" term to the contract. Although subjects in both conditions clearly would prefer a contract with an "excuse" term to one with a "no excuse" term, their preference for the former was much stronger when it was identified as the default than when it was identified as the alternative. Again, labeling a term as the default appeared to strengthen subjects' preference for it.

Form Contracts and the Power of Inertia

The results of the initial Consequential Damages and Impossibility Excuse experiments suggest that preferences for contract terms are not determined entirely exogenously to the context of the negotiations. Rather, negotiating parties are likely to prefer terms that are consistent with their perceptions of the status quo when all other things are equal. Even when all other things are not equal, the *strength* of parties' preferences for desirable terms and against undesirable terms can be affected by perceptions of the status quo.

The precise explanation for the results is obscured, however, by the fact that two possible explanatory variables are conflated in the experiments. The observed differences between conditions in both experiments could reveal a preference among subjects for terms that are identified as the legal defaults, but they also could reveal a preference for inaction over action. In both experiments, subjects displayed a bias in favor of the contract terms that would result from inertia; that is, in favor of the terms that would apply if they took no affirmative steps to contract for specific terms. To better understand the nature of the status quo bias for contract terms, it is important to determine whether a preference for default terms or a preference for inaction underlies the experimental results.

When contracting parties negotiate a term, their failure to affirmatively define the content of the term often results in the application of a legal default term to the parties' relationship (as was the case in the experiments), but this is not always the case. The relationship between inaction by the parties and application of a default term to their agreement can be disentangled by making the following plausible assumption: Parties sometimes begin contract negotiations with a standardized form contract drafted by a private entity (such as a law firm or an industry trade association) that will be operative unless the parties contract around its terms, rather than with a blank sheet of paper backstopped by a set of legally defined default rules. If an action/inaction distinction underlies the observed bias in favor of default terms, the use of a form contract as a basis for negotiations should create a similar bias in favor of the form terms.

This hypothesis was tested in a revised version of the Consequential Damages scenario. Like subjects in the original version of the scenario (conditions 1 and 2), subjects in the revised version (conditions 3 and 4) were asked to value the difference between a contract that would hold NextDay liable to Gifts, Inc. for all consequential damages caused by NextDay's failure to meet its delivery obligations and a contract that would limit NextDay's liability to damages that were reasonably foreseeable at the time that Gifts, Inc. delivered any particular package to NextDay for shipment. Unlike subjects in the original conditions, the new subjects were told that the two companies had "agreed to adopt, as a starting point in negotiations, a standard form contract prepared by attorneys for the Overnight Delivery Trade Association ('ODTA'), to which both parties are members." The form contract, the subjects were informed, "is typically used as a basis for negotiations in this type of transaction, with contracting parties making changes to the form provisions where necessary."

Condition 3 subjects were informed that the industry form contract included a term that provided for damages limited to those "reasonably foreseeable when Carrier accepted merchandise from Shipper," whereas the default rule that would govern parties in the absence of any explicit term was one of full liability. They were asked to state the minimum surcharge, per package, that they would demand Gifts, Inc. offer NextDay before they would recommend that NextDay agree to remove the favorable "limited liability" term from the form contract, thus allowing the less favorable "full liability" default term to govern. Condition 4 subjects were told that the industry form contract provided for full liability, whereas the legal default was one of limited liability. They were asked to reveal the maximum per package discount NextDay should be willing to offer Gifts, Inc. in return for Gifts, Inc. agreeing to eliminate the form contract term providing "full liability," thus permitting the "limited liability" default to govern.

From a Coasean perspective, both groups of subjects were asked to perform the same task: place a value on the difference between a contract with a limited liability term and one with a full liability term. If parties prefer inaction over action, however (the "inertia hypothesis"), condition 3 subjects should have placed a higher value on the limited liability term than condition 4 subjects, because limited liability would result from inaction for condition 3 subjects but not for condition 4 subjects.

Table 4.1. *Consequential Damages Results*

Condition	N	Default Term	Mean Valuation
1	26	Limited liability	$6.96/package
2	28	Full liability	4.46/package
3	33	Full liability (form contract = limited)	7.36/package
4	25	Limited liability (form contract = full)	4.10/package

The experimental results bear out the inertia hypothesis. Condition 3 subjects ($N = 33$) revealed that they would demand, on average, a minimum of $7.24 per package before recommending NextDay agree to remove the limited liability term from the industry form contract (leaving a full liability default to govern the contract). Condition 4 subjects ($N = 25$), in contrast, would recommend, on average, that NextDay offer Gifts, Inc. a maximum discount of $4.08 per package in return for Gifts, Inc. agreeing to remove a full liability term from the industry form contract (leaving a limited liability default). The difference between the condition 3 and 4 Consequential Damages subjects is statistically significant, and the gap between condition 3 and 4 subjects is not significantly different from the gap between condition 1 and 2 subjects. In other words, the experimental subjects showed a bias in favor of whatever damages term would govern as a result of inertia (i.e., when no action is taken by the negotiating parties). Whether the term associated with inaction was derived from a legal default rule or an industry form contract that served as the basis for contract negotiations had no significant effect on subjects' average responses.

The results suggest that the status quo bias is likely to cause contracting parties to prefer – again, all else being equal – contract terms that operate without the parties taking any affirmative steps to contract for them. In many situations, this will result in a bias in favor of legal default terms, but not because parties are biased in favor of legal defaults per se. When terms that are part of a standard form contract will apply to a transaction if the parties fail to take affirmative action to select other terms, parties' preferences are likely to be biased in the direction of the form contract terms rather than the legal default terms.

A Behavioral Theory of Inertia in Contract Negotiation

Can the observed status quo bias in negotiations over contract terms be reconciled with traditional law and economics analysis that assumes bargaining parties make decisions consistent with rational choice theory? Or can the phenomenon be understood only with a more psychologically based behavioral theory? This part argues that traditional economic approaches are insufficient to explain the experimental results presented above, and that a psychological theory based on the emotional consequences of regret provides the greatest insight into the observed valuation biases.

Traditional Law and Economics Explanations

Transaction Costs. A traditional, Coasean economic analysis would likely attempt to explain a bias in favor of inaction in terms of transaction costs. The claim that bargaining parties will tend to place a higher value on contract terms that result from inaction rather than those that can become operative only through action, standing alone, is, in fact, not at all inconsistent with traditional analysis. Terms requiring affirmative action can be more expensive to implement than terms that operate as a result of inaction. If all other things are equal, rational parties should choose contract terms that require less time and effort to negotiate and draft than alternatives.

Transaction cost explanations are unsatisfying, however, in the context of the experiments reported above. The experiments were designed so that no possible response from subjects implied longer or more complicated negotiations than any other response. In both the Consequential Damages and Impossibility Excuse scenarios, subjects were effectively told they *were* in the process of negotiating the terms in question; they were not given the choice *not* to negotiate over a term and thus save negotiation costs. In addition, no value that they might have placed on favorable terms relative to unfavorable ones would have suggested reduced negotiating costs. Finally, subjects responding to both scenarios were provided with the text of the relevant "alternative" term (i.e., the term that they could select by contracting around the default). Thus, there was no reason for subjects to think that a decision to contract around a status quo term would have entailed higher costs of drafting than accepting the status quo term.

Although transaction cost explanations are often powerful in understanding why parties select the apparent path of least resistance, something more appears to underlie the observed bias in favor of terms identified as the default.

Private Information. Traditional law and economics analysis also recognizes that parties can learn new information in the negotiation process that might rationally affect the value they place on contract terms. For example, the fact that one party proposes a certain term might signal that he has private information suggesting that the term would be advantageous to him, causing the other party to reassess (downward) his valuation of the term. To use a simple example, one party might enter a negotiation believing that a mandatory arbitration clause would be advantageous to him but interpret the other party's request for an arbitration clause as evidence that the other party had private information that he would be the one advantaged by such a clause. This could cause the original party to reconsider his initial preference.

Both experimental scenarios were constructed, however, to minimize the possibility that subjects' valuations of terms would be systematically affected by fears that Gifts, Inc. possessed private information. Consider, for example, the original version of the Consequential Damages scenario. Condition 1 subjects learned that Gifts, Inc. wished to add a term to the contract specifying full liability, whereas condition 2 subjects learned no such information about Gifts, Inc.'s preferences because full liability was described as the default term. If it were unclear ex ante whether Gifts, Inc. would desire a full liability term, the revelation of this desire might have caused condition 1 subjects (but not condition 2 subjects) to increase their preference for limited liability, assuming that full liability would be worse for NextDay than they originally believed. There was no logical reason for condition 1 subjects to react this way, however, because Gifts, Inc.'s desire for full liability was obvious – all shippers would prefer that common carriers maintain full liability for damages. In addition, both condition 1 and 2 subjects were informed that Gifts, Inc. would favor full liability, whereas NextDay would prefer limited liability.

Had condition 1 subjects been exposed to a very high offer from Gifts, Inc. to obtain a full liability clause (i.e., greater than $5 per package), those subjects might have believed full liability would be worse for NextDay than previously believed and readjusted their valuations of limited liability upward. But the scenarios were careful to present no information as to *how much* Gifts, Inc. valued full liability (which could signal private information); only that Gifts, Inc. preferred full liability (which was public information). In other words, condition 1 subjects had no reason to increase their valuation for limited liability based on information revealed to them in the hypothetical negotiating process that was not revealed to condition 2 subjects. Consequently, it seems implausible to believe that different average responses of condition 1 and 2 subjects can be attributed to private information signaled by the negotiation context as described in the hypothetical scenarios.

Network Benefits

Although transaction costs and asymmetric information are unlikely explanations of the observed status quo bias, the results are not necessarily inconsistent with an emerging economic literature on how contract terms can embody network benefits.

In recent articles Marcel Kahan and Michael Klausner[6] have theorized that contracting parties often prefer standard, or "boilerplate," terms because the widespread use of terms can actually increase the terms' value to their users. Network benefits arise when the value of a product to one of its users increases with the number of other users of the same product. For example, a telephone can be said to have large network benefits because its value to any user increases with the number of other users.

In some circumstances, contract terms may work in the same way, becoming more valuable as more parties adopt them. For example, the wider use of a particular term could lead to more judicial opinions interpreting the term, which benefits users by reducing uncertainty over how the term would be interpreted by a court in the future. Widespread use of a contract term could also create benefits for users by making lawyers and other providers of legal services more facile in drafting, negotiating, interpreting, and, if need be, litigating the term. Such facility could create value to term users by increasing the quality of legal service and/or reducing its cost. In short, widespread use of a contract term might benefit users of the term by causing complementary goods (such as judicial precedents or professional services) to become more available, cheaper, or both.

If negotiating parties believe that contract terms that will become operative as a result of inaction (i.e., the status quo terms) are most likely to be used by other contracting parties, they might rationally place a high value on such terms in recognition of the network benefits that those terms will help capture, even if other terms have a higher inherent value. Although a network benefits theory can explain the status quo bias observed in the experiments only on the assumption that the subjects were extremely sophisticated, the explanation cannot be ruled out on the basis of the results alone.

The network benefits hypothesis rests squarely on the assumption that experimental subjects assumed that the contract terms correlated with inaction would be the ones most commonly bargained for by other contracting parties; that is, subjects could have favored inaction only if they believed that the status quo terms were likely the standard terms. The following version of the Impossibility Excuse scenario tested the hypothesis by explicitly informing subjects that the most commonly used term was, in fact, the term that required affirmative action to become operative.

Subjects responding to condition 3 of the Impossibility Excuse scenario were told – like condition 1 subjects – that (1) the default rule allows impossibility as a valid excuse for nonperformance, (2) Gifts, Inc. planned to offer NextDay a side-payment if NextDay would include a term in the contract specifying that impossibility would not be a valid excuse for nonperformance, and (3) the subjects were to recommend the minimum amount NextDay should be willing to accept in return for agreeing to include the proposed term in the contract. Condition 3 subjects, however, were also given one additional piece of information: "Provisions like the one proposed by Gifts, Inc. are quite common – in fact, they are included in the vast majority of commercial shipping contracts, including the majority of NextDay's contracts with commercial shippers."

Condition 4 subjects learned – as did condition 2 subjects – that (1) the default rule was "no excuse," (2) NextDay would have to offer Gifts, Inc. a side-payment to include a term providing an impossibility excuse in the parties' contract, and (3) the subjects were to recommend a maximum amount that NextDay should offer for the inclusion of the term. Condition 4 subjects received the same additional instruction as condition 3 subjects: that contracting around the default rule is common industry and company practice. The implication of this instruction to condition 4 subjects, however, was that "excuse" terms are common in the industry and to NextDay, while the implication to condition 3 subjects was that "no excuse" terms are common for other shipping contracts, including NextDay's.

If the bias in favor of inaction observed in the initial experiments were based on perceived network benefits that might be derived by adopting the more common term, subjects in condition 3 should provide responses similar to those of condition 2 subjects (both groups might have believed that the "no excuse" term was the more common one) rather than similar to those of condition 1 subjects (who should have assumed an "excuse" term was more common). For the same reason, subjects in condition 4 should have provided responses similar to those of condition 1 subjects, not condition 2 subjects.

The results of the manipulation did not support the hypothesis that subjects would favor a common term over a term associated with inaction. Condition 4 subjects ($N = 18$) provided an average "willingness to pay" for the "common" term of $20,000, whereas condition 3 subjects ($N = 18$) on average demanded a minimum of $63,000 before they would accept the "common" term. The difference between the responses provided by condition 3 and 4 subjects is significant, and not significantly smaller than the difference between the responses of condition 1 and 2 subjects. In other words, manipulating the information subjects were given about whether the alternative was commonly used by contracting parties had no significant effect on subjects' bias in favor of inaction.

These results, then, provide support for the proposition that the bias in favor of inaction is driven by more than a sophisticated, profit-maximizing intuition that network benefits often counsel toward accepting what might be called the "terms of least resistance."

Uncertainty and Anticipatory Regret

If transaction cost, strategic behavior, and network benefits explanations are unsatisfying, why would contracting parties systematically favor contract terms that would operate in the event of inaction over those that would become operative only if affirmative steps are taken by the negotiating parties? In this section I propose an explanation rooted in the emotional consequences of actions rather than calculated cost-benefit analysis. The theoretical hypothesis, for which I will provide some empirical support, is that

Table 4.2. *Impossibility Excuse Results*

Condition	*N*	Default Term	Mean Valuation
1	22	Excuse	$188,000
2	25	No excuse	56,000
3	18	Excuse (No excuse term is common)	63,000
4	18	No excuse (Excuse term is common)	20,000

a preference for inaction is consistent with a decision-making strategy that seeks to minimize the likelihood of future regret over choices made.

Regret Theory and the Status Quo Bias. A plausible explanation of the power of inertia is that negotiators fear that they will suffer regret in the future over deciding to actively shape contract terms, and, therefore, they will act to minimize the possibility of experiencing such regret. In most situations, contracting for terms that deviate from default rules or form contracts carries the risk of suboptimal results when viewed with hindsight; that is, a negotiator knows when she contracts around a baseline or reference contract term that she is taking a gamble of sorts, which may be profitable or may not, depending upon unknown future circumstances. If a negotiator anticipates that an unprofitable outcome would cause her to regret having chosen the gamble originally, she might demand a premium above the expected value of the gamble before she would agree to it. In other words, when deciding whether to take an action with uncertain consequences, the decision maker may determine that the expected utility of *choosing* the action is lower than the inherent expected utility of the action itself.

This description could plausibly apply to both experimental scenarios described in this chapter. In the Consequential Damages scenarios, for example, subjects are informed by NextDay's accountants that costs associated with accepting full liability rather than limited liability are likely to fall between $0 and $10 per package, on average. One interpretation of this prediction is that the expected cost of agreeing to full liability when the inactive option is limited liability is approximately $5 per package. If NextDay agreed to actively add a full liability term to the contract for a $5 per-package premium, however, there would be a roughly 50 percent chance that the bargain would later appear unfavorable in hindsight. Perhaps the fear that a negative outcome would lead to regret over the decision to contract for full liability caused experimental subjects to demand more than the inherent expected value of the gamble before they would be willing to affirmatively agree to take it.

This explanation and illustration beg two difficult questions. First, why would subjects fear the possibility of contracting for full liability and having the decision turn out to be unprofitable in hindsight *more* than they would fear *not* contracting for full liability and having that decision turn out to be suboptimal in hindsight? It might be true that a person who takes what turns out to be a losing gamble would regret taking that gamble. But it is not immediately obvious why the fear of regret associated with taking action would be greater than the fear associated with failing to act when (what turns out to have been) a profitable opportunity presented itself. If parties fear the possibility of future regret when they choose to act affirmatively but fear equally the possibility of future regret when they choose not to act, there should be no bias in favor of contract terms that take effect in the event of inaction.

Second, why would the *fear* of possible regret that strikes an actor when he considers acting affirmatively not be balanced by the *hope* of rejoicing – the emotional opposite of regret – should the action yield desirable results? An actor facing a choice with uncertain results might be hesitant to act because an undesirable result could yield regret. But why would that actor not be spurred to action by the realization that a desirable outcome could yield rejoicing? That is, if an actor takes action that yields a desirable outcome, he might enjoy utility not only from the positive result but also from the knowledge that he made the decision that led to the positive result. If anticipated regret and anticipated rejoicing caused by action are roughly equal, there should be no general preference for inaction.

As to the first question, substantial experimental evidence suggests that individuals predict that greater regret will follow an action that leads to an undesirable result than will follow a failure to act that leads to the same undesirable result. Thus, acts and nonacts are likely to be psychologically distinguishable, even if they lead to the same material consequences.

Consider the following, well-known experiment conducted by Daniel Kahneman and Amos Tversky.[7] Experimental subjects were told a story of two hypothetical actors who had both made unfortunate investment decisions. Mr. Paul owned stock in Company A. He considered switching his holdings to Company B but decided not to do so. Subsequently, he learned that he would have been $1,200 better off had he made the switch. Mr. George owned stock in Company B. He considered switching to Company A and made the switch. Consequently, he was $1,200 worse off than he would have been had he not made the switch. More than 90 percent of experimental subjects surveyed believed that Mr. George would feel more regret about his decision than would Mr. Paul.

The regret that arises from the occurrence of undesirable events can be understood as a response to what is known as "counterfactual thinking." The occurrence of a negative event can cause people to attempt to mentally avoid the outcome by comparing the event to a counterfactual alternative; that is, to some conception of "what might have been." If the counterfactual event is perceived by the subject as more favorable than the experienced event, the subject is likely to experience regret. In order to understand what type of events are likely to lead to the most regret, then, it is important to understand the process by which counterfactual alternatives are mentally constructed.

Daniel Kahneman and Dale Miller[8] developed "norm theory" to provide just such an explanation. They theorized that counterfactual alternatives are constructed by beginning with the circumstances of the experienced event and then changing one or more elements of the factual predicate of the experienced event to create a different outcome. Individuals will tend to alter what Kahneman and Miller call the most "mutable" elements of the experienced event's factual predicate. Elements of the experienced event that are considered abnormal or exceptional by a subject are most mutable, whereas elements that are perceived as normal or usual are less mutable. At the extreme, some very normal elements might be immutable. Judgments of abnormality, in turn, are based on the availability of possible alternative events in the subject's mind. When elements of an experience seem normal and, thus, relatively immutable, counterfactual comparisons will be less available and outcomes will often seem inevitable. In contrast, when an element is mutable and a change in that element would avoid the negative event, that mutable element is likely to be perceived as the cause of the negative event.

The link between norm theory and the tendency of individuals to favor choices correlated with inaction over action is the prediction that actions are more mutable than failures to act; that is, "it is usually easier to imagine oneself abstaining from actions that one has carried out than carrying out actions that were not in fact performed."[9] Consequently, parties who actively shape contract terms might feel more regret if their actions turn out to be unprofitable than parties who inertly accept the status quo terms.

A related explanation of the preference for inaction over action is that individuals often perceive greater personal control over actions. Researchers in social psychology have identified controllability of an element as an important determinant of mutability; that is, an individual is more likely to mentally alter an element of an event to produce a counterfactual alternative when that element is within his control. Actions, thus, tend to be more mutable than failures to act, both because they are contrary to the norm *and* because they tend to be perceived as being within greater control of individual actors.

But even if the risk of regret is greater for actions than for failures to act, there should not be a behavioral bias in favor of inaction if the potential psychological *benefits* of action relative to inaction are significant enough to compensate for the higher risk action entails. Psychological evidence suggests, however, that anticipation of regret over actions that yield disappointing results is usually stronger than the anticipation of rejoicing over actions that yield desirable results. For example, Janet Landman[10] found that experimental subjects believed that a student who changed classes and received a high grade would feel more elated than a student who did not change classes and received a high grade. But, importantly, she found that this effect was much weaker than subjects' judgments that a student who changed classes and received a low grade would feel more regret than a student who did not change classes and received the same low grade.

That anticipated regret is likely to be stronger than anticipated rejoicing is consistent with the well-established theory of "loss aversion."[11] Loss aversion theory posits that the utility consequences to individuals of suffering a "loss" from a reference point will be greater than an equivalent "gain" from the same reference point. If losses loom larger than gains, it follows logically that anticipated regret would loom larger than anticipated rejoicing. The primacy of regret over rejoicing is also consistent with the predictions of norm theory. Desirable events are likely to be more mentally available than undesirable events. Consequently, an individual experiencing an undesirable event will likely have an easier time constructing a positive counterfactual alternative (and thus generating feelings of regret) than an individual experiencing a desirable event will have constructing a negative counterfactual alternative (and thus generating feelings of rejoicing).

Explaining the Contract Negotiation Experiments. Norm theory and the differential amount of regret that potentially can be experienced from action and inaction can serve as the basis for an explanation of the preference for inertia observed in the contract negotiation experiments. Subjects in condition 1 of the Consequential Damages scenario had to determine how much money they would demand before they would agree to place a full liability term in NextDay's contract with Gifts, Inc. The actuarially expected cost of such a term (relative to a limited liability term) was approximately $5. But if agreeing to the full liability term (action) carried with it a risk of greater future regret than did not agreeing to the term (inaction), subjects would be expected to demand a premium above the term's $5 expected cost before agreeing to add the term. Conversely, subjects in condition 2 had to determine how much they would be willing to pay to convince Gifts, Inc. to actively add a limited liability term to the contract. For these subjects, the expected actuarial benefit of a limited liability term (relative to a full liability term) was approximately $5. But if (1) adding the limited liability term (action) could lead to a greater fear of ex post regret than passing up the opportunity to add the limited liability term (inaction), and (2) the possibility of ex post regret were not compensated for by the possibility of ex post rejoicing, then subjects would be expected to offer something less than full actuarial value in order to offset the increased risk of ex post regret. The results were, of course, consistent with this explanation. Subjects in condition 1 demanded considerably more than $5 to act, while condition 2 subjects offered less than $5 for action.

Thus, the preference for inertia in contract negotiation can be plausibly explained by a desire to minimize the risk of ex post regret if a decision turns out to be suboptimal in hindsight. This explanation assumes that the subject negotiators did not attempt to maximize the expected profits of their client, but traded off profit potential against the negative utility consequences of potential ex post regret. Subjects' desire to minimize the fear of regret is not infinite, of course; subjects are willing to accept the risk of more ex post regret for a price. But the key to this explanation of the bias in favor of inaction is that subjects do demand a premium to take on the added risk of ex post regret that action implies.

Testing the Regret Avoidance Hypothesis. The regret avoidance hypothesis provides an explanation for why negotiators might not arrive at the same distribution of contract rights regardless of how the alternatives are presented. The explanation remains plausible even when Coasean explanations (e.g., transaction costs, strategic behavior) and other explanations consistent with profit maximization (e.g., the desire to capture network benefits) are not. At its root is the prediction that individuals will mentally assess the results of opportunities actively taken differently than they assess the results of opportunities not taken.

The theory, though, can only potentially describe negotiating behavior under conditions of uncertainty: that is, when parties cannot be sure at the time they are bargaining over contract terms which of the alternative terms will be most beneficial in the future. If parties can be certain of both the value of what they are giving up or foregoing in negotiations and the value of what they receive in return, then there would be no reason to fear future regret over the choice. In such a situation, the regret avoidance theory would lead to the prediction that there would be no inertia effect in contract negotiations. In a world of no uncertainty, parties should bargain to identical contract terms regardless of which terms will govern in the case of inaction, at least in the absence of transaction costs, asymmetric information, or network benefits to be gained from following other contracting parties.

The regret avoidance hypothesis can be tested in the contract negotiation context by asking experimental subjects to value contract terms where there is no uncertainty associated with actively agreeing to a particular contract term. The theory predicts that in such a situation there should be no observable preference for inaction. The following version of the Impossibility Excuse scenario eliminates the outcome uncertainty present in the original manipulations of the scenario in an effort to test this prediction. The results provide preliminary support for the regret avoidance hypothesis.

Subjects assigned to condition 5 of the Impossibility Excuse scenario, like those assigned to condition 1, were told that the legal default provided an excuse for a common carrier's failure to meet its delivery obligations when an unexpected contingency arises that makes delivery either impossible or commercially impracticable. Also like condition 1 subjects, they were asked how much money NextDay should demand before agreeing to add a term to the contract that would negate the impossibility excuse. But whereas condition 1 subjects were asked to place a value on a risky choice – that is, it was unclear how much an "excuse" term might increase NextDay's liability under the contract for delivery failures – condition 5 subjects were told that the financial consequences to NextDay of adding such a term to the contract were certain: NextDay, these subjects were told, carries liability insurance that pays all claims for delivery failures. The consequence of NextDay's agreeing to a contract with Gifts, Inc. that did not provide for an impossibility excuse would be a $75,000 increase in NextDay's annual liability insurance premium. Thus, although accepting a contract term that would negate the impossibility excuse would increase NextDay's business risk, that risk could and would be ceded to a third party for a fixed price. The insurance contrivance established that NextDay would face no uncertainty by agreeing to a full liability term.

Condition 6 subjects, like condition 2 subjects, learned that the legal default rule provided for no impossibility excuse. Also like condition 2 subjects, condition 6 subjects were asked how much NextDay should be willing to pay Gifts, Inc. to convince Gifts, Inc. to agree to add a term to the contract that would provide for such an excuse. Unlike condition 2 subjects (but like condition 5 subjects), condition 6 subjects learned that there was a *certain* benefit associated with the addition of such a term: NextDay's liability insurance carrier would reduce its annual premium by $75,000 to compensate for NextDay's reduced business risk. Again, the presence of insurance eliminates the uncertainty present in the initial Impossibility Excuse scenario manipulations.

If the regret avoidance hypothesis is correct, the addition of the third-party insurance carrier that accepted for a fixed price all the risk associated with the presence or absence of an impossibility excuse term should have eliminated the inertia observed in the original manipulation of the Impossibility Excuse scenario; that is, the large, statistically significant difference between the responses of condition 1 and 2 subjects should disappear. Condition 5 and 6 subjects should provide approximately identical responses to each other. The results support this prediction. Condition 5 subjects ($N = 29$) provided a mean response of $39,000, while condition 6 subjects provided a mean response of $69,000. These two sets of responses are not significantly different. Moreover, the gap between the responses of condition 5 and 6 subjects *is* significantly different from the gap between condition 1 and 2 subjects. In other words, removing uncertainty from the Impossibility Excuse scenario neutralized subjects' preferences for inaction, just as the regret avoidance hypothesis would predict.[12]

Prescriptive Implications

Negotiation and the Power of Reference Points

The psychological power of inertia suggests that negotiators who are able to define the status quo position, against which all proposed terms are judged, are likely to enjoy an important bargaining advantage. Before negotiating terms of a contract, a strategic negotiator should evaluate which of many plausible reference points for negotiations is most advantageous to her client's interests. Efforts to convince the opposing negotiator that the advantageous reference point is the most natural or reasonable from which to begin negotiations may have a large impact on the outcome of those negotiations. The initial terms, however established, are likely to be perceived as the terms that will govern the parties' relationship if no further action takes place. Thus, they are likely to be perceived as the status quo.

The prescriptive advice that negotiators should invest time and resources in attempting to control the reference point of contract negotiations is, of course, hardly a unique recommendation. But the underlying reasoning for this advice – that terms understood as the status quo, or baseline, are likely to be sticky because negotiators will prefer inaction over action – differs from conventional wisdom on this point. Often implicit in the usual recommendation to negotiators to control the beginning point of negotiations is the Coasean notion of the power of transaction costs. When contracting is expensive or difficult, an initial proposal is likely to find its way into the final version of the contract. Another common justification is rooted in the information asymmetries that commonly exist in negotiating situations. Since a negotiator is usually unaware of the precise value his counterpart places on reaching an agreement, he may be wary of suggesting terms that depart drastically from what appears to be the status quo, for fear that the resulting proposal might be inferior to the opponent than the opponent's alternatives. Thus, proposing a drastic departure from the status quo could lead to a bargaining impasse. Finally, any proposal favorable to the negotiator, whether or not it serves as an initial reference point, is likely to affect the final agreement if there is a strong social norm or convention, requiring that parties "split the difference" between conflicting positions.

The psychological power of inertia, in contrast, suggests that a reference point for contract negotiations will affect the intrinsic preferences of bargaining parties. Negotiators will prefer an advantageous term more strongly (or oppose a disadvantageous term less strongly) if the term is perceived to result from inaction rather than from action. Traditional accounts of the power of reference points in negotiation emphasize factors external to the negotiator that might impose costs on deviations from the perceived status quo and, therefore, make parties more likely to adopt status quo terms. The power of inertia suggests the negotiator's internal response to the status quo, which can actually increase the parties' underlying preferences for contract terms.

Policy Making and Efficient Default Rules

The Importance of Default Rules. Coasean law and economics analysis, based on the preference exogeneity assumption, assumes that the content of default terms will not affect parties' underlying preferences for contract terms. A corollary is that unless transaction costs are high or strategic behavior caused by the presence of asymmetric information prevents parties from bargaining for the terms they prefer, the choice of default rules by legal policy makers will have no effect on the outcome of contract negotiations. The evidence of the status quo bias requires an important revision of this assumption. The most fundamental insight for contract theory provided by evidence of the status quo bias is that the choice of default rules is always relevant, not just in situations of high transaction costs or asymmetric information. If lawmakers' choice of default terms alters parties' preferences for contract terms – causing an increase in the strength of their preferences for the default term and a decrease in the strength of their preferences for alternative terms – the choice of default terms has the potential to affect *any* private contract. The status quo bias suggests that the difference between default contract rules and immutable contract rules – rules that parties may not contract around – might be one of degree rather than of kind. Default rules can be seen as "quasi-immutable."

Consider, again, a negotiation concerning a consequential damages term and assume the legal default term limits damages for breach of contract to those that were "reasonably foreseeable" at the time of contracting. Under traditional economic analysis, if parties implicitly adopt a default term, that term is presumed to be the most efficient alternative for the parties (i.e., it maximizes their joint wealth) unless they face high costs of negotiating or drafting alternative terms or one party has a strategic motive to withhold private information. If there are neither high transaction costs nor asymmetric information, traditional analysis would conclude that the parties would have contracted for another term if the default did not efficiently allocate the risk of damages between the parties.

But the status quo bias makes it impossible to be sure that the failure of parties to contract around a default rule signifies that the default term is efficient for them, even absent of transaction costs and private information. It is possible that a full liability term would be efficient for a pair of negotiating parties but that the parties might fail to contract around the "reasonably foreseeable" default term because the value that they implicitly place on maintaining the status quo exceeds the gains in trade that they could capture by agreeing to a full liability term.

The status quo bias also requires theorists to adjust their interpretation of situations in which parties do bargain around default terms. Under traditional economic analysis, such a scenario would indicate that the difference in joint value to the parties between the explicitly adopted term and the default term exceeds the transaction costs of contracting around the default term plus any strategic benefit one party might be able to capture by not revealing information inherent in an attempt to contract around the default term. The status quo bias suggests that when parties contract around a default term, the value of the difference between the alternative term and the default term must be greater than traditional economic analysts would conclude: the difference must exceed (1) the parties' joint transaction costs, (2) the value to either party of not revealing information they must reveal in order to contract around the default term, and (3) the parties' joint preference for the status quo.

Local Versus Global Efficiency. Why should lawmakers care if contracting parties prefer the status quo to wealth-maximizing contract terms in marginal cases? Although such a choice fails to maximize the parties' joint wealth, it apparently maximizes their joint utility. In the context of contract terms, law and economics scholars often equate wealth maximization with utility maximization, but nowhere is it written that parties are required to consider only the best methods to create wealth when they negotiate contract terms. If parties prefer inaction over action, one might argue, it is not inefficient for them to indulge this preference when negotiating against a backdrop of legal default terms.

This argument, though, confuses local and global efficiency. Given a specific legal default term, it is neither irrational nor inefficient for bargaining parties to prefer inaction to action and to sacrifice some degree of wealth in order to be inert. In such a situation, however, it would be more efficient for lawmakers to have initially created an alternative status quo. Put another way, given the establishment of "default term A," it might well be *locally efficient* for two parties to adopt term A rather than contracting around it in favor of term B, which would require sacrificing the value to them of maintaining the status quo. But the parties might have enjoyed a higher combined utility if lawmakers had established "term B" as the default instead, thus allowing the parties to have both the wealth-maximizing contract term *and* the status quo, rather than having to choose one or the other.

The conclusion that follows is this: Parties who choose not to contract around a default term that fails to maximize their joint wealth are not necessarily behaving irrationally, but this does not mean that the default rule itself is optimal. By choosing a different default rule (and thus creating a different perceived status quo), lawmakers might steer the contracting parties to a more desirable equilibrium and, in so doing, promote private contracting that is closer to optimal efficiency. The next three subsections discuss how lawmakers might accomplish this task.

Mimicking Versus Facilitating the Market for Contract Terms. Although evidence of the status quo bias adds an element to the discourse on contract default rules that goes beyond the boundaries of traditional law and economics analysis, it has implications for an important policy debate within that paradigm. Traditional law and economics theorists disagree over whether policy makers should select "majoritarian" default terms or "penalty" default terms.[13] Majoritarian defaults mimic the terms most contracting parties would select in a world without transaction costs. Penalty defaults favor the party likely to have less information (whether or not the term is efficient for most parties) in order to encourage the informed party to reveal information in the course of bargaining for a more desirable term. Evidence of the status quo bias adds strength to the case for majoritarian defaults.

Supporters of penalty defaults concede that it is dangerous policy to set default rules that are not majoritarian in circumstances in which transaction costs are likely to be high. The reason is that, in such circumstances, barriers to negotiation will cause many parties to accede to default terms that are inefficient in the context of their transaction, rather than contract around such terms. The status quo bias has a similar effect on bargaining: If there is a strong bias in favor of the status quo, parties will often fail to contract around suboptimal default terms. This problem, like the problem of high transaction costs, can be mitigated if policy makers select default terms that the fewest number of parties need to contract around in order to achieve optimally efficient agreements.

While the status quo bias provides an argument in favor of majoritarian defaults, at least relative to penalty defaults, it simultaneously casts doubt on the conventional wisdom for how lawmakers can identify majoritarian defaults. Identifying majoritarian defaults is usually understood to require lawmakers to look at the contracting behavior of actual parties. Since efficient contract terms are Pareto superior to inefficient terms (because the parties can use side-payments to divide the additional value created by efficient terms so as to make both parties better off), legal economists assume that contracting parties will settle on them, except in situations of high transaction costs. It follows from this assumption that if few parties contract around a default rule, it must be efficient and should be retained. In contrast, if most parties contract around the default, it must be inefficient and should be changed. In a textbook example of this way of thinking, J. Hoult Verkerke recently argued that a default employment contract term of dismissal "at will" is majoritarian, as opposed to a default term requiring "cause" for dismissal, because only 15 percent of employers and employees contract around the standard "at will" default.[14]

Evidence of the status quo bias suggests that this methodology is highly suspect. If parties do not contract around an existing default term, this does not necessarily prove that the default is optimal, even if transaction costs are low. In order to identify majoritarian default terms, lawmakers must imagine a counterfactual world – one without any defaults – and attempt to predict what term most parties would agree upon in such a world. Such an approach obviously carries a high risk of error. Fortunately, their are superior approaches to avoiding inefficient contracting that can result from the status quo bias.

The Case for Tailoring. The discussion so far has implicitly assumed (as do most discussions of default rules) that whatever the applicable default contract term, it will be applied by courts to all contracting parties who fail to explicitly provide a contrary term in their contract: that is, *all* sellers will be liable for either all damages proximately caused by its breach or only reasonably foreseeable damages (unless they contract around the default term). Such terms can be characterized as "untailored" defaults, in the sense that they apply to all affected parties regardless of the unique characteristics of the parties or their circumstances.

Default rules need not be untailored, however. Rather than favoring all carriers or shippers, all buyers or sellers, "tailored" default rules require lawmakers – generally judges – to create default terms to govern a relationship between contracting parties based on the specific characteristics and circumstances of those parties. For example, the U.C.C.'s default price term – a "reasonable" price[15] – is a tailored default, because it requires a judge to consider the circumstances of the parties and the transaction before determining a price term instead of applying a uniform term to all parties. While the content of untailored defaults is clear to all contracting parties ex ante through statutory text or judicial precedent, the content of tailored defaults is unclear to parties prior to contracting. Because of the situation-specific inquiry that they demand, tailored default terms cannot be given content until after the parties complete their contract and a contingency occurs for which the contract does not explicitly provide. The lawmaker charged with determining a tailored default term must ask not what term *most* contracting parties would have agreed to had they made provisions for a contingency – a question that does not require an inquiry into the specifics of any one transaction – but what term two *particular* parties would have agreed to had they provided for the contingency.

When contracting parties prefer the status quo to alternative states of the world, all else equal, they will choose not to contract around an untailored default rule in some instances even when the rule is suboptimal for them. Lawmakers can use tailored defaults, in contrast, to avoid the contractual inefficiencies created by the status quo bias. Because the exact content of a tailored default term is unknown to parties at the time of contracting, parties are unable to clearly perceive a status quo term. If parties do not know whether, in the absence of an explicit contract term, a court forced to resolve a later dispute between them would find that the carrier is liable for all damages flowing from its breach or only foreseeable damages, there is no status quo position to anchor the parties' preferences for either of the potential contract terms. Contract default rules cannot be neutral – they must favor some terms over others – but tailored defaults can shroud the law's preference at the time of contracting, when the status quo bias operates.

Nonenforcement Defaults. Although contract default rules usually specify how courts will fill certain gaps in private contracts, they can announce instead that courts simply will refuse to enforce contracts with such gaps. The most notable example of such a "nonenforcement" default rule in contract law is section 2-201 of the Uniform Commercial Code, which provides that contracts for the sale of goods that do not specify a quantity term are not enforceable.[16]

Lawmakers can use nonenforcement defaults, like tailored defaults, to reduce the impact of the status quo bias on the content of negotiated contract terms. While tailored defaults avoid the status quo bias by not creating a status quo term, nonenforcement defaults neutralize the status quo bias by literally overwhelming it: They create a status quo term (nonenforcement) that is so strongly disliked by all contracting parties that even parties with a strong preference for the status quo will affirmatively contract for a different term. The status quo bias will affect the contracts of parties that only marginally prefer an alternative term to the default, but it will not affect the contracts of parties with a strong preference for an alternative term. Since all parties who go to the trouble of negotiating and drafting contracts presumably have a strong preference for enforcement of the contract over nonenforcement, there will be few if any parties that only *marginally* disprefer a nonenforcement default and thus fail to contract around it because of a preference for the status quo.

Since tailored and nonenforcement defaults, in theory, can be equally successful at neutralizing the status quo bias, lawmakers concerned with minimizing the bias should choose between these two options on the basis of their relative costs along other dimensions. The most significant downside of nonenforcement defaults is the harsh consequences that occur if they are ever invoked. Because of this, nonenforcement defaults will be an appropriate means of minimizing the status quo bias when the relevant contract term relates to a high-probability contingency or highly salient aspect of the contract, such that the chance of the parties' failing to contract around the nonenforcement default are low. The most important shortcoming of tailored defaults is that they impose high ex post costs on courts forced to determine highly individuating default terms. Accordingly, tailored defaults will be an appropriate response to the problem of the status quo bias where a contract term relates to a low-probability contingency, such that courts will have to create party-specific default terms only infrequently.

Conclusion

This chapter has attempted to suggest ways that behavioral analysis can improve upon traditional law and economics approaches to contract formation and contract law, both positive and prescriptive. The evidence presented suggests that negotiating parties are likely to value contract terms differently if they perceive the terms to be consistent with the status quo than if they perceive the terms to be inconsistent with the status quo. The systematic bias in favor of the status quo suggests opportunities for negotiators to secure more desirable terms for their clients and challenges for policy makers who wish to create legal rules that will maximize the allocative efficiency of private contracting behavior.

While there is compelling evidence of a status quo bias in the context of negotiations over contract terms, further research is indicated in a number of directions. First, our understanding of when and under what conditions bargaining parties are likely to perceive specific terms to be consistent with the status quo is incomplete. The evidence is convincing that, in some situations, parties will view legal default terms as the status quo terms. But it is unclear under what conditions parties will perceive other terms – such as form contract terms – as more representative of the status quo than legal default terms. Understanding the different manifestations of the status quo bias is likely to require a clearer understanding of what motivates the bias. Although the regret avoidance hypothesis is theoretically promising and consistent with the evidence collected to date, it remains only a hypothesis in need of more careful study.

Second, the policy prescriptions suggested as methods of confronting the negative impact that the status quo bias can have on the efficiency of private contracting need to be integrated into a more comprehensive framework, one that simultaneously considers other barriers to efficient contracting, such as transaction costs and asymmetric information. While highly tailored defaults and nonenforcement defaults might reduce some of the ill-effects of the status quo bias, more theoretical and empirical work needs to be done before policy makers can feel confident that these approaches will not cause damage that outweighs their benefits.

Finally, experimental and empirical work are necessary to verify that the impact of the status quo bias on student subjects role playing in a highly stylized laboratory environment can be generalized to attorneys and business professionals operating in the context of real-world commercial transactions. Controlled experiments are an excellent way to initially test theories and to hone hypotheses. Standing alone, however, they provide a thin basis to support the enactment of legal policy.

Notes

1 See R. H. Coase, The Problem of Social Cost, 3 *J.L. & Econ.* 1 (1960).
2 Daniel Kahneman, Jack L. Knetsch, and Richard H. Thaler, Experimental Tests of the Endowment Effect and the Coase Theorem, 98 *J. Pol. Econ.* 1325 (1990).
3 Jack L. Knetsch and J. A. Sinden, Willingness to Pay and Compensation Demanded: Experimental Evidence of an Unexpected Disparity in Measures of Value, 99 *Q.J. Econ.* 507 (1984).
4 William Samuelson and Richard Zeckhauser, Status Quo Bias in Decision Making, 1 *J. Risk & Uncertainty* 7 (1988).
5 Cass R. Sunstein, Endogenous Preferences, Environmental Law, 22 *J. Legal Stud.* 217 (1993).
6 See Marcel Kahan and Michael Klausner, Standardization and Innovation in Corporate Contracting (or "The Economics of Boilerplate"), 83 *Va. L. Rev.* 713 (1997); Michael Klausner, Corporate Law and Networks of Contracts, 81 *Va. L. Rev.* 757 (1995).
7 Daniel Kahneman and Amos Tversky, The Simulation Heuristic, in *Judgment Under Uncertainty: Heuristics and Biases* 201 (Kahneman et al. eds., 1982).
8 Daniel Kahneman and Dale T. Miller, Norm Theory: Comparing Reality to Its Alternatives, 93 *Psychol. Rev.* 136 (1986).
9 Ibid. at 145.
10 Janet Landman, Regret and Elation Following Action and Inaction: Affective Responses to Positive Versus Negative Outcomes, 13 *Pers. & Soc. Psychol. Bull.* 524 (1987).
11 See Amos Tversky and Daniel Kahneman, Loss Aversion in Riskless Choice: A Reference Dependent Model, 106 *Q.J. Econ.* 1039 (1991).
12 It is important to point out that, while this experiment supports the regret avoidance hypothesis, it is not dispositive. This version of the Impossibility Excuse experiment introduced a confounding variable of numerical focal points (i.e., the $75,000 figure), which could have anchored subjects' responses and swamped a still-existing status quo bias.
13 See Ian Ayres and Robert Gertner, Filling Gaps in Incomplete Contracts: An Economic Theory of Default Rules, 99 *Yale L. J.* 87 (1989).
14 J. Hoult Verkerke, An Empirical Perspective on Indefinite Term Employment Contracts: Resolving the Just Cause Debate, 1995 *Wis. L. Rev.* 837, 867–75.
15 U.C.C. §2-305(1) (1995).
16 U.C.C. §2-201 cmt. 1 (1995).

5 Organized Illusions: A Behavioral Theory of Why Corporations Mislead Stock Market Investors (and Cause Other Social Harms)

Donald C. Langevoort

Rationality is a strong assumption in the legal literature about how corporations and other organizations behave in market settings. The modern transaction-cost economics on which most contemporary corporate scholarship is based concedes that the rationality of officers, directors, and other managers is "bounded" (that is, that they do not have perfect information or unlimited time, skill, and attention) and acknowledges that these agents have self-interests that differ from those of their firms' owners.[1] Because of these limits and the imperfection of contractual and other mechanisms for resolving them, firms will not always act in a way that maximizes shareholder wealth. But within such limitations, the world that is portrayed is still one of guileful rationality. Firms that depart too far or too often from this norm will lose needed capital and succumb to their more savvy competitors. Managers are presumed to understand this and act accordingly.

Borrowing from an explosion of work by social scientists on human judgment and decision making, legal scholars have been increasingly willing to rethink strong assumptions of rationality in the context of individual behavior, even within markets. They have not yet mined to any depth, however, any equally rich vein of research on organizational rationality.[2] Yet here we find the skeptic's mother lode: empirical accounts – grounded in sociology and social psychology, but increasingly integrated with economic analysis – for why organizations so often behave in the myopic, rigid manner that we seem to observe in the real world. This literature seeks to identify the social cognitions and norm structures[3] within organizations that can lead to a "loose coupling" between day-to-day activities and instrumental rationality for reasons that go well beyond managerial opportunism.[4] It works from the assumption that these social forces are sufficiently natural and ingrained that they cannot readily be eliminated by structural or contractual design, and sufficiently contingent on the personnel in place at any given time and the situation in which the firm finds itself that they cannot easily be learned away. Competitive forces are not irrelevant but are only part of a complex set of institutional influences that operates over the entire marketplace.

This research affects a good bit of what is taught as organizational behavior in business schools. There, managerial rationality tends to be treated more as a holy grail than as an observable reality. Empirical case studies abound of systemic decision-making flaws, with many of the examples drawn from companies hardly destined for Darwinian extinction. Take, for instance, Robert Burgelman's study of Intel Corporation's loss of a strong competitive advantage over a twenty-year period (roughly 1971–91) in the dynamic random access memory market.[5] Ultimately, Intel recognized the error and successfully repositioned itself in the microprocessor business. In the end, then, Intel did adapt; no doubt market discipline drove the hard lesson. But the interesting questions are why it took so long, and whether it could happen to Intel again in some different context. To offer answers to these questions here would be to give away too much of what is to follow. Suffice it to say that many organizational theorists suggest that the cognitive and informational difficulties that overcame Intel are pervasive and commonplace. Much of their theory is social constructionist, going to how organizations perceive themselves, their goals, and their environment, and the potential for myths in conditions of high ambiguity.

My immediate interest in this scholarship stems from a continuing fascination with a fundamental question in securities regulation: Why do companies falsely portray themselves to the capital markets in filings with the Securities and Exchange Commission and through other publicity? The most common sort of large-scale class-action lawsuit alleging securities fraud is one brought against a public corporation and its senior management for concealing bad news from investors, even though the company was not in the process of selling its own shares at the time. This nonprivity "fraud-on-the-market" case typically involves some form of product or financial degeneration kept from public view until the last possible moment, leading to a rapid decline in the market price of the stock once the adverse information is disclosed, and a set of unhappy investors who bought at a time, they suspect, when the issuer's managers knew of the problems but nonetheless kept an optimistic public face.

There are very good – but confined – explanations for this kind of fraud within the framework of conventional economic analysis, particularly the thesis advocated by Jennifer Arlen and William Carney[6] that in the face of the sort of liability now imposed for securities fraud (which is almost exclusively vicarious), open-market lies are predictable if (but largely only if) the top managers see themselves as facing a "last period problem" wherein the disclosure of the truth would result in insolvency and hence the loss of their jobs. But my intuition is that stories like Intel have something else to say. Organizations are not the product of preexisting or stable preferences of a group of individual actors; instead, the structures and norms that have already evolved *determine* what those actors prefer and how they make sense of what is happening around them. Here we see the possibility that managers simply might not recognize problems or risks because of systematic "perceptual filters"[7] that play crucial protective roles in the smooth functioning of the firm. My most provocative hypothesis is that corporate cultural biases, particularly optimistic ones, can be adaptive mechanisms for encouraging trust and cooperation, and for deflecting the selfishness-inducing last-period problem that arises in times of stress and threat. If so, then such cultures should be commonplace and persistent.

Biased Inference and Corporate Cultures

The Sources of Bias

The organizational and social environment in which the decision maker finds himself determines what consequences he will anticipate, what ones he will not; what alternatives he will consider, what ones he will ignore. In a theory of organization these variables cannot be treated as unexplained independent factors, but must themselves be determined and predicted by the theory.[8]

As this quotation from James March and Herbert Simon's seminal work on organizational behavior implies, there are crucial differences in how organization theorists who do not work from the standard economic paradigm view organizational cognition as compared to more orthodox economists. In many ways, these differences boil down to an emphasis on organizational culture that is distinct from the immediate performance demands of the profit-seeking enterprise. Culture – the norms, routines, and shared understandings and expectations of those who participate in the firm's activities – is central because performance demands are often highly ambiguous once basic success has been achieved and the set of routines supporting the firm's basic technology is in place. In the face of external ambiguity with respect to further strategic decision making, organizations may turn inward to find explanations for action and the pursuit of legitimacy.

Some of this inwardness has a perfectly rational agency-cost explanation. Basic technological success creates vested political interests within the firms that are upset by strategic or technological change. As in all aspects of society, process and routine are inherently conservative. As March and Simon suggest, however, culture also has a strong cognitive dimension that does not simply reflect the self-interests of individual power bases. A basic premise in work on organizational behavior is that institutions develop belief systems – shared ways of interpreting themselves, their environments, their pasts, and their prospects. These belief systems are functionally important because they facilitate interaction and communication between managers and employees, simplifying the task of coordinating the diverse activities of large numbers of people. The failure of company employees to operate on a shared set of assumptions about their environment makes internal negotiation difficult and coherent operations impossible.[9] Equally important are useful belief systems that are essential to the task of gaining support from employees and other key constituents of the firm. This is not to say that all employees become true believers in all that management says or that corporate norms suggest. Consciously, some employees will often complain or criticize the corporate belief system. But few doubt that, on average (and even with respect to some of the apparent cynics), these belief systems are powerful normative influences once a coherent culture evolves.

We need not treat even this as a wholly noneconomic construct, of course. Economists have increasingly become interested in cultures as reputational mechanisms for generating trust within organizations and making the firm's external commitments more credible.[10] The primary points of departure, however, are cognitive and behavioral. Cultures can have strong elements of myth in them; they do not depend on (and may find counterproductive) too strong a dose of reality. Myths reduce the fear and stress that uncertainty often generates. Consequently, there are strong arguments within the literature on organizational cognition that predictable biases operate within corporate belief systems in a way that causes managers to *misperceive* events and risks, allowing them in good faith to perpetuate an unrealistic belief system in the face of external stress.[11] If so, we have another plausible explanation for deceptive corporate disclosure, with interesting legal implications. Disclosure will reflect not what an objective observer would see, but what someone embedded in the corporate culture would perceive.

To be sure, there are no fixed behavioral rules that inevitably blind corporate managers; the standard claim here is that there is a loose coupling between beliefs and productivity, not a complete separation.[12] Much information is sufficiently unambiguous that its message is hard to distort. Even in the face of ambiguity, some managers, under some circumstances, will see risks more clearly, and some companies will do better than others at "debiasing." Bias is highly contextual, and I do not want to overstate the incidence of distortion in corporate perception. My claim is simply this: These biases are sufficiently well accepted in both the theoretical and empirical literature that we should take them seriously as a behavioral risk, even if we cannot determine their exact role in any given setting or estimate how often they will apply in general. Four such biases are worth particular attention.

Cognitive Conservatism and Decision Simplification. A well-documented tendency of people who must operate in noisy informational environments is to adopt heuristic forms of thought. Busy executives process extraordinarily large amounts of information in both making decisions and deciding what matters deserve further time and attention. Such processing must necessarily be simplified, sometimes oversimplified, to make the information manageable, lest the executive be overwhelmed by data and paralyzed by ambiguity.[13]

Commonly, people build schemes to provide them with "best available" interpretations. These include stock understandings of people and situations. When given enough motivation, people will revise their schemas to reflect new information. But processing limits lead to a bias against revision: The normal cognitive strategy is to construe information and events in such a way as to confirm prior attitudes, beliefs, and impressions. Like all biases, this "cognitive conservatism" occurs unconsciously.

From this, we can see how even a single manager, acting alone, would tend unconsciously to resist the significance of information calling into question the viability of a course of action – something particularly troubling given the tendency in many companies to have as a norm that information is to be passed upward to supervisory managers *only* if it is both significant and unusual. Successful companies naturally produce positive schemas: previous challenges overcome, financing obtained, and products successfully brought to market. A new product is begun in an environment where the decision makers agree that there is a sound basis for its development. That becomes the schema (or "script"), and potentially troubling bits of information are subject to dismissal or rationalization, without much conscious deliberation, if they can be processed consistently with the original belief.[14] The tendency to ignore evidence of change in one's environment is likely to be especially strong when, as they usually do, the bits of information came sequentially in small doses rather than aggregated in some salient event.

While we can explain cognitive conservatism simply in terms of bounded rationality, it also has the motivational role of reducing stress. Revising a schema is anxiety-provoking, especially if it opens up a host of troubling possibilities. Subconsciously, busy executives do not want to be bothered with disconfirming information, and so will seek to minimize the threat. Like most everyone (except the neurotic, who do not thrive in business settings), they will tend to ignore risks that appear to have little probability of occurring. Again, the preferred course is dismissal or explanation in conformity with the existing schema; it takes a fairly visible or salient threat to prompt revision. In general, then, we can predict that most managers will systematically underestimate external threats to success.

These tendencies are strengthened when managers work in teams or share decision-making responsibility. Because of the demands of communication and negotiation, groups can attend to even less information than individuals, leading to a tendency to simplify agendas in order to make decisions tractable.[15] This is frequently done by focusing the group's attention only on immediate, first-level effects, putting out of mind the more complicated and unpredictable – though potentially important – second-level and systematic consequences. Ambiguous information tends to be dismissed as unmanageable:[16] There is an excessively high test of materiality. In an intriguing article on ethical decision making, David Messick and Max Bazerman note both the tendency of many managers to be intolerant of uncertain data – for example, the "tough-minded executive," who, in evaluating potential hiring discrimination, will accept only *specific* instances of demonstrable bias, not statistics and probabilities – as well as a tendency toward circumscribed information searches in reaching decisions, thereby forcing an underestimation of the impact on secondary stakeholders and a failure to appreciate the risk that strategic forms of "cheating" will be detected.[17] Here we see how risks that might meet the lawyer's test for materiality in a disclosure environment would be given less weight, and less attention, in the primary business setting.

Groups are also motivated to preserve cohesiveness (and the efficacy of their decision-making norms and procedures), and this too can sometimes result in the underestimation of risk. When a member brings up some information that suggests that the group's decision making has failed to consider something troubling, a threatening form of stress is introduced into the environment. Without realizing it, each member is inclined to dismiss or ignore danger signals, leading to less informed decision making that more closely resembles collective rationalization than prudent choice. Moreover, even if a group member privately wonders whether some bit of information is troubling, the fact that other group members do not appear to be concerned is a reason to let the matter drop, a process of social learning that has a dangerous circularity to it. This is especially powerful when there is a diffusion of responsibility among group members such that none feels compelled to lead and each can justify silence. The term given to the group-cohesion phenomenon by Irving Janis is "groupthink,"[18] and it is commonly used as an explanation for myopic corporate and political behavior. A group of senior managers that unconsciously deflects threatening information to preserve internal solidarity might well then disseminate inaccurate corporate publicity.

Overoptimism and the Illusion of Control. We now move more squarely into the motivational sphere. One of the most robust findings in the literature of individual decision making is that of the systematic tendency of many people to overrate their own abilities, contributions, and talents. This egocentric bias readily takes the form of excessive optimism and overconfidence, coupled with an inflated sense of ability to control events and risk.[19] In explaining good and bad fortune, people are asymmetric: Positive events are the product of their skill, negative ones of external circumstances. Furthermore, people filter self-referential information with the same asymmetry to bolster or maintain self-esteem. As with the biases discussed in the previous subsection, these are largely unconscious ones. While some outward expressions of optimism and confidence are deliberate forms of impression management, psychologists believe that most often the person truly accepts the excessively positive self-schema. Self-deception is necessary to sustain the illusion effectively, diminishing the anxiety produced by too much self-doubt.[20]

Evidence suggests that groups can increase optimistic biases,[21] and, in fact, overconfidence in business organizations is predictable and frequently observed in field studies of particular firms. Optimists are prized in the hiring process. For example, one of the leading research psychologists in this area, Martin Seligman of the University of Pennsylvania, has designed hiring tests to assess high levels of optimism for numerous corporations, including Metropolitan Life's sales force.[22] And there is good reason to believe that the tournament-like competition for promotion up the executive ladder overweights optimism and its associated behavioral traits, inflating such behavior toward the top of the hierarchy. This is especially so in industries, like many service ones, where a sales and marketing culture dominates.

For obvious reasons, the prevalence of illusory control in many businesses can become systematic, infecting the company's overarching belief system. Numerous studies offer evidence of it. Edward Zajac and Max Bazerman, for example, contend that these cognitive biases are the primary explanation for a host of suboptimal strategic decisions of the type chronically observed in industry: overbidding for assets, plant overexpansion, and foolish entry into new lines of business.[23] As much as anything, they say, systematic overcommitment derives from the inculcated and persistent belief – one that tends not to be eroded by learning and experience – that one's own company is superior to its competitors, leading to an underestimation of the competitors' likely responses to a strategic move. This explanation also underlies much of the work on the so-called winner's curse: the tendency for the winner of any auction to find later that he has overpaid. As a number of scholars have noted in explaining why tender offers so often turn out to be unprofitable to the acquirer, there is significant hubris in believing that the person who has placed the highest value on an asset is likely to have made the most accurate valuation.[24]

If overoptimism and the illusion of control come to affect a company's belief system, then the tendency to underestimate or rationalize risk in preparing publicity and disclosure will surely be exacerbated. Faced with some evidence that a product under development is failing and market share is eroding, managers in many companies will honestly believe that these are minor challenges that can readily be overcome. They will draw on inflated schemas of past successes and underrate their competitors' ability to capitalize.

Furthermore, a "can-do" culture built on these adaptive biases will prize the dismissal of risk and reject any effort to accept and acknowledge their seriousness publicly. Belief systems are powerful and need nurturing. Moreover, disconfirming information is stress-inducing, and the need to protect the management group's cohesion will result in the dismissal or rationalization of problems if there is a plausible basis for so doing. Such belief systems may not easily tolerate forms of publicity or disclosure that are at odds with the corporate self-image.

Commitment. Commitment is one of the foundational concepts of both individual and organizational psychology. Once a person voluntarily commits to an idea or course of action, there is a strong motivation to resist evidence that it was ill-chosen. Self-confidence and external image are threatened both by introducing a troubling awareness of the possibility of mistake and by raising the need to consider a reversal of one's position, which, in turn, calls into question one's reputation for consistency, a highly valued asset in our economic culture. Cognitive-dissonance theory predicts that once a commitment is made, attitudes and beliefs will shift to preserve consistency.[25] Sales people and negotiators know well that once a person takes a few steps toward some purchase or deal, the likelihood of agreement increases.

The management literature strongly suggests that once executives have committed to a course of action, their subsequent survey of information is strongly biased to bolster their choice – especially when their choice is public, and they can be held accountable for their decisions.[26] Bolstering evidence is actively sought, while disconfirming information is subconsciously resisted. Although we can see a possible rational basis here grounded in the last-period problem, the weight of authority supports the position that managers come to believe in the efficacy of projects for which they are responsible, objective evidence often notwithstanding. Hence, the phenomenon of "throwing good money after bad." Various scholars have identified the commitment bias as a primary cause of the chronic overcapacity often observed in industry.

Self-serving Beliefs. Both the optimistic and commitment biases raise a troubling concern. Beliefs that lead to throwing good money after bad in an effort to avoid acknowledging a mistake to one's self or to the public seem to be fairly selfish forms of inference.[27] This presents the possibility that certain forms of managerial beliefs may not necessarily be molded in the company's best interests – though that may be the outward impression – but rather they reflect the self-serving biases of its senior managers.

The notion of self-serving inference is another fundamental construct in social cognition.[28] When there is enough ambiguity to permit it, people naturally "see what they want to see." And what they want to see is something that is in their self-interest, not a threat to either their self-esteem or career prospects. That threat is stressful and, to a small group, upsets cohesion.[29] It is, therefore, resisted. This is not to say that management control groups live in settings of blissful ignorance. Much information is too unambiguous to deflect: Corporations do have regular feedback in the form of sales data, cash flow, and the like. Self-serving inference is an anxiety buffer, not an anxiety eliminator. Management groups may subconsciously perceive information in a way, if at all possible, that permits them to maintain consistency with their self-image of efficacy and control, thereby justifying (to themselves and others) preservation of their positions and status. They will be adept at the self-deception that leads them to persuasively articulate the corporate interest in full consistency with their personal goals.

Thus, we can see an optimistic culture as two-headed. On the one hand, it may be very useful to the firm as a motivator. On the other hand, optimism has a dark side, justifying the preservation of the status quo, and hence can also serve as an entrenchment mechanism. If the future is rosy, senior managers deserve not only to keep their jobs, but also to receive additional perquisites. This suggests that highly optimistic forms of belief may well strengthen in the face of increasingly disconfirming information as fed by the strong personal needs of the senior managers. In all likelihood, one way that we can measure the self-serving tendencies of top management is to examine how well they diffuse within the firm. Natural optimism should find a willing audience; more strained versions will be greeted with increasing levels of skepticism among midlevel managers, who are just as likely to engage in self-serving construal, although with different conclusions.

The notion that self-serving inferences are pervasive and hard to disentangle from business justifications indicates an interesting connection between social psychology and conventional economics. Though a clear violation of the standard rationality assumption, this form of inference offers a reason to expect people to behave the way economists predict – in the pursuit of self-interest – even though they deny in good faith that they are acting in anything but a fair and reasonable fashion. As ethicists increasingly recognize, antisocial behavior in business settings may be less the product of base moral corruption than of the ability of normal people in stressful environments to distort and rationalize.[30] In this sense, self-serving inferences may be particularly useful in understanding the nature and persistence of agency costs and the moral hazards in organizational economics.

Bundling the Stories. Although each of the foregoing behavioral biases is interesting by itself, the practical implications follow from their interplay. Burgelman's story about Intel recounted earlier is essentially one of senior management's inertial resistance to the disconfirmation of a highly success-oriented schema, albeit in a setting where learning ultimately did occur. As such, accounts of why companies make misleading disclosures should seek to integrate the various biases. And from these biases, it is easy to tell a generic story behind the kind of fraud allegations involving Apple Computer,[31] Time-Warner,[32] Polaroid,[33] and many other defendants in the "false optimism" cases. In most of these cases, a highly successful organization undertook a course of action with respect to some product or financial strategy and was sued for not disclosing some bits of adverse information later found in the company's files. This is precisely the kind of situation where each of the biases can readily operate: The firm was successful and no doubt had a good deal of aggregate self-esteem; the adverse bits of information were slow in coming and inconsistent with well-established schemas; and there was a heavy commitment to the success of the projects. It is perfectly plausible that, especially in the first small steps toward committing to the project – a point of very high ambiguity – individual managers were particularly optimistic. In the early stages of the project, this optimistic schema was resistant to the first (still ambiguous) bits of potentially disconfirming information. By the time their seriousness started to become clearer, there was a high degree of commitment to strengthen the prevailing beliefs, not to mention strong political reasons for preserving the status quo. Moreover, by that time the managers were committed to their publicly expressed optimism, from which they could not easily step away, even as the signs of trouble became palpable. Only at that late stage was there a truly deliberate form of dissembling. The temporal interplay between initial overoptimism (leading one to underestimate the risk of later dilemmas at the beginning of a course of action) and the commitment bias (leading toward continuation once those first steps are completed) – an optimism-commitment "whipsaw" – is an especially interesting explanation for why otherwise good people often find themselves responsible for bad behavior.[34]

Can Biases Persist?

The tension between the orthodox economic and the alternative social-science accounts of organizational behavior is most clearly posed in a single question: If business firms exist in competitive environments, will not market forces weed out those firms that act in a less-than-rational, and hence inefficient, fashion? In other words, should we not expect those firms with unrealistic belief systems that do not learn from their errors to disappear, leaving only those that have successfully countered the problem of cognitive bias? This Darwinian question is particularly apt because the problems of management myopia and excessive optimism are hardly unknown within the business community: Scores of books, consultants, and educational programs exist to alert mangers to them and point to ways of avoiding them. Many companies have adopted structures designed specifically to avoid biases in the decision-making process.

Answering this question is the most important item on the behavioral-research agenda. Before turning to a set of responses, however, it should be emphasized that even if competitive forces do gradually weed out firms that generate unrealistic belief systems, the process of decision making remains descriptively interesting. Our immediate effort is to explain why companies might deceive the stock markets, and to see what this says about securities law. Unless we make the strong and unrealistic assumption that overly optimistic or otherwise biased organizations never even enter markets in which more rational competitors exist, the category of companies that might be charged with fraud will always include some that are at risk of being eliminated because of their bias, but have not yet been. This "temporary entrant" category – with some hyperbole, the corporate equivalent of Barnum's new sucker born every minute – would still be of significance to understanding the nature and sources of corporate deception. Indeed, given that corporate failure of some sort or another is a common precursor to class-action litigation, it may be a particularly important category. We need not rest here, however, for there are other survivability accounts that deserve careful consideration, each interesting by itself but, like the biases themselves, probably most powerful in combination.

Contingency, Imperfect Competition, and the Limits of Learning from Experience. The first possible answer to the question of why competition does not assure organizational rationality is an obvious one: There is no such thing as a fixed or immutable organizational belief system. Although corporate cultures do allow for a certain degree of stability even when there is substantial turnover of key personnel, they can and do shift over time. The most obvious example of this is what March and his colleagues refer to as a competency trap.[35] A firm may act with savvy in the early stages of its development and achieve a fair level of market success. At that point, it establishes a reputation and perhaps a protectable market niche (through intellectual-property protection or proprietary internal knowledge) that give it a natural advantage over its competition. As the firm ages, this advantage may generate free cash flow that provides an additional buffer from marketplace forces.

Even orthodox economists recognize that at this point, the power of competitive forces can diminish and the firm will turn inward in its behavior. Under the standard account, that facilitates managerial entrenchment and selfish behavior by incumbent executives (to which we can add, based on the self-deception discussion in the previous section, the possibility of self-serving inference perceived by the incumbent managers *as if* it were good business judgment). With product-market forces blunted, labor-market forces become less pressing, especially if the managers have invested much human capital in the particular firm. And, as is increasingly well recognized, the third principal kind of market force – capital-marketplace influence – can be marginal, at least until a crisis. Eventually, of course, the firm that is too inward looking may fail as technology evolves and competitors are able to alter the competitive environment. The point, however, is that because of variations in the intensity of competition, we cannot assume that firms with bias-filled cultures will necessarily die quickly. Their biases may persist for unusually long periods of time. The result, for our purposes, is an enlargement of the category of companies that at any given time might be susceptible to the kinds of disclosure distortion that come from cognitive bias. Indeed, there is a strong strand in the "organizational ecology" literature that suggests that eventually nearly all successful firms are destined for failure as their perceptions and routines ill-prepare them for changes in technologies and market conditions.[36]

Quite separately, we should also take note of the difficulties associated with organizational learning and rational choice. Once a firm has exploited some technology and established itself in its market, it becomes increasingly difficult to discern what the best strategic option is. And when some choice is made, it is difficult to tell whether it was successful or not. Signals from the environment are highly ambiguous and often delayed. Nearly all failures can be ascribed, if observers are so inclined, to intervening and unforeseen situational factors rather than flaws in the decision. Such environments frustrate organizational learning and rational decision making. In this kind of setting, rational choice readily gives way to superstitious learning, and decisions and processes that are more symbolic than real, not because the company is not motivated to act rationally, but rather because environmental signals leave a void soon filled in the pursuit of other, more inward-looking needs.

Adaptive Biases. The second set of explanations for why biases might persist is different and potentially more profound. Put simply, there is reason to suspect that firms that inculcate certain types of belief systems may in many settings be competitively superior to those that are more doggedly "realistic." Though counterintuitive, this possibility finds a great deal of support in the social-psychology research relating to individual and group behavior.

As noted, there are essentially two classes of bias. One is the kind of bias arising naturally from bounded rationality and constraints on cognitive-processing ability. At the level of the firm, it is quite possible that stable perceptions and routines are necessary to allow it to focus on an objective and exploit it fully, even if the resulting tunnel vision eventually poses significant risks in times of external change.[37] This is the virtue of organizational cognitive conservatism. It can be adaptive in two senses: First, it simplifies thinking by allowing the firm to dismiss large amounts of information; second, it is often accurate insofar as stability is more common than change. In an ambiguous environment, too much willingness to shift directions and consider new possibilities makes reciprocal commitment difficult. Conversely, in a stable atmosphere, individual managers and employees, as well as such external constituencies as customers and suppliers, can rely on the firm to stick to a set of routines and so are more willing to "invest" in it for the intermediate-term future. In sum, one adaptive quality of narrow organizational perception is to focus the firm's resources and attention on what it has for the time being found that it can do well[38] and avoid the informational paralysis that often comes from seeing and thus dwelling on too many risks or opportunities.

The other kind of bias is the motivated one, and here we see a more fascinating possibility. Much research on individual cognition indicates that the most successful person, on average, tends not to be the realist, but rather the optimist. As we have seen, high levels of self-esteem and self-efficacy are associated with aggressiveness, perseverance, and optimal risk taking.[39] These biases may be particularly adaptive in business settings, where decisiveness and aggressiveness are considered indicators of a successful manager.[40] Certainly, overconfidence at times leads to disaster and severe career failure. Those who fail too visibly are often weeded out. However, there is little evidence that successful managers learn humility very well.[41] Instead, they recharacterize their minor failures in self-serving terms. They take the apparent absence of major failures, maybe from luck as much as anything else, as proof of superior skill. High levels of optimism and confidence are not only good internal motivators but also influence others; exhibitions of confidence and optimism make people more persuasive and influential.

There is no reason to believe that the same would not be true for organizational cultures generally.[42] In the same vein as David Kreps's hypothesis that a culture that emphasizes trust can allow the organization to signal more effectively the credibility of its commitments,[43] we observe that an optimistic culture can have a number of adaptive virtues. It is an ideal motivator, creating the expectation of future growth and profitability that leads individuals to invest their human capital in the firm more willingly and to defer present consumption in favor of future rewards. Firms with "can-do" cultures will thereby generate higher levels of internal effort and, by projecting self-confidence, be more successful in attracting external resources. Conversely, an optimistic culture can blind managers to the kind of anxiety about the future that might otherwise trigger both the sort of self-serving inference and the selfish "last period" kind of behavior that might operate to a firm's detriment. Faced with risk or trouble, agents will more likely persist in normal, functional activity than act self-protectively if the firm has successfully inculcated a belief system that rests on images of efficacy and control.

Of particular interest here is the relationship between optimism and trust. In recent years scholars have come to recognize that the pervasiveness of trust within an organization is positively correlated with efficiency and productivity. In any joint enterprise the potential for opportunistic behavior must be balanced against the rewards for cooperation. The greater the sense of future well-being from joint effort, the less likely opportunism becomes. Observable (and hence cascading) patterns of cooperation can then emerge, facilitating the development of a culture that has a higher-than-normal level of trust.

In light of the potentially adaptive virtue of optimism and related biases (for instance, the illusion of control), we can see how social forces that lead groups of managers not to see some risks (or to construe them unrealistically) could have a positive payoff on average. While there are serious costs associated with ignoring danger signs in a small subset of cases, these costs may be outweighed by the profitability produced by the benign influences of organizational self-deception in others. When we couple this with the other virtue of risk deflection, the ability to maintain consistency and focus, we can see at least a plausible response to the "survival of the rational" claims of conventional economics. Indeed, although little of it relates specifically to organizational behavior, much of the work on the persistence of unrealistic optimism has been generated by sociobiologists working from strong Darwinian assumptions.[44]

The Legal Implications of Bias

If corporations habitually tend toward cognitive conservatism, overcommitment, overoptimism, and selfish inference, there is a considerable likelihood that the subjective forward-looking elements of their disclosure and publicity will have the potential to mislead. Of course, market professionals and other savvy investors will discount many kinds of corporate hype, and, at least in those settings where efficiency properties predominate, such disclosures may have minimal market-price impact. On the assumption, however, that managers do have unique access to certain kinds of risk-related information such that some marketplace dependency on managerial inference is inevitable, the possibility of socially inefficient market-price distortion remains. The normative question then looms: What changes to the prevailing rules of securities regulation might we consider in light of this heretofore unexplored possibility?

The most natural response is that if we are seriously interested in deterring corporate deception, then fraud liability should not turn on conscious awareness by the specific senior executives responsible for corporate communications of the misleading nature of their misstatements or omissions. I have doubts about how often, in hindsight, judges and juries would actually recognize an instance of cognitive blindness and refuse to impose liability. At least in principle, however, an awareness requirement much too readily protects the kinds of marketplace distortions that securities regulation wants to prevent.

To overcome this, the law would want to create incentives (if not direct requirements) to force the "debiasing" of corporate inference. Within the scienter-based regime of Rule 10b-5, the first step toward achieving this end would be to develop a definition of corporate scienter that focuses on the attribution of knowledge to the firm. In response, corporations wishing to avoid liability would have an incentive to bring into the disclosure process persons not subject (or less subject) to the same biases. Depending on the type of information in question, management consultants, accounting firms, and law firms could offer a useful, though by no means fail-safe, therapeutic intervention.[45]

In areas of special concern, the law could go one step further and mandate such intervention. In essence, the due-diligence requirement for underwriters and accountants under section 11 of the Securities Act of 1933 is based on a mistrust of management as the exclusive source of firm-specific information, thereby requiring a "bonding" of disclosure completeness and accuracy by outside professionals (who in turn also have their own reputational interests at stake). While this historic mistrust is probably based more on the fear of deliberate cheating than cognitive bias, the independent evaluation of data involved in a due-diligence investigation provides a useful antidote to bias in initial public offerings and other settings where it is both required and practicable.

But this is all extremely costly. One is also entitled to ask, moreover, whether biases built on overoptimism, at least, are ones with which we really want to interfere through legal intervention, even if we could. If optimism is adaptive in that companies do better if they develop belief systems that deflect awareness of the seriousness of some kinds of risk, is it really the kind of belief system we want to discourage? Social psychology suggests that the class of persons least prone to excessive optimism and the illusion of control is the clinically depressed. We run the risk of having third-party interventions causing official company statements that, if successful, dampen the internal morale of the senior managers and perhaps the company culture as a whole. Those that fall short of success simply operate as expensive and disruptive monitoring systems with little to show in the way of improved disclosure.

Those uncomfortable with these various costs might be tempted to move to the opposite extreme and seek to immunize overoptimism from legal attack. Indeed, there has been a fascinating line of case in the twentieth century, beginning with the Fourth Circuit's decision in *Raab v. General Physics Corp.*,[46] that goes substantially in this direction. Under this view, general corporate statements of optimism are immaterial as a matter of law. While at base this is just common sense – a statement of optimism may be so general and contentless (for example, "This is a great company with a great future") that we can hardly imagine any investor seriously relying on it alone, or even a cluster of similar platitudes – the cases themselves protect statements that are far from standard puffery. *Raab* and its progeny create the ability to weed out – without the need for fact-intensive discovery into corporate state of mind – the kinds of cases where optimistic bias, rather than intentional deceit, is particularly likely to have driven the allegedly misleading disclosure.

Beyond Corporate Disclosure: Other Social Harms

From the foregoing prediction that a corporation's disclosure to investors may sometimes be distorted, not in bad faith, but rather because cognitive forces and information-flow problems lead to a skewed perception of reality by senior officials, we can extend the same story to other sorts of social harms with little difficulty. At the risk of some repetition, the following account is a generic story of "wrongdoing" that is more a failure of rationality than an example of venality. My aim here is simply to suggest that this genre of organization theory has the potential to inform a broad range of issues in civil and criminal law, where the anthropomorphic conception of the firm still weighs heavily as well.

Responding to strong internal and external pressures both to grow and to increase profitability, most management groups search continually for new technologies to exploit, such as a new product line or new mechanisms for producing current ones more efficiently. An auto manufacturer, for example, might determine that it is worthwhile to introduce a highly inexpensive automobile to play in the market for young or low-income purchasers (such as the Pinto, manufactured by Ford in the 1970s). Alternatively, a textile manufacturer might purchase more efficient, high-speed looms to respond more efficiently to foreign competition. Predictably, some of those judgments will turn out to be socially harmful – for example, a decision to lower the safety level of a car to passengers and other motorists, or increasing the noise level of looms, causing gradual hearing loss to workers. The normal, culturally conditioned response is to say that these corporations have chosen profits over social responsibility deliberately. Yet, in many cases, the ultimate costs (monetary and reputational) after being caught and penalized exceed the gains that reasonably could have been predicted at the time.

Sometimes firms do simply discover some patentable new product or technology and enter the development and marketing stage completely confident of success. But this rarely occurs. Most strategic steps are taken in an atmosphere of extremely high ambiguity, especially in the early stages. A new product or manufacturing process is an interesting possibility, but answers to questions of successful manufacture, time frame, cost, market impact, and risk are all highly uncertain. The high-level executive decision to move ahead with such a project is a political act, for it will place resources and opportunities in the hands of some managers rather than others. The political battling for resources requires careful impression management (most effective, as we have seen, if the proponents believe their own self-serving representations). Here natural optimism, coupled with impression-management demands, leads to presentations to top officials that put aside risks (which are highly indeterminate anyway at this early stage) and overstate the project's potential.[47] The senior executives faced with the resource-allocation decision probably recognize the likely bias, and other managers competing for the same resources will try to pick at the idea's soft spots. "Go ahead" decisions are not easy to elicit. Even so, most senior executives also recognize that decisions must be made, even in the face of high ambiguity. Their social role prizes decisiveness and action, and they recognize that waiting for ambiguity to be resolved before committing to any significant course of action invites organizational paralysis. For these reasons, choices are made, typically with a commitment to monitor the chosen project in its early stages so that it can be abandoned at relatively low cost should difficulties or risks surface.

Once the project begins, those closest to the situation (the winners) have ample motivation to believe in its efficacy; their natural optimism has now been rewarded by positive feedback from the top. They are committed to a positive schema, and they recognize the political reality that the project can still be killed, so they wish to manage the flow of information to prevent this from happening.[48] An environment is thus created that leads those with immediate access to information to sense, with full awareness necessarily, that risk-related information will provoke stress and potential loss. Common defense mechanisms are employed. After all, it is still early in the project, so that any risks that surface at a conscious level remain speculative and temporarily remote and thus are still susceptible to rationalization. It becomes easy to explain them away and preserve the aura of optimism. As a result, either the risks are not reported at all, or they are communicated upward in a way that dulls them. Even if there should be some conscious shading of the truth in reports to superiors, it is probably not in bad faith, given the winners' optimistic schema. Omission of certain information can be readily justified as a means of avoiding disclosure that superiors might take out of context, overreact to, or otherwise misunderstand. Higher-ups are then unlikely to sense serious cause for concern.

To the extent that there is significant diffusion of responsibility for surveying incoming information for danger signs, the ability to deflect signs of risk increases. Diffusion increases the ambiguity associated with one's own stock of data, and the act of raising a red flag threatens the newly established (and probably quite strong) group cohesion. If the private information is ambiguous and no one else acts troubled, the pressure is strong to dismiss the information.

Now let us assume that more significant, and less ambiguous, danger signs gradually appear to those with the most direct access to the information. Here, of course, the biases are likely to shift even more from the cognitive to the motivated. Postdecisional commitment becomes stronger: The winners are not only emotionally, but also economically, invested in the project, the unwinding of which is likely to have very troublesome career implications for those who find themselves in this particular "probationary crucible."[49] They may well be in something of a personal "last period." Their psychological resistance hardens, and the temptation to distort disconfirming information increases – still, however, not necessarily in bad faith (though, at this point, some background awareness of trouble may surface). The competition between conscience and motivated rationalization continues until the information becomes so clear-cut that its implications are unavoidable. Once again, to the extent that access to information is highly diffused, that may take quite some time. Presumably there comes a time, however, at which an awareness of the project's risks or dangers crystallizes. At that point, an active cover-up might begin, though at the same time the once-thought-to-be winners may well also start believing in a self-serving fashion that sufficient disclosure of the risks was made such that responsibility for continuing the project rests more with those higher up than with them. The important point, of course, is that the final awareness of the risk or harm occurs somewhat after the point in time at which, both practically and legally, the responsible actors are likely to be held accountable. This is the optimism-commitment whipsaw effect. As one of the more polite sayings goes, the managers find themselves "knee-deep in the big muddy."[50]

As to supervisory executives a step or two removed from the project itself, their ability to monitor is compromised by two basic factors. The first is the likely distortion of information. Even if some senior managers have private suspicions about the possibility of bias from below, there are often no alternative sources of data in order to test for it. As Chris Argyris argues, many corporate cultures discourage open expressions of doubt and skepticism, which skews the information flow.[51] The second is the increasing commitment of the superior who approved the project as the investment in the project increases.

Nearly all firms do have accountability or internal-control systems designed to prevent information distortion of a gross sort. Accounting-control systems are well suited to monitor the use and disposition of corporate assets, but on a basis that emphasizes current and historic reporting, not future trends. Information relating to product and technology risks shows up only very late in budgetary or financial controls. There may be other compliance functions as well, but these all tend to lack direct access to information about subjective matters such as product development and engineering defects. What information senior managers do see is likely to be fairly ambiguous, and their own biases (cognitive conservatism if nothing else) can readily lead to their ignoring some kinds of risks. Dennis Gioia's study of the failure of Ford's recall departments to become aware of the Pinto's danger to consumers in light of its heavy workload (such that limited time and attention could be given to any particular matter), and the ease with which initial crash information could be explained away in terms that suggested minimal, containable danger, provides a good example of the limits of external monitoring.[52]

Now that we have a plausible account that can fit many sorts of "corporate misconduct" cases, from the manufacture of defective products to the disposal of toxic waste to the adoption of manufacturing processes that threaten worker health or safety – all potential torts or crimes – we might ask of what significance it all is. Because both tort and criminal law pursue so many competing objectives, I could not hope to offer a single answer. The attribution of blame is a social act for which blameworthiness must sometimes be manufactured to maintain the illusion of a controllable world, especially when there are identifiable victims.[53]

But some observations may be useful, if not dispositive. For instance, from an economic standpoint, we see from the above how difficult it might be for companies to price rationally to cover the risk of future harms from new products. In terms of deterrence, to say that organizations have natural biases hardly argues by itself for a shift from vicarious to individual actor-based liability; individuals are biased as well, maybe more so. While groups sometimes exacerbate biases, that is not always the case, and there is always the potential to build into the corporate system checks and balances that reduce the likelihood that one or a small number of biased managers will cause significant social harm.

What does seem likely is that highly *indeterminate* legal standards – such as those based on "reasonableness" or "good faith" – will have a less direct impact on firm behavior than we would like to think. The managerial bias is to perceive the firm's actions as both reasonable and in good faith. In this light, a legal rule mandating that a company face a penalty if it acts unreasonably will not be all that potent in affecting day-to-day activity. A rule mandating "reasonableness" or "good faith" ignores the many reasons that managers, and thus organizations, resist becoming aware of either unreasonableness or bad faith. Because managers fail to perceive unreasonableness and bad faith, they do not modify their conduct in response to the legal rule.[54]

There are thus grounds to fear organizational insensitivity to certain kinds of legal dictates. The natural response for the law would be to increase the sanctions, hoping to make the law salient enough to break through the organization's thick cognitive defenses. As sanctions grow more draconian, however, we encounter the familiar problem of overprecaution. Firms will add layers of legal audit, product testing, and other compliance units, which impose a burden on productivity, slowing down research and development timetables, and making it more likely that the company will forego attractive competitive opportunities. The risks associated with the overlegalized corporation are well noted in the literature,[55] and without a more sophisticated empirical understanding of organizational behavior, it is hard to predict whether any given high sanction will tend to overdeter rather than strike the right balance.

Notes

1 See, e.g., Oliver E. Williamson, *Economic Institutions of Capitalism* 43–52 (1985).

2 In criminal law, organization theory has had a considerable impact due largely to the long-standing interest of sociologists in white-collar crime. See, e.g., Christopher D. Stone, *Where the Law Ends* 35–6 (1972); John C. Coffee Jr., Beyond the Shut-Eyed Sentry: Toward a Theoretical View of Corporate Misconduct and an Effective Legal Response, 63 *Va. L. Rev.* 1099, 1101 (1977).

3 Both individual ("micro") and broad social behaviors ("macro") are the subject of inquiry within this literature; the micro-macro distinction, though fuzzy, is a common one. The macrobehavioral accounts (which traditionally have been dominant) are largely sociological in nature, emphasizing the cultural forces that dominate the cognitions and behaviors of individual actors. See Alison Davis-Blake and Jeffrey

Pfeffer, Just a Mirage: The Search for Dispositional Effects in Organizational Research, 14 *Acad. Mgmt. Rev.* 385, 397 (1989). The microbehavioral emphasis, which draws heavily from the social-cognition branch of psychology that is having such an impact in law and economics, looks at individual cognitive traits to see how these can affect the behavior of the larger organization. For an effort at integration, see Barry M. Staw and Robert I. Sutton, Macro Organizational Psychology, in *Social Psychology in Organizations* 350 (J. Keith Murnighan ed., 1993).

4 Good overviews can be found in W. Richard Scott, *Organizations: Rational, Natural, and Open Systems* (3d ed. 1992), and The New Institutionalism, in *Organizational Analysis* (Walter W. Powell and Paul J. DiMaggio eds., 1991). For efforts to interest legal academics in these materials, see Walter W. Powell, Fields of Practice: Connections Between Law and Organizations, 21 *L. & Soc. Inquiry* 959 (1996), and Mark C. Suchman and Lauren B. Edelman, Legal Rational Myths: The New Institutionalism and the Law and Society Tradition, 21 *L. & Soc. Inquiry* 903 (1996).

5 See Robert A. Burgelman, Fading Memories: A Process Theory of Strategic Business Exit in Dynamic Environments, 39 *Admin. Sci. Q.* 24, 26 (1994). For a critique, see Chris Argyris and Donald Schön, *Organizational Learning II*, at 211–21 (1996).

6 See Jennifer H. Arlen and William J. Carney, Vicarious Liability for Fraud on Securities Markets: Theory and Evidence, *U. Ill. L. Rev.* 691, 724–7 (1992).

7 See William H. Starbuck and Frances J. Milliken, Executives' Perceptual Filters: What They Notice and How They Make Sense, in *The Executive Effect* 35, 38 (Donald C. Hambrick ed., 1988).

8 James G. March and Herbert A. Simon, *Organizations* 160 (2d ed. 1993); see also Mark C. Suchman, Managing Legitimacy: Strategic and Institutional Approaches, 20 *Acad. Mgmt. Rev.* 571, 573 (1995) (discussing the importance of social values in the organizational structure).

9 See Martha S. Feldman, *Order Without Design* 136–7 (1989). This is an extremely important point. Imagine two people who must work out a commercial relationship. The first task is to come to some common understanding of the existing situation and then move on to understand the means necessary to carry out their mutual objective. That is often a difficult and time-consuming task. Add a third person, and so on, and the task becomes exponentially more complex. In a large organization, there are hundreds, perhaps thousands, of key stakeholders. If each transaction within the firm must be preceded by this process of mutual orientation and agreement, the ability to conduct intrafirm business will be slowed considerably.

10 See David M. Kreps, Corporate Culture and Economic Theory, in *Perspectives on Positive Political Economy* 90, 100–11 (James E. Alt and Kenneth A. Shepsle eds., 1990).

11 See William H. Starbuck, Congealing Oil: Inventing Ideologies to Justify Acting Ideologies Out, 19 *J. Mgmt. Stud.* 3, 8 (1982) (describing studies that show managerial beliefs that depart substantially from objective measures of reality, sometimes falling into the category of the "utterly fantastic"); Starbuck and Milliken, supra note 7, at 36. For specific examples, see Paul Shrivastava et al., Nonrationality in Organizational Actions, 17 *Int'l Stud. Mgmt. & Org.* 90, 91–5 (1987) (discussing how corporate belief systems contributed to disasters for Texas Instruments, Citibank, and International Harvester), and Shaler A. Zahra and Sherry S. Chaples, Blind Spots in Competitive Analysis, *Acad. Mgmt. Executive*, May 1993, at 7, 9–21 (identifying six flaws in companies' analyses of their competitive market).

12 See Daniel A. Levinthal and James G. March, The Myopia of Learning, 14 *Strategic Mgmt. J.*, Special Issue, winter 1993, at 95, 110 (1993).

13 See Sara Kiesler and Lee Sproull, Managerial Responses to Changing Environments: Perspectives on Problem Sensing from Social Cognition, 27 *Admin. Sci. Q.* 548, 549 (1982).

14 A fascinating account of the influence of script-based cognitive conservatism on Ford's Pinto experience – written by a psychologist who, prior to becoming an academic, was one of Ford's recall managers – is given in Dennis A. Gioia, Pinto Fires and Personal Ethics: A Script Analysis of Missed Opportunities, 11 *J. Bus. Ethics* 379 (1992). Another illuminating discussion, concentrating on Boise Cascade's ill-fated expansion in the area of retail building supplies, is Erhard K. Valentin, Anatomy of a Fatal Business Strategy, 31 *J. Mgmt. Stud.* 359 (1994).

15 On the organizational need to simplify, see Danny Miller, The Architecture of Simplicity, 18 *Acad. Mgmt. Rev.* 116 (1993).

16 See Craig D. Parks and Rebecca A. Cowlin, Acceptance of Uncommon Information into Group Decisions When That Information Is or Is Not Demonstrable, 66 *Org. Behav. & Hum. Decision Processes* 307 (1996). This is not to say that under some particular circumstances group-decision processes cannot improve decision making. Groups, for instance, are good at filtering out nonsystematic kinds of errors to which a particular member might be inclined. The point is simply that group dynamics can intensify the influence of motivations that are shared among group members.

17 David H. Messick and Max H. Bazerman, Ethical Leadership and the Psychology of Decision Making, *Sloan Mgmt. Rev.*, winter 1996, at 9, 10–11.

18 Irving Janis, *Victims of Groupthink* (1972).

19 See Max H. Bazerman, *Judgment in Managerial Decision Making* 37–39 (3d ed. 1994). For instance, a sample of people who indicated near total certainty (1000- to-1 odds) that their judgments were right were in fact right only about 81 to 88 percent of the time. See ibid. at 38.

20 See Jeff Greenberg et al., Why Do People Need Self-esteem? Converging Evidence That Self-esteem Serves an Anxiety Buffering Function, 63 *J. Personality & Soc. Psychol.* 913, 913–21 (1992).

21 See Chip Heath and Forest J. Jourden, Illusions, Disillusions and the Buffering Effects of Groups, 69 *Org. Behav. & Hum. Decision Processes* 103, 104–6 (1997).

22 See Martin E. P. Seligman, *Learned Optimism* 100–12 (1991).

23 See generally Edward J. Zajac and Max H. Bazerman, Blind Spots in Industry and Competitor Analysis: Implications of Interfirm (Mis)perceptions for Strategic Decisions, 16 *Acad. Mgmt. Rev.* 37 (1991).

24 See Bernard S. Black, Bidder Overpayment in Takeovers, 41 *Stan. L. Rev.* 597, 624–26 (1989) (discussing overpayment as the result of managers' overoptimism and ignorance); Richard Roll, The Hubris Hypothesis of Corporate Takeovers, 509 *J. Bus.* 97, 197 (1986) (arguing that bidding firms infected by hubris pay too much for their targets). For an excellent survey of this phenomenon from a behavioral perspective, see Matthew L. A. Hayward and Donald C. Hambrick, Explaining the Premiums Paid for Large Acquisitions: Evidence of CEO Hubris, 42 *Admin. Sci. Q.* 103 (1997). The finance literature increasingly points to the risk of hubris and overconfidence as well: see, e.g., David Hirshleifer et al., Securities Analysis and Trading Patterns When Some Investors Receive Information Before Others, 49 *J. Fin.* 1664, 1686 (1994) (arguing that "because some investors receive information earlier than others, overconfidence will promote herding"); Raghuram Rajan and Henri Servaes, Analyst Following of Initial Public Offerings, 52 *J. Fin.* 507, 517 (1997) (examining the effects of analyst optimism on the performance of initial public offerings).

25 See Elliott Aronson, *The Social Animal* 178–9 (7th ed. 1995).

26 Postdecisional bolstering takes place in settings of accountability, even though accountability otherwise tends to improve decision quality. See, e.g., Philip E. Tetlock et al., Social and Cognitive Strategies for Coping with Accountability: Conformity, Complexity and Bolstering, 57 *J. Personality & Soc. Psychol.* 632, 638 (1989). I have suggested that this commitment bias may prevent lawyers from fully appreciating the risk of client wrongdoing, making them less than fully competent gatekeepers. See Donald C. Langevoort, Where Were the Lawyers? A Behavioral Inquiry into Lawyer Responsibility for Clients' Fraud, 46 *Vand. L. Rev.* 75, 111 (1993).

27 Not so, of course, if this commitment bias simply reflects cognitive conservatism and inflated self-efficacy, especially if derived from the organization's own biases. The point here is that disentangling self-serving and business-oriented biases may not be so easy. See Andrew D. Brown, Narcissism, Identity and Legitimacy, 22 *Acad. Mgmt. Rev.* 643, 648 (1997) (noting both the functional and dysfunctional elements of organizational egocentrism).

28 See, e.g., Dennis A. Gioia, Self-serving Bias as a Self-sensemaking Strategy: Explicit vs. Tacit Impression Management, in *Impression Management in the Organization* 219, 230–3 (Robert A. Giacalone and Paul Rosenfeld eds., 1989); George Loewenstein, Behavioral Decision Theory and Business Ethics: Skewed Trade-offs Between Self and Other, in *Codes of Conduct* 214, 221 (David M. Messick and Ann E. Tenbreusel eds., 1996).

29 We can thus include "in-group" biases within this framework. For a seminal effort to integrate in-group bias theory and corporate-law principles, see James D. Cox and Harry L. Munsinger, Bias in the Boardroom: Psychological Foundations and Legal Implications of Corporate Cohesion, 48 *Law & Contemp. Probs.* 83 (1985).

30 See Russel Hardin, The Psychology of Business Ethics, in *Codes of Conduct*, supra note 28, at 342, 359 ("At first cut, it is plausible that there is far more failure of rationality than morality in organizations"); Barry A. Stein and Rosabeth M. Kanter, Why Good People Do Bad Things: A Retrospective on the Hubble Fiasco, *Acad. Mgmt. Executive*, Nov. 1993, at 58, 62 (using the Hubble Telescope project as a paradigm for "normal accidents" in organizations and concluding that "the Hubble project failed because of faulty mental images; images reified in the project organization, in the relationships it fostered and thus, in the very process of operationalizing the total concept of a space telescope").

31 See In re *Apple Computer Sec. Litig.*, 886 F.2d 1109, 1119 (9th Cir. 1989).

32 See In re *Time-Warner Sec. Litig.*, 9 F.3d 259, 261 (2d Cir. 1993).

33 *Backman v. Polaroid Corp.*, 910 F.2d 10, 16 (1st Cir. 1990) (en banc).

34 See John M. Darley, How Organizations Socialize Individuals into Evildoing, in *Codes of Conduct*, supra note 28, at 13, 16–25.

35 See Barbara Levitt and James G. March, Organizational Learning, 14 *Ann. Rev. Soc.* 319, 322 (1988) ("[A] competency trap can occur when favorable performance within an inferior procedure leads an organization to accumulate more experience with it, thus keeping experience with a superior procedure inadequate to make it rewarding to use"); see also Danny Miller, What Happens After Success? The Perils of Excellence, 31 *J. Mgmt. Stud.* 325, 326 (1994). Levitt and March also stress, as do many other theorists, the difficulties associated with learning from experience in any situation where feedback is not both unambiguous and prompt, something rarely observed in business settings.

36 See Michael T. Hannan and John Freeman, Structural Inertia and Organizational Change, 49 *Am. Soc. Rev.* 149 (1984). More recently, there has been greater attention to the possibility of organizational adaptation to new environments, although the substantial likelihood that success (ultimately) breeds failure is still recognized.

37 In Kenneth Arrow's words, "the very pursuit of efficiency may lead to rigidity and unresponsiveness to further change." Kenneth J. Arrow, *The Limits of Organizations* 49 (1974). For a good expression of this in the managerial literature, see Danny Miller, *The Icarus Paradox* (1990). This is also a common theme in the industrial-evolution literature. See, e.g., Rebecca M. Henderson and Kim B. Clark, Architectural Innovation: The Reconfiguration of Existing Product Technologies and the Failure of Established Firms, 35 *Admin. Sci. Q.* 9, 16–19 (1990).

38 See Richard R. Nelson, Recent Evolutionary Theorizing About Economic Change, 33 *J. Econ. Literature* 48, 79 (1995) ("[T]he set of things a firm can do well at any given time is quite limited, and . . . while firms certainly can learn to do new things, these learning capabilities are also limited").

39 The efficacy of positive illusions is not uncontroversial. See Heath and Jourden, supra note 21, at 113 (finding that positive illusions make people overly sensitive to environmental feedback). It may be affected by matters of timing (for example, a lull in the illusion immediately after a task). See Thomas Gilovich et al., Effect of Temporal Perspective on Subjective Confidence, 64 *J. Personality & Soc. Psychol.* 552, 555 (1993) (discussing the potential impact of accountability for assessments immediately following the task being assessed). From a research perspective, it is hard to determine whether such illusions are the cause of positive behavior, or whether initial success leads to high levels of optimism and control, thereby becoming a self-fulfilling prophecy.

40 See James G. March and Zur Shapira, Managerial Perspectives on Risk and Risk Taking, 33 *Mgmt. Sci.* 1404, 1414 (1987).

41 See ibid. at 1414 (noting that because managers believe that they can change the odds, they are more prone to accept risks than they might otherwise be).

42 There is support for the view that the role of positive illusions is enhanced in group settings; groups may accentuate positive feedback and offer forms of rationalization to avoid the negative. See Heath and Jourden, supra note 21, at 114; see also Yechiel Klar et al., Nonunique Invulnerability: Singular Versus Distributional Probabilities and Unrealistic Optimism in Comparative Risk Judgments, 67 *Org. Behav. & Hum. Decision Processes* 241, 299 (1996).

43 See generally Kreps, supra note 10, at 106–8.

44 See generally Lionel Tiger, *Optimism* (1979).

45 Some doubts about the accountants' motivation to detect fraud are expressed in Max H. Bazerman et al., The Impossibility of Auditor Independence, *Sloan Mgmt. Rev.*, summer 1997, at 89.

46 4 F.3d 286, 291 (4th Cir. 1993); see also *Eisenstadt v. Centel Corp.*, 113 F.3d 738, 746 (7th Cir. 1997) (holding that "investors would have expected no less" than optimistic statements).

47 For a case study on this problem, see Andrew D. Brown, Politics, Symbolic Action and Myth Making in Pursuit of Legitimacy, 15 *Org. Stud.* 861 (1994).

48 This portion of the story borrows from Darley's account (see Darley, supra note 34, at 21–2, 28–36) of corporate misbehavior, especially his recounting, from a social-psychological perspective, of B. F. Goodrich's production of faulty brake assemblies for military aircraft, based on Kermit Vandivier, Why Should My Conscience Bother Me? in *Corporate Violence* 145 (Stuart L. Hills ed., 1987).

49 Robert C. Jackall, *Moral Mazes* (1986).

50 Barry M. Staw et al., Knee-Deep in the Big Muddy: A Study of Escalating Commitment to a Chosen Course of Action, 16 *Org. Behav. & Hum. Performance* 27 (1976).

51 See supra note 5.

52 See Gioia, supra note 14, at 386–8. Of course, companies could build more intrusive and effective monitoring systems, but these are likely to be very expensive and imperfect, threatening to overall corporate morale (and hence efficiency), and subject to manipulation in any event.

53 See, e.g., Mary Douglas, *Risk and Blame* 6 (1992).

54 While insensitivity is the problem on which we are focusing, sensitivity may also become an issue. Scholars are increasingly willing to recognize "overlegalized" organizational responses. These are most likely to occur either when the legal dictate is highly salient and unambiguous, or when peer organizations have responded visibly so that a claim to legitimacy is at stake. See Donna M. Randall and Douglas D. Baker, The Threat of Legal Liability and Managerial Decision Making: Regulation of Reproductive Health in the Workplace, in *The Legalistic Organization* 169, 181 (Sim B. Sitkin and Robert J. Bies eds., 1994).

55 See, e.g., Jeffrey Pfeffer, The Costs of Legalization: The Hidden Dangers of Increasingly Formalized Control, in *The Legalistic Organization*, supra note 54, at 329.

6 Reluctance to Vaccinate: Omission Bias and Ambiguity*

Ilana Ritov and Jonathan Baron

Subjects are reluctant to vaccinate a (hypothetical) child when the vaccination itself can cause death, even when this is much less likely than death from the disease prevented. This effect is even greater when there is a "risk group" for death (with its overall probability held constant), even though the test for membership in the risk group is unavailable. This effect cannot be explained in terms of a tendency to assume that the child is in the risk group. A risk group for death from the disease has no effect on reluctance to vaccinate. The reluctance is an example of omission bias,[1] an overgeneralization of a distinction between commissions and omissions to a case in which it is irrelevant. Likewise, it would ordinarily be prudent to find out whether a child is in a risk group before acting, but in this case it is impossible, so knowledge of the existence of the risk group is irrelevant. The risk-group effect is consistent with Frisch and Baron's interpretation of ambiguity.[2]

The present study concerns the role of two biases in hypothetical decisions about vaccinations. One bias is the tendency to favor omissions over commissions, especially when either one might cause harm. We show that some people think that it is worse to vaccinate a child when the vaccination can cause harm than not to vaccinate, even though vaccination reduces the risk of harm overall. The other bias is the tendency to withhold action when missing information about probabilities is salient – such as whether the child is in a risk group susceptible to harm from the vaccine – even though the missing information cannot be obtained. We show that this bias is found even when the overall probability of each outcome is clearly constant across the conditions compared. We take both of these effects to be overgeneralizations of principles or heuristics that are generally useful to situations in which they are not useful.

* This work was supported by grants from the National Institute of Mental Health (MH-37241) and from the National Science Foundation (SES-8509807 and SES-8809299). We thank John C. Hershey and Howard Kunreuther for comments.

Consider first what we shall call "omission bias," the tendency to favor omissions (such as letting someone die) over otherwise equivalent commissions (such as killing someone actively). In most cases, we have good reasons for the distinction between omissions and commissions: omissions may result from ignorance, and commissions usually do not; commissions usually involve more malicious intentions than the corresponding omissions; and commissions usually involve more effort, itself a sign of stronger intentions. In addition, when people know that harmful omissions are socially acceptable, they look out for themselves; this self-help principle is, arguably, sometimes the most efficient way to prevent harm.

In some cases, however, these relevant differences between omissions and commissions seem to be absent. For example, choices about euthanasia usually involve similar intentions whether the euthanasia is active (e.g., from a lethal drug) or passive (e.g., orders "not to resuscitate"). In such cases, when knowledge and intentions are held constant, omissions and commissions are morally equivalent.[3] Yet many people continue to treat them differently – not everyone, to be sure, but enough people to influence policy decisions. We suggest that these people are often overgeneralizing the distinction to cases in which it does not apply.

The intuition that commissions are worse, valid as it may be in most cases, is no longer valid when knowledge and intention are known to be the same for both omission and commission or when a decision maker must choose between an omission and a commission, knowing the consequences of both (as in the studies reported here). If you have a choice of killing five or letting ten people die, assuming (for present purposes) that all are drawn at random from the same population, you should kill the five. Each member of the population has twice the chance of death from your omission than from your commission, and each would therefore prefer you to act. If you choose not to act, you are hurting all by going against their preferences.

Any principle that tries to justify the omission here would have to have a strong justification, for that principle will have a price in lives. When attempts are made to formulate a principle that can justify a bias toward omissions, the very distinction between omission and commission becomes unclear, and the distinctions that can be maintained have no clear moral significance.[4] Arguments in favor of the distinction fall back on intuitive judgments about cases.[5] The correctness of intuition, however, is exactly what is at issue: To appeal to intuition is to beg the question.

One might argue that intuition is relevant because it affects the regret that people feel about different outcomes. Active killing of one person might cause more regret than passive killing of two. Our answer to this is that the regret is felt by the decision maker, not those who die, so the use of this argument as a justification is a kind of selfishness. In addition, the difference in regret might not be inevitable; it might disappear with a change in the person's view of omissions and commissions, so a general change in this view might still be justified.

Spranca et al. found that many subjects considered commissions that caused harm to be morally worse than omissions that caused harm, even with intention held constant.[6] For example, active deception was considered morally worse than withholding the truth, even when the actor's intention to deceive was judged to be the same in the two cases.[7] Subjects were also asked to evaluate two options from a decision maker's point of view: a treatment that would cure a disease but cause death with a .15 probability, or no treatment, with the disease itself causing death with a .20 probability. In 13 percent of the cases, subjects chose no treatment because (they said) they did not want to be responsible for causing deaths through their decision. (When the probabilities were reversed, subjects preferred the treatment in only 2 percent of the cases, and, in general, when subjects rated the desirability of both options, the relative desirability of the lower death rate was higher when it was associated with inaction than when it was associated with action.) This result was equally strong whether the decision was made from the point of view of a physician, a patient (deciding for himself), or a public-health official deciding for many patients. In the present study, we extend this result, using different examples and a different method.

This omission bias is related to other phenomena. Kahneman and Miller point out that commissions lead to greater regret than do omissions when a fortuitous bad outcome occurs.[8] Demonstrations of the status quo bias and related biases usually confound the status quo with an omission.[9] For example, when the willingness to pay to remove a risk is less than the willingness to accept payment to bear the risk, changing the status quo requires an action (accepting or paying) in both cases. Ritov and Baron have unconfounded the status quo effect from omission bias in both of these contexts by asking subjects whether they would act in order to prevent a change from the status quo or whether they would feel worse when a bad outcome resulted from failure to take such action (versus acting to maintain the status quo).[10] In both of these situations, we found that the omission-commission distinction is the critical one, not the preservation of the status quo.

We do not mean to suggest that people are always biased toward omissions. Under some conditions, for example, when the decision maker is in a position of responsibility, people show the opposite bias.[11] Most subjects in the studies of Spranca et al., and in the studies reported here, show no bias. A substantial minority, however, can influence public policy (e.g., on active vs. passive euthanasia) or can affect overall rates of cooperation, as in a vaccination program.

The bias toward omissions does not seem to have a single explanation.[12] Many subjects justify the distinction by arguing that omissions are not causes (despite the fact that they affect the probability of outcomes relative to the alternative option). Some of these subjects do not hold themselves responsible for outcomes that would have occurred if they were absent or ignorant, despite the fact that they were not absent and not ignorant. The use of omissions as a reference point also seems to play a small role, so that harms caused by omissions are seen as foregone gains, which are less aversive than pure losses caused by commission (as is consistent with norm theory,[13] and the loss aversion assumption of prospect theory).[14]

Consider next the effect of salient missing information. Frisch and Baron have argued that the effects of "ambiguity" on decision making can be described in terms of the salience of missing information.[15] For example, in a situation first described by Ellsberg, people told that they will win a prize if a red ball is drawn will prefer to draw from an urn with fifty red balls and fifty blue balls, rather than an urn with an unknown proportion of red and blue balls.[16] Here the proportion of red balls is a salient piece of missing information in the second case. Subjects do not think about other missing information that would be just as useful, for example, information about the proportion of red balls in the region of the first urn from which the ball will be drawn. The perception of missing information can incline people toward inaction because they feel a desire to seek the information before doing anything else. When the information is not available, however, this desire must be left unsatisfied.

Frisch and Baron argue that the tendency to withhold action when information is missing can account for other effects of ambiguity, such as the effects of conflict among experts who estimate probabilities.[17] Brun and Teigen recently provided some evidence consistent with this view: Subjects prefer guessing the outcome of an uncertain event before it has occurred to guessing after it has occurred but before they know it.[18]

In the present experiments, we test the effects of missing information directly by holding constant the probability of the outcome, a vaccine-related injury. We simply call attention to one factor that can influence the probability of such an injury, membership in a "risk group" for the injury. "Ambiguity" is therefore manipulated even though the probability of the outcome in question remains exactly known.

Previous studies of the effect of ambiguity on decision making have often failed to inform subjects explicitly that the probability of the outcome was unaffected by the ambiguity manipulation. Frisch has found that subjects in experiments such as Ellsberg's often do not know that the expected probability is constant across the conditions being compared.[19] In the present experiments we test the effects of missing information directly by holding constant the probability of the outcome, a vaccine-related injury. We simply call attention to one factor that can influence the probability of such an injury, membership in a "risk group" for the injury. "Ambiguity" is therefore manipulated even though the probability of the outcome in question remains exactly known. We therefore test the role of ambiguity itself, unconfounded by subjects' beliefs about the effects of ambiguity on probability.

Both omission-commission and missing information are involved in public policy. A classic case in which the bias toward omissions affected policy was the argument that not seeding a hurricane could be justified, even though seeding would lead to less damage, because the damage would be felt by different people, to whom the decision makers would be "responsible."[20] Our legal system, as well, honors the distinction even when it seems irrelevant: We hold manufacturers strictly liable for damages that result from their decisions to make certain products, but we do not hold them liable at all for decisions not to produce the products (e.g., new vaccines). Similarly, we seem to put more effort into reducing risk when the risk is not well known but small (e.g., products of genetic engineering) than when the risk is well known and large (e.g., radon).

In all the experiments reported here, the basic task was the following: Subjects were presented with a hypothetical situation in which they had to make one of two decisions, either whether to vaccinate their child against an epidemic disease, or whether to support a law requiring that all children be vaccinated. Naturally, the vaccine itself carries some risk.

The vaccination problems we present are modeled on the real case of DPT vaccine (diphtheria, pertussis, tetanus), which causes a serious, permanent neurological injury in one dose out of 310,000, far less than the damage formerly caused by pertussis (whooping cough) alone in infants. In 1987 the only manufacturer of DPT vaccine in the United States (Lederle) set aside 70 percent of the price of the vaccine as a reserve against tort claims.[21] Likewise, the Sabin vaccine occasionally causes polio, although it is on the whole safer than the Salk vaccine, which sometimes fails to prevent polio. The producer of the Sabin vaccine has been held liable for such cases,[22] although no suits have been brought against the producer of the Salk vaccine. More generally, manufacturers are liable for harmful effects of their actions but not for harmful effects of their inactions.[23] Ambiguity about possible side effects further reduces the willingness of companies and their insurers to move forward with new products.[24]

Experiment 1

Method

Subjects were fifty-three undergraduates recruited with a sign placed on a prominent campus walkway and paid $5 per hour.

Subjects were presented with a situation in which a disease kills 10 out of 10,000 children. A vaccine, which costs $2 per child, can prevent the disease in everyone, but the vaccine itself has side effects that kill some children. The children that die from the side effects are not necessarily the same ones who would die from the disease. Subjects were given a table of different possible values of the risk of death from side effects, ranging from 0 to 9 out of 10,000, the "net decrease in probability of death" provided by each level of risk, and the "cost per life saved." The "net decrease" and "cost per life", respectively, ranged from 10/10,000 and $2,000, when the death rate from side effects was 0, to 1/10,000 and $20,000, when the death rate from side effects was 9. Subjects were asked the maximum level of risk that should be tolerated by the government in order to institute a compulsory vaccination program.

In a "same children" condition, subjects were told, "Suppose it were discovered that the children who are susceptible to death from flu are the same ones who are susceptible to death from the side effects of the vaccine. Thus, ... the 'net decrease' would represent actual lives saved, children who would have died from flu if they had not been given the vaccine. There would be no children who would die from the vaccine who would not have died anyway." Two other items were identical except that the cost was $10 instead of $2 per child, with corresponding increases in the cost per life. Additional items addressed other issues that are not relevant.

Results

In the basic condition, in which the children who died from the vaccine were not necessarily the same as those who would die from the disease, 57 percent of the answers ranged between 1 and 8 per 10,000; 23 percent thought that no risk should be tolerated; and 9 percent gave answers of 9 (or 10, the maximum possible risk). (The remaining six gave uninterpretable answers or failed to answer this item.)

In the "same children" condition, 47 percent of the subjects (in contrast to 9 percent in the basic condition) said that the vaccine should be given at the maximum risk (9 per 10,000). In all, 68 percent tolerated higher risk in this same-children condition than in the condition with the same cost, and only 4 percent tolerated lower risk in the same-children condition than the control ($p < .001$). Several subjects pointed out that the difference between these conditions was in whether the vaccine killed children who would not die from the disease in any event. Subjects who tolerated very little or no risk in the basic condition, or who said (in answer to another question) that they thought that the government had no right to compel anyone to have the vaccine, often commented that giving the vaccine on a large scale would involve causing the deaths of some children, which was wrong even if it meant that a greater number of children would be saved. For example, "You can't force parents to give their kid a drug or vaccine that could cause the kid to die!" Subjects apparently are not inclined to consider deaths caused by failure to vaccinate (that would not occur in any case) as results of a decision, although they do consider deaths caused by vaccination as results of the decision, if they would not occur anyway.

Price had no effect on the results despite a fivefold change in cost per life. Four out of 53 subjects were less willing to vaccinate when the price was high, three were more willing, and the rest were equally willing. The bias toward omission therefore cannot be explained in terms of vaccination being more costly.

Experiment 2

The present experiment adds ambiguous situations in which the final outcome of the vaccination is dependent upon an unknown intermediate state. We expect that the subjective feeling of missing information will be more salient in such a situation, leading, in turn, to a stronger omission bias.

As before, subjects were presented with a hypothetical situation, in which they had to decide whether to vaccinate their child against an epidemic flu. Several conditions were described, differing in the presence (or absence) of "risk groups" in the population, with regard either to the flu or to the vaccine. In all cases, however, the information whether the child belongs to any of the risk groups was not available to the decision maker. We predicted that the presence of risk groups would make subjects less inclined to vaccinate, in spite of our emphasizing the fact that the overall probability of death is identical in all conditions.

We also compared the effect of ambiguity (missing information) with regard to risk of death from the vaccine to ambiguity with regard to death from the flu. To that end, we included two conditions: one condition with information only about a risk group for the vaccine and another condition with information only about a risk group for the flu.

Finally, we compared decisions for a hypothetical child of one's own with decisions concerning a hypothetical law requiring vaccination for all children.

Method

Twenty-eight students were solicited as in Experiment 1.

Subjects went through all cases twice: once to make a personal decision whether they would vaccinate their child, and once to indicate their support of a law requiring vaccination. Half the subjects did the policy decision before the personal one.

The instructions to the questionnaire read:

In the state you live in, there had been several epidemics of a certain kind of flu, which can be fatal to children under 3. The probability of each child getting the flu is 1 in 10, but only 1 in 100 children who get the flu will die from it. This means that 10 out of 10,000 children will die.

A vaccine for this kind of flu has been developed and tested. The vaccine eliminates the probability of getting the flu. The vaccine, however, might cause side effects that are also sometimes fatal.

In the personal decision, subjects were instructed: "Imagine that you are married and have one child, a one-year-old. You wonder whether you should vaccinate your child. Your child will have a 10 in 10,000 chance of dying from the flu without the vaccination." In the policy decision, they were instructed:

> Suppose that the state government is thinking of passing a law to require vaccination for all children, unless a physician thinks it is dangerous to the child's health. (Such laws exist in Pennsylvania and other states.) The question now is whether you would support such a law. If the law is not passed, the vaccine will not be offered, and 10 out of 10,000 children will die from the flu.

For each case, subjects were asked to indicate the maximum overall death rate for vaccinated children for which they would be willing to vaccinate their child (or to support the law), using the following scale:

> Would you vaccinate your child [support a law requiring vaccination] if the overall death rate for vaccinated children were (check those in which you would vaccinate [support the law]):

__ 0 in 10,000
__ 1 in 10,000
__ 2 in 10,000
__ 3 in 10,000
__ 4 in 10,000
__ 5 in 10,000
__ 6 in 10,000
__ 7 in 10,000
__ 8 in 10,000
__ 9 in 10,000
__10 in 10,000

Eight different versions of the vaccination problem were used (with titles included):

1. Basic case. "The children who die from the side effects of the vaccination are not necessarily the same ones who would die from the flu."

2. Risk group for flu. "Suppose it were discovered that 100 out of every 10,000 children were susceptible to death from the flu. Children who were not susceptible do not experience any adverse effects. The test to determine who is susceptible is not generally available and cannot be given. The overall probability of death from the flu is still 10 out of 10,000 (with all 10 included in the 100 who are susceptible)."

3. Risk group for vaccine. "Suppose it were discovered that 100 out of every 10,000 children were susceptible to death from the side effects of the vaccine (if any such deaths occur). Children who were not susceptible do not experience any adverse effects. The test to determine who is susceptible is

not generally available and cannot be given. The overall probability of death from the flu is still 10 out of 10,000."

4. Same risk group for flu and vaccine. "Suppose it were discovered that 100 out of every 10,000 children were susceptible to death from the flu, and the same children were susceptible to death from side effects (if any such deaths occur). Children who were not susceptible do not experience any adverse effects. The test to determine who is susceptible is not generally available and cannot be given. This, of course, does not mean that a child who died from side effects of the vaccination would have died anyway, since he may not have contracted the flu at all. The overall probability of death from the flu is still 10 out of 10,000 (with all 10 included in the 100 who are susceptible)."

5. Different risk groups for flu and vaccine. "Suppose it were discovered that 100 out of every 10,000 children were susceptible to death from the flu, and 100 out of every 10,000 children were susceptible to death from side effects, but they were not necessarily the same children. Children who were not susceptible to death from the flu never die from the flu, and children who are not susceptible to death from side effects never die from side effects. The tests to determine susceptibility are not generally available and cannot be given. The overall probability of death from the flu is still 10 out of 10,000 (with all 10 included in the 100 who are susceptible to death from the flu)."

6. Chemical risk group for vaccine. "Suppose it were discovered that death from the vaccine is caused by the interaction of the vaccine with a certain chemical normally produced by the body. The interaction can occur when the level of this chemical goes above a certain point. 100 out of every 10,000 children have a chemical above this point. These children are at risk of death from the vaccine. No other children are at risk. The test for the chemical is not generally available and cannot be given. The overall probability of death from the flu is still 10 out of 10,000."

7. Vaccine might cause flu. "Suppose that the vaccine consists of a certain dose of weakened bacteria, which would encourage the body to produce specific antibodies to combat the flu. The dosage given in the vaccine is the minimum that would activate the production mechanism of the antibodies. What is considered death from 'side effects' in item A is actually death from the flu, caused by the vaccine. The overall probability of death from the flu is still 10 out of 10,000."

8. Vaccine failure. "Suppose that an alternative vaccine were developed. In this case, the vaccine causes no deaths, but it could be less effective. Of children who are given this vaccine, some could die from the flu, because the vaccine will fail. The death rate from the flu is still 10 out of 10,000, as in case A. In this case, of course, there are no side effects, but vaccinated children can die from the flu if the vaccine fails."

Table 6.1. *Mean Maximal Death Rate (Out of 10,000) for Vaccinated Children (N = 20)*

Case	Personal Decision	Support of Law
1 Basic case	5.458	5.750
2 Risk group for flu	5.458	6.250
3 Risk group for vaccine	4.350	4.625
4 Same risk group	4.000	3.917
5 Different risk groups	3.667	3.500
6 Chemical risk group for vaccine	3.208	3.125
7 Vaccine might cause flu	5.167	5.542
8 Vaccine failure	7.125	6.833

Results

Four subjects out of 28 were excluded from the analysis because their answers indicated that they had not understood the task (e.g., they were more willing to vaccinate when the death rate from the vaccine was high than when it was low). Eight subjects gave the same response for all cases. Table 6.1 shows the means across subjects of the maximal death rate for which subjects still decide to vaccinate and of the maximal death rate for which subjects still support the law requiring vaccination.

The results for policy decisions were the same as those for personal decisions. We found no significant difference in overall level of vaccination for policy versus personal decisions ($t = .431$, $p = .67$). The ordering of the cases in the personal decisions did not differ from their ordering in the policy decisions either: Friedman analysis of variance of the differences in ranking of cases for the two types of decisions did not yield a significant result (Friedman test statistic = 6.698, $p = .461$). We therefore averaged the results for the two types of decisions.

To test the hypothesis that presence of risk groups for vaccinated children affects the decision, we compared the cases with a risk group for the vaccine (Cases 3 and 5) to the otherwise equivalent cases without a risk group for the vaccine (Cases 1 and 2). Indeed, the presence of a risk group for the vaccine significantly reduced subjects' willingness to vaccinate: Twelve subjects were less willing to vaccinate in Case 3 than in Case 1, and only two subjects went the other way ($p < .02$); fifteen subjects were less willing to vaccinate in Case 5 than in Case 2, and none went the other way ($p < .001$).

Our description of the risk group might have aroused suspicion. Subjects might have thought that sufficient effort would yield the missing information.

To test this possibility, we ran an additional experiment in which we made clear why the information was unavailable. Twenty-two subjects were given the basic case plus a new vaccine risk-group version, identical to version 3, except that subjects were told: "A test to determine who is susceptible is available now, but it must be done when the child is born, and it was not available when your child was born." Results were essentially unchanged. Eight subjects were less willing to vaccinate in the risk-group condition than in the basic case versus one who went the other way ($p < .02$), six gave the maximum rating (9 or 10) to both versions, and seven gave equal ratings, less than 9, to the two versions.

Returning to the main experiment, the decisions in cases with a risk group for the flu (Cases 2 and 5) did not significantly differ from the decisions in the matched cases without it (Cases 1 and 3). Four subjects were more willing to vaccinate in Case 2 than in Case 1, while four other subjects were less willing to vaccinate in this case ($p = 1$); two subjects were more willing to vaccinate in Case 5 than in Case 3, and nine subjects went the other way ($p = .065$, but here the risk group increases rather than decreases willingness to vaccinate). In sum, a risk group for the vaccine makes subjects reluctant to vaccinate, but a risk group for the flu has no significant effect.

The difference between Case 4 (same risk group for flu and vaccine) and Case 5 (different risk groups) is not significant: Seven subjects were less inclined to vaccinate in Case 5 than in Case 4, and two subjects went the other way ($p = .180$). This is consistent with the general lack of effect of the risk group for flu.

Making the missing information more salient caused subjects to be still less willing to vaccinate. Comparing Case 3 (risk group for the vaccine) with Case 6 (chemical risk group for the vaccine), we find that the additional information given in Case 6 caused ten subjects to give a lower answer in this case than in Case 3. None of the subjects went the other way ($p < .01$). Information concerning the mechanism by which the vaccine causes death does not seem to matter (seven subjects gave a higher response in Case 1 than in Case 7, and three subjects went the other way; $p = .344$).

Finally, subjects are willing to accept a higher death rate of vaccinated children when the death is a result of vaccine failure rather than vaccine side effects (ten subjects were more willing to vaccinate in Case 8 than in Case 1, and only one subject went the other way; $p < .02$). When death results from vaccine failure, the decision to vaccinate does not cause death: This condition is analogous to the "same children" in Experiment 1. This finding is consistent with the finding of Spranca et al. that omission bias is determined by belief that the commission itself causes a bad outcome, which would not have occurred if the decision maker were unaware of the possibility of making a decision.[25]

Experiment 3

The lack of flu risk-group effect in the previous experiment suggests that missing information is weighed differently when it concerns the effects of omission or the effects of commission. However, it could also result from the correspondence between the missing information and the response mode: Subjects responded in terms of number of deaths from the vaccine, so they may have been more sensitive to information concerning death from the vaccine. To test this alternative hypothesis, we designed the following experiment.

As before, subjects were presented with a hypothetical situation, in which they had to decide whether to vaccinate their child against an epidemic flu. They were first asked how willing they were to vaccinate their child in the basic case, in which no risk group was mentioned. Then they were asked whether they would be more (or less) inclined to vaccinate their child if they knew of a risk group for the vaccine, and whether they would be more inclined to vaccinate if they knew of a risk group for the flu.

Two basic cases were used. In one case the death rate from the vaccine was given, and the subjects were asked to give the minimal death rate from the flu that will make them decide to vaccinate their child. In the second case the death rate from the flu was given, and subjects were asked for the maximal death rate from the vaccine that would still make them decide to vaccinate. For each of these basic cases two versions of risk-group questions, for the vaccine and for the flu, followed.

Method

Thirty students were solicited as in previous experiments.

The instructions to the questionnaire repeated almost exactly the description of the hypothetical situation given in Experiment 2, except that the probability of death from the flu was not given. Then subjects were told, "In each of the following cases you are given some information concerning the vaccine or the flu." The cases were as follows:

Case 1: Basic case, flu response mode. Subjects were given the information that 10 out of 100,000 children will die from the vaccine, and they were asked to complete the following sentence: "I will vaccinate my child if more than ________ out of 100,000 children will die from the flu."

Case 2: Vaccine risk group, flu response mode. Subjects were asked to assume that a risk group for the vaccine has been discovered, although the tests to determine susceptibility are not generally available and cannot be given. They were asked whether, in this case, they would be more or less likely to vaccinate their child than in Case 1.

Table 6.2. *Number of Subjects Affected by Presence of Risk Groups in Experiment 3* ($N = 30$)

Risk Group	Response Mode in Basic Case	Less Likely to Vaccinate	More Likely to Vaccinate
Vaccine	Death rate from flu (Case 2)	19	5
	Death rate from vaccine (Case 6)	21	5
Flu	Death rate from flu (Case 3)	12	13
	Death rate from vaccine (Case 5)	13	13

Case 3: Flu risk group, flu response mode. This case was parallel to Case 2 with a risk group for the flu instead of the vaccine.

Case 4: Basic case, vaccine response mode. This was like Case 1, except that the available information was death rate from the flu (40 out of 100,000 children will die from the flu). Subjects were asked to complete the following sentence: "I will vaccinate my child if no more than ______ out of 100,000 children will die from the vaccine."

Case 5: Flu risk group, vaccine response mode. This was like Case 3 except that subjects were asked to refer their decision to Case 4.

Case 6: Vaccine risk group, vaccine response mode. This was like Case 2 except that subjects were asked to refer their decision to Case 4.

Results

Table 6.2 shows, for each relevant case, the number of subjects who would be affected by the knowledge of a risk group and the direction of change in their decision (relative to the corresponding basic case).

Note first that knowledge of the risk group had nearly identical effects in the two response modes. This was true for both the risk group for vaccine and the risk group for flu. To examine the effect of risk group, we averaged the numerical responses across the two cases with the risk group and the two cases without it. For the vaccine risk group (Cases 2 and 6), we find that eighteen subjects were less likely to vaccinate when they knew of a risk group for the vaccine (relative to the basic case, without mention of a risk group), and only three subjects were more likely to vaccinate ($p < .001$). The presence of a risk group for the flu did not have a systematic effect on subjects' decisions: Eight subjects were less inclined to vaccinate when they knew of a risk group for the flu (Cases 3 and 5), and ten subjects were more inclined to vaccinate ($p = .815$).

We have therefore replicated the result of Experiment 2 and eliminated an alternative explanation of this result. Subjects are less inclined to vaccinate their child when they know of a risk group for vaccinated children but are not similarly affected by existence of a risk group for children who get the flu. This finding does not seem to result from having the information concerning death rates from the vaccine made more salient by the response mode.

Experiment 4

It is evident from the previous experiments that presence of a risk group for vaccinated children decreases the willingness to vaccinate when there is no way of knowing who belongs to the risk group, even when the overall risk from the vaccine is kept constant. One possible reason for this effect may be that when faced with ambiguity, people tend to assume the worst; that is, if they know of the existence of a risk group, and have no way of finding out whether they belong to this group, they will be inclined to assume that they do. If this is true, then we should expect people to be less inclined to vaccinate as the death rate within the risk group increases.

Experiment 4 tested this hypothesis by varying the size of the risk group relative to the population and the vaccine-caused death rates of children who are in the risk group. Specifically, the risk group was either small (1,000 out of 100,000) or large (10,000 out of 100,000), and the death rate for children in the risk group was either high (10 percent) or low (1 percent). Accordingly, we had three levels of overall death rate in the population: high (1 percent), medium (.1 percent), or low (.01 percent). Obviously, the probability of death from the vaccine in the population as a whole is equal to the product of the relative size of the risk group and the death rate within this group.

As in the previous experiments subjects were told that it is not possible to determine in advance who belongs to the risk group. Subjects were asked to indicate the minimal number of deaths from the flu in the population that will make them decide to vaccinate their child. As the death rate from the vaccine was not kept constant across the different conditions, we introduced three control conditions with the corresponding overall vaccine-caused death rates, but without risk groups. Thus, the risk-group effect can be determined at each level of overall death rate.

Method

Forty subjects were solicited as in previous experiments.

Subjects went through all the cases. To control for order effects, two different orders of the cases were used, with about half of the subjects assigned to each of them. However, in both orders the control conditions preceded the risk-group conditions.

The instructions to the questionnaire were identical to the instructions in Experiment 2, except for the description of the task, which read: "In each of the following cases you are given some information concerning the vaccine of the flu, and you are asked to decide what is the minimal death rate from the flu (how many children out of every 100,000 will die) that will make you decide to vaccinate." The subjects had to fill in the blank in the following sentence: "I will vaccinate my child if more than ______ out of 100,000 will die from the flu."

Seven different versions of the vaccination problem were used. In the three control cases, 10 (in Case 1), 100 (Case 2), or 1,000 (Case 3), "out of 100,000 children will die from the vaccine." The risk-group cases were:

> Case 4. 1,000 children are at risk, 10 of them will die from the vaccine.
> Case 5. 1,000 children are at risk, 100 of them will die.
> Case 6. 10,000 children are at risk, 100 of them will die.
> Case 7. 10,000 children are at risk, 1,000 of them will die.

The exact wording of the risk-group cases was (we give Case 4 as an example): "Suppose it were discovered that 1,000 out of 100,000 children are susceptible to death from the vaccine. This means that outside of these 1,000 children no one is in danger of death from the vaccine. Of the children in the risk group, 10 out of 1,000 will die from the vaccine. The tests to determine susceptibility are not generally available and cannot be given."

Results

Table 6.3 shows the mean response for each version. Examining the control conditions first, we find an immense omission bias: the minimal number

Table 6.3. *Mean Minimal Death Rates from Flu for Giving the Vaccine* (N = 40)

Case	Risk Group Size (Out of 100,000)	Vaccine Deaths (Out of 100,000)	Mean Minimal Flu Death Rate (Out of 100,000)
1	–	10	2,584
2	–	100	4,316
3	–	1,000	10,693
4	1,000	10	8,139
5	1,000	100	7,739
6	10,000	100	7,287
7	10,000	1,000	14,435

Table 6.4. *Mean Log of the Ratio: Response to Risk Group Case over Response to Corresponding Control Case* ($N = 40$)

Case	Risk Group Size (Out of 100,000)	Vaccine Deaths (Out of 100,000)	Control Case	Log of Ratio
4	1,000	10	1	1.465
5	1,000	100	2	0.848
6	10,000	100	3	1.073
7	10,000	1,000	4	0.702

of deaths from the flu that would cause subjects to vaccinate their child is at least ten times the number of deaths from the vaccine. This result extends the results of previous experiments through the use of a free-response format. A comparison between the three control conditions shows that as the number of deaths caused by vaccination increases, the ratio between the number of deaths from the flu and the number of deaths from the vaccine decreases.

For the risk-group versions we computed the log of the ratio between the response to each version and the response to the corresponding control version. (Positive logs indicate less willingness to vaccinate with the risk group.) The means of those logs, across all subjects, are reported in Table 6.4. Each of the cells in Table 6.4 is significantly larger than zero. Thus, we replicated here the "vaccine risk group" effect found in earlier experiments: the presence of a risk group for the vaccine results in an augmentation of the omission bias. Other things being equal, subjects are even less inclined to vaccinate when they know the risk is "unevenly" spread across the population.

A multivariate test of the differences between the cells yielded a significant result ($F(4, 36) = 4.61$, $p < .01$). However, the only significant pairwise comparison is the comparison between the two extreme cases, Cases 4 and 7 ($F(1, 39) = 11.34$, $p < .01$): Willingness to vaccinate was affected more by a small risk group with low risk than by a large risk group with high risk. It is likely that this distinction is due to the difference in overall death rates rather than the independent effect of risk-group size or death rate within this group. Indeed, a comparison of the large risk group with low risk and the small risk group with high-risk cases did not show a significant difference ($F(1, 39) = .25$, $p = .61$).

These results suggest that as the overall risk gets higher, subjects are less sensitive to the presence of a risk group. The results do not support the "worst case" hypothesis, which holds that subjects who do not know whether they belong to the risk group tend to assume that they do.

General Discussion

Subjects are reluctant to vaccinate when the vaccine can cause bad outcomes, even if the outcomes of not vaccinating are worse. This is true regardless of whether the outcomes concern an individual child, in which case the difference is expressed in probabilities, or whether they concern a large population, in which case the outcomes differ in the number of children affected. Some subjects make an absolute rule and will accept no risk whatsoever that they will "cause" a death even in return for complete elimination of the risk of death from other causes.[26] These findings show a strong bias toward omissions of the sort found by Spranca et al., who discuss at greater length the determinants of this bias.[27]

In a pilot study we asked subjects to explain their reasons for deciding not to vaccinate at the optimal level. Many subjects did not write any arguments, hence we cannot subject the list of arguments to a quantitative analysis. However, it is worth noting that many of the arguments that were given revolved around the issue of responsibility.

One subject wrote, "I feel that if I vaccinated my kid and he died I would be more responsible for his death than if I hadn't vaccinated him and he died – sounds strange, I know. So I would not be willing to take as high a risk with the vaccine as I would with the flu." Another subject wrote, "I'd rather take my chance that the child will not catch the flu than to be responsible for giving my child a vaccine which could be fatal." A third subject wrote, "I did not want to risk killing the child with a vaccine that is optional. It would have been my fault if the child died from the vaccine." These arguments illustrate the main concern of subjects regarding the vaccine: One is perceived to be more responsible for outcomes of commissions than for outcomes of omissions.

Reluctance increases when we call to subjects' attention a piece of missing information about the existence of a risk group for death from the vaccine. This finding supports the proposal of Frisch and Baron that the perception of missing information can make people reluctant to act, even when the information is unobtainable.[28] In the present experiments, unlike previous experiments on ambiguity effects, the salience of missing information is varied independently of subjects' knowledge of the final probability. Frisch has found that subjects in experiments such as Ellsberg's often do not know that the expected probability is constant across the conditions being compared.[29] We tell subjects this explicitly.

It is interesting to note that the missing information is, in a sense, nothing new. If subjects thought about it, they could easily imagine that death from a vaccine is predicted by a great many factors. Subjects have typically heard about risk factors for most diseases. If the information is unavailable, knowing of its potential existence cannot affect action. We therefore suggest that the ambiguity effect we have found is a kind of framing effect,[30] a result of our calling the information to subjects' attention rather than a result of the existence of the information itself (which subjects might well imagine).

The effect of ambiguity does not appear to result from a tendency to assume that the missing information is necessarily bad. In the vaccination problems we used, a tendency to assume the worst would mean presuming that one's child belongs to the relevant risk group. This would imply greater willingness to vaccinate when subjects know of a risk group for the flu, and a decreasing willingness to vaccinate as the risk for the children in the vaccine risk group increases. We found no support for either of those predictions.

Ambiguity (salient missing information) is considered relevant only in the case of commissions. Consistent with the view that one feels more responsible for results of commission than for results of omission, subjects seem to think of the effect of missing information on the consequences of their action (vaccinating), not the consequences of their inaction (not vaccinating). Ambiguity concerning the consequences of action increases the reluctance to act, but there is no corresponding effect of the omission option. A possible explanation of this result is that ambiguity increases the feeling of responsibility for a bad outcome that a decision maker causes. Ambiguity therefore has no effect on omissions because those subjects who are affected by feelings of responsibility do not feel responsible for the results of omissions.

Our findings were obtained in certain hypothetical situations, so their generality is unclear. They do show that the patterns of inference we have found are fairly easy to detect, and it therefore seems likely that these patterns are found elsewhere, including some real situations. Parallels with real cases, such as pertussis vaccine, reinforce our findings. We and our colleagues have begun to study real decisions about vaccination as well, and these results will be reported separately.

Notes

1 See M. Spranca, E. Minsk, and J. Baron, Omission and Commission in Judgment and Choice, 27 *J. Exper. Soc. Psychol.* 76 (1991).

2 See Daniel D. Frisch and Jonathan Baron, Ambiguity and Rationality, *J. Behav. Decision Making* 49 (1988).

3 See Spranca et al., supra note 1.

4 See, e.g., Jonathan Bennett, Whatever the Consequences, 26 *Analysis* 83 (1966) (arguing one distinction is that there are more ways of not doing something than doing it, yet the number of ways of doing something has no normative significance). See also Jonathan Bennett, Morality and Consequences, 2 *The Tanner Lectures on Human Values* 45 (1981).

5 See, e.g., Shelly Kagan, The Additive Fallacy, 99 *Ethics* 5 (1988); Frances M. Kamm, Harming, Not Aiding, and Positive Rights, 15 *Phil. & Pub. Aff.* 3 (1986); *Killing and Letting Die* (Bonnie Steinbock ed., 1980).

6 See Spranca et al., supra note 1.

7 Ibid.

8 Daniel Kahneman and Dale T. Miller, Norm Theory: Comparing Reality to Its Alternatives, 93 *Psychol. Rev.* 136 (1986).
9 See Daniel Kahneman, Jack L. Knetsch, and Richard H. Thaler, Experimental Tests of the Endowment Effect and the Coase Theorem, 98 *J. Pol. Econ.* 1325, 1327 (1990); William Samuelson and Richard Zeckhauser, Status Quo Bias in Decision Making, 1 *J. Risk & Uncertainty* 7 (1988); W. Kip Viscusi, Wesley A. Magat, and Joel Huber, An Investigation of the Rationality of Consumer Valuations of Multiple Health Risks, 18 *Rand J. Econ.* 465 (1987).
10 See Ilana Ritov and Jonathan Baron, Status-Quo and Omission Biases, 5 *J. Risk & Uncertainty* 49 (1992).
11 See Ilana Ritov et al., Biases in Decisions about Compensation for Misfortune, manuscript, Dept. of Psychol., Univ. of Penn. (1989).
12 See Spranca et al., supra note 1.
13 See Kahneman and Miller, supra note 8.
14 See Daniel Kahneman and Amos Tversky, Choices, Values, and Frames, 39 *Am. Psychol.* 341 (1984).
15 See Frisch and Baron, supra note 2.
16 See Daniel Ellsberg, Risk, Ambiguity, and the Savage Axioms, 75 *Q.J. Econ.* 643 (1961).
17 See Howard Kunreuther and Robin M. Hogarth, Risk, Ambiguity and Insurance, 2 *J. Risk & Uncertainty* 5 (1989).
18 See W. Brun and K. H. Teigen, Prediction and Postdiction Preferences in Guessing, 3 *J. Behav. Decision Making* 17 (1990).
19 See D. Frisch, The Effect of Ambiguity on Judgment and Choice, unpublished Ph.D. dissertation, Dept. of Psych., Univ. of Penn. (1988).
20 See R. A. Howard, J. E. Matheson, and D. W. North, The Decision to Seed Hurricanes, 176 *Science* 1191 (1972).
21 See J. K. Inglehart, Compensating Children with Vaccine-Related Injuries, 316 *New England J. Med.* 1283 (1987).
22 Ibid.
23 See Peter W. Huber, *Liability: The Legal Revolution and Its Consequences* (1988).
24 See Kunreuther and Hogarth, supra note 17.
25 See Spranca et al., supra note 1.
26 See Jonathan Baron, Tradeoffs Among Decisions for Action, 16 *J. Theory of Soc. Behav.* 173 (1986).
27 See Spranca et al., supra note 1.
28 See Frisch and Baron, supra note 2.
29 See Frisch, supra note 19.
30 See Frisch and Baron, supra note 2.

7 Second-Order Decisions

Cass R. Sunstein and Edna Ullmann-Margalit

According to one picture of practical reasoning, people are decision-making animals, assessing the advantages and disadvantages of proposed courses of action and choosing in accordance with that assessment. This picture plays a familiar role in economics and decision theory; in various forms it is central to leading descriptions of reasoning in law and politics. Even in psychology, where models of bounded rationality are pervasive and where it is common to speak of "satisfying" rather than optimizing, the deviations can be understood only against the background of this picture.

As many people have noticed, this understanding of practical reasoning is quite inadequate.[1] An important problem is that it ignores the existence of simplifying strategies that people adopt well before on-the-spot decisions must be made. A central point here is that people seek to overcome their own shortcomings – calculative, moral, or otherwise – by making some metachoice before the moment of ultimate decision. Both rational and boundedly rational people attempt to minimize the burdens of choice and the likelihood of error.

By *second-order decisions* we refer to decisions about the appropriate strategy for reducing the problems associated with making a first-order decision. Second-order decisions thus involve the strategies that people use in order to avoid getting into an ordinary decision-making situation in the first instance. In law, for example, some judges favor a second-order decision in favor of rules, on the ground that rules promote predictability and minimize the burdens of subsequent decisions. In politics, legislatures often adopt a second-order decision in favor of a delegation to some third party, like an administrative agency. But there are various alternative strategies, and serious ethical and even democratic questions are raised by rule-bound decisions (as opposed, for example, to small, reversible steps) and by delegations (as opposed, for example, to rebuttable presumptions).

We aim here to clarify the choice among second-order strategies. These strategies differ in the extent to which they produce mistakes and also in the extent to which they impose informational and other burdens on the agent and on others, either *before* the process of ultimate decision or *during* the process of ultimate decision. There are three especially interesting kinds of cases. The first involves second-order decisions that greatly reduce burdens at the time of ultimate decision but require considerable thinking in advance. Decisions of this kind, which we call High-Low, may be difficult to make before the fact; the question is whether the burdens are worth incurring in light of the aggregate burdens, moral, cognitive, and otherwise, of second-order and first-order decisions taken together. The second we call Low-Low. Some second-order strategies impose little in the way of decisional burdens either before or during the ultimate decision. This is a great advantage, and a major question is whether the strategy in question (consider a decision to flip a coin) produces too much unfairness or too many mistakes. The third we call Low-High. Some second-order strategies involve low ex ante decisional burdens for the agents themselves, at the cost of imposing possibly high subsequent burdens on someone else to whom the first-order decision is "exported"; a delegation of power to some trusted associate, or to an authority, is the most obvious case.

We attempt to understand these different kinds of cases by drawing on actual practices, individual and institutional. The result is to provide some guidance for seeing when one or another strategy will be chosen, when one or another makes best sense, and how both rational and boundedly rational persons and institutions might go about making the relevant choices. There are two central lessons. The first is that no particular strategy can be said to be better in the abstract; the second is that it is possible to identify, in the abstract, the factors that push in favor of one or another strategy, and also the contexts in which each approach makes sense. In the process we address a range of ethical, political, and legal issues that are raised by various second-order decisions.

Decisions and Mistakes

Strategies

The following taxonomy is intended to be exhaustive of the possible second-order decisions, but the various items should not be seen as exclusive of one another; there is some overlap between them.

Rules. People anticipating hard or repetitive decisions may adopt a rule. A key feature of a rule is that it amounts to a full, or nearly full, ex ante specification of results in individual cases. People might say, for example, that they will never cheat on their taxes or fail to meet a deadline; a legislature might provide that judges can never make exceptions to the speed-limit law, or that everyone who has been convicted of three felonies must be sentenced to life imprisonment.

Presumptions. Sometimes ordinary people and public institutions rely not on a rule but instead on a presumption, which can be rebutted. The result, it is hoped, is to make fewer mistakes while at the same time incurring reasonable decisional burdens.[2] An administrative agency might presume, for example, that no one may emit more than X tons of a certain pollutant, but the presumption can be rebutted by showing that further reductions are not feasible.

Standards. Rules are often contrasted with standards. A ban on "excessive" speed on the highway is a standard; so is a requirement that pilots of airplanes be "competent," or that student behavior in the classroom be "reasonable." These might be compared with rules specifying a 55 mph speed limit, or a ban on pilots who are over the age of seventy, or a requirement that students sit in assigned seats.

Routines. By this term we mean something similar to a habit, but more voluntary, more self-conscious, and without the pejorative connotations of some habits (like the habit of chewing one's fingernails). Thus a forgetful person might adopt a routine of locking his door every time he leaves his office, even though sometimes he knows he will return in a few minutes; thus a commuter might adopt a particular route and follow it every day, even though on some days another route would be better. Courts and legislatures typically follow routines.

Small Steps. One way of simplifying a difficult situation at the time of choice is to make a small, incremental decision, and to leave other questions for another day. When a personal decision involves imponderable and apparently incommensurable elements, people often take small, reversible steps first.[3] For example, Jane may decide to live with Robert before she decides whether she wants to marry him; Marilyn may go to night school to see if she is really interested in law. A similar "small steps" approach is the hallmark of Anglo-American common law.[4] Judges typically make narrow decisions, resolving little beyond the individual case; at least this is their preferred method of operation when they are not quite confident about the larger issues, not just in the common law but in constitutional law too.

Picking. Sometimes the difficulty of decision, or symmetry among the options, pushes people to decide on a random basis. They might, for example, flip a coin, or make some apparently irrelevant factor decisive ("It's a sunny day, so I'll take that job in Florida"). Thus they might "pick" rather than "choose" (taking the latter term to mean basing a decision on preference).[5] A legal system might use a lottery to decide who serves on juries or in the military, and indeed lotteries are used in many domains where the burdens of individualized choice are high, and when there is some particular problem with deliberation about the grounds of choice, sometimes because of apparent symmetries among the candidates.

Delegation. A familiar way of handling decisional burdens is to delegate the decision to someone else. People might, for example, rely on a spouse or a friend, or choose an institutional arrangement by which certain decisions are made by authorities established at the time or well in advance. Such arrangements can be more or less formal; they involve diverse mechanisms of control, or entirely relinquished control, by the person or people for whose benefit they have been created.

Heuristics. People often use heuristic devices, or mental shortcuts, as a way of bypassing the need for individualized choice. For example, it can be overwhelming to figure out for whom to vote in local elections; people may therefore use the heuristic of party affiliation. A great deal of attention has been given to heuristic devices said to produce departures from "rationality."[6] But often heuristic devices are fully rational, if understood as a way of producing pretty good outcomes while at the same time reducing cognitive overload or other decisional burdens.

Costs of Decisions and Costs of Errors

Under what circumstances will, or should, an agent or institution make some second-order decision rather than making an all-things-considered judgment on the spot? And under what circumstances will, or should, one or another strategy be chosen?

We have said that second-order strategies differ in the extent to which they produce mistakes and decisional burdens. In what follows, we suggest that second-order strategies should be chosen by attempts to minimize the sum of the costs of making decisions and the costs of error, where the costs of making decisions are the costs of coming to closure on some action or set of actions, and where the costs of error are assessed by examining the number, the magnitude, and the kinds of mistakes. We understand "errors" as suboptimal outcomes, whatever the criteria for deciding optimality; thus both rules and delegations can produce errors. If the costs of producing optimal decisions were zero, it would be best to make individual calculations in each case, for this approach would produce correct judgments without compromising accuracy or any other important value. This would be true for individual agents and also for institutions. It is largely because people (including public officials) seek to reduce decisional burdens, and to minimize their own errors, that they would sometimes like not to have *options* and sometimes like not to have *information*; and they may make second-order decisions to reduce either options or information (or both).[7]

Three additional points are necessary here. The first involves responsibility: People sometimes want to assume responsibility for certain decisions even if others would make those decisions better, and people sometimes want to relieve themselves of responsibility for certain decisions even if other people would make those decisions worse. The second point comes from the fact that multiparty situations raise distinctive problems. Above all, public institutions (including legislatures, agencies, and courts) may seek to promote *planning* by setting down rules and presumptions in advance. The need for planning can argue strongly against on-the-spot decisions even if they would be both correct and costless to achieve. The third and most important point is that a reference to the "sum" of decision costs and error costs should not be taken to suggest that a straightforward cost-benefit analysis is an adequate way to understand the choice among second-order strategies. Of course, there is no simple metric along which to align the various considerations. Important qualitative differences can be found between decision costs and error costs, among the various kinds of decision costs, and also among the various kinds of error costs. Thus for any agent the costs of decision may include time, money, unpopularity, anxiety, boredom, agitation, anticipated ex post regret or remorse, feelings of responsibility for harm done to self or others, injury to self-perception, guilt, or shame. We refer to decision costs and error costs in order to start with a relatively simple framework by which to assess the various alternatives; additional considerations will be introduced as the discussion proceeds.

Things become differently complicated for multimember institutions, where these points also apply, but where interest-group pressures may be important, and where there is the special problem of reaching a degree of consensus. A legislature, for example, might find it especially difficult to specify the appropriate approach to global warming, given the problems posed by disagreement, varying intensity of preference, and aggregation issues; for similar reasons a multimember court may have a hard time agreeing on how to handle an asserted right to physician-assisted suicide. The result may be strategies for delegation or for deferring decision, often via small steps.

An institution facing political pressures may have a distinctive reason to adopt a particular kind of second-order decision, one that will *deflect responsibility for choice*. Jean Bodin defended the creation of an independent judiciary, and thus provided an initial insight into a system of separated and divided powers, on just this ground; a monarch is relieved of responsibility for unpopular but indispensable decisions if he can point to a separate institution that has been charged with the relevant duty.[8] This is an important kind of *enabling constraint*, characteristic of good second-order decisions. In modern states the existence of an independent central bank is often justified on this ground.

Table 7.1. *Burdens Ex Ante and Burdens on the Spot*

	Low Ex Ante Burdens	High Ex Ante Burdens
Low on-the-spot Burdens	Low-Low: picking, small steps, various heuristics, some standards (1)	High-Low: rules, presumptions, some standards, routines (2)
High on-the-spot Burdens	Low-High: delegation (3)	High-High: some characters in Henry James novels, dysfunctional governments (4)

Burdens Ex Ante and Burdens on the Spot

Some second-order strategies require substantial thought before but little thought during the process of ultimate choice, whereas others require little thought both before and during the process of choice. Thus there is a temporal difference in the imposition of the burdens of decision, which we describe with the terms "High-Low" and "Low-Low." To fill out the possibilities, we add "Low-High" and "High-High" as well. By the term "decision costs" we refer to the overall costs, which may be borne by different people or agencies: the work done before the fact of choice may not be carried out by the same actors who will have to do the thinking during the process of ultimate choice.

Consider Table 7.1. Cell 1 captures strategies that seem to minimize the overall burdens of decision (whether or not they promote good overall decisions). These are cases in which agents do not invest a great deal of thought either before or at the time of decision. Picking is the most obvious case. Small steps are somewhat more demanding, since the agent does have to make some decisions, but because the steps are small, there need be comparatively little thought before or during the decision. The most sharply contrasting set of cases is High-High, cell 4. As this cell captures strategies that maximize overall decision costs, it ought for our purposes to remain empty.

Cell 2 captures a common aspiration for national legislatures and for ordinary agents who prefer their lives to be rule-bound. Some institutions and agents spend a great deal of time choosing the appropriate rules; but once the rules are in place, decisions become extremely simple, rigid, even mechanical. Legal formalism – the commitment to setting out clear rules in advance and mechanical decision afterwards, a commitment defended by Supreme Court Justices Hugo Black and Antonin Scalia – is associated with cell 2. When a large number of decisions must be made, cell 2 is often the best approach, as the twentieth-century movement toward bureaucracy and simple rules helps to confirm. Individual cases of unfairness may be tolerable if the overall result is to prevent the system from being overwhelmed by decisional demands. Cell 2 is also likely to be the best approach when a large number of people is involved and it is known in advance that the people who will have to carry out on-the-spot decisions constantly change. On the other hand, the fact that life will confound the rules often produces arguments for institutional reform in the form of granting power to administrators or employees to exercise "common sense" in the face of rules.

Cell 3 suggests that institutions and individuals sometimes do little thinking in advance but may fail to minimize the aggregate costs of decision. As we have seen, delegations may require little advance thinking, at least on the substance of the issues to be decided; the burdens of decision will eventually be faced by the object of the delegation. Of course some people think long and hard about whether and to whom to delegate, and of course some people who have been delegated power will proceed by rules, presumptions, standards, small steps, picking, or even subdelegations. It is also possible to urge High-High, where the issue is extremely important; consider the decision to wage or to terminate a war.

It is an important social fact that many people are relieved of the burdens of decision through something other than their own explicit wishes. Consider prisoners, the mentally handicapped, young children, or (at some times and places) women; in a range of cases, society or law makes a second-order decision on someone else's behalf, often without any indication of that person's own desires. The usurpation of another's decisions, or second-order decisions, is often based on a belief that the relevant other will systematically err. This of course relates to the notion of paternalism, which can be seen as arising whenever there is delegation without consent.

In some cases, second-order decisions produce something best described as Medium-Medium, with imaginable extensions toward Moderately High–Moderately Low, and Moderately Low–Moderately High. After understanding the polar cases, analysis of these intermediate cases is straightforward, and hence we will not undertake that analysis here. We now turn to the contexts in which agents and institutions follow one or another of the basic second-order strategies.

Low-High (with Special Reference to Delegation)

Informal and Formal Delegations

As a first approximation, a delegation is a second-order strategy that reduces the delegator's burdens both before and at the time of making the ultimate decision, through exporting those burdens to the delegate. Such delegations often occur because the burdens of decision are high for the delegator but low for the delegate, who may have specialized information, who may lack relevant biases or motivational problems, or who may not mind (and who may even enjoy) taking responsibility for the decision in question. (These cases may then be more accurately captured as special cases of Low-Low.) The intrinsic burdens of having to make the decision are often counterbalanced by the benefits of having been asked to assume responsibility for it (though these may be costs rather than benefits in some cases). And there is an uneasy line, raising knotty conceptual and empirical questions, between a delegation and a division of labor (consider the allocation of household duties). A key issue is whether the recipient of the delegation has the authority to decline.

Government itself is a large recipient of delegated decisions, at least if sovereignty is understood to lie in the citizenry. On this view, various public institutions – legislatures, courts, the executive branch – exercise delegated authority, and there are numerous subdelegations, especially for the legislature, which must relieve itself of many decisional burdens. A legislature may delegate because it believes that it lacks information about, for example, environmental problems or changes in the telecommunications market; the result is an Environmental Protection Agency or a Federal Communications Commission. Or the legislature may have the information but find itself unable to forge a consensus on underlying values about, for example, the right approach to affirmative action or to age discrimination. Often a legislature lacks the time and the organization to make the daily decisions that administrative agencies are asked to handle; consider the fact that legislatures that attempt to reconsider agency decisions often find themselves involved in weeks or even months of work and fail to reach closure. Or the legislature may be aware that its vulnerability to interest-group pressures will lead it in bad directions, and it may hope and believe that the object of the delegation will be relatively immune. Interest-group pressures may themselves produce a delegation, as where powerful groups are unable to achieve a clear victory in a legislature but are able to obtain a grant of authority to an administrative agency over which they will have power. The legislature may even want to avoid responsibility for some hard choice, fearing that decisions will produce electoral reprisal. Self-interested representatives may well find it in their electoral self-interest to enact a vague or vacant standard ("the public interest," "reasonable accommodation" of the disabled, "reasonable regulation" of pesticides), and to delegate the task of specification to someone else, secure in the knowledge that the delegate will be blamed for problems in implementation.

When to Delegate

Delegation deserves to be considered whenever an appropriate and trustworthy delegate is available and there is a sense in which it seems undesirable for the agent to be making the decision by himself. But obviously delegation is sometimes a mistake – an abdication of responsibility, an act of unfairness, a recipe for more rather than fewer errors, for even higher (aggregate) costs of decision. And since delegation is only one of a number of second-order strategies, an agent should usually consider other possibilities before delegating.

Compared to a High-Low approach, a delegation will be desirable if the legislature, or the delegator, is unable to generate a workable rule or presumption (and if anything it could come up with would be costly to produce) and if a delegate would therefore do better on the merits. This may be the case on a multimember body that is unable to reach agreement, or when an agent or institution faces a cognitive or motivational problem, such as weakness of will or susceptibility to outside influences. A delegation will also be favored over High-Low if the delegator seeks to avoid responsibility for the decision for political, social, or other reasons, though the effort to avoid responsibility may also create problems of legitimacy, as when a legislator relies on "experts" to make value judgments about environmental protection or disability discrimination.

As compared with small steps or picking, a delegation may or may not produce higher total decision costs (perhaps the delegate is slow or a procrastinator). Even if the delegation does produce higher total decision costs, it may also lead to more confidence in the eventual decisions, at least if reliable delegates are available. In the United States, for example, the Federal Reserve Board has a high degree of public respect, and hence there is little pressure to eliminate or reduce the delegation. But a delegate – a friend, a spouse, an Environmental Protection Agency – may prove likely to err, and a rule, a presumption, or small steps may emerge instead. Special issues are raised in technical areas, which create strong arguments for delegation, but where the delegate's judgments may be hard to oversee (even if they conceal controversial judgments of value, such as those by the EPA).

There is also the independent concern for fairness. In some circumstances, it is unfair to delegate to, for example, a friend or a spouse the power of decision, especially but not only because the delegate is not a specialist. Issues of gender equality arise when a husband delegates to his wife all decisions involving the household and the children, even if both husband and wife agree on the delegation. Apart from this issue, a delegation by one spouse to another may well seem inequitable if, say, it involves a child's problems with alcohol, because it is an abdication of responsibility, a way of transferring the burdens of decision to someone else who should not be forced to bear them alone.

In institutional settings, there is an analogous problem if the delegate (usually an administrative agency) lacks political accountability even if it has relevant expertise. The result is the continuing debate over the legitimacy of delegations to administrative agencies. Such delegations can be troublesome if they shift the burden of judgment from a democratically elected body to one that is insulated from political control. What we are adding here is that the longstanding debate over delegations offers a far too limited sense of the alternatives. A legislature is not confronted only with the choice whether or not to delegate; if the legislature wants to avoid the degree of specificity entailed by rule-bound law, it might instead enact a presumption or take small steps (as, for example, through an experimental pilot program). Related issues are raised by the possibly illegitimate abdication of authority when a judge delegates certain powers to law clerks (as is occasionally alleged about Supreme Court justices) or to special masters who are expert in complex questions of fact and law (as is alleged in connection with a proposed delegation in the Microsoft litigation).

Complications

Three important complications deserve comment. First, any delegate may itself resort to making second-order decisions, and it is familiar to find delegates undertaking each of the strategies that we have described. Sometimes delegates prefer High-Low and hence generate rules; this is the typical strategy of the Internal Revenue Service. Alternatively, delegates may use standards or proceed by small steps. This is the general approach of the National Labor Relations Board, which (strikingly) avoids rules whenever it can and much prefers to proceed case-by-case. Or a delegate may undertake a subdelegation. Confronted with a delegation from her husband, a wife may consult a sibling or a parent. Asked by Congress to make hard choices, the president may and frequently does subdelegate to some kind of commission, for some of the same reasons that spurred Congress to delegate in the first instance. Of course, a delegate may just pick.

The second complication is that the control of a delegate presents a potentially serious principal-agent problem. How can the person who has made the delegation ensure that the delegate will not make serious and numerous mistakes, or instead fritter away its time trying to decide how to decide? There are multiple possible mechanisms of control. Instead of giving final and irreversible powers of choice to the delegate, a person or institution might turn the delegate into a mere consultant or advice giver. A wide range of intermediate relationships is possible. In the governmental setting, a legislature can influence the ultimate decision by voicing its concerns publicly if an administrative agency is heading in the wrong direction, and the legislature has the power to overturn an administrative agency if it can muster the will to do so. Ultimately the delegator may retain the power to eliminate the delegation, and to ensure against (what the delegator would consider to be) mistakes, it may be sufficient for the delegate to know this fact. In informal relations, involving friends, colleagues, and family members, there are various mechanisms for controlling any delegate. Some "delegates" know that they are only consultants; others know that they have the effective power of decision. All this happens through a range of cues, which may be subtle.

The third complication stems from the fact that at the outset, the burdens of a second-order decision of this kind may not be so low after all, since the person or institution must take the time to decide whether to delegate at all and if so, to whom to delegate. Complex issues may arise about the composition of any institution receiving the delegation; these burdens may be quite high and perhaps decisive against delegation altogether. A multi-member institution often divides sharply on whether to delegate, and even after that decision is made, it may have trouble deciding on the recipient of the delegated authority.

Intrapersonal Delegations and Delegation to Chance

Thus far we have been discussing cases in which the delegator exports the burdens of decision to some other party. What about the intrapersonal case? On the one hand, there is no precise analogy between that problem and the cases under discussion. On the other hand, people confronted with hard choices can often be understood to have chosen to delegate the power of choice to their future selves. Consider, for example, such decisions as whether to buy a house, to have another child, to get married or divorced, to move to a new city; in such cases agents who procrastinate may understand themselves to have delegated the decision to their future selves.

There are two possible reasons for this kind of intrapersonal delegation, involving timing and content respectively. You may believe you know what the right decision is, but also believe it is not the right time to be making that decision, or at least not the right time to announce it publicly. Alternatively, you may not know what the right decision is and believe that your future self will be in a better position to decide. You may think that your future self will have more information, suffer less or not at all from cognitive difficulties, bias, or motivational problems, or be in a better position to assume the relevant responsibility. Perhaps you are feeling under pressure, suffering from illness, or not sure of your judgment just yet. In such cases, the question of intrapersonal, intertemporal choice is not so far from the problem of delegation to others. It is even possible to see some overlapping principal-agent problems with similar mechanisms of control, as people impose certain constraints on their future selves. There are close parallels for judges and legislators, who care a great deal about both timing and content, and who may wait for one or another reason.

High-Low (with Special Reference to Rules and Presumptions)

We have seen that people often make second-order decisions that are themselves costly, simply in order to reduce the burdens of later decisions in particular cases. This is the most conventional kind of precommitment strategy.

When this process is working well, there is much to do before the second-order decision has been made, but once the decision is in place, things are greatly simplified. Many people have noticed this point, but the implications have not been sufficiently explored by those interested in the general problem of precommitment.[9]

Diverse Rules, Diverse Presumptions

We have suggested that rules and presumptions belong in this category, and frequently this is true. But the point must be qualified; some rules and presumptions do not involve high burdens of decision before the fact. For example, a rule might be picked rather than chosen: drive on the right-hand side of the road, or spoons to the right, forks to the left. Especially when what is important is to allow all actors to coordinate on a single course of conduct, there need be little investment in decisions about the content of the relevant rule. A rule might even be framed narrowly, so as to work as a kind of small step. A court might decide, for example, that a law excluding homosexuals from the armed services is unconstitutional, and this decision might be framed as a rule; but the court's opinion could be issued in such a way as to leave undecided most other issues involving the constitutional status of homosexuals. Rules often embody small steps. Of course, the same points can be made about presumptions, which are sometimes picked rather than chosen and which might be quite narrow.

For present purposes we focus on situations in which an institution or an agent is willing to deliberate a good deal to generate a rule or a presumption that, once in place, turns out greatly to simplify (without impairing and perhaps even improving) future decisions. This is a familiar aspiration in law and politics. A legislature might, for example, decide in favor of a speed limit law, partly in order to ensure coordination among drivers, and partly as a result of a process of balancing various considerations about risks and benefits. People are especially willing to expend a great deal of effort to generate rules in two circumstances: (1) when planning and fair notice are important and (2) when a large number of decisions will be made.[10]

In most well-functioning legal systems, for example, it is clear what is and what is not a crime. People need to know when they may be subject to criminal punishment for what they do. The American Constitution is taken to require a degree of clarity in the criminal law, and every would-be tyrant knows that rules may be irritating constraints on his authority. So, too, the law of contract and property is mostly defined by clear rules, simply because people could not otherwise plan, and in order for economic development to be possible they need to be in a position to do so. When large numbers of decisions have to be made, there is a similar tendency to spend a great deal of time to clarify outcomes in advance. In the United States, the need to make a large number of decisions has pushed the legal system into the development of rules governing Social Security disability, workers' compensation, and criminal sentencing. The fact that these rules produce a significant degree of error is not decisive; the sheer cost of administering the relevant systems, with so massive a number of decisions, makes a certain number of errors tolerable.

Compared to rules, standards and "soft" presumptions serve to reduce the burdens of decision ex ante while increasing those burdens at the time of decision. This is both their virtue and their vice. Consider, for example, the familiar strategy of enacting rigid, rule-like environmental regulations while at the same time allowing a "waiver" for special circumstances. The virtue of this approach is that the rigid rules will likely produce serious mistakes – high costs, low environmental benefits – in some cases; the waiver provision allows correction in the form of an individualized assessment of whether the statutory presumption should be rebutted. The potential vice of this approach is that it requires a fair degree of complexity in a number of individual cases. Whether the complexity is worthwhile turns on a comparative inquiry with genuine rules. How much error would be produced by the likely candidates? How expensive is it to correct those errors by turning the rules into presumptions?

Of Planning and Trust

Often institutions are faced with the decision whether to adopt a High-Low strategy or instead to delegate. We have seen contexts in which a delegation is better. But in three kinds of circumstances the High-Low approach is to be preferred. First, when planning is important, it is important to set out rules (or presumptions) in advance. The law of property is an example. Second, there is little reason to delegate when the agent or institution has a high degree of confidence that a rule (or presumption) can be generated at reasonable cost, that the rule (or presumption) will be accurate, and that it will actually be followed. Third, and most obviously, High-Low is better when no trustworthy delegate is available, or when it seems unfair to ask another person or institution to make the relevant decision. Liberal democracies take these considerations as special reasons to justify rules in the context of criminal law: The law defining crimes is reasonably rulelike, partly because of the importance of citizen knowledge about what counts as a crime, partly because of a judgment that police officers and courts cannot be trusted to define the content of the law. Generally legislatures tend in the direction of rulelike judgment when they have little confidence in the executive; in America parts of the Clean Air Act are a prime example of a self-conscious choice of High-Low over delegation.

When would High-Low be favored over Low-Low (picking, small steps)? The interest in planning is highly relevant here and often pushes in the direction of substantial thinking in advance. If the agent or institution has faith in its ability to generate a good rule or presumption, it does not make much sense to proceed by random choice or incrementally. Hence legislatures have often displaced the common law approach of case-by-case judgment with clear rules set out in advance. In England and America, this has been a great movement of the twentieth century, largely because of the interest in planning and decreased faith in the courts' ability to generate good outcomes through small steps. Of course mixed strategies are possible. An institution may produce a rule to cover certain cases but delegate decision in other cases; or a delegate may be disciplined by presumptions and standards; or an area of law, or practical reason, may be covered by some combination of rule-bound judgment and small steps.

Private Decisions: Ordinary People, Intrapersonal Collective Action Problems, and Recovering Addicts

Thus far we have been stressing public decisions. In their individual capacity, people frequently adopt rules, presumptions, or self-conscious routines in order to guide decisions that they know might, in individual cases, be too costly to make or be made incorrectly because of their own motivational problems. Sarah might decide, for example, that she will turn down all invitations for out-of-town travel in the month of September, or John might adopt a presumption against going to any weddings or funerals unless they involve close family members. Some especially important cases involve efforts to solve the kinds of intertemporal, intrapersonal problems that arise when isolated, small-step first-order decisions are individually rational but produce harm to the individual when taken in the aggregate. These cases might be described as involving "intrapersonal collective action problems."[11] Consider, for example, the decision to smoke a cigarette (right now), or to have chocolate cake for dessert, or to have an alcoholic drink after dinner, or to gamble on weekends. Small steps, which are rational choices when taken individually and which produce net benefits when taken on their own, can lead to harm or even disaster when they accumulate. As a self-control strategy, a person might adopt a rule: cigarettes only after dinner; no gambling, ever; chocolate cake only on holidays; alcohol only at parties when everyone else is drinking. Well-known private agencies designed to help people with self-control problems (Alcoholics' Anonymous, Gamblers' Anonymous) have as their business the development of second-order strategies of this general kind. The most striking cases involve recovering addicts, but people who are not addicts, and who are not recovering from anything, often make similar second-order decisions. When self-control is particularly difficult to achieve, an agent may seek to delegate instead. Whether a delegation (Low-High) is preferable to a rule or presumption (High-Low) will depend in turn on the various considerations discussed above.

Low-Low (with Special Reference to Picking and Small Steps)

Equipoise, Responsibility, and Commitment

Why might an institution or agent pick rather than choose? When would small steps be best? At the individual level, it can be obvious that when you are in equipoise, you might as well pick; it simply is not worthwhile to go through the process of choosing, with its high cognitive or emotional costs. As we have seen, the result can be picking in both low-stakes (cereal choices) and high-stakes (employment opportunities) settings. Picking can even be said to operate as a kind of delegation, where the object of the delegation is "fate," and the agent loses the sense of responsibility that might accompany an all-things-considered judgment. Thus some people sort out hard questions by resorting to a chance device (like flipping a coin).

Small steps, unlike a random process, are a form of choosing. Newspapers and magazines offer trial subscriptions; the same is true for book clubs. Often advertisers (or for that matter prospective romantic partners) know that people prefer small steps and they take advantage of that preference ("no commitments"). On the institutional side, consider lotteries for both jury and military service. The appeal of a lottery for jury service stems from the relatively low costs of operating the system and the belief that any alternative device for allocation would produce more mistakes, because it would depend on a socially contentious judgment about who should be serving on juries, with possibly destructive results for the jury system itself. The key point is that the jury is supposed to be a cross section of the community, and a random process seems to be the best way of serving that goal (as well as the fairest way of apportioning what many people regard as a social burden). For military service, related judgments are involved, in the form of a belief that any stated criteria for service might be morally suspect, and hence a belief that random outcomes produce less in the way of error.[12]

Change, Unintended Consequences, and Reversibility

Lotteries involve random processes; small steps do not. We have said that Anglo-American judges often proceed case-by-case, as a way of minimizing the burdens of decision and the consequences of error. In fact, many legal cultures embed a kind of norm in favor of incremental movement. They do this partly because of the distinctive structure of adjudication and the limited information available to the judge: In any particular case, a judge will hear from the parties immediately affected, but little from others whose interests might be at stake. Hence there is a second-order decision in favor of small steps.

Suppose, for example, that a court in a case involving a particular patient seeking a "right to die" finds that it has little information; if the court attempted to generate a rule that would cover all imaginable situations in which that right might be exercised, the case would take a very long time to decide. Perhaps the burdens of decision would be prohibitive. This might be so because of a sheer lack of information, or it might be because of the pressures imposed on a multimember court consisting of people who are unsure or in disagreement about a range of subjects. Such a court may have a great deal of difficulty in reaching closure on broad rules. Small steps are a natural result.

When judges proceed by small steps, they do so precisely because they know that their rulings create precedents; they want to narrow the scope of future applications of their rulings given the various problems described above, most importantly the lack of sufficient information about future problems. A distinctive problem involves the possibility of too *much* information. A particular case may have a surplus of apparently relevant details, and perhaps future cases will lack one or more of the relevant features, and this will be the source of the concern with creating wide precedents. The existence of (inter alia) features X or Y in case A, missing in case B, makes it hazardous to generate a rule in case A that would govern case B. The narrow writing and reception of the Supreme Court's decision in the celebrated Amish case, allowing an exemption of Amish children from mandatory public schooling, is an example.

Small steps can also make special sense if circumstances are changing rapidly. Perhaps relevant facts and values will change in such a way as to make a rule quickly anachronistic even if it is well suited to present conditions. Thus it is possible that any decision involving the application of the First Amendment to new communications technologies, including the internet, should be narrow, because a broad decision, rendered at this time, would be likely to go wrong. On this view, a small step is best because of the likelihood that a broad rule would be mistaken when applied to cases not before the court.

In an argument very much in this spirit, Joseph Raz has connected a kind of small step – the form usually produced by analogical reasoning – to the special problems created by one-shot interventions into complex systems.[13] In Raz's view, courts reason by analogy in order to prevent unintended side effects from large disruptions. Similarly supportive of the small-step strategy, the German psychologist Dietrich Dorner has done some illuminating computer experiments designed to see whether people can engage in successful social engineering.[14] Participants are asked to solve problems faced by the inhabitants of some region of the world. Through the magic of the computer, many policy initiatives are available to solve the relevant problems (improved care of cattle, childhood immunization, drilling more wells). But most of the participants produce eventual calamities, because they do not see the complex, system-wide effects of particular interventions. Only the rare participant is able to see a number of steps down the road, to understand the multiple effects of one-shot interventions on the system. The successful participants are alert to this risk and take small, reversible steps, allowing planning to occur over time. Hence Dorner, along with others focusing on the problems created by interventions into systems,[15] argues in favor of small steps. Judges face similar problems, and incremental decisions are a good way of responding to the particular problem of bounded rationality created by ignorance of possible adverse effects.

From these points we can see that small steps may be better than rules or than delegation. Often an institution lacks the information to generate a clear path for the future; often no appropriate delegate has that information. If circumstances are changing rapidly, any rule or presumption might be confounded by subsequent developments. What is especially important is that movement in any particular direction should be reversible if problems arise. On the other hand, a small steps approach embodies a kind of big (if temporary) decision in favor of the status quo; a court that tries to handle a problem of discrimination incrementally may allow unjust practices to continue, and so too with a state that is trying to alleviate the problem of joblessness in poor areas. A small steps approach might also undermine planning and fail to provide advance notice of the content of law or policy. Thus it cannot be said that a small steps approach is, in the abstract, a rational approach to bounded rationality;[16] whether it is a (fully optimal) response to bounded rationality, or a (suboptimal) reflection of bounded rationality, depends on the context.

The analysis is similar outside of the governmental setting. Agents might take small steps because they lack the information that would enable them to generate a rule or presumption, or because the decision they face is unique and not likely to be repeated, so that there is no reason for a rule or a presumption. Or small steps may follow from the likelihood of change over time, from the fact that a large decision might have unintended consequences, or from the wish to avoid or at least to defer the responsibility for large-scale change.

Summary and Conclusions

Second-Order Strategies

The discussion is summarized in Table 7.2. Recall that the terms "low" and "high" refer to the overall costs of the decision, which are not necessarily borne by the same agent: With Low-High the costs are split between delegator and delegate; with High-Low they may be split between an institution (which makes the rules, say) and an agent (who follows the rules).

There are two principal conclusions. The first is that no second-order strategy can reasonably be preferred in the abstract. The second is that it is possible to identify the settings in which one or another is likely to make sense, and also the factors that argue in favor of, or against, any particular approach.

Table 7.2. *Second-Order Strategies*

Strategies	Examples	Potential Advantages	Potential Disadvantages	Appropriate Context
Low-High: delegation	Spouses and friends, administrative agencies	Relief from direct responsibility for ultimate decisions, increased chance for good outcomes	Problems relating to trust, fairness, and responsibility; possible high costs in deciding whether and to whom to delegate	Availability of appropriate and trustworthy delegate; high burdens of, or perceived likelihood of error in, decision by delegator
Low-Low: picking, small steps, various heuristics	Anglo-American common law, lotteries, big personal decisions	Low overall costs, reversibility, coping with change and with unintended consequences	Difficulty of planning, high aggregate decision costs, multiple mistakes	Equipoise/symmetry of preferences or values, reasonable aversion to drastic changes, reasonable fear of unanticipated consequences
High-Low: rules, presumptions, routines	Speed limit laws, legal formalism, criminal law, recovering addicts, rigid people	Low costs of numerous decisions once in place, uniformity, facilitates planning	Difficulty of generating good rules or presumptions, mistakes once in place	Sheer number of anticipated decisions/decision makers, repetitive nature of future decisions, need for planning, confidence in ability to generate ex ante decisions
High-High	Certain Henry James characters, dysfunctional governments	None (unless decision costs are actually pleasant to incur and decisions end up being good)	Paralysis; unpopularity, individual or institutional collapse	Agency or institution cannot do otherwise

Do People Actually Make Second-Order Decisions? Should They?

An important underlying issue remains: Do people, or institutions, actually make a self-conscious decision about which second-order strategy to favor, given the menu of possibilities? Sometimes this is indeed the case. A legislature may, for example, deliberate and decide to delegate rather than to generate rules; a court may choose, self-consciously, to proceed incrementally; having rejected the alternatives, a president may recommend a lottery system rather than other alternatives for admitting certain aliens to the country. An institution or a person may well make an all-things-considered decision in favor of one or another second-order strategy.

Sometimes, however, a rapid assessment of the situation takes place, rather than a full or deliberative weighing of alternative courses of action. This is often the case in private decisions, where judgments often seem immediate. Indeed, second-order decisions might be too costly if they were a product of an optimizing strategy; so taken, they would present many of the problems of first-order decisions. As in the case of first-order decisions, it sometimes makes sense to proceed with what seems best, rather than to maximize in any systematic fashion, simply because the former way of proceeding is easier (and thus may maximize once we consider decision costs of various kinds). For both institutions and individuals, the salient features of the context usually suggest a particular kind of second-order strategy; there is no reason to think long and hard about the second-order decision.

These are intended as descriptive points about the operation of practical reason. But there is a normative issue here as well; we often say that people's second-order decisions go wrong. For example, legal formalists, most prominently Justice Antonin Scalia, argue for a High-Low strategy, but they do so on an a priori basis, without engaging the pragmatic and empirical issues at stake, and without showing that this strategy is preferable to the realistic second-order alternatives.[17] The same can be said about those who favor incrementalism, or small steps, in political or legal reasoning.[18] There are many ways of handling decisional burdens, and others may be better. Pathologically rigid rules can be a serious problem for law and policy; the Sentencing Guidelines are often criticized on this ground, and whether or not the criticism is just, pathological rigidity is a problem for societies as well as individuals. Sometimes delegation is a most unfortunate route to travel. At the political level, and occasionally at the individual level too, it would be much better to be more explicit and self-conscious about the diverse possibilities, so as to ensure that societies and institutions do not find themselves making bad second-order decisions, or choosing a second-order strategy without a sense of the candidates. We have attempted to systematize the underlying considerations here.

Rationality and Bounded Rationality

Second-order decisions are often a response to a particular source of bounded rationality: limited information. As we have emphasized, each of the second-order strategies is a potentially optimal solution to the problems posed by unanticipated side effects and the difficulty of obtaining knowledge about the future. Or second-order decisions may respond to an institution's awareness that it is prone to use unreliable heuristic devices when a decision must be made on the spot. In addition, second-order strategies may be a response to motivational rather than cognitive problems; people try, for example, to counteract their own tendencies toward impulsiveness, myopia, and unrealistic optimism[19] through rules and presumptions. In these ways second-order decisions can be seen as entirely rational responses by rational actors making those decisions with full awareness of the costs of obtaining information and of their own propensities for error.

Although rational actors make second-order decisions to overcome their own bounded rationality, bounded rationality can affect those decisions as well. A lack of information often presses people and institutions in the direction of suboptimal second-order strategies; an inadequately informed court, for example, may choose small steps even though rules would be far better. We suspect that the availability heuristic – by which people make judgments by asking what similar cases come readily to mind – underlies some erroneous judgments about appropriate second-order strategies.[20] Bad second-order decisions can also be a result of motivational problems. An impulsive or myopic institution may fail to see the extent to which rules will be confounded by subsequent developments; an unrealistically optimistic institution may overestimate its capacity to make optimal small steps; using simple heuristics, people may choose second-order strategies that badly disserve their own goals, even when the stakes are high.[21]

Conclusion

Ordinary people and official institutions are often reluctant to make on-the-spot decisions; they respond with one or another second-order strategy. The diverse candidates raise separable ethical and political problems. Some such strategies involve high initial burdens but generate a relatively simple, low-burden mechanism for deciding subsequent cases. These strategies, generally taking the form of rules or presumptions, seem best when the anticipated decisions are numerous and repetitive and when advance notice and planning are important. Other strategies involve both light initial burdens and light burdens at the time of making the ultimate decision. These approaches work well when a degree of randomization is appealing on normative grounds (perhaps because choices are otherwise in equipoise, or because no one should or will take responsibility for deliberate decision), or when a first-order decision is simply too difficult to make (because of the cognitive or emotional burdens involved in the choice) or includes too many imponderables and a risk of large unintended consequences.

Still other strategies involve low initial burdens but high, exported burdens at the time of decision, as when a delegation is made to another person or institution, or (in a metaphor) to one's future self. Delegations take many different forms, with more or less control retained by the person or institution making the delegation. Strategies of delegation make sense when a delegate is available who has relevant expertise (perhaps because he is a specialist) or is otherwise trustworthy (perhaps because he does not suffer from bias or some other motivational problem), or when there are special political, strategic, or other advantages to placing the responsibility for decision on some other person or institution. Delegations can raise serious ethical or political issues and create problems of unfairness, as when delegates are burdened with tasks that they do not voluntarily assume, or would not assume under just conditions, and when the delegation is inconsistent with the social role of the delegator, such as a legislature or a court. Hence delegations can be troubling from the point of view of democracy or the separation of powers.

The final set of cases involve high burdens both before and at the time of decision, as in certain fictional characters, and in highly dysfunctional institutions. We have merely gestured in the direction of this strategy, which may make sense under extreme circumstances, but which generally can be considered best only on the assumption that bearing high overall burdens of decision is an affirmative good (perhaps for moral reasons) or even something to relish. This assumption might appear peculiar, but it undoubtedly helps explain some otherwise puzzling human behavior, behavior that often provides the motivation to consider the other, more promising second-order decisions discussed here.

Notes

1 See, e.g., Jon Elster, *Solomonic Judgments: Studies in the Limitations of Rationality* (1989); John Rawls, Two Concepts of Rules, 64 *Phil. Rev.* 3 (1955); Edward F. McClennen, *Rationality and Dynamic Choice* (1990). Within economics, see, e.g., Thomas C. Schelling, Enforcing Rules on Oneself, 1 *J.L. Econ. & Org.* 357 (1985); Louis Kaplow, Rules Versus Standards: An Economic Analysis, 42 *Duke L. J.* 557 (1992); Richard H. Thaler, *Quasi-rational Economics* (1991).

2 It is important here to distinguish between a presumption and a rule with exceptions. A rule with exceptions has the following structure: "Do X – except in circumstances A, in which case you are exempt from doing X." For example, "Observe the speed limit – except when you're driving a police car or an ambulance in an emergency, in which cases you may exceed it." By contrast, a typical presumption says something like "Act on the assumption that P – unless and until circumstances A are shown to obtain, in which case, do something else." The two amount to the same thing when the agent knows whether or not circumstances A obtain. The two are

quite different when the agent lacks that information. With a presumption, you can proceed without the information; with a rule with exceptions, you cannot proceed, that is, you are justified neither in doing X nor in not doing X.

3 See Edna Ullmann-Margalit, Opting: The Case of "Big" Decisions, in *The 1985 Yearbook of the Wissenschaftskelleg zu Berlin*.

4 See Edward H. Levi, *An Introduction to Legal Reasoning* (1949). In political science, see Charles E. Lindblom, The Science of Muddling Through, 19 *Pub. Admin. Rev.* 79 (1959), which offers an influential and relevant argument about incrementalism. See also Charles E. Lindblom, Still Muddling, Not Yet Through, 39 *Pub. Admin. Rev.* 517 (1979).

5 See Edna Ullmann-Margalit and Sidney Morgenbesser, Picking and Choosing, 44 *Soc. Res.* 757 (1977).

6 See, e.g., John Conlisk, Why Bounded Rationality? 34 *J. Econ. Literature* 669 (1996).

7 See Edna Ullmann-Margalit, On Not Wanting to Know, in *Reasoning Practically* (1999); Gerald Dworkin, Is More Choice Better Than Less? in *Autonomy* (1991).

8 See Stephen Holmes, *Passions and Constraint: On the Theory of Liberal Democracy* (1995).

9 See, e.g., Elster, supra note 1, and Schelling, supra note 1, who see that precommitment strategies are often appropriate, but who do not discuss the choice between rules and alternative candidates, or whether some other second-order strategy might be better.

10 See Kaplow, supra note 1.

11 Cf. Thomas C. Schelling, Self-command in Practice, in Policy, and in a Theory of Rational Choice, 96 *Am. Econ. Rev.*, May 1984, Papers & Proceedings, at 1.

12 On ethical and political issues associated with lotteries in general, see Elster, supra note 1, at 36–122.

13 Joseph Raz, *The Authority of Law: Essays in Law and Morality* (1979).

14 See Dietrich Dorner, *The Logic of Failure: Why Things Go Wrong and What We Can Do to Make Them Right* (1996).

15 See James C. Scott, *Seeing Like the State: How Certain Schemes to Improve the Human Condition Have Failed* (1998).

16 In one form or other, small steps are favored in Scott, supra note 15; Levi, supra note 4; Alexander M. Bickel, *The Least Dangerous Branch* (1962).

17 See Antonin Scalia, *A Matter of Interpretation: Federal Courts and the Law* (1997).

18 See Levi, supra note 4.

19 See Neil D. Weinstein, Unrealistic Optimism About Susceptibility to Health Problems: Conclusions from a Community-Wide Sample, 10 *J. Behav. Med.* 481 (1987) for a general discussion.

20 Cf. Itzhak Gilboa and David Schmeidler, Case-Based Decision Theory, 110 *Q.J. Econ.* 605 (1995); Daniel Kahneman and Dan Lovallo, Timid Choices and Bold Forecasts: A Cognitive Perspective on Risk Taking, 39 *Mgmt. Sci.* 17 (1993).

21 See Yuen Foong Khong, *Analogies at War: Korea, Munich, Dien Bien Phu, and the Vietnam Decisions of 1965* (1992) for suggestive examples.

Part III

Valuation: Values and Dollars in the Legal System

8 Experimental Tests of the Endowment Effect and the Coase Theorem*

Daniel Kahneman, Jack L. Knetsch, and Richard H. Thaler

The standard assumptions of economic theory imply that when income effects are small, differences between an individual's maximum willingness to pay for a good (WTP) and minimum compensation demanded for the same entitlement (willingness to accept or WTA) should be negligible.[1] Thus, indifference curves are drawn without reference to current endowments, any difference between equivalent and compensating variation assessments of welfare changes are in practice ignored,[2] and there is wide acceptance of the Coase Theorem assertion that, subject to income effects, the allocation of resources will be independent of the assignment of property rights when costless trades are possible.

The assumption that entitlements do not affect value contrasts sharply with empirical observations of significantly higher selling than buying prices. For example, Thaler found that the minimal compensation demanded for accepting a .001 risk of sudden death was higher by one or two orders of magnitude than the amount people were willing to pay to eliminate an identical existing risk.[3] Other examples of similar reported findings are summarized in Table 8.1. The disparities observed in these examples are clearly too large to be explained plausibly by income effects.

Several factors probably contribute to the discrepancies between the evaluations of buyers and sellers documented in Table 8.1. The perceived illegitimacy of the transaction may, for example, contribute to the extraordinary high demand for personal compensation for agreeing to the loss of a public good.[4] Standard bargaining habits may also contribute to a discrepancy between the stated reservation prices of buyers and sellers. Sellers are often rewarded for overstating their true value, and buyers for understating theirs.[5] By force of habit they may misrepresent their true valuations even

* Financial support was provided by Fisheries and Oceans Canada, the Ontario Ministry of the Environment, and the behavioral economics program of the Alfred P. Sloan Foundation. The authors wish to thank Vernon Smith for encouraging us to conduct these experiments and for providing extensive comments on earlier drafts.

Table 8.1. *Summary of Past Tests of Evaluation Disparity*

	Means			Medians		
Study and Entitlement	WTP	WTA	Ratio	WTP	WTA	Ratio
Hypothetical Surveys:						
Hammack and Brown (1974)						
Marshes[37]	$247	$1,044	4.2	n.a.	n.a.	n.a.
Sinclair (1976)						
Fishing[38]	n.a.	n.a.	n.a.	35	100	2.9
Banford et al. (1979)						
Fishing pier	43	120	2.8	47	129	2.7
Postal service[39]	22	93	4.2	22	106	4.8
Bishop and Heberlein (1979)						
Goose hunting permits[40]	21	101	4.8	n.a.	n.a.	n.a.
Rowe et al. (1980)						
Visibility[41]	1.33	3.49	2.6	n.a.	n.a.	n.a.
Brookshire et al. (1980)[42]						
Elk hunting[a]	54	143	2.6	n.a.	n.a.	n.a.
Heberlein and Bishop (1985)						
Deer hunting[43]	31	513	16.5	n.a.	n.a.	n.a.
Real Exchange Experiments:						
Knetsch and Sinden (1984)						
Lottery tickets[44]	1.28	5.18	4.0	n.a.	n.a.	n.a.
Heberlein and Bishop (1985)						
Deer hunting[45]	25	172	6.9	n.a.	n.a.	n.a.
Coursey et al. (1987)[46]						
Taste SOA[b]	3.45	4.71	1.4	1.33	3.49	2.6
Brookshire and Coursey (1987)[47]						
Park trees[b,c]	10.12	56.60	5.6	6.30	12.96	2.1

[a] Middle-level change of several used in study.
[b] Final values after multiple iterations.
[c] Average of two levels of tree plantings.

when such misrepresentation confers no advantage, as in answering hypothetical questions or one-shot or single transactions. In such situations the buying-selling discrepancy is simply a strategic mistake, which experienced traders will learn to avoid.[6]

The hypothesis of interest here is that many discrepancies between WTA and WTP, far from being a mistake, reflect a genuine effect of reference positions on preferences. Thaler labeled the increased value of a good to an individual when the good becomes part of the individual's endowment the *endowment effect*.[7] This effect is a manifestation of *loss aversion*, the generalization that losses are weighted substantially more than objectively commensurate gains in the evaluation of prospects and trades.[8] An implication of this asymmetry is that if a good is evaluated as a loss when it is given up, and as a gain when it is acquired, loss aversion will, on average, induce a higher dollar value for owners than for potential buyers, reducing the set of mutually acceptable trades.

There are some cases when no endowment effect would be expected, such as when goods are purchased for resale rather than for utilization. A particularly clear case of a good held exclusively for resale is the notional token typically traded in experimental markets commonly used to test the efficiency of market institutions.[9] Such experiments employ the *induced value technique* in which the objects of trade are tokens to which private redemption values that vary among individual participants have been assigned by the experimenter.[10] Subjects can obtain the prescribed value assigned for the tokens when redeeming them at the end of the trading period; the tokens are otherwise worthless.

No endowment effect would be expected for such tokens, which are valued only because they can be redeemed for cash. Thus, buyers and sellers should both value tokens at the induced value they have been assigned. Markets for induced value tokens can therefore be used as a control condition to determine whether differences between the values of buyers and sellers in other markets could be attributable to transaction costs, misunderstandings, or habitual strategies of bargaining. Any discrepancy between the buying and selling values can be isolated in an experiment by comparing the outcomes of markets for real goods with those of otherwise identical markets for induced value tokens. If no differences in values are observed for the induced value tokens, then economic theory predicts that no differences between buying and selling values will be observed for consumption goods evaluated and traded under the same conditions.

The results from a series of experiments involving real exchanges of tokens and of various consumption goods are reported in this paper. In each case, a random allocation design was used to test for the presence of an endowment effect. Half of the subjects were endowed with a good and become potential sellers in each market; the other half of the subjects were potential buyers. Conventional economic analysis yields the simple prediction that one-half of the goods should be traded in voluntary exchanges. If value is unaffected by ownership, then the distribution of values in the two groups should be the same except for sampling variation. The supply-and-demand curves should therefore be mirror images of each other, intersecting at their common median. The null hypothesis is, therefore, that half of the goods provided should change hands. Label this predicted volume

V^*. If there is an endowment effect, the value of the good will be higher for sellers than for buyers, and observed volume V will be less than V^*. The ratio V/V^* provides a unit-free measure of the undertrading that is produced by the effect of ownership on value. To test the hypothesis that market experience eliminates undertrading, the markets were repeated several times.

A test for the possibility that observed undertrading was due to transaction costs was provided by a comparison of the results from a series of induced value markets with those from the subsequent goods markets carried out with identical trading rules. Notice that this comparison can also be used to eliminate numerous other possible explanations of the observed undertrading. For example, if the instructions to the subjects are confusing or misleading, the effects should show up in both the induced value markets and the experimental markets for real goods. The second section describes studies of trading volume in induced value markets and in consumption goods markets. The third section provides a further test for strategic behavior and demonstrates that the disparity findings are not likely to be due to this cause. The fourth section investigates the extent to which the undertrading of goods is produced by reluctance to buy and reluctance to sell, and the fifth section examines undertrading in bilateral negotiations and provides a test of the Coase Theorem. The sixth section describes an experiment that rules out income effects and a trophy effect as explanations of the observed valuation disparity. Implications of the observed effects are discussed in the final section.

Repeated Market Experiments

In Experiment 1, forty-four students in an advanced undergraduate law and economics class at Cornell University received a packet of general instructions plus eleven forms, one for each of the markets that were conducted in the experiment. (The instructions for all experiments are available from the authors.) The first three markets were for induced value tokens. Sellers received the following instructions (with differences for buyers in brackets):

> In this market the objects being traded are tokens. You are an owner, so you now own a token [You are a buyer, so you have an opportunity to buy a token] which has a value to you of $x. It has this value to you because the experimenter will give you this much money for it. The value of the token is different for different individuals. A price for the tokens will be determined later. For each of the prices listed below, please indicate whether you prefer to: (1) Sell your token at this price, and receive the market price. [Buy a token at this price and cash it in for the sum of money indicated above.] (2) Keep your token and cash it in for the sum of money indicated above. [Not buy a token at this price.] For each price indicate your decision by marking an X in the appropriate column.

Part of the response form for sellers follows:

At a price of $8.75 I will sell ____ I will not sell ____
At a price of $8.25 I will sell ____ I will not sell ____

The same rectangular distribution of values – ranging from $0.25 to $8.75 in steps of 50 cents – was prepared for both buyers and sellers. Because not all the forms were actually distributed, however, the induced supply-and-demand curves were not always precisely symmetrical. Subjects alternated between the buyer and seller roles in the three successive markets and were assigned a different individual redemption value in each trial.

Experimenters collected the forms from all participants after each market period and immediately calculated and announced the market-clearing price,[11] the number of trades, and whether or not there was excess demand or supply at the market-clearing price.[12] Three buyers and three sellers were selected at random after each of the induced markets and were paid off according to the preferences stated on their forms and the market-clearing price for that period.

Immediately after the three induced value markets, subjects on alternating seats were given Cornell coffee mugs, which sell for $6.00 each at the bookstore. The experimenter asked all participants to examine a mug, either their own or their neighbor's. The experimenter then informed the subjects that four markets for mugs would be conducted using the same procedures as the prior induced markets with two exceptions: (1) One of the four market trials would subsequently be selected at random, and only the trades made on this trial would be executed. (2) On the binding market trial, *all* trades would be implemented, unlike the subset implemented in the induced value markets.[13] The initial assignment of buyer and seller roles was maintained for all four trading periods. The clearing price and the number of trades were announced after each period. The market that "counted" was indicated after the fourth period, and transactions were executed immediately: All sellers who had indicated that they would give up their mug for sums at the market-clearing price exchanged their mugs for cash, and successful buyers paid this same price and received their mug. This design was used to permit learning to take place over successive trials and yet make each trial potentially binding. The same procedure was then followed for four more successive markets using boxed ballpoint pens with a visible bookstore price tag of $3.98, which were distributed to the subjects who had been buyers in the mug markets.

For each goods market subjects completed a form similar to that used for the induced value tokens, with the following instructions:

You now own the object in your possession. [You do not own the object that you see in the possession of some of your neighbors.] You have the option of selling it [buying one] if a price, which will be determined later, is acceptable to you. For each of the possible prices below indicate whether you wish to: (1) Sell your object and receive this price, [Pay this price and receive an object to take home with you], or (2) Keep your object and take it home with you. [Not buy an object at this price.] For each price indicate your decision by marking an X in the appropriate column.

The buyers and sellers in the consumption goods markets faced the same incentives as they had experienced in the induced value markets. Buyers maximized their potential gain by agreeing to buy at all prices below the value they ascribed to the good, and sellers maximized their welfare by agreeing to sell at all prices above the good's worth to them. As in the induced value markets, it was in the best interest of the participants to act as price takers.

As shown in Table 8.2, the markets for induced value tokens and consumption goods yielded sharply different results. In the induced value markets, as expected, the median buying and selling prices were identical. The ratio of actual to predicted volume (V/V^*) was 1.0, aggregating over the three periods. In contrast, median selling prices in the mug and pen markets were more than twice median buying prices, and the V/V^* ratio was only .20 for mugs and .41 for pens. Observed volume did not increase over successive

Table 8.2. *Results of Experiment 1*

Induced Value Markets (Expected Trades = 11)			
Trial	Trades	Price	Expected Price
1	12	$3.75	$3.75
2	11	4.75	4.75
3	10	4.25	4.25

Trial	Trades	Price	Median Buyer Reservation Price	Median Seller Reservation Price
Mugs (Expected Trades = 11)				
4	4	$4.25	$2.75	$5.25
5	1	4.75	2.25	5.25
6	2	4.50	2.25	5.25
7	2	4.25	2.25	5.25
Pens (Expected Trades = 11)				
8	4	1.25	.75	2.50
9	5	1.25	.75	1.75
10	4	1.25	.75	2.25
11	5	1.25	.75	1.75

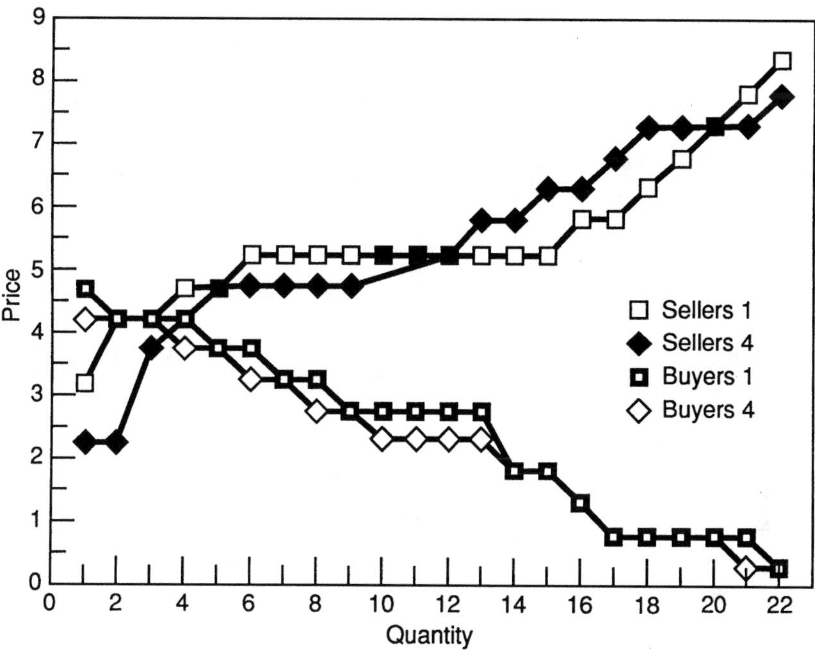

Figure 8.1. Supply and Demand Curves, Markets 1 and 4.

periods in either the mug or pen markets, providing no indication that subjects learned to adopt equal buying and selling prices.

The results of the first and last markets for coffee mugs are also displayed in Figure 8.1. There are five features to notice in this figure. (1) Both buyers and sellers display a wide range of values, indicating that in the absence of an endowment effect there would be enough rents to produce gains from trade. Indeed, the range of values is similar to that used in the induced value markets, which had near perfect market efficiency. (2) The distribution of selling prices has a single mode, unlike some recent results in which an evaluation discrepancy could be explained by a bimodal distribution of compensation demanded.[14] (3) The payment of a small commission for trading, such as \$0.25 per trade, would not significantly alter the results. (4) The mugs were desirable. Every subject assigned a positive value to the mug, and the lowest value assigned by a seller was \$2.25. (5) Neither demand nor supply changed much between the first and last markets.

Experiment 2 was conducted in an undergraduate microeconomics class at Cornell ($N = 38$). The procedure was identical to that of Experiment 1, except that the second consumption good was a pair of folding binoculars in a cardboard frame, available at the bookstore for \$4. The results are reported in Table 8.3.

Table 8.3. *Results of Experiment 2*

Induced Value Markets				
Trial	Actual Trades	Expected Trades	Price	Expected Price
1	10	10	$3.75	$4.25
2	9	10	4.75	4.25
3	7	8	4.25	4.75
Trial	Trades	Price	Median Buyer Reservation Price	Median Seller Reservation Price
Mugs (Expected Trades = 9.5)				
4	3	$3.75	$1.75	$4.75
5	3	3.25	2.25	4.75
6	2	3.25	2.25	4.75
7	2	3.25	2.25	4.25
Binoculars (Expected Trades = 9.5)				
8	4	1.25	.75	1.25
9	4	.75	.75	1.25
10	3	.75	.75	1.75
11	3	.75	.75	1.75

In Experiments 3 and 4, conducted in Simon Fraser University undergraduate economics classes, the subjects were asked to provide minimum selling prices or maximum buying prices rather than answer the series of "yes or no" questions used in Experiments 1 and 2. The induced value markets were done with no monetary payoffs and were followed by four markets for pens in Experiment 3 and five markets for mugs in Experiment 4. In Experiment 3 subjects were told that the first three markets for pens would be for practice, so only the fourth and final market would be binding. In Experiment 4, one of the five markets was selected at random to count, as in Experiments 1 and 2. Other procedures were unchanged. The results are shown in Table 8.4.

Experiments 2–4 all yielded results similar to those obtained in Experiment 1. Summing over the induced value markets in all four experiments, the V/V^* index was .91. This excellent performance was achieved without participants having the benefit of experience with the trading rules, with limited monetary incentives in Experiments 1 and 2, and with no monetary incentives in Experiments 3 and 4. In the markets for consumption goods,

Table 8.4. *Results of Experiments 3 and 4*

	Trial	*N*	Object	Actual Trades	Expected Trades	Ratio of Seller MV* to Buyer MV*
Experiment 3	1	26	Induced	5	6.5	n.a.
	2	26	Pen	2	6.5	7.2
	3	26	"	2	6.5	7.2
	4	26	"	2	6.5	5.6
	5	26	"	1	6.5	6.7
Experiment 4	1	74	Induced	15	18.5	n.a.
	2	74	"	16	18.5	n.a.
	3	74	Mug	6	18.5	3.8
	4	74	"	4	18.5	2.8
	5	72	"	4	18	2.2
	6	73	"	8	18	1.8
	7	74	"	8	18.5	1.8

* Mean Value

with all participants facing monetary incentives and having gained experience with the market rules from the induced value markets, V/V^* averaged .31, and median selling prices were more than double the corresponding buying prices. Trading procedures were precisely identical in markets for goods and for induced value tokens. The high volume of trade in money tokens therefore eliminates transaction costs (or any other feature that was present in both types of markets) as an explanation of the observed undertrading of consumption goods.

It should be noted that subjects in the position of buyers were not given money to use for purchases, but rather had to make transactions using their own money. (Subjects were told to bring money to class, and that credit and change would be available if necessary. Some subjects borrowed from friends to make payments.) The aim was to study transactions in a realistic setting. While the present design makes potential sellers slightly wealthier, at least in the first market, the magnitude of the possible income effect is trivial. In one of the markets the equilibrium price was only 75 cents, and the prices in other markets were never above a few dollars. Also, as will be shown in Experiments 7 and 8, equal undertrading was found in designs that eliminated the possibility of an income effect or cash constraint.

As shown in Tables 8.2–8.4, subjects showed almost no undertrading even on their first trial in an induced value market. Evidently neither bargaining habits nor any transaction costs impede trading in money tokens. On the other hand, there is no indication that participants in the markets for goods learned to make valuations independent of their entitlements. The discrepant evaluations of buyers and sellers remained stable over four, and in one case five, successive markets for the same good and did not change systematically over repeated markets for successive goods.

A difference in procedure probably explains the apparent conflict between these results and the conclusion reached in some other studies that the WTA-WTP discrepancy is greatly reduced by market experience. The studies that reported a disciplinary effect of market experience assessed this effect by comparing the responses of buyers and sellers in preliminary hypothetical questions or nonbinding market trials to their behavior in a subsequent binding trial with real monetary payoffs.[15] In the present experiments, the markets for consumption goods were real and potentially binding from the first trial, and the WTA-WTP discrepancy was found to be stable over a series of such binding trials.

It should be stressed that previous research did not actually demonstrate that the discrepancy between buyers and sellers is eliminated in markets. Although the discrepancy between the final selling and buying prices in the experiment of Coursey et al.[16] was not statistically significant, the ratio of median prices of sellers and buyers was still 2.6.[17] If the buyers and sellers had been allowed to trade according to their final bids, a total of nine advantageous exchanges would have occurred between the two groups, compared to the theoretical expectation of sixteen trades.[18] This V/V^* ratio of .56 is quite similar to the ratios observed in Experiments 1–4. In the study by Brookshire and Coursey,[19] the ratio of mean prices was indeed reduced by experience, from a high of 77 for initial hypothetical survey responses to 6.1 in the first potentially binding auction conducted in a laboratory. However, the ratio remained at 5.6 in the final auction.

Testing for Misrepresentation

As previously stated, subjects faced identical incentives in the induced value and consumption goods phases of Experiments 1–4. Therefore, it seems safe to attribute the difference in observed trading to the endowment effect. However, some readers of early drafts of this paper have suggested that because of the way market prices were determined, subjects might have felt they had an incentive to misstate their true values in order to influence the price, and perhaps this incentive was perceived to be greater in the consumption goods markets. To eliminate this possible interpretation of the previous results Experiment 5 was carried out in a manner similar to the first four experiments, except that subjects were told that the price would be selected at random. As is well known, this is an incentive-compatible procedure for eliciting values.[20]

Each participant received instructions that read in part (with appropriate alternative wording in the buyers' forms):

> After you have finished, one of the prices listed below will be selected at random and any exchanges will take place at that price. If you have indicated you will sell at this price you will receive this amount of money and will give up the mug; if you have indicated that you will keep the mug at this price then no exchange will be made and you can take the mug home with you. . . . Your decision can have no effect on the price actually used because the price will be selected at random.

The experiment was conducted in a series of six tutorial groups of a business statistics class at Simon Fraser University. The use of small groups helped assure complete understanding of the instructions, and the exercises were conducted over the course of a single day to minimize opportunities for communication between participants. Each group was divided equally, and half the subjects were designated as sellers by random selection, and the other half became buyers. A total of fifty-nine people took part.

Two induced value markets for hypothetical payoffs and a subsequent third real exchange market for money and mugs were conducted with identical trading rules used in all three. All participants maintained the same role as either buyers or sellers for the three markets. As in Experiments 1 and 2, the prices that individuals chose to buy or to sell were selected from possible prices ranging from $0 to $9.50 listed by 50 cent increments.

The results of this experiment were nearly identical to the earlier ones in which the actual exchanges were based on the market clearing price. Even though possibly less motivating hypothetical values were used in the two induced value markets, nearly all participants pursued a profit-maximizing selection of prices to buy or sell the assets. Fourteen exchanges at a price of $4.75 were expected in the first induced value market on the basis of the randomly distributed values written on the forms. Thirteen trades at this price were indicated by the prices actually selected by the participants. The results of the second hypothetical induced value market were equally convincing with sixteen of the seventeen expected exchanges made at the expected price of $5.75. The procedures and incentives were apparently well understood by the participants.

Mugs, comparable to those used in other experiments, were distributed to the potential sellers after the induced value markets were completed. A mug was also shown to all of the potential buyers. The following form with instructions, nearly identical to the ones used in the induced value markets, was then distributed (with the alternative wording for buyers in brackets):

> You now [do not] have, and own a mug which you can keep and take home. You also have the option of selling it and receiving [buying one to take home by paying] money for it.
>
> For each of the possible prices listed below, please indicate whether you wish to:
>
> (1) Receive [pay] that amount of money and sell your [buy a] mug,
>
> or
>
> (2) Not sell your [buy a] mug at this price.

After you have finished, one of the prices listed below will be selected at random and any exchanges will take place at that price. If you have indicated you will sell [buy] at this price you will receive this amount of money [a mug] and will give up the mug [pay this amount of money]; if you have indicated that you will keep the [not buy a] mug at this price then no exchange will be made and you can take the mug home with you [do not pay anything].

Notice the following two things: (1) Your decision can have no effect on the price actually used because the price will be selected at random. (2) It is in your interest to indicate your true preferences at each of the possible prices listed below.

For each price indicate your decision by marking an X in the appropriate column.

	I Will Sell [Buy]	I Will Keep [Not Buy] the Mug
If the price is $0	———	———
If the price is $0.50	———	———
. . .		
If the price is $9.50	———	———

After the instructions were read, reviewed by the experimenter, and questions answered, participants completed the forms indicating either their lowest selling price or highest buying price. A random price, from among the list from $0 to $9.50, was then drawn, and exchanges based on this price were completed.

The results again showed a large and significant endowment effect. Given the twenty-nine potential buyers, thirty potential sellers, and the random distribution of the mugs, 14.5 exchanges would be expected if entitlements did not influence valuations. Instead, only six were indicated on the basis of the values actually selected by the potential buyers and sellers ($V/V^* = .41$). The median selling price of $5.75 was over twice the median buying price of $2.25, and the means were $5.78 and $2.21 respectively.

Reluctance to Buy Versus Reluctance to Sell

Exchanges of money and a good (or between two goods) offer the possibilities of four comparisons: a choice between gaining either the good or money; a choice between losing one or the other; buying (giving up money for the good); and selling (giving up the good for money).[21] The endowment effect results from a difference between the relative preferences for the good and money. The comparison of buying and selling to simple choices between gains permits an analysis of the discrepancy between WTA and WTP into two components: reluctance to sell (exchanging the good for money) and reluctance to buy (exchanging money for the good).

Experiments 6 and 7 were carried out to assess the weight of reluctance to buy and reluctance to sell in undertrading of a good similar to the goods used in the earlier experiments. The subjects in Experiment 6 were seventy-seven Simon Fraser students, randomly assigned to three groups. Members of one group, designated Sellers, were given a coffee mug, and were asked to indicate whether or not they would sell the mug at a series of prices ranging from $0 to $9.25. A group of Buyers indicated whether they were willing to buy a mug at each of these prices. Finally, Choosers were asked to choose, for each of the possible prices, between receiving a mug or cash.

The results again reveal substantial undertrading: While 12.5 trades were expected between Buyers and Sellers, only three trades took place ($V/V^* =$ 0.24). The median valuations were: Sellers, $7.12; Choosers, $3.12; and Buyers, $2.87. The close similarity of results for Buyers and Choosers indicates that there was relatively little reluctance to pay for the mug.

Experiment 7 was carried out with 117 students at the University of British Columbia. It used an identical design except that price tags were left on the mugs. The results were fully consistent with those in Experiment 6. Nineteen trades were expected on the basis of valuation equivalence, but only one was concluded on the basis of actual valuations ($V/V^* = .05$). The median valuation of Sellers was $7.00, Choosers $3.50, and Buyers $2.00.

It is worth noting that these results eliminate any form of income effect as an explanation of the discrepant valuations since the positions of Sellers and Choosers were strictly identical. The allocation of a particular mug to each Seller evidently induced a sense of endowment that the Choosers did not share: The median value of the mug to the Sellers was more than double the value indicated by the Choosers even though their choices were objectively the same. The results imply that the observed undertrading of consumption goods may be largely due to a reluctance to part with entitlements.

Bilateral Bargaining and the Coase Theorem

According to the Coase Theorem, the allocation of resources to individuals who can bargain and transact at no cost should be independent of initial property rights. However, if the marginal rate of substitution between one good and another is affected by endowment, then the individual who is assigned the property right to a good will be more likely to retain it. A bilateral bargaining experiment (Experiment 8) was carried out to test this implication of the endowment effect.

The subjects were thirty-five pairs of students in seven small tutorials at Simon Fraser University. The students were enrolled either in a beginning economics course or an English class. Each student was randomly paired with another student in the same tutorial group, with care taken to ensure that students entering the tutorial together were not assigned as a pair. A game of Nim, a simple game easily explained, was played by each pair of participants. The winners of the game were each given a 400 gram Swiss chocolate bar and told it was theirs to keep.

An induced value bargaining session was then conducted. The member of each pair who did not win the Nim game, and therefore did not receive the chocolate bar, was given a ticket and an instruction sheet that indicated that the ticket was worth $3 because it could be redeemed for that sum. The ticket owners were also told they could sell the ticket to their partner if mutually agreeable terms could be reached. The partners (the chocolate bar owners) received instructions indicating that they could receive $5 for the ticket if they could successfully buy it from the owner. Thus there was a $2 surplus available to any pair completing a trade.

The pairs were then given an unlimited amount of time to bargain. Subjects were told that both credit and change were available from the experimenter. Results of the bargaining sessions were recorded on their instruction sheets.

Of the thirty-five pairs of participants, twenty-nine agreed to an exchange ($V/V^* = .83$). The average price paid for the twenty-nine tickets was $4.09, with twelve of the exchange prices being exactly $4. Payments of the redemption values of the tickets were made as soon as the exchanges were completed. These payments were made in single dollar bills to facilitate trading in the subsequent bargaining session. After the ticket exchanges were completed, owners of the chocolate bars were told they could sell them to their partners if a mutually agreeable price could be determined. The procedures used for the tickets were once again applied to these bargaining sessions.

An important effect of the preliminary induced value ticket bargains was to provide the ticket owners with some cash. The average gain to the ticket owners (including the six who did not sell their tickets) was $3.99. The average gain to their partners (the chocolate bar owners) was only $0.76. Thus the potential chocolate bar buyers were endowed with an average of $3.23 more than the owners, creating a small income effect toward the buyers. Also, to the extent that a windfall gain such as this is spent more casually by subjects than other money, trading of chocolate bars should be facilitated.

Results of the chocolate bar bargains once again suggest reluctance to trade. Rather than the 17.5 trades expected from the random allocations, only 7 were observed ($V/V^* = .4$). The average price paid in those exchanges that did occur was $2.69. (The actual prices were: $6.00, 3.10, 3.00, 2.75, 2.00, 1.00, and 1.00). If the six pairs of subjects who did not successfully complete bargains in the first stage are omitted from the sample on the grounds that they did not understand the task or procedures, then 6 trades are observed where 14.5 would be expected ($V/V^* = .414$). Similarly, if two more pairs are dropped because the prices at which they exchanged tickets was outside the range of $3.00–5.00, then the number of trades falls to 4, and V/V^* falls to .296. (No significant differences between the students in the English and economics classes were observed.)[22]

To be sure that the chocolate bars were valued by the subjects, and that these valuations would vary enough to yield mutually beneficial trade, the same chocolate bars were distributed to half the members of another class at Simon Fraser. Those who received chocolate bars were asked the minimum price they would accept to sell their bar, while those without the bars were asked the maximum price they would pay to acquire a bar. The valuations of the bars varied from $0.50 to $8.00. The average value ascribed by sellers was $3.98, while the buyers' average valuation was $1.25. (The median values were $3.50 and $1.25.)

The Endowment Effect in Choices Between Goods

The previous experiments documented undertrading in exchanges of money and consumption goods. A separate experiment establishes the same effect in exchanges between two goods.[23] Participants in three classes were offered a choice between the same two goods. All students in one class were given a coffee mug at the beginning of the session, as compensation for completing a short questionnaire. At the completion of the task, the experimenters showed the students a bar of Swiss chocolate, which they could immediately receive in exchange for the mug. The students in another class were offered an opportunity to make the opposite exchange after first being given the chocolate bar. The students in a third class were simply offered a choice, at the beginning of the session, between a chocolate bar and a mug. The proportion of students selecting the mug was 89 percent in the class originally endowed with mugs ($N = 76$), 56 percent in the class offered a choice ($N = 55$), and only 10 percent in the class originally endowed with chocolate bars ($N = 87$). For most participants a mug was more valuable than the chocolate when it had to be given up, but less valuable when the chocolate had to be given up. This experiment confirms that undertrading can occur even when income effects are ruled out. It also demonstrates an endowment effect for a good that was distributed to everyone in the class and, therefore, did not have the appeal of a prize or trophy.

Discussion

The evidence presented in this paper supports what may be called an instant endowment effect: The value that an individual assigns to such objects as mugs, pens, binoculars, and chocolate bars appears to increase substantially as soon as that individual is given the object.[24] The apparently instantaneous nature of the reference point shift and consequent value change induced by giving a person possession of a good goes beyond previous discussions of the endowment effect, which focused on goods that have been in the individual's possession for some time. While long-term endowment effects could be explained by sentimental attachment or by an improved technology of consumption in the Stigler-Becker sense,[25] the differences in preference or taste demonstrated by more than seven hundred participants in the experiments reported in this paper cannot be explained in this fashion.

The endowment effect is one explanation for the systematic differences between buying and selling prices that have been observed so often in past work. One of the objectives of this study was to examine an alternative explanation for this buying-selling discrepancy, namely, that it reflects a general bargaining strategy[26] that would be eliminated by experience in the market.[27] Our results do not support this alternative view. The trading institution used in Experiments 1–7 encouraged participants to be price takers (especially in Experiment 5), and the rules provided no incentive to conceal true preferences. Furthermore, the results of the induced value markets indicate that the subjects understood the demand-revealing nature of the questions they were asked and acted accordingly. Substantial undertrading was nevertheless observed in markets for consumption goods. As for learning and market discipline, there was no indication that buying and selling prices converged over repeated market trials, though full feedback was provided at the end of each trial. The undertrading observed in these experiments appears to reflect a true difference in preferences between the potential buyers and sellers. The robustness of this result reduces the risk that the outcome is produced by an experimental artifact. In short, the present findings indicate that the endowment effect can persist in genuine market settings.

The contrast between the induced value markets and the consumption goods markets lends support to Heiner's conjecture that the results of induced value experiments may not generalize to all market settings.[28] The defining characteristics of the induced value markets is that the values of the tokens are unequivocally defined by the amount the experimenter will pay for them. Loss aversion is irrelevant with such objects because transactions are evaluated simply on the basis of net gain or loss. (If someone is offered $6 for a $5 bill, there is no sense of loss associated with the trade.) Some markets may share this feature of induced value markets, especially when the conditions of pure arbitrage are approached. However, the computation of net gain and loss is not possible in other situations, for example, when risky prospects are traded for cash, or in markets where people sell goods that they also value for their use. In these conditions, the cancellation of the loss of the object against the dollars received is not possible because the good and money are not strictly commensurate. The valuation ambiguity produced by this lack of commensurability is necessary, although not sufficient, for both loss aversion and a buying-selling discrepancy.

The results of the experimental demonstrations of the endowment effect have direct implications for economic theory and economic predictions. Contrary to the assumptions of standard economic theory that preferences are independent of entitlements,[29] the evidence presented here indicates that people's preferences depend on their reference positions. Consequently, preference orderings are not defined independently of endowments: Good A may be preferred to B when A is part of an original endowment, but the reverse may be true when initial reference positions are changed. Indifference curves will have a kink at the endowment or reference point,[30] and an indifference curve tracing acceptable trades in one direction may even cross another indifference curve that plots the acceptable exchanges in the opposite direction.[31]

The existence of endowment effects reduces the gains from trade. In comparison to a world in which preferences are independent of endowment, the existence of loss aversion produces an inertia in the economy because potential traders are more reluctant to trade than is conventionally assumed. This is not to say that Pareto optimal trades will not take place. Rather, there are simply fewer mutually advantageous exchanges possible, and so the volume of trade is lower than it otherwise would be.

To assess the practical significance of the endowment effect it is important to first consider some necessary conditions for the effect to be observed. Experiments 6 and 7 suggest that the endowment effect is primarily a problem for sellers; we observed little reluctance to buy, but much reluctance to sell. Furthermore, not all sellers are afflicted by an endowment effect. The effect did not appear in the markets for money tokens, and there is no reason in general to expect reluctance to resell goods that are held especially for that purpose. An owner will not be reluctant to sell an item at a given price if a perfect substitute is readily available at a lower price. This reasoning suggests that endowment effects will almost certainly occur when owners are faced with an opportunity to sell an item purchased for use, which is not easily replaceable. Examples might include tickets to a sold-out event, hunting licenses in limited supply,[32] works of art, or a pleasant view.

While the conditions necessary for an endowment effect to be observed may appear to limit its applicability in economic settings, in fact these conditions are very often satisfied, and especially so in the bargaining contexts to which the Coase Theorem is applied. For example, tickets to Wimbledon are allocated by means of a lottery. A standard Coasean analysis would imply that in the presence of an efficient ticket brokerage market, winners of the lottery would be no more likely to attend the matches than other tennis fans who had won a similar cash prize in an unrelated lottery. In contrast, the experimental results presented in this paper predict that many winners of Wimbledon tickets will attend the event, turning down opportunities to sell their tickets that exceed their reservation price for buying them.

Endowment effects can also be observed for firms and other organizations. Endowment effects are predicted for property rights acquired by historic accident or fortuitous circumstances, such as government licenses, landing rights, or transferable pollution permits. Owing to endowment effects, firms will be reluctant to divest themselves of divisions, plants, and product lines even though they would never consider buying the same assets; indeed, stock prices often rise when firms do give them up. Again, the prediction is not an absence of trade, just a reduction in the volume of trade.

Isolating the influence of endowment effects from those of transaction costs as causes of low trading volumes is, of course, difficult in actual market settings. Demonstrations of endowment effects are most persuasive where transaction costs are very small. This was – by design – the case in the experimental markets, where the efficiency of the induced value markets demonstrated the minimal effect of transaction costs, or other impediments, on exchange decisions, leaving the great reluctance to trade mugs and other goods to be attributable to endowment effects.

Endowment effects are not limited to cases involving physical goods or to legal entitlements. The reference position of individuals and firms often includes terms of previous transactions or expectations of continuation of present, often informal, arrangements. There is clear evidence of dramatically asymmetric reactions to improvements and deteriorations of these terms and a willingness to make sacrifices to avoid unfair treatment.[33] The reluctance to sell at a loss, owing to a perceived entitlement to a formerly prevailing price, can explain two observations of apparent undertrading. The first pertains to housing markets. It is often observed that when housing prices fall, volume also falls. When house prices are falling, houses remain on the market longer than when prices are rising. Similarly, the volume for stocks that have declined in price is lower than the volume for stocks that have increased in value,[34] although tax considerations would lead to the opposite prediction.

Another manifestation of loss aversion in the context of multiattribute negotiations is what might be termed "concession aversion," a reluctance to accept a loss on any dimension of an agreement. A straightforward and common instance of this is the downward stickiness of wages. A somewhat more subtle implication of concession aversion is that it can produce inefficient contract terms owing to historic precedents. Old firms may have more inefficient arrangements than new ones, because new companies can negotiate without the reference positions created by prior agreements. Some airlines, for example, are required to carry three pilots on some planes while others – newer ones – operate with two.

Loss aversion implies a marked asymmetry in the treatment of losses and of foregone gains, which plays an essential role in judgments of fairness.[35] Accordingly, disputes in which concessions are viewed as losses are often much less tractable than disputes in which concessions involve foregone gains. Court decisions recognize the asymmetry of losses and foregone gains by favoring possessors of goods over other claimants, by limiting recovery of lost profits relative to compensation for actual expenditures, and by failing to enforce gratuitous promises that are coded as foregone gains to the injured party.[36]

To conclude, the evidence reported here offers no support for the contention that observations of loss aversion and the consequential evaluation disparities are artifacts, nor should they be interpreted as mistakes likely to be eliminated by experience, training, or "market discipline." Instead, the findings support an alternative view of endowment effects and loss aversion as fundamental characteristics of preferences.

Notes

1 See Robert D. Willig, Consumer's Surplus Without Apology, 66 *Am. Econ. Rev.* 589 (1976).

2 For example, the conventional prescription for assessing environmental and other losses is that "practically speaking, it does not appear to make much difference which definition is accepted." A. Byron Freeman, *The Benefits of Environmental Improvement* 3 (1979).

3 Richard Thaler, Toward a Positive Theory of Consumer Choice, 1 *J. Econ. Behav. & Org.* 39 (1980).

4 See, e.g., Robert D. Rowe, Ralph C. d'Arge, and David S. Brookshire, An Experiment in the Economic Value of Visibility, 7 *J. Envtl. Econ. & Mgmt.* 1 (1980).

5 Peter Knez, Vernon L. Smith, and Arlington W. Williams, Individual Rationality, Market Rationality and Value Estimation, 75 *Am. Econ. Rev.* 397 (May 1985).

6 See Don L. Coursey, John L. Hovis, and William D. Schulze, The Disparity Between Willingness to Accept and Willingness to Pay Measures of Value, 102 *Q.J. Econ.* 679 (1987); David S. Brookshire and Don L. Coursey, Measuring the Value of a Public Good: An Empirical Comparison of Elicitation Procedures, 77 *Am. Econ. Rev.* 554 (1987).

7 See Thaler, supra note 3.

8 See Daniel Kahneman and Amos Tversky, Prospect Theory: An Analysis of Decision Under Risk, 47 *Econometrica* 263 (1979); Amos Tversky and Daniel Kahneman, Loss Aversion and Risky Choice, unpublished working paper, Stanford University (1989).

9 See Vernon L. Smith, Microeconomic Systems as an Experimental Science, 72 *Am. Econ. Rev.* 923 (1982); Charles R. Plott, Industrial Organization Theory and Experimental Economics, 20 *J. Econ. Literature* 1485 (1982).

10 See Vernon L. Smith, Experimental Economics: Induced Value Theory, 66 *Am. Econ. Rev.* 274 (1976).

11 The instructions stated that "*It is in your best interest to answer these questions truthfully.* For any question, treat the price as fixed. (In economics jargon, you should act as 'price takers.')" All the subjects were junior and senior economics majors, so they were familiar with the terms used. If subjects asked how the market prices were determined, they were told, truthfully, that the market price was the point at which the elicited supply-and-demand curves intersected. The uniformity of the results across many different experiments suggests that this information had no discernible effect on behavior. Furthermore, the responses of the subjects in the induced value portion of the experiments indicate that nearly all understood and accepted their role as price takers. See also Experiment 5 in which a random price procedure was used.

12 When this occurred, a random draw determined which buyers and sellers were accommodated.

13 The experimental design was intended to give the markets for consumption goods every possible chance to be efficient. While in the induced value markets not

everyone was paid, in the consumption goods markets everyone was paid. Also, the consumption goods markets were conducted after the induced value markets and were repeated four times each, to allow the subjects the maximum opportunity for learning.

14 Rebecca R. Boyce et al., An Experimental Examination of Intrinsic Values as a Source of the WTA-WTP Disparity, 82 *Am. Econ. Rev.* 1366 (1992).

15 See Knez et al., supra note 5; Coursey et al., supra note 6; Brookshire and Coursey, supra note 6.

16 See Coursey et al., supra note 6.

17 The ratio of the mean selling and buying prices is 1.4 if all subjects are included. However, if one buyer and one seller with extreme valuations are excluded, the ratio is 1.9. These numbers were reported in an earlier version of Coursey et al., supra note 6.

18 For detail see Jack L. Knetsch and J. A. Sinden, The Persistence of Evaluation Disparities, 102 *Q.J. Econ.* 691 (1987).

19 Brookshire and Coursey, supra note 6.

20 See Gordon M. Becker, M. H. DeGroot, and J. Marshak, Measuring Utility by a Single-Response Sequential Method, 9 *Behav. Sci.* 226 (1964).

21 See Tversky and Kahneman, supra note 8.

22 We conducted two similar bargaining experiments that yielded comparable results. Twenty-six pairs of subjects negotiated the sale of mugs and then envelopes containing an uncertain amount of money. Buyers had not been given any cash endowment. These sessions yielded six and five trades respectively, where thirteen would be expected. Also, some induced value bilateral negotiation sessions were conducted in which only 50 cents of surplus was available. (The seller's valuation was $1.50 and the buyer's was $2.00.) Nevertheless, twenty-one of a possible twenty-six trades were completed.

23 Jack L. Knetsch, The Endowment Effect and Evidence of Nonreversible Indifference Curves, 79 *Am. Econ. Rev.* 1277 (1989).

24 The impression gained from informal pilot experiments is that the act of giving the participant physical possession of the good results in more consistent endowment effects. Assigning subjects a chance to receive a good, or a property right to a good to be received at a later time, seemed to produce weaker effects.

25 See George J. Stigler and Gary S. Becker, De Gustibus Non Est Disputandum, 67 *Am. Econ. Rev.* 76 (1977).

26 See Marc Knez and Vernon L. Smith, Hypothetical Valuations and Preference Reversals in the Context of Asset Trading, in *Laboratory Experiments in Economics: Six Points of View* 131 (Alvin E. Roth ed., 1987).

27 See Coursey et al., supra note 6; Brookshire and Coursey, supra note 6.

28 See Ronald A. Heiner, Experimental Economics: Comment, 75 *Am. Econ. Rev.* 260 (March 1985).

29 Although ownership can affect taste in the manner suggested by Stigler and Becker, in the absence of income effects it is traditional to assume that the indifference curves in Edgeworth Box diagrams do not depend on the location of the endowment point.

30 See Tversky and Kahneman, supra note 8.

31 See Knetsch, supra note 23.

32 See R. Bishop and T. Heberlein, Measuring Values of Extra Market Goods: Are Indirect Measures Biased? 61 *Am. J. Agric. Econ.* 926 (1979).

33 See Daniel Kahneman, Jack L. Knetsch, and Richard Thaler, Fairness as a Constraint on Profit Seeking: Entitlements in the Market, 76 *Am. Econ. Rev.* 728, 729–30 (1986).

34 See Hersh Shefrin and Meir Statman, The Disposition to Sell Winners Too Early and Ride Losers Too Long: Theory and Evidence, 40 *J. Fin.* 777 (1985); Stephen P. Ferris, Robert A. Haugen, and Anil K. Makhija, Predicting Contemporary Volume with Historic Volume at Differential Price Levels: Evidence Supporting the Disposition Effect, 43 *J. Fin.* 677 (1988).

35 See Kahnemanl et al., supra note 33.

36 See David Cohen and Jack Knetsch, Judicial Choice and Disparities Between Measures of Economic Values, 30 *Osgoode Hall L. J.* 737 (1992).

37 Judd Hammack and Gardner Mallard Brown Jr., *Waterfowl and Wetlands: Toward Bioeconomic Analysis* (1974).

38 William F. Sinclair, 5 *Kemano II Environmental Studies: The Economic and Social Impact of the Kemano II Hydroelectric Project on British Columbia's Fisheries Resources* (1976).

39 Nancy D. Banford et al., Feasibility Judgements and Alternative Measures of Benefits and Costs, 11 *J. Bus. Admin.* 25, 29–32 (1979).

40 Bishop and Heberlein, supra note 32.

41 Rowe et al., supra note 4.

42 David S. Brookshire et al., Valuing Increments and Decrements in Natural Resource Service Flows, 62 *Am. J. Agric. Econ.* 478, 482–7 (1980).

43 Thomas Heberlein and Richard Bishop, Assessing the Validity of Contingent Valuations (paper presented in Italy 1985, at an international conference).

44 Jack L. Knetsch and J. A. Sinden, Willingness to Pay and Compensation Demanded: Experimental Evidence of an Unexpected Disparity in Measures of Value, 99 *Q.J. Econ.* 507 (1984).

45 Heberlein and Bishop, supra note 43.

46 Coursey et al., supra note 6.

47 Brookshire and Coursey, supra note 6.

9 Assessing Punitive Damages (With Notes on Cognition and Valuation in Law)

Cass R. Sunstein, Daniel Kahneman, and David Schkade

The award of punitive damages has become one of the most controversial and important uses of the tort law, extending well beyond the common law to such statutory areas as environmental protection and employment discrimination. In recent years many people have objected that punitive damages are unpredictable, even "out of control."[1] Consider, as possible examples, a punitive award of $4 million for nondisclosure of the fact that the plaintiff's new BMW had been repainted, a $6 million punitive award for tortious interference with contractual relations, a $400 million punitive award for fraud by an owner of funeral homes, a $30 million punitive award for anticompetitive conduct, and a $2.7 million award, later reduced to $480,000, to a woman who spilled coffee on herself that McDonald's knew to be too hot. These are mere anecdotes, but there is more systematic evidence as well, suggesting a far from trivial degree of randomness, especially at the high end.

Our principal interest here is in identifying some of the sources of unpredictability in jury judgments. On the basis of a study of 899 jury-eligible citizens, we offer the following major findings:

1. People have a remarkably high degree of moral consensus on the degrees of outrage and punishment that are appropriate for punitive damage cases. At least in the products liability cases we offer, this moral consensus, on what might be called *outrage* and *punitive intent*, cuts across differences in gender, race, income, age, and education. For example, our study shows that all-white, all-female, all-Hispanic, all-male, all-poor, all-wealthy, all-black, all-old, and all-young juries are likely to come to similar conclusions about how to rank and rate a range of cases.

2. This consensus fractures when the legal system uses dollars as the vehicle to measure moral outrage. *Even when there is a consensus on punitive intent, there is no consensus about how much in the way of dollars is necessary to produce appropriate suffering in a defendant.* Under existing law, widely shared and reasonably predictable judgments about punitive intent are turned into highly erratic judgments about appropriate dollar punishment. A basic source of

arbitrariness with the existing system of punitive damages (and a problem not limited to the area of punitive damages) is the use of an *unbounded dollar scale*.

3. A modest degree of additional arbitrariness is created by the fact that juries have a hard time making appropriate distinctions among cases in what we call "a no-comparison condition." When one case is seen apart from other cases, people show a general tendency to place it toward the midpoint of any bounded scale. It is therefore less likely that sensible discriminations will be made among diverse cases. This effect is, however, far less important than the effect identified in finding (2) in producing arbitrary awards.

The principal purpose of this chapter is to set out and to elaborate these findings and to use them to develop some policy reforms in the area of punitive damages. Our basic suggestion is that the legal system should enable juries to engage in tasks that they are capable of performing and should not require juries to carry out tasks that they cannot perform well. Juries are likely to produce erratic judgments about dollar amounts; their judgments are likely to be much less erratic when they are asked to rank cases or to assess the degree to which a defendant should be punished on a bounded rating scale.

Both the empirical findings and the policy recommendations have implications well beyond the problem of punitive damages. The problem of "mapping" judgments onto a dollar scale arises not only in the setting of punitive damages, but also in damages for "pain and suffering," libel actions, sexual harassment cases, intentional infliction of emotional distress, administrative penalties, and judgments about the appropriate focus of the regulatory state. Very typically, juries and judge are mapping judgments onto an unbounded dollar scale. The phenomenon of widespread and predictable judgments, combined with the demonstrable cognitive difficulty of translating preferences and values into dollar amounts, has wide-ranging implications for the operation of both private and public law.

Why Punitive Damage Awards Are Erratic

Our study was designed to examine hypotheses about three topics: (1) the psychology of the sequence of judgments and attitudes that produce individual judgments about punitive awards in particular cases, (2) the sources of variability in these judgments, and (3) the implications of these findings for the unpredictability of jury awards and for possible reforms in the tasks assigned to juries.

A total of 899 respondents were selected from the voter registration rolls of Travis County, Texas, and paid $35 to participate in the study. A set of ten vignettes of product liability cases were created in which a plaintiff (always an individual customer) sued a firm for compensatory and punitive damages.

All vignettes had versions that differed in the size of the defendant firm (medium or large). For four of the vignettes, there were also versions that differed in the harm that the plaintiff was said to have suffered, but not in the description of the defendant's actions. In total, there were twenty-eight different variations of the ten vignettes. Each respondent evaluated ten cases, composed of one variation of each of the ten basic vignettes. The respondents were told to assume in all cases that compensatory damages had been awarded in the amount of $200,000, and that punitive damages were to be considered. Three subsamples were asked to answer different questions about each scenario: how outrageous was the defendant's behavior (on a scale of 0 to 6), how much should the defendant be punished (on a scale of 0 to 6), how much should the defendant be required to pay in punitive damages. Each respondent first dealt with one case without seeing the others (the "no comparison" condition) and then received a booklet with nine new cases.

The Outrage Model

We propose a descriptive theory of the psychology of punitive awards, called the *outrage model*. The essential claim is that the moral transgressions of others evoke an attitude of outrage, which combines an emotional evaluation and a response tendency. The rules that govern outrage present an important problem that we do not address in this chapter. We assume that outrage is governed largely by social norms. Judged by reference to these norms, a particular person's expressions of indignation may be deemed too intense for its cause or not intense enough. Social as well as legal norms also regulate the mapping from transgressions to punishment.

An attitude is a mental state and is not directly observable. The various aspects of an attitude can, however, be "mapped" onto diverse responses, which might include facial expressions, verbal statements of opinion, gestures – even physical assault. Response "modes" might include a judgment about outrageousness on a numerical scale. Under the outrage model, punitive damages are considered an expression of an angry or indignant attitude toward a transgressor. The evaluative aspect of the attitude is labeled outrage; the response tendency is labeled punitive intent. Outrage is basic, and punitive intent is measured by outrage and additional factors, such as harm. As we will see, the verbal indication of the desired severity of punishment (punitive intent) is affected both by the outrage that an action evokes and by the severity of its consequences ("harm"). This retributive aspect of punishment is incorporated in many aspects of the law, such as the large discrepancy between sentences for murder and for attempted murder. The relationship between victim and juror was manipulated in an experiment by Reid Hastie, David Schkade, and John Payne.[2] Under experimental conditions, larger awards were made when the defendant was from a remote location. We speculate that this factor affects punitive intent: The retributive urge is stronger when the victim belongs to one's group than when the victim is a stranger. The amount demanded by the plaintiff also affected the size of the awards, most likely an anchoring effect, which influences the award directly, independently of punitive intent.

In some situations the expression of an attitude is restricted to a particular scale of responses. For example, in the situation with which we are concerned here, the responses of juries are restricted to a scale of dollars. Dollar amounts of punitive awards (like the length of prison sentences in criminal cases) are only one of a number of possible scales on which outrage might be expressed. By adopting a particular response "mode," the legal system, in a sense, constructs the relevant values. A bounded numerical scale would be another obvious possibility. We propose that some factors affect the mapping of punitive intent onto the dollar scale, but that these factors do not affect punitive intent on a bounded numerical scale. For example, the size of the defendant firm is an important factor in translating punitive intent into dollars; a judgment that appears severe when the defendant is a small firm may appear grossly inadequate when the defendant is a giant. Thus firm size will affect dollar awards even if it does not affect punitive intent as measured on a bounded numerical scale.

In summary, the outrage model assumes an internal state of outrage, which can be mapped onto different response scales. These scales vary not only in their complexity, but also in the precision and reliability of the measurement that they support: Some scales are "noisier" than others. As we will see, the dollar scale is an extremely noisy expression of punitive intent.

Hypotheses

Our two central hypotheses were that jurors would exhibit shared outrage, but that dollar awards would be erratic. The basis for the shared outrage hypothesis is the belief that a bedrock of broadly shared social norms governs the outrage evoked by different scenarios of tortious behavior. With respect to outrage and punitive intent, we thus predicted that randomly selected juries are likely to be similar to one another. In addition, we predicted that rankings of different scenarios would be generally similar for different demographic groups, at least in the context of the personal injury cases given here. The erratic dollar amounts hypothesis was that, in contrast to outrage and punitive intent, which are measured on bounded scales, punitive awards denominated in dollars are susceptible to large individual differences, which could be a significant cause of the unpredictability of jury determinations. We tested this prediction by comparing the extent of variations in judgments about outrageousness and appropriate punishment with the extent of variations in judgments about appropriate dollar awards.

We also examined three other hypotheses. First, we considered the "harm effect." We hypothesized that punitive intent – as measured on a bounded numerical scale – is determined by the outrageousness of the defendant's behavior and by other factors, prominently including the harm suffered by the defendant. The prediction that harm affects punitive intent but not outrage was tested by presenting alternative versions of some scenarios, in which the severity of the harm suffered by the plaintiff varied. Second, we tested whether the defendant firm's size was relevant. We hypothesized that damage awards are determined by punitive intent, and by other ascertainable factors, prominently including the size of the defendant firm. We tested this prediction by presenting each scenario in two versions, in which the size of the defendant varied. Third, we considered the effect of having comparison cases. In a "no-comparison" condition, we hypothesized that there is a cautious tendency to place cases toward the middle of a bounded numerical scale, and hence people will not make appropriate distinctions among cases. We tested this hypothesis by giving respondents cases in isolation and in the context of other cases.

Results

Shared Outrage. Our first question was whether the degree of outrage is consistent across individuals and across possible juries. A simple way to answer this question is to examine whether rankings of different scenarios are generally similar for different demographic groups. We therefore computed the means of the three responses (outrage, punitive intent, and dollar awards) separately for groups of respondents defined by demographic variables (men, women, whites, Hispanics, African Americans, different levels of income, and education). To measure the level of agreement across disjoint categories (e.g., men and women) we computed the correlation between their average responses over the set of twenty-eight cases.

The correlations were remarkably high for judgments both of outrage and of punitive intent (see Table 9.1). In particular, there was essentially perfect agreement among groups in the ranking of cases by punitive intent: the median correlation was .99. Men and women, Hispanics, African Americans, and whites, and respondents at very different levels of income and education produced almost identical orderings of the twenty-eight scenarios used in the study. Judgments of intent to punish in these scenarios of product liability cases evidently rest on a bedrock of moral intuitions that are broadly shared in society. We also looked for differences among groups in the average severity of their judgments (i.e., the level of the average rating) and here too found no significant differences (with the one exception of gender, to be taken up below).

This striking finding may not generalize to all domains of the law. We might expect to find larger differences between communities and social categories in other domains of the law, perhaps including attitudes toward civil rights violations and environmental harms; at least it is possible that,

Table 9.1. *Correlation Between Demographic Groups on Intended Severity of Punishment*[a]

Gender

	Men
Women	.974

Ethnicity

	Black	White
White	.975	
Hispanic	.963	.988

Household Income

	30,000	30,000–50,000
30–50K	.991	
> 50K	.986	.986

Age

	< 30	30–39	40–49
30–39	.994		
40–49	.992	.994	
> 50	.991	.993	.987

[a] Entries are correlations between mean responses to scenarios by respondents in the indicated demographic categories.

for example, African Americans would *rate* civil rights cases more severely than whites do. We expect, however, that within the same category of cases, *rankings* may remain the same across different groups, so that different demographic groups would agree on which defendants have behaved least and most egregiously. Here there is a great deal of room for further empirical work.

The (Modest and Partial but Interesting) Exception of Gender Ratings. As noted, the only statistically significant difference in average ratings was between women and men. While women and men ranked the scenarios identically (as indicated by the extremely high correlations), men were somewhat more lenient and women were somewhat more severe: Women rated the defendant's behavior as more outrageous (a mean difference of .52 scale units, $p < .001$), expressed more punitive intent (a mean difference of .37 scale units, $p < .001$), and set higher log dollar awards ($p < .01$). There was also an interaction between scenarios and gender, in which women assigned even higher ratings of outrage and punishment (but not higher awards) to cases in which the plaintiff was female ($p < .05$).

This finding should not be overemphasized; the differences in ratings were relatively small. But it bears on legal and social disputes about jury composition, providing some empirical evidence that women do reach different conclusions from those reached by men and in particular that they seek more severe punishment of civil defendants. Our finding is in line, broadly speaking, with other research suggesting that women and men view social risks differently and, in particular, that women tend to view such risks as more serious than men do.[3]

Unpredictable Dollar Awards. With respect to dollar awards, our central hypothesis was that such awards are erratic because of individual differences in the mapping of punitive intent onto the dollar scale. To test this hypothesis we produced simulated juries by randomly sampling, with replacement, groups of twelve responses to each case for each response scale. In this manner we constructed a large number of three types of simulated juries: "outrage juries," "punishment juries," and "dollar juries." Of course, there is a large question about how a set of individual judgments will produce a jury verdict. No doubt group dynamics can push deliberations in unexpected directions, sometimes toward the most extreme member of the group. As a statistical matter, however, the experimental literature on the relationship between prior individual judgments and the outcomes of group deliberation suggests that the median judgment is a good predictor[4] and indeed may even understate our ultimate conclusion.[5] (Our subsequent experiments with deliberating juries, the basis for work now in progress, tend to confirm this judgment.)

We therefore used the median judgment of each simulated jury as an estimate of what the judgment of that jury would have been. Without losing sight of the limitations of our estimation procedure, we apply the label "jury judgment" to these estimates for simplicity of exposition. Table 9.2 summarizes the simulated jury judgments for punishment and dollar awards. Jury judgments can be considered shared and therefore predictable, in our use of that term, if there is high agreement between juries randomly selected from the population. In order to find a source of erratic judgments, we attempted to compare the predictability of the judgments made by simulated dollar juries,

Table 9.1. *Synthetic Jury Response Distributions by Scenario*

Scenario	Firm Size	Harm Level	Lower 95% Confidence Bound	Median	Upper 95% Confidence Bound	Mean Jury Punishment	Prediction Error Ratio ($/Punishment)
Joan	Large	High	$500,000	$2,000,000	$15,000,000	5.14	3.36
Joan	Medium	High	200,000	900,000	3,000,000	5.03	2.27
Thomas	Medium	–	200,000	500,000	1,575,000	5.02	1.69
Martin	Medium	High	350,000	1,000,000	4,000,000	4.98	4.01
Thomas	Large	–	200,000	560,000	2,750,000	4.95	0.50
Joan	Large	Low	175,000	1,000,000	12,500,000	4.93	13.57
Martin	Large	High	350,000	1,900,000	10,000,000	4.92	2.40
Frank	Medium	–	230,000	760,000	2,100,000	4.86	1.67
Frank	Large	–	225,000	1,000,000	4,000,000	4.82	2.62
Mary	Large	–	290,000	1,000,000	4,000,000	4.79	1.49
Joan	Medium	Low	150,000	750,000	5,500,000	4.71	9.90
Mary	Medium	–	250,000	710,000	2,100,000	4.70	2.51
Martin	Large	Low	350,000	1,000,000	5,000,000	4.47	3.63
Martin	Medium	Low	200,000	675,000	2,250,000	4.16	2.53
Susan	Large	–	100,000	300,000	1,000,000	3.27	1.78
Susan	Medium	–	50,000	225,000	800,000	3.03	0.93
Janet	Medium	High	100,000	200,000	690,000	2.79	1.37
Carl	Medium	–	15,000	155,000	375,000	2.78	1.59
Carl	Large	–	50,000	200,000	750,000	2.64	1.59
Janet	Medium	Low	0	150,000	650,000	2.49	2.00
Janet	Large	High	0	287,500	1,500,000	2.39	4.41
Janet	Large	Low	12,500	200,000	1,000,000	2.38	1.30
Jack	Large	High	0	0	350,000	1.24	2.10
Jack	Medium	High	0	45,000	225,000	1.07	1.30
Jack	Medium	Low	0	0	112,500	1.03	0.89
Jack	Large	Low	0	2,550	500,000	0.95	2.91
Sarah	Large	–	0	0	1,000	0.51	1.12
Sarah	Medium	–	0	0	13,000	0.46	∞
						MEDIAN	2.18

outrage juries, and punishment juries. First, we imagined that all of our case scenarios were tried on the same day by independent juries, analogous to how jury judgments for different cases are produced in practice. We then asked the question, "If these same cases were tried again independently, how likely are we to get the same ratings and rankings as in this first set of trials?"

To answer this question we conducted an analysis requiring four steps. (1) We created a randomly selected jury for each of the twenty-eight cases and computed the median judgment for each. (2) We then imagined that a time machine allowed us to replay each case again independently of the first trial, including the random selection of a new jury. We therefore created a second set of twenty-eight randomly selected juries and corresponding median judgments. The correlation between these and the first set of jury judgments is a measure of how erratic or consistent juries are. (3) To get a more reliable

Table 9.2. *Median Correlations Between Sets of Simulated Juries*

	Outrage	Punishment	Dollar Awards
Outrage	.87		
Punishment	.86	.89	
Dollar Awards	.47	.51	.42
Overall Median Award	.71	.77	.69

indication of the typical correlation between juries, we performed Step 1 sixty times for each of the three response modes. This produced 180 columns of data, each of which contained one set of twenty-eight jury judgments. (4) We then computed the correlations between every pair of sets of simulated jury judgments (i.e., correlations between the columns). This computation was performed both within response (e.g., the correlation between two sets of twenty-eight outrage ratings) and across responses (e.g., the correlation between a set of twenty-eight outrage ratings and a set of twenty-eight punishment ratings). The data shown in Table 9.3 are medians of the correlations obtained for each response mode or response mode combination.

As we had hypothesized, the individual differences in dollar awards produce severe unpredictability, and highly erratic outcomes, even in the medians of twelve judgments (the results would be even more extreme with smaller samples such as six-person juries). While there is strong agreement between independent sets of outrage or punishment juries ($r = .87$ and .89), agreement between independent sets of dollar juries is quite weak ($r = .42$). The variability of individual dollar judgments is so large that even the medians of twelve judgments are quite unstable. The problem could be reduced, of course, by taking larger samples. For example, we found that the correlation between sets of dollar juries rises to .80 when the size of the juries is increased to thirty (correlations for thirty-person outrage and punishment juries rise to .95 and .97, respectively).

Context, Harm, Firm Size, and Other Findings. In this section we briefly report our findings on our other hypotheses and discuss some issues of particular relevance to punitive damage reform.

1. *The effect of context.* Unlike real jurors, who are exposed to a single case for a long time, the participants in our study responded to a total of ten product liability cases in quick succession and had an opportunity to compare most of these scenarios to each other. To examine the effect of this unusual procedure, every participant first encountered one of the first six scenarios, which was presented in a separate envelope and was evaluated in isolation from the others. The experimental design provides a comparison of

the distribution of judgments to each scenario when it is judged in isolation or in the context of other scenarios.

We examined whether the availability of a context of comparison affected the distribution of judgments; the question is important, since the legal system often forces juries to evaluate cases without a set of comparison. Our basic finding was that in a no-comparison condition there is a cautious tendency to diminished differentiation in judgments about different cases. The availability of a context apparently makes a serious case appear more serious than it would on its own and makes a milder case appear milder. Thus the most consistent effect of a context of similar cases is to increase the *range* of the judgments across different scenarios. We conclude that the availability of a context of similar cases improves people's ability to discriminate among these cases but does not affect the basic moral intuitions that the cases evoke.

2. *From outrage to punishment: The harm effect.* An action can be judged more or less outrageous without reference to its consequences. Consequences, however, are important to punishment in law, and we suspected that they would also be important to lay intuitions about the proper punishment for reprehensible actions. These predictions were tested by constructing alternative versions of four additional vignettes, which differed in the harm that the plaintiff had suffered. Note that the difference was measured qualitatively rather than in dollar terms; in all of the cases, the jury had awarded $200,000 in compensatory damages, but in some of them, the description of the injury suggested less in the way of qualitative loss, as, for example, in the case of a burned child.

As predicted, we found that the degree of outrage evoked by the defendant's behavior was not affected by the harm that occurred. In contrast, varying the harm had a small but statistically significant effect on punishment ratings, where defendants who had done more harm to the plaintiff were judged to deserve greater punishment. As predicted by the outrage model, the significant harm effect found for punishment ratings carried through to dollar awards. Thus low harm produced an average award of $727,599, and high harm an average award of a substantially greater amount: $1,171,251.

3. *The effect of firm size.* Within the academic community, opinion is sharply divided on the question whether the amount of punitive awards should depend on the size of the defendant firm. Lay intuitions, in contrast, are quite clear. People think in terms of retribution rather than deterrence, and the intention to punish is an intention to inflict pain; this means that the size of the defendant matters a good deal. Our hypothesis was that firm size would affect neither outrage nor punitive intent, but that the same degree of punitive intent would be translated into a larger amount of damages when the firm is larger than when it is smaller.

As expected, we found no statistically significant effects of firm size on either outrage or punishment judgments. But large firms were punished with much larger dollar awards (an average of $1,009,994) than medium firms ($526,398). This is substantial evidence that equivalent outrage and punitive intent will produce significantly higher dollar awards against wealthy defendants.

The Underlying Problem: "Scaling Without a Modulus." How do these findings bear on the appropriate role of juries in setting punitive damage awards? As we have seen, a conventional understanding of such awards sees the jury as a sample from the community whose function is to provide an estimate of community sentiment. If jury judgments are erratic, this function is badly compromised, for any particular jury's judgment may not reflect community sentiment at all. The bottom row of Table 9.3 presents the median correlations between sets of simulated jury judgments for the twenty-eight scenarios and the corresponding estimates of community sentiment, for which we used the overall median of dollar awards for each scenario. It is obvious that the judgments of dollar juries provide a poor estimate of overall community sentiment. *Indeed, the unreliability of dollar juries is so pronounced that the dollar awards that would be set by the larger community are predicted more accurately by punishment juries.* This is a counterintuitive finding. It leads directly to a possible recommendation, which we explore below: juries instructed to state their punitive intent could be used, in conjunction with a preset conversion function, to generate punitive awards that would accurately represent community sentiment, thus reducing much of the unpredictability of awards.

A key to our analysis is a distinction that psychologists draw between two types of scales. (1) *Category scales* are bounded and anchored in verbal descriptions at both ends; scales of this type are often used in public opinion surveys and were used here to measure outrage and punitive intent. (2) *Magnitude scales* are unbounded and are defined by a meaningful zero point. These scales are often used in the psychological laboratory, for example, to scale the brightness of lights or the loudness of sounds. Magnitude scales have occasionally been used to measure the intensity of response to socially relevant stimuli, such as the severity of crimes and the severity of punishments.[6] The dollar scale of punitive awards is obviously not a category scale; it satisfies the defining characteristics of a magnitude scale, for the zero point is meaningful and the scale is unbounded.

Although the relations between the two types of scales have been the topic of much controversy,[7] some characteristic differences between them are well established. (1) The distributions of judgments on magnitude scales are generally positively skewed, with a long right tail (this is a consequence of the fact that the scale is bounded by zero at the low end); (2) judgments on magnitude scales are often erratic, in the sense of highly variable; and (3) the standard deviations of individual judgments of different objects (a measure of variability) is often roughly proportional to the mean judgments of these objects.

The common practice in laboratory uses of magnitude scaling is to define a *modulus:* Respondents are instructed to assign a particular rating to a "standard" stimulus, defined as the modulus, and to assign ratings to other stimuli in relation to that modulus. Thus, for example, a modulus of "5" might be assigned to a noise of a certain volume, and other noises might be assessed in volume by comparison with the modulus. An experiment can, however, be conducted without specifying a modulus. In this situation of *magnitude scaling without a modulus*, different respondents spontaneously adopt different moduli, but their responses generally preserve the same *ratios* even when the moduli differ. For example, one observer may assign a judgment of 200 to a stimulus that another observer rates as 10. If the first observer now assigns a rating of 500 to a new stimulus, we may expect the second to assign to that stimulus a value of 25.

Here is the central point: Magnitude scaling without a modulus produces extremely large variability in judgments of any particular stimulus because of arbitrary individual differences in moduli. The assignment of punitive damages satisfies the technical definition of magnitude scaling without a modulus. This reasoning is what led to the central hypothesis of the present study, a hypothesis that we described and established above.

A Simple Way to Improve Predictability. Is it possible to improve the predictability of dollar awards? How might this be done? We performed a statistical analysis designed to answer these questions.

A conventional view about the role of juries in setting punitive awards is that the jury is a sample from the community, whose function it is to provide an estimate of community sentiment. In the context of our experiment, community sentiment about the punitive damages for a scenario was defined as *the median of the damages set by all the respondents who judged it.* This sentiment represents population-wide judgments about appropriate dollar awards. The findings summarized in Table 9.3 suggest a straightforward procedure for improving the accuracy with which this community sentiment can be estimated from the judgments of a sample of twelve citizens: use judgments of punitive intent and a conversion function based on the results of a large sample, one that can be taken to reflect a population-wide judgment.

To test the effect of this procedure in our data, we first estimate the conversion function separately for medium and for large firms, since there was a significant effect of firm size on dollar awards. Following Stevens,[8] power functions were estimated, which related the mean punishment jury response for each case to the corresponding overall median of individual dollar awards, our measure of community sentiment. We then generated two sets of simulated jury judgments for each case. The first set consisted of the median judgments of one hundred randomly sampled dollar juries. The second set was obtained by taking the median judgments of one hundred randomly selected punishment juries, and transforming this value to dollars, separately for each jury, by the appropriate conversion function (depending on whether the defendant firm was large or medium-sized). To measure the accuracy of a simulated jury as an estimate of the population median, we computed the discrepancy between the dollar award set by a jury (for punishment juries we used the dollar value from the conversion function) and the overall median dollar award for that case. From these discrepancies we can compute the root-mean-squared error (RMSE), which is a conventional measure of accuracy of estimation and is analogous to the standard error of the estimate in a regression model.

This analysis provides two values of RMSE for each of the twenty-eight cases in our study, one from dollar juries and one from punishment juries. In twenty-five of the twenty-eight cases, RMSE is smaller (indicating higher accuracy) for estimates derived from punishment juries. To assess the magnitude of the effect, we computed the ratio of the two values of RMSE for each scenario (listed in the last column of Table 9.2). The median ratio was 2.18, which is interpreted to mean that for the median case, using dollar juries leads to over *twice* as much prediction error than using punishment juries and a conversion function. For example, for the case of Joan with a medium firm size and high harm, the ratio is 2.27, the median award is $1,000,000, and the estimates of dollar juries have an average error from this value of $913,481 compared to $402,414 for estimates based on punishment juries.

In simple language, this means that unpredictability could be greatly reduced, and population-wide judgments about dollar awards would be far more likely to be found, if the legal system used punishment juries and a conversion function rather than dollar juries. Indeed, as can be seen in Table 9.2, the median probably understates the decisive overall advantage of using predictions based on punishment ratings, since for some individual cases the reduction in error is extremely large.

One note of caution is in order here. The fact that punitive damages share the known deficiencies of magnitude scaling is likely to be a significant cause of unpredictable punitive awards – but it is not the only one. Other factors include regional differences, plaintiff's demand, anchors of various sorts, differences in social norms over both time and space, the quality of the lawyers on both sides, and doubtless others. We take up some of these points below.

Policy Reforms: Community Judgments with Meaning and Without Noise?

Preliminary Observations, Anchoring, and the Rule of Law

1. *Anchors and their effects.* Our study did refer to compensatory damages and to firm size, but it did not contain two usual "anchors":[9] plaintiff's demand and the jury's own prior determination of compensatory damages. Such anchors are likely to matter a great deal to actual awards. There is experimental evidence that the plaintiff's demand has considerable importance,[10] and experimental evidence too of the effect of anchors in pain and suffering cases, which are analogous.[11] There is real-world as well as experimental

evidence of an anchoring effect from the compensatory award.[12] Other anchors may well emerge during the lawyers' advocacy.

How does the existence of real-world anchors affect our findings? The answer is that anchors may or may not increase predictability. If it is hard to know in advance what will be used as the anchor, predictability will be absent; if everyone knows what the anchor is likely to be, there will be less in the way of unpredictable outcomes. But if this is so, predictability comes with a cost of its own: introducing an additional layer of arbitrariness, if (as is likely) the anchor is itself arbitrary on normative grounds. There is no reason to think that the plaintiff's demand should carry a great deal of weight in determining the that proper punitive award. And if the compensatory award that anchors the punitive award, there is a kind of arbitrariness to the extent that anchor is arbitrary, as deterrence theory suggests that it is.

2. *The rule of law and how to obtain (and how not to obtain) its virtues.* Many concerns about punitive damage awards point to their apparently arbitrary character, and many proposed remedies attempt to promote rule-of-law values through, for example, more careful and more specific judicial instructions. Contrary to the common view, the problem does not lie in insufficiently clear instructions to juries. The problem is instead the effort to measure attitudes in dollars. Even general and open-ended instructions can produce a high degree of predictability *if the response mode is appropriate.* Even specific and tailored instructions are likely to produce a high degree of unpredictability *if the wrong response mode is used.* For purposes of obtaining the virtues associated with the rule of law, the solution lies in counteracting the arbitrariness that comes from the unbounded dollar scale of dollars.

3. *Deterrence and retribution.* Our findings here strongly support the conclusion that if optimal deterrence is the purpose of the award of punitive damages, the jury system is an extremely bad institution. This is so for two reasons. The first has to do with the jury's motivations. The second has to do with the jury's capacities.

First, ordinary people do not spontaneously think in terms of optimal deterrence when asked questions about appropriate punishment, and it is very hard to get them to think in these terms. Even if focused on deterrence, a jury will be influenced by moral judgments with a retributive dimension, and these judgments will point in the direction of high awards for conduct that is outrageous but likely to be detected (perhaps a murder or an environmental disaster). Second, jurors are not likely to be good at the task of promoting optimal deterrence even if this is what they are seeking to do. If, for example, punitive damage awards are supposed to be grounded in the probability of escaping detection, it is sufficient to say that ordinary people are very bad at making post hoc probability judgments. In order to assess the probability of detection with any precision, people have to master a high degree of technical knowledge about a wide variety of subjects. Hindsight bias will almost inevitably confuse the assessment. If optimal deterrence is the goal, some institution other than a jury, probably an administrative body composed of experts and charged with the specific task, would be much better.

4. *Isolating objections to the current system.* Punitive damages reform should attempt to ensure that juries are charged with performing tasks that they can perform well and should relieve juries from having to perform tasks that they perform poorly, in a way that produces excessive unpredictability, confusion, and arbitrariness. And it would be reasonable to react to our study by suggesting a simple reform: Juries should decide questions of civil liability, just as they do questions of criminal liability. But judges should decide on the appropriate level of punitive damages, just as they do criminal punishment, subject, in both cases, to guidelines laid down in advance. Of course, there is a possible problem with judicial judgments about punitive awards, just as in the case of judicial choice of criminal sentences: In both cases, judges are scaling without a modulus, and different judges will reach different conclusions, thus producing arbitrariness. Hence there is good reason for guidelines and constraints on judges. In any case our study provides strong support for the practice, found in some courts, of reviewing punitive awards to ensure that they are consistent with general outcomes in other cases. Judges need not fear that this practice is antipopulist, for as we have seen, the award of any particular jury may well fail to reflect the community's sentiment on the topic of appropriate dollar award.

To evaluate these and other possible reforms, it is important to distinguish, more carefully than we have thus far, among three possible objections to the idea of using the juries' dollar amounts, as the legal system currently does.

The first objection emphasizes *sheer unpredictability.* The problems here are that potential defendants are not given fair notice and similarly situated people are not treated similarly, in large part because *any particular jury's judgment about the appropriate dollar award is unlikely to reflect the judgment of the community as a whole about the appropriate dollar award.* The second objection points to *defective calibration,* that is, to a poor translation of punitive intent into dollars. The problem is that juries lack the information that would enable them to undertake a good or accurate translation, since ordinary people cannot know the effects of a particular dollar award on a particular class of defendants. The third objection is directed against punitive intent and points to *improper grounds for judgment.* Here the complaint is that the jury is focusing on irrelevant factors, giving undue weight to relevant factors, giving insufficient weight to relevant factors, or ignoring relevant factors.

Punitive Damages Reform, I: Predictable Populism

From what we have said thus far, the most modest reform proposal is straightforward, and it is modest indeed. The goal of the modest reform is to get a true understanding of community judgments – true in the sense that it filters out the noise and arbitrariness that come from asking random groups of twelve people to come up with (the community's judgments about) dollar amounts. If this could be done successfully, it would, in one simple stroke, reduce the problem of unpredictability by a large factor (in the illustrative data used here, by a factor of 2.18). The result would be a form of *predictable populism.*

We have seen that if particular juries are asked to produce a dollar award, as an indicator of community sentiment, there will be a great deal of variability, and that there is also a degree of susceptibility to anchors that have little or no normative weight. But if juries are asked to produce not dollar amounts but either punishment ratings or punishment rankings, the number that results can be turned into what we might call "true dollar awards," by the simple step of taking the jury's rating or ranking and using a population-based calibration function like that described above to produce a dollar value.

Because this approach does what the current system seeks to do with so much less noise and arbitrariness, it should be counted as a nearly unambiguous improvement. It accepts the sovereignty of community judgments with respect to punitive damages, even dollar awards, and it uses the jury to obtain an estimate of what the population as a whole, if equally informed, would want to have done. Through this route it would be possible to produce much more predictability without sacrificing anything else.

Punitive Damages Reform, II: Technocratic Populism

The second kind of reform would attempt to elicit the jury's punitive intent, or its judgment about appropriate punishment, but would not ask the community to make decisions about dollar amounts. On this view, it is agreed that the jury's *intention to punish* is what should govern punitive damage awards. In this way, the outrage model is accepted on normative grounds. The problem is that the most modest reform proposal, just described, perpetuates the crucial defect of the current system; that is, it relies on the abilities of ordinary citizens and hence the community to translate punitive intention into dollars (which, we have argued, results largely in stabs in the dark). A remedy for this defect would use the community's intention to punish but allow experts to translate that intention into dollar amounts. The result would be a form of *technocratic populism.*

For those who favor this approach, it is important to emphasize that ordinary people are unlikely to know what it takes to hurt different people of different means through financial punishment. They certainly do not know what it takes to hurt an organization. Whether or not an organization is involved, they are also using unbounded dollar scales, lacking a modulus that would give meaning to their estimates of different magnitudes. Hence it would be necessary to devise a translation formula that depends on the community's normative judgments about intended punishment, which are not only predictable but also worth using, and not on community judgments about dollar amounts, which can be made more predictable but which may not be worth using. To do this well, it would be desirable to translate the jury's intention to punish with expert assistance; the experts would know what various amounts would mean, or do, to various defendants.

Punitive Damages Reform, III: Bureaucratic Rationality

Should more dramatic reforms be considered? From the discussion thus far, it would be reasonable to conclude that if punitive damages are designed to produce optimal deterrence, juries should be eliminated, for it is doubtful that they can be made to carry out that task. If this is the goal of punitive damages, surely it would be better for the judgment to be made by a judge or (better still) by a specialized regulatory agency entrusted with precisely that task. The result would be a form of *bureaucratic rationality.*

If we agree that the intention to punish is relevant to the punitive award, but not decisive, there is a simple response: Use the jury's intention to punish as one among a set of factors for judicial consideration in imposing punitive damage awards. The judge might be required to consider as well the size of the defendant, the probability of detection, the illicit character of the defendant's gains, and other factors. A risk with such an approach arises from the fact that weights have not been given to the various factors; the absence of weights raises the danger that judicial determinations will also suffer from unpredictability. Hence the legislature or commission might attempt to give greater guidance, by, for example, offering scenarios accompanied by dollar awards, creating ranges, or providing floors and ceilings.

Certainly more dramatic alternatives can be imagined, including those that dispense with a jury entirely. An administratively operated schedule of fines and penalties would seem better than juries at producing deterrence, for such a system would reduce the costs of decision and probably reduce the costs of error as well. There are many analogies. Discussion of pain and suffering awards has included "technocratic" suggestions designed substantially to reduce the jury's role in the interest of more consistent and more expert judgments. In the context of damages to natural resources, it has been suggested that contingent valuation should be replaced by a schedule of damages based on categories of harm;[13] in this way an antecedent set of administrative or legislative judgments would form the backdrop for judgments by a trustee, thus making it unnecessary to ask what may be hopelessly uninformative questions of individuals about their willingness to pay. Radical changes of this kind cannot, of course, be evaluated without a comparison of the likely performance of different governmental institutions.

Mixed Approaches, Caps, and Multipliers

It is possible to imagine mixed approaches, drawing on different aspects of our proposals. For example, a jury might be provided with a preselected set of exemplar cases, accompanied by the damages actually or reasonably awarded in these cases; its job might be to assess damages by comparing the case at hand to the preselected cases. This approach would not take the whole subject of dollar awards away from the jury; it would attempt to root punitive awards in a set of antecedents judgment that could reasonably be compared with the case at hand. Other mixed approaches might attempt to supply a kind of modulus. Juries might, for example, be given average dollar awards for the type of injury at issue, or intervals (showing where a certain percentage of awards for similar injuries fell), or both average dollar awards and intervals.

We do not have sufficient information to evaluate all the possible alternatives here. But we can offer two general conclusions. First, there is much to be said on the behalf of an incremental step, building on current practice: ensuring, in every jurisdiction, a serious oversight role for judges, calling not for individual judicial judgments about individual cases, but for judicial comparisons among various similar cases, so as to ensure against dramatic outliers. Second, the ideal system of punitive damage awards would not involve juries or even judges, but specialists in the subject matter at hand, who are able to create clear guidelines for punitive awards. These guidelines would be laid down in advance and based on a clear understanding of different forms of wrongdoing and of the consequences, for defendants, of different awards. The practical question is whether it is possible to design that ideal system. Experiments in this direction can be found in the workers' compensation system and in the system of administrative penalties and fines.

Consider, by way of summary of what has been a complicated discussion, Table 9.4; our overall evaluations must be tentative because much depends on some answered empirical questions about the likely operation of the different systems.

Implications, Extensions, Speculations

Our central finding – about the difficulty of mapping normative judgments onto an unbounded dollar scale – is relevant to a number of issues now facing law and policy. In this section we briefly describe areas on which our data directly bear.

Difficult Damage Determinations

Many damage determinations require juries to undertake magnitude scaling without a modulus, and to do so in settings that lack clear market measures. A basic underlying question has to do with the appropriate role of normative judgments in settling on the apparently but – as we shall see – controversially "factual" question of what amount would provide "compensation." Thus there are serious issues about the populist and technocratic dimensions of compensatory awards in these domains of the law.

Table 9.3. *Punitive Damage Reform Possibilities*

	Description	Analogies	Virtues	Vices	Overall Evaluation
1. Current system	"Ad hoc populism"	"Kadi justice" (as discussed by Max Weber)	Allows a role for popular convictions	Unpredictability, susceptibility to arbitrary anchors, jury ignorance about effects of dollar awards	Hard to defend from any standpoint; the best that can be said is that the current problems are not so serious
2. Caps	Prevents the most excessive awards	Current civil rights statutes, which also impose a cap	Easy to administer, would prevent egregiously large awards	May increase variability; crudely tailored to any view of the problem or the purpose of punitive awards	In some ways an improvement, but unlikely to make things much better and may in some ways make things worse
3. Damage multipliers	Ties punitive awards to compensatory awards	Sherman Antitrust Act	More flexible than caps; also easy to administer	Crude, since compensatory award is a rough guide to appropriate punitive award	In some ways a little better than caps, but not much better
4. Provide juries with other cases and their accompanying punitive awards, in dollars	Retains jury authority over dollars	Proposals in the area of pain and suffering awards	Should improve predictability and increase rationality	Unclear how jury will respond to prior awards if it disagrees with them; unclear how to make sure the prior awards contain the right amounts	Promising way of providing context and cabining judgment, but may be too complex
5. Strengthened or exclusive judicial control	"Civil sentencing" model	Current system of criminal justice	May reduce unpredictability; may also produce more overall rationality	May also involve scaling without a modulus; eliminates or reduces populist elements; need to ensure judicial comparison of cases	Modest but quite promising response to problems of unpredictability and irrationality
6. Population-wide calibration function	A form of "predictable populism"	None	Reduces variability, increases predictability	Complicated administrative task	Intriguing, but could be too complex and novel
7. Expert calibration function	A form of "technocratic populism"	None	Solves problem of jury ignorance about effects of punitive awards while preserving centrality of punitive intent	Might not trust either punitive intent of juries or the experts	Intriguing and promising, but less feasible than 5 and probably less promising than 8

(continued)

Table 9.4. *(continued)*

	Description	Analogies	Virtues	Vices	Overall Evaluation
8. Ask jury for punitive intent with comparison cases; convert to dollars via 6 or 7	Combination of 4 and 6 or 7; improved predictable populism, improved technocratic populism	None	Has advantage over 4 in supplying comparisons to avoid problems that can come from isolated examination of cases	Might not trust punitive intent of juries; conversion has the problems of 6 and 7	More complex than 4, but a better task for jury, and some promise and problems of 6 or 7
9. Administrative penalties	Bureaucratic rationality	Workers' compensation system; Social Security "grid"; administrative penalties and fines	Could produce both predictability and rationality	Experts may not be trustworthy	In principle, the most promising of all, as a way of reducing decision costs and error costs

1. *Pain and suffering.* Awards for pain and suffering raise many of the same questions as punitive damages. To be sure, and importantly, such awards are nominally compensatory rather than punitive; they ask the jury to uncover a "fact." But they also involve goods that are not directly traded on markets and require a jury to turn into dollars a set of judgments that are, at the very least, hard to monetize. Judgments about pain and suffering require juries to make a decision about harm (with a likely ingredient, in practice, of intended punishment) and to map that judgment onto a dollar scale. In the absence of uncontroversial market measures to make the mapping reliable, the resulting verdicts are notoriously variable, in a way that raises questions very much like those in the punitive damage setting.[14] Our study suggests one of the sources of the variability. A judgment about harm, perhaps made in a predictable way on a bounded numerical scale, becomes unpredictable and arbitrary when translated into an unbounded dollar scale lacking a modulus.

2. *Libel.* Similar issues arise in the law of libel, which notoriously lacks clear measures of damages. Juries are asked to decide how much loss has been inflicted as a result of reputational injury; thus plaintiffs are able to recover both for identifiable pecuniary loss ("special damages") and for damages, stemming from general reputational harm, that cannot be easily correlated with monetary measures ("general damages"). Libel awards are likely to reflect effects similar to those we have discussed here.

3. *Intentional infliction of emotional distress and sexual harassment.* The latter half of the twentieth century has witnessed the rise of two important new legal wrongs: intentional infliction of emotional distress and sexual harassment. Both of these are accompanied by damage remedies. With respect to such remedies, the basic story should be familiar. Monetization is extremely

difficult. Significant arbitrariness is entirely to be expected; similar cases may well give rise to dramatically different awards. In both of these contexts, compensatory and punitive damages are likely to be entangled, in the sense that juries probably do not sharply separate the one from the other. A principal source of unpredictability is likely to involve the translation of the underlying moral judgments into dollar amounts.

4. *Compensatory vs. punitive damages: general considerations.* We can bring together some of the strands of this discussion by noting how the reform proposals discussed above may or may not bear on compensatory damage awards that are especially likely to be erratic. The most important feature of compensatory damages is that they are intended to restore the status quo ante. Punitive damages, by contrast, are intended to reflect a normative judgment about the outrageousness of the defendant's conduct (together with a judgment about deterrence). Thus the compensatory decision, far more than the punitive decision, reflects an assessment of *fact* (at least in theory). At first glance this is a sharp distinction between the two. In this light would it make sense to consider reforms designed respectively to (1) capture a population-wide judgment about appropriate compensation, (2) capture a "compensatory intent" that would be mapped, by experts, onto dollar amounts, and (3) dispense partly or entirely with juries on the ground that juries are unlikely to have the competence to make accurate judgments about the factual questions involved?

To answer this question it is necessary to ask why juries are now charged with the task of making judgments about appropriate compensation in cases in which that inquiry strains their factual capacities. The most straightforward answer is self-consciously populist. In cases involving libel, pain and suffering, sexual harassment, and the intentional infliction of emotional distress, no institution is likely to be especially good at uncovering the "fact" about compensation, if there is indeed any such "fact." Moreover, it is appropriate, on this view, to let the underlying decision reflect not merely facts but also the judgments of value that are held by the community as a whole. Whatever fact-finding deficiencies the jury may have – as compared to, say, a specialized agency – are overcome by the value of incorporating community sentiments into the decision about appropriate compensation for injuries that are not easily monetized. On this view, compensatory judgments, at least in these contexts, are not so different from punitive judgments after all; both of them have important normative components.

Thus the simplest argument on behalf of jury judgments about compensation is that any such judgment is – perhaps inevitably and certainly appropriately – not solely compensatory. It has evaluative dimensions, both in deciding what compensation properly includes and in imposing burdens of proof and persuasion and resolving reasonable doubts. The evaluative judgments, it might be thought, should be made by an institution with populist features and virtues. The point may well apply to judgments about compensation for pain and suffering, libel, intentional infliction of emotional distress, and sexual harassment. A populist institution, on this view, should be permitted to undertake evaluative judgments about what amount would "compensate" someone who has suffered as a result of an improper medical procedure, a lie about his private life, or an unwanted sexual imposition by an employer or teacher.

In the relevant cases, however, the problem of erratic judgments, emerging from magnitude scaling without a modulus, remains. This problem would not be severe (indeed, it would not be a problem at all) if what appeared to be erratic judgments were really a product of careful encounters with the particulars of individual cases, producing disparate outcomes that are defensible as such because they are normatively laden. But our study suggests grave reasons to doubt that this is in fact the case. Thus there is a serious question of reform strategies. How would the proposals discussed above work here? The first point to notice is that for compensatory damages, ranking is far preferable to rating along a bounded scale; it is certainly useful to see how a jury believes that the injury at issue compares with other injuries, but far less useful, when punishment is not involved, to get a sense of the jury's numerical rating. A ranking might be used in various ways. If the basic problem is erratic judgments in the context of compensatory damages, it might be desirable to use a conversion formula to obtain a population-wide judgment about appropriate compensation.

A problem with this approach is that a population-wide judgment about appropriate dollar compensation might be ill-informed; it might not reflect "true" compensation. If the normative dimensions of that judgment seem to deserve a good deal of weight – if we see the jury's judgment about compensation as appropriately reflecting considerations not involving the apparently factual question of "compensation" – this approach might well make sense. But if the factual dimensions deserve to predominate, the jury's ranking might be understood as a kind of "compensatory intent," to be converted to compensatory awards not by population-wide data but instead by an administrative or legislative conversion formula, rooted in a judgment of the appropriate treatment of the cases against which the case at hand has been ranked. This kind of reform seems somewhat awkward, for the notion of "compensatory intent," supposedly rooted in a judgment about the facts, is less straightforward than that of "punitive intent," which is an unmistakably normative judgment. But it would mix populist and technocratic elements in a way that is mildly reminiscent of the treatment of Social Security disability cases – though there the jury is not of course given a role, displaced as it is by an administrative law judge.

If the social security disability cases are really taken as a good analogy, technocratic considerations should predominate, and the third kind of reform proposal might seem best. On this view, an administrative or legislative body might create a kind of "pain and suffering grid," "libel grid," or "sexual harassment grid," combining the basic elements of disparate cases into presumptively appropriate awards. A judge would produce a dollar award by seeing where the case at hand fits in the grid and perhaps by making adjustments if the details of the case strongly call for them. A technocratic approach of this kind could eliminate or at least greatly reduce the problem of erratic awards. Whether it is desirable depends on the value of incorporating populist elements in the way that the more modest reforms promise to do. Elements of these various approaches can be found in reform proposals, thus far restricted to the pain and suffering context, that attempt to cabin the jury's judgment by requiring it to decide in accordance with damage schedules and to place the case at hand in the context of other cases.

Regulatory Expenditures

In the last decade there has been a great deal of interest in the problem of setting priorities for regulatory expenditures, both public and private. The "pollutant of the month" syndrome has given rise to a fear that priorities are set in a random fashion, and hence that expenditures per life saved are unpredictable. Disparities between different life-saving programs are quite common and very substantial. Arbitrariness results partly from the difficulty of mapping normative judgments onto dollar amounts, and many regulatory problems are assessed in a no-comparison condition. We can imagine initiatives that would ensure a greater role for population-wide normative judgments while also promoting more expert "mapping" onto dollars.

Mapping onto a Scale of Years

Our emphasis throughout has been on an unbounded dollar scale, but the legal system makes use of another scale: years. Criminal punishment of course requires a decision about how to map a normative judgment onto a scale of years. That scale is not unbounded, in the sense that capital punishment, or life imprisonment, may be taken as extreme ends; but it presents a similar difficulty of scaling without an obvious modulus.[15] Thus the use of the scale of years presents some of the same questions as magnitude scaling in the absence of a modulus. Before the enactment of the Sentencing Guidelines, there were serious problems of arbitrary and unpredictable sentences, leading to dissimilar treatment of the similarly situated. It is reasonable to think that some of these problems resulted from the difficulty of mapping normative judgments onto a scale of years. Those who challenge the Sentencing Guidelines might be taken to be complaining, among other things, about the absence of an appropriate modulus around which to organize diverse sentences.

A Note on Contingent Valuation

The topic of contingent valuation raises the question whether people can turn their judgments about regulatory goods into nonarbitrary dollar awards. The goal of contingent valuation methods is of course to decide how much to value goods that are not traded on markets. Rather than looking at actual choices, these methods ask people hypothetical questions about how much they would be willing to pay to avoid certain harms or conditions.

Despite their apparent promise, contingent valuation methods have serious limitations, involving the difficulty of mapping normative judgments onto dollars and the problems created by framing effects. A special problem is that of indifference to quantity, or inadequate sensitivity to scope. Consider the fact that Toronto residents are willing to pay almost as much to maintain fishing by cleaning up the lakes in a small area of Ontario as they are willing to pay to maintain fishing in all Ontario lakes.[16] Relatedly, the valuation of a resource is affected by whether it is offered alone or with other goods. Willingness to pay for spotted owls drops significantly when the spotted owl is asked to be valued with and in comparison to other species. When asked for their willingness to pay to preserve visibility in the Grand Canyon, people offer a number five times higher when this is the first question than when it is the third question.[17]

What unifies contingent valuation and punitive damage assessment is the problem of mapping a normative judgment onto an unbounded dollar scale. As with punitive damages, it may well make sense to consider substitutes for the current system of contingent valuation, perhaps rooted in the same considerations that we have discussed here.[18] Perhaps policy makers could develop a small number of scenarios for environmental damages, or use public judgments on a bounded scale, to begin a process by which such judgments might be translated into dollar amounts.

Conclusion

Why are jury determinations about punitive damages sometimes erratic and arbitrary? A large part of the answer lies in the difficulty of "mapping" normative judgments, including those of outrage and punishment, onto dollar amounts. This answer operates against an important backdrop: With respect to judgments of both outrage and punishment, important domains of law show substantial agreement in normative judgments, and the consensus operates across differences of gender, race, age, education, and income.

When the legal system translates punitive intent into dollars, it must answer questions about the extent to which the law should incorporate, qualify, or work against the jury's determination. We have suggested reforms that embody different answers to those questions. Any ultimate conclusion depends on a specific assessment of what is wrong with current punitive damage awards. We have suggested three general possibilities: sheer variability; inadequate assessment, by ordinary people, of what different dollar awards will accomplish; or a focus, by ordinary people, on improper factors as the foundation for punitive awards. Thus an assessment of the normative issues requires an identification of the nature of the populist ideals that underlie the institution of the jury, and a judgment about what place, exactly, those ideals deserve to have in light of juror psychology.

Our study shows that the characteristics of jury judgments include high sensitivity to outrage (and likely low sensitivity to the probability of detection), substantial sensitivity to harm, substantial sensitivity to firm size, susceptibility to anchors, and a backward-looking focus on retribution. A translation phase might incorporate or reject one or all of these characteristics; it may or may not be founded on the jury's punitive intention. At a minimum, our study strongly suggests that appellate judges and district courts should continue the practice, found in some courts, of rejecting punitive awards that are out of line with general practice and relevant comparison cases[19] – especially because, as we have shown, the dollar awards of any particular jury are not likely to reflect the population's judgment about appropriate dollar awards. A more dramatic approach – probably the best for the long term, though not without risks of its own – would involve the development of a system of administrative penalties for serious misconduct, based on judgments made in advance and subject to democratic control.

Notes

1 See, e.g., John Calvin Jeffries Jr., A Comment on the Constitutionality of Punitive Damages, 72 *Va. L. Rev.* 139 (1986).

2 See Reid Hastie, David A. Schkade, and John W. Payne, Juror Judgments in Civil Cases: Effects of Plaintiff's Requests and Plaintiff's Identity on Punitive Damage Awards 23 "Law and Human Behavior" 445 (1999).

3 See Paul Slovic, Trust, Emotion, Sex, Politics, and Science: Surveying the Risk Assessment Battlefield, *U. Chi. Legal F.* 59, 71, 73–4 (1997).

4 See James H. Davis, Group Decision Making and Quantitative Judgments: A Consensus Model, in *Understanding Group Behavior* 35, 47 (Erich Witte and James H. Davis eds., 1996). Clearly, the appropriateness of this measure may depend on the task structure of the group (e.g., whether a unanimous decision is required). In our study, replacing the median of jurors' individual judgments as the group decision with the mean had little effect on the results for outrage and punishment but made dollar awards even more unpredictable.

5 See ibid. at 48–9; Shari Diamond and Jonathan Casper, Blindfolding the Jury to Verdict Consequences, 26 *L. & Soc'y Rev.* 513, 553 (1992); Martin F. Kaplan and Charles E. Miller, Group Decision Making and Normative Versus Informational Influence, 53 *J. Personality & Soc. Psychol.* 306, 309 (1987). Note, however, the existence of an "amplification of bias," by which a group process, involving a set of individuals biased in one direction or another, may push awards in extreme directions, in fact, more extreme than that of any individual before deliberation began. Cf. Norbert

L. Kerr et al., Bias in Judgment: Comparing Individuals and Groups, 103 *Psychol. Rev.* 687 (1996) (finding an amplification of bias in settings other than punitive damage determinations). We are indebted to Robert MacCoun for suggesting this possibility. The possibility of extremes resulting from group deliberation would fortify our conclusion by showing even greater variance.

6 See Stanley S. Stevens, *Psychophysics* 252–8 (1975).

7 See, e.g., ibid. at 26–31; R. Duncan Luce and Carol L. Krumhansl, Measurement, Scaling, and Psychophysics, in 1 *Stevens' Handbook of Experimental Psychology* 3 (Richard C. Atkinson et al. eds., 2d ed. 1988); Lawrence E. Marks, Magnitude Estimation and Sensory Matching, 43 *Perception & Psychophysics* 511 (1988).

8 For experimental evidence that the plaintiff's demand has considerable importance, see Gretchen B. Chapman and Brian H. Bornstein, The More You Ask for, the More You Get: Personal Jury Verdicts, 10 *Applied Cognitive Psychol.* 519, 537 (1996). For evidence about anchors in awarding damages for pain and suffering, see Michael J. Saks et al., Reducing Variability in Civil Jury Awards, *Law & Hum. Behav.*, spring 1997, at 253–5. For real-world evidence about the anchoring effects of compensatory awards, see Theodore Eisenberg et al., The Predictability of Punitive Damages, 26 *J. Legal Stud.* 623, 637 (1997).

9 With the exception of firm size and compensatory damages, both of which might serve as an anchor, but probably less in our experiment than in real-world cases, where those damages are chosen by deliberating juries and thus may have special salience.

10 See Chapman and Bornstein, supra note 8.

11 See Saks et al., supra note 8.

12 See Eisenberg et al., supra note 8.

13 See Richard B. Stewart, Liability for Natural Resource Injury: Beyond Tort, in *Analyzing Superfund: Economics, Science, and Law* 219, 241–4 (Richard L. Revesz and Richard B. Stewart eds., 1995); see also Murray B. Rutherford et al., Assessing Environmental Losses: Judgments of Importance and Damage Schedules, 22 *Harv. Envtl. L. Rev.* 51 (1998) (advocating a damage schedule for environmental losses that is derived from pairwise comparisons of the relative importance of different adverse environmental outcomes or events).

14 See U.S. Gen. Accounting Office, *Medical Malpractice: Characteristics of Claims Closed in 1984*, at 2–3, 18–19, 23–4, 40–2 (1987); Randall R. Bovbjerg et al., Valuing Life and Limb in Tort: Scheduling Pain and Suffering, 83 *Nw. U. L. Rev.* 908, 919–28 (1989); Mark Geistfeld, Placing a Price on Pain and Suffering: A Method for Helping Juries Determine Tort Damages for Nonmonetary Injuries, 83 *Cal. L. Rev.* 773 (1995); W. Kip Viscusi, Pain and Suffering in Product Liability Cases: Systematic Compensation or Capricious Awards? 8 *Int'l Rev. L. & Econ.* 203, 204–8, 214–19 (1988).

15 See Stevens, supra note 6, at 31–3 (using magnitude scaling on jail sentences and using cross-modality matching against the severity of crimes).

16 See Daniel Kahneman and Jack L. Knetch, Valuing Public Goods: The Purchase of Moral Satisfaction, 22 *J. Envtl. Econ. & Mgmt.* 57, 58–9 (1992).

17 See ibid.

18 See Daniel Kahneman and Ilana Ritov, Determinants of Stated Willingness to Pay for Public Goods: A Study in the Headline Method, 9 *J. Risk & Uncertainty* 5, 29–30 (1994); Rutherford et al., supra note 13, at 63–71.

19 See, e.g., *Kimzey v. Wal-Mart Stores, Inc.*, 107 F.3d 568, 576–8 (8th Cir. 1997); *Lee v. Edwards*, 101 F.3d 805, 809–12 (2d Cir. 1996); *Stafford v. Puro*, 63 F.3d 1436, 1444–5

(7th Cir. 1995); *Allahar v. Zahora*, 59 F.3d 693, 696–7 (7th Cir. 1995); *Klein v. Grynberg*, 44 F.3d 1497, 1504–5 (10th Cir. 1995); *King v. Macri*, 993 F.2d 294, 298–9 (2d Cir. 1993); *Ross v. Black & Decker, Inc.*, 977 F.2d 1178, 1189–90 (7th Cir. 1992); *Vasbinder v. Scott*, 976 F.2d 118, 121–2 (2d Cir. 1992); *Michelson v. Hamada*, 36 Cal. Rptr. 2d 343, 356–9 (Ct. App. 1994); *Baume v. 212 E. 10 N.Y. Bar Ltd.*, 634 N.Y.S.2d 478, 480 (App. Div. 1995); *Parkin v. Cornell Univ., Inc.*, 581 N.Y.S.2d 914, 916–17 (App. Div. 1992). As noted, our evidence suggests that if community-wide judgments are the goal, it is important to have a mechanism for additur as well as remittitur.

10 Framing the Jury: Cognitive Perspective on Pain and Suffering Awards

Edward J. McCaffery, Daniel J. Kahneman, and Matthew L. Spitzer

Scholars working in various areas of cognitive psychology and decision theory have long noted that there is a difference in how one values an item based solely on how one perceives it relative to the status quo: whether one views a given matter as a gain or a loss, say. In the case of jury instructions, a relevant difference may be between how much one needs to be paid to be made whole, once an injury has already taken place (a "making whole" perspective), versus how much one would have to be paid to subject herself to the injury in the first place (a "selling price" perspective). While there is a growing literature on the psychology of the jury, we are aware of no study that has examined how the framing of jury instructions in accordance with these perspectives might affect monetary awards for pain and suffering.

A parallel omission characterizes the legal literature on tort theory. Until fairly recently there has been a greater focus on liability rules than on the determination of damages. The emergent literature on damages has tended to focus on the sometimes competing rationales of compensation, insurance, corrective justice, deterrence, or efficiency. This general literature has been supplemented with periodic complaints of a torts "crisis" featuring overly generous damage awards; critics sometimes focus more particularly on pain and suffering or so-called nonpecuniary damages. The related psychological literature, which has for some time explored the relevance for damage awards of extra-evidentiary or logically irrelevant factors, such as gender, race, or the physical appearance of the legal parties, has also begun to look recently at the roles of compensation versus consequentialism in setting damages. In all of this literature there has been little deeper exploration of what "compensation" in fact even *means*, especially as to nonpecuniary losses, and virtually no such exploration outside of the limiting case of death; that is, there has not been much attention paid to what has recently been termed the "measurability problem."[1] This chapter intends to begin filling that gap.

Setting the Stage: Two Background Influences

Our project reflects the confluence of two bodies of thought: contemporary tort law and theory, and cognitive decision theory. This section gives some background for the experimental surveys to follow by considering each subject in turn.

Tort Law and Theory

Damages are obviously extremely and often critically relevant in individual cases to the actual parties involved. Damages also stand at the center of tort theory and practice. For example, the prevalent means of determining negligence liability is the so-called Hand formula, or the rule that a nonnegligent defendant must be willing to make any safety-enhancing expenditure if the cost of the expenditure is less than the expected harm thereby eliminated: $B \leq pL$, in formal terms, where B is the burden (or cost), p the probability of harm, and L the extent of liability or, in our terms, the damages generated by a possible accident. The exclusive focus of our studies is on pain and suffering, or (equivalently) "nonpecuniary" damages. This category of damages accounts for perhaps one-half of the total tort damages paid out in the important cases of products liability and medical malpractice.

In the real world, the determination of damages for "nonpecuniary" or pain and suffering losses tends to be left to juries with vague charges to be "reasonable." Section 905 of the Restatement (Second) of Torts simply allows compensation to be awarded "without proof of pecuniary loss" in the cases of "bodily harm" and "emotional distress," without any elaboration as to the means for computing such losses. An accompanying Comment adds, rather unhelpfully, that "there is no rule of certainty with reference to the amount of recovery permitted for any particular type of emotional distress; the only limit is such an amount as a reasonable person could possibly estimate as fair compensation." In this rote incantation of mantras like "fair" and "reasonable," the Restatement Comment echoes actual jury instructions. For example, approved jury instructions in California for nonpecuniary losses are as follows:

> No definite standard or method of calculation is prescribed by law by which to fix reasonable compensation for pain and suffering. Nor is the opinion of any witness required as to the amount of such compensation. In making an award for pain and suffering you shall exercise your authority with calm and reasonable judgment and the damages you fix shall be just and reasonable in the light of the evidence.[2]

Relative inattention, abstraction, and conservatism characterize these practical outlooks on pain and suffering damages.

As a matter of fact, actual awards for pain and suffering damages tend to vary a great deal from case to case. The vast majority of filed personal injury cases settle, of course, and the vast majority of these feature rather low settlements in absolute dollars. In such cases, settlements tend to exceed economic damages. In larger settlements, the opposite is true; settlement awards are a fraction of claimed economic damages, suggesting that nonpecuniary damages are not obviously significant. In cases that result in actual jury verdicts, pain and suffering damages frequently account for a large percentage of the total award, although the variance is quite high. The most statistically significant way of sorting the awards tends to be by type and severity of injury.

Cognitive Decision Theory

The central relevant body of cognitive decision theory research for our project has been variously termed the "endowment effect," the "status quo bias," or the "willingness to pay versus willingness to accept" differential. Standard microeconomic theory, as embodied in such familiar doctrines as the Coase Theorem, would hold that the valuation of an object should be independent of its ownership, assuming correction for wealth effects. One should value a coffee mug at $5, say, whether one owns it or not; certainly, there should not be a large gap between what one would pay to acquire it and the price at which one would sell it. So much for standard microeconomic theory: The well-documented endowment effect refers to the fact that people indeed must be paid more to give up a good than they would pay to get the very same good in the first instance. The effect has been tested in a variety of thought and actual experiments, where it has been robustly found that people insist on being paid about twice as much for a good as they would pay to acquire it: about $10, say, for a mug that they could readily buy for $5.

The endowment effect can be decomposed into various constituent elements. Three particularly important factors are the ideas of "carriers of utility," "loss aversion," and "framing effects." The idea of carriers of utility is that decision utility – we say "decision" utility to begin to mark a distinction with "experienced" utility, to be explored further below – is impacted by events, not states. For example, gains or losses, generally conceived of with reference to the status quo, loom larger than final asset values in the determination of subjective utility assessments. This is important because end states are often the same although the means of arriving at them are different; we shall see this distinction in the experiments to follow, where the putative plaintiffs always end up with both an injury and a sum of money, albeit by different mental "routes." Loss aversion refers to the phenomenon that gains are less valued, in absolute terms, than losses are disvalued. The subjective utility of losing a good exceeds that of gaining it, even controlling for wealth effects. In our particular case, "losing" health will be cashed out into a higher dollar value than actors would be willing to spend to "buy" the very same objective unit of health. Finally, framing effects refer to the fact that the very same choice can be perceived as a gain or a loss based purely on its formal presentation. For example, individuals will perceive a penalty for using credit cards as a loss and a bonus for using cash as a gain; this will lead individuals to use cash if and only if the "penalty" tack is taken, although the two situations are, from an economic and end-state perspective, identical. Once again, in our case, the loss of health is in some objective sense equivalent to the absence of a cure for ill-health, but the two situations are not subjectively perceived as being the same. Putting all three elements together roughly yields the endowment effect: Individuals evaluate choices based on absolute changes in value, from a baseline that is typically the status quo, attaching more disutility to losses than utility to gains, and being highly subject to purely formal or semantic manipulation, as in the specification of the status quo, throughout.

The endowment effect and the related literature hold out the promise of rethinking a good many legal and economic problems. In our immediate case, these ideas set us to thinking about a parallel problem involving juries and pain and suffering damages. Here we distinguish between the making whole price and a selling price. The difference is between how much one would need to receive to be made whole again, once an injury has occurred – how much one would pay to "buy" good health – and what one would "sell" the corresponding good health for. The making whole perspective is ex post the injury; the selling price, ex ante. In the parallel language of cognitive decision theory, the ex post, making whole perspective establishes the *injured* state as the reference point, baseline, or status quo. The ex ante, selling price perspective instead makes the *healthy* state into the reference point. Cognitive decision theory yields a very definite prediction here: Since the specification of status quo matters (decisions are evaluated vis-à-vis a fixed reference point), losses are more costly than are gains, and framing can have real effects, we expected the ex post, making whole perspective to yield values below the ex ante, selling price perspective. The sense of losing health generates a higher dollar amount than the idea of buying it back – even though the end states (money and lost health) are the same in the two cases.

As we explore at some length in our second round of experiments, the selling price also involves an element of choice or responsibility not present in the making whole perspective. In addition to having the healthy state as the reference point, the selling price perspective might be thought to implicate volitional choice in accepting personal injury. Cognitive decision theory has also suggested that such a "responsibility" component can affect valuation, and we aimed to address this variable in our second round of experiments. In sum, standard economic and psychological theory might predict little or no difference between purely formal, perspectival manipulations of the way that damages are sought, but we suspected otherwise.

The Main Event: Two Experimental Surveys

This section presents the heart of our effort: two experimental surveys, administered to sizeable groups of law students and a general lay public, respectively, exploring how the choice of frame affects compensation awards for pain and suffering.

Round I

Our first round of surveys was administered to a group of 283 law students at the University of Southern California Law School, after several pretests had been given to small groups of Yale Law School students and changes made to improve the forms. This survey featured a control group and two other groups receiving different jury instructions, one using a making whole and the other a selling price perspective. We found a dramatic and significant increase when the selling price instruction was used.

Survey Design and Administration. All subjects were given the same initial page and asked for their name and optional phone number; they were told that the phone number was in case we had any follow-up questions. This initial page explained that the subject was to imagine that she was a juror in a trial. All minimally necessary facts except the nature of the injury were stipulated. Thus, the subject was told that the injury had already happened and was expected to last for about three years, that liability had been fixed, that there was no effect on earnings capacity, and that she was being asked only to choose an "appropriate amount of compensation" for pain and suffering damages.

The initial page went on to explain that there would be two ways of specifying damages: first, by placing a mark on a base ten, logarithmic scale, with choices running from $1,000 to $10,000,000, and, second, by filling in the amount in a blank space next to the scale. We decided to have this two-part technique after initial pretests indicated that, without prompting, students simply had no idea of a relevant range of awards, so that the responses showed a wide variance. The scale and blank combined made sure that some care was taken in answering, allowed us to check for internal consistency and, most importantly, gave all subjects a similar, if quite wide, range within which to operate; we were only interested, after all, in relative differences. The initial page concluded with an example.

Following this initial page, the basic instructions were repeated on page 2. Once again, all aspects of a personal injury trial were stipulated except for the precise nature of the injury. Six descriptions of injuries followed. We chose injuries that we considered neither too severe nor trivial; recall that we had specified that each was to last for about three years. Examples included "experience extreme stiffness in the upper back and neck" and "have intermittent migraine headaches, lasting for one hour at a stretch." All subjects were given precisely the same six descriptions, in precisely the same order, but were divided into three groups based on the form of jury instruction. The control group was given nothing except the six injury descriptions and thus were left with the simple charge to find an "appropriate" level of compensation. In fact, this is fairly close to what actual jurors are told, as evidenced by the generic jury instructions quoted earlier.

The other two groups, after the first two questions, were given a specific jury instruction on page 3. This format allowed us to use the first two questions as covariates, or terms to calculate the subject's general tendencies to award money damages, and to isolate out a within-subject multiplier. Each of these two groups was told that the judge had given them a specific instruction regarding how to view the question of damages, which was to be used in answering Questions 3–6. One group was given the following making whole instruction:

To determine the appropriate compensation, imagine that you are the plaintiff. You have already suffered the described injury. What amount of money is needed to make you "whole" again – that is, as fortunate as if nothing (i.e., neither the injury nor the payment) had happened?

This instruction simply emphasized the ex post nature of the setting ("you have already suffered") and quite literally invoked the making whole perspective. In contrast, the final group was given the following selling price instruction:

To determine the appropriate compensation, imagine that you are the plaintiff. Before any injury has taken place, the defendant offers you a sum of money to suffer the described injury exactly as it is later experienced. What amount of money would you demand to willingly accept the injury?

In contrast to the making whole instruction, this one emphasized the ex ante nature of the setting ("before any injury has taken place"), or, equivalently, the healthy state as baseline, and used the device of a counterfactual market transaction to drive home the selling price idea. Thus the juror *qua* putative plaintiff was given a choice of undergoing the injury or not. In both cases we took care to be simple and direct; a major focus in our early pretests was to ensure the clarity of these instructions.

Each of these two groups, along with the control group, was then given the same injury descriptions in Questions 3–6. All subjects were given a final page, in which both instructions were listed, and the subjects were asked which version they expected to yield higher values, which they believed to be closer to commonsense intuitions about fair compensation, and which they thought was proper. To control for a possible "anchoring" effect of the order of the instruction on this final page, each of the three groups (control, making whole, and selling price) were further divided in two, with one-half of each group getting the making whole instruction first and the other one-half the selling price, as we explain further below.

The survey was administered on a single morning to four large classes of law students at the University of Southern California Law School; two were first-year and two were upper-division classes. The classes met either simultaneously or in immediate sequence, so that no subject was aware of any other running of the experiment. One of the coauthors, a professor at the Law School, was present during each administration and read the first page of instructions out loud. There were no apparent difficulties in understanding the form; students generally completed it in five to ten minutes.

Results. There are several ways to look at the data, and technical reasons to prefer one over another. We used various methods to get at the differences between the making whole and selling price instructions. We took the means and medians of each of the three groups, using raw data; we transformed the data into natural logarithms, to reduce the influence of "outliers," or unusually large responses, and then took the means of the logarithms; we looked at the "multiplier," or by how much the average answer to Questions 3–6 increased over the average answer to Questions 1–2, as a way of factoring out varying tendencies to award money damages; we performed ordinary least-square-regression analysis, with the instruction as the explanatory variable and the average answer to Questions 3–6 as the dependent one. All of these techniques told the same basic story: The selling price instruction yielded higher values than did the making whole one, which in turn yielded higher values than the control group. Under various tests for statistical significance, all of these differences were significant.

The different techniques all have something to recommend them, so that it is difficult to find any single metric with which to communicate the data to a general audience. Table 10.1 presents the multiplier, the antilogarithm of the logarithmic or geometric mean, and the raw data median for each of the three groups. In plain words, the first column, the multiplier, indicates by how much the answers to Questions 3–6 increased, on average, over those to Questions 1–2; the multiplier uses the means of the raw data for the two

Table 10.1. *Basic Results from Round I*

Instruction	Multiplier	Logarithmic Mean	Median
Control	2.15	$72,113	$93,750
Making Whole	4.20	151,448	290,000
Selling Price	10.41	331,042	527,500

sets of questions. This approach takes into account the different views of the appropriate range of money damages; we were interested, after all, only in the effect of the jury instruction, and this instruction came after Questions 1–2. Another way to think about this multiplier is that it gives a look at an intrasubject, as opposed to a between-subject, comparison. The multiplier tells us what effect the instruction had on the average individual subject within a given pool, as compared with the cross-subject pool comparisons used in the next two columns. The second column resulted from transforming the raw data for Questions 3–6 into natural logarithms, taking the mean of each, then the mean of the means, and finally converting back into dollar figures by taking an antilog. This seemingly cumbersome procedure is a simple but relatively standard way of taking into account outliers; it is exactly equivalent to taking a geometric mean, for those readers with some statistical background. Finally, the last column gives the median of the raw data. This is simply the middle value when the values are arranged from highest to lowest; one-half of the group gave higher values, and one-half lower ones.

The results in Table 10.1 make clear that the selling price perspective yielded larger awards than did the making whole one. Under all three statistics, the selling price perspective is around two times the making whole one; specifically, the ratios are 2.48, 2.19, and 1.82 for the three statistics. This result is precisely in line with the findings from the general endowment effect literature, discussed above. We should emphasize that the dollar figures, alone, have little significance; in fact, they are greatly higher than actual pain and suffering awards tend to be. We would expect that in a real trial these figures would become more restricted, in part because of the collective decision-making process of the jury and the constraining effects of a real trial setting. It is the relationship between the figures that most interests us; the selling price is consistently and significantly higher than the making whole one.

The multiplier figure is especially interesting. The control group doubled its answers to Questions 3–6, indicating both that these injuries were deemed to be more serious and that the subjects were focusing on differentiating among injuries. The making whole instruction pool increased awards by four times (we discuss the control – making whole difference below). The selling price perspective pool increased their awards more than tenfold. Among other things, this indicates that the selling price perspective is not a particularly natural one; left on their own as to what "appropriate compensation" meant, subjects in the control group gave damages much more in line with a making whole perspective.

Two additional points are worth noting before moving on to analysis of the follow-up fairness questions and the related Round II experiment. First, neither the gender nor the class of respondents (first-year or upper-division law student) had significant explanatory power. Aside from the instruction given, which had strong power, only the average response to Questions 1–2 had any explanatory power, as one would expect; generous subjects were generous both before and after the instruction. Second, the difference between the making whole and the control group, about a factor of 2, was consistently significant. There are several possible explanations for this multiplier effect: for example, perhaps any instruction at all is likely to increase awards. But we believe that the main determinant of this effect was that even our making whole instruction was *subjective*; it had the subject imagine herself as the plaintiff/victim. We thought that this language was innocent enough – a way of giving simple instructions – but we found out later that such a charge to place oneself in the shoes of the plaintiff violates the so-called (perhaps inaptly) golden rule from actual trial practice in America. The golden rule bars an attorney from arguing that a juror should imagine herself in the plaintiff's situation and is defended in part as a means of keeping a check on the size of damage awards. In a descriptive regard, the practice seems correct; an inadvertent by-product of our research is confirmation that making a juror think of herself as the plaintiff does have a significant, positive effect on damage awards – approximately doubling them.

Recall that all subjects were given a follow-up page, in which both the making whole and the selling price instruction were set out. The students were asked, on a scale ranging from "certainly" through "probably" making whole (at one pole) to "about the same" and then "probably" through "certainly" selling price (at the other pole), which instruction they thought (1) was likely to yield higher values, (2) seemed "closer to what you believe to be commonsense intuitions about fair compensation," and (3) "in your personal opinion ... comes closer to a proper standard for measuring compensation." As a control against any possible "anchoring" effect – the tendency of subjects to cling to their first impression on a subject – we alternated the order of the instructions as version A and B (and thus had to transpose half of the answers so that all conformed to the same scale). Thus, there were six forms: control, making whole, and selling price formed three large pools, with the order of instructions on page 5 further dividing each group into two smaller ones. An anchoring effect could have occurred based either on the initial instruction given, on page 3, or on the order of instructions appearing on page 5.

The first step in our analysis, however, was to rule out any possible anchoring effect. Subjects did not significantly differ in their page 5 responses based either on which, if any, instruction they had previously been given, or on the order of instructions appearing on page 5 itself. This, in itself, is an interesting finding, because our survey of real-world actors, discussed below, indicates that practitioners often think that the way things are done, using vague and abstract instructions, is the fair or appropriate way – suggesting an anchoring effect as a possible explanation for ideas of "fairness." It is possible, of course, that law students had *already* formed opinions on the issue; that is, that an anchoring had already transpired. This becomes a point of comparison with the lay subjects in Round II, where, interestingly, some weak anchoring is present but there is less favoring of making – whole-type instructions. In any event, the finding of no anchoring allowed us to group together all of the approximately three hundred subjects. We also found that the answers to Question 2, which was intended to get at what the subject thought a typical juror might think, and Question 3, which asked for a subjective evaluation of fairness, were not significantly different. Thus, we look only at Questions 1 and 3 below.

The best way to present the data on the follow-up questions is probably through a histogram or bar chart, simply showing the actual range of responses. In our figures we assign values from 1 to 5, with 1 representing "certainly the making whole instruction" and 5 representing "certainly the selling price instruction." The middle value, 3, represents "about the same." There is nothing significant about these particular numbers, and thus averaging across them is not especially meaningful. Such averaging would also obscure important issues of the distributions of answers. For example, an average answer of 3, as we in fact approximately found for Question 1, could mean either that most respondents thought that the values would be about the same for either instruction, or that there was a wide divergence of opinion, as we in fact found. Figure 10.1 presents the distribution of answers to Question 1, on which instruction was likely to yield higher values.

Figure 10.1 reveals the large split in responses between subjects who thought that the making whole or selling price instructions were, respectively, likely to yield higher values. Although the average response was in

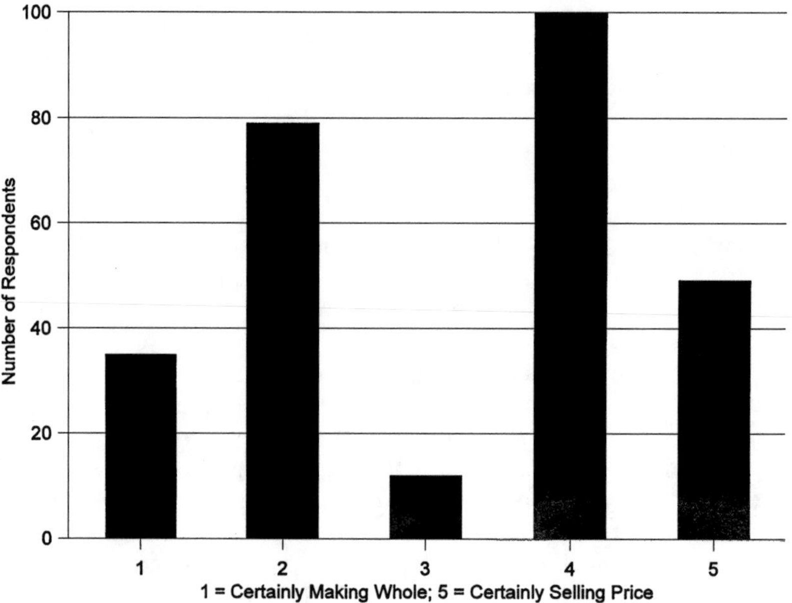

Figure 10.1. Prediction of higher values.

fact close to the neutral answer, 3, surprisingly few students actually chose this option, only 12 out of 275. (Perhaps this demonstrates that law students just have strong opinions, one way or another.) Over 40 percent of respondents thought that the making whole perspective would certainly or probably yield higher values; less than 18 percent were certain that the selling price would be higher. What is interesting here, of course, is that the making whole answers are demonstrably wrong, in light of the evidence presented above. The selling price perspective in fact yields significantly higher values, two to three times higher than the making whole perspective. At a minimum, these responses suggest that, when we turn to the subjective fairness Question 3, the answers are not motivated by a strong belief in the higher magnitude of the selling price perspective; that is, subjects do not seem to be choosing what is appropriate based on a strong or at least accurate reading of the magnitudes involved.

Figure 10.2 presents the responses to Question 3, asking what the subjects, in their personal opinions, thought was a more appropriate instruction.

Question 3 reveals a pull toward the making whole perspective. Over 68 percent of respondents considered this rule either "certainly" or "probably" more appropriate. But the opinion was neither uniform nor especially dogmatic. Less than 15 percent were certain that the making whole price was more appropriate; over 30 percent thought either that there was no difference or that the selling price was more appropriate. Especially as these results

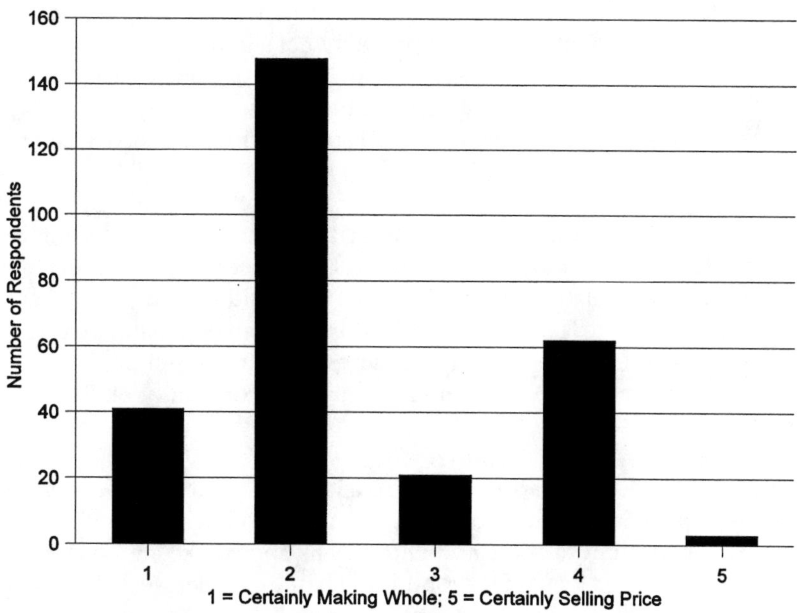

Figure 10.2. Evaluation of proper standard.

obtain with virtually no tutoring or motivation for the no doubt more counterintuitive selling price instruction (as we give in Round II), we interpret them as supporting only a weak conclusion that law students are inclined toward making – whole-type instructions. Some further evidence for the appeal of the making whole perspective to this pool of subjects can be deduced from the fact, noted above, that the uninstructed control group was clearly far closer to the making whole perspective in its valuations; our sense is that these two groups (making whole and control) would have been nearly identical but for the subjective aspect of the making whole instruction.

Round II

The first round of experimental surveys left us with one large question and several smaller ones. The major question concerned two possible determinants of the selling price–making whole differential, the existence of which was our principal finding in Round I. One possible element can be called the temporal or reference-dependent component. The making whole instruction sets the perspective ex post the injury, creating an injured baseline or reference point, whereas the selling price perspective is ex ante, with a healthy state as baseline. A second possible element can be called a volitional or responsibility component. The selling price involves an exercise of free choice; it involves the putative victim in the act of deciding between well-being and money, whereas the making whole perspective does not. (We knew from the extensive literature and earlier surveys that a third possible influence, wealth effects or state-dependent utility, was probably not significant, although we indirectly take this into account in Round II anyway.) We wondered about the relative contributions to damage awards of the reference and responsibility elements and designed a new experimental survey with the task in mind of sorting through the difference.

Running a second round allowed us to explore other, lesser questions. Thus we decided to run Round II with a lay audience, to see how it might differ from law students. We softened the subjective feature of the jury instructions that had violated the "golden rule" in Round I. We used different follow-up questions to get different takes on the perceptions of fairness. We also laid the foundation for further studies regarding the significance of plaintiffs' wealth or income level on assessments of compensation for nonpecuniary harms.

Survey Design and Administration. The basic outline and approach of the forms was substantially similar to those used in Round I, with some changes made based on the nature of the audience (lay as opposed to law students), because of the different focus of the round, and based on what we had learned from Round I. An initial page asked for the respondent's gender and age and was otherwise completely anonymous. This initial page explained that the subject was to imagine herself as a juror and proceeded to describe the scale. For this round, we made the scale larger and easier to read and included the space for writing in the amount below the scale, rather than beside it as in Round I.

Page 2 then began with a description that specified all minimally relevant legal facts except the nature of the injury. Thus, subjects were told that the injury had already occurred, that it was expected to last about three years, that it was caused by a drug company whose liability had been established, and so on. The subjects were told that the injured party or plaintiff was a person of the same gender as the subject, thirty years old, and whose family had a combined income of $40,000, an approximately median figure. As in Round I, the subjects were told that earnings were unaffected by the injury, and that they were being asked "to consider only the appropriate payment for the injured person's pain and suffering." The focus was thus once again on nonpecuniary damages only.

The same descriptions of six injuries as had been used in Round I then followed. After the first two questions we inserted a jury instruction on page 3. We did not use an uninstructed control in Round II, since our main concern was to get at the determinants of the differential between the making whole perspective and the selling price one. One group was given the following making whole instruction, analogous to that used in Round I:

> To determine the appropriate sum of money, imagine the following situation from the injured person's point of view. You have recently suffered the injury, and expect to live with it for three full years. What amount of money would be just enough to make you, on balance, as fortunate as you were before the injury happened?

The use of the qualifying phrase "from the injured person's point of view" was intended to mitigate the "golden rule" violation noted in Round I; otherwise, these instructions were simply designed as a more accessible, less legalistic variant of the making whole instruction. Note that the second sentence clearly establishes the ex post, injured reference point. A second group was given the following selling price instruction:

> To determine the appropriate sum of money, imagine the following situation from the injured person's point of view. Before anything happens, you are offered a sum of money to experience the injury exactly as it later occurs, for the full three years. What amount of money would be just enough to make you accept the injury?

Once again, except for the change in the narrative perspective to mitigate the golden rule problem and the removal of certain legalistic language, this instruction is parallel to the selling price perspective instruction used in Round I. It uses the same first sentence as the prior making whole instruction, but then continues in a manner that is clearly ex ante the injury, that is, with a healthy state as baseline, and has an element of choice. The juror is putatively being asked to decide between an injury and a sum of money, a choice that does not exist in the making whole setting. Thus this instruction has both the reference point and the responsibility element of the selling price perspective.

To split the difference – that is, to employ an instruction that made only one of the changes on the way to a making whole perspective – we came up with the following instruction:

To determine the appropriate sum of money, imagine the following from the injured person's point of view. You have recently suffered the injury, and expect to live with it for three full years. A complete cure for the injury exists. You are offered enough money to buy an immediate cure, or you could instead decide to keep the money and live with the condition. What amount of money would be just enough to make you willing to live with the injury?

We refer to this third instruction as the "hybrid" one. The first two sentences are virtually identical to those in the making whole perspective. By specifying that the injury has already occurred, these sentences establish the reference point dimension as being injured, or ex post the injury. The final sentence of the hybrid instruction, in contrast, is virtually identical to the final sentence in the selling price instruction. Here an element of choice preserves the responsibility component. To motivate the element of choice notwithstanding the ex post setting, we used the counterfactual of an existing cure. The putative injured person can choose between a cure and a sum of money. It may at first seem odd that the price of the cure implicitly rises with the alternative sum of money, but this is in fact an accurate description of the opportunity cost of the cure; by choosing the cure, one forgoes the sum.

What is important to see is the fact that, in terms of end states, this hybrid instruction offers a choice set that is *exactly* the same as that obtaining under the selling price perspective. In both cases, the putative plaintiff is given the choice of being healthy *or* being injured but having a sum of money of the juror's choosing. This choice does not exist under the making whole perspective, where all that can be offered is money. The fact that the final states are the same as between the selling price and the hybrid indirectly takes care of wealth effects; in both cases, as with the making whole one, the monetary alternative is accompanied by the injury. Relatedly, the equivalence of the end states would lead standard economic, rational actor theory to predict no difference between the results; the experienced utility should look the same in each instance. But the hybrid instruction is situated after the accident has happened, and, in this regard, looks more like the making whole perspective. Thus, these three instructions, taken together, were intended to help us decompose the reference point and responsibility components from our Round I findings.

Finally, the subjects each received two follow-up pages. The first repeated the instruction that they had been given and, after giving a short motivational explanation, asked, essentially on a scale of 1–5, whether or not the instruction was fair. The next page presented a different instruction and explanation, with the same question and scale. The survey was administered outside the Exploratorium, a science museum open to the public in San Francisco. A psychology graduate student set up a table, and volunteer subjects were paid $3 to complete the survey. A total of 175 subjects participated.

Results. The basic results showed that the hybrid instruction yielded values in the middle of the making whole and the selling price instructions. Table 10.2 presents the same three statistics for Round II as were used in Round I. The principal finding from Table 10.2 is that the results from the hybrid instruction fall almost exactly in the middle between the results from the making whole and selling price perspectives. The hybrid instruction yielded statistics 2.4, 2.41, and 1.63 times the making whole one, whereas the selling price increased the hybrid yield even more, by 3.48, 1.63, and 1.94 times. These findings indicate that both the reference and responsibility components are doing work in pulling down the making whole perspective, in almost equal measures.

The large gap between the selling price and the making whole perspectives in Round II is a bit puzzling. We do not make too much of this fact because of the high variance in Round II answers, and because it is too difficult to aggregate results across the two pools. (That is, it is difficult, because of the differences in population and experimental instruments, to make meaningful comparisons using both rounds at the same time.) Nonetheless, one interesting possibility is that the correction for the golden rule violation was more effective in the case of the making whole instruction than in the selling price one. That is, the results from the objective making whole instruction from Round II approached those obtained from the uninstructed control group in Round I. This suggests that the making whole perspective is the default mental perspective from which individuals are naturally inclined to view pain and suffering damages. In contrast, Round II's selling price instruction carried an implicit subjective message; working through the act of choice made putative jurors consider themselves in the shoes of the victim. Thus, in addition to the 2 times tendency observed in Round I due to the shift from the making whole to the selling price perspective, we were also observing a further compounding due to the implicit golden rule violation. Although

Table 10.2. *Basic Results from Round II*

Instruction	Multiplier	Logarithmic Mean	Median
Making Whole	2.14	$110,084	$245,000
Hybrid	5.13	265,401	400,000
Selling Price	17.87	431,490	775,000

we lack enough data to pin this result down formally, the fact that, in practice, selling price and subjective techniques often merge together lends some support to this hypothesis.

As noted above, all subjects were given two follow-up pages. Each follow-up page asked, on a scale ranging from "definitely fair" through "probably fair" and "unclear" to "definitely unfair" (a scale we transpose to 1–5 in the figures), what they thought of the fairness of a certain instruction. Each subject was first given, on page 5, the precise instruction she had been given earlier on page 3; each was then given, on page 6, a new instruction. Those who had been given a making whole instruction were given a selling price one as a new test; those who had been given selling price or hybrid instructions were now given making whole ones. After each instruction was given (that is, on both pages 5 and 6) but before the question, a brief motivational explanation was given. The making whole instruction was explained as follows:

> The idea behind this instruction is that, since the injury has already happened, the best that any jury can do is to make the injured person as well off as he or she was before the injury.

The selling price instruction was explained as follows:

> The idea behind this instruction is that the defendant has deprived the injured person of the choice of remaining healthy. The payment should therefore be determined with reference to the values of the injured person when he or she was still healthy. It is not intended, of course, to suggest that any such deal would ever take place; it is a mental exercise to help get you, the juror, thinking about compensation in the right way.

Finally, the hybrid instruction was explained as follows:

> The idea behind this instruction is that, since the injured person cannot in fact be made healthy, the most that any jury could do is to give him or her the amount of money that would make the person willingly accept living with the injury. The instruction is not intended, of course, to suggest that any such deal would ever take place; it is a mental exercise to help get you, the juror, thinking about compensation in the right way.

The purpose of these short explanations was to give a simple and hopefully unbiased common basis for understanding the purpose of instructions that might have seemed odd, perhaps especially to a lay audience.

As in Round I, we first tested for anchoring. Since the making whole and the selling price pools were symmetric – that is, each pool was given both instructions on the follow-up pages – we focused on these two groups. We found no anchoring in evaluating the making whole perspective: that is, whether or not the subjects had been given this instruction in working through their quantitative answers to Questions 3–6, they were equally likely to think that the instruction was fair. On the other hand, we found a slightly significant anchoring with regard to the selling price instruction. Those subjects who had initially been given the selling price perspective were more likely to think that it was fair. This anchoring tendency lends support to the idea that one tends to think more highly of what one has done or experienced in some sense.

What is interesting about the Round II follow-up fairness questions, however, is the fact that subjects were almost equally likely to think that *any* of the *three* instructions was fair. Since we detected only a slight anchoring tendency, we lumped together all of the subject responses to each particular instruction: all 175 addressed the making whole instruction, either as a given or a new instruction; two-thirds, or 120, of the subjects addressed the selling price instruction; and 55 addressed the hybrid instruction. Figure 10.3 shows how these various pools rated the fairness of the instructions. The figures are presented as percentages (i.e., are normalized) to get them all on the same scale, despite the different absolute numbers.

Figure 10.3 is striking in demonstrating how similar the evaluations of fairness are, although these are three very different jury instructions, and although each subject was given two different instructions that could be used as points of comparison. Indeed, the most salient fact about Figure 10.3 is the strong modality of answer 2, "probably fair," to each instruction; this answer accounted for almost half of all answers to each question. Recall also that the selling price instruction is pulled toward unfairness by the subjects seeing it

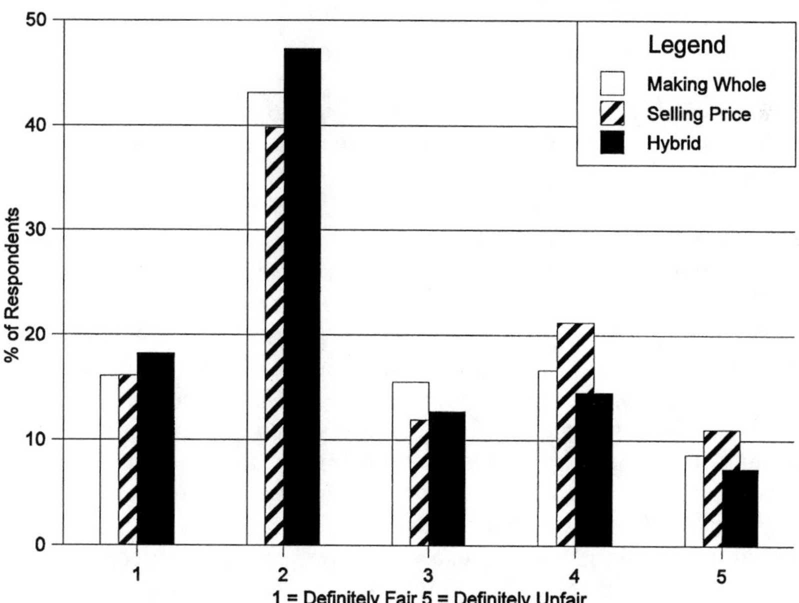

Figure 10.3. Evaluation of fairness of instructions.

for the first time on page 6, and that the hybrid instruction was only given to fifty-five subjects. Thus, the relative frequencies are virtually identical. It appears that lay subjects do not have strong fairness preconceptions, and/or that the brief motivational explanations were equally sufficient to convince all groups of the fairness of each instruction.

Summary and Analysis

The general conclusion from the experimental surveys, in both Rounds I and II, is that the framing of requests for pain and suffering damages matters a great deal. It is hardly a natural mental exercise to engage in valuing nonpecuniary items such as pain and suffering, and so it is not surprising that much should turn on how the question is posed. Our findings are very consistent with cognitive decision theory, although not in keeping with standard economic or rational actor models. The experiments confirmed our most general presupposition, namely that the making whole–selling price differential, or, equivalently, the specification of the status quo ante, matters. Specifically, we found, consistent with the extensive literature on the endowment effect in other settings, that the ex ante selling price perspective yielded a value twice as large as the ex post making whole perspective did.

We also reached other conclusions, several of which ought to be of interest to the broad cognitive decision theory literature as well as to the legal audience. The making whole–selling price differential decomposed into two almost equal components. One, a reference effect, indicated that viewing the situation ex ante the injury, with a healthy reference point, increased awards as compared to an ex post, injured reference point baseline. A second, responsibility effect, did likewise; focusing on a putative choice between remaining or becoming healthy and receiving a sum of money – that is, drawing attention to the exercise of free will – increased awards over a more traditional focus on coming up with a sum of money to attempt to make a plaintiff/victim whole again. Each effect contributed in apparently equal parts to the overall factor of 2 effect manifested by the selling price over the making whole perspective. This finding may at first seem puzzling, since the factor of 2 effect has been observed in a wide range of buying-selling price experiments, such as those involving coffee mugs. On reflection, however, some element of the responsibility or choosing effect may be present in all such settings. Selling an item, even a minor one, may be thought to involve choice in a deeper or more vivid sense than buying; after all, selling is a far rarer activity for the average individual, so that the choice to sell or not may seem rather weighty. In contrast, the decision whether to buy or not is made by individuals nearly constantly, in a wide variety of highly impersonal settings. Another way of seeing this point is that the act of selling seems more permanent than that of not buying, so that one is more reluctant to sell than not to buy. In both cases, the phenomenon is compatible with the "carriers of utility" idea, that individuals attach a disproportionate weight to short-term transitions and transitional processes, as opposed to focusing on the persistent end state.[3] The responsibility or choice component may thus explain at least part of the reference component effect. Here, as we found, both effects seem present and significant, independently of the other.

Finally, we found that respondents did not have strong intuitions on the relative fairness of different approaches. The law student subjects were rather inaccurate in their descriptive estimations of the effects of different perspectives and were only mildly likely to see the making whole rule as a fairer instruction than the selling price one. The lay subjects, given a brief motivational explanation for each of three different instructions, were almost equally likely to think that any of them were fair.

An Encore: One Real-World Survey

To find out more about what occurs in actual courtrooms, we mailed out a questionnaire to approximately five hundred participants in the legal system. We selected approximately two hundred each of plaintiff and defense personal injury lawyers, using computerized databases of lawyers in Connecticut, New Hampshire, Massachusetts, and Rhode Island. We determined their area of expertise from listed specialties, using "insurance defense" as a screen to select defense lawyers, and we limited our search to attorneys who had gotten their bar degree between ten and twenty years before. Finally, we added one hundred trial judges.

The purpose of the questionnaire was to learn, in a general way, about trial practices in personal injury cases. Unlike our work discussed in the prior section, we were not aiming here to conduct a scientific survey, and we do not engage in sophisticated statistical analysis in this section. Rather, we indicate general trends and themes, of an anecdotal nature, and quote extensively from the various responses we received. These were, in general, enormously helpful: Many of the respondents were very thorough. The survey allowed us, for example, to learn about the golden rule, discussed above and to be discussed in greater detail below.

We received back ninety-five completed questionnaires, and an additional thirty-five were returned because of improper address or because the addressee was not engaged in civil trial work (this often happened because the judges served only on the criminal docket). Thus, we had a response rate of approximately 20 percent. Because of both limited funds and the nature of our inquiry, we did not follow up the initial mailing. Nonetheless, the completed responses gave us a wide range of useful and pertinent information.

The questionnaire was accompanied by a cover letter, written on law school stationery, explaining the nature of our project and assuring complete anonymity. At the top of page 1, we asked whether the respondent was a trial judge, a plaintiff or defense attorney, or other. Out of the ninety-five completed questionnaires, we received back fifteen from trial judges, thirty-two from plaintiff attorneys, thirty-four from defense attorneys, and fourteen that were either mixed plaintiff-defense or did not identify themselves.

The questionnaire proceeded to describe the selling price perspective and to ask five open-ended questions. Question 1 asked whether or not the respondent had observed the selling price perspective in practice, and whether or not jury instructions ever adopted it. Question 2 asked about other means of measuring pain and suffering damages. Question 3 asked which perspective the respondent thought was most fair or appropriate. Question 4 explained a concern of ours, deliberately minimized in our experimental surveys, about a possible "legitimacy" effect. We were worried that in certain types of cases, a juror might consider a selling price perspective especially illegitimate; for example, being paid to suffer an occasional headache is one thing, whereas actually selling a body part is another. In our experimental surveys, we deliberately chose temporary conditions that, in our opinion, did not raise great legitimacy issues. Question 4 asked if a sense of legitimacy might constrain the selling price perspective. Finally, Question 5 asked for any general thoughts or comments about the respondent's experience with selling price perspectives in trials.

A solid majority of respondents, fifty-seven out of ninety-five (60 percent), stated that they had *never* seen or used the selling price perspective in practice. A very large percentage of this group, in turn, opined that such a perspective would be categorically barred in their jurisdiction; a good many of these respondents mentioned the golden rule specifically, and several even cited cases or gave us excerpts from relevant legal materials. The most common answer to Question 1 from this pool of respondents was "no" or "I have never seen this done." Representative answers included:

> No – in Rhode Island, this is objectionable and violates the "golden rule." Arguing explicitly in this way could cause a mistrial or a reversal.

> In Connecticut practice, it [is] viewed as highly improper/to the extent of mistrial/to invite the jury to answer that question.

> You cannot ask such a question under Massachusetts state law.

> No because it is an improper argument and unethical. This would be prohibited, at least in New Hampshire.

All of these particular answers were reiterated by other respondents. Since we only mailed the questionnaire out to lawyers in those four states – Connecticut, Rhode Island, Massachusetts, and New Hampshire – the assertiveness of these answers would seem to lay things to rest; the selling price perspective is simply never used in practice. Interestingly, all ninety-five respondents agreed that jury instructions never adopt a selling price perspective. From what we can tell – several judges gave us their instructions, generally reproduced from standard form books, and we have since had many conversations with practicing lawyers, all confirming this point – actual jury instructions seem to follow the California form quoted above, emphasizing impartial and abstract "reasonableness." These instructions in turn track the Restatement approach. Those who had never seen or used the selling price perspective were fairly evenly distributed across our categories of lawyers: they included eight trial judges, twenty-two plaintiff lawyers, and nineteen defense attorneys. Our most vehement answer came from a plaintiff lawyer: "Never! Absurd premise to expect or suggest that you would 'sell' yourself into a personal injury."

Perhaps our most interesting general finding, then, given the above, was simply that a significant minority – the remaining thirty-seven out of ninety-five respondents (40 percent) – had indeed seen a selling price perspective in practice, although only a handful admitted to using it themselves. Some of these answers, no doubt, may be traceable to confusion over what we meant by a selling price perspective. (This might also explain some of the negative answers as well.) Many of the positive answers, however, indicated a clear and correct comprehension of the perspective; two good examples include the following:

> I have seen one or two plaintiff lawyers ask, rhetorically, "How much money would you accept to suffer this pain?" or words to that effect.

> I have been involved in trials where plaintiff's attorney has raised the selling perspective by asking jurors to consider how much someone would have to be paid to voluntarily undergo what the plaintiff had to undergo in that particular case.

A good many of the positive responses to Question 1 indicated that respondents were quite aware that the practice was officially improper under the golden rule, and several even suggested ways around the rule. These positive answers spanned all four jurisdictions at issue. A typical response along these lines was "Yes, I have seen lawyers attempt to advance the 'selling price' point of view in closing arguments. However, that is an improper argument under Massachusetts law." A defense attorney commented, "I have seen it. I know it is marginal in terms of propriety."

Several respondents indicated that a selling price perspective was a *common* litigation strategy:

> Plaintiff attorneys frequently use this approach to get jurors to consider pain and suffering in terms of monetary compensation. (defense attorney)

> Yes, lawyers often use this common technique. (trial judge)

> Yes – the attempt to personalize injury is common. (defense attorney)

> This approach is *always* used by good and effective plaintiff trial lawyers, without expressly positing a "golden rule" argument. This tactic is particularly useful in cases where human injury is great, but economic loss may be small (e.g., facial scarring). (trial judge) (emphasis in original)

One trial judge wrote:

In recent years I have noticed a distinct falling-off of the use of "selling price" arguments to juries to the extent that I can't recall the last time I heard it. During the time I was a litigator, although I never used it in the direct form, I did hear it from time to time. I preferred a more indirect form.

One respondent even included an excerpt from a trial practice manual, indicating a not-all-too-subtle way to smuggle in a selling price perspective around the golden rule. As in the case of negative responses to Question 1, positive responses spanned the spectrum of categories of respondents: they included seven trial judges, ten plaintiff attorneys, and fourteen defense attorneys.

What is going on? How can it be that a sizeable majority of respondents had never seen the selling price perspective used, and a good many of them stated in unequivocal terms that it would be impermissible to do so, while at the same time a significant minority claim to have seen it, in some cases to have used it themselves, and several thoughtful responses even averred that a selling price perspective is *common*? A reader untutored in the ways of the law may conclude that something must be terribly wrong with our questionnaire, the respondents, or both. For those of us with experience in legal matters, however, the apparent contradiction is not surprising. In practice, there is wide room for interpretive maneuvering in the law. What appears to be a categorical, hard and fast rule against selling price perspectives can be subtly avoided, often, no doubt, in ways that leave one side ignorant of the evasion. This is, after all, the point of the techniques that we were given as ways around the golden rule.

It also appears that narrowly local factors can explain some of the divergence. Lawyers seem to be well attuned to what will or will not work before jurors in their particular areas; many answers suggested that the respondent thought that a selling price perspective risked backfiring before jurors, and often these answers were quite locality-specific:

I think most lawyers up here would fear juror (generally conservative Yankee-type) negative reactions and thus simply don't engage in it.

I am from a very conservative area, resort town, with many retirees. I like to stick to the basics.

Other respondents had a more general aversion to using the selling price perspective:

I think that this would be offensive as well as objectionable.

Selling price perspective appears absurd, inhumane.

[M]ost jurors would be alienated by such an argument.

A trial judge stated that, in the rare instances he had seen a selling price perspective used, the results had been "disastrous."

Of course, these reactions were by no means universal. Some respondents seemed to have a good intuitive feel for what our experimental studies were to show. One plaintiff attorney wrote, in answering the final question:

> I personally feel that the selling price argument is probably the strongest.
>
> I think when Plaintiff counsel merely suggests this in a closing statement (even if the comment is stricken), it forces the jury to look at the case in an entirely different way.

Another plaintiff attorney noted in closing that the selling price perspective "sounds like an interesting concept which I have not had much experience with." Perhaps the best way to sum up the varying responses is in the words of a trial judge, who took the time to write us a most thoughtful letter. This judge initially noted that "[o]ver the past nearly ten years I have presided over hundreds of civil jury trials in which damages have been claimed for bodily injuries. Before that for some thirty years I represented both plaintiffs and defendants in personal injury trials." The judge then went on to note, as we quoted above, that he has seen a falling off in the use of the selling price perspective and that he, personally, in practice had preferred a more indirect form. The judge's final comment nicely captures the sense with which we, as naive outsiders, came to regard actual practice: "If you and your colleagues develop meaningful empirical data I would be most interested in reviewing it. Most of us really know very little about the juries we work with every day."

What do we make of these general responses? Clearly the selling price perspective is highly constrained in actual practice, both by legal standards that block its explicit invocation and by a sense of propriety and decorum that prevents at least some plaintiff attorneys from appearing too aggressive in front of juries by invoking it. Jury instructions never employ the approach and seem always to use an abstract and impersonal language of fairness and reasonableness. Equally clearly, the selling price perspective is indeed used, and its actual incidence ranges from occasional, in certain types of cases, to frequent. The facts of the matter seem to vary by jurisdiction and may be difficult to ascertain. Many of the uses of selling price perspectives are subtle, implicit, perhaps even "subliminal." A predominantly defense attorney who had not seen the selling price perspective used formally, and who noted that it was not permitted in his state of Massachusetts, went on to comment that "[c]learly this is the subliminal message that I think most attorneys try to convey with an overlay of the plaintiff's own subjective perspective." Another defense attorney, who also wrote that she had not seen the selling price perspective used formally, added that "[t]his is a subliminal theme used by plaintiffs, quite effectively." Most interesting was a trial judge, who answered Question 1 by writing: "I have not observed attorneys using this technique but I know from speaking with jurors (post trial) that they consider this at times."

Paired with our empirical findings from the second section, the significant variance in practices helps to explain the actual variance in pain and suffering awards that has helped to trigger reform efforts such as those to generate schedules for damages. Lawyer skill, personality, and relative risk aversion would seem to matter a good deal under these conditions. In terms of fairness, we note that most lawyers think that the way things are done – using abstract and impersonal jury instructions and emphasizing a mechanical "per diem" approach to damage assessments – is fair; in this regard, actual participants in the legal system mimic the law students of Round I. On the other hand, a very sizeable minority of respondents thought that there was no one "fair" approach, or that *any* approach was fair, or, perhaps equivalently, that all approaches were arbitrary; in these regards, responses mimicked those of the lay audience in Round II. Virtually no answers indicated any awareness of the potential empirical dimensions of the issue, and one seasoned veteran of over forty years in the personal injury arena told us, directly, that most people who work with juries have little idea of how they actually think. In this ignorance, at least, there is a rare degree of convergence between the academic literature and real people.

A Critical Review

We consider our project to be largely positive or descriptive. We were concerned to show the magnitude of the effects that various frames or perspectives can have on pain and suffering awards. We believe that we have established that a selling price perspective yields awards approximately twice as great as a making whole one does, and that this effect decomposes into two roughly equal, constituent elements, a reference-dependent or temporal dimension and a responsibility or volitional one. We also have reason to believe that a subjective perspective, violating the golden rule, doubles awards, and that selling price instructions naturally tend toward this subjective stance. The untutored mental default seems to favor an impersonal making whole perspective. Legal practices officially bar a subjective frame and tend toward impersonal, abstract, making whole perspectives, but a large number of lawyers have found more or less direct ways around the official rules. All of these we take as facts, at least until additional research extends or refines them.

But these are facts that call out for further, deeper normative analysis. At a minimum, they are facts that suggest a set of questions not yet formally addressed in the scholarly literature on tort damages. Standard economic and psychological theory would have left us with the impression that large differences in value based solely on the choice of frame or perspective would not exist. Combined with the evidence of actual practices from our questionnaire discussed in the third section, the empirical dimensions of framing help to explain the great variance in pain and suffering damages observed in actual cases. Once scholars have been made aware of certain empirical determinants of these differences, namely that some lawyers and perhaps some types of cases are better than others at getting away from an impersonal making whole perspective and moving toward a subjective selling price one, some thought has to be given to what the legal system ought to do. This section aims simply to frame those questions for later, broader, and deeper analysis.

Getting at the Truth: Half Empty or Half Full?

Once the fact of an injury has been established, there are at least two ways to look at nonpecuniary damages. On the one hand, we can consider that there was once a healthy plaintiff who has now lost her health; we can ask how much she has lost from the baseline of her healthy self. On the other hand, we can consider that there is now only an injured plaintiff, and that the best we can do is to give her some money to attempt to "make her whole"; that is, we can adopt the baseline of the injured party and look at her loss from "below," as it were. Neither perspective is more "accurate" than the other. Standard economic theory and untutored intuitions might suggest that there is no real difference between the two perspectives, just as these approaches would suggest that there ought not to be a large buying/selling price differential. Our findings from the second section indicate, however, that there can be a dramatic difference in the magnitudes of awards depending on which referential frame is adopted. The responsibility or volitional component adds yet another dimension to the same issue. If we adopt a fully ex ante perspective, we can consider that one of the incidents of good fortune inhering in the healthy plaintiff is the free will to become injured or not; if our baseline is ex post the injury, that one particular freedom is forever gone. The question, of course, is what to do.

Decision Versus Experienced Utility

We mean to mark a distinction between "decision" and "experienced" utility. Most economic theory presumes that decisions are made on the basis of subjective assessments of actual, underlying utility. A person thinks that she decides to order chocolate rather than vanilla ice cream based on an accurate assessment of the utility to be had at the moment of tasting each flavor; one has, as it were, a correspondence theory of utility. But an increasingly large body of experimental evidence has arisen to challenge the correlation between the utility levels used in making decisions and actual *experienced* utility; it appears that individuals are often poor predictors of their very own preferences or hedonic states, and that their memories are often similarly flawed. The gap may suggest grounds for paternalistic intervention, say, in "informed consent" choices over medical care.

A thoroughgoing, Benthamite hedonic utilitarianism – that is, a belief in real and measurable psychological states corresponding to varying levels of utility or pleasure – that gave weight only to experienced utility would thus suggest that the lower, making whole perspective, measured off the ex post injury baseline, is the proper social response to the variance we have observed. The reasoning for this position is simple. Assume that all we care about is "utiles"; we are Benthamites and believe in the possibility and normative propriety of interpersonal cardinal utility comparisons. The making whole perspective asks how much money we need give to the injured plaintiffs to make her whole: that is, to give her the same utility level she had before the accident. If we in fact do this, then the plaintiff is, *ex hypothesi*, no worse off for the accident, and the lower making whole perspective should set the correct level of compensation. Any *greater* damages would compel defendants (and those to whom they pass on the costs) to overcompensate plaintiffs; part of the damage payments, again *ex hypothesi*, would serve the purpose of bringing plaintiffs victims to a higher utility level than they had occupied before the accident.

A way of making this same point, namely that the ex post, making whole perspective is more correct from a certain hedonic utilitarian philosophy, through the language of cognitive decision theory, is to see that parties giving the higher, ex ante, selling price perspective are *wrong* under a Benthamite psychology. These parties, acting under the pervasive influence of the status quo bias, are change averse; they overestimate the disutility that actual injuries or other harms might bring. In fact, individuals seem far more adaptable after suffering unpleasant turns of fortune than they had predicted they would be beforehand.[4] This resilience may suggest that, from a normative perspective, society should not give too much weight to the exaggeratedly high ex ante, selling price values. People are forever dreading changes that they come not to find as bad as they feared, or not to mind at all, or even to appreciate. Decision utility places too much stress on fleeting transitional concerns as carriers of utility and grossly misstates actual experienced utility levels.

To note the gap between experienced and decision utility, however, is by no means to solve the normative questions. The decision/experienced differential may at first suggest a case for paternalistic overriding of individual decisions. But even if we are to stick within a utilitarian construct, it is not always clear that we ought to give in to the temptation toward paternalism. After all, decision utility is utility, and it has long been noted that people have important "second-order" preferences, or preferences over preference formation. Disrespecting people's choices, even in their own best interests, involves a cost to their autonomy, self-regard, and well-being; any parent knows all too well the importance – indeed, the necessity – of sometimes ceding to their child's preferences, knowing full well that these preferences are sometimes apt to lead the young one astray on the child's own lights, as later appraised.

Beyond Utility: A Note on Commensurability

Traditional utilitarian theory does not necessarily counsel for the making whole perspective, but it at least suggests it; absent strong second-order preference effects, a hedonic utility maximizer would be suspicious of jury damages, which are necessarily set in an abstract realm, and she would be especially suspicious of a selling price frame. On the other hand, we are not all, for better or worse, thoroughgoing Benthamite utilitarians. Indeed, phenomena such as state-dependent utility or adaptability to adverse conditions, each of which may undergird and at least partially explain the decision/experienced utility gap, may be strong reasons to reject Benthamite psychology as a basis for *social* rules. As Amartya Sen has pointed out, we would expect individuals – we count it as virtuous and healthy – to adapt in the face of adversity and to conform their expectations and preferences accordingly. But this does not mean that, when they are healthy, we should devalue their freedom because we have reason to believe that, having lost aspects of it, they would not be all that bad off in a cardinal, hedonic utilitarian sense.

This brings us to the idea of "commensurability," currently a hot topic in legal academia and a useful concept, in part on that account, through which to discuss nonutilitarian approaches to tort damages. We do not mean to deal extensively with this topic, but we note that "incommensurability" can have both a subjective and an objective meaning. Subjectively (within an individual agent's mind) some things may simply be incomparable, so that individual choice mechanisms break down. Faced with a choice of careers or a choice between simultaneous commitments to two equally dear friends, for example, an individual agent may simply have no rational way to compare alternatives. Objectively, society may not want certain things to be compared; there can be incommensurability by fiat. Money, health, and well-being are often in this latter camp; it may be possible to make trade-offs – we do so, implicitly, all the time – but there may be settings in which society does not want to do so publicly.

It is precisely because money and health are in some sense incommensurate that we must face, more pressingly, the question of perspective. If money were commensurate with health, then the Benthamite position would become appealing; it would "really" be the case that the compensated plaintiff had been made whole, and that she was no worse for the wear. If we do not believe this fiction – and it seems that we generally do not – then the ex post, making whole perspective loses its quasi-scientific appeal along with its logical and ethical force. We must face the deeper normative questions raised by an awareness of perceptual differences.

Putting It All Together: Different Strokes for Different Torts?

The making whole–selling price differential parallels a well-noted potential gap between compensation and deterrence. Even if we believed that the lower, ex post making whole value adequately compensated an injured plaintiff once an injury had occurred, it does not follow that the damages faced by putative defendants, for purposes of calibrating their ex ante incentives and expressing society's values, should also be set at this making whole level. Once again, we are not engaging in the contemporary tort theory debate over the ideal role of and scope for damages. Rather, we simply note that setting damages at the higher selling price perspective would force rational defendants to take into account in their actions the value of health and free will to the pre-injury plaintiff. These defendants would have to consider the loss of utility or well-being in going from the healthy to the unhealthy state. They would have to value freedoms and abilities not necessarily valued by individuals once they have lost them; putative defendants would not be internalizing a thoroughly Benthamite psychology. They would have to exert greater care, because society would place a value on the well-being or freedom forever lost in going away from a healthy baseline.

We are not addressing all of the issues entailed in developing a complete theory of tort damages. One important bottom line is simply that we have to think about the issues raised by an awareness of the consequences of perceptual distinctions from a normative perspective. There is no right answer to the question of half full or half empty, except, perhaps, one that involves questioning the question. Like the rhetorical question, there is no definite right answer to the question of making whole versus selling price perspectives for pain and suffering damages. Quite unlike the rhetorical example, however, the making whole-selling price differential really does matter – it has demonstrable consequences. It is a question we need to learn how to ask.

We mean to stress, therefore, not only that our suggestions are preliminary, but also that they are for the consideration of society at large. No principle of cognitive decision theory, and no detailed study of extant legal rules, can answer the question of how we *should* think about nonpecuniary damages in those settings where we want them at all. We have shown that it matters, a good deal, whether one takes the healthy or the injured plaintiff as a baseline, and whether one considers the loss of free will to remain healthy as a component of value. Once we have seen that these choices matter, that they must be made, and that our practices have implicitly answered them in a generally conservative fashion that also leaves a wide scope for varying practical answers, the normative social inquiry is only at its beginning.

Notes

1 Mark Geistfeld, Placing a Price on Pain and Suffering: A Method for Helping Juries Determine Tort Damages for Nonmonetary Injuries, 83 *Cal. L. Rev.* 773 (1995). Professor Geistfeld's fine article was developed simultaneously with but independently of our effort. Geistfeld provides a very helpful summary and discussion of current scholarly positions regarding pain and suffering damages in a wide range of contexts.

2 *Book of Approved Jury Instructions [BAJI], California Jury Instructions: Civil*, (8th ed. 1994). Judges from Connecticut and New Hampshire sent us their jury instructions in conjunction with the questionnaire discussed in the third section; these were each nearly identical to the California version.

3 See, e.g., Daniel Kahneman, New Challenges to the Rationality Assumption, 150 *J. Inst. & Theoretical Econ.* 18 (1994).

4 See generally ibid. at 25–32, and sources discussed therein (summarizing a range of experiments establishing that individuals are poor predictors of their own future hedonic states and, similarly, often fail to remember events accurately; these studies tend to involve both pleasant and unpleasant activities).

11 Behavioral Economic Analysis of Redistributive Legal Rules*

Christine Jolls

This chapter offers a behavioral economic analysis of redistributive legal rules. Redistributive legal rules are rules chosen for their effects in shifting wealth from high-income to low-income individuals (progressive redistribution). The desirability of such rules has been the subject of intense debate within the legal community. Many law and economics scholars have urged that legal rules be chosen solely with an eye toward Kaldor-Hicks efficiency (which I will call simply "efficiency" for the remainder of this chapter); these scholars often urge that distributional considerations be addressed (if they are to be addressed at all) exclusively through the tax and welfare systems.[1] On this view, distributive goals do not provide a basis for choosing an inefficient legal rule – although they might, it seems, provide a basis for choosing between two efficient rules.[2] Other legal scholars have argued that the selection of legal rules should be informed by distributional considerations even at the expense of efficiency.[3] I will call a rule "redistributive" if it makes such a trade-off between distributive objectives and efficiency.

A recurring theme in the debate over redistributive legal rules has been the relative cost of redistributing wealth through legal rules (defined to mean rules other than those that directly relate to the tax and welfare systems) and redistributing wealth through the tax and welfare systems (which I will call simply "the tax system" or "taxes" for the remainder of this chapter).

* This chapter is a shortened version of an essay with the same title that appeared in a symposium issue of the *Vanderbilt Law Review* (Christine Jolls, Behavioral Economic Analysis of Redistributive Legal Rules, 51 *Vand. L. Rev.* 1653 [1998]). Omitted from this version are discussions of (1) the possibility that market forces will correct departures from rationality as defined by neoclassical economics; (2) (a related point) the focus of my analysis on individual rather than firm behavior; (3) a numerical example illustrating and expanding upon various points about the effect of insurance on my analysis; (4) the effect on the analysis of valuation of uncertain outcomes based on prospect theory rather than expected utility theory; (5) the prospect of probabilistic (or randomized) taxation; and (6) other considerations (apart from effects on work incentives) that bear on the choice between redistributive legal rules and taxes. The reader is referred to the original essay for a discussion of these topics.

Under the assumptions of neoclassical economics, any desired level of redistribution can be achieved at lower cost through the tax system than through legal rules.[4] This is not because the tax system can redistribute wealth costlessly; the animating feature of both lawyers' and economists' analyses of tax schemes is their potential to distort people's work incentives. Higher taxes on the wealthy will tend to discourage people from earning high incomes. But from the perspective of neoclassical economics, precisely the same is true of redistributive legal rules: "[U]sing legal rules to redistribute income distorts work incentives fully as much as the income tax system – because the distortion is caused by the redistribution itself."[5] Thus, for example, a 30 percent marginal tax rate, together with an inefficient legal rule that redistributes an average of 1 percent of high earners' income to the poor, creates the same distortion in work incentives as a 31 percent marginal tax rate coupled with an efficient, nonredistributive legal rule.[6] However, the former regime also entails costs due to the inefficient legal rule. (For example, under a redistributive tort rule, potential defendants may be excessively cautious and thus may be discouraged from engaging in socially valuable activities.) Thus, whatever the desired level of redistribution, it can always be achieved at lower cost by choosing the efficient legal rule and increasing the degree of redistribution through the tax system than by choosing an inefficient rule because of its distributive properties.[7]

A basic premise about human behavior underlies this analysis: Work incentives will be distorted by the same amount as a result of a probabilistic, law-based mode of redistribution (such as tort law) as they will be as a result of a tax. Thus, for example, if high-income individuals face a .02 probability of incurring tort liability for an accident, then a redistributive legal regime that imposes $500,000 extra in damages (beyond what an efficient rule would call for) would distort work incentives by the same amount as a tax of $10,000; $10,000 is the expected cost of both the tax and the redistributive tort rule. (Of course, risk-averse actors may choose to purchase insurance against tort liability in such situations; the role of insurance in this analysis is discussed below.)

Why should redistributive legal rules and taxes have the same effects on work incentives? "[W]hen an individual . . . contemplates earning additional income by working harder, his total marginal expected payments [out of that income] equal the sum of his marginal tax payment and the expected marginal cost on account of accidents."[8] The expected costs of the two forms of redistribution are the same, and thus behavior is affected in the same way. At least that is the assumption that neoclassical economics makes.

Is this assumption valid? Would an individual typically experience the same disincentive to work as a result of a more generous (to victims) tort regime as would be experienced as a result of a higher level of taxation? Behavioral law and economics suggests that the answer may be no (although, as emphasized below, only empirical evidence that we do not yet have can definitively resolve the question). One reason for this conclusion stems from the fact that uncertain events – such as incurring tort liability – are often processed very differently from certain events. And taxes, to paraphrase Ben Franklin, are (along with death) nothing if not certain. A second reason for the difference between the two forms of redistribution is that they may be charged to different "mental accounts." As described below, some costs may be viewed as direct charges against income, while others may be viewed as different sorts of "expenditures," which may affect work incentives differently.

These points about redistributive legal rules do *not*, I will argue, suggest that people sometimes overestimate, but other times underestimate, the effects of such rules. If this were true, then on average the errors might cancel, or, at least, there would be no good way to predict the direction of the errors. Indeed, a suggestion along just these lines has been offered by Professors Louis Kaplow and Steven Shavell: If people "misestimat[e] the extent of redistribution [through legal rules], there is no compelling reason to assume that their guesses [will] be too low rather than too high."[9] This chapter advances the contrary view that the costs of redistributive legal rules are more likely to be *underestimated* than to be *overestimated*, and, thus, that work incentives may be distorted less by redistributive legal rules than by taxes.[10]

Distortionary Effects of Redistributive Legal Rules and Taxes

For two major reasons, described below, behavioral law and economics suggests that work incentives may be distorted less by redistributive legal rules than by taxes.

The Processing of Uncertain Events

Estimation of Probabilities. A salient feature of redistributive legal rules in the tort context is the uncertainty of their application to any given actor. The effect of such rules "tends to be limited to those few who become parties to lawsuits."[11] While one knows that one will have to pay taxes every year, one knows that one is quite likely *not* to become involved in an accident. In such settings, it becomes important to consider how people estimate the probability of uncertain events.

In general, people may either underestimate or overestimate the probability of an uncertain event.[12] Underestimation is common (strokes and auto accidents, for example, are underestimated),[13] but overestimation may occur when a risk becomes highly visible or salient to people.[14] This pattern of underestimation and overestimation seems to hold true across a range of different cultures and different times.[15] Although a full account of what risks are underestimated and overestimated by a given group of people at a given time may require consideration of social and cultural factors beyond the scope of individual psychology and, thus, behavioral economics as presently understood,[16] behavioral economics seems to provide significant insight into the basic pattern of underestimation and overestimation of risks.

An amazingly robust finding about human actors – and an important contributor to the phenomenon of risk underestimation – is that people are often unrealistically optimistic about the probability that bad things will happen to them. A vast number of studies support this conclusion.[17] Almost everyone thinks that his or her chances of having an auto accident, contracting a particular disease, or getting fired from a job are significantly lower than the average person's chances of suffering these misfortunes; estimates range from 20 to 80 percent below the average person's probability.[18] Likewise, on a more anecdotal level, if one surveys students anonymously at the beginning of a course, very few (if any) will predict that their final grade will be below the average grade in the course. Of course, these beliefs cannot all be correct; if everyone were below (or above) "average," then the average would be lower (or higher).

The phenomenon of unrealistic optimism is not, as one might initially speculate, an artifact of using college undergraduates as subjects in studies of the phenomenon. (One might think that undergraduates have a more positive outlook than most postgraduates, and perhaps a more positive outlook than those who do not have the opportunity to attend college.) Unrealistic optimism is also evident in studies of people taken from the general population.[19] Unrealistic optimism is also apparent for both low-probability and high-probability events.[20] And unrealistic optimism appears to reflect not *overestimation* of the probability that negative events will happen to others, but rather *underestimation* of the probability that they will happen to oneself; for instance, people not only think (as noted above) that the probability of their being involved in an auto accident is lower than the average person's probability,[21] but also think that their probability is lower than the *actual* probability.[22] (They also appear to think that the probability of an auto accident in the general population – that is, for others rather than for themselves – is less than the actual probability;[23] this provides further support for the conclusion that people are underestimating their own probability as opposed to overestimating the average person's probability.) Finally, there is evidence that people's real-world behavior in certain areas tracks the predictions of unrealistic optimism; for instance, many people fail to buy insurance against negative events such as floods and earthquakes despite massive federal subsidies and heavy marketing efforts by insurers[24] (and federal aid in the event of a flood or earthquake is not a convincing explanation for this phenomenon, since most of those who fail to buy insurance expect no federal aid). Of course, people in other contexts do buy insurance (for instance, against auto accidents); the relationship between this fact and the unrealistic optimism findings is discussed in the next section.

What explains unrealistic optimism? The explanation seems to be that by thinking things will turn out well, people often increase the chance that they will turn out well. Unrealistic optimism, from this perspective, is generally a highly adaptive behavior (although it may harm people in particular instances). Consistent with the adaptiveness hypothesis, unrealistic optimism tends to correlate with happiness, contentment, and the ability to engage in productive, creative work.[25] Also, there is evidence (although this is subject to debate) that those with accurate, as opposed to excessively favorable, impressions of their personal abilities (impressions that may in turn be correlated with their impressions of the probability that a negative event will occur) tend to be clinically depressed.[26] The adaptiveness explanation for unrealistic optimism provides further support for the conclusion that this phenomenon reflects not overestimation of the average person's probability of a negative event, but underestimation of one's own probability.

People offer unrealistically optimistic assessments of the probability of negative events in areas directly related to the effects of redistributive legal rules. For example, most people think that they are less likely than the average person to be sued.[27] Likewise, people think that they are less likely than the average person to cause an auto accident.[28] They also think that their own probability of being caught and penalized for drunk driving is lower than the average driver's probability of being apprehended for such behavior.[29]

What does unrealistic optimism about the probability of negative events imply for the distortionary effects of redistributive legal rules as opposed to taxes? People will tend to underestimate the probability that they will be hit with liability under a redistributive legal rule; therefore, their *perceived* cost of the rule will be lower. As a result, their work incentives will tend to suffer a lesser degree of distortion than under a tax yielding the same amount of revenue for the government. For instance, in the numerical example from the introduction, people may not attach an expected cost of $10,000 to a .02 (objective) probability of having to pay $500,000 extra in damages under a redistributive tort rule; they may tend to underestimate the probability that they will incur liability – and thus they may tend to underestimate the expected cost of the rule – as a result of unrealistic optimism.[30]

In some cases, however, people may tend to *overestimate* the probability of a negative event. Overestimation may often occur when an event is highly salient, threatening, or otherwise highly "available"; familiar examples include nuclear power plant accidents and environmental issues such as contamination from toxic waste dumps.[31] An event is "available" if it comes readily to people's minds; events that are highly available are typically ones that have received a great deal of media attention, and are often ones that are intrinsically vivid or memorable, or have a technological nature. People may significantly exaggerate the probability of such events. But this phenomenon is unlikely to affect the assessment of redistributive legal rules, at least insofar as individuals (the focus of this chapter) rather than firms are concerned. Consider the quintessential event that can expose an individual to tort liability: the auto accident. As noted above, people appear to underestimate the probability that they will be involved in an auto accident (relative to the actual probability);[32] this presumably results from a combination of underestimation of the general probability of an accident (by approximately 50 percent according to the leading study)[33] and further underestimation of people's *own* probability relative to the average person's.[34] The situation would likely be different, of course, for an event such as a nuclear power plant accident, the probability of which might be overestimated due to its availability. But highly available events (consider also the example of contamination from a toxic waste dump) tend to involve firm, not individual, liability. It is difficult to come up with examples of events giving rise to individual liability, the probability of which is likely to be overestimated rather than (as suggested above) underestimated. And with underestimation of the probability of liability, work incentives will be distorted less by redistributive legal rules than by taxes.

The Effect of Insurance. How is the analysis offered above affected by the availability of insurance? Because insurance almost always involves some combination of deductibles, copayments, and experience rating (to mitigate problems of moral hazard), even with insurance there will still be *some* uncertainty about the degree to which a redistributive legal rule will affect a given individual, just as there is uncertainty under a redistributive legal rule without insurance. Part of the redistributive cost will thus be incurred only probabilistically, depending on whether an accident occurs. And, based on the analysis offered above, individuals will tend to underestimate the probability of being affected, and thus their work incentives may again be less distorted than with a tax (although the effect will be less pronounced).

The opposite conclusion might hold, however, if the carrying costs of insurance were large enough to outweigh the effect of underestimation of the probability of causing an accident. The larger the carrying costs, the larger the expected cost of the redistributive legal rule, and at some point this effect would begin to outweigh the effect of underestimation of the probability of causing an accident. However, even if insurance completely undoes the effect described above, the phenomenon of mental accounting, discussed in the following section, provides a separate reason that work incentives may be distorted less by redistributive legal rules than by taxes.[35]

One final comment about insurance is necessary here. One might wonder whether the fact that many people purchase insurance undermines the conclusion that people often underestimate the probability of negative events. For if they think such events are unlikely to happen, why would they buy insurance against them? There are several responses. First, as noted earlier, people sometimes do not buy insurance in circumstances in which it would seem that a rational decision maker would be likely to do so.[36] Second, with regard to situations in which people do buy insurance, it may be that a high level of risk aversion toward large losses causes them to want to insure against such losses despite their underestimation of the probability that such losses will occur. Even if people underestimate the probability of a loss, risk aversion may cause insurance to remain attractive. Note that this does not necessarily imply that people are risk averse toward the probabilistic losses that remain *after* the purchase of insurance (due to deductibles, copayments, and experience rating); there is in fact some evidence that people are risk *seeking* toward moderate losses.[37] So the fact that people choose to insure against some portion of the losses to which they are exposed does not imply that their perceived cost of the losses to which they *remain* exposed after the purchase of insurance is greater than the objective expected value of these losses. (For instance, if the probability of incurring liability is .02 and the extra liability under a redistributive legal rule is $500,000, the fact that a person finds it in his or her interest to pay $8,000 for coverage against $400,000 of the $500,000 in liability [coverage with an objective expected value of $8,000] does not imply that the perceived cost of the remaining probabilistic loss [a .02 (objective) probability of incurring $100,000 in liability] is greater than or equal to a sure payment of $2,000 [the objective expected value of this loss].) Of course, it also does not imply the opposite; we simply do not know why people on the one hand appear to be unrealistically optimistic and also often risk seeking, but on the other hand often purchase insurance. For those who have found my attempt to reconcile these features of human behavior unpersuasive, I note again that the section just below, on mental accounting, provides a separate reason (unrelated to the processing of uncertain events) that work incentives may be distorted less by redistributive legal rules than by taxes.

Mental Accounting

The second major reason that work incentives may be distorted less by redistributive legal rules than by taxes is that the costs imposed by the two approaches to redistribution may be attributed to different "mental accounts." The idea behind "mental accounting" is that people do not always view a dollar spent in the same way; it may matter very much from which "account" the dollar is coming. Money is not fungible in the way that standard economics assumes.

Consider this example:

Case 1: Imagine that you have decided to see a play for which admission is $10 per ticket. As you enter the theater you discover that you have lost a $10 bill. Would you still pay $10 for a ticket to the play?

Case 2: Imagine that you have decided to see a play and paid the admission price of $10 per ticket. As you enter the theater you discover that you have lost the ticket. The seat was not reserved, and the ticket cannot be recovered. Would you pay $10 for another ticket?

Standard economic theory predicts no difference between these two situations. Either it is worth paying $10 to see the performance, notwithstanding the loss of $10 (or something worth $10) discovered on the way into the theater, or it is not. What actually happens? Eighty-eight percent of respondents in Case 1 would still pay $10 for a ticket, but only 46 percent of respondents in Case 2 would buy a new ticket.[38] These results may be explained by mental accounting. In the first situation, the $10 ticket cost is "charged" to the "entertainment" account; the loss of a $10 bill is charged to a different account. But in the second situation, the $10 lost ticket is charged to the entertainment account, and thus if a new ticket is purchased, $20 in entertainment costs will have been incurred – perhaps more than the individual wishes to spend.

Mental accounting may also occur in the context of redistributive legal rules and taxes. When taxes are used to redistribute wealth, taxes go up solely on account of earning more income; as one earns more, one pays more. In this circumstance, it is reasonable to imagine that people view the cost of taxes as a direct charge against their incomes. Consider the receipt of an academic honorarium. My guess is that most people view a $500 honorarium as something like $300 in income; the tax liability is simply subtracted off the top.

In contrast, the costs of redistributive legal rules may be viewed as expenditures out of income (rather than direct charges against income); and heightened expenditures out of income may produce fewer work disincentives than direct charges against income. Why would the costs of redistributive legal rules be viewed as heightened expenditures rather than direct charges against income? What occasions the cost of a redistributive legal rule is not *just* that a person has earned a high income, but also that the person has caused an accident. The expenditure is not one with a sole cause – earning more income – but rather is one with dual causes – earning more income and being a tortfeasor (the latter of which may well loom larger in the actor's mind). Indeed, the first cause (earning a higher income) is not even a direct cause of the expenditure; the chain of causation is that earning more income led the person to engage, or be more likely to engage, in an activity (say, driving an automobile) than the person otherwise would have been, and this in turn produced greater exposure to tort liability. (Earning more income would be a direct cause of the expenditure associated with a redistributive legal rule if the rule explicitly conditioned damages on income – say, $250,000 in liability for defendants below a certain income level and $750,000 for those above that level; but such rules have commanded little support among commentators.)[39]

Interestingly, the fact that redistributive legal rules do their work based not only (and not even directly) on income level but also on accident-related behavior has been a significant source of criticism in the law and economics literature. If redistribution is the goal, it is said, then it is best achieved by directly targeting those with high incomes. For "[i]t may be that higher income persons are more likely to be drivers than pedestrians, but certainly there are many low-income drivers and high-income pedestrians. Thus, liability rules regarding driver-pedestrian accidents are not very precise instruments for accomplishing income redistribution."[40] What this account may overlook, I suggest, is that directly targeting high-income individuals may increase the level of distortion in work incentives caused by the redistribution. Again, this could not be true from the perspective of conventional economics, but a mental accounting phenomenon may suggest that it is. The possible cost of redistributive legal rules in targeting less precisely the parties from whom redistribution is sought must be balanced against the possible benefit of such rules along the dimension of minimizing the distortion of work incentives.

Of course, the degree to which a redistributive legal rule or tax is viewed as a direct charge against income, and hence a direct disincentive to work, may be influenced by the way in which it is presented. If W-2 forms listed expected tort obligations under a redistributive legal rule, then the costs of the rule might be more likely to be charged directly against income. This would make redistributive legal rules more like taxes. What about the reverse – making taxes seem less like charges against income; would this be possible? One might imagine strategies such as not reporting amounts withheld on pay stubs, having the government rather than individuals prepare tax returns, or making taxes more "hidden" in some other way (for example, by structuring them as sales taxes rather than income taxes).[41] But it seems unlikely, for the reason given just below, that strategies such as these would produce a situation in which taxes would be perceived no differently from redistributive legal rules (although taxes might be perceived differently from the way they are perceived under the present system) by those whose work incentives we are seeking not to distort.

In considering the comparison between redistributive legal rules and taxes from a mental accounting perspective (including the issue just raised), it is useful to think about how the *beneficiaries* of each of these forms of redistribution are regarded. Often the beneficiaries of legal rules (even, I think, redistributive ones) are regarded as having *rights* to what they receive; for instance, the tort victim has a *right* to the damages paid by the tortfeasor. In contrast, beneficiaries of redistributive taxes often are not regarded in this way; instead, they are living off government largesse (it is thought). Just as the beneficiaries of redistributive legal rules and taxes are viewed differently, I want to suggest, those on the paying end will often respond differently to the two regimes in terms of the degree of distortion of work incentives, even if the tax regime is implemented in a manner designed to diminish the sense that taxes are direct charges against income.

Much more would be necessary, of course, before reaching any sort of final conclusion about the effects of redistributive legal rules and taxes from a mental accounting perspective. The empirical evidence discussed above (and the other empirical evidence of which I am aware on the topic of mental accounting) involves contexts that are quite different from the one addressed in this chapter, and it may be that mental accounting is a highly context-specific phenomenon. As an illustration, the likelihood that work incentives would be distorted less by redistributive legal rules than by taxes as a consequence of mental accounting might depend critically on the prevalence of redistributive rules in the legal system. At the current status quo, the costs of redistributive legal rules might be accounted for differently from the costs of taxes, but under a system in which massive redistribution occurred through legal rules, it is conceivable that people would begin to view the costs of redistributive legal rules as direct charges against income.[42] One might also argue that, even in today's system, the costs of redistributive legal rules are viewed as "losses," whereas the costs of taxes are viewed as "foregone gains"; in this case behavioral economics would suggest that the costs of redistributive legal rules could weigh more heavily on people's minds (due to their characterization as losses).[43] Here redistributive legal rules would lead to greater distortion of work incentives than taxes would. But it is unclear why the costs of taxes would be viewed as foregone gains rather than losses; my own hunch is that people typically experience them as clear losses. In any event, future empirical work may help to disentangle the different strands of analysis; my only purpose in this subsection has been to suggest the intuitive plausibility of the idea that under our current legal and tax systems, work incentives may be distorted less by redistributive legal rules than by taxes as a consequence of mental accounting.

Work Incentives of Redistribution's Beneficiaries

Until now, this chapter has focused on the work incentives of those who may be burdened by redistribution; it has asked whether work incentives are likely to be distorted as much by redistributive legal rules as by taxes. Redistribution, however, may affect not only the incentives of those burdened by it, but also the incentives of those benefited by it. Neoclassical economics would suggest that the effects on beneficiaries – like the effects on those burdened – will be the same under redistributive legal rules and taxes; for example, if low-income individuals face a .02 probability of becoming tort victims, then a redistributive legal rule that imposes $500,000 extra in tort damages (above what an efficient rule would call for) will distort the work incentives of low-income individuals by the same amount as a welfare or transfer payment of $10,000 would (assuming for simplicity that beneficiaries are risk neutral).

How do redistributive legal rules and taxes compare in terms of their effects on beneficiaries' work incentives from the perspective of behavioral law and economics? The discussion just above (of mental accounting) hinted at one difference between the two forms of redistribution: What occasions receiving the benefit of a redistributive legal rule is not *just* that a person has a low income, but also that the person was the victim of an accident, and the latter cause may well loom larger in the beneficiary's mind. Thus, beneficiaries' work incentives may be distorted less by redistributive legal rules than by taxes, just as the distortion may be less for those *burdened* by redistribution when redistributive legal rules as opposed to taxes are used (as discussed above).

Uncertainty provides another reason that work incentives of beneficiaries may be distorted less by redistributive legal rules than by taxes. As discussed earlier in the chapter, in settings of uncertainty, unrealistic optimism may lead people to underestimate the probability of negative events. Assuming that being a tort victim is viewed as a negative event even under a redistributive legal rule (under which recovery is likely to be greater than it would be under an efficient rule), underestimation of the probability of negative events would imply less distortion of beneficiaries' work incentives from redistributive legal rules than from taxes. Certainly in the case of nonmonetary harm (for example, losing a limb), it seems reasonable to assume that being a tort victim is viewed as a negative event even under a redistributive legal rule. In the case of purely monetary harm, whether it would be viewed as a negative event would depend on the magnitude of the redistribution as compared with the costs of litigation and the limitations (if any) on recovery of damages; these together would determine whether a victim would be better or worse off as a result of the tort, and, hence, whether the occurrence of the tort would be viewed as a negative event. At least for nonmonetary harm, however, underestimation of the probability of harm is likely to reinforce the effects of mental accounting in making redistributive legal rules more attractive than taxes from the perspective of minimizing the distortion of beneficiaries' work incentives.

Conclusion

What effect do redistributive legal rules and taxes have on work incentives? Neoclassical economics suggests a clear answer: the two forms of redistribution have identical effects.[44] Behavioral law and economics suggests a different answer: work incentives may be distorted less by redistributive legal rules than by taxes, due both to the uncertainty associated with redistributive legal rules (tempered to some degree by insurance) and to the different ways in which the two forms of redistribution may be treated from a mental accounting perspective. This analysis of redistributive legal rules is of course only suggestive; in my view, the question whether redistributive legal rules or taxes cause greater distortion in work incentives is ultimately an empirical one and cannot be definitively resolved by the sort of analytic argument offered in the existing law and economics literature and in this chapter. My only purpose here has been to examine and, I hope, call into question the confident prediction in the prior literature that work incentives are distorted as much by redistributive legal rules as by taxes.

The question whether redistributive legal rules or taxes cause greater distortion in work incentives is fundamentally a positive question (and has been approached as such in this chapter), but the inquiry raises a pressing normative issue as well: If redistributive legal rules distort work incentives less than taxes do (and if this is so for the reasons suggested by behavioral law and economics), then is it proper for government to rely on redistributive legal rules to achieve its distributive objectives? The advantage of these rules over taxes stems from the fact that citizens do not perceive the same degree of redistribution as with taxes, but is it proper for government to make use of this error in citizens' perception?[45] If the suggestion of behavioral law and economics that work incentives may be distorted less by redistributive legal rules than by taxes ultimately proves to be correct (or at least persuasive), then these normative questions about redistributive legal rules will require our attention.

Notes

1 See, e.g., A. Mitchell Polinsky, *An Introduction to Law and Economics* 124–7 (2d ed. 1989); Louis Kaplow and Steven Shavell, Why the Legal System Is Less Efficient Than the Income Tax in Redistributing Income, 23 *J. Legal Stud.* 667 (1994).

2 See Duncan Kennedy, Law-and-Economics from the Perspective of Critical Legal Studies, in 2 *The New Palgrave Dictionary of Economics and the Law* 465, 469–70 (Peter Newman ed., 1998).

3 See, e.g., Guido Calabresi, The Pointlessness of Pareto: Carrying Coase Further, 100 *Yale L.J.* 1211, 1224 n. 36 (1991); Kennedy, supra note 2, at 469–71.

4 See Kaplow and Shavell, supra note 1; Steven Shavell, A Note on Efficiency vs. Distributional Equity in Legal Rulemaking: Should Distributional Equity Matter Given Optimal Income Taxation? 71 *Am. Econ. Rev.* 414 (1981). The point is originally due to the Shavell article.

5 Kaplow and Shavell, supra note 1, at 667–8.

6 See ibid. at 668.

7 See ibid.

8 Ibid. at 671.

9 Ibid. at 671 n. 5.

10 Throughout the chapter I focus on the particular context of redistributive tort rules that operate between strangers (as opposed to between, say, firms and the consumers of their products – parties in a preexisting contractual relationship). This focus tracks that of much of the existing literature on redistributive legal rules. See, e.g., Kaplow and Shavell, supra note 1; Thomas J. Miceli and Kathleen Segerson, Defining Efficient Care: The Role of Income Redistribution, 24 *J. Legal Stud.* 189 (1995). The analysis of redistributive legal rules in settings such as contract law differs in important respects from that offered here; these other settings are not discussed in this chapter. (For a discussion of efficiency and distributional goals in the contract setting, see Richard Craswell, Passing on the Costs of Legal Rules: Efficiency and Distribution in Buyer-Seller Relationships, 43 *Stan. L. Rev.* 361 [1991].)

11 Kaplow and Shavell, supra note 1, at 675.

12 See Colin F. Camerer and Howard Kunreuther, Decision Processes for Low Probability Events: Policy Implications, 8 *J. Pol'y Analysis & Mgmt.* 565, 566 (1989) (describing

divergence in both directions from actual probabilities or [where actual probabilities are difficult to compute] expert judgments of probabilities).

13 See W. Kip Viscusi, *Fatal Tradeoffs: Public and Private Responsibilities for Risk* 150 (1992); sources cited infra note 22.

14 See Viscusi, supra note 13, at 150.

15 See Vincent T. Covello and Branden B. Johnson, The Social and Cultural Construction of Risk: Issues, Methods, and Case Studies, in *The Social and Cultural Construction of Risk: Essays on Risk Selection and Perception* vii, viii–ix (Branden B. Johnson and Vincent T. Covello eds., 1987).

16 See ibid. at viii–xii.

17 A bibliography (unpublished, on file with the author) containing nearly two hundred articles on unrealistic optimism is available from Neil Weinstein, one of the early contributors to this literature.

18 See David M. DeJoy, The Optimism Bias and Traffic Accident Risk Perception, 21 *Accident Analysis & Prevention* 333, 336–7 and tbl. 3 (1989); John P. Kirscht, Don P. Haefner, S. Stephen Kegeles, and Irwin M. Rosenstock, A National Study of Health Beliefs, 7 *J. Health & Hum. Behav.* 248, 250–1 (1966); Neil D. Weinstein, Unrealistic Optimism About Future Life Events, 39 *J. Personality & Soc. Psychol.* 806, 809–12 (1980).

19 See Andrew Guppy, Subjective Probability of Accident and Apprehension in Relation to Self-Other Bias, Age, and Reported Behavior, 25 *Accident Analysis & Prevention* 375, 377–8 and tbl. 1 (1993); Neil D. Weinstein, Unrealistic Optimism About Susceptibility to Health Problems: Conclusions from a Community-Wide Sample, 10 *J. Behav. Med.* 481, 487–9 (1987).

20 See Weinstein, supra note 18, at 810 tbl. 1 (finding unrealistic optimism for a wide range of unlikely and much-more-likely events).

21 See DeJoy, supra note 18, at 336–7 and tbl. 3; Ola Svenson, Baruch Fischhoff, and Donald MacGregor, Perceived Driving Safety and Seatbelt Usage, 17 *Accident Analysis & Prevention* 119, 121, 122 tbl. 1 (1985).

22 See Richard J. Arnould and Henry Grabowski, Auto Safety Regulation: An Analysis of Market Failure, 12 *Bell J. Econ.* 27, 34–5 (1981); Camerer and Kunreuther, supra note 12, at 566.

23 See Sarah Lichtenstein, Paul Slovic, Baruch Fischhoff, Mark Layman, and Barbara Combs, Judged Frequency of Lethal Events, 4 *J. Exper. Psychol.* 551, 564 tbl. 5, 566 fig. 11 (1978).

24 See Howard Kunreuther, Limited Knowledge and Insurance Protection, 24 *Pub. Pol'y* 227, 231–9 (1976).

25 See Shelley E. Taylor and Jonathan D. Brown, Illusion and Well-being: A Social Psychological Perspective on Mental Health, 103 *Psychol. Bull.* 193 (1988).

26 See Peter M. Lewinsohn, Walter Mischel, William Chaplin, and Russell Barton, Social Competence and Depression: The Role of Illusory Self-perceptions, 89 *J. Abnormal Behav.* 203, 207–8, 210–11 (1980). For a critical discussion of these findings, see James C. Coyne and Ian H. Gotlib, The Role of Cognition in Depression: A Critical Appraisal, 94 *Psychol. Bull.* 472, 479 (1983).

27 See Weinstein, supra note 18, at 810 tbl. 1.

28 See DeJoy, supra note 18, at 336 tbl. 1 (people think they are less likely than the average person to [1] cause a serious accident while intoxicated, [2] lose control of their vehicles and hit another vehicle, and [3] bump another vehicle while pulling from a parking space); Svenson et al., supra note 21, at 121 (people think they are safer behind the wheel than the average driver); Ola Svenson, Are We All Less Risky

and More Skillful Than Our Fellow Drivers? 47 *Acta Psychologica* 143, 144–6 (1981) (same).

29 See Guppy, supra note 19, at 378–80.

30 Note that underestimation of the probability of liability would affect not only the distortion of work incentives from a redistributive (and thus, by the definition given above, inefficient) legal rule, but also the determination of what the efficient legal rule would be. If potential tortfeasors underestimate the probability of liability, the efficient (meaning optimal-deterrence-achieving) legal rule would be more generous to tort victims than the efficient legal rule without underestimation of probabilities would be. But the newly generous rule would not be "redistributive" in the relevant sense, since it would not be sacrificing efficiency to achieve distributive goals. The focus of this chapter, as stated in the introduction, is on legal rules that redistribute wealth at the expense of efficiency.

31 See Viscusi, supra note 13, at 150; Christine Jolls, Cass R. Sunstein, and Richard Thaler, A Behavioral Approach to Law and Economics, 50 *Stan. L. Rev.* 1471, 1518–22 (1998).

32 See sources cited supra note 22.

33 See Lichtenstein et al., supra note 23, at 564 tbl. 5.

34 See DeJoy, supra note 18, at 336–7 and tbl. 3; Svenson et al., supra note 21, at 121–2 tbl. 1.

35 For a much fuller discussion of the effect of insurance on the foregoing analysis, see Christine Jolls, Behavioral Economic Analysis of Redistributive Legal Rules, 51 *Vand. L. Rev.* 1653, 1664–6 (1998).

36 See supra note 24 and accompanying text.

37 See Jolls, supra note 35, at 1668–9.

38 See Amos Tversky and Daniel Kahneman, The Framing of Decisions and the Psychology of Choice, 211 *Science* 453, 457 (1981).

39 See Kaplow and Shavell, supra note 1, at 675. As this discussion suggests, neither Kaplow and Shavell's analysis nor the analysis in this chapter assumes a situation in which damages are explicitly conditioned on income.

40 Polinsky, supra note 1, at 126.

41 See Edward J. McCaffery, Cognitive Theory and Tax, 41 *UCLA L. Rev.* 1861, 1874–86 (1994), for a discussion of some of the possibilities.

42 Cf. ibid. at 1876–7 ("hidden" taxes may become visible as they become more widespread).

43 See Daniel Kahneman and Amos Tversky, Prospect Theory: An Analysis of Decision Under Risk, 47 *Econometrica* 263, 279 (1979) (citing Eugene Galanter and Patricia Pliner, Cross-modality Matching of Money Against Other Continua, in *Sensation and Measurement* 65 [Howard R. Moskowitz, Bertram Scharf, and Joseph C. Stevens eds., 1974]) (losses are weighted more heavily than gains).

44 See supra notes 5–6 and accompanying text.

45 McCaffery, supra note 41, at 1942–3, raises similar questions about tax structures that exploit cognitive errors.

12 Do Parties to Nuisance Cases Bargain After Judgment? A Glimpse Inside the Cathedral

Ward Farnsworth

The Question

Nuisance cases have figured prominently in the literature of law and economics because they present simple and sometimes charming fact patterns in which courts must pick between awarding property rights to parties and awarding them money. A nuisance suit arises when a plaintiff complains to a court that his neighbor is interfering unreasonably with the use and enjoyment of his property – usually because the neighbor is engaging in some activity that is noisy, noisome, or otherwise offensive to the plaintiff. A typical example of a nuisance case that has figured prominently in law and economics scholarship is the old English case of *Bryant v. Lefever*. The plaintiff and the defendants were neighbors. The defendants began rebuilding their house and built a high wall with timber stacked on top of it; the wall ran alongside the plaintiff's chimney and caused some of the smoke from it to back up into the plaintiff's house. The plaintiff sued, claiming the wall was a nuisance. The court rejected the claim. Coase used this case to illustrate his analysis in *The Problem of Social Cost*:

> The smoke nuisance was caused both by the man who built the wall *and* by the man who lit the fires. . . . On the marginal principle it is clear that *both* were responsible and *both* should be forced to include the loss of amenity due to the smoke as a cost in deciding whether to continue the activity which gives rise to the smoke. And given the possibility of market transactions, this is what would in fact happen. Although the wall-builder was not liable legally for the nuisance, as the man with the smoking chimneys would presumably be willing to pay a sum equal to the monetary worth to him of eliminating the smoke, this sum would therefore become for the wall-builder, a cost of continuing to have the high wall with the timber stacked on the roof.[1]

For the most part the legal literature has been based on speculation of this sort about how parties might be expected to behave after judgment. Calabresi and Melamed, for example, observe that "[n]uisance or pollution is one of the most interesting areas where the question of who will be given an entitlement, and how it will be protected, is in frequent issue";[2] and the authors illustrate the argument in their paper by describing a nuisance dispute between two neighbors, Taney and Marshall. Taney creates pollution offensive to Marshall. The authors' general suggestion is that a property right – an injunction against Taney's pollution, or a finding of no liability for Taney at all – is a sensible remedy from an efficiency standpoint if the court thinks that the loser is the one who most cheaply can eliminate the problem. But of course a court might be wrong in making such an assessment, and the possibility of such mistakes makes it important to consider the likelihood that the parties can bargain after judgment:

> If we were wrong in our judgments and if transactions between Marshall and Taney were costless or even very cheap, the [property right for one side or the other] would be traded and an economically efficient result would occur in either case. If we entitled Taney to pollute and Marshall valued clean air more than Taney valued the pollution, Marshall would pay Taney to stop polluting even though no nuisance was found. If we entitled Marshall to enjoin the pollution and the right to pollute was worth more to Taney than freedom from pollution was to Marshall, Taney would pay Marshall not to seek an injunction or would buy Marshall's land and sell it to someone who would agree not to seek an injunction.... Wherever transactions between Taney and Marshall are easy, and wherever economic efficiency is our goal, we could employ entitlements protected by property rules even though we would not be sure that the entitlement chosen was the right one. Transactions as described above would cure the error.[3]

Is this analysis based on good behavioral assumptions? How do parties to nuisance cases react to a judicial judgment? Do they try to bargain around it? If not, why not?

Methodology

In setting out to learn whether the behavior of parties to real nuisance cases after judgment resembles the behavior envisaged in the literature, I began by searching online databases of reported judicial decisions for recent nuisance cases that involved simple, classic fact patterns. The cases had to involve ongoing private nuisances: lawsuits arising from conduct of one neighbor that typically was bothersome to the eyes, ears, or nose of another. They had to involve few parties: suits involving just two neighbors, or perhaps a handful of families living near each other – and in no case involving more than forty people. They had to be cases in which a court entered a final judgment consisting of a property right for one side or the other (an injunction, or a judgment of no liability for any reason). They had to be cases where there were no other claims between the parties, or at least none that were entangled with the nuisance claims. And I looked for cases several months old (to give the parties time to bargain) but preferably no more than a year or so old (so that the cases still would be fresh in the minds of the lawyers who handled them). I located twenty cases that fit these criteria. All involved appeals, since those tend to be the cases that generate reported decisions in the state courts. Most involved a dispute between two homeowners or between a homeowner and a small business, usually owned and run by one person or a family.

After identifying these cases, I contacted the attorneys of record, seeking to interview them either by telephone or in writing about what happened between the parties after judgment. I asked whether the rights the court awarded had changed hands after judgment, and if not, whether there were any negotiations over that possibility. If there were no negotiations, I asked why not, and whether the lawyers thought there would have been bargaining after judgment if the court had decided the case the other way (that is, if the loser had won). This last question was important, because it addressed the possibility that there was no bargaining only because the court had assigned a property right to the side that would have paid the most for it anyway. The implication of such an assignment is that if it had been made the other way – in other words, if the loser had won – then perhaps the loser would have bought the rights from the winner, or at least would have tried. Usually I communicated with lawyers for both sides (and told each of them that I was doing so). All of the lawyers I was able to reach were willing to talk about their cases.[4]

Results

To summarize the reports the lawyers offered in response to these inquires, none of the parties in the twenty cases considered made trades after judgment. They generally did not negotiate at all after judgment. The lawyers in these cases did not think there would have been bargaining if the litigation had ended with a judgment in the opposite direction, either.

Two types of impediments to bargaining after judgment figured prominently in the lawyers' reports. First, in almost every case the lawyers said that acrimony between the parties was an important obstacle to bargaining. The parties in these cases often thought that their adversaries were behaving in ways that were unreasonable, discourteous, and unneighborly, and frequently were not on speaking terms by the time the case was over (sometimes much earlier).

The second recurring obstacle involves the parties' disinclination to think of the rights at stake in these cases as readily commensurable with cash. The lawyers often would say that their clients "didn't want money. They wanted to get rid of the noise" created by the defendants, or that the "money wasn't important" to their clients in this context, or that "[t]he case had to do with your right to use your land as you damn well please," or that the lawyer's clients "weren't out to make a buck over the whole thing[; t]hey were concerned about their rights." Other lawyers remarked on the difficulty their clients would have had in putting a price on the rights at issue in the case. The attorneys would concede on reflection that their clients might have been amenable to a cash bargain if the price were extraordinarily attractive, but they said that no such price would have been offered by either side.

One goal of this paper is to offer a realistic picture of the attitudes of parties to nuisance cases that are litigated to judgment, and of their behavior afterwards. Here I will describe five illustrative cases.

Thomsen v. Greve.[5] The Thomsens (Elmer and Phyllis) and the Greves (Ron and Nancy) were neighbors in Pender, Nebraska. The Greves moved there in 1973; the Thomsens moved in next door in 1990. Starting in 1986, the Greves used a wood-burning stove as their primary means of heating their house. In 1992 the Thomsens began to complain to the Greves that smoke from the stove was finding its way into their house, bringing "rotten," "unbearable" smells with it and making the Thomsens physically ill. The Greves suggested that the Thomsens keep their windows and doors shut. Eventually the Thomsens filed a lawsuit seeking to enjoin the Greves' use of their stove as a nuisance. The trial court denied the Thomsens damages but ordered the Greves to increase the height of their chimney by 36 inches; the court of appeals reversed in part, both awarding damages and ordering the Greves to abate the nuisance, whether or not this could be accomplished by extending the chimney. On remand, the trial court modified the injunction to allow the Greves to use their stove when the wind was from the west, southwest, or northwest at a rate of at least 10 miles per hour, which would be sufficient to blow the smoke away from the plaintiffs' house.

The lawyers reported that after judgment the defendants stopped using their stove altogether rather than try to adapt their use to the conditions the court had set. There was no discussion after judgment of the possibility that the defendants might pay the plaintiffs for the right to continue using their stove as before; negotiations "did not occur because the defendants are the most unreasonable people in the community" (according to the plaintiffs' lawyer) or because "hard feelings resulting from this litigation prohibited any reasonable resolution" (according to the defendants' lawyer).

The lawyers for both sides agreed that if the *defendants* had won the case, there would have been no bargain struck in which the plaintiffs paid the defendants not to use their stove: "If the Court had found no nuisance, the defendants would have continued burning garbage and whatever else they burned." "The feelings in the matter were such that nothing was going to end this dispute short of ridiculous sums of money changing hands to buy the other side's house," the defendants' lawyer said. The plaintiffs' lawyer had a similar view of the situation: "They hate each other. They'll flip each other off as they drive by." The plaintiffs' lawyer had heard that the Greves' defense was financed by their homeowners' insurance company, which he thought must have spent more than $30,000 on the case. I asked him whether the plaintiffs would have accepted $30,000 in cash to settle the case, and he said probably yes; but no such offer was made. What the defendants did offer to do at one point was buy the plaintiffs' house outright for the price the plaintiffs had paid to acquire it, but the plaintiffs "weren't interested in moving," and the defendants weren't interested in paying the plaintiffs a large enough sum to dislodge them.

Tichenor v. Vore.[6] Carl Vore lives near Wheaton, Missouri, a semirural area; his house is just beyond the official town line, in an unincorporated region. He raises dogs for the purpose of eventually showing them and selling them. Next to his house he built a kennel in 1995, constructed of cinder blocks and a wood shingle roof, to house his Australian Shepherd show dogs. The kennel contained pens for the dogs and runs along its sides where they could be exercised. He kept about sixteen dogs there.

Five neighboring families brought a nuisance suit against Vore, complaining about the barking of the dogs. Charles Tichenor, the lead plaintiff, testified that Vore's dogs would "[b]e barking hard enough, constant enough, you can't go back to sleep... you lay there and listen to them dogs." At trial Tichenor also said that he had been a "royal grouch" for the past year; "[t]he dogs has finally just got me – my nerves shook. There ain't no place to get away from it." Tichenor's wife put into evidence a fifty-page typewritten diary of the aggravation the barking caused her and her husband. The Tichenors said they "were often unable to perform yard work, plant flowers, work in the garage or enjoy their back porch because of the constant 'roar' of dog barking." Other neighbors who lived nearby, though not quite as close as the Tichenors, testified to substantial but lesser degrees of annoyance.

The trial court entered an injunction against the operation of the kennel, permitting Vore to keep just two dogs. The court of appeals affirmed. Since then the injunction has been enforced; there have been no discussions between the parties of the possibility that Vore might purchase from the defendants the right to continue housing his dogs in the kennel. The plaintiffs' lawyer predicted that if Vore had made such overtures, his clients' reaction would have been to say "not only 'No' but 'Hell, no: Get your dogs out of there.'" Mr. Vore's lawyer agreed: The plaintiffs "would not have agreed to do anything for the benefit of the defendant for any amount of money." But then what if Vore had won the case – would the plaintiffs have paid *him* to get rid of the dogs? Both lawyers thought not. "It was obvious that both sides were pretty strong-willed," the plaintiffs' lawyer said; he thought that offers to pay Vore "would have fallen on deaf ears." "Money wasn't important to [Vore]. The case had to do with your right to use your land as you damn well please," he said.

The plaintiffs' lawyer compared this case to others where a landowner builds a fence ten feet over his neighbor's property line. In these situations, he said, one might think the land would be easy to value and that a deal might be struck, but in his experience this was not so: "Generally the emotions are so strong, they're almost like the emotions in a divorce, because it's land involved that's dear to their hearts ... particularly in rural Missouri, where land is important."

This is not to say that there has been no movement at all on Mr. Vore's side. Though he has not been negotiating with the plaintiffs, he has been considering other ways that he might be able to avoid trouble under the injunction and still bring back his dogs. His lawyer wrote that "Mr. Vore is deciding whether to have his show dogs 'de-barked' (a surgical procedure of severing the vocal chords, thereby reducing the bark of the dog to a whisper)."

Payne v. Skaar.[7] Idaho Falls is a town on the Snake River in Idaho populated by about 50,000 people. In 1971 Keith Skaar bought a cattle feedlot on the north side of the town. At the time it contained between 500 and 1,000 cows. The number grew to 5,000 by 1990. Neighbors living in homes nearby became unhappy with the smell. About ten couples and a few others in the neighborhood established an organization dedicated to eradicating the feedlot. They sued Skaar, his wife, and the corporation they had formed. On the recommendation of an advisory jury, the judge entered an injunction ordering Skaar to make various improvements in sanitation and to reduce the number of cows to the level that he maintained prior to the complaints. After an enforcement proceeding (and an unsuccessful appeal by Skaar on several essentially technical grounds), the feedlot went out of business. Skaar blames the lawsuit.

The lawyers agreed on the following points: there were no discussions between Skaar and the plaintiffs, or among the plaintiffs, about the possibility that Skaar might pay them for permission to continue operating his feedlot at full strength. There would have been no interest in such a transaction if it had been suggested. The lawyers said that the plaintiffs did not want to be bought out. They were focused on getting rid of the smells the feedlot created and did not think of the situation in terms of money. In their view Skaar in effect was dumping manure onto their property without permission; they considered him a bad neighbor whose discourtesy was offensive. The plaintiffs' lawyers described the suit as a "contest of wills." The residents pressed hard for the enforcement of every line of the injunction, even when it became clear that Skaar could not feasibly comply; Skaar's lawyer thus concluded that the basis for the suit was "vendetta" rather than principle and for that reason agreed with the plaintiffs' lawyers that negotiations to temper the terms or enforcement of the injunction would have been futile.

If Skaar had won, would the neighbors have paid him to scale back his feedlot? The lawyers thought not; they described it as a "neighborhood dispute" with too much bad blood to overcome. From the plaintiffs' perspective, Skaar would have been too stubborn to accept a deal; "people were threatened with firearms and shovels at times," and Skaar was a "truculent, obdurate man." From the defendant's perspective, in addition to the problems created by the personalities involved, Skaar was uninterested in taking money to scale back. He was trying to grow his business and claimed it would cost him a million dollars to relocate.

Ball v. Jorgenson.[8] Mrs. Ball owned property adjacent to land owned by a family named Jorgenson in Josephine County, Oregon. A stream ran through the Jorgensons' property on a seasonal basis, and when flooding became heavy their horses were in danger of contracting "hoof rot" from standing in water. The Jorgensons therefore dug ditches to channel the water diagonally across their property line onto Mrs. Ball's land. Some of the water already flowed in that direction; the ditches increased and intensified the flow of water onto her property. Mrs. Ball used piles of dirt to block the flow of the water, and brought a lawsuit seeking to enjoin its diversion onto her land (she wanted the flow restored to its state before the ditches were added); the Jorgensons counterclaimed for an injunction requiring Mrs. Ball to remove the dirt she had placed in the water's path. The trial court found for the Jorgensons. The court of appeals affirmed (on the ground that Mrs. Ball's trial lawyer had not objected properly at trial to the jury instructions that were the subject of the appeal).

Mrs. Ball did not go on to pay or otherwise induce the Jorgensons to stop channeling the water onto her property. The lawyer who handled her appeal wrote that "my impression was that trial counsel on both sides had little or no client control. The parties were so polarized by trial that any compromise post-judgment was impossible." He said that the parties "disliked each other intensely" and thought this might have been an aberration caused by some unique features of Josephine County in southern Oregon, a region he described as heavily populated with "survivalists and crazy right-wingers" who are "retreating from something," are "very intolerant of their neighbors," and "take an extreme view of property rights." "I really feel that the litigants couldn't be expected to reach an agreement, not because it wouldn't have been reasonable, but because their views were so extreme." Mrs. Ball's lawyer said the parties' positions were made more intractable by the defendants' failure to ask the plaintiff for permission before diverting the water onto her land; he said that in this region, incursions by one property owner onto the land of another sometimes seemed to ignite "something akin to 'road rage' – people just snap." He thought that had happened here and said that the negotiations that did occur before judgment consisted of "histrionics on both sides."

The lawyers did not think there would have been bargaining if Mrs. Ball had won. The defendants' lawyer said he thought his clients would have been ready to make an offer to Mrs. Ball but thought "she would not have accepted anything"; he characterized her as "exceptionally hard-headed" and said that settlement discussions had not been fruitful: She "wrote long, scathing letters saying she recognized no authority but the Lord." Mrs. Ball's appellate lawyer likewise said that "she would have planted her feet" if she had won and would not have authorized him to negotiate. The appellate lawyer thought it possible there might have been an opening for a compromise of some sort if the case had been remanded for retrial, because then he would have taken over the case from the previous trial counsel, and he had a good relationship with the lawyer on the other side of the case. He thought that perhaps he and the other lawyer could have persuaded the parties to accept some sort of agreement rather than go through another trial. But he said that a victory for either side, as occurred here, foreclosed negotiation.

BAGKO Development Co. v. Damitz.[9] A building company called BAGKO, owned by a man named Bagley and run by Bagley and his son, bought property in Kokomo, Indiana, and developed a subdivision there called Willowridge. The first buyers in Willowridge were Charles and Nila Damitz. They had three young sons, and Charles Damitz was a little league baseball coach. In addition to the lot for the house, the Damitzes bought a neighboring parcel of land and spent about $45,000 building a regulation-size baseball diamond there. The diamond included lights, a pitching machine, and a batting cage, and Mr. Damitz used it from 4:00 p.m. until 7:30 two or three times a week from April through June to coach two teams. Some other children from the neighborhood played whiffle ball and other games on the diamond during the off-season. There were no reports of balls flying onto anyone else's property.

Mr. Damitz said that he obtained permission to build the baseball diamond from the junior Bagley, who had agreed to allow it because Damitz also had agreed to buy an expensive lot and build an expensive house there. But when the senior Bagley learned of this he strongly disapproved. He believed that the property in the development should be used for residential purposes only, and along with a neighbor next door to the diamond he sued Damitz on nuisance and other theories. In fact, nine residents of Willowbrook complained about the lights from the diamond; for eight of them, however, it was enough that Damitz agreed to reduce his use of them. He offered to take down the lights on the field altogether to get rid of the complaints from the remaining resident and from Bagley, but Bagley was adamant that the diamond must go. After a two-day bench trial, the court gave judgment to the Damitzes, finding among other things that the baseball diamond was not a nuisance; the court of appeals held this not to be clearly erroneous.

There were no negotiations at all after judgment. The baseball diamond remains in place. Mr. Damitz gets along fine with his neighbors now, and by all accounts is reasonable in his dealings with the Bagleys (aside from the matter of the diamond). Both lawyers characterized the parties as "hard-headed" and did not think negotiations after judgment would have gone anywhere no matter who had won the rights in court. If Bagley won, the diamond would have gone (and presumably the land would be sold to someone else). The lawyer noted that Bagley did not ask for damages. He wanted an injunction or nothing. If Damitz won, the ballfield would stay (and has stayed). Damitz was unwilling to consider selling out to Bagley, his lawyer said, because he felt that he had been promised he could have the diamond, and it meant a lot to him.

Interpretation and Implications

The sample of cases considered here is too small, and the methodology too informal, to support aggressive generalizations about how courts should resolve nuisance disputes. But the consistency of the results in these cases is striking and seems sufficient to support a more modest conclusion: Stylized economic descriptions of nuisance litigation and its aftermath have omitted consequential dimensions of human attitudes and behavior. The omissions are important because they have caused the models to generate potentially misleading predictions about behavior after judgment. So while it is not possible to say that parties never bargain after judgment in nuisance lawsuits, it is possible to say that there are serious and potentially fatal obstacles to bargaining after judgment in such cases – obstacles that deserve consideration in the literature of remedies, and that courts interested in efficiency would ignore at their peril. Acrimony and a distaste for bargaining tend to eat away any bargaining surplus that otherwise might be expected to exist between the positions of two parties to a case. If the stakes of a case are large enough, there may be gains to be had from trade even in the presence of those difficulties; in the cases considered here, however, it appears that the amounts each side would have demanded to "get over" their hostility and distaste for bargaining were larger than any monetary surplus that the courts' assignments of rights could have created.

The Function of Markets

This section examines the practical and cognitive obstacles to bargaining found in these cases and explores the possibility that they might be understood as resulting from the absence of vigorous markets for the rights at stake in them. By an absence of vigorous (or "thick") markets, I am referring to the fact that the parties in these cases were able to deal only with each other, and that there often were no good substitutes for the goods involved in their disputes; in a robust market, as I will use the term, there is competition for goods, and the goods have ready substitutes. In suggesting that the lack of bargaining in these cases may be related to the absence of markets for the rights involved, I am not referring only or even primarily to the problems usually thought to be presented by thin markets, such as the possibility that an absence of competition might permit either side to hold out for payments much greater than their true reservation prices. The problems in these cases – or at least at the forefront of them – do not appear to have involved such strategic behavior or the fear of it. Rather, my argument is that markets may reduce the incidence and significance of the acrimonious attitudes the parties held in these cases, and that markets bring with them (and are made possible by) a set of values and way of thinking about entitlements that the parties in these cases did not share. The cognitive and normative function of markets, as well as the practical function of them, is to encourage the kinds of transactions that did not occur after judgment in these cases.

1. *Acrimony.* The first obstacle to bargaining identified by the lawyers was acrimony, grudges, or bad chemistry between the parties; lawyers who had handled a number of nuisance cases sometimes remarked on their "rancorous" nature and on the frequently rancorous nature of property litigation between neighbors generally. If two people are not on speaking terms, it may seem easy enough to understand why they do not bargain. On reflection, however, it might seem a little odd that ill will should play such an important role in the parties' unwillingness to bargain, since the parties had lawyers to handle their negotiations, and since in some business contexts parties may bargain despite not liking each other at all. Why is acrimony important here?

Perhaps the answer has to do with the function of markets and their absence in these cases. As a practical matter markets make transactions quicker and thus reduce the need for personal interaction between buyers and sellers; nor do buyers and sellers usually need to be in close proximity either before or after their business is done. Vigorous markets thus tend to make transactions less personal and more faceless; purchasers are focused on what they are buying, not the identity of the seller. Neighbors in nuisance disputes do not have those advantages. Judgment arrives after a long series of previous moves between the parties – frequently antagonistic moves, if the parties are litigating. And while the parties may have lawyers who can bargain on their behalf, this only avoids one sort of face-to-face contact between them. They enjoy no anonymity of any other sort, and they usually will have to assume that they are stuck with each other for the foreseeable future. The identities of the buyers and sellers are uppermost in each others' minds.

The nature of the right makes it still more difficult to separate from the person selling it. A bargain after judgment often would resemble a kind of personal service contract, a contract in which one party agrees to perform or not perform some activity, rather than a contract that provides for the simple exchange of a thing. It is harder to depersonalize this kind of service contract than a contract for goods, because the subject of the contract is the seller's own behavior. The rights involved here also were personalized on their other end – the receiving end, as it were. Where the issue is the allocation of a simple good, one party can end up with it and the other can move on. Here the right at stake consists in part of one neighbor's right to inflict disutility on another. It is not just A's right to a given stick in the bundle that is at issue; it is A's right to poke B with it.

Sometimes a lack of anonymity between parties to a bargain can be an advantage, of course, as in situations where one neighbor makes an "off-market" transaction to sell some property to another when they are on friendly terms, or where a budding nuisance dispute is nipped with a phone call to the neighbors asking them to turn the music down. The bargain in turn may even improve their relationship; it may amount to an exchange of favors that adds to the goodwill between neighbors. Bargains outside of markets thus may have communicative components and other meanings to the participants, meanings that robust markets might otherwise have diluted. But of course not everyone is equally accommodating, and inevitably some neighbors will be radically unaccommodating. (And one neighbor perceived as falling into that category may incite others to follow suit.) In these instances the personalization of the bargain, and the side meanings it conveys, can become a great disadvantage. A bargain requires a compromise, which often entails a show of respect for the importance of another's interests. That respect may be wanting. Either party may be eager to avoid making the other better off.

Finally, strong markets may soften the impact of prickly people even in situations where the parties to an exchange do care a lot about the identities of their trading partners. Those who feel strongly about their partners can choose among many; the significance of their idiosyncrasies likely will be washed out by the offsetting idiosyncrasies of others. And there may be possibilities for arbitrage: In the perfectly functioning markets of economists' models, an intermediary would be able to do business with each of the parties without their needing to do business with each other. If the parties' views of each other are not idiosyncratic – in other words, if a player earns a general reputation as a bad egg – the bad egg will be punished by the market and perhaps driven from it altogether. But in a neighborhood nuisance dispute, the significance of prickles and other idiosyncrasies is magnified. There is no market that can punish and thus curb the expression of temperamental inflexibility, and likewise no market into which one can escape from it by resorting to other buyers or sellers.

2. *Distaste for bargaining*. The other thread that runs persistently through the lawyers' accounts is that their clients would have found the prospect of a cash exchange altogether distasteful, apart from the identity of the partner to the exchange. The precise nature of this distaste is difficult to pinpoint, since it often was expressed imprecisely in remarks to the effect that the parties weren't "in it for the money" or weren't "thinking of their rights in

that way." While any attempt to explain these attitudes must therefore be somewhat speculative, I will suggest that they may be related in interesting ways to the absence of markets for the rights at stake in these cases. More specifically, I will consider the possibility that the parties' attitudes may be a result of the lack of close substitutes for the rights involved in these cases; or it may be that putting the rights up for sale would have seemed to degrade the rights, or degrade the parties, in ways that would have made the parties uncomfortable. These two possibilities may be related, and both may be connected – as causes as well as effects – to the absence of markets here.

Sources of Distaste for Bargaining: Problems of Substitution and Commensurability. First, there tended not to be ready substitutes for the rights involved in these cases. If I obtain an injunction requiring you to get rid of your barking dogs (or perhaps have them "de-barked"), and you offer me cash to dissolve the injunction, I cannot use the cash to buy peace and quiet to replace the peace and quiet I have sold away. Perhaps I could buy earplugs, or louder dogs of my own; but these are quite inferior alternatives to being rid of the barking. If I could sell you my whole house, that would be a little different: then I could buy a different house, which while not a perfect substitute might at least be close. (Accordingly, mention of the possibility of buying a neighbor's house occasionally occurred before judgment in the cases considered here.) That there are no close substitutes for an entitlement does not make it either infinitely valuable or entirely incommensurable with cash, of course. Trade-offs between goods that are imperfectly commensurable necessarily are made often by individuals on their own, as when Mr. Vore decided whether to keep, sell, or de-bark his dogs. But making such deals with others, explicitly and for cash, may make people uncomfortable for several reasons.

First, an absence of close substitutes makes it hard to put a price on an entitlement, and its holder may feel most comfortable erring on the side of caution and saying that it's "not for sale" (or in any event would be for sale only at some very high price), thus minimizing the risk that he will feel regret once the unique good is lost. The agony of putting a price on a unique good is likely to be most severe when part of the reason for the good's uniqueness is that its owner is emotionally involved with it. Ordinary homeowners thus may be reluctant to make distressing determinations of how much they would demand to put up with obnoxious odors in their homes on a regular basis. So if a price were requested, the prospective seller might react to this unease by declining to name one, or by naming one so high that it seems unthinkable that it could be met (and so high that if somehow it were met, the seller would make the deal without any fear of remorse).

Additionally, apart from the danger of regret, some parties may regard their rights in ways that make them poor candidates for a cash exchange. The act of putting rights up for sale requires a decision to think of them as commodities, which parties may resist. Compare two situations: one in which A offers B $5,000 for B's family heirloom, and B declines, saying that it is not for sale and that he has no interest in bargaining over it; the other in which A accidentally destroys the heirloom, and the two parties agree that $5,000 is reasonable compensation for it. In the latter case the decision to "sell" the heirloom has been forced upon B; to accept cash in return for the heirloom requires no distasteful decision by B to treat it as suitable for sale. In short, people's ability to make trade-offs between poorly commensurable goods does not imply that their valuation of those goods is stable or easily reduced to cash terms. It may not be possible to state one price that the owner of an entitlement places on it; its value may depend on who is asking and why, and on what sort of statement the parties would be making about the right, and about themselves, by entering into a cash transaction for it. These are instances of human complexity. Whether they are instances of irrationality in either a lay or economic sense is another and more difficult question.

The application of this principle to the nuisance cases considered here is that for the parties, the very act of entering into cash bargains with their enemies over their families' rights to comfort, or their right to carry on their livelihoods, might itself have entailed sacrifices. The "price" that the holder would state in such a situation is not a price for the rights per se, but rather reflects the cost of selling rights to a particular neighbor against the background of a particular history or context of beliefs and norms that makes cash bargaining uncomfortable. The parties were not thinking of their rights as bargaining chips and did not want to think that way about them. Their preferences and sense of value could have been flattened onto an accountant's spreadsheet, Mercator fashion, but would have been distorted by the process in a way that obliterated any bargaining range.

Sources of Distaste for Bargaining: Meanings of Bribery. I want to explore now one particular source of the parties' distaste for bargaining that some of the lawyers mentioned: the aversion their clients would have felt toward the prospect of paying their adversaries not to do things they didn't want them to do. One of the lawyers referred to this as the prospect of a "bribe," which seems a fair enough characterization; the "best briber" has made frequent appearances in the literature of economic analysis. But not everyone is comfortable with the idea of paying bribes, even broadly defined. How often do we offer cash to other people to stop engaging in conduct that we do not like? Not often, at least not in this culture at this time. The parties thus may have been up against a set of manners and norms, both external and internalized, that regulate the appropriateness of a cash exchange. They tended to have strong views about the righteousness of their positions, and about their right to enjoy their property as they saw fit. Offering thousands of dollars to their enemies to do what the enemies were supposed to do for free would have been hard on the parties' sense of themselves. It also might have been hard on the parties, and perhaps on their local reputations, to reveal themselves as being "in it for the money." Like most things, perhaps, those sensibilities have their price, but it was too high to contemplate in this setting. As noted in the discussion of acrimony, the communicative component of a cash payment – here, the dash of humiliation that may accompany it, whatever the origins of such a reaction may be in this culture at this time – can go a long way toward preventing a bargain.

These observations may help us understand the types of negotiations that occurred *before* judgment in the cases considered here. First, there were adjustments made for "free" (i.e., without any exchange of money) to make the dispute go away (another form of compensation); an example is the reduced use of the lights on the baseball diamond in the Damitz case. Second, there were all-or-nothing offers to buy or sell the property at issue. There is an established market for entire pieces of property, so offering to buy a neighbor's house to resolve a dispute is not so novel or offensive and is done occasionally. I did not find any cases where either side offered to pay or take money in return for a change in conduct, or for an incremental adjustment of their rights. I believe that such offers would have given offense to prevailing norms about appropriate uses of cash.

The Absence of Markets as Cause and Effect of the Distaste for Bargaining. If these ways of thinking about the parties' attitudes have merit, might they be understood as resulting from the absence of markets for the rights at issue? The answer was easier when the obstacle under consideration was acrimony between the parties, because as a practical matter a robust market may allow parties to avoid each other. Here the answer is more complex, because markets have a number of features that might bear on the parties' attitudes toward bargaining. And the parties' attitudes toward bargaining may help explain the absence of markets, rather than the other way around.

First, I suggested that the parties' reluctance to bargain resulted in part from the lack of good substitutes for the rights involved in these cases. In a thick market that would not be a problem, though it is difficult to visualize a thick market for the rights at stake here. First, we would have to imagine a situation in which parties on either side of a nuisance case are in competition with others to sell their rights. And we would have to imagine good substitutes for the rights: a world where, as suggested earlier, the plaintiff's peace and quiet or the defendant's dogs readily are replaceable, or in which units of sentimental value and emotional attachment are experienced by the parties as fungible. Under those circumstances we would have thick markets for the rights in these cases, which might indeed have made bargaining after judgment more likely. But to imagine such a state of affairs is not just to imagine some logistical changes that would make bargaining more efficacious. It is to imagine the goods at stake altered in fundamental ways.

Or perhaps it is to imagine the parties themselves altered in fundamental ways. To say there are no substitutes for a good is to make a statement about the way people feel about the good, not about the good itself. People decide whether they think that goods have substitutes. If Vore had thought that one place for raising his dogs was as good as the next, or if he felt ready to substitute freely between dogs and cats, there would have been no substitution problem in *Tichenor v. Vore*; if Damitz felt that other uses of his land were just as satisfactory as using it as a baseball diamond, there would have been no substitution problem in *BAGKO v. Damitz*. No doubt there are many cases in which parties do feel roughly that way about their rights. For *those* parties, compromises are easy enough to make; the goods involved – which may, from an objective standpoint, look similar to the goods at stake in the cases recounted here – do have substitutes, so far as their owners are concerned. The cases considered in this chapter, however, are precisely those in which the parties doubted that, so far as *they* were concerned, there were satisfactory substitutes for the entitlements at issue. The absence of markets, in the sense of plentiful chances to make substitutions, thus may not be the most powerful way of explaining the lack of bargaining after judgment in the cases considered here. Since substitutability is a subjective conclusion, rather than an inherent property of entitlements, that explanation would amount to saying that the parties would have bargained after judgment if they had felt differently about their rights. One could as well reverse the propositions and say that if the parties had felt differently about their rights, there would have been plenty of substitutes for them – and, in effect, thick markets.

It would risk a similar tautology to say that robust markets would have removed the other reasons I have suggested for the parties' reluctance to bargain: their discomfort toward the prospect of treating their entitlements as commodities, or toward the prospect of bribing their adversaries. No doubt those impediments to bargaining would have dissolved if the parties were operating in a well-functioning market, rather than being forced to deal only with each other. Markets consist in part of signals indicating when and where and what it is appropriate to exchange; they grease the cognitive skids that enable people to make substitutions between what they own and dollars, and between dollars and what they want. Markets also consist in part of norms that make the purchase and sale of entitlements seem ordinary. They strip bargaining of its communicative aspect, and in particular of the malodorous social meaning that may attach to suggestions outside of a market that someone pay their neighbor to behave better. So if the parties had been operating in robust markets, they might well have felt differently about bargaining. But the point here resembles the one made above: where an offer of cash would entail a loss of face, to say this would not be a problem if there were a robust market amounts to little more than saying there would have been no obstacle to bargaining if the parties had felt differently about their rights or about bargaining. Likewise, to say that norms disfavoring certain types of cash offers would have presented no difficulties if markets had been well functioning may be little more than a truism, akin just to saying that norms would not have been obstacles if they had been different.

Limitations and Objections

I now consider some objections to the methods used in this study and some limits on the conclusions that can be drawn from it.

Cases Litigated to Judgment

This study might be said to suffer from a sampling bias: it considers only cases that were litigated to final judgment. What about cases that settle? This is an important point, though when framed as a sampling bias it reflects a misunderstanding of the study and its conclusions. I am not purporting to ask or answer any questions about what happens in cases that settle, so excluding them is just a limitation on what the study means. Cases litigated to judgment are, of course, only the tip of an iceberg consisting of all nuisance disputes, most of which are resolved without lawyers; some large proportion of the rest surely are settled without filing suit, or without a trial, or without an appeal. It should not be terribly surprising that in cases that make it to final judgment – to the bitter end, so to speak – the parties often will not be interested in trying to bargain afterwards.

Perhaps discussions of nuisance remedies therefore ought to be reoriented away from the analysis of bargaining after judgment by parties and should be focused instead on ways that a court's decisions affect settlement negotiations by those who come later. That is a promising idea, but such a move should be made cautiously. First, we do not know anything about settlement patterns in nuisance cases. We know some things about the rates of settlement in civil litigation generally, but nothing about whether nuisance cases, once they enter the court system, settle as often as other kinds of cases do – as often as, say, auto accident cases. Nuisance cases differ from most other tort cases in a potentially important respect: In a typical tort suit the damage has been done, leaving the plaintiff with nothing to do but seek money; since the amount of money that will change hands is the only question in the case, some of the obstacles to bargaining discussed in this paper will not arise. The reluctance to enter into a transaction is not at issue. A transaction has been forced, and the stage is set for bargaining over a dollar amount. That is not true in a nuisance case. The plaintiff has hope of winning an injunction and avoiding a forced transaction altogether. This may result in fewer cash bargains in nuisance suits than we see elsewhere, since parties disinclined to trade their rights for cash are not obliged to do so.

In nuisance cases that are compromised, we know little about the character of the bargaining and adjustments involved, or about what influences those arrangements and to what degrees. Do the compromises involve exchanges of cash, or do they involve noncash bargaining in the form of other adjustments the parties can make (including unilateral adjustments by the defendant just to be rid of the lawsuit)? When parties do hammer out a compromise, how closely are they trying to predict what a court would do if the case were litigated to judgment? It is easy enough to create assumptions about these matters, but then it also has been easy enough to make assumptions about how parties to nuisance cases that go to judgment behave afterwards.

Appealed Cases

There is another form of possible sampling bias in this study, and this time the term potentially is apt: The study only includes cases that generated opinions published on Westlaw or Lexis, which here meant cases that generated an appeal. It is possible that appealed cases tend to involve parties more stubborn than those who accept the trial court's judgment without appealing; maybe the latter parties make the kinds of trades not made by the parties in the cases studied here. While I doubt this is a strong source of bias (I doubt, in other words, that the difficulties described by the attorneys in these cases are much less formidable in cases litigated to judgment but where no appeal is taken), I cannot rule it out and flag it for the reader.

The Courts Are Even Better Than We Thought

Another possible reading of the results of this study is that it shows only that courts are doing a perfect job by economic lights: They always are assigning rights to the parties that value them the most, thus obviating the need for any bargaining. (Or at least courts are only using property rights to protect entitlements in cases where the assignment of the entitlement seems efficient.) It is important to tread carefully here, because there are many possible definitions of efficiency and they can cause confusion. One way to define efficiency is to say that an assignment of rights is inefficient if it results in unexhausted gains from trade. Given that definition, I agree that courts routinely make efficient assignments of rights in these cases: There will be no unexhausted gains from trade no matter which way the court assigns the rights; regardless of who wins and loses, the price the winner will demand to relinquish the rights usually will be more than the price the loser is willing to pay. Perhaps that is the best way to understand these results. In order to be at odds with what I am saying, by contrast, the criticism I am identifying must be a claim that of the two general ways a court can assign rights, one will be efficient and the other will not be; that the courts in these cases assigned the rights efficiently; and that if the courts here had not done so, the parties would have bargained after judgment, or at least that bargaining would not have been foreclosed by the obstacles described in this paper. If this interpretation is correct, then the absence of bargaining would show only that courts are skillful in awarding property rights to whichever party would pay the most for them. ("The courts are even better than we thought," the economist might say.)

I do not think the account just presented is a good description of how courts decide nuisance cases, but it will not be fruitful to debate here whether judges try to award the rights in nuisance cases to the party that would pay the most for them. For even if it could be shown that courts do not make such assignments deliberately, one still could argue that courts sometimes do it inadvertently, and since we cannot know for sure when courts are doing so, we cannot know whether and when the parties' failure to bargain after judgment has any significance. But the suggestion of this paper is not that parties fail to bargain regardless of whether the courts assign the rights efficiently or inefficiently. Rather, the suggestion is that this way of thinking about the assignment of rights – as "efficient or inefficient" in some helpful sense – in fact is unhelpful here because "the party that would have paid the most for the rights" is not as stable a concept as it is assumed to be in economic models. The parties' valuations depend on the context in which they are asked for them (when, and by whom, and for what purpose), and on which party was assigned the rights in the first place.

Put differently, the criticism I have been describing would reflect a disagreement with (or disbelief of) what the lawyers said about their cases. The lawyers said that the obstacles to bargaining that they described would have foreclosed the possibility of negotiations even if the rights had been assigned the other way. The critic I am anticipating would say the lawyers are mistaken or are trying to give accounts of their cases that make themselves or their clients look good; there *would* have been bargaining between their clients if the case had been decided the other way. While conventional transaction costs might have frustrated the process, the critic would say, there at least would have been a will to bargain; statements to the contrary by lawyers are just talk. I consider that argument less plausible than the competing hypothesis, which is that the lawyers accurately perceived and described their clients' likely behavior. The dynamics of the cases here are foreign to economic models, but are they foreign to human experience? If two parties detest each other and would find a cash exchange somewhat bizarre or offensive under the circumstances, it seems reasonable enough to suppose that those considerations would make bargaining after judgment unlikely regardless of what the court does. This would be obvious if the cases involved requests for injunctions against protests outside abortion clinics: One would not expect bargaining around the court's judgment, both because of the parties' likely feelings toward each other and because of their attitudes toward the rights at stake. Feuding neighbors are capable of developing broadly comparable attitudes. Or so their lawyers say; but then what evidence is on the other side, militating against the lawyers' accounts?

Conventional Transaction Costs

Another possible argument is that the *real* obstacles to bargaining in these cases were conventional transaction costs: the bilateral monopolies, freeloader and hold-out problems, and private information that have been much discussed in the literature. The conventional transaction costs just enumerated essentially are varieties of strategic behavior that tend to frustrate attempts at bargaining. They do not seem prominent in these cases and were not the types of problems the lawyers described. Here there were no attempts to bargain, and the lawyers generally did not mention strategic behavior (or fear of it) as an impediment to making a deal.

Conclusion

The aftermath of the nuisance cases considered here raises a number of questions worthy of further exploration. Why might parties have the attitudes toward cash exchanges that the lawyers in these cases describe? To what extent do similar attitudes toward cash exchanges exist in other nonmarket contexts? What stance should the law take toward the parties' feelings in cases like these? One possibility is to treat acrimony or distaste for bargaining as types of transaction costs. But transaction costs normally are defined as practical obstacles to the parties' ability to effectuate their consent to a bargain; and in these cases there is no such consent to effectuate. Treating these impediments to bargaining as transaction costs therefore would require a more general normative model of human behavior in which acrimony and distaste for bargaining are considered the sort of unattractive human behavior that legal institutions are intended to help overcome. Perhaps such a model can be constructed, but it is not the model that economists ordinarily use.

The importance of these issues extends beyond nuisance cases. Nuisances often involve situations where conventional transaction costs are low, and the stories told about them thus have served in some instances as sources of ideas about how the law should handle the many other situations where transaction costs are prohibitive. One proposition to emerge from this literature is that where bargaining between legal actors is not feasible as a practical matter, the law should try to re-create the outcomes that would emerge if bargaining were easier. But if it turns out that parties do not bargain over their rights when transaction costs are low (or if we know they wouldn't because we see them refusing to bargain for reasons that have nothing to do with transaction costs in the sense of feasibility problems), then the broad project of using law to create bargains for parties when transaction costs are high becomes more complicated to defend.

In the meantime, however modest the sample and methodology used here may be, I hope the accounts presented in this paper will encourage a measure of caution on the part of economic modelers who propose to generalize about the consequences of using property rights and liability rules as remedies.

Notes

1 R. H. Coase, The Problem of Social Cost, 3 *J.L. & Econ*. 1, 13 (1960).
2 Guido Calabresi and A. Douglas Melamed, Property Rules, Liability Rules and Inalienability: One View of the Cathedral, 85 *Harv. L. Rev.* 1089, 1115 (1972).
3 Ibid. at 1118.
4 I communicated by telephone, mail, or both with lawyers for both sides in sixteen of the cases; in the other four I have relied on one side's account.
5 See 550 N.W.2d 49 (Neb. Ct. App. 1996). This account is based on the opinion in the case, questionnaires filled out by both lawyers, and telephone interviews with the lawyers for the plaintiffs and the defendants on February 11, 1998.
6 See 953 S.W.2d 171 (Mo. App. 1997). This account is based on the opinion in the case, a questionnaire filled out by the defendant's lawyer, and a telephone interview with the plaintiffs' lawyer on March 13, 1998.
7 See 900 P.2d 1352 (Id. 1995). This account is based on the opinion in the case and on telephone interviews with the lawyers for the plaintiffs (May 21, 1996) and defendants (Sept. 12, 1996).
8 See 934 P.2d 634 (Or. App. 1997). This account is based on the opinion in the case, a questionnaire filled out by the plaintiff's lawyer, and telephone interviews with the lawyers for the plaintiff (Feb. 18, 1998) and defendants (Feb. 12, 1998).
9 See 640 N.E.2d 67 (Ind. App. 1994). This account is based on the opinion in the case and on telephone interviews with the lawyers for the plaintiff (May 22, 1996) and defendants (May 22, 1996).

Part IV

The Demand for Law: Why Law Is As It Is

13 Some Implications of Cognitive Psychology for Risk Regulation

Roger G. Noll and James E. Krier

Beginning with a set of books and articles published in the 1950s,[1] cognitive psychologists have developed a new descriptive theory of how people make decisions under conditions of risk and uncertainty. A dominant theme in the theory is that most people do not evaluate risky circumstances in the manner assumed by conventional decision theory – they do not, that is, seek to maximize the expected value of some function when selecting among actions with uncertain outcomes.

The purpose of this paper is to consider some implications of the cognitive theory for regulatory policies designed to control risks to life, health, and the environment. The first section describes the theory and outlines the key differences between it and conventional decision theory. The next two sections then address, in turn, two central questions about the uses of the theory. First, if people behave in the manner described by the cognitive psychologists, how will this shape the *demands* that citizens make, through the political system, for risk regulation, and how (if at all) might these demands differ from those that would be expected if citizens behaved, instead, in the manner assumed by conventional decision theorists? Second, if citizens make demands as predicted by the cognitive theory, how (if at all) might their behavior affect the regulatory responses that political actors *supply*?

These questions are not entirely new to the risk assessment literature, but our approach to them is novel in that we seek to integrate the cognitive psychologists' theory of decision making under uncertainty with the political economists' theory of policy making and implementation in a representative democracy. Thus far, the literature on cognitive psychology and risk regulation has mostly focused on two concerns: (1) redefining the normative criteria used to evaluate risks and policy responses to them[2] and (2) examining how citizen opinion on risk policy issues is affected (and perhaps manipulated) by the manner in which the issues arise and are discussed in the political arena.[3] The primary aim of the first kind of work has been to enrich the methods of risk analysis; the primary aim of the second has been to augment our understanding of how political rhetoric influences the process of issue information.[4]

Our concerns are different. We seek to identify how, in a democratic society, public attitudes about risk might influence the kinds of risk regulation programs that will be enacted, given that political officials, in their quest for electoral security, seek to satisfy the preferences of constituents. This task presents us with something of a dilemma. Like much of life generally, politics itself is a risky business. If the cognitive psychologists are correct in describing how people perceive and make decisions about hazards to their well-being, then their model may also apply just as fully to political actors – actors who will be mindful, after all, that their policy decisions will have an (uncertain) effect on their desire to secure reelection or otherwise advance their careers. Alternatively, political competition may cause people who use decision theory to win more elections than people who behave as the cognitive theory describes. A comprehensive treatment of the questions we pose would thus have to consider how the cognitive theory alters our understanding of the behavior of both citizens *and* elected political officials, compared to the conventional view.

For now, though, this task is too ambitious. We choose to proceed on the assumption that while cognitive theory accurately describes how citizens make decisions about risks to life and health, traditional decision theory can be aptly applied to the political actor's problem of calculating the best response to citizen demands for action. That said, let us state here a point expanded on in our concluding remarks. Cognitive theory offers a number of apparent insights into human behavior and regulatory policy that differ from or go beyond those generated by the standard decision-theoretic model of the economics and politics of regulation. The insights are derived from experiments and surveys, many of which are controversial because of their design. We do not attempt to assess the strength and validity of the insights here, our chief concerns being description and elaboration. We are struck, though, by the large number of insights from the cognitive theory that *are* consistent with conventional analysis. In other words, although the cognitive theory is novel for its hypotheses about how people perceive risk and act in response to it, the hypotheses themselves have few novel implications for regulatory policy.

Cognitive Decision Theory

In this section our purpose is simply to describe some empirical findings by cognitive psychologists that are inconsistent with the general assumptions of conventional decision theory. We shall not deal in detail with the attempts of others to incorporate the cognitive theory into standard decision analysis.[5] Moreover, we are not concerned with observations by the cognitive psychologists that have to do with how people evaluate events as a function of the details of the risks they pose. (Examples include evaluations based on distinctions between types of risk, such as voluntary vs. involuntary, identifiable vs. statistical, and concentrated vs. diffuse. Factors like these, which ultimately hinge on the risk attributes people care most about, can easily – if tautologically – be included in the traditional decision-theoretic model, though commonly they are not.)

Our focus is on three elements of cognitive theory: prospect theory, heuristics and biases, and cognitive pathologies. *Prospect theory* refers to a set of hypotheses about the mathematical form of the functions describing how individuals evaluate risky outcomes; cognitive theorists offer the hypotheses as alternatives to the mathematical forms used in decision theory. *Heuristics and biases* refer to cognitive shortcuts people use to solve complex problems. The shortcuts cause "mistakes" in the sense that they lead to decisions inferior to the decisions that would have been reached had the shortcuts not been used. Use of the shortcuts is not necessarily irrational, however, because it saves information-processing and decision-analysis costs. If the errors induced by heuristics and biases are sufficiently small on average, and if the information and decision costs are sufficiently large, then the use of shortcuts can yield net benefits to decision makers. *Cognitive pathologies* are systematic, repeated decision methods (not random errors) that are simply irrational and mistaken. They consist of presuppositions and calculation methods that do not conserve on information and decision costs and that can be expected to impose losses on decision makers.

In comparing these elements of cognitive theory to conventional decision theory, we do not attempt to include literally every aspect of them that has been identified or talked about in the literature. Instead, we try to capture the thrust of cognitive theory by revealing its essentials and dwelling on the aspects that have the most important implications for risk-management policy.

The baseline for our comparative treatment is conventional expected utility theory, which has the following core assumptions.[6]

First, people evaluate any action in terms of the level of welfare it produces. Welfare is usually conceptualized as the unmeasurable value of a utility function, whose arguments are quantitative measures of economic variables such as wealth, income, or consumption. The utility function is typically assumed to obey the law of diminishing marginal utility, which implies risk aversion on the part of the decision maker.

Second, if the outcomes of an action are uncertain, people evaluate the action according to its expected value. To perform such an evaluation, the decision maker is said first to envision outcomes as a set of mutually exclusive, collectively inclusive events and then to assign to each event an estimate of its relative likelihood that obeys the laws of probability. Then the decision maker calculates the expected value, or probability-weighted sum, of all of the possible outcomes of a given action.

Third, estimates of the probabilities and values of the outcomes of each action are efficiently calculated, making the best use of available information. For example, new information about the likelihood outcomes leads to a recalculation of the probabilities according to Bayes's Rule.

A formal representation of these three assumptions facilitates a comparison of expected utility with the cognitive theory. Suppose that some action can lead to one of three possible wealth outcomes, X, Y, and Z, having probabilities p, q, and r, respectively, where $p+q+r=1$ and where p, q, and r are all nonnegative. Let $v(\cdot)$ be the evaluation (utility) function of wealth. For purposes of decision analysis, the evaluation, V, of the action in question is given by

$$V = pv(X) + qv(Y) + rv(Z).$$

Moreover, if some level of wealth W satisfies

$$V = v(W),$$

then, because of the law of diminishing marginal utility,

$$W < pX + qY + rZ.$$

Suppose there exists some event that, if it occurs, means the final wealth state will be either X or Y. If the event occurs, the probabilities of the wealth states must be recalculated, and their new values, p', q', and r', are

$$p' = p/(p+q), \qquad q' = q/(p+q), \qquad r' = 0.$$

The revised value of the action is then

$$V' = [pv(X) + qv(Y)]/(p+q).$$

Finally, an important property of decision theory is that the evaluation process exhibits rational expectations. Essentially, this means that intervening events that either have been anticipated or are irrelevant to the consequences of a subsequent action will not alter the decision maker's choice of subsequent actions. A formal example that proves useful for comparative purposes is as follows. Suppose a decision maker can select either of two actions, A and B, with evaluations V_A and V_B, where $V_A > V_B$. Suppose also that the decision maker faces two problems that are identical, save that in the first the valuations of actions A and B are as described above, while in the second the values of each action will be available only if some other event (with a probability p) occurs. In the case of the first problem, the decision maker selects action A because V_A is larger than V_B. In the case of the second problem, the expected values are as follows:

$$V_A^* = pV_A + (1-p)0,$$

and

$$V_B^* = pV_B + (1 - p)0.$$

Obviously, if V_A is larger than V_B, then V_A^* is also larger than V_B^*; hence, the choice of actions should be independent of an intervening probabilistic event. The decision maker would make the same choice whether the decision between A and B is made before or after this event. The reason is that the event provides no information about the relative values of the two actions.

The attack by cognitive psychologists on the traditional decision-theoretic model sketched above has three components. First, empirical evidence indicates that people do not use valuation functions over outcomes of the form $v(X)$ described above. Second, other empirical evidence indicates that decisions about actions are not based on probability-weighted sums of even descriptively more accurate forms of the valuation function. Third, people do not respond to new information in the ways described by Bayes's Rule and rational expectations.

Outcome Valuation Functions

From their experimental evidence, cognitive psychologists hypothesize that valuation functions do not contain only the outcomes of actions. Thus, they propose a function exhibiting a "reference effect," where the valuation of an outcome depends on the sign and magnitude of the change in the status quo that the outcome would produce.[7]

The reference effect has two components, loss aversion and the reflection effect.[8] *Loss aversion* refers to the fact that people ascribe additional negative value to an outcome if it represents a negative change from the status quo. Thus, the valuation function contains the status quo, the direction of change, and the magnitude of change and has the property that, for baseline Y and change X,

$$v(Y, 0) > v(Y + X, -X).$$

The *reflection effect* works in a direction opposite to that of loss aversion but is never fully offsetting. It postulates that, for increases in income, v obeys diminishing marginal utility, but, for decreases in income, v exhibits increasing marginal utility. Thus, descriptively, people are risk averse as to gains but risk taking as to losses. Consider a lottery with probability p of being at a level of wealth $(Y + X)$ and with probability $(1 - p)$ of being at wealth Y. According to the cognitive theory, there must be some level of wealth W, between Y and $Y + X$, such that

$$v(W) < (1 - p)v(Y, 0) + pv(Y, X),$$

and

$$v(W) > (1 - p)v(Y + X, -X) + pv(Y + X, 0).$$

Using traditional decision theory, the right side of each of these expressions collapses to $(1 - p)v(Y) + pv(Y + X)$, so that both inequalities cannot be true simultaneously.

Another observation of cognitive psychologists is that people are not particularly effective in estimating outcome values. The process by which people go from the description of an outcome to its evaluation is affected by a phenomenon called *coding*, or the use of various heuristics as evaluation shortcuts.[9] (The notion is that people like to avoid careful consideration of alternatives and so seek ways to simplify the process.) Although coding has many aspects, two are especially important in considering behavioral responses to risk. One of these is the *representativeness* heuristic, which refers to a tendency to reason by analogy to previous circumstances.[10] Thus, if on superficial observation an outcome Y appears to be similar to an outcome X, people tend to set $v(Y) = v(X)$. This is not particularly problematic when outcomes can be aptly expressed in a single dimension; the representativeness heuristic is troublesome, however, when outcomes have multiple attributes because equating the outcomes on the basis of only some attributes can lead to evaluation errors. Moreover, because errors vary as a function of the attributes actually inspected, the errors themselves are random and unpredictable in the absence of a systematic search method (but predictable when a systematic search procedure is used).

The other important aspect of coding is the tendency to ignore small differences through the use of rounding[11] and ratio-difference principles.[12] *Rounding* refers to the practice of regarding some complex quantity as the nearest simple one (for example, forty-nine and fifty-one are both rounded to fifty). *Ratio difference* refers to thinking of changes in magnitude in percentage terms and treating a given percent of a big number as equivalent to the same percent of a small number.

An important element of the cognitive psychological theory of outcome valuation is called the *framing effect*.[13] The manner in which people value outcomes depends on how an outcome is characterized or presented ("framed"): Is it a gain or a loss? Is it the result of a sequence of small changes or one summary large change? Is the baseline against which change is measured defined narrowly, making the change large in percentage terms, or defined expansively, making the change small in percentage terms? In economic analysis, the appropriate concept for calculating the costs of an action is the value of the benefits (opportunities) forgone by taking that action rather than the next best alternative. When dealing with certain costs and benefits, of course, the convention concerning which action is the "status quo" (and hence the source of opportunity costs) and which is the "proposed action" (and hence the source of benefits) is unimportant. But when benefits and costs are uncertain, cognitive decision theory predicts that the convention of presentation, or framing, does matter.

The Calculation of Action Values

Cognitive decision theory also claims that evaluating actions on the basis of the expected values of outcomes is incorrect, even if the valuation functions are altered to take into account the factors described above. The claim has two major components. First, people are said to systematically misestimate probabilities. Second, the weights they place on outcomes are not equal to their probability estimates.

The first assertion is based on observations of a variety of circumstances in which people do not make the best use of available information in estimating probabilities. One persistent source of error in this regard arises from the *availability* heuristic, whereby people are influenced in estimating the probability of an event by whether an event similar to that in question comes readily to mind.[14] A similar event might come readily to mind because it occurred recently; for example, plane crashes are thought to be more probable by people who have just heard of one. Or a similar event might come readily to mind even though it occurred long ago because of selective recollection of, say, pleasant memories (nostalgia). In this way, people believe old movies are likely to be better than new ones because all of the old movies they remember were good ones. Another source of error is *anchoring*, referring to a tendency to resist altering (to the extent required by Bayes's Rule) a probability estimate, once formed, when pertinent new information comes to light.[15] Finally, a third source of error arises from *overconfidence*: People tend to underestimate the degree to which their own knowledge and judgments are imperfect.[16] An important example of overconfidence is neglecting possible events and outcomes that might influence the value of an action and then (because all probabilities sum to one) overestimating the probabilities associated with the outcomes that do come to mind.

To summarize, people will tend to overestimate the probability of an outcome if an example of the event has recently been called to their attention or otherwise comes readily to mind, if recent information indicates that the outcome has become less likely, or if a large number of other outcomes could occur but each is quite unlikely by itself and infrequently comes to mind. Probabilities will tend to be underestimated if the opposite of each of these instances is the case.

Once people form probability estimates, cognitive decision theory holds that they will not use them directly to calculate the expected value of actions. Instead, they will behave as though they were using another set of weights. Moreover, the precise weighting method that is used will depend on the characteristics of the decision to be made. These ideas are drawn together under the name *prospect theory*.[17]

Prospect theory begins by addressing how the weights used in evaluating actions are calculated. If p represents a person's belief about the actual value of a probability (perhaps calculated incorrectly, as described above), then $P(p)$ is the weighting function that translates p into the weights used in calculating the value, V, of an action. In general, $P(p)$ has the following properties.[18] (1) $P(p) > p$ if p is very small, but for other p's, $P(p) < p$. (2) Nonconcatenation: for probabilities p and q, $P(pq) > P(q)P(p)$ for small values of p, but $P(pq) < P(q)P(p)$ otherwise. (3) Subcertainty: if $p, q > 0$ and $p+q = 1$, $P(p)+P(q) < 1$. (4) Certainty effect: $P(0) = 0$ and $P(1) = 1$. In properties 1 and 2, "small" is not precisely defined but is generally thought to apply to probabilities below approximately 10 percent.

The implications of these assumptions are as follows. First, people behave as if they think that low-probability events are more likely than their own beliefs about the probabilities would suggest; for all other larger probabilities less than unity, however, they behave as if the events were less likely than they believe. Moreover, if an event of given probability is the consequence of *one* source of uncertainty, people behave as if it is more likely to occur than if it is the consequence of *several* sources of uncertainty but has the same concatenated probability. Conceptually, nonconcatenation suggests that people apply an added discount to concatenated probabilities because "there are so many ways to lose" compared to the "one way to lose" from a single event with the same objective probability. Finally, subcertainty is a mechanism whereby risk aversion can enter action evaluations other than through the outcome valuation functions. Not only do valuation functions satisfy "loss aversion" and, for gains, diminishing marginal utility, but, in addition, weighted sums of outcomes are further depressed by a tendency to have their weights sum to less than their actual probabilities.

Two other implications of the prospect function, P, are potentially important but have not been examined in the literature on prospect theory. One implication is that the degree of subcertainty (that is, the difference between unity and the sum of the weights) is not completely independent of the values taken by the probabilities. The general shape of the function $P(p)$ is assumed to be linear, except that, to satisfy all of the conditions placed on it, the function must have some nonlinear regions. For example, $P(p)$ must be relatively flat for low values of p, but more steep for high values of p, in order to satisfy all of the conditions placed on it (as described in our preceding discussion). This implies that, for lotteries involving one very unlikely event plus some events with higher probabilities, the sum of the weights on outcomes declines as the probability of the unlikely event increases. Consequently, people behave as if they assign a value nearer to the actual expected value of a lottery if it contains a highly unlikely event. Thus, the "extra" risk aversion implied by the form of the $P(p)$ function is greater when all of the events are regarded as sufficiently likely that $P(p) < p$ for all outcomes.

A second unnoticed aspect of the presumed shape of the $P(p)$ function is that it works in a direction opposite to that of the overconfidence hypothesis. Specifically, if the sum of outcome weights is less than unity, the effect behaviorally is as if the decision maker had assigned a positive probability to another possible outcome that is not incorporated into the decision problem. The valuation of this "phantom" outcome is not necessarily zero, but to explore this issue requires examining how prospect theory hypothesizes that weights and outcomes are combined to evaluate action.

Contrary to conventional decision theory, prospect theory does not assume that actions are evaluated simply by summing the weighted values of outcomes. Only if at least one possible outcome preserves the status quo, or if at least two outcomes entail changes from the status quo of opposite sign, will decision makers evaluate actions analogously to calculating expected value. In this case, if an action can produce three possible changes in the status quo, X, Y, and Z, with probabilities p, q, and r, respectively ($p + q + r = 1$), and if I is the status quo, then the evaluation of the action is given by

$$V = P(p)v(I, X) + P(q)v(I, Y) + P(r)v(I, Z) + [1 - P(p) - P(q) - P(r)]v(I, 0). \tag{1}$$

If an action leads to outcomes that all change the status quo in the same direction, then decision makers are assumed to proceed as follows. First, they determine which outcome involves the smallest departure from the status quo. Second, they assume that the outcome involving the smallest departure will occur with certainty. Third, they calculate the value of the other outcomes as uncertain departures from the status quo. The effect of this procedure is to overstate the relative contribution to the value of the action that is caused by the outcome producing the smallest departure. Formally, for an action involving an initial position I, three possible changes in the status quo (X, Y, and Z, all of which are either strictly positive or strictly negative, and among which X has the smallest absolute value), and probabilities p, q, and r (which sum to one), prospect theory proposes that actions will be evaluated according to the following calculations:[19]

$$V = v(I, X) + P(q)[v(I, Y) - v(I, X)] + P(r)[v(I, Z) - v(I, X)] + [1 - P(q) - P(r)]v(I, 0). \tag{2}$$

An interesting feature of both of the foregoing formulas is that they accord weight to the status quo even though, by assumption, the status quo has zero probability of continuing. Technically, this appears to create a logical inconsistency in the theory since the certainty effect requires $P(0) = 0$. However, this exception to the certainty effect reflects another essential component of the theory, the reference effect, according to which the value of all uncertain actions depends on the value the decision maker places on the status quo.

The implication of equation (2) is that the outcome involving the smallest departure from the status quo is given more weight than $P(p)$. The reason is that, with subcertainty, $P(p) < 1 - P(q) - P(r)$; however, the latter weight is implicitly given to $v(I, X)$ in the first expression. If q and r are "not small," this implies that the weight accorded to $v(I, X)$ is larger than the subjective probability. If p is "small," then $v(I, X)$ is doubly overweighted – partly because $P(p)$ exceeds p, and partly because $[1 - P(q) - P(r)]$ exceeds $P(p)$. Finally, if q or r is "small," the implicit weight on the smallest change may be larger or smaller than its subjective probability. The reason is that the overweighting of the low-probability event is offset to an unknown extent by the substitution for $P(p)$ in the evaluation function.

The bearing of the preceding observations is that, if all outcomes of an action involve some loss, two types of outcomes are accorded excessive weight in the evaluation of actions. First, for outcomes in which the loss is small, there occurs what might be called the "optimism effect." Given a range of possible catastrophes, the best among a bad lot will tend to have too much influence on the evaluation of an action. Second, as emphasized above, large catastrophic outcomes with nontrivial probabilities will be undervalued, whereas large catastrophic outcomes with low probabilities will be overvalued. Note that, in the second case, the valuation function over losses already has a shape that encourages risk-taking behavior, so the action evaluation process serves to enhance the likelihood that people will be willing to take relatively high chances of very large losses.

The evaluation function when events do not produce results of the same sign has a similar but slightly different implication. If one alternative say X, is zero (that is, it maintains the status quo), then the first formula accords the status quo a weight of $1 - P(q) - P(r)$, which is not only larger than $P(p)$ but is also larger than p unless both q and r are "small." Two kinds of plausible action-outcome relations fit this case. In one, an action may have "large" probabilities of both gain and loss, in which case both outcomes are relatively undervalued compared to the status quo. This has the effect of offsetting risk aversion (including loss aversion); however, it has no necessary implication concerning the willingness to undertake such an action. In the other action-outcome relation, the so-called Faustian bargain in which a high probability of small gain is paired with a low probability of catastrophe, the latter is overweighted relative to the former (this might be called the "pessimism effect"). Note, then, an interesting implication of prospect theory: People may be excessively prone to avoid actions that can have both good and bad consequences, but when faced with the certainty of some loss, they may be excessively prone to take actions involving a reasonably large chance of a catastrophic outcome.

An important prediction from prospect theory is an aversion to "probabilistic insurance," meaning an action that reduces but does not eliminate the probability of a loss.[20] In general, the theory predicts a dislike for insurance because of the risk-taking shape of the valuation function over losses. Moreover, because insurance converts a risk from a situation in which one outcome is good (a loss of zero) to a situation in which all outcomes entail a loss (the smallest of which is loss of the insurance premium), the presence of loss aversion and, in the former case, an overweighting of the status quo further militate against insurance.[21] In addition, if probabilistic insurance reduces a "large" risk to a "small" one, the weighting of the bad outcome will not be reduced in proportion to its reduced probability. For all of these reasons, people are likely to prefer either no insurance at all or insurance that always protects totally against the loss. In particular, insurance that reduces the probability of loss from a reasonably large one to a very small one will be relatively undervalued. Of course, here, "insurance" can mean any costly action that reduces the chance of a bad event.

Prospect theory also predicts actions inconsistent with the idea of rational expectations. This can be demonstrated by a simple example. Suppose a person has an initial position I and is indifferent between the certainty of X or a chance p of Y, implying that $v(I, X) = P(p)v(I, Y) + [1 - P(p)]v(I, 0)$. (In this example, we will henceforth suppress argument I for ease of notation.) Now consider a case with two probabilistic events. In the first event, a person receives either nothing with probability q, or, with probability $(1 - q)$, the chance to experience the second event, which entails receiving either X or a chance p of Y. The choice between X and p of Y must be made before the outcome of the first event is observed. To select between these options requires a comparison between the following values:

$$V_x = P(1-q)v(X) + [1 - P(1-q)]v(0),$$

and

$$V_y = P[(1-q)p]v(Y) + \{1 - P[(1-q)p]\}v(0).$$

If V_x and V_y are equal, as rational expectations theory requires, then, with rearranging, the following must hold:

$$v(X) \stackrel{?}{=} \frac{P[(1-q)p]v(Y) + \{P[(1-q) - P(1-q)p]\}v(0)}{P(1-q)}.$$

But from the first problem,

$$v(X) = P(p)v(Y) + [1 - P(p)]v(0).$$

Hence, both of these relationships can hold only if

$$P[(1-q)p] = P(1-q)P(p).$$

But this violates the nonconcatenation property of prospect theory; hence, both equalities cannot hold.

This significance of the preceding example is this. In some cases, people will prefer a guaranteed outcome to a lottery. However, if they must decide whether to play the lottery or take the certain outcome, they may express the opposite preference and commit to a lottery in advance of knowing whether the commitment will ever amount to anything. But then, if events transpire such that their choice has a bearing and their commitment is binding, they will regret not having taken the certain outcome. The implication is that people will be prone not to protect in advance against risks that may not emerge, even though, if the risks do emerge, people will regret their decision, notwithstanding that the objective relative merits of the safe and risky options have not been affected.

Implications Regarding the Demand for Risk Regulation

To consider how the cognitive theory of decisions under risk translates into demands for political action, we first must specify the theory of political processes that maps citizen preferences into incentives to act on the part of government officials. We will begin by exploring the implications of the "positive responsiveness" of majority-rule electoral processes, then amend the treatment to take account of "mobilization bias." Our interest in both cases will focus on two inquiries: First, how citizen demands, given the cognitive view, will depart from those predicted by traditional decision theory; and second, what kinds of decisions are especially susceptible to the possibility of preference reversal with the unfolding of time. The second inquiry has to do with circumstances in which citizens change their minds about the appropriateness of some policy, even though the objective conditions surrounding the policy choice have not changed. These circumstances are especially important to government officials because they create the possibility for intertemporal inconsistencies in citizen demands. A political leader caught in such circumstances has to make a trade-off between disappointing citizens today and disappointing them tomorrow, when their preferences have changed. How politicians might deal with these problems is the subject of the next section.

Pure Majority-rule Democracy: Positive Responsiveness

One characteristic of majority-rule decision processes is that the likelihood of a policy being adopted does not decline as the number of citizens who favor it increases, a property called *positive responsiveness*.[22] In analyzing the policy implications of cognitive decision theory, we first focus on this property. We will not deal extensively with the other major property of majority rule – its fundmental instability. In general, the outcome of a system of pairwise, majority-rule votes depends on the particular sequence in which the alternatives are considered.[23] Without restrictions on sequence, majority rule can usually lead to essentially any policy outcome, and any policy that wins at one moment can be defeated at the next vote.[24]

The importance of the instability of voting mechanisms for our purposes is that it provides risk-averse voters and political leaders with an incentive to design political systems in which policies are difficult to change once adopted. Such an idea, called *structure-induced equilibrium*,[25] has been offered as one rationale for the complexity of the American federal system (multiple independent levels of government, checks and balances in the federal structure) and the rules of procedure governing elections and legislative processes. The key point is that political institutions designed to combat the inherent instability of majority-rule democracy also attenuate the responsiveness of policy to changes in citizen preferences. Hence, if citizens exhibit intertemporal inconsistencies in preferences regarding risk regulation, modifications in policy are unlikely fully to reflect these changes in preferences.

The first type of risk-management problem that arises involves an ongoing, valued activity that also carries with it the possibility of causing serious harm. Here cognitive theory indicates that people will tend to value the activity more highly than its objective expected value as long as the probability of the damaging event is not too low. They will take risks contraindicated by conventional decision theory. But if the probability of the damaging event becomes sufficiently small, the opposite result is obtained. People will seek to terminate an activity that traditional decision theory indicates should be continued. The overall effect, from the perspective of decision theory, is to take too many risks of high probability and too few of low probability.

This effect influences expenditures to ameliorate risks, that is, to bear the costs of some measure that would reduce the probability or magnitude of damage. In general, as the probability of a damaging event increases, so too will the amount that citizens are willing to spend to ameliorate it. But, unlike traditional decision theory, the willingness to pay for amelioration rises less rapidly than the rate of increase in the probability of the damaging event. From the decision theory perspective, citizens are willing to spend relatively too much on low-probability events as compared to ones of higher probability.

If the foregoing preferences are based on accurate estimates of probabilities and outcome values, then they are unlikely to present intertemporal instability problems for government officials. In essence, those sorts of problems arise because true preferences persistently and systematically diverge from the evaluations arising from the application of traditional decision theory. In this case, the occurrence of a damaging event at a frequency consistent with its objective probability will not cause a citizen's evaluation of policies for dealing with it to change over time.

Circumstances change if citizen preferences are affected by the cognitive pathologies discussed earlier, such as availability, anchoring, representativeness, and overconfidence. The occurrence (or lack of occurrence) of a damaging event can alter the estimates of probabilities, the valuation of outcomes, or both. Moreover, the extent to which preferences are likely to shift over time is predictable.

Consider, for example, the effect of availability, which predicts that people will systematically overestimate the probability of an event if similar events come readily to mind but will systematically underestimate them otherwise. The implication is that, immediately following a widely publicized disaster, citizens will place unusually great demands on their government to take action against recurrence, but as attention subsides, so too will the demand for action.

An interesting implication of prospect theory is that intertemporal instability is less of a problem in the case of events with small probabilities. The reason is that the weighting function $P(p)$ is less sensitive to changes in p when p is small; if citizens alter their estimates of p because of recent experience, relatively small changes in the evaluation of policies for dealing with the risk will result. Thus, policies regarding low-probability events are likely to be more resistant to changes in perceptions about the underlying risk than policies dealing with more likely events.

A second set of risk regulation issues is related to the violation of rational expectations in cognitive decision theory. Imagine the decision to develop a viable new technology that, after the research and development (R & D) phase, can be implemented in either a risky form (high economic returns but a chance of catastrophe) or a safe form (lower returns but few, if any, risks). One possibility is to postpone the development decision until after the R & D phase. The other possibility is to make a decision between the safe or risky form during the R & D phase. The first strategy allows the decision about safety to be taken after the technology is known to be commercially interesting, whereas the second strategy requires commitment to a decision about safety before commercial feasibility is established. As discussed above, interposing the uncertainty of commercial feasibility may well reverse the choice between safe and risky options, such that, after the R & D phase is complete, citizens will regret the commitment made before R & D began, even though no new information about the nature of the risk and the cost of ameliorating it has become available.

The underlying inconsistency here can result in regretting either choice. The safe alternative can be regretted, ex post, because resolving the uncertainty about commercial feasibility increases the expected value of the risky option, as calculated by prospect theory. Recall that, at the low end, an increase in objective probability causes a less-than-proportional increase in the outcome weight for evaluating options, whereas, for higher probabilities, this relationship is more nearly proportional. For this rather common case – a high probability of no accident, a small probability of damage – risk policy would be expected to exhibit greater caution before commercial uncertainties are resolved than after. This provides a reason why greater caution is generally exercised in licensing new industrial ventures than in regulating established ones.

But preference reversal can work the other way too. Before the fact, a new technology may be regarded as a lottery with both good and bad outcomes; after the technology has been put in place, all of the outcomes may be perceived as favorable. The reason is that, initially, the R & D cost may be lost if the technology turns out to be commercially infeasible; however, if commercial feasibility is demonstrated, then the possibilities can become (1) a risky plant that has no accidents; (2) a risky plant that has an accident but that, nevertheless, proves to be, on balance, a social benefit; or (3) a safe plant with a net benefit intermediate between the two. The second case demonstrates more risk aversion than the former, according to prospect theory, such that, in stage 1, the risky strategy may be preferred. In stage 2, if commercial feasibility is proved, that decision may be regretted. This tendency would be amplified by the availability heuristic if the damaging event occurred after a plant was put into operation.

A third issue affected by the cognitive theory is the trade-off between making a decision now and postponing the decision until more information is acquired. The motivation to wait is to obtain new information to resolve uncertainties about probabilities, the magnitude of damages, or the costs of protection against risks. Cognitive theorists have not fully explored this issue, but a natural interpretation is that people will calculate the value of information in much the same way as in decision theory, except that the calculations will be based on updated outcome weights (not updated probabilities) using the evaluation formulas of prospect theory. The key observations here are that the outcome weights do not change in proportion to the changes in probabilities and that the nature of the lottery can change if information is received that switches the applicable evaluation formula.

Outcome weights increase relatively slowly for low-probability events and have discontinuities at probabilities of zero and one – with the following implications. First, information that serves to refine estimates of low probabilities will be accorded less value than in decision theory, given the less-than-proportional relationship between outcome weights and actual probabilities at the low end. Second, information conclusively showing that an event is either certain or of zero probability has an accentuated value, relative to decision theory, owing to the discontinuities in the weighting function at extreme probabilities. Third, for issues that do not involve low probabilities, both good and bad outcomes will be treated in a roughly symmetrical fashion;

however, because probability weights are less than probabilities across the board and sum to less than one, the general tendency is to undervalue information. Refining these probabilities (assuming that certainty is not obtained) will still change values by less than would be the case if all calculations were based on actual probabilities.

The conclusion to be reached is that, in general, the value of information is likely to be lower if people behave as cognitive theory claims rather than according to traditional decision theory. Complete certainty is an unlikely product of any search for more information; so, in most realistic cases, information will be accorded too low a value. This tendency is reinforced by some other behavioral characteristics identified by cognitive theory. For example, anchoring implies that probabilities are updated less than they ought to be as new information appears, and overconfidence suggests that people underestimate the extent to which there are uncertainties to be resolved. The implication of these considerations is that information will be given a still lower value than that suggested by the formal calculations of prospect theory.

Even if information is acquired, the consequences are not likely to be what one might conventionally expect. Essentially, information theory asks people to examine what decision they will make after an uncertainty has been resolved. Rational expectations theory can be invoked to argue that people can accurately assess how they will behave in such circumstances, but prospect theory says people violate rational expectations. Even if information is acquired, people might renege on their agreements about how they would respond to it. The acquisition of information presents basically the same problem as the decision about a safe or risky technology prior to knowledge about its commercial feasibility. Resolving the uncertainty about the results of the information search can reverse people's preferences.

A final aspect of the cognitive theory that affects preferences regarding risk-management problems involves the path dependence of preferences. Path dependence arises from the hypothesis that individual valuations of changes in outcomes (or utility functions) are asymmetrical around the status quo, exhibiting risk aversion in gains and risk acceptance in losses. Thus, as the outcomes moves away from the status quo in either direction, the ratio of the change in value (utility) to the change in outcome is largest for the smallest changes. The implication is that both the shape and the position of the valuation function depend on the status quo – that is, individual valuations of a particular outcome depend on the status quo ante from which that outcome was obtained. The nature of path dependence in the cognitive theory, and its implications for behavior, can be clarified by a diagram.

Figure 13.1 depicts the valuation function over outcomes under prospect theory. Note that "loss aversion" over the entire range of feasible changes from the status quo requires that the actual valuation function over losses must always lie below the projection of the valuation function over gains into

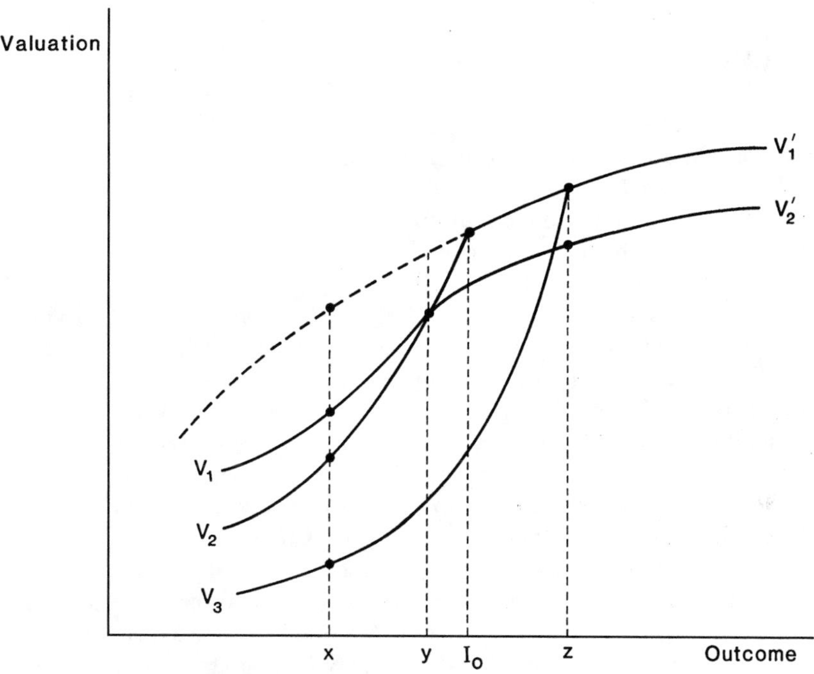

Figure 13.1. Prospect Theory.

the range of losses. In the figure this projection is the dotted line between initial state I_0 and outcomes producing worse outcomes, such as X and Y; that is, the actual valuation function $V_1 V_1'$ lies below the dotted projection for all feasible outcomes below I_0. Moreover, it has a shape that bows in a direction opposite that of the projection.

Note also the effect of an actual bad outcome, which replaces I_0 with Y. The latter outcome becomes the new status quo, and the valuation function is redefined from this baseline, as depicted in line $V_2 V_2'$. The implication is that, after Y has transpired, all feasible outcomes except Y now have a lower value than they had when I_0 was the initial point. Likewise, if a good outcome transpires – such as point Z – the portion of the valuation function below Z is altered to reflect loss aversion below that point, so that the new valuation function becomes $V_3 V_1'$. Thus, the bad outcome X produces a lower valuation if it is reached from a higher initial point. More generally, the valuation of a bad outcome keeps getting worse as the value of the status quo increases, and the value of a good outcome is lower for lower values of the status quo.

Figure 13.1 reveals the path dependence of outcome values: precisely the same risk can produce different evaluations, depending on the status quo *and* on the sequence of events that produced the status quo. Suppose, in the figure, that the comparison is between a lottery of X or Z and the certainty of I_0. Clearly, the valuation of the relative merits of these choices depends on whether the status quo is I_0 or Y (after a fall from I_0). In the latter case, the valuation of the lottery has fallen relative to the certainty of I_0 because the shape of the valuation function causes larger drops in the valuation of X and Z than in the valuation of I_0. Alternatively, if the choice is between the same lottery and the current status quo (I_0 or Y), the lottery has been made more attractive owing to the fall from I_0 to Y. After this fall, the lottery gives the person more to gain and less to lose.

In most instances, the outcomes of policy decisions regarding environmental risk take time to materialize. Hence, a citizen will evaluate a policy with reference to the status quo prevailing at the time of the evaluation. If, for example, incomes are increasing (or citizens, for other reasons, regard themselves as better off as time progresses), an environmental risk that appears worth taking today will lead to regret in the future. Moreover, if environmental risk policy consists, in general, of a series of alternating gains and setbacks, people will regard themselves as becoming steadily worse off in some cases where, by objective measures of outcome, they are actually becoming better off. Note that, in the figure, the outcome Z along V_2V_2' is objectively superior, but subjectively worse, than the outcome I_0 along V_1V_1'. Hence, the sequence I_0:Y:Z makes people feel worse off than they would had they remained at I_0. Obviously, this means that, if the cognitive theory is correct, environmental risk policy must either avoid significant setbacks altogether or be very good indeed, overall, if people are to perceive policy progress. The result is somewhat analogous to the distaste for probabilistic insurance: policies that serve to reduce (but not to eliminate) the losses due to occasional damaging events can simultaneously increase the average value of realized outcomes as measured objectively but leave people with the perception that, on balance, they are worse off. The reason is the extra welfare cost associated with any loss – a cost that, according to the cognitive theory, has a permanent depressing effect on a person's future ability to derive welfare from good outcomes.

Political Economy and the Cognitive Theory

Real representative democracies are more complex than the simple majority-rule system hypothesized in the preceding section. Decision-theoretic models of the political process emphasize two key elements of political participation: rational ignorance and mobilization bias.[26] Rational ignorance refers to the lack of incentives on the part of citizens to be fully informed about the policy positions a candidate advocates in an election campaign. The incentive problem is caused, first, by the mismatch between the complexity of policy and the simplicity of the signal a voter can send (yes, no, or abstain) and, second, by the powerlessness of a single vote. To acquire and digest information requires time and effort, yet after exhaustive analysis a voter can send only a very weak signal, one that is not sensitive to the intensity of the voter's preferences, and one that is highly unlikely to influence the outcome of an election. In consequence, there is little incentive to compare candidates and their policies carefully. Voters are likely to pay relatively little attention to campaigns and will usually base their decisions primarily on information freely available in an entertaining form (TV sound bites) – and even then will pay attention only to messages concerning a small number of issues that they regard as especially important (such "salient" issues as the state of the economy and of international relations, plus a few more specific matters of particular interest to a given voter). Voting behavior should be especially likely to exhibit the kinds of cognitive shortcuts described above.

Mobilization bias refers to the fact that some preferences tend to be more effectively represented in political processes than others. One way to overcome rational ignorance is to rely on someone else to perform issue analyses, then to vote as instructed. Similarly, one way to overcome voter powerlessness is to act in concert with other like-minded individuals.[27] Collectively, a group of voters might have a substantial chance of swinging an election to one candidate or another. Moreover, through campaign contributions, a group can help preferred candidates provide the free entertaining information that might lead others to vote as the group desires. But forming groups, devising strategies, and coordinating efforts also require time, effort, and money. Hence, small, homogeneous groups with high per capita stakes in an issue are more likely to organize successfully than are large, heterogeneous groups with small per capita stakes.[28]

We can now consider how the cognitive theory provides some insights into the bearing of rational ignorance and mobilization bias on risk policies. Framing, discussed in the first section, suggests that, in a world of rational ignorance, the way political actors describe issues will alter a voter's evaluation of policy options. For example, if an issue is put as one involving alternative ways to obtain gains, voters will exhibit risk aversion; whereas, if the same issue is framed in terms of various ways to experience losses, voters will exhibit loss aversion with risk-taking behavior.[29] Hence, the way an issue is stated can influence outcomes. Consider the case of a proposal to make seat belts mandatory, with a mandatory fine if one is caught unbelted. Outcomes could be expressed variously as follows:

1. A large benefit from driving without a belt, not being caught, and having no accident
2. A somewhat smaller net benefit from driving belted and having no accident
3. A smaller net benefit still from driving unbelted, getting caught and fined, and having no accident
4. A small negative net benefit from wearing a belt and having an accident

5. A more negative net benefit from driving unbelted and having an accident, and
6. A slightly more negative net benefit from driving unbelted, having an accident, and being fined to boot (adding insult to injury).

Facing these possibilities, a voter is likely to exhibit risk aversion because some possibilities are expressed positively.

Alternatively, one could put the seat-belt issue in terms that start with a status quo in which driving safely, unbelted, and unfined is the baseline, so that all other outcomes are negative. This would induce risk-taking behavior and a propensity to search for accident-reduction policies that reduce risks to zero (to avoid probabilistic insurance). In short, adeptness at characterizing issues can go a long way in determining the policy preferences expressed by the electorate.[30]

Issue salience is also related to issue presentation. According to the representativeness heuristic, one can induce preferences concerning policies about one risk by presenting it as being like another risk. Then, voters will evaluate the two risks as though they were the same. Therefore, if one environmental risk becomes salient (because, say, a damaging event has recently occurred), political actors may piggyback other environmental risks on the first by presenting them as essentially identical to the salient one.

The availability effect accentuates the importance of salience. A damaging event, if timed appropriately and if widely publicized, induces people to behave as if the likelihood of such events had increased. If the effect makes the issue politically salient – makes it one of the few issues that can animate political participation – then it can serve, for a time, to help overcome mobilization bias. With regard to environmental risk policy, risk producers will normally be the better-organized, more effective participants in the political process. But a highly publicized environmental catastrophe can cause some citizens to overestimate the degree of risk they face and thus to be spurred to mobilize for political action. Moreover, other political actors may enhance the success of their own mobilization efforts by clever use of representativeness in the presentation of other issues. Mobilization bias may be temporarily overcome – temporarily because, if the probability of some damaging event is truly low, then events of that sort are likely gradually to subside from public consciousness and lose their salience.[31]

The mechanics of how availability and mobilization bias work on a class of risk policy issues are complex, but a few prototypical examples provide some insight into the general process. Consider three types of low-probability risk circumstances. One is a low-probability catastrophic event that, if it occurs, will harm a large number of people simultaneously, such as the Bhopal or Chernobyl disasters. The second is an event in which the probability of a disaster at a facility is again low, but where there are a large number of facilities. Assume here that the number of people harmed per disaster would be much lower than in the first case, but large enough to make for a newsworthy event. Examples are airline or bus accidents, where between a few and a few hundred people are killed or injured. Events of the second type occur more frequently than those of the first type; assume that the lower damage per event is exactly offset by the greater exposure, so that the average annual number of deaths would be the same in the two cases. The third type of event is one presenting a risk to only a single person or a very small group. Events of this sort again have low probability, but a very large number of exposures causes frequent occurrences – so frequent that, with such small losses per event, they are not newsworthy.

Availability suggests a different politics for each of the three types of events, even if they have the same expected losses. Regarding the first, most of the time the issue is not before the public, so policy questions are not salient. The dominant form of politics here will be mobilization bias, with well-represented groups who have atypically high stakes in the issue serving as the major drivers of policy. But immediately after an event actually occurs, it will become very salient because of the large amount of damage, and this will cause more broad-based political demand for substantial ameliorative action.

In the second case, the higher frequency of events, all of which pass the availability threshold, will tend to keep the issue perpetually salient to people other than those already well organized into groups. Policy here is less likely to be prone to alternating periods of hectic corrective fire drills and quiescence. Organized interests will be influential in the quiescent periods, but frequent periods of salience, anticipated by political actors, will tend to work against complete capture even in quiet times.

In the third case, risks are never salient, so policy will either be nonexistent or dominanted entirely by interests with atypical stakes.

We can think of examples for each of these extremes. Great earthquakes are very low probability events (even in California) that threaten large disasters. Yet even in areas that are relatively earthquake prone, enforcement of building standards (especially their retroactive application to old structures) is lax. Airline crashes are relatively frequent, newsworthy events, and airline safety regulation is especially stringent, making it by far the safest mode of transportation in terms of expected annual fatalities per unit of exposure. By contrast, safety standards and their enforcement are quite lax in the case of automobiles and motorcycles, resulting in higher accident rates than those of other modes of transportation in which greater numbers of people are at risk in any given accident.

In the view of some observers, comparisons like these reveal a citizen preference for greater safety when large numbers of people are simultaneously at risk. This may be true, but, even in the absence of that particular preference, the cognitive theory would predict the same pattern of political demands – except in the case of truly calamitous outcomes. In this instance, the theory is rather ambiguous. On the one hand, availability will suppress the demand for policy in this arena most of the time. On the other hand, the tendency to overweight low-probability events in calculating action values will have a compensating effect. How these two effects balance out is, of course, not predicted by the theory. What the theory does predict is intertemporal inconsistency in the demand for policy, with the occurrence of an event causing a temporary surge of demand.

Summary of Political Demands for Risk Policy

The preceding discussion leads to several generalizations about the kinds of demands citizens collectively will make on government with regard to risk policies.

1. The intensity of demand for policies to ameliorate risks will tend to be higher for low-probability risks and lower for high-probability risks than is predicted by conventional decision theory.

2. The intensity of demand for policies to ameliorate risks will depend on whether the risk is perceived as a lottery among different levels of improvement, among different levels of losses, or among a mixture of gains and losses.

Imagine that a previously unsuspected potential source of risk is suddenly discovered, say, through the invention of a beneficial, but risky, new technology. Suppose that, without controls, the technology offers a lottery between small and large gains but, with controls, brings the certainty of a moderate gain. Here demand will tend to reflect risk-averse behavior. Suppose now, in the alternative, that new information appears about previously unsuspected dangers from an established valuable technology. The choice of what to do requires selection among a range of costly controls that would reduce, but not eliminate, the amount or likelihood of damage, or both. In this case, demand will tend to exhibit risk-taking behavior. Consider, finally, a new technology that may bring benefits but may also bring net reductions in welfare. Here loss aversion will tend to overcome risk taking in losses. If, however, the possible gains and losses are both very large, citizen preferences may exhibit risk-taking behavior in the selection between partial and total control.

3. The intensity of demand for risk policies will diverge from the predictions of conventional decision theory depending on the frequency and magnitude of consequential events, holding constant the expected and the actual long-term average losses.

The demand for policy will be affected, first, by the fact that the weights assigned to outcomes increase less than proportionately to outcome probabilities, so that events with lower frequency but with outcome values of compensatingly greater magnitude are not evaluated equally. In addition, availability will mitigate against demand for risk-avoidance policies at two extremes: very bad outcomes of very low probability and very frequent events with very small damages.

4. Policy preferences will exhibit intertemporal instability, even if underlying information about outcomes and probabilities does not change.

Intertemporal instability has two sources. First, decision evaluations depend on whether there are intervening inconsequential events between the decision and the outcome and, incidentally, on the status quo (which determines which outcomes are net gains and which are net losses). Second, intertemporal instability arises from framing effects in political discourse because people's perceptions of risks and policies to ameliorate them are determined by the language used to describe the issues.

5. The effect of new information on policy preferences depends on how familiar citizens are with the risk – with overreaction to new information in the case of unfamiliarity and underreaction in the case of considerable familiarity. Essentially, if people update expectations as the cognitive theory assumes, one consequence is that expectations are subject to the availability effect when an event is unfamiliar and to overconfidence or anchoring when it is familiar.

6. Rational ignorance (nonsalience) and mobilization bias are offset to some degree for low-probability events by the form of the weighting function and for all harmful events by the availability effect (temporarily after an event transpires). In other periods, the absence of an occurrence enhances the effects of rational ignorance and mobilization bias.

Implications Regarding the Supply of Risk Regulation

The premise of the following discussion is that, if the cognitive decision theory presents an accurate picture of human behavior, then elected political officials will take into account its effects on the political preferences of their constituents when making policy. We assume that officials seek to secure reelection and that they adopt policies with that end in mind. Political actors may, of course, have their own personal objectives to pursue, but first they have to succeed with the electorate. So we will focus on reelection-maximizing strategies, given the lessons of cognitive theory about electorate behavior.

The first challenge facing elected political officials is to institutionalize systematic differences in the stringency of risk regulation among types of risks so as to reflect the different evaluations of the risks by citizens. (Some risks will be more intensively controlled than others, as measured, say, in terms of expenditures per unit of reduction in expected harm.) One way to accomplish this end would be through a statutory specification of differential objectives. This approach can, however, create problems in several respects. First, changes in preferences, knowledge of risks, or technological developments can quickly make the original policy targets obsolete, requiring time-consuming and sometimes unpredictable policy reauthorization.[32] Second, the intertemporal inconsistencies predicted by prospect theory guarantee that a specific statement of a policy objective will be regarded as suboptimal either now or in the future (and perhaps both). Third, if different risks affect different members of the electorate, explicit differences in the commitment to protecting them may provide effective ammunition for future political challengers who can use the issue to appeal to disfavored groups.[33]

A more effective means for producing differential policy outcomes is to specify ambitious targets in all programs but vary resource allocations and the procedural requirements for adopting regulations among various risk-reduction programs.[34] For example, one way to make airline safety standards more rigorous than auto safety standards is simply to give the agency regulating airlines a much larger budget and much more statutory authority, relative to the problem it is asked to solve, than that given to auto regulators. In the case of toxic chemicals,[35] the Food and Drug Administration (FDA) has, in the Delaney amendment, a very strong and easily invoked tool for removing man-made carcinogens from foods, whereas the Toxic Substances Control Act (administered by the Environmental Protection Agency [EPA]) provides only a weak mechanism for keeping off the market new toxic chemicals used in industrial processes. The government bears the burden of proving that a substance is carcinogenic in both cases, but the standard of proof is lower for the FDA than for the EPA. Of course, these differences do not necessarily have their basis in cognitive decision theory; they merely demonstrate how resource allocations and statutory language could lead to policies of quite different stringency among different categories of risk.

Procedural tools are also a potentially useful way to deal with intertemporal instability in preferences. For example, if the demand for policy reflects availability – because it arises from some catastrophic event unlikely to recur soon – strong policy rhetoric, combined with a protracted process and an understaffed agency, assures that the actual standards for ameliorating the risk will be adopted by the implementing agency only long after the event in question has occurred. Detailed regulatory procedures administered by a resource-poor agency thus allow politicians to "lash themselves to the mast" while waiting out the temporary siren calls for immediate overreaction; they allow an agency to "strike when the iron is cold," after the issue has lost its political salience.

The strategies of lashing to the mast and striking when the iron is cold are politically effective but not necessarily normatively correct. The normative problem arises from the fact that, as salience wanes in the course of the agency's developing its regulatory strategy, participation in the policy process will come to be dominated by organized interests, usually the industries subject to regulation. Hence, a publicly interested policy enacted in the midst of public outcry and relatively free of mobilization bias will end up being implemented through a regulatory process hidden from view and subject to special interest favoritism. This may appear to be politically advantageous to elected officials in that it allows them to serve public demands today and special interest desires tomorrow, but even here a problem arises. If an event similar to that in question is likely to recur sometime during the career of politicians responsible for the regulatory policy, then they risk being blamed for unsuccessful regulation. Given this risk, the best political strategy might be to enact rather rigorous and explicitly specified policy targets but set up a process of implementation that provides distributive benefits to participants in the process. An example would be a cumbersome process for setting industry standards, combined with differentially more rigorous standards for new sources of risk than for old ones – so that the costs to industry of the tough standards will be offset (perhaps more than offset) by barriers to competitive entry.[36] A move like this (which happens to reflect regulatory reality) might satisfy political demands in all three periods: There would be an apparently strong response to availability-driven demand for instant overreaction to some incident; there would be a means to cater to the mobilization bias of industrial interests as salience subsides; there would be a reduction in the likelihood that a disastrous event will recur during one's political career.

The choice between strict legislative policy, on the one hand, and delegation of policy objectives to an administrative agency, on the other, turns on the duration of the availability effect as well as the probability of a damaging event recurring. The theory of availability owing to recency does not specify the rate at which overly intense feelings decay as the event recedes into the past, but this rate and the frequency of the sort of event in question determine two critical elements of the delegation/no delegation decision. The first is the proportion of the time that the issue will be salient and thus protected to some degree from mobilization bias. The second is the chance that today's elected officials will later be held accountable for some damaging event. If an event is unlikely to recur within the time horizon of a politician, and the politician (unlike constituents) is free of cognitive pathologies that lead to overestimation of the probability of recurrence, then the politically optimal policy is to do little or nothing of substance with respect to regulation but to cater to the overreaction and temporary mobilization of citizens who seek action. If the duration of the availability effect is short, lashing to the mast through delegation works for the reasons described above. But if the duration of the availability effect is sufficiently long that overreacting citizens remain mobilized throughout the protracted process of developing a policy through an administrative proceeding, there is likely to be excessive regulation. Thereafter, as the availability effect recedes, the politician is left with no political support from previously overreacting citizens (the issue is no longer salient for them) but with a residue of opposition from an industry that remains organized and has had to comply with unnecessary regulations.

One potentially safe escape for a politician facing these circumstances is to seek government subsidies for the risk-abatement policy. Subsidies will soften industry opposition and provide phantom benefits that overreacting citizens might see as larger than the costs. Perhaps the Superfund program for dealing with toxic waste dumps is an example of this strategy. Toxic chemicals are linked to cancer, and cancer and cancer policy seem to be perpetually salient issues. Environmental groups can rely on the representativeness heuristic to link toxic dumps to cancer and to extend the period of salience that follows some newsworthy event involving pollution from a dump. If relatively few dumps are really threats to public health, but large numbers of dumps are politically salient because of availability and representativeness, then the subsidization strategy keeps industry operating profitably, placates citizens, and avoids disaster. (Of course, the factual premises of this example are a matter of controversy, and there are other plausible explanations for a vigorous policy on toxic dumps. We are simply trying to illustrate one of the implications of cognitive theory for policy making. There is, though, a major puzzle about toxic waste policy. If dumps are a major threat to public health, why has the government not been more active in passing clean-up costs on to industry – as it has been in the case of air and water pollutants and nuclear radiation? The cognitive theory suggests an answer.)

The last case to be considered is where the frequency of recurrence, assuming no regulatory intervention, is shorter than the time horizon of a politician. Here the politician has to trade off demands for excessive regulation against the self-interest of those responsible for creating the risk (they, presumably, want underregulation). If the duration of the availability effect is short, the politician's best available strategy is likely to be a compromise between these interests that is explicitly stated in legislation. Delegation to an agency would be attractive only if the agency could act rather quickly – before salience wanes and before another damaging event occurs. Thus, if delegation is observed, it should be accompanied by strict deadlines for decisions and a commitment to the agency of sufficient resources to make the deadline feasible.

If the period of salience is longer, delegation becomes more attractive, for it can result in an arrangement whereby the representatives of overreacting citizens, and those of self-interested risk producers, are forced to negotiate a compromise under the watchful eye of agencies and the courts. If the duration of the availability effect is long, participation in the policy development process in a regulatory agency will be likely to include both regulated firms and the most intense demanders for risk regulation. Thus, more balanced mobilization will encourage elected political officials to delegate the question of the overall stringency of a policy to an agency.

Our final observation about the optimal political strategy for dealing with risks is the general attractiveness of formulating policy choices in terms of risks of loss rather than as lotteries over gains. In part, loss aversion implies that citizens are easier to motivate when the issue is the threat of loss as opposed to the opportunity for gain. In addition, overreaction by citizens, if it can be orchestrated, is beneficial to political actors. If citizens can be made to attack a problem more intensively than its probability and the gravity of its damage warrant, the ultimate outcome – which is likely to be little or no damage – will cast favorable light on the responsible politicians. In other words, the very nonoccurrence of events will result in greater thanks to the politicians than they deserve. Moreover, by casting risk issues in negative, loss-aversive terms, a political leader is protected against effective challenge by someone adopting the same strategy. This argument is not symmetric: a negative formulation cannot as easily be attacked by a positive formulation because the shape of a citizen's valuation function depends on whether outcomes are gains or losses. That is, gains promise smaller changes in welfare than do losses; thus, they are less likely to be salient to the electorate and less likely to lead to the mobilization of political activity.

Concluding Remarks

The cognitive theory of choice under uncertainty offers two sorts of insights of some relevance to analysts interested in the regulation of risk. First, people take shortcuts (use heuristics) that lead them to make mistakes about variables (such as probability) relevant to evaluating risk. Second, putting the mistakes aside, they approach risk in ways that depart from the norms and assumptions of conventional decision analysis.

The latter category of insights is, of course, much more interesting than the former because the observation that people make mistakes is hardly fresh or startling. Moreover, the cognitive theory seems to contain examples of all kinds of mistakes: for example, while availability may account for overreaction to a catastrophe, anchoring may explain underreaction. As yet, the theory cannot tell us very much about which mistakes are likely to occur in any given circumstance. Even at that, though, the cognitive psychologists' catalog of judgmental errors is a useful contribution, for several reasons. First, knowing something of the types, range, and causes and consequences of misjudgment can guide efforts toward more fruitful communication between the public and policy makers on matters of risk and its regulation, a matter currently (and righly) of much importance. Second, understanding that judgmental error is fairly regular can help avoid some policy pitfalls. Error is predictable as to kinds of mistakes and their direction, and it is likely to plague *any* decision maker, even a professional risk assessor. Recognizing these problems guards against such easy answers to problems of risk regulation as faithfully delegating the whole business to "experts." At the same time, an awareness of the problems enables experts to be sensitized to judgmental shortcomings in the course of their training, so as to make them more worthy of their name.

Points like these are surely beyond contention, something that cannot be said of the implications of the other chief contribution of the cognitive theory – its claim that people think about risk, even when they do so free of miscalculation, in ways that depart from conventional decision theory. What the cognitive psychologists describe, after all (and as they well know),[37] are citizens who are, from the conventional perspective, plainly irrational.

Here, the cognitive theory poses a real problem for conventional decision theorists and policy makers alike. For the first group, there seems to be "little hope for a theory of choice that is both normatively acceptable and descriptively adequate."[38] For the second group, policy makers, the problem is that the measure of good policy becomes ambiguous: Is it what the electorate persistently wants, or is it what conventional analysis persistently dictates?[39]

There is a way out of both of these binds, of course. Theorists and policy makers could simply accept the cognitive theory as the privileged viewpoint, such that the conventional ideas about rationality would become something of an anomaly, rather than (as at present) the other way around. Yet oddly enough, even the cognitive psychologists who have identified the binds in the first place appear to find such an alternative unattractive, perhaps even inappropriate.[40] In any event, so long as there is fundamental disagreement about whether we *should* follow the norms of conventional decision theory or instead accede to the norms at least implicit in prospect theory and other parts of the cognitive psychologists' descriptive picture, there will be fundamental disagreement about just what amounts to "good" regulation of risk.

Policy makers, all politicians included, are likely to have a little less difficulty with this kind of disagreement than are those in more academic positions. True, political actors may at times "face the hard choice between going against their better judgment by using the public's assessment of risk (in which they do not believe) or going against the public's feeling by imposing policies that will be disliked."[41] On some occasions, though, they will surely be able to convince themselves that the most important thing, in the end, is that they act in a way that keeps them in their jobs. On even more occasions, they will find ways to satisfy the public and their own consciences all at the same time. As we suggested above, means can be devised to give the public what it wants while, at the same time, answering to the rationality norms of conventional theory (or is it to the demands of another part of a policy maker's constituency?).

These last conclusions, it should be noticed, follow from our own application of conventional decision theory and its implications for the politics of regulation. Whatever the novel contributions of cognitive theory to the demand side of risk regulation, standard analysis readily suggests the sorts of policies that will be supplied in response. It is possible, of course, that our standard picture is simply wrong – possible, in particular, because it works from an assumption that, while citizens behave according to the cognitive psychologists' description of the world, politicians do not. What cuts in the other direction is that conventional theory does predict rather accurately the behavior of the regulatory system. Perhaps this is because it already incorporates, though sometimes in different jargon, a set of concepts similar to some of those devised by the cognitive theorists. "Availability," after all, is in many respects just another name for the "salience" of standard political theory, and to elaborate such heuristics as "representativeness" and "anchoring" might just be to codify what every successful politician (and every successful political analyst) knew long ago. But then again, maybe much was known long ago precisely because the research undertaken by the cognitive psychologists had seeped unnoticed into the common consciousness.

Notes

1 Identifying the origins of a line of research is always somewhat arbitrary, but we believe that the beginnings of the literature under review here are found in Herbert A. Simon's work on "bounded rationality." See his *Models of Man: Social and Rational* (1957). A compendium is *Judgment Under Uncertainty: Heuristics and Biases* (Daniel Kahneman, Paul Slovic, and Amos Tversky eds., 1982).
2 See, for example, Paul Slovic, Baruch Fischhoff, and Sarah Lichtenstein, Regulation of Risk: A Psychological Perspective, in *Regulatory Policy and the Social Sciences* 241 (Roger G. Noll ed., 1985).
3 See, for example, Baruch Fischhoff, Ola Svenson, and Paul Slovic, Active Responses to Environmental Hazards, in 2 *Handbook of Environmental Psychology* 1089 (D. Stokols and I. Altman eds., 1987).
4 See esp. George A. Quattrone and Amos Tversky, Contrasting Rational and Psychological Analyses of Political Choice, 82 *Am. Pol. Sci. Rev.* 719 (1988).
5 Mark J. Machina has written an informative survey of this work. See his Choice Under Uncertainty: Problems Solved and Unsolved, I *J. Econ. Persp.* 121 (1987).
6 For a comparison of the key assumptions of expected utility and much of cognitive theory, see ibid.
7 Daniel Kahneman and Amos Tversky, Prospect Theory: An Analysis of Decision Under Risk, 47 *Econometrica* 263, 286–8 (1979).
8 Ibid. at 268, 287; Quattrone and Tversky, supra note 4, at 720–1.
9 Kahneman and Tversky, supra note 7, at 274.
10 David Grether, Bayes' Rule as a Descriptive Model: The Representativeness Heuristic, 95 *Q.J. Econ.* 537 (1980).
11 Kahneman and Tversky, supra note 7, at 275.
12 Quattrone and Tversky, supra note 4, at 727–8.
13 Ibid. at 727–30.
14 Slovic et al., supra note 2, at 245–7.
15 Grether, supra note 10.
16 Slovic et al., supra note 2, at 247–8.
17 Kahneman and Tversky, supra note 7.
18 Ibid. at 275–6, 280–4.
19 Ibid. at 276.
20 Ibid. at 269–71.

21 Howard Kunreuther et al., *Disaster Insurance Protection: Public Policy Lessons* (1978).
22 William H. Riker, *Liberalism Against Populism*, ch. 3 (1982).
23 Ibid., ch. 5.
24 Kenneth Arrow, *Social Choice and Individual Values* (1951).
25 Kenneth A. Shepsle and Barry R. Weingast, Structure-Induced Equilibrium and Legislative Choice, 37 *Pub. Choice* 503 (1978).
26 Anthony Downs, *An Economic Theory of Democracy* (1957).
27 Mancur Olson, *The Logic of Collective Action* (1965).
28 Roger G. Noll and Bruce M. Owen, *The Political Economy of Deregulation*, ch. 3 (1983).
29 Quattrone and Tversky, supra note 4.
30 We do not know how voters choose the status quo.
31 For examples of these observations, drawn from the history of air pollution control efforts in Los Angeles in the years after World War II, see James E. Krier and Edmund Ursin, *Pollution and Policy* 263–77 (1977) (discussing the effect of salient "crises" on pollution policy and how they wane over time).
32 Mathew D. McCubbins, Roger G. Noll, and Barry R. Weingast, Structure and Process, Politics and Policy: Administrative Arrangements and the Political Control of Agencies, 75 *Va. L. Rev.* 431 (1989).
33 Riker, supra note 22, ch. 8.
34 Roger G. Noll, The Political Foundations of Regulatory Policy, 139 *Zeitschrift für die gesamte Staatewissenchaft* 377 (1983).
35 Mathew D. McCubbins, Roger G. Noll, and Barry R. Weingast, Administrative Procedures as Instruments of Political Control, 3 *J.L. Econ. & Org.* 243, 268–9 (1987).
36 The 1977 amendments to the Clean Air Act's new source performance standards are commonly interpreted as an application of this approach. See Bruce A. Ackerman and William T. Hassler, *Clean Air Dirty Coal* (1981); and McCubbins, Noll, and Weingast, supra note 35.
37 See, for example, Quattrone and Tversky, supra note 4, at 734–5 (psychological account of political decision making describes behavior that diverges from standard definitions of rationality).
38 Ibid. at 735.
39 See, for example, Slovic et al., supra note 2, at 278.
40 So Quattrone and Tversky, supra note 4, at 735, say that the "descriptive failure of normative principles [drawn from conventional decision theory] . . . does not mean that people are unintelligent or irrational. The failure merely indicates that judgment and choice – like perception and memory – are prone to distortion and error." But why should the cognitive theorists label the behavior they study as revealing "distortion and error" simply because it departs from conventional norms? To say that is to say that the conventional norms are the "right ones," the privileged viewpoint. One could as well say that conventional theory simply has an otherwordly view of rationality.
41 Slovic et al., supra note 2, at 278.

14 Explaining Bargaining Impasse: The Role of Self-serving Biases

Linda Babcock and George Loewenstein

A major unsolved riddle facing the social sciences is the cause of impasse in negotiations. The consequences of impasse are evident in the amount of private and public resources spent on civil litigation, the costs of labor unrest, the psychic and pecuniary wounds of domestic strife, and in clashes between religious, ethnic, and regional groups. Impasses in these settings are not only pernicious, but somewhat paradoxical, since negotiations typically unfold over long periods of time, offering ample opportunities for interaction between the parties.

Economists, and more specifically game theorists, typically attribute delays in settlement to incomplete information. Bargainers possess private information about factors such as their alternatives to negotiated agreements and costs to delay, causing the bargainers to be mutually uncertain about the other side's reservation value. Uncertainty produces impasse because bargainers use costly delays to signal to the other party information about their own reservation value.[1] However, this explanation for impasse is difficult to test because satisfactory measures of uncertainty are rare. With only a few exceptions,[2] most field research in this area has been limited to testing secondary hypotheses such as the relationship between wages and strike duration.[3] Experimental tests of incomplete information accounts of impasse have been hindered by the difficulty of completely controlling important aspects of the experimental environment such as the beliefs maintained by the subjects,[4] and those that have been conducted have generally not provided strong support for the specific models under examination.

This paper identifies a different and relatively simple psychological mechanism as a major cause of bargaining impasse: the tendency for parties to arrive at judgments that reflect a self-serving bias – to conflate what is fair with what benefits oneself. Such self-serving assessments of fairness can impede negotiations and promote impasse in at least three ways. First, if negotiators estimate the value of the alternatives to negotiated settlements in self-serving ways, this could rule out any chance of settlement by eliminating the contract zone (the set of agreements that both sides prefer to their reservation values). Second, if disputants believe that their notion of fairness is impartial and shared by both sides, then they will interpret the other party's aggressive bargaining not as an attempt to get what they perceive of as fair, but as a cynical and exploitative attempt to gain an unfair strategic advantage. Research in psychology and economics has shown that bargainers care not only about what the other party offers, but also about the other party's motives.[5] Third, negotiators are strongly averse to settling even slightly below the point they view as fair.[6] If disputants are willing to make economic sacrifices to avoid a settlement perceived as unfair and if their ideas of fairness are biased in directions that favor themselves, then bargainers who are "only trying to get what is fair" may not be able to settle their dispute.

The evidence we review shows that the self-serving bias and the impasses it causes occur even when disputants possess identical information, which suggests that private and incomplete information may not be as critical for nonsettlement as is commonly believed. The bias is also present when bargainers have incentives to evaluate the situation impartially, which implies that the bias does not appear to be deliberate or strategic.

We begin by reviewing some evidence from the psychology literature that demonstrates the existence of the self-serving bias in different domains. We then present results from experimental and field research, conducted by ourselves and several coauthors (Colin Camerer, Samuel Issacharoff, and Xianghong Wang), which establishes the connection between self-serving bias and impasse and helps to pinpoint the cognitive and motivational mechanisms underlying the bias. Finally, we review previous experimental economics research on bargaining and show that some of the results can be interpreted as manifestations of the self-serving bias.

Psychological Research on the Self-serving Bias

Although psychologists debate the underlying cause of the self-serving bias, its existence is rarely questioned. The self-serving bias is evident in the "above average" effect, whereby well over half of survey respondents typically rate themselves in the top 50 percent of drivers,[7] ethics,[8] managerial prowess,[9] productivity,[10] health,[11] and a variety of other desirable skills. It is also evident in the large body of research showing that people overestimate their own contribution to joint tasks. For example, when married couples estimate the fraction of various household tasks they are responsible for, their estimates typically add to more than 100 percent.[12] People also tend to attribute their successes to ability and skill, but their failures to bad luck.[13]

The self-serving bias affects individuals' evaluations of not only themselves, but also of groups they are affiliated with. For example, in one early study, Hastorf and Cantril examined individuals' judgments of penalties committed during a football game between Princeton and Dartmouth.[14] Students at these schools viewed a film of the game and counted the number of penalties committed by both teams. Princeton students saw the Dartmouth team commit twice as many flagrant penalties and three times as many mild penalties as their own team. Dartmouth students, on the other hand, recorded an approximately equal number of penalties by both teams. While the truth probably lies somewhere in between, the researchers concluded that it was as if the two groups of students "saw a different game."

A subset of research on the self-serving bias has shown that people tend to arrive at judgments of what is fair or right that are biased in the direction of their own self-interests. For example, Messick and Sentis divided subjects into two groups: One group was told to imagine that they had worked seven hours at a task and the others had worked ten hours.[15] Subjects who worked seven hours were always paid $25. Subjects were asked how much the subjects who had worked ten hours should be paid. Seven-hour subjects, on average, thought the ten-hour subject should be paid $30.29. However, the ten-hour subjects thought they should be paid $35.24. The difference between $30.29 and $35.24 – $4.95 – was cited as evidence of a self-serving bias in perceptions of fairness.

This experiment also yielded insights about the underlying cause of the bias. The perceived fair wage for the ten-hour workers was bimodal: Some people thought it was fair to pay both parties equally, regardless of hours worked; others thought it was fair to pay both an equal hourly wage (which would mean paying the ten-hour workers approximately $35.70). The difference between the seven- and ten-hour subjects resulted from the higher fraction of ten-hour subjects who believed that an equal hourly wage was fair. This research suggests that self-serving assessments of fairness are likely to occur in morally ambiguous settings in which there are competing "focal points," that is, settlements that could plausibly be viewed as fair.[16]

An Experimental Investigation: A Texas Tort Case

To investigate the role of self-serving assessments in bargaining, we designed an experimental paradigm, which we then used in a number of experimental studies. We developed a tort case that is based on a trial that occurred in Texas, in which an injured motorcyclist sued the driver of the automobile that collided with him, requesting $100,000. Subjects are randomly assigned to the role of plaintiff or defendant and attempt to negotiate a settlement. Subjects first receive a page explaining the experiment, the sequence of events, rules for negotiating, and the costs they would face if they failed to reach an agreement. Both subjects then receive the same twenty-seven pages of materials from the original legal case in Texas. The materials included witness testimony, police reports, maps, and the testimony of the parties.[17] Subjects are informed that we gave the identical case materials to a judge in Texas, who reached a judgment between $0 and $100,000 concerning compensation to the plaintiff.

Before negotiating, subjects are asked to write down their guess of what the judge awarded. They are told they will receive a bonus of $1 at the end of the session if their prediction is within $5,000 (plus or minus) of the actual judge's award. They are also asked what they considered a fair amount for the plaintiff to receive in an out-of-court settlement "from the vantage point of a neutral third party." Subjects are told that none of this information will be shown to the other party. The two subjects are then allowed to negotiate for thirty minutes. Delays in settlement were made costly to the subjects by imposing "court costs" that accumulate in each period in which the subjects fail to settle. If they fail to reach a voluntary settlement within thirty minutes, then the judge's decision determines the defendant's payment to the plaintiff and legal costs are levied on the parties.

At the beginning of a session, both subjects are paid a fixed fee for participating (e.g., $4) and the defendant is given an extra $10. Ten thousand dollars is equivalent to $1 for the subjects. For example, if the subjects reach a $60,000 settlement and each side owes court costs of $10,000, the defendant keeps $4 and gives $6 to the plaintiff, and both parties give $1 to the experimenter in court costs. If the parties fail to settle, the defendant pays the plaintiff $3.06, representing the judgment of $30,560 actually awarded by the judge (that was unknown to the subjects during the negotiation), and both parties pay legal costs of $2.50 for not settling.

The experiment was designed to test for the effect of the self-serving bias in a contextually rich and controlled experimental setting. Since both parties are given the same case information and neither party has private information about the judge, differences in estimates between defendant and plaintiff cannot be attributed to differences in information.

Our first experiment with this framework found strong evidence that the negotiators formed self-serving assessments of the judge's award, and that the discrepancy between the plaintiffs' and defendants' assessments was correlated with the parties' ability to reach voluntary settlements.[18] The subjects were eighty undergraduates from the University of Chicago and eighty law students at the University of Texas at Austin. Subjects were assigned randomly to roles as either the defendant or plaintiff immediately upon entering the experiment.

The self-serving bias was clear in that plaintiffs' predictions of the judge averaged $14,527 higher than defendants', and plaintiffs' fair settlement values averaged $17,709 higher than defendants', with both differences statistically different from zero ($p < .0001$). Table 14.1 presents a median split of the discrepancy in the parties' assessments of the judge and summarizes the percent of pairs that reached an impasse for each group. The first row of the table shows that in this experiment, nonsettlement was strongly related to

Table 14.1. *Probability of Impasse by Discrepancy Between Plaintiffs' and Defendants' Assessments of the Judge*

	Pairs in Which the Discrepancy Is:	
	Below the Median	Above the Median
Loewenstein et al. (1993) ($n = 80$)	.03 (.03)	.30 (.09)
Babcock et al. (1995) ($n = 94$)	.04 (.03)	.28 (.06)
Babcock et al. (1996) ($n = 49$)	.04 (.04)	.36 (.10)

Note: Standard errors are in parentheses. All differences are significant at the .05 level.

Sources: Loewenstein, George, Samuel Issacharoff, Colin Camerer, and Linda Babcock, Self-serving Assessments of Fairness and Pretrial Bargaining, 22 *J. Legal Stud.* 135–59 (January 1993). Babcock, Linda, George Loewenstein, Samuel Issacharoff, and Colin Camerer, Biased Judgments of Fairness in Bargaining, 85 *Am. Econ. Rev.* 1337–43 (1995). Babcock, Linda, Xianghong Wang, and George Loewenstein, Choosing the Wrong Pond: Social Comparisons That Reflect a Self-serving Bias, 111 *Q. J. Econ.* 1–19 (February 1996).

the discrepancy between the plaintiffs' and defendants' predictions of what the judge would award.

One limitation of this study was that it does not necessarily demonstrate that the self-serving bias *causes* impasse. It is possible, for example, that there is a third factor, perhaps some element of personality such as aggressiveness, that causes certain subjects to misestimate the judge and to be unwilling to settle. To avoid this problem, in a new study we introduced a manipulation to diminish the magnitude of the discrepancy in expectations without changing other key features of the experiment. The manipulation involved changing the order of the events in the experiment. In the control condition, the participants learned whether their role would be defendant or plaintiff *before* they read the case materials and offered their anonymous assessments of the judge and a fair settlement; in the experimental condition, they learned which role they would play *after* reading the case materials and offering their estimates of the judge and a fair settlement. Our prediction was that the discrepancy between the plaintiffs' and defendants' assessments would be smaller for those who learned their role after reading the case, because, not knowing their role when they read through the case, they would process the information in an unbiased fashion.

The experiment was run with 38 public policy students at Carnegie Mellon University, 120 law students from the University of Texas, and 30 business

Table 14.2. *Discrepancy in Assessments of the Judge and Rates of Impasse by Condition*

Babcock et al. (1995)	Learned Roles Before Read Case	Learned Roles After Read Case
Discrepancy in assessments of the judge	$18,555 (3,787)	$6,936 (4,179)
Impasse rate	.28 (.07)	.06 (.03)
Babcock et al. (1996)	**Control**	**Learned About and Listed weaknesses**
Discrepancy in assessments of the judge	$21,783 (3,956)	$4,674 (6,091)
Impasse rate	.35 (.10)	.04 (.04)

Note: Standard errors are in parentheses. All differences are significant at the .05 level.
Sources: Babcock, Linda, George Loewenstein, Samuel Issacharoff, and Colin Camerer, Biased Judgments of Fairness in Bargaining, 85 *Am. Econ. Rev.* 1337–43 (1995). Linda Babcock, George Loewenthal, and Samuel Issacharoff, "Debiasing Litigation Impasse," unpublished paper (1996).

students from the University of Pennsylvania.[19] Consistent with a causal relationship running from the self-serving bias to impasse, when the subjects did not learn their roles until after they read the case and made their assessments of the judge and fairness, only 6 percent of the negotiations were resolved by the judge; however, when the subjects knew their roles initially, 28 percent of negotiations had to be resolved by the judge (this statistically significant difference is shown in the first row of Table 14.2). As in the previous experiment, the discrepancy in the parties' assessments of the judge's decision was related to settlement; only 4 percent of the negotiations in which the discrepancy was below the median ended in impasse, while 28 percent of pairs above the median discrepancy failed to settle (see the second row of Table 14.1).

Prior research on self-serving biases[20] and on biased processing of information in general[21] suggests that the bias results from selective information processing. As Danitioso, Kunda, and Fong argue, "People attempt to construct a rational justification for the conclusions that they want to draw.[22] To that end, they search through memory for relevant information, but the search is biased in favor of information that is consistent with the desired conclusions. If they succeed in finding a preponderance of such consistent information, they are able to draw the desired conclusion while maintaining an illusion of objectivity." We explored this explanation by giving subjects a questionnaire at the end of the bargaining session in which they were asked to rate the importance of a series of eight arguments favoring the plaintiff and eight favoring the defendant.[23] Consistent with the psychology research, plaintiffs tended to weight arguments favoring the plaintiff as much more compelling than those favoring the defendant and vice versa. This provides evidence that the self-serving bias results from role-dependent evaluation of information.

Might other experimental manipulations offer suggestions for practical ways of reducing the discrepancy in the parties' expectations and thus avoid impasse? Obviously, our experiment that gave subjects their role after reading the case materials has no practical implication, since parties to a dispute usually know their own roles from the outset.

We experimented with several interventions that were designed to "de-bias" the disputants' judgments as a way to promote settlement. In one experimental treatment subjects read a paragraph describing the extent and consequences of the self-serving bias after they were assigned their roles and read the case, but before they recorded their assessments of fairness and their predictions of the judge's decision. They also took a short test to make sure that they had understood the paragraph explaining the bias. However, being informed of the bias had no effect on the discrepancy in the parties' expectations, nor on the likelihood of settlement. One interesting result, however, did emerge from this study. In addition to asking their perception of fairness and the judge, we asked subjects to guess their opponent's prediction of the judge. Our results indicate that informing subjects of the bias made them more realistic about the predictions of the other party. However, it did not cause them to modify their own prediction of the judge. When they learned about the bias, subjects apparently assumed that the other person would succumb to it, but did not think it applied to themselves.

In another treatment, before they negotiated, subjects were instructed to write an essay arguing the opponent's case as convincingly as possible. This intervention was inspired by research that has suggested that people with better perspective-taking ability resolve disputes more efficiently.[24] This did change the discrepancy in expectations, and in a way that was marginally statistically significant, but opposite to the intended direction. Again, there was no significant impact on the settlement rate.

Finally, we turned to research in psychology showing that biases are diminished when subjects question their own judgment. Slovic and Fischhoff,[25] for example, found that the "hindsight bias" (the tendency to view the past as having been more predictable than it actually was) was reduced when subjects were instructed to give reasons for why outcomes other than the one that actually occurred could have occurred. Koriat, Lichtenstein, and Fischhoff found that a bias called "overconfidence" was reduced by having subjects list counterarguments to their beliefs.[26] They conclude that "overconfidence derives in part from the tendency to neglect contradicting evidence and that calibration may be improved by making such evidence more salient."[27] Research on other biases has produced similar debiasing success stories when subjects are instructed to "consider the opposite."[28]

Based on this common finding, we designed an intervention in which subjects, after being assigned their role and reading the case materials, were informed of the self-serving bias (as in the previous experiment) and told that it could arise from the failure to think about the weaknesses in their own case.[29] They were then asked to list the weaknesses in their own case. The effect of this intervention was to diminish the discrepancy in the parties' expectations about the judge (see the third row of Table 14.2): the discrepancy averaged $21,783 in the control condition, where neither party received this intervention, but only $4,674 when the subjects received the debiasing procedure ($p < .05$). The debiasing treatment also reduced the rate of impasse from 35 to 4 percent ($p < .01$). Notice that this intervention can be implemented after an individual realizes that he or she is involved in a dispute. It thus holds a possibility of serving as a practical tool in mediation.

Our research on debiasing begs the question of whether the self-serving bias is indeed "self-serving." In fact, one reviewer commented that it was more of a "self-defeating" bias since it caused individuals to make systematic errors that made them worse off. However, psychologists have argued that these biases are clearly beneficial to well-being in some domains. For example, Taylor and Brown argue that unrealistically positive self-evaluations promote happiness as well as other aspects of mental health.[30] Furthermore, they suggest that individuals that have more accurate self-evaluations are either low in self-esteem, moderately depressed, or both. However, it is clear from our research that, in negotiations where the costs of impasse are high, the self-serving bias hurts both parties economically. An unresolved issue, which we are exploring in our current research, is whether it benefits a party to be less biased, holding constant the beliefs of the other party. While this will help to reduce impasse, it may also cause that party to be less persuasive in a negotiation, leading to an inferior outcome should a settlement be reached.

A Field Study: Public School Teacher Negotiations

In presenting these findings at seminars and conferences, we are often questioned as to whether experienced negotiators would succumb to the self-serving bias. To address this point, we conducted a study to examine the bias and its impact on bargaining in a real-world setting – public school teacher contract negotiations in Pennsylvania.[31] Since 1971 approximately 8 percent of all teacher contract negotiations have ended in a strike, with an average strike duration of 16.4 days.

In public-sector contract negotiations, it is commonplace for both sides to make references to agreements in "comparable" communities. We hypothesized that both sides would have self-serving beliefs about which communities were comparable, and that impasses would be more likely as the gap between their beliefs widened. To explore this hypothesis, we surveyed union and school board presidents from all school districts in Pennsylvania to obtain a list of districts that they viewed as comparable for purposes of salary negotiations.[32] We linked the survey data to a data set that included district-level information about strikes, teachers' salaries, community salary levels, and other demographic and financial information. The combination of survey and field data allows us to examine the relationship between strike activity and the subjective perceptions of the respondents.

Considering only the districts in which both the union and school board returned the survey, we found that both sides listed about the same number of districts as being comparable (about 4.5). However, the actual districts listed by the two sides differed in a way that reflected a self-serving bias. The average salary in districts listed by the union was $27,633, while the average salary in districts listed by the board was $26,922. The mean difference of $711 is statistically and economically significant; it is equivalent to about 2.4 percent of average teacher salary at a time when salary increases averaged less than 5 percent per year.

To test for the effect of self-serving bias on strikes, we regressed the percent of previous contract negotiations that ended in a strike against the difference in the average salaries of the two parties' lists of comparables. The regression also included variables controlling for district wealth and local labor market conditions. This regression produced a significant effect of differences in the lists of comparables on strike activity. The point estimate suggests that a district where the average salary of the union's list is $1,000 greater than the board's list will be approximately 49 percent more likely to strike than a district where the average salaries of the union's and board's lists are the same.

We also found that the difference in the list of comparables was correlated with the variance in the salaries of teachers in the neighboring districts. Apparently, larger variation in neighboring salaries provides more opportunity for each side to choose self-serving comparison groups. However, the difference in the lists of comparables was unrelated to the level of experience of either the union or board presidents. Experience with bargaining does not seem to inoculate one against the self-serving bias.

Reinterpreting Findings from Previous Bargaining Experiments

The existence of the self-serving bias offers a useful tool for reinterpreting a number of past findings in the research on bargaining. In one study, for example, two subjects bargained over how to distribute one hundred tickets for a lottery.[33] One subject would receive $5 for winning the lottery, while the other would receive $20. Given this setup, there were two focal points for splitting the chips: fifty chips to each (equal chance of winning) or twenty chips to the $20-prize player and eighty chips to the $5-prize player (equal expected value). When neither player knew who would receive which payoff, subjects generally agreed to divide the chips about equally, and only 12 percent of pairs failed to reach an agreement and ended up with no payoff. However, when both subjects knew who was assigned to which payoff, 22 percent failed to reach agreement. A likely interpretation is that both sides viewed as fair the focal settlement that benefited themselves, so the $20-prize player was likely to hold out for half of the chips, while the $5 player demanded equal expected values.

Another well-known bargaining framework is the so-called shrinking pie game, in which one subject (the "proposer") is presented with a sum of money and asked to divide it with another subject (the "responder"). If the responder rejects the offer, the amount of money to be divided (the "pie") shrinks, the players switch roles, and the game continues either until an offer is accepted, or until a specified number of rounds have been played. In this game it is common to see a responder reject a lopsided offer and then propose a counteroffer that gives them less than the offer they just rejected but is more equitable because the other side's amount has been reduced by even more. In one investigation of this game, Weg, Rapoport, and Felsenthal found that when the pie shrank at the same rate for both individuals, the rejection rate was only 12 percent in the first round, but when the pie shrank at different rates for each subject, the rejection rate was 57 percent in the first round.[34] Again, consistent with the self-serving bias, perhaps subjects whose pies shrank relatively slowly viewed this as justification for requesting a large fraction of the pie, but subjects whose pies shrank quickly rejected the rate of pie shrinkage as a criterion for allocating the pie.

A special case of the shrinking pie game is the "ultimatum" game in which there is only a single round. In this case, if the responder rejects the proposer's offer in the first round, the pie shrinks to zero and neither side gets any payoff. If proposers care only about self-interest, and if they believe responders do too, the proposer should offer a trivial amount (like 1 cent), and it should be accepted. But in practice, the modal offer is typically half the pie, and smaller offers are often rejected.[35]

Although ultimatum experiments have been used by economists to illustrate the importance of fairness considerations, rejections in these experiments can be explained by self-serving biases. Proposers, who view themselves in a powerful role, believe that they deserve more than half of the pie, whereas responders do not believe that role should affect the division of the pie. Beyond the simple fact of nonsettlement, certain variants of the standard ultimatum game have produced results that provide more direct evidence of the role of self-serving biases. In one variant of the game, the roles of proposer and responder were determined either randomly or by the outcome of a trivia contest with the winner playing the role of proposer.[36] Offers in the contest condition were lower than in the chance condition, and the rejection rate was substantially higher. It seems that proposers in the contest condition felt self-servingly entitled to a higher payoff, but responders did not view the contest as relevant to the fair division of the pie.

In another variant of the ultimatum game, Knez and Camerer conducted experiments in which players earned a known dollar amount if the responder rejected the proposer's ultimatum offer.[37] For example, if the amount to be divided is $10 and if the offer was rejected, proposers earned $4 and responders earned $3. There are two obvious fair divisions: to simply divide the $10.00 evenly, giving both parties an equal payoff of $5.00, or to divide the surplus over the outside offers evenly; in this example, an offer of $4.50 would give the responder a surplus of $1.50 ($4.50 – $3.00) and the proposer an equal surplus of $1.50 ($5.50 – $4.00). These alternative definitions create scope for self-serving assessments of fairness, and indeed respondents in this situation consistently demanded more than half the "pie," and about half of the offers were rejected – a rate of disagreement much higher than previous ultimatum studies.

Two studies of labor negotiations have produced similar evidence that can be interpreted as showing self-serving biases. In an experimental study of labor-management negotiations, Thompson and Loewenstein found that management estimates of a fair settlement were significantly lower than those provided by the union and observed a significant positive correlation between the difference in assessments of fairness and the length of strikes.[38] They also manipulated the complexity of information provided to the two sides and found that complexity had a small but significant effect in increasing the discrepancy between the union and management's self-serving perceptions of the fair wage.

In a field study examining the use of arbitration in contract negotiations for public school teachers in Wisconsin, Babcock and Olson found that increases in the variation of wage settlements within a district's athletic conference increased the probability that the district failed to negotiate a contract and ended up using arbitration.[39] This evidence can be interpreted in the same way as our field study of Pennsylvania teachers mentioned earlier; when there are numerous potential comparison groups to assess fairness, the parties focus on those that favor themselves.

Discussion

Taken as a body, the research discussed here presents strong evidence that the self-serving bias is an important determinant of bargaining impasse. As a general lesson, the research suggests that, for the bias to occur, there needs to be some form of asymmetry in how the negotiation environment is viewed. This should not be taken to mean that the bias comes from asymmetric information. Instead, what we have in mind is that the parties – even with complete information – interpret the situation in different ways. Few subjects placed in a symmetric bargaining setting in which they are instructed to divide $10 with another party will believe that anything other than an even split is fair. However, even in a very simple setting like this, as soon as asymmetries are introduced between the parties – for example, different nonagreement values or costs of nonsettlement, or subtle differences in roles – both parties' notions of fairness will tend to gravitate toward settlements that favor themselves. They will not only view these settlements as fair but also believe that their personal conception of fairness is impartial.

We have attempted to show that the self-serving bias provides an account of impasse that has greater explanatory power than models based on incomplete information. Moreover, the self-serving bias may also help explain other important economic phenomena, such as unemployment. If job searchers have inflated evaluations of their productivity, they will have unrealistically high reservation wages, leading to longer unemployment spells. Research has found that job search assistance programs lead unemployed workers to find jobs more quickly. One reason these programs are successful may be that, like our debiasing treatment described above, they deflate expectations, causing individuals to be more objective about their alternatives. Self-serving biases may also help to explain the low take-up rate for unemployment insurance (the percentage of eligible individuals that use the program). Again, if workers have inflated expectations regarding their job search, they will believe that they will quickly find a good job, reducing the incentive to apply for assistance. Other research has found that self-serving biases contribute to the "tragedy of the commons" problems. When individuals evaluate their "fair share" of the scarce resource in a self-serving way, they will deplete the resource at a faster rate.[40] A closely related bias, overconfidence, may help to explain what some researchers view as excessive trading in foreign exchange markets and on the New York Stock Exchange. Odean develops a financial market model in which traders are overconfident about the precision of their private information.[41] This leads to a quasi-rational expectations equilibrium in which there is excessive trading volume.

The self-serving bias has other wide-ranging ramifications. Whenever individuals face trade-offs between what is best for themselves and what is morally correct, their perceptions of moral correctness are likely to be biased in the direction of what is best for themselves.[42] In making the trade-off, then, self-interest enters twice: directly, when it is traded off against moral correctness, and indirectly, via its impact on perceptions of moral correctness. Transplant surgeons, for example, must often decide how to allocate scarce organs between potential recipients. To maintain favorable statistics, their self-interest may not be to transplant those who would benefit most in terms of *increased* survival, but instead those where the probability of a successful operation is highest. Based on the research we have reviewed, it seems likely that transplant surgeons' views of who benefits most from the transplant will be distorted by their interest in "cream skimming." Similarly, we suspect, doctors who change to a remuneration system that compensates them less for conducting medical tests are likely to alter their views concerning the medical value of testing. In a different domain, it seems likely that the judgments of auditors, who ostensibly represent the interests of shareholders but are hired (and fired) by the people they audit, are likely to be blinded to some degree by the incentive for client retention.

Will Experience and Learning Minimize the Bias?

When we have presented this work, three issues are commonly raised, all relating to the importance of the self-serving bias in the real world. First, it is suggested that, while naive experimental subjects might exhibit such a bias, trained professionals, such as lawyers, would be resistant. Besides the evidence from our field study of Pennsylvania teachers, which shows that seasoned negotiators are subject to the bias, other evidence also shows that professionals are not immune. For example, Eisenberg analyzed a survey conducted with 205 experienced bankruptcy lawyers and 150 judges involved in bankruptcy cases that asked a series of questions about lawyers' fees, such as how long it takes judges to rule on fee applications and the fairness of fees.[43] Comparisons of judges' and lawyers' responses revealed a self-serving bias in virtually every question in the survey. For example, 78 percent of judges reported that they rule on interim fee applications at the fee hearing, but only 46 percent of lawyers report that the judges rule so quickly. Thirty-seven percent of judges reported that they most frequently allow reimbursement at the "value of the services," while only 15 percent of lawyers reported that judges reimburse at such rates. Sixty percent of lawyers report that they always comply with fee guidelines, but judges reported that only 18 percent of attorneys always comply. Whether the lawyers or judges or, most likely, both, are responsible for these discrepancies, this evidence certainly does not suggest that professionals are immune to the self-serving bias.

A second criticism raised is that the stakes involved in our experiments are too low – that our subjects are insufficiently motivated to process the information in an unbiased way. This criticism fails on several grounds. First, these biases are observed in real-world settings in which the stakes are extremely high such as the teacher contract negotiations described above. Second, individuals are unlikely to be conscious of their biased processing of information so that increases in incentives will not cause them to be more conscientious. Third, "high stakes" experiments, such as those conducted by Hoffman, McCabe, and Smith, have not produced substantively different behavior than those with lower stakes.[44]

A third criticism of the experiments is that they fail to allow for learning. While our experiments were "one-shot," in most economics experiments it is common to run subjects through the same procedure multiple times to allow for learning. It is not at all obvious, however, that the real world allows for anything like the opportunities for learning that are present in economics laboratory experiments. Most people find themselves only sporadically involved in bargaining, and each bargaining situation differs from past situations on numerous dimensions. Undoubtedly, all of our experimental subjects, especially the law and business school students, had numerous experiences with bargaining prior to participating in our experiment, but this experience did not seem to alert them even to the existence of the self-serving bias, let alone actually give them the capacity to counteract it. We should also note that our results from the Pennsylvania field study are not consistent with the notion that experience will eliminate the bias.

In fact, there is reason to be concerned that experience and real history almost always contain the kind of ambiguous information and competing claims that are breeding grounds for self-serving assessments of fairness. In a study by Camerer and Loewenstein, subjects bargained over the sale of a piece of land, knowing only their reservation value.[45] All pairs agreed on a sale price. In a second phase, the same pairs of students negotiated the identical situation again, after learning their partners' reservation value. Twenty percent of pairs failed to settle on this second round, despite the fact that they possessed more information. Students who did poorly in the first round felt that they deserved to be compensated for the previous bad outcome. Those who did well in the first round viewed the first round as irrelevant to the second. One important implication of these results for mediation is that recriminations about the past should be excluded from negotiations to the greatest extent possible. If the adage "let bygones be bygones" applies to economic decision making, it applies doubly to negotiations.

Methods: Psychology and Economics

Experimental economists find several features of the studies discussed in this paper to be unusual. The first is the inclusion of a rich legal context in the experiment. Experiments in economics often deliberately limit the context of the interaction, with generic labeling of roles and rigidly controlled communications between the parties. As Cox and Isaac write, experiments in economics do not normally involve "role playing" by subjects, that is, "experiments in which the instructions, context, and/or motivation of the experimental design draw upon subjects' knowledge of economic agents or institutions outside the laboratory."[46] In contrast, in our Texas tort experiment subjects took the role of a party in a realistic law case with unstructured face-to-face communication. As our choice of method implies, we think the emphasis among economists on expunging context in experiments is a mistake. Human thinking, problem solving, and choice are highly context-dependent. Psychologists have found that there are many problems that people are unable to solve in the abstract, but are able to solve when placed in a real-world context.[47]

One classical illustration is the Wason "four card problem." Subjects are shown a deck of cards, each with a number on one side and a letter on the other. The exposed sides they see are X, Y, 1, and 2. They are asked which cards need to be turned over to test the rule that "If there is an X on one side there is a 2 on the other." When the problem is given to people in the abstract form just described, very few people give the correct answer, which is "X" and "1." However, when the task is put into a familiar context, almost everyone answers correctly. For example, when the rule is "If a student is to be assigned to Grover High School, then that student must live in Grover City," and students are shown cards that read "lives in Grover City," "doesn't live in Grover City," "assigned to Grover High School," and "not assigned to Grover High School" (with the relevant information on the other side of the card), 89 percent of subjects state correctly which cards need to be turned over.[48]

The notion of a "context-free" experiment is, in any case, illusory. Experiments using the ultimatum game have shown that seemingly subtle variations in procedure that should not matter from a strictly economic point of view – for example, the mechanism that determines the roles, whether the game is framed as an offer game or a demand game, and the timing and method of eliciting an offer – all have powerful effects on how people play the game.[49] Researchers who subscribe to the illusion that their particular experiment is "context-free" are likely to come away with an exaggerated sense of the generalizability of their findings.

A second nonstandard feature of the Texas tort experiments and the Pennsylvania teachers field study is that we measured subjects' perceptions. Economists, like behaviorist psychologists, sometimes pride themselves on measuring behavior, rather than perceptions. As a practical matter, we often delude ourselves by this distinction. Much of the data on "behavior" used in economic analyses comes from surveys, such as the National Longitudinal Survey and Current Population Survey, in which respondents provide information on such things as jobs, wages, spells of unemployment, and so on. However, such self-reports of behavior are highly fallible, because of biases, limitations in memory, and deliberate misreporting. Indeed, Akerlof and Yellen have shown that people do not even seem able to remember with any great accuracy whether they were employed or unemployed during the past year.[50]

Moreover, failure to collect data on psychological constructs robs us of information that can contribute to more nuanced tests of theory. For example, Tracy finds a positive relationship between investor uncertainty (a proxy for the union's uncertainty about the firm) and strike activity and cites this as evidence consistent with an asymmetric information model of impasse.[51] However, there are undoubtedly many theories that could predict this positive correlation. Only by actually collecting data on the unions' perceptions of firm profitability before and after contract negotiations can one directly test the notion that firms are using delay in settlement to signal information about their profitability to the union. Because of the reluctance to collect and analyze data on intervening variables, economists have sometimes been forced into very coarse tests of their models' predictions.

Some economists are concerned that incorporating psychology would complicate economic analysis or force an abandonment of the traditional tools of constrained maximization. Nothing could be further from the truth. Models that incorporate individuals' preferences for "fair" outcomes still use traditional methods yet lead to predictions with more empirical support than conventional models.[52] Recent attempts to model self-serving interpretations of fairness,[53] we hope, will help persuade more economists that psychological factors can be incorporated into formal economic analyses.

All economics involves psychology. Bayes's Rule, the rational expectations assumption, and the theory of revealed preference are all *psychological* assumptions about how people form expectations and what motivates them. The question for economics is not whether to include or exclude psychology, but rather what type of psychology to include.

Notes

1 See John Kennan and Robert Wilson, Strategic Bargaining Models and Interpretation of Strike Data, 4 *J. Applied Econometrics* 87 (1989); Peter C. Cramton, Strategic Delay in Bargaining with Two-Sided Uncertainty, 59 *Rev. Econ. Stud.* 205 (1992).

2 See Joseph S. Tracy, An Investigation into the Determinants of U.S. Strike Activity, 76 *Am. Econ. Rev.* 423 (1986); Joseph S. Tracy, An Empirical Test of Asymmetric Information, 5 *J. Lab. Econ.* 149 (1987).

3 See Henry S. Farber, Bargaining Theory, Wage Outcomes, and the Occurrence of Strikes: An Econometric Analysis, 68 *Am. Econ. Rev.* 262 (1978); David Card, Strikes and Wages: A Test of an Asymmetric Information Model, *Q.J. Econ.* 625 (1990); Sheena McConnell, Strikes, Wages and Private Information, 79 *Am. Econ. Rev.* 801 (1989); John Kennan, The Economics of Strikes, in 2 *Handbook of Labor Economics* 1091 (Orley Ashenfelter and Richard Layard eds., 1986); John Kennan, The Duration of Contract Strikes in U.S. Manufacturing, 28 *J. Econometrics* 5 (1985).

4 See Alvin E. Roth, Bargaining Experiments, in *The Handbook of Experimental Economics* 253 (John H. Kagel and Alvin E. Roth eds., 1995).

5 See Sally Blount, When Social Outcomes Aren't Fair: The Effect of Causal Attributions on Preferences, 63 *Org. Behav. & Hum. Decision Processes* 131 (1995); Elizabeth Hoffman et al., On Expectations and Monetary Stakes in Ultimatum Games, 25 *Int'l J. Game Theory* 289 (1996), offers an empirical investigation of this point. Matthew Rabin, Incorporating Fairness into Game Theory, 83 *Am. Econ. Rev.* 1281 (1993), provides a literature review and a theoretical analysis.

6 See George F. Loewenstein et al., Social Utility and Decision Making in Interpersonal Contexts, 57 *J. Personality & Soc. Psychol.* 426 (1989).

7 See Ola Svenson, Are We All Less Risky and More Skillful Than Our Fellow Drivers? 47 *Acta Psychologica* 143 (1981).

8 See R. C. Baumhart, *An Honest Profit: What Businessmen Say About Ethics in Business* (1968).

9 See L. Larwood and W. Whittaker, Managerial Myopia: Self-serving Biases in Organization Planning, 62 *J. Applied Psychol.* 194 (1977).

10 See P. Cross, Not Can but Will College Teaching Be Improved, 17 *New Directions for Higher Education* 1 (1977).

11 See Neil D. Weinstein, Unrealistic Optimism About Future Life Events, 39 *J. Personality & Soc. Psychol.* 806 (1980).

12 See Michael Ross and Fiore Sicoly, Egocentric Biases in Availability and Attribution, 37 *J. Personality & Soc. Psychol.* 322 (1979).

13 See M. Zuckerman, Attributions of Success and Failure Revisited, or: The Motivational Bias Is Alive and Well in Attribution Theory, 47 *J. Pers.* 245 (1979).

14 See Albert H. Hastorf and Hadley Cantril, They Saw a Game: A Case Study, 4 *J. Abnormal & Soc. Psychol.* 129 (1954).

15 See David Messick and Keith Sentis, Fairness and Preference, 15 *J. Exper. Soc. Psychol.* 418 (1979).

16 See Thomas C. Schelling, *The Strategy of Conflict* (1979).

17 In some of the experiments subjects were given a week to read the case, and in other experiments they were given thirty minutes.

18 See George Loewenstein, Samuel Issacharoff, Colin Camerer, and Linda Babcock, Self-serving Assessments of Fairness and Pretrial Bargaining, 22 *J. Legal Stud.* 135 (1993).

19 See Linda Babcock, George Loewenstein, Samuel Issacharoff, and Colin Camerer, Biased Judgments of Fairness in Bargaining, 85 *Am. Econ. Rev.* 1337 (1995).

20 See D. Dunning, J. A. Meyerowitz, and A. D. Holzberg, Ambiguity and Self-evaluation: The Role of Idiosyncratic Trait Definitions in Self-serving Assessments of Ability, 57 *J. Personality & Soc. Psychol.* 1082 (1989).

21 See John M. Darley and Paget H. Gross, A Hypothesis-Confirming Bias in Labeling Effects, 44 *J. Personality & Soc. Psychol.* 20 (1983).

22 See R. Danitioso, Z. Kunda, and G. T. Fong, Motivated Recruitment of Autobiographical Memories, 59 *J. Personality & Soc. Psychol.* 229 (1990).

23 See Babcock et al., supra note 19.

24 See Max H. Bazerman and Margaret A. Neale, Improving Negotiation Effectiveness Under Final Offer Arbitration: The Role of Selection and Training, 67 *J. Applied Psychol.* 543 (1982).

25 See Paul Slovic and Baruch Fischhoff, On the Psychology of Experimental Surprises, 3 *J. Exper. Psychol.: Hum. Perception & Performance* 544 (1977).

26 See Asher Koriat, Sarah Lichtenstein, and Baruch Fischhoff, Reasons for Confidence, 6 *J. Exper. Psychol.: Hum. Learning & Memory* 107 (1980).

27 Ibid. at 113.

28 See Charles G. Lord et al., Considering the Opposite: A Corrective Strategy for Social Judgment, 47 *J. Personality & Soc. Psychol.* 1231 (1984); Craig A. Anderson, Abstract and Concrete Data in the Perseverance of Social Theories: When Weak Data Lead to Unshakable Beliefs, 19 *J. Exper. Soc. Psychol.* 93 (1983); Craig A. Anderson, Inoculation and Counterexplanation: Debiasing Techniques in the Perseverance of Social Theories, 1 *Soc. Cognition* 126 (1982).

29 See Linda Babcock, Xianghong Wang, and George Loewenstein, Choosing the Wrong Pond: Social Comparisons in Negotiations That Reflect a Self-serving Bias, 111 *Q.J. Econ.* 1 (1996).
30 See Shelley E. Taylor and Jonathan D. Brown, Illusion and Well-being: A Social Psychological Perspective on Mental Health, 103 *Psychol. Bull.* 193, 202 (1988).
31 See Babcock et al., supra note 29.
32 The response rate for returning the survey was 57 percent for the union presidents and 35 percent for the school board presidents. See Babcock et al., supra note 29, for details on the response rate and issues of selectivity bias.
33 See Alvin E. Roth and J. Keith Murnighan, The Role of Information in Bargaining: An Experimental Study, 50 *Econometrica* 1123 (1982).
34 See Eythan Weg, Amnon Rapoport, and Dan S. Felsenthal, Two-Person Bargaining Behavior in Fixed Discounting Games with Infinite Horizons, 2 *Games & Economic Behavior* 76 (1990).
35 For a brief discussion of the game and an overview of findings from various permutations, see Colin Camerer and Richard H. Thaler, Anomalies: Ultimatums, Dictators, and Manners, 9 *J. Econ. Persp.* 209 (1995).
36 See Elizabeth Hoffman et al., Preferences, Property Rights and Anonymity in Bargaining Games, 7 *Games & Econ. Behav.* 346 (1994).
37 See Marc Knez and Colin Camerer, Outside Options and Social Comparison in Three-Player Ultimatum Game Experiments, 10 *Games & Econ. Behav.* 65 (1995).
38 See Leigh Thompson and George Loewenstein, Egocentric Interpretations of Fairness and Interpersonal Conduct, 51 *Org. Behav. & Hum. Decision Processes* 176 (1992).
39 See Linda C. Babcock and Craig A. Olson, The Causes of Impasses in Labor Disputes, 31 *Indus. Rel.* 348 (1992).
40 See Kimberly Wade-Benzoni, Ann Tenbrunsel, and Max Bazerman, Egocentric Interpretations of Fairness in Asymmetric, Environmental Social Dilemmas: Explaining Harvesting Behavior and the Role of Communication, 62 *Org. Behav. & Hum. Decision Processes* 111 (1996).
41 See Terrance Odean, *Volume, Volatility, Price, and Profit When All Traders Are Above Average* (1995).
42 See George Loewenstein, Behavioral Decision Theory and Business Ethics: Skewed Trade-offs Between Self and Other, in *Codes of Conduct* 214 (David M. Messick and Ann E. Tenbreusel eds., 1996).
43 See Theodore Eisenberg, Differing Perceptions of Attorney Fees in Bankruptcy Cases, 72 *Wash. U. L. Q.* 979 (1994).
44 See Hoffman et al., supra note 5.
45 See Colin F. Camerer and George Loewenstein, Information, Fairness, and Efficiency in Bargaining, in *Psychological Perspectives on Justice: Theory and Applications* 155 (Barbara A. Mellers and Jonathan Baron eds., 1993).
46 See James C. Cox and R. Mark Isaac, Experimental Economics and Experimental Psychology: Ever the Twain Shall Meet? in *Economic Psychology: Intersections in Theory and Application* (A. J. MacFadyen and H. W. MacFadyen eds., 1986).
47 See William M. Goldstein and Elke U. Weber, Content and Discontent: Indications and Implications of Domain Specificity in Preferential Decision Making, in *The Psychology of Learning and Motivation*, vol. 32, 83 (J. R. Busemeyer, R. Hastei, and D. L. Medin eds., 1995).
48 See Leda Cosmides, The Logic of Social Exchange: Has Natural Selection Shaped How Humans Reason? Studies with the Wason Selection Task, 31 *Cognition* 187 (1989).

49 See Blount, supra note 5; Hoffman et al., supra note 5.

50 See George Akerlof and Janet L. Yellen, Unemployment Through the Filter of Memory, 99 *Q.J. Econ.*, 747–773 (1986).

51 See Tracy, supra note 2.

52 See, e.g., Gary Bolton, A Comparative Model of Bargaining: Theory and Evidence, 81 *Am. Econ. Rev.* 1096 (1991); Rabin, supra note 5.

53 See, e.g., Matthew Rabin, *Moral Ambiguity, Moral Constraints, and Self-serving Biases* (1995).

15 Controlling Availability Cascades*

Timur Kuran and Cass R. Sunstein

The purpose of this chapter is to identify a set of interlinked social mechanisms that have important, possibly desirable, but sometimes harmful effects on risk regulation. The harmful effects range from inconsistent health regulations to mass anxiety about foods with no scientifically confirmed health hazards. The underlying mechanisms help shape the production of law through their effects on legislators, administrative agencies, and courts.

The mechanisms outlined below are mediated by the availability heuristic, a pervasive mental shortcut whereby the perceived likelihood of any given event is tied to the ease with which its occurrence can be brought to mind. Cognitive psychologists consider the availability heuristic to be a key element of individual judgment and perception. They demonstrate that the probability assessments we make as individuals are frequently based on how easily we can think of relevant examples.[1] Our principal claim here is that this heuristic interacts with identifiable social mechanisms to generate *availability cascades*: social cascades, or simply cascades, through which expressed perceptions trigger chains of individual responses that make these perceptions appear increasingly plausible through their rising availability in public discourse. Availability cascades may be accompanied by countermechanisms that keep perceptions consistent with the relevant facts. Under certain circumstances, however, they will generate persistent *collective availability errors*: widespread mistaken beliefs grounded in interactions between the availability heuristic and the social mechanisms described below. The resulting mass delusions may last indefinitely, and they may produce wasteful or even harmful laws and policies.

An availability cascade subsumes two of the special cascades that recently have received considerable attention in the social sciences: informational cascades[2] and reputational cascades.[3] An informational cascade occurs when

* This chapter is a much abbreviated version of an article by the same authors, "Availability Cascades and Risk Regulation," 51 *Stanford Law Review* 683 (1999).

people with little personal information on a particular matter base their own beliefs on the apparent beliefs of others. Specifically, when the words and deeds of certain individuals give the impression that they accept a particular belief, other insufficiently informed individuals accept that belief by virtue of its acceptance by others. As long as members of the relevant group are heterogeneous along one or more dimensions (e.g., initial personal information, dependence on society for information, timing of social contacts), the transformation of the distribution of beliefs can take the form of a cascade, known also as a bandwagon or snowballing process. Not every member of a society experiencing an informational cascade need be influenced; those with reliable private information may remain unswayed. Under the right conditions, however, most of the society's members, even all, will end up with essentially identical beliefs, which may well be fanciful. Insofar as society is socially fragmented, it may exhibit *local informational cascades*. A local informational cascade is one limited, for example, to a geographical area, a demographic subgroup, or a core of activists who share a political objective.

Like an informational cascade, a reputational cascade is driven by interdependencies among individual choices. It differs, however, in the underlying personal motivations. In the case of a reputational cascade, individuals do not subject themselves to social influences because others may be more knowledgeable. Rather, the motivation is simply to earn social approval and avoid disapproval. In seeking to achieve their reputational objectives, people take to speaking and acting as if they share, or at least do not reject, what they view as the dominant belief. As in the informational case, the outcome may be the cleansing of public discourse of deviant perceptions, arguments, and actions. Just as informational cascades may be limited in their reach, there may exist *local reputational cascades*: self-reinforcing processes that reshape the public pronouncements of particular subgroups without affecting those of the broader population.

Reputational and informational cascades are not mutually exclusive. Ordinarily, they exhibit interactions, even feed on one another.[4] The resulting composite process is what we are calling an availability cascade.

Social agents who understand the dynamics of availability cascades and seek to exploit their insights may be characterized as *availability entrepreneurs*. Located anywhere in the social system, including the government, the media, nonprofit organizations, the business sector, and even households, availability entrepreneurs attempt to trigger availability cascades likely to advance their own agendas. They do so by fixing people's attention on specific problems, interpreting phenomena in particular ways, and attempting to raise the salience of certain information. Such *availability campaigns* often produce social benefits by overcoming public torpor and producing debates on long-festering though rarely articulated social problems. At the same time, availability campaigns sometimes do great harm by fueling collective availability errors. This danger points to the need for institutional safeguards designed to ensure better priority setting and fuller use of scientific knowledge.

Our major illustrations of availability cascades involve the regulation of risks, a topic especially well suited to exploring interactions between democracy and law. However, with suitable refinements the general framework can be applied to a wide variety of other areas. Among the diverse social transformations that exhibit striking examples of availability cascades are: the rise and decline of McCarthyism; the struggle for black civil rights; the spread of affirmative action and the recent explosion of public opposition to it; the rise of feminism, the antitax movement, and the religious right; ongoing campaigns against pornography, hate speech, smoking, health maintenance organizations, and the burning of black churches; the persistence and sudden fall of communism; the global turn toward market-friendly government policies; and finally, the spread of ethnic and religious separatism across the world.

Three Costly Availability Errors

We now present three examples of collective availability errors, which will then form a background for the subsequent analysis.

Love Canal

Between 1942 and 1953, the Hooker Chemical Company filled Love Canal, an abandoned waterway that feeds into the Niagara River in New York State, with chemical waste.[5] It then covered the waste with dirt and sold it to the Niagara Falls Board of Education. The local government developed the area, turning it into a neighborhood. The neighborhood was settled in 1957, and the site of the old canal, which many of the new homes bordered, became a school and a playground.

Following several years of unusually heavy rain, in 1976 a commission responsible for monitoring the Great Lakes found the insecticide Mirex in Lake Ontario fish. Shortly thereafter the New York Department of Environmental Conservation identified Love Canal as a major contributor. The local press began reporting that area residents were worried about the health effects of Love Canal. Frightening tales spread quickly: children being burnt, omnipresent odors inducing nausea, undrinkable water, black sludge everywhere. Residents feared that the buried chemicals had resurfaced, making their neighborhood unlivable.

At this stage no government official attempted to reassure the residents about the dangers, probably because any attempt at reassurance would have been met with considerable distrust. Newspapers continued to fan the flames. A key development was a set of frightening stories in June 1978, which came to the attention of Lois Marie Gibbs, a housewife. Gibbs would become a central figure in publicizing residents' fears of adverse health effects and in mobilizing public attention.[6] Gibbs eventually appeared on national television programs and was invited to both the state capitol and the White House. Initially, her reaction to the newspaper articles led her to go door-to-door in the area, organizing a petition.[7] Partly as a result of such efforts, the residents became essentially immune to counterevidence.

Responding to the outcry, New York State Health Commissioner Robert Whalen declared a public health emergency in the area. Characterizing Love Canal as a "great and immediate peril," he urged area residents to stay out of their basements and to avoid eating anything from their gardens. He also sought the temporary relocation of twenty-five pregnant women and children under age two, whereupon residents whom the plan would leave behind inquired why their health should be treated as "less important." A month later, Whalen published a report, "Love Canal: Public Health Time Bomb," which described Love Canal as a "modern day disaster, both profound and devastating."[8] The federal government, too, responded to the growing sense of crisis. The director of the Federal Disaster Assistance Administration toured the area very visibly around the same time, and two days later President Jimmy Carter declared a national emergency.

Mounting public concern discouraged officials and even ordinary citizens from questioning the reality of the danger. With alarming information flowing rapidly from one group to another, anyone who challenged the alarmist interpretation of Love Canal risked severe public criticism. In early 1980, at a time when Love Canal was prominently featured in network newscasts almost every day, Governor Carey established a blue-ribbon panel to review the scientific evidence. Remarkably, in view of the state of public opinion, the panel endorsed none of the reports of serious health effects. But its evaluation had no appreciable influence on subsequent events. Soon after, President Carter decided to relocate an additional seven hundred families at a cost of at least $3 million.

The Love Canal "time bomb," as press reports called it, was not the original source of government concern about abandoned hazardous waste dumps. But there is no doubt that publicity about Love Canal was crucial to the creation of a huge program to clean them up. In 1980 *Time* magazine made the topic of waste sites a cover story, and new network documentaries followed suit. Congress responded quickly with the Comprehensive Environmental Response and Liability Act (CERCLA), generally known as "Superfund," which called for $1.6 billion in expenditures over five years.[9]

The perceptual and attitudinal transformation that occurred between 1978 and 1980 has proved enduring. Since that period Americans have consistently ranked waste sites among the country's top environmental problems. In a highly publicized 1987 study, the EPA found that Americans rank hazardous waste sites *first* among all environmental problems: above pesticides, acid rain, indoor air pollution, radioactive waste, water pollution, exposure to work site chemicals, tap-water contamination, and thinning of the ozone layer, among many others.[10] This preeminence was confirmed by public opinion polls in 1987 and 1988.[11] To this date, moreover, American presidents and serious presidential candidates of both major parties invoke abandoned waste dumps as a leading environmental problem. Congress has continued to spend vast sums on clean-up campaigns. By 1994 it had allocated a total of $13.6 billion to the cause.[12]

Yet it remains unproven that the contamination of Love Canal, inasmuch as it happened, ever posed a significant risk to anyone. A follow-up study published in 1984 found the frequency of altered chromosomes to be the same in Love Canal as in other areas of Niagara Falls. Equally significant, no subsequent study discovered any link between the identified chromosome alterations and the contamination in question. An exhaustive 1982 study by the EPA, based on six thousand samples of soil, air, and groundwater from the evacuated area and other sampling regions, found "no evidence of environmental contamination" at Love Canal. And in the same year the Department of Health and Human Services found that the emergency zone was "as habitable as the control areas with which it was compared."

Alar

Alar is a pesticide long used on apples. About 1 percent of Alar is composed of UDMH, a carcinogen. Alar's manufacturer, the Uniroyal Company, embarked on a two-year study of its effects, completing the initial year of investigation in January 1989. Preliminary results indicated a greater incidence of tumors in rodents exposed to high levels of UDMH. On the basis of these tentative findings, the Natural Resources Defense Council (NRDC) made a series of extrapolations, which it interpreted as implying that about one out of every forty-two hundred preschool children exposed to Alar will develop cancer by age six.

The television show "60 Minutes" publicized the allegation against a background consisting of a red apple overlaid with a skull and crossbones. The program instigated a public outcry, complete with protests from many celebrities, including actress Meryl Streep, who founded an activist group called Mothers and Others for Pesticide Limits. The NRDC's self-conscious agenda was "to create so many repetitions of [its] message that average American consumers (not just the policy elite in Washington) could not avoid hearing it – from many different media outlets within a short time. The idea was for the 'story' to achieve a life of its own, and continue for weeks and months to affect policy and consumer habits."[13]

The EPA reviewed the evidence and interpretations and concluded that the risk was vastly exaggerated: one in 111,000 rather than in 4,200. However, by the time the EPA made its announcement, the demand for apples had plummeted. In desperation, the nation's apple growers asked Uniroyal to withdraw Alar from the market. Before the year was out, but after the EPA announcement, Uniroyal agreed to stop producing Alar, evidently to avoid the costs of contested cancellation proceedings.

The EPA's initial risk estimate has turned out to be too high. According to its subsequent analyses, only one in 250,000 children exposed to Alar will develop cancer, doubtless a nontrivial risk, but less than half the initial EPA figure, and lower than that of the NRDC by a factor of sixty.[14] Thus a 1991 editorial in *Science* argues that "a clearly dubious result about possible carcinogenicity by a special interest group was hyped by a news organization without the most simple checks on its reliability or documentation."[15] A United Nations panel, along with others who have investigated the data, found that even the EPA's revised figure is too high. Alar does not cause cancer in mice, it concluded, and it is not dangerous to people.[16]

Reflecting on this episode, one observer writes, "Words fail on Alar. The most charitable interpretation is that an environmental group . . . decided to take matters into its own hands by writing a report and orchestrating its release to the media in so forceful a manner as to compel governmental action. The syndrome its report played out is by now distressingly familiar: a few suggestive tests involving tiny quantities raised way above the actual amount by extreme assumptions about children's eating habits, expanded further by statistical manipulations, extrapolated against huge populations to create row-upon-row of child cancer victims."[17]

TWA Flight 800

A striking example of a quick availability cascade involves reactions to the 1996 crash of TWA flight 800, which killed all 230 people on board. With about 95 percent of the wreckage now recovered, the cause of the accident remains unknown, although none of the evidence implicates a bomb or a missile. Nevertheless, the public outcry that followed the crash quickly led to heightened security measures at airports all across the United States and to the formation of the White House Commission on Aviation, Safety, and Security.[18]

There are indications that the relevant government officials did not believe that the crash resulted from terrorism; with wild rumors circulating, and with denials of terrorist activity seeming callous or reckless, they simply pretended to take the claims seriously when expressing themselves publicly. A mere forty-five days after its creation the White House commission proposed extensive additional safeguards against terrorism. And within a month of this initial report, President Clinton signed most of the commission's recommendations into law. The direct cost to taxpayers is estimated to be $400 million per year. The total price tag, including all costs to consumers and producers, apparently exceeds an estimated $6 billion.[19]

Yet the new security measures may not save any lives. On the contrary, they may even cost lives. Having made airline travel more expensive and more cumbersome, these measures have reduced the relative attractiveness of flying. Flying, however, is far less dangerous than driving. Between 1960 and 1995 the fatal accident rate in commercial aviation dropped from .011 fatal accidents per million aircraft miles flown to .0005, to the point where flying is now the safest mode of transportation.[20] By making people substitute car travel for air travel, the adopted measures may well increase, rather than decrease, the number of unnatural deaths.[21]

Additional examples from recent years include mass outcries over Agent Orange, asbestos in schools, breast implants, and automobile airbags that endanger children. Their common thread is that people tended to form their risk judgments largely, if not entirely, on the basis of information produced through a social process, rather than personal experience or investigation. In each case, a public upheaval occurred as vast numbers of players reacted to each other's actions and statements. In each, moreover, the demand for swift, extensive, and costly government action came to be considered morally necessary and socially desirable – even though, in most or all cases, the resulting regulations may well have produced little good, and perhaps even relatively more harm.

Interpreting Mass Scares About Minor Risks

What explains widespread fixations on unthreatening waste dumps, nearly harmless chemicals, and unlikely causes of a tragic airplane crash, when for years on end far more serious health hazards, such as breast cancer, indoor air pollution, "junk food" consumption, and asthma in the inner city have commanded comparatively little attention? At first blush, the episodes in question confirm an essential finding of cognitive psychology: As individuals we are capable of developing and retaining beliefs that are scientifically unjustified, even unjustifiable. Being boundedly rational, we rely on mental shortcuts that leave us misinformed in many contexts, even seriously wrong.[22] The episodes are consistent also with one of the central themes of the public choice school, namely, that citizens of a large polity have incentives to remain "rationally ignorant."[23] Why should the residents of Love Canal, or the rest of us, devote time and effort to learning the full truth about the alleged contamination when as individuals we each have only one voice and one vote to influence policies that the choices of many millions will help shape?

It would be a mistake, however, to treat these episodes merely as additional manifestations of bounded rationality and rational ignorance. Both interpretations raise the question of why, in each case, millions of Americans fell victim to exactly the *same* delusion. People evidently formed their perceptions interdependently, with each individual's expressed perceptions helping to shape those of others. Equally important, invoking bounded rationality or rational ignorance sidesteps the challenge of explaining why people came to believe *what* they did.

Cognitive Processes

In each of these episodes what Americans "knew" depended, in the first instance, on their predispositions to believe certain claims more readily than others. For our purposes here, the most critical cognitive predisposition is the *availability heuristic*, a mental shortcut that involves estimating the probability of an event on the basis of how easily instances can be brought to mind. This heuristic can produce substantial judgmental distortions whenever certain alternatives are easier to imagine than others. Thus, a person may overestimate the incidence of AIDS simply because many of his acquaintances have the disease and he can easily think of AIDS cases. Alternatively, a person may underestimate the incidence of AIDS because he cannot think of anyone who is among its victims. In certain contexts, of course, the availability heuristic yields benefits by economizing on decision costs. But the benefits should not be overstated. People systematically err in assessing the number of lives lost as a result of various risks. While underestimating dangers that are not highly publicized (heart disease, strokes, asthma), they grossly overestimate risks to which the media pays a great deal of attention (accidents, electrocution).[24]

Interactions Between Social and Cognitive Influences

The extent to which a risk is publicized is neither exogenous to the social system in which individuals operate nor fixed. It depends on a circular process. In particular, *identifiable social mechanisms govern the availability of information; and through the mediation of the availability heuristic, this availability shapes, on the one hand, judgments about the magnitudes of various risks and, on the other, the acceptability of these risks. Simultaneously, the consequent individual actions and expressions affect the availability of information.* There are thus two-way interactions between social outcomes and individual cognitive processes. These interactions form an *availability cascade* whenever individual uses of the availability heuristic raise the public availability of data pointing to a particular interpretation or conclusion, and this increase in availability then triggers reinforcing individual adjustments.

In contexts subject to availability cascades, the distribution of beliefs across the relevant population may entail multiple equilibria. In other words, the same objective information may be capable of sustaining different, even highly different, belief patterns, depending on whether a cascade occurs and, if so, which of many possible cascades is initiated. Thus, one risk may gain salience, receive an enormous amount of attention, and become the object of tight regulation, while another risk, which experts deem equivalent, is treated as "part of normal life."

Against this background, it is unsurprising that culturally and economically similar nations can display dramatically different reactions to identical risks. Whereas nuclear power enjoys widespread acceptance in France, it arouses considerable fear in the United States. Another implication of multiple equilibria is that any given risk assessment may change suddenly and dramatically even in the absence of any major change in the relevant scientific evidence. Over a short time, people convinced that their environment is perfectly livable may come to think, because everyone else seems to be getting alarmed, that it is replete with dreadful carcinogens. And insofar as people lack independent means of judging a claim's validity, there is a danger that the beliefs generated by a cascade will be factually incorrect. Millions of individuals may develop erroneous beliefs simply by giving each other reasons to adopt and preserve them.

Private and Public Aspects of Availability Cascades

An analysis of any mass upheaval that triggers political and legal responses to perceived risks must take into account two sets of influences. The first consists of the effects that social variables have on personal ones. The social variable of greatest interest here is *public discourse,* which is the ensemble of publicly expressed or conveyed sentiments, ideas, and information that individuals use as gauges of what others know and want. Policy initiatives and enactments, including steps taken by official agencies, are also relevant. Public discourse and other social variables influence three sets of individual variables: people's *risk judgments,* which are their perceptions of the risks they face; their *risk preferences,* which are their orderings of alternative risks; and finally, their risk-policy preferences, or simply their *policy preferences,* which are their orderings of possible ways of regulating risks.

In terms of these variables, the first set of influences runs from social variables to personal ones. The second set goes the opposite way. It consists of the impact that individuals have on public discourse through their own personal transformations. The two sets of influences form a circular process. Public discourse shapes individual risk judgments, risk preferences, and policy preferences; and the reshaped personal variables then transform the public discourse that contributed to their own transformations.

In ordinary language, the term "public" is employed to connote both openness and collectiveness. It is the former sense that we are conveying here. Unlike a "private" variable, a public variable is one that is generally visible. Strictly speaking, a private characteristic, such as a private perception of a chemical spill's risk, is known only to the person who holds it, although people close to the individual, including his relatives and close friends, may have good insight into what he is thinking and feeling. Because of its visibility, the transformation of a public variable can have sudden and direct effects on individual thoughts and dispositions. If a newspaper report suggests that a water supply is safe, thousands of readers may instantly feel reassured.

By contrast, the immediate effects of private variables are necessarily limited, although, as we shall see, they have important effects over longer time spans, albeit through less direct channels. If an official investigates scientific reports about a waste dump and becomes convinced that worries are unjustified, this knowledge itself will have no impact on the information available to concerned residents. What will influence the perceptions of residents is what he says publicly. It is critical to recognize that the official's public pronouncements are manipulable. Indeed, they can diverge from the thoughts that he carries within his head and from the knowledge he conveys to a confidante. To avoid charges of insensitivity, even to avoid having to justify an unpopular position, he may make speeches and promote policies that convey deep concern about the very waste spill that he actually considers harmless.

Just as an official may tailor his public pronouncements to protect his reputation, so, too, may the other individuals who contribute to public discourse and public activity. Let us distinguish, therefore, between the private and public variants of the variables that characterize individuals. A given resident of Love Canal has a *private risk judgment* and also a corresponding *public risk judgment*. Depending on the reputational costs and benefits associated with alternative public acts and expressions, the latter may differ from the former. In particular, she may convey an interpretation that under- or overstates what she would express privately. Likewise, in any given context the resident's *private risk preference* and *private policy preference* may differ from her corresponding *public risk preference* and *public policy preference*. Whenever she chooses to express different preferences than those that she holds in her own mind, she engages in a form of preference falsification. And by misrepresenting her risk judgment in public, she engages in a form of knowledge falsification.

Informational and Reputational Mechanisms

As mentioned in the introduction, availability cascades are ordinarily driven by a combination of informational and reputational processes that interact with one another. It will be instructive to examine each of these processes in isolation. An integrated analysis will follow.

Let us first abstract, then, from the social pressures that cause people's private characteristics to diverge from their public characteristics. A strictly informational cascade occurs when people start attaching credibility to a proposition P (e.g., the claim that a certain abandoned waste dump is dangerous) merely because other people seem to accept P. Suppose that Ames signals that he believes P. Barr, who would otherwise have major reservations, believes P because Ames appears to do so. Cotton, who would have dismissed the proposition as silly, begins taking it seriously upon discovering that not just Ames but *both* he and Barr are believers. Noticing that Ames, Barr, and Cotton *all* seem alarmed, Douglas then accepts P without further thought. When Entin learns that all of his friends believe P, he joins the pack of believers on the grounds that their shared understanding cannot be wrong.

Ordinarily, individuals differ in their preconceptions, the reliability of their personal sources of information, their openness to public discourse, and their sensitivity to changes in the apparent views of others. These differences fulfill a precondition of any cascade: *variations in individual responsiveness to social signals*. In the absence of such variations, everyone would adjust simultaneously to new information, producing not an informational cascade but a sudden shift by independent actors. With a cascade, adjustments come at different times, with some individuals becoming convinced of a serious danger at the earliest sign of adverse health effects, but others remaining skeptical to varying degrees until more information becomes available.

This process contributed to the three episodes discussed above, though it is not the whole story. In each of these cases, many people lacked the means to form their own judgments, so they came to consider the alleged problem serious by accepting the dominant opinion. In the course of an informational cascade, the perceived validity of a claim grows progressively stronger with the number of apparent believers, and people's doubts weaken, possibly even disappear. In accepting a belief, each individual strengthens the case for acceptance, which results in additional acceptances that strengthen the case even further. The ultimate outcome can be a widely shared judgment based on error.

By abstracting from social pressures, informational cascades disregard the possibility that people will distort what they think in order to accommodate the perceived agendas of others. But only rarely are cascades *purely* informational. In practice, each public signal or communication will differ from its private counterpart insofar as people seek to protect or improve their social standing through preference and knowledge falsification. Depending on the apparent social pressures, a group of officials may endorse reports that Love Canal poses a huge threat to nearby residents, when they know of data that make the reports suspect; and they may feign approval of a relocation plan even though they consider the step ludicrous. The first case of insincerity constitutes a case of knowledge falsification. It signals to others an exaggerated risk judgment, one that inflates the corresponding private perception. The second act provides a case of preference falsification, in the sense that it makes the support for relocation greater than one would find if officials were polled through a secret ballot. Simply because of reputational influences people may echo a popular sentiment, even though they have not made up their minds and feel confused, or a popular judgment, even though they are clueless about its veracity. Plainly, all such forms of falsification were present in the Love Canal episode.

Knowledge and preference falsification are common because people want to be regarded and treated well, and, equally important, this desire is common knowledge. These conditions provide individuals and groups opportunities to advance their agendas merely by expressing approval of those individuals who lend them public support and disapproval of those who deny them support. The granting of approval operates as a "subsidy" to supporters and that of disapproval as a "tax" on opponents. Insofar as some individuals' need for social approval outstrips their other needs – more precisely, "reputational utility"[25] looms large in their total utility – they will tailor their expressed beliefs and conveyed dispositions to their audiences. A related means of earning the affection, support, and goodwill of a group is to help punish its enemies and reward its friends. Accordingly, a common form of preference falsification entails criticizing people whose expressions one does not dislike, or even likes. For instance, a New Yorker aware of the lack of scientific evidence for serious danger may, in the interest of bolstering her reputation, intimate that an official who counsels calm should be reprimanded or even removed from office, perhaps on the ground that he is lamentably "weak on the environment." Through such actions, preference and knowledge falsification contribute to the very social pressures that produce and reproduce them.

Availability entrepreneurs actively encourage the statement of views favorable to these options and discourage the statement of unfavorable views. A precondition for a reputational cascade is thus the possibility of inducing splits between many people's private and public "selves." Such a split requires a willingness on the part of many citizens to shade their public expressions and tailor their public behaviors in the interest of protecting their social standings.

Once initiated by groups with a financial or ideological stake in policy control, social pressures may grow through the assistance of the broader population. For this reason, such groups confer reputational benefits on individuals who support particular positions and impose reputational costs on those who oppose them. They make individuals seem altruistic or selfish, virtuous or vicious, depending on what preferences and beliefs they express. People ordinarily want to be perceived as standing on high moral ground, so in the presence of sufficiently strong pressures, they will adjust their expressions accordingly. Suppose that questioning the wisdom of relocating the Love Canal residents is generally equated with obtuseness and cold-heartedness, and calling for further scientific study is construed as giving anti-environmentalist firms time to develop a strong defense. Under these circumstances, residents, observers, and policy makers will all think twice before expressing misgivings about the dominant diagnoses or policies.

Earlier we performed a thought experiment that abstracted from social pressures and, hence, the reputational consequences of people's expressive choices. Going to the opposite extreme, let us now suppose that the choices of individuals are driven entirely by efforts to protect their social standings. We are thus imagining that people's private judgments and preferences play no role at all in their expressive choices; like puppets under a puppeteer's command, they express themselves simply to accommodate social pressures. If everyone was equally aware of the prevailing social pressures, interpreted threats and promises identically, and cared equally about maintaining a good reputation, they would do so in unison at the first hint that someone wanted them to support a particular agenda. In reality, all such factors vary across individuals. People differ, for instance, in the attention they pay to the news, the circles in which they move, their experiences with taking unpopular positions, and the importance they attach to being admired and accepted. Such differences guarantee variations in responsiveness to social pressure.

Imagine, then, that when a waste spill is reported, journalists seeking a career break that will make them famous, or politicians aiming to build up their pro-environmental credentials, take to denigrating the responsible industry. Sensing an opportunity to appear virtuous, the first people to witness this campaign participate in the denunciations. In so doing, they raise the volume of criticism, which makes additional people aware of the ongoing transformation in public discourse. The latter join the chorus of criticism to build their own reputations, which raises the volume further, and in this manner the vilification campaign grows through a reputational cascade. The cascade completes its course when news of the campaign has reached everyone who cares sufficiently about maintaining a good reputation.

Socialization and Its Limits

The personal motives that underlie a purely reputational cascade differ fundamentally from those of a purely informational one. In the reputational variant people ask themselves, "How will my community think of me if I fail to endorse its dominant position?" and they fall in line upon gaining awareness of the prevailing political mood. In the informational variant, poorly informed people ask themselves, "What is the dominant view within my society?" and they base their views on those of others. In the former case they are motivated solely by social approval, in the latter only by knowing the truth.

Of these pure types, the reputational variant presents an oversocialized view of human nature. Although certain individuals' expressions are sometimes ruled solely by reputational concerns, most people ordinarily balance these concerns against the desire to be truthful to others and to themselves. At the opposite extreme, a purely informational cascade presents an undersocialized conception of the individual. Only highly abnormal people convey knowledge and preferences without any regard for the possible effects on their reputations.[26] A realistically socialized view of human nature will treat individuals as social beings who generally seek acceptance but also as knowledge seekers and as expressive agents who develop individualities by speaking their minds. To be sure, people differ from one another along these dimensions; some care enormously about their reputations, while others depend minimally on what others think of them.[27]

The balanced perspective offered here implies that when a possible risk, such as the contamination of a canal, is characterized as a dangerous problem or, alternatively, as no threat whatsoever, there will be two distinct influences on listeners. On the one hand, the characterization will shape their private risk judgments, risk preferences, and policy preferences. On the other, it will teach them something about the evolving political climate, thus shaping their perceptions of the reputational costs and benefits associated with the possible public expressions. The public counterparts of the foregoing variables – the judgments and preferences that people choose to convey in social settings – will reflect a combination of these two influences. When public discourse on the contamination undergoes a change, the transformation will reflect partly modifications in people's actual thoughts and dispositions, and partly their efforts to preserve or gain social status by adjusting to perceived shifts in social pressures.

In principle, these influences may counteract one another. When a claim of "no danger" comes from a notoriously unscrupulous yet politically powerful lobbyist, the source of the information may generate skepticism, making listeners less willing to endorse the lobbyist's claim. But it may also cause them to perceive a reputational advantage to endorsing the claim publicly, thus enhancing their willingness to do so. In the cases of greatest concern here, however, these influences are mutually supportive. The multiplicity of individual sources of information makes the claim hard to dismiss as the concoction of greedy troublemakers. Consequently, its credibility grows even as it becomes increasingly prudent to endorse publicly.

Populist Firestorms and Democratic Risk Regulation

Availability cascades create serious problems for democracy and raise important issues for democratic theory. They create a danger that apparently democratic outcomes will rest on misinformation and be unrepresentative, in any normatively attractive sense, of citizens' actual beliefs, desires, and judgments.

Above all, the argument thus far indicates that "public opinion" about the regulation of risks (the distribution of public policy preferences) constitutes a highly problematic basis for government policy. This is partly because publicly expressed demands for regulation are likely to conceal doubt, ambivalence, and concern. But even the corresponding "private opinion" (the distribution of private policy preferences) might constitute a poor foundation for policy, because availability cascades often spread falsehoods that overwhelm sound scientific reports.

Our call for caution about populist firestorms evokes two time-honored themes of the American tradition of public law. The first involves the ideal of deliberative democracy, which elaborates on the principle of democratic decision making by insisting that policies be based on careful deliberation and reflection rather than mechanical reactions to citizen preferences. A principal point of the original Constitution was to ensure that representatives "refine and enlarge" popular sentiment, rather than automatically translate it into law. The key institutions of the American system of government were designed to promote the desired filtering.

The second and more modern theme is that policy choices should rest on sound knowledge of relevant evidence. In the context of risk regulation, this objective requires a measure of deference to the purely factual judgments of scientific experts. It also requires democratic policy makers to discount regulatory demands rooted in availability errors, to pay special attention to trained experts who have had time to put claims in perspective, and to show initiative in responding to significant problems that the citizenry happens to be overlooking.

Many features of the prevailing system of checks and balances offer protection against availability cascades. For example, the bicameral legislature prevents cascades within one chamber from creating legislation on their own. Still, as matters now stand, the American government is ill-equipped to provide meaningful resistance against social pressures grounded in misinformation. When there is an upsurge of interest in addressing a particular risk, the government loses its ability to set sensible priorities, undertake long-range planning, and enforce intertemporal consistency. It has been estimated that the American government could save an additional sixty thousand lives per year at no additional cost or, alternatively, save the lives it currently does for as much as $31 billion less than it now spends.[28] The reforms proposed below would provide instruments for achieving such gains.

Product Defamation Laws

The Texas lawsuit that pitted beef producers against television talk show host Oprah Winfrey brought into sharp relief one possible measure against harmful availability cascades: civil actions to deter individuals and groups from instigating or aggravating such cascades in the hope of profiting from the ensuing panic. Conscious of the potential advantages, thirteen states have already enacted product disparagement laws. As one might expect, many observers consider such laws to be constitutionally unacceptable devices designed to placate powerful economic actors intent on suppressing legitimate doubts about the safety of their products. But the underlying issues are more complicated. For one thing, it is unclear that product disparagement laws violate the First Amendment. For another, their beneficiaries would hardly be limited to industries trying to block reports about the defects of their products. Just as ordinary libel law serves to discourage the articulation of falsehoods about individuals, product disparagement laws discourage false statements about products. In each case, the purpose is to prevent availability cascades from doing irreparable damage.

When a product is "libeled," the news may spread rapidly, bringing harm to a wide range of people. And when an availability cascade is under way, the liberty to counter false charges will not necessarily provide a corrective, and this is what product disparagement and ordinary libel laws acknowledge. Indeed, predictable social forces may reinforce rather than dampen sensational charges. One such force involves the mass media. The typical newspaper, magazine, or television station incurs a large penalty whenever it falls behind its rivals in reporting "breaking news."[29] A complementary social force is that evolving reputational pressures can make it personally costly for individuals to defend a disparaged product. The consequent individual reticence will contribute to the growth and spread of availability errors.

To identify certain advantages of product disparagement laws and to defend their constitutionality is not, of course, to prove that on balance they are beneficial or desirable. This is ultimately an empirical matter.

Congress

Congress is currently quite vulnerable to availability cascades, partly because its members feel compelled to respond to mass demands for legislation simply to keep their seats, and partly because they have incentives to serve as availability entrepreneurs who work in concert with diverse individuals to further parochial agendas. As an institution, Congress is poorly equipped to place risks in comparative perspective. Its committee system keeps Congress highly balkanized and increases its susceptibility to short-term pressures.

1. *Risk oversight.* A possible method for insulating Congress from such pressures is to create a risk regulation committee entrusted with compiling information about a wide range of risk levels and empowered to help set priorities. This committee would have authority over both substantive statutes and the appropriations process. It would thus operate as a check on short-term pressures by putting particular concerns in a broader context. Its basic goal would be to rank risks, publicize misallocations, and initiate legislative corrections. In its ideal form, the committee would rely heavily on prevailing scientific knowledge. At the same time, it would recognize that risk judgments and preferences constitute legitimate considerations in the determination of priorities and selection of policies. Thus, its essential function would be to prevent myopic, unduly quick, and poorly reasoned responses, not to insulate risk regulation from evolving social values. Helping to slow down, limit, and possibly even prevent availability cascades, the committee's hearings would enable Congress to "strike when the iron is cold."[30]

Like any government body, the risk regulation committee would most certainly become the target of well-organized lobbies intent on molding policies to their own advantage. But it should be possible to dampen the incentives for rent seeking by altering the culture of congressional risk regulation and, in particular, guaranteeing that risks are put in a comparative light. The very act of comparing risks and publicizing the obtained rankings would provide a measure of protection against well-organized special interests. If the social costs of accommodating a particular lobby's demands gain widespread recognition, counterlobbying might neutralize this lobby's political effectiveness.

2. *Cost-benefit analysis.* Congress has debated a number of bills designed to require agencies to engage in cost-benefit analysis. The use of cost-benefit analysis as the basis for regulatory decisions has been highly controversial, partly because of conceptual and empirical obstacles to quantifying either costs or benefits, and partly because no agency is widely trusted to undertake a fair analysis. Although we cannot resolve these problems here, it is clear that availability cascades provide a new and distinct reason for some kind of cost-benefit mandate, not as a way of obtaining an uncontroversial assessment of policy options, not as a foundation for every decision, and not because economic efficiency is the only legitimate ground for regulation, but as a commonsensical brake on measures that would do little good and possibly considerable harm.

Wherever some salient event might trigger a cascade in favor of speedy regulation, there are good reasons to support mechanisms that help identify and quantify actual risks, and for putting "on screen" the various possible disadvantages of attempting to reduce them. Cost-benefit analysis might therefore serve as a check on ill-advised availability campaigns. Consider, for example, the very different implications of cost-benefit analysis for a lead phasedown (amply justified) and for eliminating asbestos (a decidedly mixed picture).[31] An understanding of availability cascades certainly does not establish the usefulness of cost-benefit analysis; the proof would lie in its implementation. Yet such an understanding offers a new basis for requiring cost-benefit analysis as a means of widening the viewscreens of political actors and containing availability errors.

The Executive Branch

Other possible safeguards against harmful availability cascades would involve the executive branch, which is probably in the best position to analyze risks comprehensively. Here are three complementary proposals, each of which can contribute to the prevention of mass scares driven by misperceptions.

1. *Peer review.* Several recent bills would require executive agencies to use peer review as a means of corroborating the evidence that underlies the regulations they institute. Under peer review, agency proposals are subject to scrutiny by informed outsiders. Many agencies have already experimented with this procedure. The argument developed in this chapter provides systematic reasons for expanding the ongoing experiments. The most critical function of peer review would be to identify and correct the misperceptions spread through availability cascades. While an availability cascade is in

progress, but even after it has run its course, peer review provides an important safeguard against policy responses that the facts do not justify. The Love Canal and Alar scares might have been contained at an early stage had the claims that fueled fears been subjected to peer review in a timely manner and the findings given wide publicity.

2. *Risk information site on the internet*. Among the reasons why people turn to nonexperts for information on various risks is that they lack easy access to statistically accurate and scientifically up-to-date judgments. This handicap limits their capacity to compare risks and develop sound understandings of dangers associated with, for example, air travel, automobile driving, poor diet, and infrequent exercise. To be sure, most such information may be found in publications shelved in any good library or bookstore. Alas, people seeking to educate themselves might have to read dozens of books to make the necessary comparisons; not only that, they would first have to identify the appropriate sources and learn how to standardize disparate pieces of information. There exist huge potential gains, then, from making the most current and scientifically most credible information easily accessible to the widest possible audience. In the computer age in which we now live, the internet may serve as the requisite medium.

We thus propose the creation of a central *risk information site* (RIS) on the internet. This site would be dedicated to the listing of various risks and the identification of the probabilities, or range of probabilities, associated with each of them. The technology of the internet allows the nesting of multiple levels of detail. The most elementary level ought to be extremely simple to follow – simple enough, perhaps, for a high-school dropout to check the latest scientific knowledge on, say, the risks associated with Alar or Love Canal; below this layer there would lie progressively more sophisticated layers, each accessible at the click of a mouse. Where the scientific community is divided on a particular risk matter, as it is on the thinning of the ozone layer, the RIS should make the substance of the controversy as clear as possible, allowing web surfers to review the opposing arguments. The proposed website could be set up and operated by a nongovernmental *risk information center* (RIC), along the lines of *Consumer Reports*. It could even be a profit-oriented enterprise; after all, there exist profit-driven credit bureaus that enjoy an exemplary reputation because they have a stake in their maintenance.[32] Only if no nongovernmental entity is willing or able to undertake the task should the federal government take the lead, because a government-operated RIC would have a harder time rising above partisan politics and establishing its trustworthiness.

Counteracting the irrational attitudes and counterproductive policy demands caused by cognitive biases and the distortions of public discourse, an RIS would allow individuals to form their risk preferences and judgments more rationally than is currently possible. It would offer information on how other countries are dealing with particular risks, thus alerting people to possible over- or underreactions. It might also allow parties to a controversy to make their case as well as rebut their opponents. Had an RIS existed during the Love Canal episode, both Lois Marie Gibbs and her skeptics within the scientific world might have been given opportunities to post evidence supporting their respective cases as well as their reasons for doubting the other side's account. Equally important, the proposed RIS would feature systematic information on possible discrepancies between public and private opinion on current controversies.

3. *Office of Information and Regulatory Affairs.* In 1980 President Reagan created a new agency, an Office of Information and Regulatory Affairs (OIRA), that would oversee risk regulation to ensure both coordination and rationality. Since that time, the functions of OIRA have undergone changes. Under Reagan and Bush, OIRA operated essentially as a "cost-benefit" monitor that intervened in an ad hoc way to force the reconsideration of inefficient or excessive regulations. President Clinton, who has taken steps of his own to "reinvent government" so as to ensure greater attention to results than to processes, has de-emphasized this particular function.

In view of the dangers of availability (and unavailability) cascades, OIRA should be reinvigorated and its powers extended and strengthened. This measure would serve both to deter unreasonable regulations and to encourage reasonable ones. Specifically, OIRA should have, and be known to have, authority over both priority setting and cost-benefit balancing. It should be committed to mitigating the most unfortunate effects of availability cascades, not only by keeping small risks from consuming huge resources but also by ensuring that major risks receive attention. Where experts working under OIRA lacked confidence in risk judgments spreading through a cascade, they would conduct fact-finding exercises, and where necessary, they would publicize any inaccuracies of the popular beliefs. Likewise, where a scientific study suggested a revision in a particular risk judgment, OIRA would examine the study's methodology, check whether its results can be replicated, and disseminate its findings. Thus OIRA's mission should also include the dissemination of systematic information concerning risks, including changes in what scientists know about particular risks and the methods for controlling them. Finally, it should conduct systematic comparisons with other societies in the interest of finding cross-country differences that might provide clues to misperceptions or policy flaws at home. OIRA would constitute one of the information sources for the RIS discussed above.

Courts

Courts, too, have a role to play in preventing excessive reactions to availability cascades. Most naturally, they can undertake the judicial review of administrative actions alleged to be "arbitrary" or "capricious" within the meaning of the Administrative Procedure Act. The ban on arbitrary or capricious action is increasingly being understood as requiring agencies to produce plausible evidence that their actions produce "more good than harm."[33] This notion would appear to embody a presumptive requirement that costs not be grossly disproportionate to benefits.[34] Thus, existing doctrine authorizes courts to invalidate the most extreme and the most poorly conceived regulatory proposals, at least if they are not required by statutes. Courts can hardly be expected to identify availability cascades or to invalidate regulatory initiatives merely for being the outcome of a cascade. But if regulators are required to demonstrate, taking account of all relevant variables, that their policies would plausibly make things better rather than worse, we will have a potentially valuable safeguard against harmful cascades.

Conclusions and Extensions

In this chapter we have tried to substantiate the following claims:

1. In a broad array of contexts that call for risk judgments, individuals lack reliable or first-hand knowledge. In such contexts, they assess probabilities with the help of the availability heuristic. Insofar as this heuristic influences the information that individuals store, retrieve, and process, it interacts with all other judgmental heuristics and with all cognitive biases that distort their judgments.

2. The availability heuristic, which has been studied in isolation, is in practice frequently amplified by socially shaped informational cues and reputational incentives. People often believe something because others appear to believe it; or they pretend to believe it to avoid reputational harm.

3. The informational and reputational processes that shape public discourse ordinarily feed on one another. Under the right conditions, they generate availability cascades that spread and deepen misperceptions. As a result, the perceived collective wisdom may bear little, if any, relation to reality.

4. Availability entrepreneurs try to trigger availability cascades likely to advance their causes, and they work to extend those already in progress. Acting selfishly or altruistically, they focus attention on isolated events, select information to support their preferred interpretations, and make anyone who questions their objectives seem ignorant, duped, or depraved.

5. Insofar as the availability heuristic helps shape individual perceptions, public opinion about the relative magnitudes of risks will exhibit multiple expressive equilibria. This implies the possibility of sudden shifts in public discourse on any given matter, inconsistencies across contexts, and discrepancies across countries at any given time.

6. Availability cascades should be an important element in the positive analysis of legislation and regulation. An emphasis on interest-group pressures alone, or the availability heuristic standing by itself, leaves important gaps in understanding.

7. Availability cascades that spread empirically baseless information create formidable political pressures in support of wasteful and counterproductive regulations. Given the possibility of undesirable policy outcomes, the political process through which risk policies are selected and revised should take account of the behavioral mechanisms at work. These measures might be mitigated by equipping the political system with "circuit breakers" to slow availability cascades and encourage the reconsideration of the demands they spawn. Without removing the right to select risk policies democratically, all three branches of government should be required to resist demands driven by misinformation about risks and to seek consistency among risk policies.

Availability cascades are relevant not only to routine legislative struggles but also to the making and exercise of constitutional law. Consider first the matter of constitutional design. The rules for Constitution making and Constitution amending provide safeguards against bad cascades. In particular, they call for extended deliberation to prevent rushed, myopic, or misinformed judgments. Under Article V of the United States Constitution, amendments require laborious procedures. Proposed amendments succeed only by surviving a complex process of "peer review" by many people in various institutional settings. Like the rules that govern constitutional design, the checks and balances of the Constitution are designed to counteract the potentially destructive social forces that we have highlighted here.

The courts themselves are not immune to the social mechanisms examined in this chapter. Judges rely on the availability heuristic, and they are subject to informational biases and reputational incentives. As such, they are open to the influences of availability cascades.[35] Occasionally, a single legal decision – *Dred Scott v. Sandford*,[36] *Plessy v. Ferguson*,[37] *Lochner v. New York*,[38] *Brown v. Bd. of Education*,[39] *Roe v. Wade*[40] – comes to signal how an entire area of law should be understood. By virtue of the salience it acquires, it is taken to convey a relatively simple moral or institutional lesson. For precisely this reason, Americans with strong views on a possible, pending, or actual legal decision try to show that it is, or could become, "another Lochner," "another Brown," or "another Roe." Social struggles over the meaning of great legal cases should be understood in this light.

Availability cascades can help or hinder the tasks of governance by shaping social norms and determining compliance levels. Behavioral research shows that changes in the availability of information about compliance with a prevailing norm may influence the extent to which it is followed. For instance, taxpayers are far more likely to comply with the prevailing tax laws if they believe that most people fulfil their tax obligations than if they think that noncompliance is widespread.[41] Another example involves the problem of controlling drinking on college campuses. Students with a penchant for "binge drinking" tend to overestimate the number of binge drinkers; when informed of the actual numbers, their likelihood of continuing the behavior diminishes.[42] The tax evasion and binge drinking examples suggest that antisocial behavior may be curbed simply by controlling the information available to relevant actors, or alternatively, correcting the collective availability errors responsible for the undesirable conduct.[43] Laws that have produced compliance with little or no enforcement, such as those that relegate smoking to designated areas and those that require people to clean up after their dog, have much to do with the informational and reputational mechanisms discussed above.

Our arguments constitute a challenge to both the economic analysis of law and branches of cognitive psychology that are beginning to influence legal scholarship. With few exceptions, economists have ignored critical interdependencies that govern people's preferences, choices, and beliefs; even the public choice school, which focuses on the sources of legislation, typically neglects the interdependencies at the heart of the foregoing analysis. Yet, as we have emphasized, there is no inherent conflict between the rational actor framework and the mechanisms that this chapter has highlighted. Indeed, certain economists, along with legal scholars interested in economics, have derived valuable insights by recognizing that utility-maximizing individuals are also social beings who care about status and look to others for knowledge. For their part, cognitive psychologists have made large contributions to our understanding of information-processing mechanisms. But they have done so without examining how these cognitive mechanisms interact with the social construction, communication, and suppression of knowledge; and this tendency has carried over to the areas of legal scholarship that make use of cognitive psychology.

This chapter has shown that social processes compound the effects of cognitive heuristics and biases whose importance may appear trivial when individual decisions are observed in isolation. It has also demonstrated that the interactions in question affect the content of law in important ways. The challenge for the future is to translate our knowledge of availability cascades into improvements of a regulatory system that remains so vulnerable to them.

Notes

1 Amos Tversky and Daniel Kahneman, Judgment Under Uncertainty: Heuristics and Biases, in *Judgment Under Uncertainty* 3 (Daniel Kahneman, Paul Slovic, and Amos Tversky eds., 1982).

2 For analyses of purely informational cascades, see Sushil Bikchandani, David Hirshleifer, and Ivo Welch, A Theory of Fads, Fashion, Custom, and Cultural Change as Informational Cascades, 100 *J. Pol. Econ.* 992 (1992); idem, Learning from the Behavior of Others: Conformity, Fads, and Informational Cascades, 12 *J. Econ. Persp.* 151 (1998). W. Brian Arthur and David A. Lane, Information Contagion, in *Increasing Returns and Path Dependence in the Economy* 69 (W. Brian Arthur ed., 1994); David Hirshleifer, The Blind Leading the Blind: Social Influence, Fads, and Informational Cascades, in *The New Economics of Human Behavior* 188 (Mariano Tommasi and Kathyrn Ierulli eds., 1995); Lisa Anderson and Charles Holt, Information Cascades in the Laboratory, 87 *Am. Econ. Rev.* 847 (1997); Abhijit Banerjee, A Simple Model

of Herd Behavior, 107 *Q.J. Econ.* 797 (1992); idem, The Economics of Rumours, 60 *Rev. Econ. Stud.* 309; and Vai-Lam Mui, Information, Civil Liberties, and the Political Economy of Witch-hunts, 15 *J.L. Econ. Org.* 503 (1999).

3 For examples of reputational cascades, see George A. Akerlof, The Economics of Caste and of the Rat Race and Other Woeful Tales, 90 *Q.J. Econ.* 599 (1976); Timur Kuran, Sparks and Prairie Fires: A Theory of Unanticipated Political Revolution, 61 *Pub. Choice* 41 (1989); idem, Now Out of Never: The Element of Surprise in the East European Revolution of 1989, 44 *World Politics* 7 (1991); idem, Ethnic Norms and Their Transformation Through Reputational Cascades, 27 *J. Legal Stud.* 623 (1998).

4 Some of these interactions are analyzed in Timur Kuran, *Private Truths, Public Lies: The Social Consequences of Preference Falsification* (1995).

5 Our account draws on independent research and on Lois Marie Gibbs, *Love Canal: My Story* (1982); Aaron Wildavsky, *But Is It True?* (1996); M. Landy et al., The *Environmental Protection Agency: Asking the Wrong Questions* (2d ed. 1994).

6 See Gibbs, supra note 5, at 9.

7 Ibid. at 19.

8 Ibid.

9 Comprehensive Environmental Response, *Compensation and Liability Act of 1980*, Pub. L. No. 96-510, 94 *Stat.* 2767, 42 *U.S.C.* §9601.

10 Table 2.4 in W. Kip Viscusi, *Rational Risk Policy* 22 (1998). See also Stephen Breyer, *Breaking the Vicious Circle* 21 (1993).

11 See ibid. at 21.

12 Congress authorized an additional $6.9 billion in 1986 and $5.1 billion more in 1990.

13 See Wildavsky, supra note 5, at 204.

14 See Robert V. Percival, Alan S. Miller, Christopher H. Schroeder, and James P. Leape, *Environmental Regulation: Law, Science, and Policy* 524 (2d ed. 1996), at 528.

15 See Daniel Koshland, Credibility in Science and the Press, *Science* 254 (Nov. 1, 1991), at 629.

16 Wildavsky, supra note 5, at 221.

17 Ibid. at 222.

18 For general discussion, see Robert Hahn, The Economics of Airline Safety and Security: An Analysis of the White House Commission's Recommendations, 20 *Harv. J. L. & Pub. Pol'y* 791 (1997).

19 See ibid. at 800–1.

20 Ibid. at 794.

21 See ibid.

22 For a highly influential variant of this argument, see Herbert A. Simon, Theories of Bounded Rationality, in *Decision and Organization: A Volume in Honor of Jacob Marschak* 161 (C. B. McGuire and Roy Radner eds., 1972); idem, Rationality as Process and as Product of Thought, 68 *Am. Econ. Rev.: Papers & Proc.* 1 (1978). See also John Conlisk, Why Bounded Rationality? 34 *J. Econ. Literature* 669 (1996); Christine Jolls, Cass R. Sunstein, and Richard Thaler, A Behavioral Approach to Law and Economics, 50 *Stan. L. Rev.* 1471, 1477–9 (1998).

23 The foundations of the underlying logic were laid by Walter Lippmann, *Public Opinion* (1922). For its classic rendition, see Anthony Downs, *An Economic Theory of Democracy*, chs. 11–14 (1957).

24 See Jonathan Baron, *Thinking and Deciding* 217–19, 230–3 (1994).

25 For a full definition of reputational utility and a discussion of how it relates to other sources of utility, see Kuran, supra note 4, chap. 2.

26 For critiques of the two extreme positions, see Dennis Wrong, The Oversocialized Conception of Man in Modern Sociology, 26 *Am. Soc. Rev.* 183 (1961); Mark Granovetter, Economic Action, Social Structure, and Embeddedness, 91 *Am. J. Soc.* 481 (1985); and James S. Coleman, A Rational Choice Perspective on Economic Sociology, in *Handbook of Economic Sociology* 166 (Neil Smelser and Richard Swedberg eds., 1994).

27 These differences across individuals are related to differences in "social intelligence," which is the ability to navigate in social waters. Antonio R. Damasio, *Descartes' Error: Emotion, Reason, and the Human Brain* (1994), esp. p. 169, traces such skill variations to differences in brain functions. See also Howard Gardner, *Frames of Mind: The Theory of Multiple Intelligence* (1983); and Daniel Goleman, *Emotional Intelligence* (1995).

28 See Harvard Group on Risk Management Reform, *Reform of Risk Regulation: Achieving More Protection at Less Cost* 16 (1995), citing Tammy O. Tengs, Optimizing Societal Investments in Preventing Premature Death (Ph.D. dissertation, Harvard School of Public Health, 1994).

29 See Robert H. Frank and Philip J. Cook, *The Winner-Take-All Society* 189–95 (1995).

30 See Roger G. Noll and James E. Krier, Some Implications of Cognitive Psychology for Risk Regulation, 19 *J. Legal Stud.* 747 (1990), at 774.

31 See Richard Morgenstern, *Economic Analyses at EPA* (1997).

32 Daniel B. Klein, Promise Keeping in the Great Society: A Model of Credit Information Sharing, 4 *Econ. & Pol.* 117 (1992). For many related works, see idem ed., *Reputation: Studies in the Voluntary Elicitation of Good Conduct* (1997).

33 See Edward Warren and Gary Merchant, More Good Than Harm: A First Principle for Environmental Agencies and Reviewing Courts, 20 *Ecology L.Q.* 379 (1993); Howard Margolis, *Dealing with Risk* (1996).

34 See *Corrosion Proof Fittings v. EPA*, 947 F.2d 1201 (5th Cir. 1991); *Industrial Union Dep't v. American Petroleum Inst.*, 448 U.S. 607, 671 (1980); *Natural Resources Defense Council, Inc. v. EPA*, 824 F.2d 1146 (D.C. Cir. 1987) (en banc).

35 For many related ideas, see Thomas J. Miceli and Metin M. Coşgel, Reputation and Judicial Decision-Making, 23 *J. Econ. Behav. & Org.* 31 (1994).

36 60 U.S. 393 (1857).

37 163 U.S. 537 (1896).

38 198 U.S. 45 (1905).

39 347 U.S. 483 (1954).

40 410 U.S. 113 (1973).

41 James Q. Wilson, *The Moral Sense* (1993), gives many additional examples.

42 See H. Wesley Perkins, College Student Misperceptions of Alcohol and Other Drug Norms Among Peers, in *Designing Alcohol and Other Drug Prevention Programs in Higher Education* 177–206 (1997).

43 Each of these cases shows also that the availability of information about compliance levels affects behavior through two channels: by signaling what is socially acceptable and by providing clues as to what is good for one's own happiness. The channels in question, reputational and informational, are thus of critical importance to understanding why social cooperation is more common in some contexts than in others.

16 Cognitive Theory and Tax

Edward J. McCaffery

Introduction

Overview

Legal academia has been overrun by a torrent of interdisciplinarism. Law and economics, philosophy, literature, feminist studies, sociology, history, and just about any other recognized discipline have become new fields, new approaches to gaining insight into law's meanings and possibilities. For the most part, this movement has been salutary. Its health is based on the simple fact that other disciplines are relevant to law – to what law is, to how it affects people and institutions, and to what it can and should be. But legal scholars must always be careful to use the new disciplines wisely. We must be sensitive to the particulars of the legal cases at hand, to the structure of the other discipline, and to the terms of the interaction. Interdisciplinary scholarship can as easily descend into superficiality as it can rise to perspicacity.

In the case of my chosen area of legal academia, taxation, the interdisciplinary contributions have been dominated by economists, who have made many invaluable contributions to the field. Philosophy and political science, which once had a good deal to say about matters of tax, have become less frequent but still important contributors. But other social sciences, such as psychology, have not been incorporated into the general tax academic's worldview. To be sure, there have been some moves to bring psychology into the study of tax, but these attempts have not been systematic and do not approach the growing level of attention paid to psychology in other legal fields, such as regulatory and environmental law.

The simple thesis of this chapter is that cognitive psychology in particular has much to offer the study of taxation, in both its positive and normative dimensions, and vice versa. Cognitive psychology is the study of how the mind works – of how human agents process information. Practitioners such as Daniel Kahneman and Amos Tversky have been able to show that people think in ways that have systematic biases and distortions. For example, people are likely to overweigh the possibility of highly publicized events, such as airplane crashes, recurring, and people react dramatically to the purely formal way in which a question is raised or "framed."

My central theme is that cognitive biases can help explain major structural features of our existing tax system that are otherwise difficult to understand, and that they must be taken into account in developing any general normative theory of tax. This is different from the more traditional psychological focuses on taxpayer compliance, or general attitudes toward taxes and their relative fairness, or fiscal illusion. The idea here is that cognitive tendencies have played an important role in the particular evolution of our actual tax system, because the people, through democratic input and popular opposition, have created powerful constraints on what practical tax systems emerge. More specifically, the role of cognitive tendencies can come from one of two directions. One is passive and evolutionary: Cognitively favored tax systems are more apt to survive and become stable fixtures of a tax regime than are cognitively disadvantaged ones. A second is active and conscious: Taxing authorities might seek to exploit cognitive biases in maximizing their revenue intake. In either case, however – and it will often be impossible to say just which case we are in, and the two can also obtain at the same time – there are certain problems that a detached observer will confront in developing the relationship between cognitive theory and tax, largely relating to the underdeterminacy of cognitive theory itself.

Gaps, Problems, and Possibilities

If cognitive theory in fact describes the real tendencies of real people – as it purports to do, and as it must do if it is to succeed on its own terms – then the relevance of cognitive theory to tax is inescapable. People care about tax and act on the basis of these concerns, politically, personally, economically, psychologically. If cognitive error characterizes people's thinking about tax, then such error pervades all of those actions for which ideas about tax are a predicate, such as voting on tax issues or on candidates based on their tax-related positions, or making tax-sensitive decisions regarding work, saving, and the like.

I proceed with certain qualifications in mind. I have chosen to advance the current project by discussing a wide range of examples from tax. These are meant to illustrate the breadth of the appeal of cognitive theory, to illustrate some of its central terms and concepts, and to highlight some questions for cognitive psychology itself. I have deliberately chosen this strategy over an alternative one, of concentrating on a small number of examples at greater depth, because I believe that we need more refined tools than we yet have for deeper investigations.

A Brief Sketch of Cognitive Theory

A clarification worth noting is that most of cognitive theory has been developed with probabilistic situations in mind. Perhaps because of its historic basis as a critique of expected utility theory (EUT), cognitive theory has studied how agents approach issues of uncertainty over future outcomes; it tends to be about decision making in the face of risk. It is perhaps not surprising, therefore, that what legal applications have been suggested to date deal directly with matters of risk. Most of the cognitive traits studied generalize, however, to other conditions of uncertainty, including static ones. We often approach issues of fact the same as we approach questions of risk; we do not know what the facts are, and we make some guess. An especially interesting feature of tax systems is that cognitive theory is relevant even to those areas of tax where the uncertainty itself is a function of a cognitive tendency. Thus, a "hidden" tax can actually be quite certain and knowable; that individuals systematically pay more attention to certain kinds of taxes rather than others illustrates that people remain uncertain about certain knowable things and not others. In this regard, I am proposing a significant extension of the domain of legal relevance for cognitive theory, to features of the world not necessarily involving risk in the classic sense. The ideas are that the structure of our tax system reflects cognitive tendencies, because this system has evolved in the face of cognitive error, and that the activities induced by the tax system are influenced by cognition.

This ought to be enough background to get the project started. To summarize, cognitive theory to date has two principal components: one, a catalog of coding errors, or heuristics and biases, that leads to inaccurate perceptions of reality; two, alternative evaluatory structures that do not correspond to normative ideals such as EUT. There remain very large gaps, ambiguities, and tensions in cognitive theory; as I note throughout, cognitive theory tends to be underdeterminative and only weakly explanatory. For this reason, consideration of real-world examples from tax might lend as much insight into cognitive theory as vice versa. In any event, below I shall discuss various aspects of cognitive theory, as well as their interrelations, in the context of tax.

Looking at Examples

This section looks at several classes of examples of cognitive psychological biases at work in the tax laws. The purposes of this inquiry are to illustrate the general theme that cognitive psychology is relevant for understanding the positive and normative dimensions of tax, to indicate what tax can tell us about cognition, and to indicate certain specific areas for further study. Each section pairs an aspect of the cognitive literature with at least one example from tax.

Hidden Taxes and Loss Aversion

A standard lesson from prospect theory in particular and cognitive psychology more generally is that people are especially averse to losses. For example, people will not use credit cards if a merchant advertises a 3 percent penalty for using them, but they will do so if the same merchant advertises a 3 percent bonus for using cash: Being penalized appears worse than forsaking a bonus, although the two outcomes are economically equivalent. Similarly, people consistently attach more disutility to losing a sum of money or a valuable possession than they do to failing to gain the same sum or good, even controlling for wealth effects. A related phenomenon is that people insist on being paid more for giving up something they already own than they would be willing to pay to acquire it in the first place. All of these effects may be captured in the phrase "loss aversion," often employed in prospect theory. The idea of loss aversion is that people are especially sensitive to losses, above and beyond the particular dollars involved.

The relevance of loss aversion to taxation comes in the form of the tax law's propensity for "hidden" taxes. The idea is that it will appear to be better to "pay" a tax imputedly, by never receiving money in the first place, rather than directly, by first receiving money and then having to give some of it back. I should hasten to qualify that by "better," I mean preferable from the point of view of a hypothetical tax-maximizing legislator or a tax-averse taxpayer; later I shall discuss the interesting and open normative implications of the interface between politics, tax, and cognition.

The term "hidden" is prevalent in discussions of tax, but ambiguous. There are actually different degrees and types of hidden taxes. One type, which I shall call "partially" hidden, simply involves taking money from taxpayers' pockets without necessarily telling them that they are paying a tax. A typical sales tax often works in this manner. Although the nominal incidence of the tax is on the seller, it is common practice to mark up the price of goods by the amount of the tax; a $1.00 item becomes $1.08 with the tax. Partially hidden taxes can thus vary by degree. Consider, for example, taxes that are even more deeply buried in the good (i.e., items for which the public is given a single "tax included" price), as is typical of gasoline, cigarette, and alcohol taxes. Partially hidden taxes are in fact very common, and all of the taxes considered in this section may be said to be "hidden" in some sense – the point of all of the examples is that taxpayers somehow do not notice a de facto tax. A question for cognitive theory to address is why taxpayers notice some taxes and not others, or react against certain taxes disproportionately to their narrow economic burden.

A second type of tax, which I shall call "fully" hidden, involves appropriating the money before it ever reaches the hands of its contingent owner. The two particular examples I explore below, the employer share of Social Security contributions and the corporate income tax, exhibit this fully hidden pattern. In each case, money is diverted from what would otherwise be its course in private commerce and sent to the government, without the potential recipient of the value ever necessarily being aware of the levy. In the more common case of partially hidden taxes, there is an initial giving followed by a surreptitious taking away. In fully hidden taxes, there is no giving in the first place; deceit precedes receipt, so to speak. It is generally well known that any hidden tax has certain advantages for the government; cognitive effects such as prominence and framing are relevant here. Loss aversion suggests that fully hidden taxes are especially advantaged. Like partially hidden taxes, fully hidden ones also have degrees, as the two examples I shall consider at length illustrate. Thus, the employer portion of payroll taxes is fairly readily traceable to each individual employee, whereas the true incidence of the corporate income tax is deeply obscure.

Social Security Contributions. The largest payroll tax, the Social Security system, is typically labeled a "contribution," not a tax, although the system was never intended as an actuarial one. The image of contributions suggests individuals contributing to *their own* retirement accounts, but, almost from the outset, the Social Security system was a pay-as-you-go one; current workers paid in the sums withdrawn by then current retirees. For many years, however, the "contribution" label stuck, and these payments appeared not to be viewed as hostilely as the dreaded income tax. Other features of the payroll tax, most notably the fact that the tax is completely withheld at the source and involves, on behalf of payees, no filing of forms or other paperwork, no doubt contributed to this benevolent view. This social perception seems to be breaking down, as the Social Security system has grown in size to account for 85 percent as much annual revenue intake as the income tax and to be, for most individual Americans, a larger source of payments. Pessimism over the future soundness of the system has also led many to be skeptical of ever receiving their "contributions" back; the pay-as-you-go aspect of the system has become more transparent.

There are interesting political and psychological stories to be told about the labeling and procedural aspects of Social Security payments. There may well be a phenomenon of "tax aversion," akin to but distinct from loss aversion, whereby individuals attach disproportionate disutility to government extractions perceived or labeled as "taxes." I want to focus attention on another aspect of the story: the feature whereby the employer "matches" the employee's payment. Presently, the combined Social Security and Medicare payment per worker is 15.3 percent of salary, up to a ceiling of $60,600 in 1994. Rather than this all coming out of an employee's paycheck, however, the Social Security system is set up such that the employee pays half of the tax, or 7.65 percent, and the employer kicks in the balance. Economically, the standard (indeed, nearly universal) assumption is that the entire 15.3 percent in fact comes out of each employee's paycheck. The reasoning is elementary:

The costs to the employer are employee specific and thus must come out of salary.

An example helps to illustrate these principles. Assume an employee, Alice, who is paid $10,000 in taxable salary. To this $10,000, the employer must under current law add $765 in Social Security and Medicare contributions. If Alice were not worth at least $10,765 to the employer, she would not be hired; if she were worth more than this, she should be paid more, or some competitive employer would bid her away. In perfect competition, the total wage reflects the marginal physical productivity of labor; the employer draws no distinction between money wages, noncash benefits, and taxes paid on behalf of any individual employee. Now assume that the law were changed, and the employer's obligation to pay one-half of the Social Security contribution were eliminated. Looking at the matter only in partial equilibrium, Alice's wage should rise to $10,765; if it did not, a competitive employer would have an opportunity to lure her away. But then this means that, as it is, the employer's contribution in fact comes out of the employee's pocket.

Why do we do things this way? Note that it is *not* simply a matter of collectibility, or liability for the tax. As it stands, the employer is required to withhold the employee's 7.65 percent share and is legally responsible for payment of the same amount. It would be a simple expedient to "gross up" salaries, levy the full 15.3 percent share from the employee, and still have the employer do all of the withholding. Instead of Alice's being "paid" $10,000, contributing $765, and taking home $9,235, she would instead be "paid" $10,765, contribute $1,530, and take home $9,235 – exactly the same bottom line. (There would be a difference flowing from the income tax consequences, but this could be settled rather easily.) Table 16.1 summarizes these figures.

Table 16.1 reflects the bottom-line equivalence of the two approaches: Social Security contributions and take-home pay are the same as between the two cases. Why then does the law choose the first technique rather than

Table 16.1. *Social Security Contributions With and Without Employer "Matching"*

Item of Salary or Tax	Case I	Case II
Gross salary	$10,000	$10,765
Employee contribution	765	1,530
Employer contribution	765	0
Total contributions	1,530	1,530
Net salary	9,235	9,235

the latter? My hypothesis is that loss aversion has much to do with this choice. While the two arrangements are economically or objectively equivalent, this is precisely a situation where cognitive psychology would predict a subjective difference. Getting paid and then losing the $765 is subjectively worse than never having received the $765 in the first place. Cognitive psychology predicts a more favorable taxpayer response to the Case I approach.

I am not necessarily claiming that politicians, like Madison Avenue executives, consciously manipulate taxpayer perceptions and take advantage of various heuristics and biases. For now, my claim is a more modest one: It is the passive and evolutionary idea mentioned above. Whatever the reasons why the matching form of financing was first adopted, cognitive psychology predicts that it has an advantage, in terms of subjective utility assessments, over the more direct, pay-it-yourself, Case II method. (Later I shall discuss what I take to be more conscious and active manipulations by government.) This advantage might translate into a greater tendency on the part of the government to rely on Social Security taxes, which has, indeed, transpired. Figure 16.1 shows the relative percentages of total federal revenues accounted for by individual income taxes and Social Security contributions, over five-year intervals from 1950 to 1990.

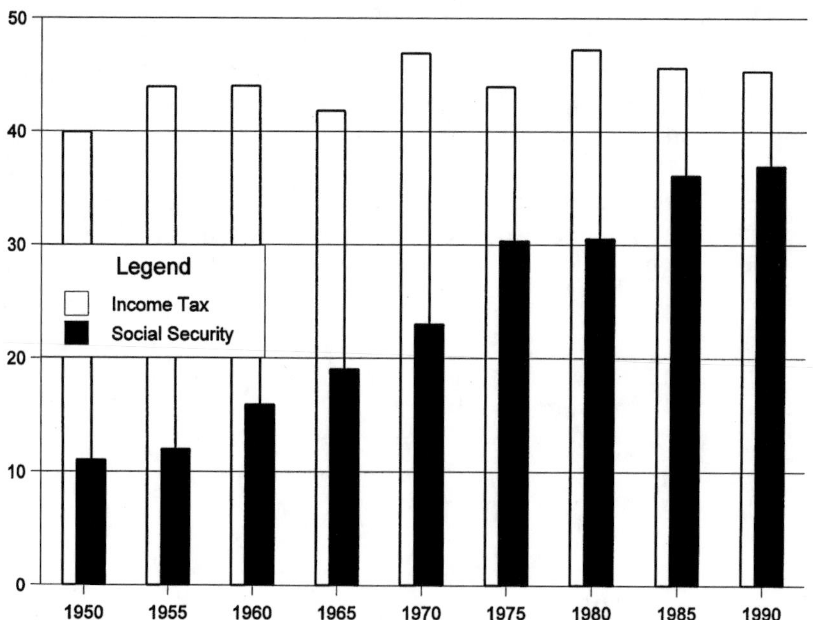

Figure 16.1. Individual income and Social Security taxes. *Source*: Budget of the U.S. government, historical tables, FY1994, at 23, tbl. 22 (1993).

Figure 16.1 reveals that, whereas the contribution of individual income taxes has been fairly steady, at the low to mid-40 percent range, that of Social Security taxes has grown dramatically, from just over 10 percent of federal revenues in 1950 to almost 40 percent in 1990. If the Clinton health reform plan were to go into effect, with its heavy reliance on "employer-mandated" payroll taxation, the balance would be shifted even more dramatically toward such taxes over income-based ones. That the employer-paid payroll tax is a widely popular – and apparently widely misunderstood – aspect of the Clinton proposal is fully consistent with the above discussion. Of course, other factors, most notably the rise in the benefit structure of Social Security and Medicare itself, have much to do with the Social Security phenomenon. Even at this point, though, we should hesitate a bit, because there is no necessary reason to link the benefit and contribution structures up; we could, for example, finance Social Security payments out of general income tax revenues. In any event, the basic thesis is that the differing cognitive consequences of income and payroll taxes has had something to do with the clear trend.

A natural question may be that, if the cognitive story told here has validity, why has the law stayed at a mere 50 percent contribution level? One answer is that 50 percent itself has a certain prominent pull: It reinforces an idea, present in early Social Security discussions, of the program as a "partnership" between employer and employee. Second, the law was put into place in the 1930s, at a time when the dominant model of cognitive tendencies in the tax laws was apt to be the passive and evolutionary one; Congress did not necessarily know how successful the gambit would be, if, indeed, they even understood it as a gambit. Finally, any move to *increase* the percentage would itself be prominent and would run the risk of killing a goose laying an abundance of golden eggs. But the fact that the recent Clinton proposals for employer mandates in the medical insurance context have featured an 80-20 split, with the larger share going to the employer, may indicate that the times have changed. In any event, the basic cognitive claim is that the success and dramatic increase in Social Security is due at least in part to cognitive factors that ought to affect the normative evaluation of the program.

The Corporate Income Tax. The corporate income tax has long been an enigma among the academic tax community, both economists and lawyers. The trouble, simply put, is that no one is quite sure who pays the tax. Corporations may be "legal persons," but they are certainly not flesh-and-blood ones – and they do not really pay taxes. Ultimately, the dollars paid by corporations must come out of the pockets of real humans: shareholders, managers, employees, suppliers, customers, capitalists generally. A very strong case can be put that much or all of the burden, or "incidence," of the corporate tax falls on labor, although others have argued that it falls on savers generally. In any event, the revenue raised, from whatever ultimate source, comes at a considerable cost, in the form of economic distortions. Noncorporate forms of ownership are favored over corporate ones. Within the corporate sector, there is a bias in favor of debt over equity, and hence in favor of industries or businesses with greater debt capacities. Tax breaks such as accelerated depreciation schedules or the investment tax credit, pushed for by corporations and their lobbyists as a means of reducing the corporate tax burden, skew investment and other allocative decisions. To the extent the ultimate incidence of the corporate tax is on capital, savings-consumption decisions are distorted; to the extent it is on labor, work-leisure decisions are affected. And so on.

Not surprisingly, this combination of uncertain and possibly regressive incidence with severe distortions has led many in the academic community – certainly the majority of those who have focused on the issue – to advocate some move away from a separate tax on corporate income, as by "integrating" the corporate and personal income taxes. Once again, however, cognitive psychology can help explain at least the political appeal of the tax. Fully hidden by its uncertain incidence, the corporate income tax is attractive for exactly this reason. If we were to repeal it and replace it with a tax of equal net revenue, the tax burden would become manifest, and loss aversion would dictate a fall in total utility. In 1992 the federal corporate income tax produced approximately $100 billion. Repealing the tax would therefore, in the first instance, be expected to increase income by at least that much. But then, if the government were to raise taxes by that same $100 billion figure – even if it were to figure out who, precisely, the beneficiaries of the repeal had been, and to tax exactly those parties (that is, in other words, even if it were to solve the incidence question) – this would involve precisely the same giving and taking away as the alternative formulation of the Social Security system discussed above. Utility would fall.

As with the Social Security example, cognitive psychology suggests an advantage to the actual, apparently senseless, way of doing things. Note that this is *not* the same thing as saying that old taxes are good ones, although that familiar proposition has interesting psychological dimensions as well. It is, rather, a statement that fully hidden taxes have a systematic advantage over more transparent ones. A cognitive perspective therefore casts some doubt on the political possibilities of integration projects. Figure 16.2 shows the trend in reliance on corporate taxes.

Figure 16.2 presents a different story than that concerning Social Security taxes reflected in Figure 16.1. Unlike such payroll taxes, corporate income taxes have not shown a steady increase over time; in fact, corporate income tax collections as a percentage of GDP are well below their historic highs. But corporate income taxes are, from just about any normative perspective, bad taxes; they are distortionary, inefficient, and not necessarily equitable. This is not clearly true of payroll taxes, which have the structure of a flat-rate consumption tax. Traditional tax theory might suggest that corporate income taxes would not persist – that, particularly once they reached a low

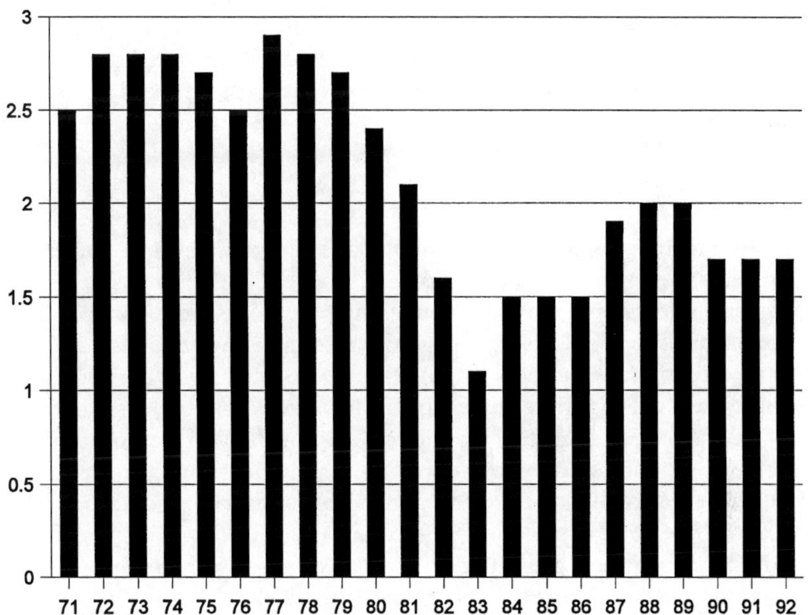

Figure 16.2. Corporate income taxes. *Source*: Budget of the U.S. Government, Historical Tables, Fiscal Year 1994 (1993).

level, as they did in 1983, they might continue to fade away. But this has not happened. The corporate income tax's contribution to federal revenues solidified and increased during the 1980s; recently the Clinton-sponsored tax reform raised the top corporate marginal tax rate to over 35 percent, and there have been some hints that it may rise again. The tax looks like it is here to stay, at least absent some cognitively savvy revolution.

Summary. We can think of two types of hidden taxes: partially hidden ones, where the fact of tax payment is obscured from the taxpayer, and fully hidden ones, where taxpayers "pay" a tax without ever receiving the money in the first place. The employer's share of Social Security contributions and the corporate income tax are both examples of fully hidden taxes. Such taxes implicate loss aversion. Standard cognitive psychology findings show that an individual suffers more disutility from having to pay something that she thinks she owns than from "merely" failing to receive an equivalent amount in the first place. In the case of Social Security taxation, the fully hidden character has led to an increasing reliance on these taxes, to the point where they are almost the dominant form of taxation in America today. In the case of the corporate income tax, the cognitive advantage has led to a steady reliance on what, by virtually all accounts, is a bad tax. Loss aversion thus helps to at least weakly explain a large segment of the actual tax systems we have adopted. There may also be a phenomenon of tax aversion, whereby taxpayers attach greater hostility to extractions readily assimilated as "taxes"; this is a phenomenon that sounds in representativeness or, more generally, prominence, which we turn to next.

Prominence and the Rate Structure

Another feature noted in the cognitive psychology literature is the effect of "prominence," sometimes also referred to as "salience" or "vividness." Prominence refers to the practice of attaching particular, and disproportionate, importance to highly visible or easily recallable events or facts. This extremely common phenomenon stands at the center of many of the heuristics and biases that cognitive psychologists have explored, such as the availability heuristic. For example, individuals are apt to overreact to disasters that are well publicized on television in predicting the future; in analyzing present facts, individuals are apt to give disproportionate weight to their own immediate, local experiences, and so on.

In the case of taxation, prominence helps to explain – again in a thin sense – why certain partially hidden taxes remain hidden: that is, why citizens fail to notice, or otherwise underreact to, certain types of taxes and tax changes. The examples considered in this section relate to the income tax rate structure. The basic idea is that the nominal income tax rate structure set out in Section 1 of the Internal Revenue Code and well publicized in the financial and general press, especially when Congress changes it, is particularly prominent. More specifically, the single highest rate bracket is socially prominent, whereas each person's individual highest rate bracket is individually prominent. Prominence creates both opportunities and constraints for the tax-maximizing legislator. The predictions are that Congress will have a hard time in raising top marginal rates, but will have more freedom in operating inframarginally, or otherwise raising taxes without raising apparent tax rates.

Rates and Crises. A simple visual inspection of the history of the marginal rate levied on the highest incomes under the income tax, from its inception in 1913 to the present day, begins the story. Figure 16.3 presents the data.

The basic message is that rates spike up during crises, such as the Great Depression and wartime, and trend down thereafter. In 1916 the top marginal rate was 15 percent; by 1918 it had jumped to 77 percent. It was not raised again until 1932, under Franklin Roosevelt and in the midst of the Great Depression; by that time, it had fallen to 25 percent and was increased, dramatically, to 63 percent. The top rate underwent another sharp, upward spike during World War II, reaching 94 percent in the war years 1944 and 1945. It then trended down a bit, but was raised again in 1950, during the Korean and Cold Wars, to 91 percent, where it effectively remained until 1964. Starting in 1964, the rate began an extended period of decline, interrupted

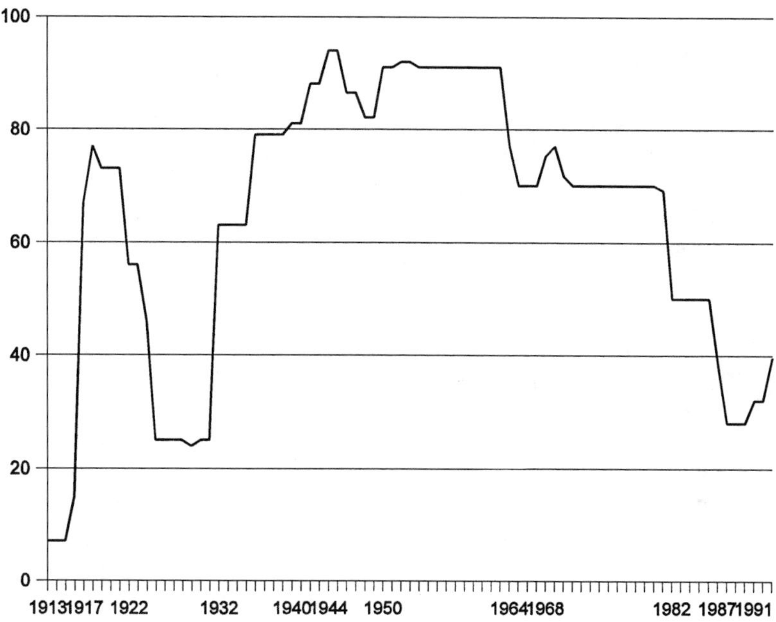

Figure 16.3. Top marginal rates. *Source*: Joseph Pechman, *Federal Tax Policy*, appendix A (5th ed. 1987) and I.R.C.

only by slight increases in 1968 and 1969, at the height of the Vietnam War, until the 1990s. In the eighty-year history of the income tax, the marginal rate on the highest incomes was increased twelve times: in 1917, 1918, 1932, 1936, 1940, 1942, 1944, 1950, 1968, 1969, 1991, and 1993. Eight of these instances occurred in the first thirty-seven years of the tax; only four have occurred in the almost fifty years since 1950.

One observation, from a prominence perspective, is that, during wartimes and other crises, citizens are either more patriotic and willing to share with the government, and/or are distracted by the crisis itself, so that Congress is able to directly raise the highest marginal tax rate. But when the crisis and its attendant revenue needs are over, Congress gives back the rate increases, although perhaps more slowly than need alone might dictate. This latter phenomenon – the gradualness of the reduction in rates – relates to the "fiscal illusion" or "Leviathan hypothesis." But loss aversion is also relevant to this latter effect. Having lost the tax rate battle during the crisis, taxpayers are relatively less concerned with winning it back. The loss is behind them; a reduction in rates is a gain, which brings less utility in absolute terms than the loss took away. In any event, it appears to be very hard to raise nominal rates in peacetime, as politicians as diverse as former President George Bush and former New Jersey Governor Jim Florio learned soon enough.

Figure 16.3 tells only part of the story, however, for many reasons. It does not factor in the definition of the income tax base, or favorable provisions on certain kinds of income such as capital gains, or maximum rates on earned income. These omissions, however, are precisely consistent with the central thesis, namely, that the highest rate bracket itself garners disproportionate attention. More important, Figure 16.3 presents only a single marginal rate at any point in time. As I have noted briefly, there are two degrees, or aspects, to the prominence story of marginal rates. At any point in time, there is a single marginal rate applied to the highest incomes in America; this socially prominent rate is what is displayed in Figure 16.3. Cognitive theory suggests that this rate has importance; the press is apt to report it, and citizens, hearing such phrases as "marginal rates as high as *x* percent," may form impressions of the income tax based, in disproportionate part, on this figure. But there is also each *individual's* highest marginal rate bracket, where prominence will also play a role. The particular bracket that a taxpayer is in matters, not only for the economically correct marginal analysis of personal financial plans, but also because the taxpayer is apt to know, from tax rate tables or the general literature, what her marginal rate bracket is. Another feature of prominence, well known to any teacher of a course in basic taxation, is that the typical taxpayer is likely to overestimate the relevance of her marginal rate bracket in assessing the real, effective income tax burden on her: that is, a taxpayer in the 25 percent *bracket* will often think that she pays 25 percent of *all* of her income in taxes; she will exaggerate the burden from the margin.

Figure 16.3 thus cannot, and does not, present the whole story. Indeed, no two-dimensional picture can present the whole story, because there are several degrees of freedom in the income tax. Marginal rates, the breadth and number of rate brackets, base definition, dependency and standard deductions are all ways of adjusting individual tax burdens. Precisely this inability to present a simple picture of tax burdens creates opportunities and constraints. Cognitive theory suggests that the best way to raise taxes, from a tax-maximizing legislator's perspective, may be to implicate neither the socially prominent single highest rate nor the individually prominent personal rate bracket; we can call this a "doubly nonprominent" move. I shall discuss in the next section that this is exactly what a failure to index can do under a simplified rate structure: It slides individuals along within their highest marginal rate bracket, or, equivalently, shrinks the effective domain of their lower, submarginal rates.

In any event, the doubly nonprominent technique, analogous to the fully hidden corporate income tax, may be the most attractive move available to the legislator. A second-best move is to expand the domain of the higher rate brackets – this implicates *only* individual prominence, not social prominence. In fact, the coverage of the highest marginal rate bracket has varied dramatically over time. Figure 16.4 illustrates the income level at which the top marginal rate bracket of Figure 16.3 kicks in, in thousands of dollars.

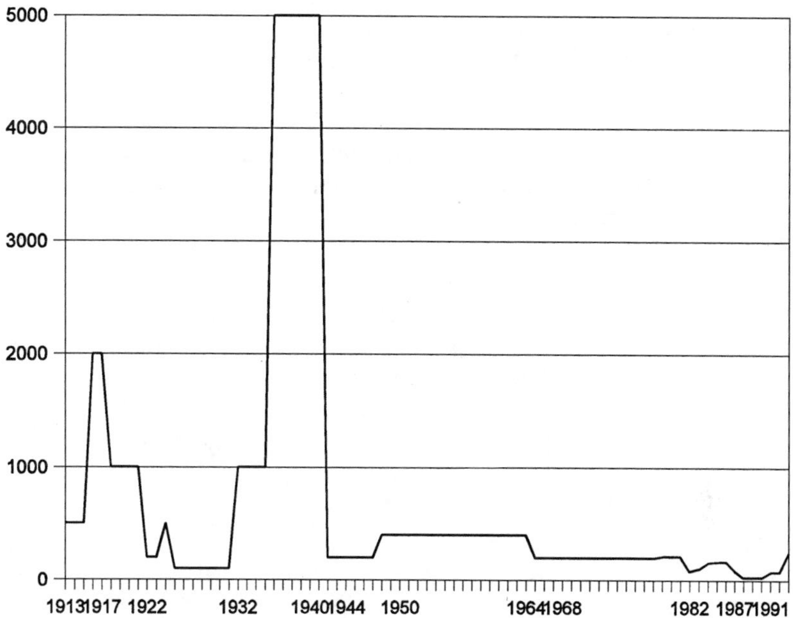

Figure 16.4. Income level of top bracket. *Source*: Pechman, *Federal Tax Policy*.

Figure 16.4 reveals the very wide sway of definition in the top income tax bracket.[1] Indeed, because the figure shows nominal dollars – that is, unadjusted for inflation – the real story is even more dramatic. When the highest rate bracket was 67 percent in 1917, only those taxpayers with income over $2,000,000 per year were in it; this corresponds to $13,000,000 in 1992. In 1936, when the rate rose from 63 to 79 percent, its jurisdiction began at $5,000,000 per year, the equivalent of nearly $48,000,000 in 1992. Even Michael Jordan does not make *that* much.

Figure 16.4 thus strongly suggests another cognitive game that was going on, from very early in the history of the income tax. During times of crises, as mentioned above, the top marginal rate did indeed increase. But the domain of these highest rates was so limited, at first, that they were really little more than symbolic. The symbolism served, at those times, an important purpose. The top marginal rate bracket was given a lot of public attention, and, in part due to its prominence, compounded by the tendency to equate marginal with effective rates, the typical citizen might have thought, erroneously, that the tax system was steeply progressive, and that the truly rich were paying most of their income to the government. (Interestingly, studies have shown a tendency on the part of citizens to equate the actual highest marginal tax rate with the ethically appropriate one.) This then might have made their own tax burdens appear to be less painful. Further, the device allowed Congress to increase taxes in the future without raising the highest rate bracket, by extending downward its domain. The ratcheting up of the top rate was a "foot-in-the-door" phenomenon. Thus, in 1942, with the revenue demands attendant on World War II escalating, the top bracket was raised from 81 to 88 percent – a rather minor change. But the income level at which this bracket kicked in plummeted, from $5,000,000 to $200,000 – a staggeringly large drop. This was a partially nonprominent move, because the citizenry had already digested, albeit more or less vicariously, the fact of high marginal tax rates.

Nonindexing. Throughout most of the history of the income tax, rate brackets have not been indexed for inflation. The issue of rate bracket indexing arises because of two factors: first, the income tax's reliance on a system of varying, and generally progressive, marginal rates; and, second, the use of fixed dollar amounts to demarcate the boundaries for such rates. In times of inflation, nominal gains in dollars earned push taxpayers into steeper brackets, or higher along within their currently top bracket, so that their real tax burden increases.

All of this is easily seen with an example. Imagine a taxpayer, Bob, who earns $30,000 in Year 0, under the rate structure in Table 16.2. Bob will pay $2,000 of taxes under the given schedule – 0 on his first $10,000, and 10 percent of the next $20,000 – for an average tax rate of 6.67 percent (2/30). If inflation rises at a 10 percent rate during Year 0, assuming no other changes and a fully indexed salary, adjusted as of the first of the year, Bob will earn $33,000 nominal dollars in Year 1. If the rate brackets are indexed to account for inflation, all of the dollar amounts in the left column of Table 16.2 will increase by 10 percent; that is, the 0 bracket will end at $11,000, the 10 percent bracket will extend up to $33,000, and so on. Under such a system, Bob will pay a tax of $2,200 – 10 percent of the difference between $11,000 and $33,000 – once again for an average tax rate of 6.67 percent (2.2/33). His tax paid, just like his salary, has risen solely to keep pace with inflation; each remains constant in real Year 0 dollars. If, however, there is no indexing, then Bob pays a tax of $2,600 under the rate schedule; all of his $3,000 inflationary gain has been taxed at the 20 percent rate. Bob's average tax rate has increased to 7.88 percent (2.6/33), although his real income has been held constant.

Table 16.2. *Hypothetical Marginal Rate Schedule*

Income	Marginal Tax Rate
$0–10,000	0%
$10,001–30,000	10
$30,001 and up	20

The example captures the effects of a failure to index, which came to be known as "bracket creep." These effects were always present under the United States income tax, which has since its inception in 1913 relied on both progressive marginal rates and fixed dollar brackets. The problem was not perceived as a severe one, at least not politically, until the 1970s, when high and unpredictable inflation became a significant concern. A proposal to index rate brackets was first put before Congress in 1976; that proposal and a subsequent one made in 1977 were each sponsored by Republicans and each widely rejected. In 1981, as part of the sweeping Reagan-sponsored ERTA bill, indexing of rate brackets finally became law, although it was not to become effective until 1985, and subsequent congressional action delayed full implementation until 1989.

The role of prominence in the story is that a failure to index generates a revenue increase without changing the publicly visible, nominal rate system and without directly compelling Congress to legislate changes in the rate brackets. Indeed, nonindexing can often result in the best of all possible worlds, from the tax-maximizing legislator's point of view – a doubly nonprominent tax increase. Absent indexing, inflation pushes one farther along *within* one's top bracket. As long as one's marginal rate is above her average rate – a necessary condition for all but those taxpayers in the lowest (i.e., zero) bracket under a system of progressive marginal rates – inflation increases the effective rate of tax, for that very reason.

To see this point, let us return to the previous example, but with a simplified rate structure (see Table 16.3). Consider another taxpayer, Cindy, who earns $20,000 in Year 0, paying a tax of $2,000 for an effective average rate of 10 percent. In Year 1, there is 10 percent inflation, and Cindy's salary rises to $22,000. With indexing, the rate bracket cutoff point increases to $11,000, and Cindy pays a tax of $2,200, keeping her effective rate at 10 percent (2.2/22). Without indexing, her tax increases to $2,400 (20 percent of $12,000), for an effective rate of 10.91 percent (2.4/22). Cindy's effective rate has gone up, without her entering into a higher rate bracket, because the entire inflationary gain has been taxed in her *highest* rate bracket, instead of being evenly distributed throughout both brackets. Inflation generated annual tax increases without even necessarily pushing taxpayers into new, higher tax brackets. The de facto tax increase could be dramatic over time,

Table 16.3. *Simplified Marginal Rate Schedule*

Income	Marginal Tax Rate
$0–10,000	0%
$10,001 and up	20

because the extra burden caused by failing to index would become part of the base for each subsequent year; each taxpayer's average tax rate would steadily increase.

Cognitive theory suggests that nonindexing might be a successful way to raise taxes, until and unless high inflation itself became prominent, and/or the combination of high inflation and multiple brackets made the individually prominent occurrence of entering a higher rate bracket more common. There is good evidence to support this general theory. Throughout our income tax history, bracket creep has been an important source of de facto tax increases. Figure 16.5 superimposes the rate of increase of the consumer price index (a proxy for inflation) and income taxes as a percentage of GDP, for the years 1961–89.

Of course, we are dealing here with a very complex story, and there are many intricate relationships between inflation, productivity, reported income, and taxation, but I mean the figure to illustrate how periods of higher inflation correlate with an increased real income tax burden. In particular, the steep rise in inflation levels during the 1970s, and even more particularly the dramatic increases from 1975 to 1981, correlate with a significant rise in the level of the income tax burden. In 1976 personal income tax collections represented 7.8 percent of GDP, a figure just slightly below the

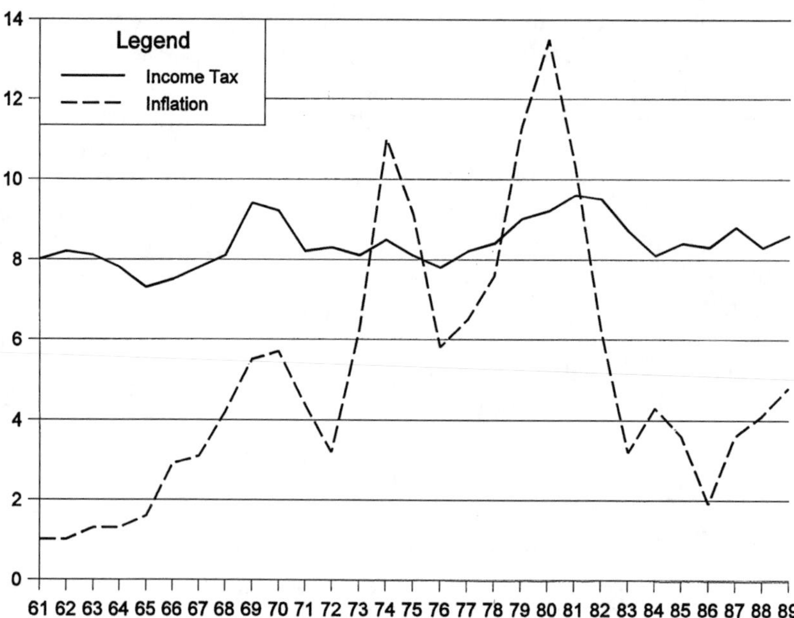

Figure 16.5. Inflation and Income Tax. *Source*: historical tables at 25–26, tbl. 23; U.S. Department of Commerce, *Statistical Abstract of the United States* (1993), at 482, tbl. 757.

average from the preceding thirty-year, postwar period, 1946–75. (The mean burden during this period was 7.86 percent, with a standard deviation of .72.) By 1981, after inflation had averaged nearly 10 percent for the five years 1977–81, reaching a high of 13.5 percent in 1980, the income tax burden reached a level of 9.6 percent – the highest ever, except for the war year 1944. The change from 1976 to 1981 represented an increase of 23 percent in the real level of the income tax burden; the 9.6 percent level reached in 1981 was nearly three standard deviations above the 1946–75 average. Yet the 1976–81 period was *not* marked by any significant statutory tax increase. Indeed, the two major Carter era tax bills, the 1977 Tax Reduction and Simplification Act and the 1978 Revenue Act, were each billed, projected, and expected to be tax *reductions*. Inflation was clearly doing a good deal of the work of increasing income taxes.

Ironically enough, for those who may feel that nonindexing was a large evil, the presence of indexing may be leading to even worse tax policy decisions, from a normative perspective, as Congress is compelled to take more visible steps to raise revenues. Nonindexing as a tax policy at least has a progressive effect; it increases reliance on the income tax, and its real burdens fall more heavily on upper-bracket taxpayers. As I discuss next, the steps taken in an age of indexing, more often than not, involve changes other than open, direct changes to the rate structure; Congress moves to exploit other degrees of freedom that income taxation generates. Having lost the particularly easy way out provided by bracket creep, Congress may have to search for the next most hidden form of tax increase. Often this makes for questionable tax policy.

Cognitive Tricks in an Age of Indexing. Cognitive theory suggests that nonindexing gave Congress an easy way out of raising nominal tax rates. The tax boost provided by inflation is relatively hidden, does not attain the social prominence of explicit changes in the rate structure, and often does not even necessarily implicate the individual prominence of moving particular taxpayers into higher marginal rate brackets. Now that the income tax is indexed, and in the absence of major crises – combined with a massive deficit, a phenomenon that may be related in interesting ways to the current discussion – Congress is left with a limited range of tools for raising revenues. The thesis of this prominence discussion is that Congress will seek to raise taxes in relatively less visible ways, and in any event will implicate the publicly visible rate structure only as a last resort.

History supports the thesis. Even before George Bush's highly celebrated "read my lips" pledge, Washington had begun to show a fondness for hidden rate increases. Thus, the Tax Reform Act of 1986 introduced the "bubble" – a 5 percent "surcharge" on upper-middle-income taxpayers designed to slowly phase out the benefits of lower rate brackets. For all intents and purposes, this device simply introduced another rate bracket; the rate structure now went 0-15-28-33-28. For a married couple filing jointly, the 33 percent "bubble" range lasted from taxable income of $71,900 to $149,250 – a range of $77,350; by the time a couple reached the upper limit of the range, more than half of their income had been taxed at the 33 percent level. But Congress did not explain the matter this way. The surcharge was buried in a separate part of the code, and the promulgators of the Tax Reform Act earnestly clung to the largely semantic claim that there were only two rate brackets: 15 and 28.

The bubble was just the tip of the iceberg, to mix metaphors, as other cognitive tricks soon followed. Social Security receipts became taxable, in part, above certain thresholds of income. Personal dependency deductions were to be phased out over a range of upper incomes under the 1990 act. So, too, were most itemized deductions. But the best illustration to date of cognitive tricks in an age of indexing has come with the Clinton-sponsored Revenue Reconciliation Act of 1993. Much of this law can be read as an obsessive attempt to maintain the appearance of low marginal rates; in particular, there seems to have been something of a Maginot Line created at the 40 percent level. Thus, the ostensible top rate is 36 percent, but a 10 percent "surcharge" on the highest incomes quickly (and obviously) pushes this up to 39.6 percent. (Interestingly, the general community seems to have learned its lesson from the failed "bubble" trick of 1986; the administration first proposed the higher rate as a 10 percent surcharge, but this was quickly picked up on as a 39.6 percent bracket, and this is how the ultimate act read.) Phase-outs continue; the percentage of Social Security contributions that are taxable for upper-income taxpayers has been raised to 85 percent; the deductibility of business meals and entertainment expenses was lowered to 50 percent; there are lower ceilings on pension plan contributions; and the ceiling on Medicare taxable income (at a 2.9 percent combined employer-employee rate) was lifted altogether. Perhaps most striking of all, from a policy perspective, is the fact that the "marriage penalty" brought about by the steeper rate structure on married couples increased dramatically under the Clinton plan.

A particular feature of the 1993 act helps to illustrate the general point. The 1993 act became law on August 10, 1993. Given this date, relatively late in the year, the tax rate increases in the bill would have had only limited revenue effects during the 1994 filing season. The administration decided it needed the revenue increase that would come from an effective implementation of the new rate structure as of January 1, 1993. There are two ways that the administration could have gotten this result. One was by making the rate increases retroactive – a risky strategy, given some legal uncertainties, and the near certainty that Republican opponents would make hay with the issue. The second option was to use a common, standard technique – that of "blended" rates, a device so well established that it is sanctioned by a specific Internal Revenue Code section. Blended rates work as follows: A single rate is formed by adding together the prior and the new tax rate, each weighted by the percentage of the year during which they held sway. For example, if the old rate had been 30 percent, and a new, 40 percent rate had taken effect precisely at midyear, the "blended" rate for the year would be 35 percent (.5[30] + .5[40]). The Clinton administration *could* have used this blended rate technique to get the new, 36 and 39.6 percent rates in effect as of January 1, while avoiding the adverse publicity and legal challenges that retroactive application entailed. But to have done so would have meant having rate brackets of 44 and 53 percent for the balance of the year – numbers well above the magic 40 percent level. Given a choice between retroactivity and higher nominal marginal rates – a choice that would have meant *no* difference in bottom-line results – the administration chose to take the retroactivity gambit.

The various changes and techniques discussed above enable the government to raise revenue without having to face the adverse publicity, and focus, of a significantly changed marginal tax rate schedule. Yet, for the most part, all of these changes are in fact changes in the rates; Congress is saying that people at certain income ranges should pay a higher percentage of their incomes in taxes, without regard to the sources of that income. (This is most obviously true in the case of the surcharge or "bubble.") Some of the changes are, in fact, rather incoherent as a matter of base definition. Why is it, for example, that we should modify lower and middle incomes with a dependency deduction for each minor child, but not upper incomes? Are the costs of dependency any *less* for the rich? When we shift from a static, distributive perspective to a dynamic, incentive-oriented one, the questions become more pressing. Are we *more* concerned about pro-natalist incentives among the wealthy? Further, the phase-outs create higher marginal rates; is there any sound reason why a family should be in a higher rate bracket because it has more children? In effect, the more children a wealthy family has, the greater is the impetus for the secondary earner, almost always the wife, to stay home and generate imputed income. Similarly, the increased marriage penalties among the wealthy do not seem to follow from any principled decision, say, about the levels of imputed income for wealthy families, and these also have the unfortunate effect of aggravating a bias against secondary earners.

The analysis from traditional tax policy indicates that many of the recent changes are poor ones: They are not readily justified under most compelling normative theories of tax, and they seem to have emerged haphazardly, without due consideration to either distributive or behavioral effects. The lesson from cognitive theory, in contrast, is that these are precisely the types of changes to be expected. Phase-outs, surcharges, floors, ceilings, and marriage taxes become the new, postbracket creep tools of tax increases.

A Case Study: State Taxes After the Tax Reform Act of 1986. The particular prominence of the income tax and its rate structure can be illustrated with one final example. Prior to the Tax Reform Act of 1986, all state and local taxes were deductible from federal income taxes, at least for those taxpayers who itemized their deductions. In the case of sales and use taxes, there were certain practical difficulties in keeping adequate records, but the federal government generously alleviated these by providing standardized tables of estimated sales taxes paid. For reasons not relevant to the current effort – and that are obscure in any event – the Tax Reform Act eliminated the deductibility of state sales taxes, but preserved a deduction for income as well as property taxes. Now, very elementary economic theory would tell us that states would then increase their reliance on income taxes and decrease sales taxes; paying income taxes meant a federal tax break, and hence the possibility of a national subsidy of at least high-bracket residents, whereas the burden of sales taxes would be unmitigated – indeed, this burden was effectively *increased* by the repeal of federal deductibility.

But this prediction has not generally come to pass. In the wake of the 1986 act, states have continued to rely heavily on sales taxes. Figure 16.6 illustrates the trends; it depicts aggregate state and local sales, property, and income taxes from 1984–91, in billions of dollars.

While Figure 16.6 reveals a slightly increased tendency to rely on property taxes, the trends in all three taxes are similar; certainly there was no dramatic shift away from sales taxes in the wake of the 1986 act, as per the naive prediction. Perhaps more interestingly, those states that did not have income

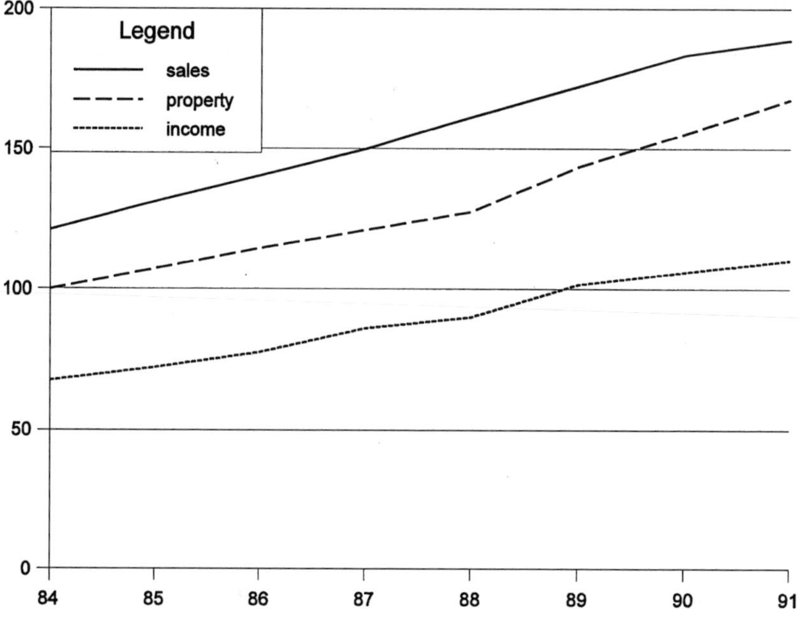

Figure 16.6. State and local taxes. *Source*: *Statistical Abstract at* 299, tbl. 476.

taxes – there were ten of them – did not generally move to adopt one after 1986. Of course, there are a good many factors at work here: The choice of taxes has distributive and allocative consequences and, most likely, effects on the size and nature of government as well. But, once again, cognitive theory adds *a* reason for what would otherwise be at least a somewhat puzzling trend: income taxes are prominent, and sales taxes are not. Citizens appear to be willing to pay a higher real burden based solely on the choice of the form of taxation.

Summary. Prominence suggests that the public will pay attention to certain aspects of taxation more than others, not in proportion to the absolute burden or extent of the tax issue itself, but based instead on the tax's relative visibility. The best examples of prominence effects relate to the marginal rate structure of the personal income tax. The single highest rate bracket is socially prominent, whereas each individual's marginal rate bracket is individually prominent. Prominence limits the ability of Congress to raise rates, globally or individually. But the prominence of the rate structure also creates opportunities for Congress to act in ways that do not impact nominal rates. The history of symbolically high marginal rates, the long-standing failure to index rate brackets for inflation, and the recent plethora of non-rate-structure cognitive tricks support the hypothesis. The general prominence of income taxes is further indicated by the failure, after 1986, for states to shift away from sales and toward income taxes, despite the deductibility of the latter. No complete discussion of tax policy can afford to overlook the psychological affects that the marginal tax rate system of the income tax helps to generate.

Conclusions

I hope to have established by now at least a prima facie case that the relevance of cognitive psychology to tax is broad and interesting. Cognitive theory suggests that cognitive misperceptions are relevant to both the size and the structure of the tax system. Hidden, especially fully hidden, and nonprominent, especially doubly nonprominent, taxes and tax increases are favored. Taxpayers make mistakes in their own dynamic behavior, confusing average and marginal rates, making "too large" charitable contribution deductions or entertainment expenses, relying too heavily on fringe benefits, falling in love with tax shelters, ignoring capitalization, and so on.

That all of these phenomena seem clear and even obvious to tax cognoscenti is hardly a reason for not pursuing them further. Formal studies of taxpayer perceptions of various structural aspects of the tax laws could add immensely to our understandings. This work could advance by some combination of experimental surveys, questionnaires, and focus group discussions.

Similarly, much work needs to be done in constructing a cognitive-political model of tax. I suggested that the tax aspects of the story add to the general insights behind such better-discussed phenomena as the Leviathan hypothesis and fiscal illusion, but I also added the caveat that any dynamic is unlikely to be smooth or completely ex ante predictable. When will a previously hidden tax become manifest? What factors inform the public's willingness and ability to pay attention to certain tax phenomena and not others? Is there anything of general interest to be learned, for example, from the at least cognitive successes of the passive activity loss rules and Stanley Surrey's tax expenditure gambit? We need a better, thicker picture of how tax politics transpires. In answering these challenging questions, it will be difficult to continue to avoid facing up to the need for a deeper theory of the individual, as well as paying attention to the institutional features of tax implementation and design.

There is thus much work to be done on the positive side, in terms of pinning down the nature, extent, and effects of cognitive errors insofar as they relate to the creation and evolution of tax systems. But there is also a great deal of work to be done on the normative side. Of course, a thicker description of reality is itself a helpful adjunct to reform. Another central question is what relevance the facts of cognition have for various possible comprehensive normative theories of tax. Does the fact of persistent cognitive error push us toward one or the other of these theories, ex ante? What modifications could or should be made internally to each approach in the face of the lessons of cognitive psychology? Can a distinction be drawn among types of paternalism in the presence of cognitive error? And, as we have discussed, cognitive theory can also help to suggest particular local reforms, such as the passive activity loss rules or the budgeting procedures suggested by Stanley Surrey, and cognitive theory can also help to suggest means for implementing independently attractive proposals. In pursuing these ideas and in answering these and other questions, I believe that the need for and relevance of a richer theory of the individual taxpayer will become even more clear.

So there is much to be done, on both the positive and the normative side, by psychologically oriented experimenters, philosophically oriented theorists, economically oriented analysts, and practically oriented tax professionals. But if there is much to be done, the ultimate prize seems well worth pursuing: a general, comprehensive theory of tax, one that can unite the diverse insights of law, psychology, economics, philosophy, and other disciplines in a manner that can help us to analyze existent tax systems and prescribe new ones. It is high time for interdisciplinarism to move beyond a fashionable way to keep academics from perishing for want of publishing, and instead toward generating insights and answers of importance to real-world people and problems.

Note

1 From 1948 forward, the figure uses the married filing jointly schedule. Because the range on Figure 16.4 is so great, it may be hard to read. Figure 16.7 compresses the range by using a logarithmic vertical axis. Figure 16.7 helps to show the dramatic variability in definition of the top marginal rate bracket.

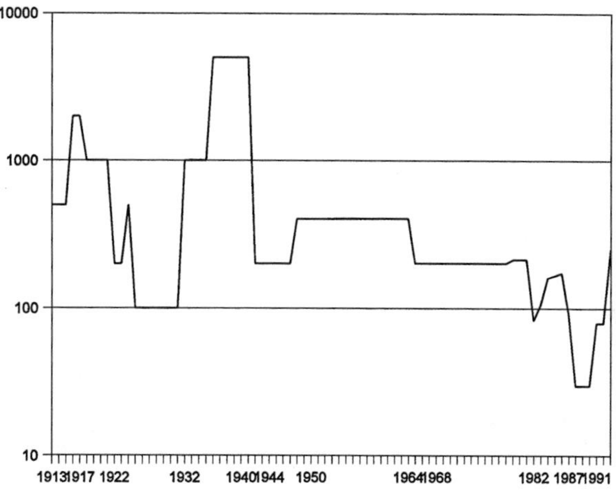

Figure 16.7. Domain of top marginal rate bracket. *Source*: Pechman, *Federal Tax Policy*.

Index